# Grappling Masters

VOLUME 2

# Grappling Masters

## Volume 2

Jose M. Fraguas

**DISCLAIMER:**

Please note that the author and publisher of this book are NOT RESPONSIBLE in any manner whatsoever for any injury that may result from practicing the techniques and/or following the instructions given within. Since the physical activities described herein may be too strenuous in nature for some readers to engage in safely, it is essential that a physician be consulted prior to training.

Published in 2021 by Empire Books/AWP LLC.

© Copyright 2021 by Jose M. Fraguas.

All rights reserved. No part of this publication may be reproduced or utilized in any form or by any means, electronic or mechanical, including photocopying, recording, or by any information storage and retrieval system, without prior written permission from Empire Books/AWP LLC.

Library of Congress Cataloging-in-Publication Data

Names: Fraguas, Jose M., author.
Title: Grappling Masters/ by Jose M. Fraguas.
Description: Los Angeles, California: Empire Books, 2021. | Description based on print version record and CIP data provided by publisher; resource not viewed.
ISBN: 978-1-949753-34-9 (pbk.: alk. paper)

1. Grappling-Masters I. Fraguas, Jose M. II. Title GV1114.M339 2020
796.815 '2' 0899103-dc22

2224012669

**EMPIRE BOOKS**
LOS ANGELES, CALIFORNIA

# Dedication

To the memory of Grandmaster Carlos Gracie, the first member of the Gracie family who trained in the art of Jiu-Jitsu. And to the memory of Helio Gracie, a true pioneer who broke barriers and put himself to test on behalf of his beloved art. His study and sacrifice paved the road for all future generations.

# Acknowledgments

Special thanks to the members of the Gracie and Machado families, whose permission to quote and peruse from personal notes has given this text its core, and to all the instructors appearing in this work for granting me access to interviewing them. I want to thank all of the students and practitioners around the world whose support and dedication to the art has helped tremendously to promote and popularize the art of Brazilian Jiu-Jitsu.

– Jose M. Fraguas

# Contents

| XII | XIV | 1 |
|---|---|---|
| *About the Author* | *Introduction* | *Carlos Baretto* |
| 13 | 39 | 59 |
| *Vitor Belfort* | *Wander Braga* | *Willie Cahill* |
| 73 | 93 | 103 |
| *Rico Chiapparelli* | *Randy Couture* | *Husi Duarte* |
| 117 | 129 | 145 |
| *Paulo Gillobel* | *Carley Gracie* | *Carlson Gracie* |
| 175 | 187 | 207 |
| *Fabio Gurgel* | *John Lewis* | *Dean Lister* |

| 219 *Cleber Luciano* | 233 *Rodrigo Medeiros* | 249 *Helio "Soneca" Moreira* |
| --- | --- | --- |
| 261 *Jason Morris* | 271 *B. J. Penn* | 283 *Antonio "Nino" Schembri* |
| 297 *Ken Shamrock* | 309 *Mike Swain* | 327 *Leo Vieira* |

# About the Author

Born and raised in Madrid, Spain, Jose "Chema" Fraguas began his martial arts studies with judo, in grade school, at age 9. From there, he moved to taekwondo and then to kenpo karate, earning a black belt in both styles. During this same period, he also studied shito-ryu karate and eventually received a fifth-degree black belt. He began his career as a writer at 16 by serving as a regular contributor to martial arts magazines in Great Britain, France, Spain, Italy, Germany, Portugal, Holland and Australia. Having a black belt in three different styles allows him to better reflect the physical side of the martial arts in his writing. "Feeling before writing," Fraguas says.

In 1980, he moved to Los Angeles, and Dan Inosanto accepted him as a student at the Kali Academy. In his first struggling years, he managed to meet numerous martial arts greats such as Gene LeBell, Hawkins Cheung, Jun Chong, Wally Jay, et cetera. Fraguas also trained at the legendary Main Street Boxing Gym in downtown L.A. to learn "boxing hands" that Dan Inosanto recommended. The open-minded mentality taught at the Kali Academy helped him to develop an eclectic approach to the martial arts. Seeking to supplement and expand his personal training, Fraguas researched other disciplines such as wing chun, savate, muay Thai, wrestling and jiu-jitsu.

In 1986, Fraguas founded his own book and magazine company in Europe, authoring dozens of books and distributing his magazines to 35 countries in three different languages. His reputation and credibility as a martial artist and publisher became well known to the top masters around the world. Considering himself a martial artist first and a writer and publisher second, Fraguas feels fortunate to have had the opportunity to interview many legendary martial arts teachers. He recognizes that much of the information given in the interviews helped him to discover new dimensions in the martial arts. "I was constantly absorbing knowledge from the great masters," he recalls. "I only trained with a few of them, but intellectually and spiritually all of them have made important contributions to my growth as a complete martial artist."

Steeped in tradition yet looking to the future, Fraguas understands and appreciates martial arts history and philosophy and feels this rich heritage is a necessary stepping stone to personal growth and spiritual evolution. His desire to promote both ancient philosophy and modern thinking provided the motivation for writing this book. "If the motivation is just money, a book cannot be of good quality," Fraguas says. "If the book is written to just make people happy, it cannot be deep. I want to write books so I can learn as well as share."

The author currently lives in Los Angeles, California.

# Introduction

I've been both lucky and fortunate. Some of my best days were spent interviewing and meeting the masters appearing in this book. There is little I enjoy more than "gnawing" on a great interview while time slows and sometimes even seems to stop. Having the opportunity to meet and interview the most relevant and prestigious martial artists of the past four decades is something that every martial artist doesn't have the chance to do. Hopefully, in some small way, this will help make up for that.

Meeting the masters and having long conversations with them that were published in magazines around the world allowed me to do more than simply "scratch the surface" of the technical aspects of their respective styles. It also allowed me to research and analyze the human beings behind the teachers. Some of the dialogues and interviews began by simply commenting about the superficial techniques of fighting and ended up turning into an uncommon spiritual conversation about the philosophical aspects of the martial arts.

Although they are all very different, considering their respective styles and backgrounds, they all share a common thread of the traditional values such as discipline, respect, positive attitude, dedication and etiquette.

For more than 25 years, I've faced the long odds of interviewing these fighters and martial arts masters, one-on-one, face-to-face and with no place to run if I asked a stupid question. Many times, it was a real challenge to not only make contact with them, but also make the interview interesting enough to bring out the knowledge that resided inside them. In every interview I tried to absorb as much knowledge as I could, ranging from their training methods, to their fighting methods, to their philosophies about life itself.

Their different origins and cultural backgrounds heavily influenced them but never prevented them from analyzing, researching or modifying anything that they considered appropriate. They always kept an open mind to improving both their arts and themselves. From a formal philosophical point of view, many of them follow the wisdom of Zen and Taoism – others just use common sense.

They devoted themselves to their arts, often in solitude, sometimes to the exclusion of other pursuits most of us take for granted. They worked themselves into extraordinary physical condition and stayed there. They ignored distractions and diversions and brought to their training a great deal of concentration. The best of them got as good as they could possibly get at performing and teaching their chosen art, and the rest of us watched them and, leading our "balanced lives," wondered how good we might have gotten at something had we devoted ourselves to whatever we did as ferociously as these masters embraced their arts. In that respect, they bear our dreams.

It would be wonderful to find a single martial artist who combined all the great qualities of these fighters, but that's impossible. That, however, was one of the things that inspired me to write this book. I wanted to preserve some things that were said a long time ago, of which not many people today are aware.

If you read carefully between the lines, you'll see that these men either trained hard to personify their personal idea of what it means to be "the best fighter in the world," or dedicated time and knowledge to create the most devastating martial arts system known to man. Interestingly enough, at the same time they also focused on how to use the martial arts to become better human beings. There are many links that once discovered open a wide spectrum of possibilities, not only to martial arts, but to a better existence as individuals.

The interviews often lasted as long as three or four hours. I would begin at their school and finish the conversation at a restaurant or coffee shop. A lot of information in these interviews had been never published and some had to be trimmed either at the master's request or edited to avoid creating senseless misunderstandings later on. It is not the questions that make an interview. An interview is either good or bad depending on the answers given. Considering the masters in this book, I had an easy job. My goal was to make these masters comfortable talking about their life and training – especially those who trained under the founders of original systems. In modern time, there are not many who have had the privilege of living and learning under the legendary founders.

"The masters are gone," many like to say. But as long as we keep their teachings in our heart, they will live forever. To understand the martial arts properly, it is necessary to take into account the philosophical and psychological methods, as well as the physical techniques. There is a deep distinction between a fighting system and a martial art, and a general feeling in the martial arts community is that the roots of the martial arts have been de-emphasized, neglected or totally abandoned. Martial arts are not a sport – they are very different. Someone who chooses to devote himself to a sport such as basketball, tennis, soccer or football – which is based on youth, strength and speed – chooses to die twice. When you can no longer do a certain sport, due to the lack of any one of those attributes, waking up in the morning without the activity and purpose that has been the center of your day for 25 years is spooky. Martial arts can and should be practiced for life. They are not sports, they are a "way of life."

A true martial arts practitioner, like an artist of any other kind – be this a musician, a painter, a writer or an actor – is expressing and leaving part of himself in every piece of his craft. The need for self-inspection and self-realization of "who" he is becomes the reason for a journey in search of that perfect technique, that great melody, that inspiring poetry, that amazing painting or that Academy Award performance. It is this motivation to reach that "impossible dream" that allows a simple individual to become an exceptional "artist" and "master" of his craft.

Many of the greatest teachers of the fighting arts share a commonly misunderstood teaching methodology. They know the words that could be used to pass their personal experience to their students have little or no meaning. They know that to try "self-discovery" in quantitative or empirical terms is a useless task. A great deal of knowledge and wisdom (the ability to use knowledge in a proper and correct way) comes from what is called the "oral traditions," which martial arts, like every other cultural aspect, has. These oral traditions have been always reserved for a certain kind of student and have been considered "secrets." I believe these secrets are such because only few very special students, perspicacious and with a keen sense of introspection, have the minds to attain them. As Alexandra David-Neel wrote: "It is not on the master that the secret depends but on the hearer. Truth learned from others is of no value. The only truth which is effective and of value is self-discovered…the teacher can only guide to the point of discovery." In the end, "The only secret is that there is no secret." Or, as Kato Tokuro, probably the greatest potter of the last century, a great art scholar, and the teacher of Spanish painter and sculptor Pablo Picasso (1881–1973) said: "The sole cause of secrets in craftsmanship is the student's inability to learn!"

As human beings, we are always tempted to follow straight-line logic towards ultimate self-improvement – but the truth is that there are no absolute truths that apply to all. You have to find your own way in life, whether it be in the martial arts, business or cherry picking. Whatever path you pursue, you have to distill your personal truths to what is right for you, according to your own life. The quest for perfection is actually quite imperfect and is not in tune with either human nature or human experience. To have any hope of attaining even a single perfection, you have to concentrate on a single pursuit and direct all your energies towards it. In this sense, perfection comes from appreciating your endeavors for their own sake – not to impress anyone – but for your own inner satisfaction and sense of accomplishment.

Martial arts are a large part of my life, and I draw inspiration from them, both spiritually and philosophically. I really don't know the "how" or the "why" of their affect on me, but I feel their influence in even my most mundane activities. It's not a complex thing in which I have to look deep into myself to find their influence. All human beings have sources or principles that keep them grounded, and the martial arts are mine. I believe that is when the term "way of life" becomes real. In bushido, the self-discipline required to pursue mastery is more important than mastery itself – the struggle is more important than the reward. A common thread throughout the lives of all the masters is their constant struggle towards self-mastery. They realized that life is an ongoing process and once you achieve all your goals you are as good as dead. But this process is not all driven by action. Often the greatest action is inaction, and the hardest voice to hear is the sound of your inner voice. You need to sit alone and collect your thoughts, free from all forms of technology and distraction, and just think. It is perhaps the only way to achieve mental and spiritual clarity.

I don't believe that great books are meant to be read fast. I've always thought that really good writing is timeless and that time spent reading doesn't detract anything from your life. Instead, it adds to it. So take your time. Approach the reading of this book with either the Zen "beginner's mind" or "empty cup" mentality and let the words of these great teachers help you to grow not only as a martial artist but as a human being as well.

# Carlos Baretto

## *The Best is Yet to Come*

CARLOS BARETTO IS WORLD-CLASS FIGHTER FROM BRAZIL WHO GIVES EVEN THE TOUGHEST OPPONENTS REASON TO PAUSE BEFORE FACING OFF AGAINST HIM. EQUALLY AT HOME ON THE GRAPPLING MAT OR IN THE NO-HOLDS-BARRED CAGE, BARETTO BUILT UPON HIS EARLY TRAINING IN JUDO AND MUAY THAI BY TAKING UP WITH THE CARLSON GRACIE COMPETITION TEAM AT THE AGE OF 17. UNDER THE MASTER TEACHER'S TUTELAGE, BARETTO WON NUMEROUS JIU-JITSU TITLES AND IS A THREE-TIME STATE CHAMPION, A TWO-TIME BRAZILIAN CHAMPION, AND A WORLD CHAMPION. WITH SEVERAL IMPRESSIVE NO-HOLDS-BARRED WINS, BARETTO IS NOW RETURNING TO HIS ROOTS AND WIDENING HIS FIGHTING SKILLS BY INCLUDING MUAY THAI, WRESTLING, AND JUDO INTO HIS PRACTICE ROUTINE TO AUGMENT HIS ALREADY IMPRESSIVE BRAZILIAN JIU-JITSU SUBMISSION SKILLS.

**Q: How did you first get started in martial arts?**
A: My first martial art was Thai boxing and then Liborio, one of the top members of the Carlson Gracie team at that time, introduced me to jiu-jitsu. He invited me to go and train at the Carlson Gracie Academy. So I went to see Carlson and try out jiu-jitsu and I became very good friends with one of the instructors there, Bolao. After a while Bolao went on to open his own school and I followed him because he was a very good instructor. Under Bolao I developed an even greater interest in jiu-jitsu. I began to lead classes and teach children's and self-defense classes and I went on to develop my skills as a teacher, also. Then Murrillo Bustamonte went on to open a school with Bolao, and then at this time that Murrillo also introduced me to no-holds-barred, or freestyle, jiu-jitsu.

**Q: How old were you when you started Thai boxing?**
A: I was 17. I did judo when I was a child – it is common in Brazil to do judo in school as a child – but I didn't really take it to any high level.

**Q: How long did you train in Thai boxing before you started jiu-jitsu?**
A: I trained muay Thai for about two years. But then when I started train-

*"I love muay Thai, and I respect muay Thai. At the time I started jiu-jitsu, however, there was a great rivalry between the different martial arts in Rio – especially jiu-jitsu and muay Thai. So I had to choose one or the other."*

ing jiu-jitsu I kept training muay Thai, also. But I gave up muay Thai completely after a few months. I love muay Thai and I respect muay Thai, but at the time I started jiu-jitsu there was a very great rivalry between the different martial arts in Rio – especially jiu-jitsu and muay Thai. So I had to choose one or the other. Today, though, the arts are coming together and the relationships between the different arts are much friendlier.

**Q: Do you ever use any muay Thai in your no-holds-barred fights?**
A: Yes, I do. I use a lot of knees, for example, from a standing position. I try to use the techniques in the muay Thai way. But I want to devote more time to muay Thai, now, because I feel good about it and I think I have a natural feel for it because I trained for it when I was younger.

**Q: When did you realize that you were good in jiu-jitsu? Were you a natural or did you have to work hard before you started to excel?**
A: I figured out that I had the talent and the ability at the purple belt level. Because before that, I had many other activities other than jiu-jitsu. I had school, I had work, and a lot of fun sports I did for enjoyment. But after I got the purple belt, I started devoting more time to jiu-jitsu. I got stronger and more dedicated and started doing more tournaments and doing well in them. What inspired me to devote this time to jiu-jitsu as a purple belt and start to see jiu-jitsu as a career was the example of Wallid

Ismail and what he accomplished as a full-time jiu-jitsu man. Although Wallid is not a Gracie, he was able to build a name for himself, get recognition, and he developed a full-time career in jiu-jitsu. So I thought that if he could do it then so could I. I wanted to follow in his footsteps as a professional.

**Q: What was your first big win that made people notice you?**
A: I cannot recall a first one because there were so many. It was more a sequence of victories that all contributed to bringing me to the attention of the public. I was a three-time state champion, I was twice the Brazilian champion and I was also the world champion. So all the victories combined, I think, made people start to remember my name and notice me.

**Q: Do you feel that you're still improving and getting better?**
A: I think that I'm getting better on many different levels, not just in jiu-jitsu. I'm improving my technique, I'm getting stronger and quickly physically, and also I'm improving psychologically – my mind is improving and gettin stronger. So all those three aspects are improving for me, all the time. For example, in the world of no-holds-barred competition today, I feel I have a lot to offer to any promoter or fighting event. My guard, for example, I consider the best guard in the world. I have a guard that is hard to pass and very dangerous to my opponents for potential submissions. I have worked hard at it and so I'm happy of my progress in that area.

*"My guard, for example, is the best guard in the world. I have a guard that is hard to pass and very dangerous to my opponents for potential submissions. I have worked hard at it and I'm happy with my progress in that area."*

*"In vale tudo, the technique has to be more objective and more offensive. You can't wait for your opponent to make a mistake, because while you're waiting there, he is pounding you even if you have him between your legs."*

**Q: Is your style of jiu-jitsu passive or active?**
A: I would rather do the guard, and use that to tap out my opponent – I am most comfortable there. I love to fight from the bottom.

**Q: Do you use that same strategy in no-holds-barred?**
A: It is completely different – the two are not related at all. In sport jiu-jitsu the guard is more loose – it's a relaxed game. In vale tudo, the technique has to be more objective and more offensive. You can't wait so much for your opponent to make a mistake because while you're waiting there, he is pounding you even if you have him between your legs. You can get hurt from the guard – especially if you're fighting a really strong wrestler with a very good base. Strength does matter and so does size in vale tudo. So you can't allow yourself to take punishment and you're better off attacking and keeping your opponent off-guard and reacting to you, instead of you reacting to him.

**Q: Describe your fight against Mark Kerr at Abu Dhabi.**
A: The main reason I went to Abu Dhabi was out of respect for Prince Tahnoon, because he wanted to see me fight. I had just arrived from a major fight against Brandon Lee Hinkle, which I won. But during the fight I was taken down and in the process I injured my shoulder. So when I arrived to Abu Dhabi, I was not able to train like I should have because I was getting therapy on my shoulder. Although I was not able to train, I

also did not expect to fight Mark Kerr in the first match in Abu Dhabi. I didn't know I was going to face him and so I did not formulate a strategy to fight him. The doctor at Abu Dhabi examined me a half-hour before the fight and suggested that I take a cortisone shot to the shoulder. I felt during the fight that Mark Kerr was very strong, and had a very solid base. I think that if I had been training to my full potential before the fight that I would have been able to tap him out.

The reason I didn't enter the Absolute division was because I had taken many shots of cortisone. So I spoke to Carlson Gracie and he told me that he did not want me to take so many shots because it would not be good for my health. So he suggested that I not fight anymore and I honored his wishes.

*"I use boxing and muay Thai as a regular part of my training. I'm also emphasizing wrestling takedowns and judo throws. Then I use jiu-jitsu for submissions that I learn from Carlson Gracie."*

**Q: What's your typical training routine?**
A: I use boxing and muay Thai as a regular part of my training. I'm also emphasizing wrestling takedowns and judo throws. Then I use jiu-jitsu for submissions that I learn from Carlson Gracie. My ultimate goal is to increase my training schedule from four hours per day to six hours per day. I enjoy lifting weights to help my power. For my endurance I like to run twice a week, and the swim three times a week. When I run, I do it at a medium pace for 40 minutes – so I go by time, not distance. In the swimming pool I use a method called water running and deep running. Water running is a method where I put on a buoyant vest and then run in the pool without touching the bottom of the pool. Deep running is where I

"Carlson is an intelligent and open-minded man with a lot of experience in no-holds-barred. He realizes that you must mix styles and that there is no more space for a specialist in the martial arts fighting world. You can't just concentrate on one thing."

am submersed. I used a diving vest with lead weights to keep myself on the bottom. Then I swim underwater from one end to the other. The bottom one is more for strength and the one on top of the water is for my wind. It is the best workout for conditioning that I have ever seen. Also, there is little stress on the joints and so you don't get injured.

**Q: Does Carlson Gracie approve of all the cross-training outside of jiu-jitsu?**
A: Carlson is an intelligent and open-minded man with a lot of experience in no-holds-barred. He realizes that you must mix styles and that there is no more space for a specialist in the martial arts fighting world. You can't just concentrate on one thing. You have to be able to do it all. Everyone knows what is coming now, and most fighters know a little of everything. So you have to prepare for everything.

**Q: Do you prefer vale tudo or jiu-jitsu?**
A: Vale tudo, without a doubt. Sport jiu-jitsu is more of a friendly thing for relaxation. Vale tudo is more extreme, with more possibilities. You have to be stronger mentally and physically.

**Q: What makes someone a champion?**

A: It is a combination of physical ability, mental ability, and spiritual ability. The spirituality comes in, and is a very important factor, because it allows you to see things objectively and to recognize that your opponent is not your enemy. Within the context of the fighting sports, nobody is better than anyone else. Each person is trained and wants to win and what is going to determine the winner is the willpower, the organization and execution of your fight plan, and the strength of the training. The winner will also be the athlete who has a good combination of experience. You can train all you want, and you can spend hours sparring in your studio, but you don't know what you have inside until you step onto the mat, or into the ring, in a real competition or fight. That experience of looking inside yourself, and seeing just who you really are, is what will determine if you are a winner or a loser.

*"Within the context of the fighting sports, nobody is better than anyone else. Each person is trained and wants to win. What is going to determine the winner is the willpower, the organization and execution of the fight plan, and the strength of the training."*

# Grappling Techniques

While on the ground, Carlos Baretto faces his opponent (1). When the opponent tries to get closer, Baretto grabs his hand (2) and pulls the arm (3). Notice that the opponent's arm is securely between Baretto's legs (3). Meanwhile, Baretto swings his body to the right so he can grab the opponent's left leg (4). This disrupts the opponent's balance, sending him on a one-way trip to the floor. This provides Baretto the opportunity to apply an armlock (5).

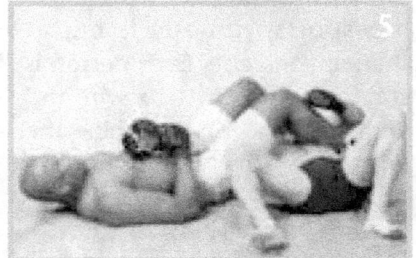

The opponent is not only on top, he has also planted his left knee squarely on Baretto's stomach (1). Using his left hand, Barrreto latches onto the opponent's left ankle (2) and then sits upright (3). Using his right hand, Baretto applies a nasty figure four anklelock (4).

## BARETTO

Baretto faces his opponent (1). The aggressor unleashes a punch with his right hand, and Baretto throws up a block (2). Baretto immediately drops his right knee (3) and then quickly circles to the left, positioning himself behind the opponent (4). Baretto hooks the opponent's right leg (5), pushes forward and brings him down (6). This provides Baretto with an opportunity to hammer his opponent with devastating elbows (7). After softening his opponent, Baretto drops down and applies a choke (8).

# Grappling Techniques

Baretto faces off with his opponent (1). To close the distance, Baretto blasts the opponent's front leg (2). Then, he follows with a solid right punch (3), circles to the right (4), positions himself behind the opponent (5) and takes his opponent to the ground (6). To get the final submission, Baretto puts his left knee on the opponent's stomach (7).

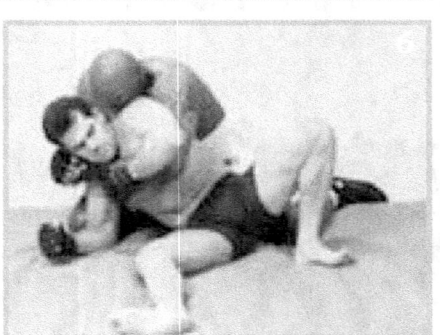

While on his back, Carlos Baretto faces his opponent (1). As soon as the opponent punches, Baretto slides inside, moves to the left (2) and quickly positions himself on the opponent's back (3). Baretto then attacks with a barrage of elbows (4-6).

# VITOR BELFORT

## A Force of One

Vitor Belfort is one of NHB's premier attractions. "The Phenom" as he is rightly called, burst onto the no-holds-barred scene in 1996 at the age of 18 with a 12 second KO over Jon Hess in SuperBrawl 2. He followed that up with three straight KO's in the UFC before losing to Randy Couture in UFC 13. fter a submission victory over Joe Charles in the UFCJ, many felt that Belfort had perhaps lost his explosive punching power. In his next fight against the "unbeatable" Vanderlei Silva in Brazil, he was considered "washed up" at the age of 19 and was widely expected to be crushed. Someone was crushed that night in Rio — but it wasn't Belfort. In a shocking turn of events, Belfort destroyed Silva in only 44 seconds in one of no-holds-barred most famous upsets. With this victory, The Phenom proved that he was more dangerous than ever and that reports of his demise had been greatly exaggerated — he hasn't lost since.

With his sculptured physique and intense fighting style, many have the impression that Belfort is nothing more than a mindless automaton of destruction. Nothing could be further from the truth. While possessing a confidence that a top athlete must have in order to compete at the highest level of any sport, Belfort is well aware of the ephemeral nature of fame and knows that anyone, on any given night, can be beaten. This feeling of vulnerability has led Belfort to train furiously in boxing, wrestling, jiu-jitsu, and judo. With such a diverse mix of skills, Belfort is unpredictable and virtually impossible to formulate an effective fight plan against.

With all of Belfort's successes, though, it is important to remember that he has not yet hit his fighting prime. "I'm just beginning," Belfort says. "People forget that I'm very young. I'm still growing and learning and developing. I'm going to get a lot better."

**Q: How did you get involved in martial arts?**
A: I got involved when I was 8 years old. I started fighting judo. Martial arts in Brazil was big all the time. Then I started learning jiu-jitsu with Jacare

"I think that God just blessed me with natural ability. I was just 18 years old for my first fight in Hawaii. Then I went to the UFC right after that and won the tournament. From then on my life has just been blessed by a higher power."

when I was 10 years old. I studied with him for a year then I left to train with one of Carlson Gracie's students because his school was closer to my house. But when I didn't do well in school, my mother took me out of jiu-jitsu and I started training in boxing. There used to be a stamp the teacher would give you to show that you had gone to school that day. I stole it so I could stamp myself, and I just went to the gym and trained boxing for a year. When my father found out he said, "Let's sit down and talk. If you want to be a fighter you have to behave in school, and if you don't then I'm going to punish you and you're not going to be able to do sports."

At that time I did a lot of sports as well as martial arts. My father was a volleyball player and my mother was also athletic. They always thought that I should do sports to keep me out of drugs and gangs and trouble. They wanted me to have sports idols instead of following bad influences. So then when I started back in jiu-jitsu and wrestling, after my father told me to behave myself, I started to do very well. I think that God just blessed me with natural ability. I was just 18 years old for my first fight in Hawaii. Then I went to the UFC right after that and won the UFC tournament. From then on my life has just been blessed by a higher power.

**Q: You have trained in judo, boxing, jiu-jitsu, and wrestling. Which of those do you enjoy the most?**
A: I like jiu-jitsu the best, followed by wrestling, and then boxing. I like judo the least because it has too many rules. The first three are all fun because you can personally express yourself without being limited by excess rules. It really just depends on the moment as to which one I like the best. Sometimes I feel like I want to box, sometimes I feel like wrestling, and sometimes I want to do jiu-jitsu.

**Q: How did your first fight happen?**
A: I was working out and training at a fitness center, and a friend who managed the club was one of the sponsors of the fighting event. His name is Donny Bender. I was supposed to fight in *Battlecade*, in *Extreme Fighting*, but I was so young that I couldn't fight because I was not yet 18. So when I turned 18 Donny knew I wanted to fight and asked me, so I said yeah. He said they were going to put up an appearance fee for me to fight. But I said instead of an appearance fee why didn't they just make the purse winner take all. So that's what they did and I was successful in that fight against John Hess in just a few seconds. I thank the Lord for the victory, and from that day my life just went up. Hess was a veteran fighter at that time, and I was just a kid. But I really punished him. I took him down, I put my knee on his belly, and then I knocked him out.

*"I like jiu-jitsu the best, followed by wrestling and then boxing. It really just depends on the moment as to which one I like the best. Sometimes I feel like I want to box, sometimes I feel like wrestling and sometimes I want to do jiu-jitsu."*

**Q: When you went into the UFC, did you have any idea you would become an overnight sensation?**
A: I knew that I had a lot of skills that people in the sport didn't have at that time, because I could punch and also grapple. A lot of people came at me to take me down because they thought I was just a puncher. You never know what is going to happen, of course, but I had a feeling that I would do well. I always say that tomorrow is a promissory note, yesterday is a cancelled check, and today is cash on hand. That is the way that we should all live our lives. When I put myself into a fight – and I really concentrate on it – I know that I can do well. But when my mind is not there, that is when I don't do as well as I should and have a bad time.

**Q: You're generally considered to have the most natural talent of any fighter. But some also say that you don't live up to that talent. Is that because you lose focus?**
A: The problem is that I get bored with the sport sometimes. That is what happened to me in the past. I'm not going to blame other people for

*"I always say that tomorrow is a promissory note, yesterday is a cancelled check and today is cash on hand. That is the way that we should all live our lives."*

what I've done or haven't done. I'm guilty. If I don't want anything to happen in my life that distracts me, then I have that choice – I decide. But when I had my loss to Randy Couture, I was totally out of focus and totally mixed up. I had a girlfriend at the time who caused a lot of confusion in my life and I was very young and I didn't know how to deal with it in a mature way. Also, I was still very young and things had happened very fast for me – too fast. Sometimes in our lives we make mistakes. And when we recognize that mistakes were made then we can correct them. God gives us free will so we can do what we want. And sometimes we forget to ask God what we should be doing. I think it is important to keep in mind that somebody, someplace, somewhere is better than you – more talented, wealthier, whatever. You have to be humble and not think that you're the best. A true champion is one who doesn't think he is the best, but yet others do. So when my mind is not there for a fight, then Vitor is not there and anything can happen. And that is what happened in the first Randy Couture fight and also the Sakuraba fight.

**Q: Many feel that when you're truly focused that you're nearly unbeatable. Do you feel that way?**
A: Nobody is unbeatable – that is the thing that I know for sure and that I remind myself of. But I think that for a guy to beat me, he really has to on his game that day and that God has to want him to win. But it will be a brawl. But when I'm not in shape – when I'm not 100 percent – then I could have trouble. The thing is that I've only fought good guys, you know. Most all of the guys I've fought have been the best and the guys I've lost to have been the best – Randy and Sakuraba. So when you fight the best, and you're not all there, then you can't expect to do well.

**Q: When you fought Sakuraba it seemed like you dominated the fight in the early going, then you just stopped fighting. What happened?**

A: A lot of people don't know that two weeks before the fight I had knee surgery. But I had made a commitment that I was going to fight and I thought that it would look bad for my career if I didn't. So I decided that I would step into the ring no matter what. A couple of months before that fight I was supposed to fight in the UFC, and I dropped out of that because of another health problem. So I felt that if I dropped out of two fights in a row that people would think badly of me. So I felt that I had to do it, even though I probably shouldn't. But people don't know what goes on in my life day to day. They only see the headlines. So I just decided to try to do my best. I didn't have time for my knee to really heal, I didn't have time to train, and I was really out of shape. I knew all that but I still went in to try to win.

*"Some fighters are just too cocky. I don't see cockiness as a sign of confidence."*

But to make it even worse, at the last minute Pride made me lose 20 pounds. That was not in the contract, but they made me do it anyway because Sakuraba was afraid to fight me heavy. He respects me a lot and so he would only fight me if I went to 199 pounds. They weighed me at 6pm the day before the fight and then they told me that if I wasn't 199 by the next day the fight was off. I was scared because I had flown all the way from Brazil and I needed the money. So even though the weight limit wasn't in the contract I signed, I decided to do it. In that way I felt that they set me up. When Sakuraba fought Royler Gracie, Pride didn't make Sakuraba lose 20 or 30 pounds the night before the fight. But I didn't want to disappoint my fans. So I lost the weight mainly just from sitting in a sauna and sweating.

Then in the first three minutes of the fight I broke my hand so badly that the bone was sticking out and I couldn't punch for the rest of the fight. But I still didn't quit and tried to grapple him. But he didn't want to

*"So, hopefully God will bless me so that I will be able to compete at the peak of my career and get into the ring and do my best. All I want is to live up to my potential – whatever that turns out to be."*

grapple, all he wanted to do was to score points and that's what he did. He was scared to grapple me but he fought smart and just scored points – that's how he fights. I tried to get a rematch after that fight so I could get in shape and train at the correct weight, but they would never give me a rematch.

**Q: It seems funny that he would fight Royler Gracie who was 50 pounds lighter.**
A: I have a lot of respect for Royler for doing that. Royler is a warrior. He didn't care how much Sakuraba outweighed him. But Sakuraba didn't want to fight me without making me lose 20 pounds. I was there with him and his manager. A lot of people who were there saw it. I went to the sauna with a jacket and just sat there. But I had to lose the weight or else I would not have gotten paid and I would have disappointed my fans. So I just wanted to be professional. To be fair to Sakuraba I don't know if this came from him. He doesn't speak English so the demand for me to drop the weight could have come from his manager. Sakuraba has fought big guys before in the Grand Prix – so you never know. But I know that whatever the reason he didn't want to step into the ring with a weight difference – but I have a lot of respect for Royler for getting into the ring with him.

**Q: It seems like every time people give up on you, you come back and surprise them.**
A: When I'm ready, I'm ready – I feel that I can take anyone. I show a lot of things. But you know, no matter what you do people will still not be satisfied. Every time there will be someone saying, "Vitor just got lucky." That's what fighting is all about. So I guess that I just got lucky 9 times in all my wins. I'm just beginning my career. I want people to know that. But I think that I should get a little more respect. I respect all fighters – even the one who are just beginning. I respect them because the fighting business is just

like having a job, you know? You have to be humble to every one who is involved – from the guy who puts up the ring to the promoters who put up the money. I respect everybody so I think that people should respect me. Some fighters are just too cocky. I don't see cockiness as a sign of confidence; I see cockiness as a sign of fear. When you have fear you're cocky, but when you're confident you're humble.

**Q: Do you feel that you've hit your fighting prime yet?**
A: In my mind, I feel that I'm just beginning – that I'm still growing and learning an developing. I exploded young – just like Mike Tyson. But Tyson spent the best years of his career in jail. He was a phenomenon in his time. He didn't even hit his peak during the time he really dominated everyone. And the time that he would have been in his prime he spent in jail. The only difference between me and Tyson is that we are in different sports and have different personalities – but our situations are very similar.

*"Vitor Belfort is unpredictable. Right now, my mind is totally on business. I want to bring the sport up, make money for it and for myself, and help to bring in new fans. The most important thing is the fans."*

I respect Mike Tyson a lot as a fighter. I don't know him personally and I never met him. But as a fighter I respect him so much because he exploded as a fighter at the age of 19 or 20, the same as me. So I think I understand him a little. But I'm different in the fact that I'm not going to spend time in jail, of course. I'm a very humble guy and I don't see myself getting set up to get into that kind of trouble. So, hopefully God will bless me so that I will be able to compete at the peak of my career and set into the ring and do my best. All I want is to live up to my potential – whatever that turns out to be.

**Q: Was there any fights in the UFC that you were afraid you were going to lose?**
A: The first time I went into the UFC I was very young – I had just turned

*"When I am in the U.S., I try to improve my skills in many different areas because there are a lot of good guys outside jiu-jitsu. So I train in boxing, wrestling and whatever."*

19. I had to fight two fights in a and so of course I was nervous. God just blessed me that day and I won. Of course, everybody gets nervous but sometimes you get more and sometimes you get less. In that first fight in the UFC I was nervous and then against Sakuraba I was nervous because I knew that I wasn't in shape. I knew I could dominate him, but when my hand broke and I couldn't punch that made me nervous.

**Q: When you fought Vanderlei Silva did it shake your confidence that everyone thought you were going to lose?**

A: I never lost confidence in myself but some people thought I did. My game is to sometimes play tricks on the other fighter. Sometimes I play like I think I will lose just so I can come out and surprise my opponent. But at the time I had a really bad headache because of a medicine I had taken. And people thought that because of that Vitor was scared. But I wasn't scared, I was just afraid to fight with the headache because I didn't know what was causing it. Anytime anything touched my head, it would make my brain throb – so of course that worried me. And people made a big thing about that. But the truth is that I was really confident about the fight itself and it showed in what I did to him. I walked through him. The day before the fight they asked Vanderlei what he thought and he said, "I'm going to knock Vitor out in 5 minutes." When they asked me though, I just said, "I think this is going to be a tough match so let's just see what happens." I didn't talk a lot with my mouth, but I just let my fists talk for me – I talk a lot through my fists. I don't need to talk outside the ring because what I do inside of it speaks for me. Talking trash is not my style. I don't need to impress anyone. I have done a lot of things in the sport and people know what I can do. But some people always think that you have something more to prove. I don't have to prove anything to anyone. I just want to step into the ring, do my best for the fans and give a good show. I fight to put on a good show and I fight for myself.

**Q: You're known as NHB's most exciting puncher. Have you always had fast hands?**
A: Well, of course I train to have fast hands but a lot of it is a gift – and I thank God for that. There are a lot of fighters in the world, but not a lot of exciting fighters. That's what I train for – to put on an exciting fight. But a lot of my fighting tools I haven't even shown yet. People are still going to see a lot of new and exciting things from me in the years to come. My career is just beginning and I have so much more to show the NHB fans. It's just a matter of time. When the time is right then you're going to see it.

**Q: Most people think of you as a pure striker. How do you think of yourself?**
A: I take every fight one at a time. In my recent Pride fights I've stayed in the guard and punched people out from there because that is how the fight went. I can dominate a fight from many positions and control it from beginning to the end. I just did that in my last two Pride fights to show that I could do that. Maybe in my next fight I will work submissions or maybe I will stand and punch. I like to be unpredictable so my opponents don't know what to expect from me. Just like Tyson. When he steps into the ring we don't know what can happen – he can even bite, you know? Anything from Tyson will be exciting. But some guys when they step into the ring we know what they're going to do and we know it is going to be boring. So with me, people don't know if I'm going to grapple, or wrestle, or box, or do jiu-jitsu. People don't know. Vitor Belfort is unpredictable. Right now, my mind is totally on business. I want to bring the sport up, make money for it and for myself, and help to bring in new fans. The most

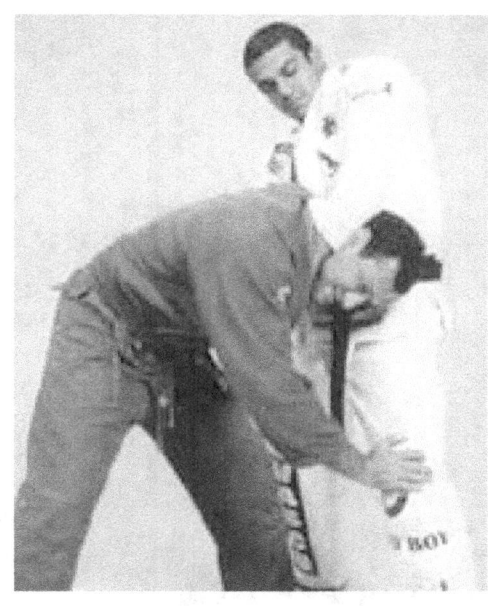

*"I think that we're here [in life] to learn. We learn until the day that we go out of this planet and move on. You don't need to be rich or famous to live good. I want to help people in ways that money cannot buy. Maybe by seeing what I do, they can see that they too can achieve their goals. I just want to live a good life."*

*"Right now, my mind is totally on business. I want to bring the sport up, make money for it and for myself, and help to bring in new fans. The most important thing is the fans. You can fight to win, but you had better fight for the fans, too. If you win the fight but lose the fans, you've lost everything."*

important thing is the fans. You can fight to win, but you had better fight for the fans, too. If you win the fight but yet lose the fans then you've lost everything. Better to lose the fight and win the fans. Winning the fans is what drives the sport forward. Of course, my goal is to win the fight and win the fans.

**Q: Against Gilbert Yvel, many said you would lose. But yet you showed enough to win and to prove your doubters wrong.**
A: I can say that I was only fighting one strategy in that fight because I knew that I could control him on the ground. So I did that from the beginning to the end. I knew that I was going to win that fight. You don't know you're going to win for sure, of course. You have to step into the ring and do your best. I'm ready for anything.

**Q: Many people think of you as a pure jiu-jitsu and vale tudo fighter. But didn't you concentrate on boxing for a while?**
A: I always loved no-holds-barred but at that time the sport was going so bad, people were treating the sport like garbage. Using it just as a way to make money and then get out. I don't think that way. I think we've got to make money of course, but first of all make our fans and the people that love the sport happy. Too many promoters were not thinking that way; they were not treating the fighters right. They just pick-up a fighter and say, "Hey, man, wanna make some money? Just come here and fight." The rules were so nasty, so bloody, so bad and I didn't like that. I said, "Hey, that's not what I want for life and that's not what I want for the sport." What I want for the sport is for it to get big again. When I decided to go to the Olympics, one week before the trails I was hurt and I couldn't go to the trials. So I missed my chance. Then Pride offered me a fight right around that time. So I said OK. So I trained for two weeks and I went to fight. And I was so happy because Pride has good rules. Now I have the chance to go

professional boxing. You see, I want to prove that I can do both. I know I can.

**Q: What is your training like now?**
A: I train Monday though Saturday. We mix it up with kicking, punching, grappling, wrestling. We put it all together and train each other. I try to do a little bit of everything everyday. Some days we do guard, kicks, and punches. Other days we do passing the guard, takedowns, and arm bars. I think that if you mix it up every day then you don't get bored and it keeps the training fun.

**Q: Do you train with any one person in particular?**
A: Just whoever is there. It depends on the day. When I am in the U.S. I try to improve my skills in many different areas because there are a lot of good guys outside jiu-jitsu. So I train boxing, wrestling, and whatever. I don't limit myself. Some schools only want you to train at their school, but I am not like that. I like to learn from everybody in order to improve. The key of training is that you can't have too many rules. You can't say don't train here, or don't train there. Of course, I'm not going to train my opponent, or the opponent of someone on my team. But I can train with other guys. I don't have rules like that.

*"I want the sport to get big again. When I decided to go to the Olympics, I hurt my shoulder one week before the trials, so I couldn't go. I missed my chance. Then Pride offered me a fight right around that time. So, I said, 'OK.' I trained for two weeks, and I went to fight. I was so happy because Pride has good rules."*

In the group of people I train with, we don't compete that way when we train. We think more about technique than about not tapping. On a certain day I might tap to a white belt if I'm in a certain position and want to put myself in danger and see if I can get out of it. We want to learn from each other so we don't have a lot of ego in the school.

*"The key to training is that you can't have too many rules. You can't say, 'Don't train here.' Or, 'Don't train there.' Of course, I'm not going to train my opponent or the opponent of someone on my team. But I can train with other guys. I don't have rules like that."*

**Q: How many hours total do you train each day?**

A: Four, six, or eight hours depending on what I'm training for – submission or vale tudo or boxing or whatever. It varies according to how close my fight is also. There are a lot of variable. Like I say, I train hard but I try to be smart and flexible. I control my training, I don't let my training control me. If I'm hurt I take it easy. If I'm tired I rest. If I'm sick I don't push it. But if I'm healthy and feeling good then I will train like a madman. I like to train with Paulo Caruso for my overall physical training. A lot of the fighters there train with him for strength, fitness, endurance, balance, and agility. Everyone who trains with him improves. I trust what he tells me 100 percent. He is the most important of all my trainers. With him I do specific training for fighting. We don't just lift weights, for example, we do specific types of training that works individual motions that you would use in the ring. He was a black belt in jiu-jitsu, then he got degrees in physical training – so he really understands the fight game and what fighters need.

**Q: Do you follow a special diet?**

A: I try to eat healthy but I do eat my junk food, too. I'm young so I don't worry about that so much. A lot of the fighters are older than me and so they worry about their diet because they need every advantage. When I'm older I will probably start to worry about it. I'm a regular person so I eat normal. The only thing I avoid is a lot of sugar and a lot of fat. I don't take a lot of supplements. Because I have a strong body a lot of people assume that I lift weights. But I don't lift anymore than I do anything else. I just try to train what I need to be a good fighter, not just to look good.

**Q: Do you think the sport of NHB can grow?**
A: I think it can as long a people work together. If everybody does a little bit to help and to bring the sport up, the sport is going to be the biggest thing in the world. Like the movie *Gladiator*. We *are* the real gladiators of the modern world. We have to let people know that this sports exists.

**Q: Which fighters do you like to watch?**
A: I like to watch Igor Vovchanchyn, Gilbert Yvel, Sakuraba, Vanderlei Silva, Tito Ortiz, Frank Shamrock, Coleman, Renzo Gracie, Pedro Rizzo – I like a lot of fighters. I'm a fan of the sport as well as someone who competes. They are all so good. When I was a kid growing up I really liked Liborio, and Murillo and a lot of people I used to train with who were black belts when I

*"I liked Rickson Gracie at that time. He was training and fighting a lot. Everyone looked up to him. I learned a lot from watching all the top fighters. Royce, of course, was a big inspiration when the UFC first started. For me, Renzo Gracie is great. He always fights the tough guys – the top guys – and he doesn't care who he fights."*

was not. I still like them a lot. When I was a kid I saw them as an inspiration. And not just them. I liked Rickson Gracie at that time, who was training and fighting a lot. Everyone looked up to him. I learned a lot from watching all the top fighters. Royce, of course, was a big inspiration when the UFC first started. For me, Renzo Gracie is great. He always fights the tough guys – the top guys – and he doesn't care who he fights. He'll fight anyone. I really like him. He doesn't lie about his record and he doesn't make excuses when he loses. He just does his thing like everyone else.

**Q: Did you feel a little like a Gracie, from being with Carlson so long?**
A: Of course, a little. I was training with him before vale tudo really took off. But I think the mentality of some of the Gracie family is wrong. Some don't like to show all the techniques, they don't like you to train hard with them, they don't want you to train with anyone else or they'll kick you out

*"Some don't like to show all the techniques. They don't like you to train hard with them, and they don't want you to train with anyone else or they'll kick you out of their school; that is not right. Jiu-jitsu should be shared – not hidden. Otherwise, how can it improve?"*

of their school – that is not right. Jiu-jitsu should be shared not hidden. Otherwise how can it improve? Just because someone is from another school, why is it wrong to train with them? So what if he is a wrestler or a sambo player and you are a guy who does jiu-jitsu. So what? Let's train hard, fight hard, and let the best guy win. Afterwards, lets have a drink. They are my opponents, not my enemies. I like that they are good because they give me someone to fight who helps me to make money. They let me enjoy my life. I have to love my opponent for what he does for me. They support my family and my needs. I want to win but I don't want to hurt anyone.

**Q: Is it difficult to live up to your reputation?**
A: I know people expect me to get a 10 second knockout every time I fight, but I try not to think about that. Everybody has an ego but I don't like to think that I'm great or wonderful or unbeatable. I like to remind myself that I'm just beginning – that I have a lot to learn still. I try to think of myself as a regular person and to live like one. I don't want to believe my own press. I want to fight and to not be part of the hype about myself. I'll leave that to other people – to the promoters and the writers. I'm just a guy who wants to live simply, enjoy life, and prove I can do good.

**Q: Where would you like to be in five years?**
A: In five years I would like to be regarded as someone who increased his learning in life and helped others to realize they could also achieve their

goals. I think that we're here in life to learn. We learn until the day that we go out of this planet and move on. I want to enjoy and learn and I want people to look at me and say, "That guy, you know, he was a great fighter and also a great person." You don't need to be rich or famous to live good. Sometimes the rich live worse than the poor. If you're rich inside with family and friends then it doesn't matter how much money you have. I want to help people in ways that money cannot buy. Maybe by seeing what I do, they can see that they can achieve their goals also. I just want to live a good life. Just don't forget that tomorrow is a promissory note, yesterday is a cancelled check, and today is cash on hand.

**Q: Tell us about your first fight with Randy Couture.**
A: I wasn't focused, and I didn't take the fight seriously. I really thought it would be an easy fight. At that time, my head was big, I was young and I was not very mature. I was also surrounded by a lot of people who were not necessarily good people, including a girlfriend. On top of everything else, I had an intestinal problem that I had been fighting for more than a year. This is something that I got from eating raw fish or from a salad. I had all those problems when I fought him. On the night that I fought him, it took me awhile to come out of the dressing room. Some people thought that I was deliberately stalling so he'd tighten up, but I actually was in the restroom because of the health problem. I had a big problem with that. At that time of my life, I thought I could take care of anything that happened, but I learned a lesson from that loss. Things happen for a reason. Randy beat me. Afterward, my mother told me, "You see? Randy has God in his life. You should look for God." She told me I was a nice kid, but my head was too big and I wasn't focused. There were so many things wrong in my life. But Randy deserved that win, and I can't take anything from him. It was the worst time in my life.

**Q: Then you lost to Sakuraba.**
A: Yes, I lost to Sakuraba. I actually had a broken hand during that fight, but I didn't tell my corner. It's not an excuse, but I just wanted people to know.

**Q: What was your strategy for the second fight with Couture?**
A: The same. I studied his game, and I knew that he could put stuff together and add things to his game. Thus, I had to be well prepared. I also had to be able to change [my strategy] at any time during the fight.

People say I was lucky in that fight, but that was not luck. He was lucky that punch didn't land on his face. Otherwise, he would have been out. I'm not taking anything away from him, but I don't like it when people try to take my credibility away, especially because I worked hard. I deserved that belt. I like him and respect him a lot. He's a legend of the sport, and he's been there for a long time.

**Q: Did you consider – even for a second – that you would have an advantage over Couture because of his age?**
A: I never think I have an advantage when I fight anyone. It's important to stay humble and focused. I just think about getting ready and not getting too confident. I just want to focus on what I'm doing and do it right. I'll let my actions in the ring do all the talking.

**Q: How difficult was it for you to stay focused on your fight with Couture with your sister missing?**
A: Very hard. Very difficult. The only way I made it through was in the strength that God gave me. He blessed me to do my job and fulfill my responsibility. In addition to that, I had a commitment. Besides, we all have problems, but these problems should not affect other people. It was through the power that God gave me that I was able to get through all these problems. In fact, he guided me from my worst days as a professional athlete to the best thing that could happen in my life – becoming a world champ. I'm thankful for that. It's also my responsibility to train hard so that I can give 100 percent when I step in the ring.

**Q: Why did you decide to fight with so much on your mind?**
A: I had a commitment to do it. A commitment with the fans, the promoters and even Randy [Couture]. The first thing I did was pray to God to give me an answer. I even asked my friends and officials with the UFC. They all said there are much more important things than fighting. Dana White [of the UFC] said he understood what I was going through and told me that life is much more important. I told him that I understood his concern, but I made a commitment, and I trained hard for five months. Besides, this is my dream and my sister's dream. I am sure that wherever she is she supports and wants me to do my best. I know that she wants the best thing for me.

**Q: Did you ever think that you would hold the UFC title again?**
A: Of course. That is why I fight and train. We are all capable of doing what we want. All it takes is hard work, discipline, determination, desire and faith in God. Everything is possible.

**Q: Your emphasis on spirituality is new. How did it come about?**
A: There always have been a lot of people, including my mother, who talked to me about Jesus Christ. That is what Jesus does. He surrounds you. You can run, but you cannot hide from him. At that time, I had a lot of people talking about Jesus, but I didn't want to hear. Anyway, one night I was drinking at a party when some guy came up to me and said, "Jesus Christ loves you man. Stop the bad things in your life." That is how Jesus talks to us. It's not a personal conversation.

**Q: How does fighting in the UFC compare to fighting in Pride?**
A: I like both and both are good, but there are some differences. Japan is an awesome country, and they provide lots of support. The fighters are respected and recognized on the street. Some do commercials and get sponsors. The fighters can't walk on the street. The money is bigger than what we get in America, too.

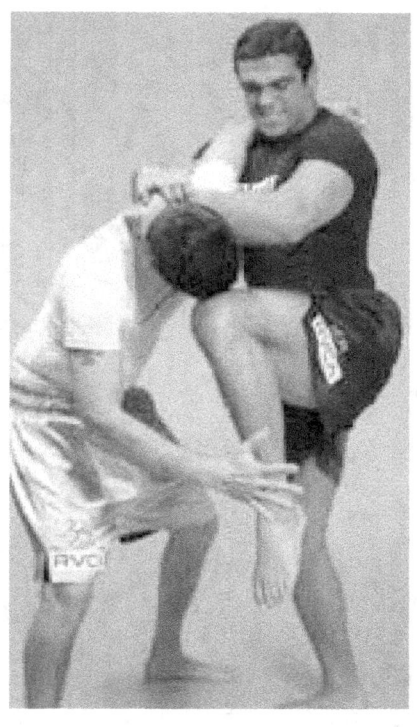

*"Japan is an awesome country, and they provide lots of support. The fighters are respected and recognized on the street. Some do commercials and get sponsors. The fighters can't walk on the street. The money is bigger than what we get in America, too."*

**Q: Do you like the shorter rounds or fewer and longer rounds?**
A: I like both, but the longer rounds give me more time to work. The longer rounds enable me to save energy, but they do require more stamina. In the UFC, you have to be in good shape because they bring the fight right on. In Pride, you have more time to work and the fans understand the fight when you're on the ground. In America, the fans want to see the KO. I fit pretty well in both.

# Grappling Masters

*"It's important to remember that the body is not a computer. You have to learn how to make your body work best. I like to work on my weaknesses. In fact, everything I have is a weakness. I want to improve things that a lot of people don't care about."*

**Q: Have you been training more stand-up or grappling lately?**
A: I have been trying to do both on a daily basis. I spend four hours per day training. It's important to remember that the body is not a computer. You have to learn how to make your body work best. I like to work on my weaknesses. In fact, everything I have is a weakness. I want to improve things that a lot of people don't care about. For example, we all have our good sides. So I work on my right [or weak] side. This lets me change sides any time during a fight. When you have a weakness, you improve something that you did not have in your game. So every time I add to my game.

**Q: What is the best mix of skills for an NHB fighter today to have?**
A: Boxing, jiu-jitsu, Thai boxing and a little wrestling.

**Q: Do you work on hand speed or is it entirely genetics?**
A: When we are born, we all have our own gift. That is the one that God gave me, and I thank him for that. I do work on it a little, but it is mostly a gift.

**Q: Do you follow the big submission and jiu-jitsu tournaments anymore?**
A: Sometimes. A good friend of mine, Leonardo Vieira, is my training and business partner, and he competes in these. He's also one of the guys who gets me ready for a fight. He's an incredible fighter. I admire him for his size and weight. He's also unpredictable. I like people who add things to their game.

**Q: Do you think you'll ever enter a submission tournament again?**
A: Yes, but don't forget that I'm a professional fighter. I'm interested in getting paid. If I want to have fun, I can roll in my gym.

**Q: Who is your all-time favorite fighter in any combat sport and why?**
A: There are several. When I was younger, I used to love watching Mike Tyson fight because of his speed, power and the way he took care of business. The determination, dedication and the glory he gave to God made me a fan of Evander Holyfield. Others I like include George Foreman, Oscar de la Hoya, Shane Mosley and Roy Jones Jr. Jones adds things to his game, and he can be dangerous.

**Q: As a fighter, or as a person, do you try to pattern yourself after anyone?**
A: Jesus. I know that I'll never be like him, but I want to follow him. I follow his words. He means everything to me. Five years ago I would not have said that, but the old Vitor is dead. Now I am not influenced by anyone. Instead, I'm influenced by the Holy Spirit. The word of Jesus Christ is like a sword. It goes deep into your heart.

**Q: What are the most important physical and mental qualities of a champion?**
A: It's important to train hard, be healthy and do the right things. Mentally, it's important for your soul to choose between the spirit and the flesh. The flesh is immediate gratification such as having a good time or sex. There's too much corruption in flesh. That is why the world is so dangerous. The spirit chooses wise things that are solid and stay forever. For some people, it's hard to stay on course.

## Grappling Techniques

Vitor Belfort faces off with his opponent (1). Vitor lowers his right knee to the ground and pulls his opponent's right sleeve (2). Immediately, Vitor changes grips, grabs the oppo-nent's collar and moves to the right (3). Vitor applies excruci-ating pressure and submits his opponent with a choke (4).

Vitor is standing while his opponent is on the ground (1). Vitor moves his left leg between the opponent's legs (2), wraps his left arm around the opponent's ankle (3) and applies an ankle lock (4).

Vitor's opponent is on the ground (1). Vitor moves his right leg close to the opponent's body and turns slightly to the right (2). He leans back, grabs the opponent's left leg with his left arm (3) and applies a nasty leglock (4).

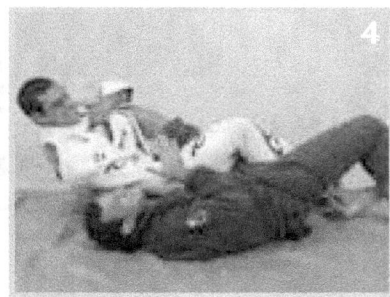

Vitor faces his opponent, who is employing an open guard (1). Vitor changes his grip and seizes the opponent's right arm (2). Next, he moves his right knee closer to the opponent (3), sits, leans back as he secures the arm (4) and applies a painful armlock (5).

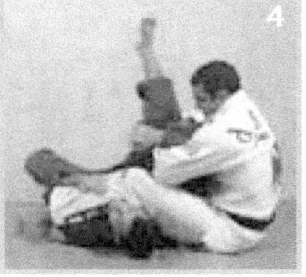

# Grappling Techniques

Vitor, who is on his back, tries to prevent his opponent from passing the guard (1). As soon as the opponent leaves space, Vitor scrambles under the opponent's right arm (2), circles to the outside (3) and applies an omoplata (4).

Vitor squares off with his opponent (1). As soon as the opponent closes the distance and gets into the clinch (2), Vitor drills him in the chin with his left knee (3). Vitor then circles his left arm around the opponent's neck (4) and applies a finishing choke (5).

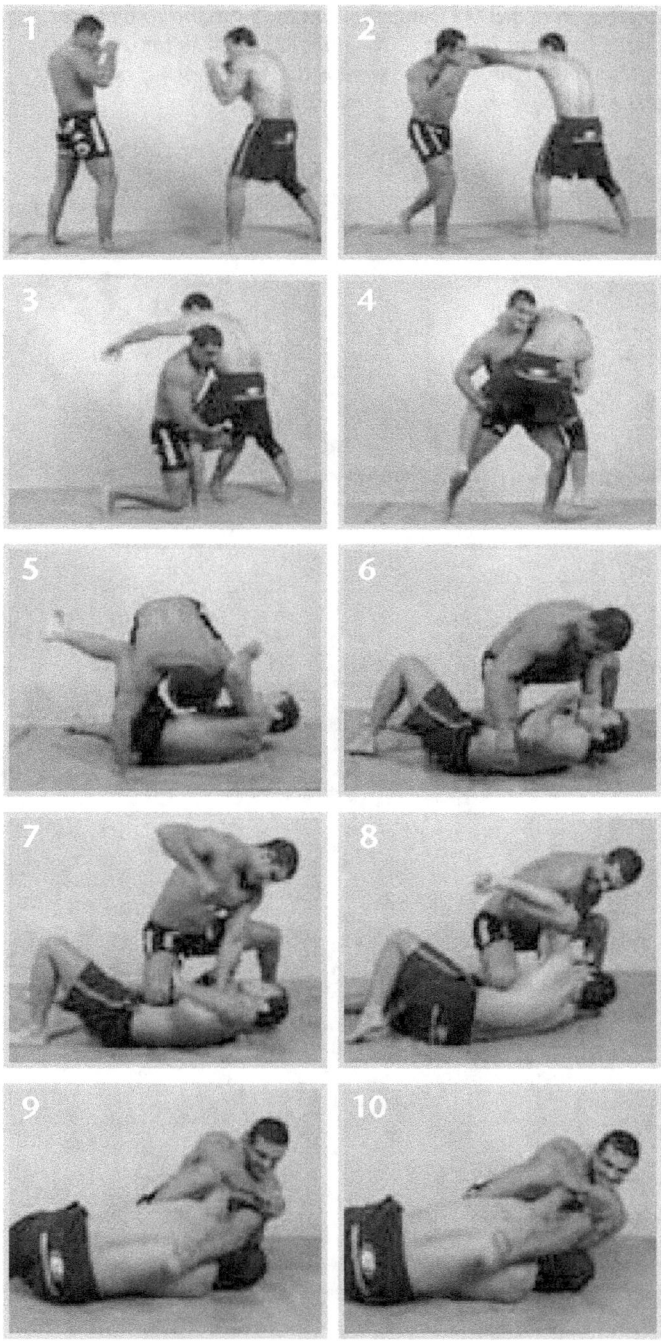

Vitor faces his opponent (1). When the opponent punches, Vitor covers (2), drops his right knee to the ground (3) and executes a flawless takedown (4-5). As soon as the opponent hits the ground, Vitor secures him with his right knee (6) and unleashes a flurry of punches (7). To cover, the opponent uses his left arm, which Vitor grabs (8). He pulls the arm back (9) and applies a straight armlock (10).

# Grappling Techniques

*Vitor has the opponent in the closed guard (1). While he uses his left hand to pull the opponent's arm across his body, he slides his hips to the right (2). Next, Vitor pulls the opponent's right sleeve (3). Using his right leg, Vitor sweeps the opponent (4) and ends up on top (5). To end the match, he applies an armlock (6).*

Vitor squares off with his opponent (1). When the opponent kicks with his right leg, Vitor closes the distance and grabs the leg and body (2). He swiftly moves his right leg inside (3) and sweeps the opponent (4). Once his opponent is on the floor, Vitor applies an anklelock (5).

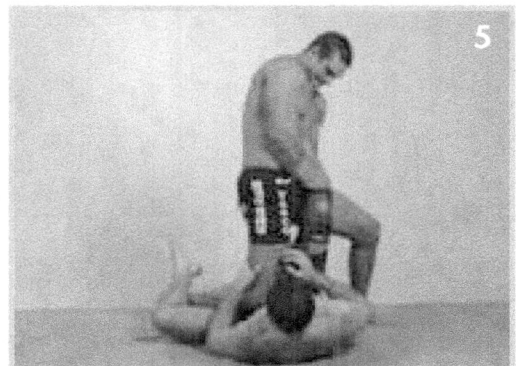

# Wander Braga

## *Quietness and Confidence*

The ancient prophet Isaiah, speaking in the Old Testament, said to his followers, "In quietness and confidence shall be your strength." Those same words definitely apply to modern Brazilian jiu-jitsu competitor and instructor Wander Braga. With a firm belief in family and friends, and a jiu-jitsu work ethic that has earned him numerous national and international upper echelon finishes, Braga is living proof that you don't have to be loud to be tough. Born and raised in Brazil, but now teaching out of Richard Allen's world famous L.A. Boxing gym in downtown Los Angeles, Braga is gaining fans and students alike drawn to his balanced and friendly approach to teaching Brazilian jiu-jitsu. But make no mistake, this winner of numerous Brazilian *vale tudo* (anything goes) matches can bring it on if he wants — but he'll be likely to shake your hand after a fight, regardless of the outcome. Humbleness, according to Braga, is the true quality of champions: "Being humble means having an open attitude to learn and gain knowledge, and to endure sweat and pain while trying to improve your skills. It means thinking that you are still a beginner and still have a lot to learn. If you have that important quality, everything else will be possible because you've got a strong foundation to build on."

**Q: How long have you been practicing Brazilian jiu-jitsu?**
A: Almost two decades – and I haven't lost any interest since the first day I stepped on the mat. It is a kind of love story. I can't think of my life without thinking of jiu-jitsu. What I am today is a direct product of the philosophy and teachings of the art. Because I started early, most of the influences that made me as a man came from my friends and teachers in jiu-jitsu. My first and only teacher is Jorge Pereira and I owe him a lot.

**Q: Have you ever trained in other martial arts?**
A: When I was very young I trained karate a little. Recently I have been practicing boxing since I teach jiu-jitsu at L.A. Boxing, one of the top gyms in the world. I believe boxing is a perfect compliment for jiu-jitsu

*"If you only want to practice self-defense, there is no reason to train in anything but Brazilian jiu-jitsu. But if you are serious about vale tudo, you should train boxing, muay Thai or other striking arts. You need to learn how to use punches and kicks as well as protect against them."*

because it teaches how to use hands effectively. I am seriously thinking about becoming a professional boxer. I really love it. It is a great sport and a very effective fighting method.

**Q: Do you think it is good to learn many martial arts styles?**
A: In general, if you learn 10 different martial arts styles you will just end up being confused. If you only want to practice self-defense then there is no reason to train in anything but Brazilian jiu-jitsu. But if you are serious about vale tudo then you should train boxing, muay Thai or other striking arts. You need to learn how to use punches and kicks as well as protect against them. If you are a jiu-jitsu man, though, don't step into the ring

and try to kickbox with a kickboxer! Stick to what you know best and what you've been practicing. That's what you'll really have a feel for.

**Q: What kind of training drills did Jorge Pereira do to help you get a "feel" for jiu-jitsu?**
A: When I was yellow belt, Jorge used to turn off the lights and we would all start to slap each other. Imagine the situation – no lights and eve ybody slapping everybody! It was fun but also a very helpful drill for you to feel what is going on around you. Human beings rely too much on sight and once this is out of the equation the whole world changes. Your body needs to read the opponent's actions by feel. Keeping your eyes open gives you a sense of location – not only of your opponent but also of your own space and position. This is very important in both jiu-jitsu and in vale tudo.

**Q: Do you remember your first vale tudo fight?**
A: I was ready to fight in a vale tudo tournament but my opponent, a capoeira fighter, backed out and so I was going to get to go to the finals without fighting. I

*"Human beings rely too much on sight. Once this is out of the equation, the whole world changes. Your body needs to read the opponent's actions by feel. Keeping your eyes open gives you a sense of location – not only of your opponent but also of your own space and position."*

thought that was pretty cool. But for some reason it made Jorge mad and so he grabbed the microphone and challenged the whole capoeira team to find someone with enough guts to face me! The bad part was that the event was in their home town and I thought the whole team was going to go after me! So they finally found another guy to fight me – there went my free trip to the finals. Jorge came to me and said: "If you don't beat this guy, we'll never be able to show our face in this town again." I fought the guy and after 15 minutes he gave up. I then won the final fight and the title. We managed to leave the town in one piece and I got

# Grappling Masters

*"Scoring points is part of the game, but I believe that submissions really exemplify the true essence of the art. But the rules of the game are the rules of the game, and you have to know how to use them to your advantage. If you don't do it, your opponent will."*

my black belt from my teacher. To this day I'm not sure if Jorge did me a favor or not!

**Q: Did jiu-jitsu movements come easy to you?**
A: I believe I had some natural skill that helped me in the beginning – but if I wouldn't have trained every day I still wouldn't have progressed. Having talent and being gifted physically only means so much. You may have all the physical ability in the world, but if you don't sweat on the mat every day you won't become a champion. In the long run it is consistency and dedication that makes the difference. Strangely enough, those who quit in the early stages of training, after only a couple of years, are the ones who have the best natural ability for the sport!

**Q: How has your jiu-jitsu evolved over the years?**
A: In the past, every time I was competing I used to go for submissions. I was more aggressive and I wanted to be in active control the whole fight. Now, I like to play more of strategic game instead of going crazy for submissions. My game now is more tactical and quiet but at the same time more dangerous. I observe what my opponent does and then act accordingly. I don't rush but neither do I hesitate when I see an opportunity to finish. Scoring points is part of the game but I believe that submissions really exemplify the true essence of the art. But the rules of the game are the rules of the game and you have to know how to use them to your advantage. If you don't do it then your opponent will.

**Q: Do you feel that you still have more to learn?**
A: Definitely. I look at jiu-jitsu as an extension of life. In life you don't stop growing and learning new things. I believe that we always have something new to learn – I don't understand those who claim otherwise. Well, maybe if you're Helio Gracie there is nothing new and better, but it doesn't mean

that you know everything he does. I like to read new books and watch videos whenever I can to absorb more information. That helps me to improve my technical level and better understand how the different aspects and elements of the art work together. I think it is very important to compete as much as possible because the art is evolving and there is always a new twist for an old technique. Competing gives you an edge that is impossible to have otherwise.

*"It is true, that many people get bored and discouraged so they start focusing more on different movements instead of working on the basics. This can be more appealing in the beginning. When the years pass by and you face an opponent who has a sound knowledge and skill of the basics, you'll find out that you are lacking something."*

**Q: What is the best way for beginning students to improve?**
A: Set goals according to each level of your training and practice consistently. Beginners should learn the basics because they need to establish a solid foundation for the more advanced techniques. It is true, though, that many people get bored and discouraged so they start focusing more on different movements instead of working on the basics. This can be more appealing in the beginning but when the years pass by and you face an opponent who has a sound knowledge and skill of the basics, you'll find out that you are lacking something. Even if new techniques and movements appear, they all are based on the fundamentals and are simply a personal expression.

**Q: As a black belt, is it hard to stay sharp in the U.S.?**
A: In America, the fighters and top instructors coming from Brazil don't have many black belts to train with. This prevents Brazilian competitors from keeping the same competition level they had in Brazil. I'm confident things will change in the near future but still there is a big technical gap.

**Q: Who do you admire in jiu-jitsu?**
A: I have always admired Rickson Gracie and I'm lucky to have had the opportunity to train with him. Honestly, everything you hear about him is

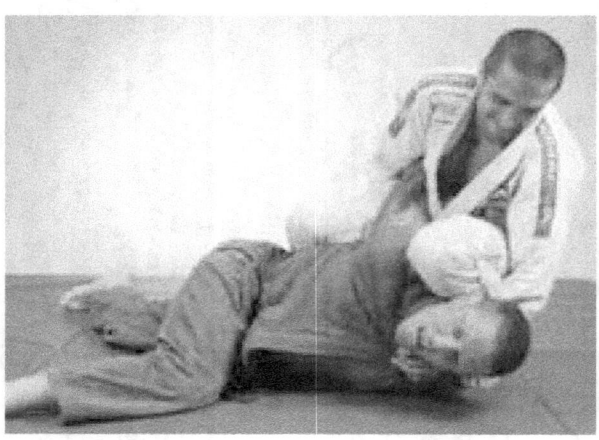

*"Every competition is a new challenge, and I train hard and give my best so I will perform at the level I expect. My students and my family are also a big motivational factor. I am a simple individual who loves simple things. In jiu-jitsu, stick to the basics and make sure you master those."*

true and sometimes what people say doesn't truly describe how good he is. Not only he is an excellent technician but he also knows how to teach any kind of student from a white belt to an advanced instructor or to a world champion. His ability to relate to any kind of student is amazing.

**Q: What would you say to someone who is interested in starting jiu-jitsu?**
A: It is important for a student to know what they are looking for and what their priorities are. Do they want to learn self-defense or just be in good physical shape? Do they want to focus on sport competition, vale tudo, or both? Once the student has an idea then visit a school and watch the teacher. Observe how he relates to the students and how he breaks down the techniques. Talk to the teacher and get a feel for what kind of individual he is. Get a feel for the students and how they act. Jiu-jitsu is a great exercise and you'll be spending a lot of time at the school. You want to make sure that the people at the school are the kind of individuals that will bring positive things into your life.

**Q: What keeps you motivated after all these years?**
A: Competition. Tournaments and competitions keep me going forward every day. Every competition is a new challenge and I train hard and give my best so I will perform at the level I expect. My students and my family are also a big motivational factor. I am a simple individual who loves simple things. In jiu-jitsu, stick to the basics and make sure you master those. In life, stick to the people that you love and who love you back and focus on things that make you grow. The important things are family, good friends, and health – put the rest aside. Good people bring good energy. And good energy brings success. Don't get me wrong, when I say "success" I don't necessarily mean money and fame! Having a family that supports you and

loves you and having good friends that you can rely on is already a great success.

**Q: How do you mentally prepare for a tournament?**
A: I'm a quiet guy so I don't get out of control. Relaxation is very important before a match, and so I will visualize how things might happen and go through different scenarios. This makes me feel more confident and prepared. I also love to go to the beach and relax there. Jiu-jitsu it is an art where you need to be relaxed in order to give your best. Of course, this is very easy to say and very hard to accomplish. Everybody talks about relaxation but they don't explain how to achieve it.

*"You need to keep your breathing pattern under control. The timing of the breath has to be steady and consistent under any circumstances. You also need to be confident of your technical ability. No confidence, no calmness. No calmness and you'll begin to gasp for air like crazy."*

**Q: How do you achieve relaxation?**
A: Number one is proper breathing. You need to keep your breathing pattern under control. The timing of the breath has to be steady and consistent under any circumstances. You also need to be confident of your technical ability. No confidence, no calmness. No calmness and you'll begin to gasp for air like crazy. In order to have confidence in your technique, you need to have proper training in the fundamentals so they become automatic reflexes. Only then can you be relaxed in a fight.

**Q: Does jiu-jitsu have a spiritual side?**
A: I think so. It definitely requires introspection. I have always tried to develop positive qualities such as humbleness, dedication, willpower and positive attitude. Don't give up when things get tough and always remember that there are many different way of achieving what you want. Don't think you are superior or better than anybody. Be realistic about your goals and your potential.

**Q: Do people sometimes set goals they can't achieve?**
A: We all have to be realistic about our own potential and abilities. We need to know our limitations so we can excel. Maybe a student doesn't

*"Humbleness. This is a basic quality that everybody talks about but few people have. Being humble means having an open attitude to learn and gain knowledge, and to endure sweat and pain while trying to improve your skills."*

have the potential to be a world champion – very few do. So the teacher needs to motivate the student and get the best out of him without making him believe impossible things. He needs to help the students to see their potential without creating false expectations. The same thing goes the other way, too. Teachers who constantly run students down also is bad. Be positive but be realistic. There is a big responsibility on the teacher's shoulders in this regard.

**Q: What is the most important mental quality of a successful jiu-jitsu fighter?**
A: Humbleness. This is a basic quality that everybody talks about but very few people have. Being humble means having an open attitude to learn and gain knowledge, and to endure sweat and pain while trying to improve your skills. It means thinking that you are still a beginner and still have a lot to learn. If you have that important quality, everything else will be possible because you've got a strong foundation to build on.

**Q: What is the most important physical quality?**
A: Try to be in good shape all the time. Keep your body clean and follow a good nutrition plan. Food is the fuel of your body. Be careful what kind of food you eat because it will directly effect the way you perform in competition and training. Keep your cardiovascular training up and eat a balanced diet.

**Q: What do you think can be done to improve the sport?**
A: I believe that Brazilian jiu-jitsu can become an Olympic sport. A lot of things need to be done to fulfill the requirements of the International Olympic Committee for the sport has to be practiced in each continent. It will take a lot of hard work to accomplish that but with the growing sup-

port from fans, practitioners, and governments around the world I don't see why can't become a reality. In mixed martial arts I believe that fighters should be taken into consideration much more than they are now. They should get paid bigger sums of money because they are the ones making everything possible. As the sport grows and the crowds get bigger in the U.S. I think it will happen.

**Q: Do you have any future plans for doing mixed martial arts fights?**
A: I spend few years away from MMA I recently decided to go back. My kids Magali and Kayan are a big inspiration for me. My wife Luana strongly supports me in everything I do, just as I try to support her. Also my teacher Jorge Pereira is extremely important in my life. I feel that I have a future in mixed martial arts and am looking forward to doing some more matches.

**Q: What does jiu-jitsu mean to you?**
A: Jiu-jitsu is an extremely important part of my life. It gave me direction when I was young, and gave me the opportunity to meet great people that I have developed close ties and relationships with. Professionally, it is my job and I put myself into it as much as I can. All my existence evolves around jiu-jitsu and only my family is more important to me. I am truly grateful to the Gracie family for developing this great art and for working hard to spread it around the world.

*"Jiu-jitsu is an extremely important part of my life. It gave me direction when I was young, and it gave me the opportunity to meet great people who I have developed close ties and relationships with."*

## Grappling Techniques

Wander Braga latches onto the opponent's belt and collar (1). Braga quickly spins, while holding firmly to the belt (2). Braga sits back, pulls the opponent head over heels (3-4) and applies an armbar (5).

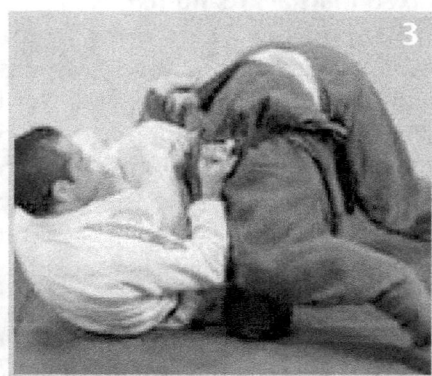

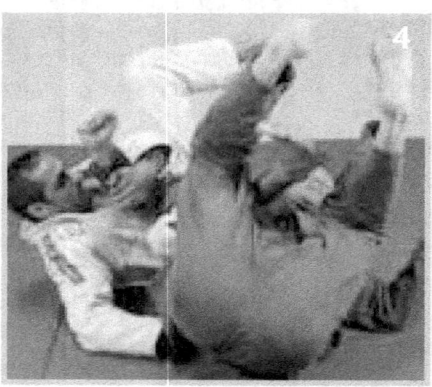

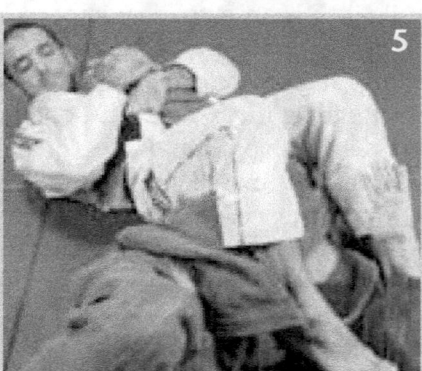

Wander Braga works from the back, trying to get the hooks in (1). He pulls his opponent over (2), grabs the ankle (3) and tries to apply a toe hold (4), which his opponent blocks (5). While putting a figure-four on the leg (6), Braga shifts his hips out (7), releases the foot (8), secures the arm (9) and flawlessly applies the finishing armlock (10).

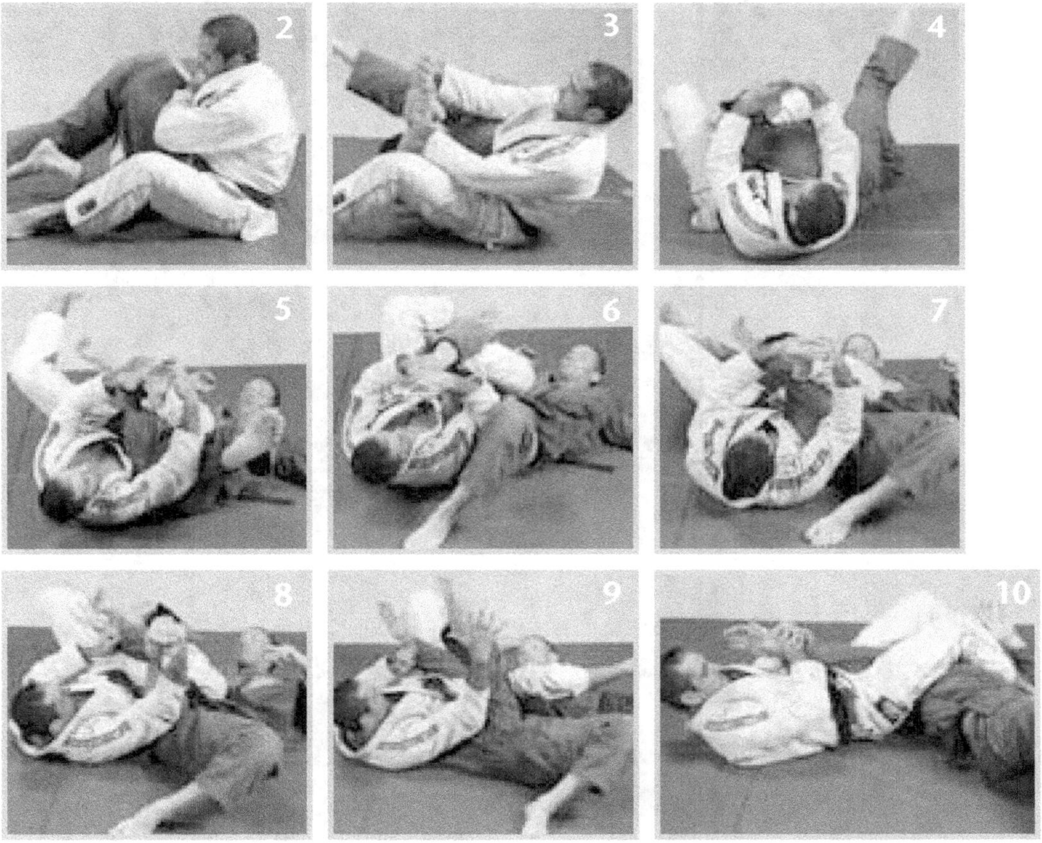

## Grappling Techniques

Wander attacks the opponent from the back (1). He uses his right hand to attempt a choke (2), but the opponent feels the attack (3), moves to the side and uses his left hand to thwart the choke (4). Wander lowers his body to the floor, moves his right leg over the opponent's head (5) and applies an armlock (6).

Wander, who is on the top of his opponent, assumes command with the side-control position (1). To begin the attack, Wander places his right knee on the opponent's chest (2). When the opponent uses both arms to block the movement, Wander swings around in a counterclockwise motion (3), placing himself on the other side (4). He secures the opponent's left arm, lowers himself to the ground (5) and applies a straight armlock (6).

## GRAPPLING TECHNIQUES

*Wander has his opponent in the closed guard (1). He uses his left hand to pull the opponent's left arm and his right to grab inside the collar (2). Attempting a sweep, Wander slides his hips to the side, but the opponent stops him cold (3). Wander immediately switches positions, moves his right leg between the opponent's and grabs the belt from the back (4). He sweeps the opponent to the right (5) and ends up on top. Here he can initiate an attack (6).*

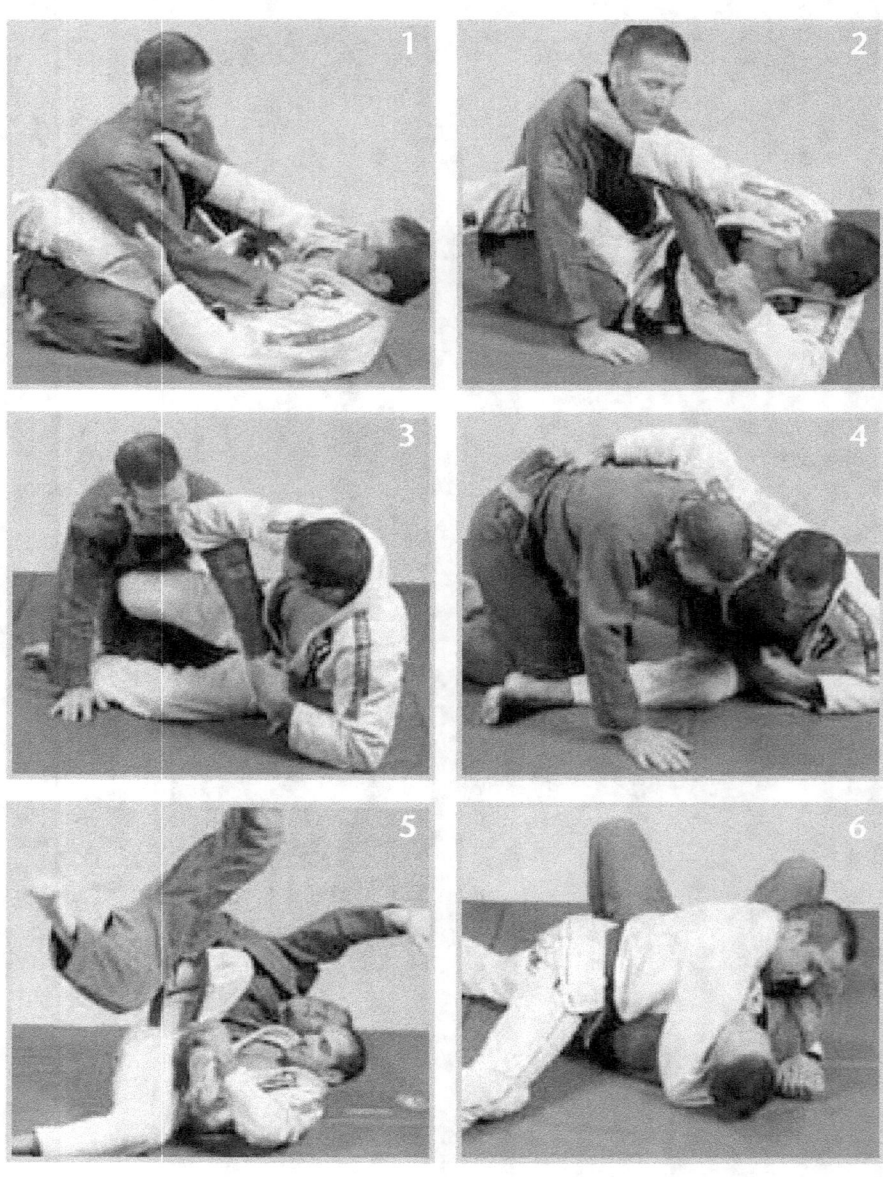

Wander has the opponent in his butterfly guard (1). As soon as the opponent feels Wander grab his left leg, he stands (2). To disrupt the action, Wander secures the left leg and pushes the opponent's right shin with his left foot. This disrupts the opponent's balance (3), sending him directly to the ground (4). Wander quickly applies a side control (5).

## GRAPPLING TECHNIQUES

Wander faces his opponent (1). He sits and places both feet on the opponent's hips (2). This prevents the opponent from getting too close as he readjusts his posi-tion. He pulls his opponent securely inside his guard (3) and applies a straight armlock (4).

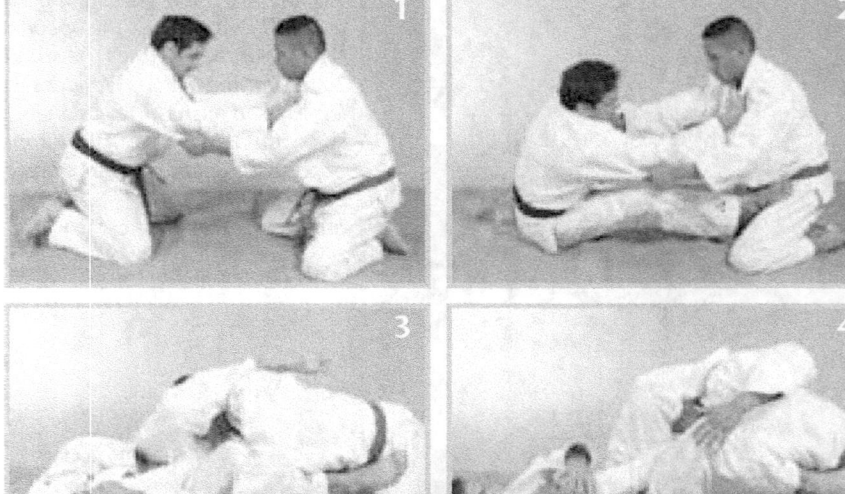

From a clinch position (1), Wander moves his left leg to the oppo-nent's right hip (2), as he secures the opponent's left arm to establish control (3). He wraps up the sequence with a straight armlock (4).

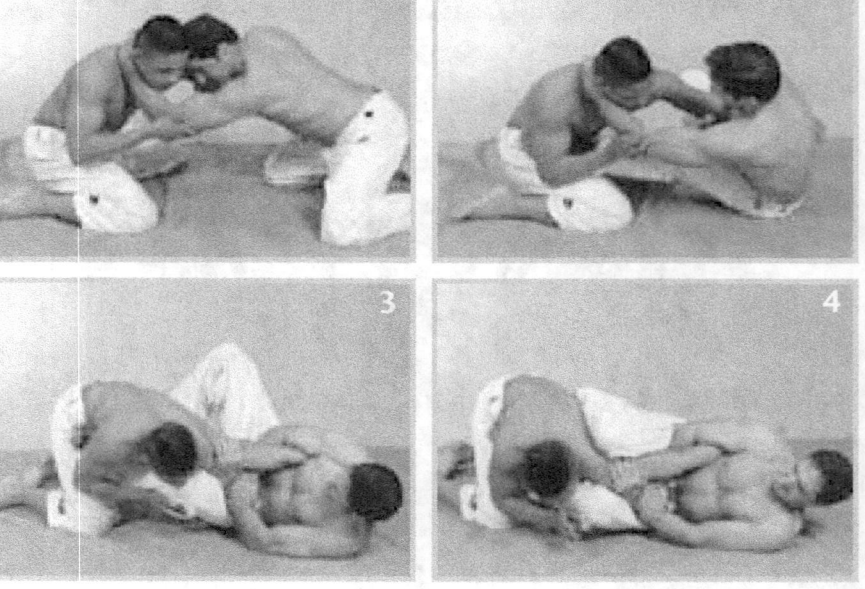

Wander faces his opponent (1). When the opponent grabs Wander's right leg (2), he moves back and sweeps the opponent's left leg (3). Wander ends up in the mount position (4). Next, Wander puts pressure on the opponent's chest (5), shifts his body quickly and applies a confrontation-ending armlock (6).

## Grappling Techniques

From a clinch position (1), Wander moves his left foot onto the opponent's right hip (2). Then, he moves his right leg over the opponent's left shoulder (3), closes the position and underhooks his left leg with his right foot (4). This enables him to apply a "triangle" choke (5).

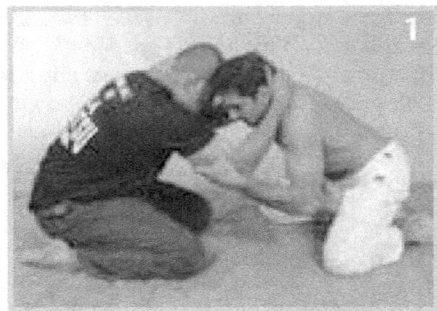

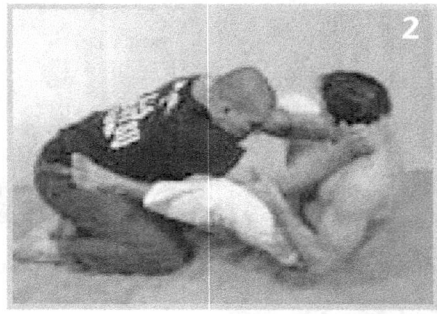

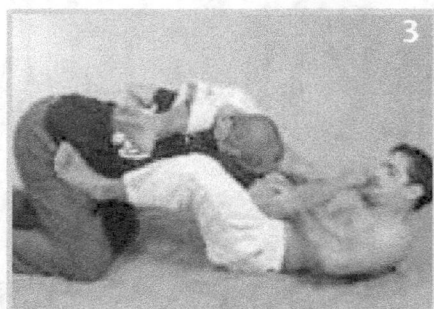

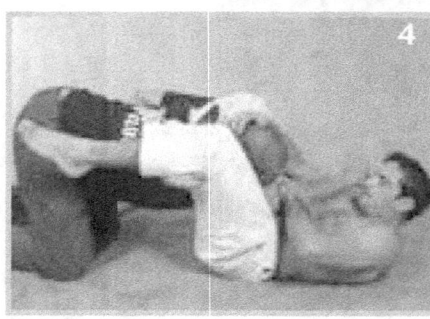

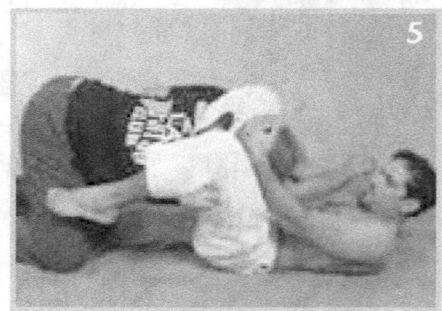

*From a clinch position (1), Wander ducks under the opponent and tries to attack the legs (2). In response, the opponent grabs Wander, who responds by securing the grip (3), turning to the side and applying a bent armlock (4).*

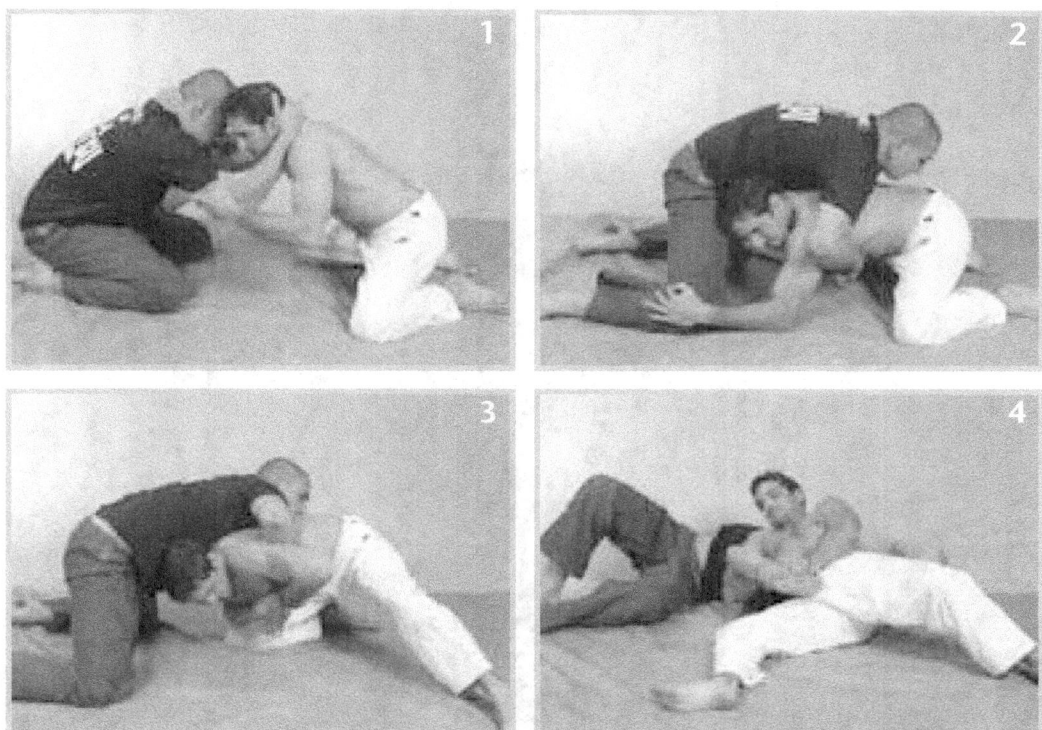

# WILLY CAHILL

## Keeping the Pace

The Cahill family tree traces its roots to John K. Cahill, Sr., who was regarded as one of the best jiu-jitsu instructors ever produced in the Kodenkan jiu-jitsu system. Willy Cahill has followed in his father's footsteps and is now known as one of the most knowledgeable men of Kodenkan kata. Described as an unselfish and dedicated instructor, Willy would often hold free sessions in jiu-jitsu for federation instructors. When asked why he did not wish any compensation, he explained that he felt obligated to Professor Okazaki and to his father, one of the early Okazaki followers. In repayment to them, Willy was willing to teach today's Okazaki followers the correct method as taught by the Professor. It is the opinion of many that the original art taught by the old Professor has been changed so many times by his followers that the kata taught at many federation clubs does not resemble what Okazaki originally set forth. It was Willy's desire to preserve and spread the original form of the kata.

Willy himself has been in judo for more than 20 years and holds high black belt ranks in both judo and jiu-jitsu. In 1964, he traveled to Japan, along with Mits Kimura, and a group of judoka from around the country and was able to train at the Kodokan and at various universities. While in Tokyo, he was a luncheon guest of Risei Kano, son of the founder of judo, and was also a guest at the home of Professor Shoichi Shimizu, an instructor at Kelo University and director of the All-Japan Student Judo Federation. This is Willy Cahill... a true grappling legend.

**Q: Cahill Sensei, would you tell us a little about the history of the arts you practice and how your father got involved in the martial arts?**
A: Kodenkan jiu-jitsu began in the early 1930s. Professor Okazaki established it in what was at that time the Hawaiian Protectorate of the United States. In those early days in Honolulu, the teaching of the secrets of jiu-jitsu to non-Orientals was practically forbidden, but Professor Okazaki broke the tradition and graduated his first five *haole* (Hawaiian slang for

*"My father, John K. Cahill, Sr., began learning jiu-jitsu in 1937 at 26 under Professor Okazaki and the "Original Five." He trained four hours a day, six days a week, to earn his black belt in two years... all the while supporting a wife and four children."*

Caucasian) black belt students. They were to become known as the "Original Five." My father – John K. Cahill, Sr. – began learning jiu-jitsu in 1937 at age 26 under Professor Okazaki and the "Original Five." He trained four hours a day, six days a week, to earn his black belt in two years... all the while supporting a wife and four children. He began teaching in 1940 at Professor Okazaki's dojo, calling the school Hui Miki Miki Judo Club. *Hui* in Hawaiian means club, while *miki miki* means lots of pep.

During the Second World War, the Japanese martial arts were curtailed, but my father continued teaching numerous servicemen and participated in the training of Special Forces personnel in the Islands. It was during these years that one of his students, Herman Wedemeyer, went on to become one of the most outstanding football players in the nation, gaining his fame as an All-American halfback at St. Mary's College in California.

**Q: When did your family decide to move to California?**
A: In 1947. We settled in the southern area of San Francisco. My father opened the first mainland dojo in Daly City the next year under the same name, Hui Miki Miki. Seven years later, he was granted permission to use the facilities at South San Francisco High School, and it was at that time the name Cahill Judo Academy was adopted. He was also the co-founder of the South San Francisco Boy's Club and co-founder of the American Judo and Jiu-Jitsu Federation. In this organization, his club would dominate every tournament and walk off with most of the trophies. But good, keen competition became very scarce, so they had to seek it elsewhere. At that time, Wally Jay, head instructor of the Island Judo and Jiu-Jitsu Club of Alameda (California), persuaded my father to join the Hokka Yudanshakai. In 1960, the Cahill Judo Academy separated from the American Judo and Jiu-Jitsu Federation to become a member of the Hokka Yudanshakai, which was part of the U.S. Judo Federation.

**Q: Sensei, you were seriously sick when you were a kid. How did this affect your motivation and interest in sports?**
A: I was about eight years old at the time, and the doctor said I would never walk again because I had polio. Imagine you can't move your legs. Not an inch. Forget about standing, throwing a baseball or chasing a butterfly. You're confined to a hospital bed with polio. It was a terrible nightmare. As you can imagine, that was pretty devastating because I could not walk. I don't think I realized how serious it was until they put me in the hospital. I could not even get out of bed. It was then when I really saw what was happening. I was pretty nervous when I could not walk without a brace, but I knew I wanted to play football. I also started judo about the same time. It was pretty depressing. Somehow, however, I knew I would walk again, but I also knew that I would need a lot of dedication. In addition to the medical care I received to combat the viral disease that inflames the brainstem and spinal cord, I had also got some help from my father's judo instructor. He used to put herbs on my legs and give me a massage while I was confined to the bed. About a year later I was out of the hospital and free of polio.

*"I was about eight years old at the time, and the doctor said I would never walk again because I had polio. I don't think I realized how serious it was until they put me in the hospital. I could not even get out of bed. It was then when I really saw what was happening."*

**Q: As a teenager, was it easy to give up all the distractions of a land like Hawaii to immerse yourself in the art of judo?**
A: I grew up in Hawaii so you might imagine that giving up the crystal blue waves of the Pacific would be too strong to resist, but I particularly loved the gridiron. I also had a fairly strong interest in the martial arts, especially since my dad was teaching judo and jiu-jitsu. But it was hard, though. Although my father was teaching all the time, he did not pressure us to participate. He was not like that. My brothers and I wanted to play football because football was our first passion. One day my father

"Although my father was teaching all the time, he did not pressure us to participate. He was also not the kind of coach or father who expected us to win. He did not put pressure on us to be victorious in competitions. He just wanted us to go out, participate and enjoy what we were doing."

said that if we wanted to play football we would have to learn how to fall, which we would learn in the martial arts. He was also not the kind of coach or father who expected us to win. Not did he put pressure on us to be victorious in competitions. He just wanted us to go out, participate and enjoy what we were doing.

**Q: Did you practice both sports at the same time?**
A: Yes. I got into both sports and truly enjoyed everything until the Army drafted me right out of high school. I spent the next two years in the service. Then my family moved to the mainland in 1947. We settled in San Francisco. My father, John, worked as a machinist and opened his first judo and jiu-jitsu school in Daly City. In 1962, when he was just 50, my father died. I was supposed to take over the school, but I was a little bit reluctant.

**Q: How did things change when your father died?**
A: On July 5, 1962 my father passed away at the age of 50, leaving my mother Abigail with four sons. His passing did not deter the progress of the Academy. I took over the responsibility of head instructor, assisted by my brothers Ben and John. When my father passed away and I had the responsibilities of the school, I decided to drop out. I didn't have the energy or motivation to carry on what my father had left. However, Wally Jay came over and told me that I had to teach. He said that it was my responsibility. He suggested that I quit competing and focus on teaching and sharing the heritage my father passed onto me. He said I owed it to my parents. Wally grew up with my dad and offered to help me in anything I needed. Another gentlemen, Bill Montera, my dad's first black belt student from Hawaii, also came out and

helped me teach until I caught up with the flow of things. Soon I felt I could teach and run the school myself.

**Q: What was the major turning point in your career as a teacher?**
A: Things started to look good in 1965 when I took some kids to the U.S. Judo Championships, and one of the kids did really well. One year later, he finished second and two others placed. I was now on a roll. In 1968, one of my students won the U.S. Championships and was voted the most outstanding competitor. That gave me confidence to keep teaching and sharing the art. That led to later success and soon I had more offers to coach than I could handle. I coached my first international team in 1976 when I took the U.S. team to Mexico City for the Junior Pan American Championships. After that, there was Stanford University, San Francisco State University, the World Championships, the Pan American Games, the Olympics, the Goodwill Games and on and on. Along the way, I have produced more than 900 national and international medal winners.

*"I believe that the U.S. has to start all over again if we really want to be among the elite of the world judo competition. Our top competitors can't lose in less than a minute. Instead of getting better, we're getting worse."*

**Q: What will it take for American judo players to start finishing first in international competitions?**
A: I believe that the U.S. has to start all over again if we really want to be among the elite of the world judo competition. Our top competitors can't lose in less than a minute. Instead of getting better, we're getting worse. I don't want to be critical of the people who are running the program because it's easy to sit back from a distance and criticize, and I am always careful not to do that. I only want to make observations that may help to get the teams back on track. Right now it just seems as if we are going

# GRAPPLING MASTERS

*"We need to look at other sports and analyze how they train. There are a lot of judo guys who work out, but they do not train. And that is a big difference. When you train, that should include weights, running, sprints, nutrition, sports psychology and a lot of drills."*

backward instead of forward. It seems like the United States feels lucky when we place someone in the Olympics or the World Championships. It shouldn't be that way. We won our first championship in 1953. Here we are down the line, and we've only got a few world champions. Therefore, the first thing we need to do is make sure all of the coaches are certified. All the coaches need to know and understand the sport. Too many coaches come in and start to teach without any background. A lot of it is still guesswork. Our first national judo championships were held at San Jose State in 1953, and now, more than 50 years later, we are still struggling to stay afloat in the international arena. We need to look at other sports and analyze how they train. There are a lot of judo guys who work out, but they do not train. And that is a big difference. When you train, that should include weights, running, sprints, nutrition, sports psychology and a lot of drills. Competitors also need to take a break, so they do not burn out. They need to plan the season. These guys should be making a graph of the whole year and set five different goals. Then you can then strive for those and peak at the right time.

**Q: The mentality should change too, right?**
A: Definitely. Let me give you an example. During international competition in Venezuela, I was the coach of the U.S. Judo Team, and we were housed along with the U.S. men's and women's swim team. Both teams were scheduled to compete the following day. The only thing that separated our dorm from theirs was a glass door. The coach asked me if we could keep the noise down because his team would be going to bed at 8 p.m. On the other hand, the judo team didn't want to go to bed until they were tired. They wanted to stay up and play cards. In essence, the

swim team, which always wins a lot of medals, came to win, and the judo players were hoping to win. The judo players were all eager to learn and try things. It was a great high. The players really had the enthusiasm. They wanted to be the first to get gold for the United States. I used to tell them that the last thing they do before they fall asleep is see themselves on the victory stand with that medal. Every night. Every morning. That is all they thought about for eight months. They also need to set specific goals that help them to improve and get better along the way.

**Q: Like little steps that the athlete can reach instead of focusing on a long-term objective.**
A: Yes. Setting goals is the most important thing, and that is what I always tell my students right in the beginning. You have to set a reachable goal. For example, I tell the white belts to strive for yellow. I tell the athletes the same thing. Making the Olympic team might be unreachable at first, but winning a national championship is certainly reasonable.

*"Setting goals is the most important thing, and that is what I always tell my students right in the beginning. You have to set a reachable goal. For example, I tell the white belts to strive for yellow. Making the Olympic team might be unreachable at first, but winning a national championship is certainly reasonable."*

**Q: How important is strength and what is the best way to train for it in judo?**
A: Muscular strength is one of the most important requirements for developing efficient expertise in judo. Skill, proper *budo* (martial way) attitude, and theoretical and practical knowledge are all indispensable in the study of the martial arts. But it is true that given two men with the same degree of

*"In sport judo as practiced today, there can be no doubt strength and conditioning play a significant part in the outcome. Even in the internal Chinese arts, where theoretically strength should not enter into a contest, I have been told that – given the same skill – the more powerful will conquer."*

skill that the stronger man will be the victor. In sport judo as practiced today, there can be no doubt strength and conditioning play a significant part in the outcome. Even in the internal Chinese arts, where theoretically strength should not enter into a contest, I have been told that – given the same skill – the more powerful will conquer.

**Q: How do you define and identify strength when mixed with pure technique and skill?**
A: It is difficult. Force generated at all points in a range of motion, force generated at different speeds of joint motion and force expended in repetitive muscular effort are all aspects of strength. Strength can be generated through the will and conscious effort or strength can be generated by an unconscious processes. Strength can also be related to a specific activity. Pushing a hand truck, throwing a ball, sprinting and distance running all depend upon different types of strength. Developing it is a truly a multi-faceted problem. The use of isometric exercises can increase strength and so can isotonic exercises. Both types of exercises have their advantages and disadvantages. Combining the two is the method of choice, and the regimen should be generated to the specific style of martial art. In any case, for strength to improve, the muscles must be used to full capacity. Just by increasing the amount of force used strength will improve. Increasing speed will also aid in developing strength. Increasing the time of expenditure of effort will also bring about strength improvements. Increasing the number of times work is done against a fixed resistance will bring about the same result. Don't forget that different methods of building strength must be applied to different needs. The training schedule must be devel-

*"The training schedule must be developed and formulated in relation to the specific requirements of the activity to be engaged in. Well, the truth is the most people in sports stick to their own particular sport. Consequently, they never tap the potential resources of vital movements and conditioning that other sports have to offer."*

oped and formulated in relation to the specific requirements of the activity to be engaged in. In short, the training program must be custom made to give maximum efficiency in developing the type of strength needed for judo, jiu-jitsu and any other grappling arts.

**Q: You mentioned that martial artists should look at the way athletes of other sports train. What did you mean by that?**
A: Well, the truth is the most people in sports stick to their own particular sport. Consequently, they never tap the potential resources of vital movements and conditioning that other sports have to offer. For example, gymnastics aid in muscular conditioning and control of one's body. Other sports develop hand-feet coordination and so on. It is smart to look into how other sports develop certain physical attributes for proper performance.

*"Strangling techniques have been an integral part of judo and jiu-jitsu training since the beginning of these arts, although it is true that other martial arts have been using them extensively. Their objective is to render the opponent unconscious and helpless without hurting him severely."*

**Q: Choking techniques have been popularized by some MMA and submission grappling events, but they have been used in judo for a very long time... long before the boom of grappling arts. What can you tell us about the proper use and technique of what is called in judo *shime-waza*?**

A: Strangling techniques have been an integral part of judo and jiu-jitsu training since the beginning of these arts, although it is true that other martial arts have been using them extensively. Their objective is to render the opponent unconscious and helpless without hurting him severely. The pressure is applied to the neck to reduce circulation to the brain and also cut off normal breathing. Interfering with brain circulation brings effects within a few seconds and is painless. Interfering with respiration is painful and brings effects in several minutes. Strangulation places direct pressure on both the carotid and vertebral arteries. It is important to have the proper supervision when practice and training these techniques. It cannot be stressed enough that the shime-waza techniques should only be applied with proper care and with an understanding of the basic physiological principles, dangers and precautions. The teacher should be fairly competent in the application of "katsu" in case something happens during the training.

**Q: Sensei Cahill, would you like to add something for the readers?**
A: I simply try to follow and maintain the Cahill tradition and the art my father John mastered under Henry Okazaki. I'm just doing my job and enjoying the process. Martial arts are a process and all practitioners should enjoy it without adding unnecessary pressure to it. Live your life truly and honestly.

*"I simply try to follow and maintain the Cahill tradition and the art my father John mastered under Henry Okazaki. I'm just doing my job and enjoying the process."*

## GRAPPLING TECHNIQUES

Matthew Midyette and Willy Cahill square off (1). When Midyette reaches over Cahill's shoulder to apply a choke, Cahill leans back (2), ties up his opponent's arm (3), pulls downward and moves his right leg closer to Midyette (4) so he can execute a throw (5). With his opponent firmly on the ground, Cahill can execute an armlock and/or strike him in the ribs (6).

Matthew Midyette (right) launches a right punch, which Willy Cahill blocks with his forearm (1). While Cahill pulls his right hand back, he pushes the attacker's right arm away with his left hand (2) and delivers a right to Midyette's ribs (3). Cahill pulls his opponent's right arm down (not visible) and simultaneously grabs him across the neck (4). Meanwhile, Cahill steps forward with his right leg as he sweeps his opponent to the ground (5).

# Rico Chiapparelli

## *Leader of Attack*

One of the most acclaimed wrestlers of our time, Rico Chiapparelli is the leader of the ultra-aggressive RAW Team. A three-time All American, an NCAA collegiate wrestling champ, a four-year member of the USA national team, a U.S. Open freestyle champion, and a World Cup champion, Chiapparelli's credentials are legitimate, impeccable, and beyond reproach. Legendary Iowa wrestling coach Dan Gable has the photograph of only one former wrestler on his wall, that of Rico Chiapparelli, the "Baltimore Butcher." He is one of the few men to have an international wrestling technique named after him — the Rico Roll. He is a grappling purist, a gifted teacher, and a skilled athlete who can create positions out of a locked box. He has been seen submitting a top Russian NHB champ in thirty seconds — and more than a few world champion Brazilian Jiu-Jitsu black belts in less time, with or without the gi. But none of these achievements have come from the lips of Chiapparelli himself. Despite his legitimate world titles and his runway good-looks, he has a monk-like modesty. Getting him to talk about himself or about his achievements is like prying open a cherrystone clam with a white pine toothpick.

When he teaches a position it looks so effortless that one is led to believe that shooting a double-leg takedown on him would be as simple as watching ice melt in the sun. Yet when you attempt the move it is akin to a bull moose trying to hump the Taco Bell Chihuahua. You have to reconcile the fact that he is world class athlete who has done it since age 8. Gifted athleticism is an obvious factor, as is years of high level training, but there is also an intangible at work — an extra gear in place that he can shift into on a moment's notice. While the average weekend grappler runs on diesel fuel, Chiapparelli runs on nuclear fusion. His flow from position to position is extraordinary to watch, and even more extraordinary to actually experience on the mat. His submission skills are so fierce that they explode out of nowhere like a Tomahawk cruise missile, and usually occur before you even hit the ground, during transition on the way to the mat. He is a grappler's grappler who has deciphered the Brazilian Jiu-Jitsu mystique and created a conundrum for those who wish to train with him.

# GRAPPLING MASTERS

*"Everybody in the college, everybody in the city, everyone in the state knew about all the wrestling matches. All the matches were televised live over statewide television. Plus, we'd get something like 16,000 fans in the arena for our home matches. It was almost like being a big-time athlete, but in a small-time sport."*

**Q: Why are you called the Baltimore Butcher?**
A: That's just a nickname that the announcer at college gave me. It was just a gimmick. There's no real or interesting story behind it. The interesting thing was just wrestling for Dan Gable – it was much more interesting than my nickname. He was just very intense in training. The thing was that Iowa was very intense about wrestling – so it was very, very good. Everybody in the college, everybody in the city, everyone in the state, knew about all the wrestling matches. All the matches were televised live over statewide television. Plus, we'd get something like 16,000 fans in the arena for our home matches. It was almost like being a big time athlete, but in a small time sport.

**Q: What made Dan Gable such a great coach?**
A: He knew how to peak people. He knew about the puritization of training. The other thing was that he could motivate anyone to be just about anything. Everybody at Iowa was training all the time. Whenever the gym was open, you could go in there any hour of the day and you'd see peo-

ple training. So you had to train hard because these guys were trying to take your position away on the team. So it was very competitive just within the wrestling room itself. So if you could get through that then you knew that you'd be able to beat just about anyone else you would face in a meet. And Dan's number one thing was conditioning – conditioning to break your opponent mentally. Once you broke the guy mentally, you could do whatever you wanted. There are certain factors you can always control, and conditioning is one of them. You can always be in great condition. So if you can control as many factors as possible, then the chances of you winning are a lot better. If you can get your technique, your fitness, your quickness, and your strength as close to 100 percent as you can, then your chances of losing come down dramatically.

*"Once you broke the guy mentally, you could do whatever you wanted. There are certain factors you can always control, and conditioning is one of them. You can always be in great condition. If you can control as many factors as possible, the chances of you winning are a lot better."*

**Q: Did Gable actually roll on the mat?**
A: When I was in college he still did. Not too many people think of Gable as a highly technical wrestler, but he actually really was. People are really surprised when they would go to different training camps and he would teach techniques and stuff and you would see these other wrestlers going, "I can't believe he just did that move." But he did. He was very well versed in the techniques of wrestling. But just like in the martial arts people think that if you know all the moves then you're going to be great – but that s meaningless to a large extent. Can you apply those techniques in a live combat situation? Technique is one very small aspect of a competition. Mental toughness, fitness, attitude, et cetera – and technique is one of them, of course, but many times in the UFC you see guys with no technique beating guys with tons of technique. You can force a guy into your position and your style.

*"The Russians would win by superior technique and superior positioning, but not with fitness; they are not known for their fitness. That's what I realized. So even through they weren't in good shape, they could play with guys because of their positions."*

**Q: What about when you first competed internationally in Russia? Were you surprised by the quality of Russian grapplers?**
A: I had always watched tapes of them so I wasn't really surprised. What I was shocked by was how everyone on the American team said how good the Russians were – and so they had lost before they ever stepped on the mat. At these international tournaments you'd have guys who were really good in college or really good in the United States and you got your eyes opened that there were people around the world who were really good. But there were people who are national champions around Iowa who get a lot of respect, but people never knew that some of these guys went to international meets and got their ass kicked a hundred times. What I was interested in was how people said the Russians were so great, but when I wrestled them I found out that they weren't so great. They're just like everyone else, you know. But there was a mystique about them. Just like a lot of teams would lose against Iowa just because they expected to lose because of the Iowa mystique. But there were certain Russian wrestlers that were just amazing technically. The Russians would win by superior technique and superior positioning, but not with fitness – they are not known for their fitness. That's what I realized. So even through they weren't in good shape, they could play with guys because of their positions. It's like me – I'm in terrible shape right now. But if you put a highly-conditioned high school wrestler with me right now I'd just play with them and not get tired because of superior position. So that's how some of the Russians were. They would play with guys who were multiple times U.S. champions. Going from high school to college is a big jump; then going from college to American freestyle is another jump – you see national collegiate champions who have never won a U.S. Ope

title. So to go from American freestyle to international competition was an equally huge jump. It's like the wrestling equivalent of single-A, double-A, and triple-A baseball. Each step up is a big jump and not many people can handle it.

**Q: Once your international career was over and you started seeing mixed martial arts, did you have to tweak your wrestling skills to adapt to it?**
A: The first time I ever saw mixed martial arts was when some guy showed me a tape of the first UFC. The first few UFCs were terrible, you know, because they hand-picked the guys so the one Gracie could win, basically. So I was looking at it and thinking that these guys were terrible – any wrestler with good position could have gone in there and beate them. Basically the opponents were expending a lot of energy in areas where a wrestler would not expend any. So since I had gotten into a lot of physical confrontations when I was younger I was like, "Hook him here. Knee him there." Use wrestling control positions to subdue them.

First of all, any top wrestler, even now, is just so much better athletically than anyone else out there in the world. You have world class athletes who are actually competing in a real sport that is contested in the Olympics. So that, number one, you have athletes who have been in thousands of competitions in front of thousands of people in many different countries – in places like Russia where they don't treat you very nice and they keep you up all night, and it's cold, and you travel for 5 days. That teaches mental toughness through hard competition that you can't get from just training casually against your own students in your own school. That is going to beat 90 percent of the guys out there. Then just the tweaks and techniques are going to take out the rest.

But then I saw the Gracies and I thought, "You know, there's something to that stuff." I always kind of rolled across my back in wrestling but I would never stay there – because in wrestling this is a very bad technique because it exposes your back to the mat for an instant. But if you need it, you can use it. But then all of a sudden it was okay to be on your back, and there were a ton of things you could do from there. I can do elevators, and that little move I used to do where I would roll across my back sometimes and set people up for a pin – people used to call it the "Rico Roll."

**Q: This was a move that was named after you by other wrestlers?**
A: Who knows who came up with that name. It's been printed in different

*"I saw the Gracies, and I thought, 'You know, there's something to that stuff.' I always kind of rolled across my back in wrestling, but I would never stay there — In wrestling, this is a bad technique because it exposes your back to the mat for an instant. But if you need it, you can use it. All of a sudden it was ok to be on your back, and there were a ton of things you could do from there."*

articles and stuff – in *Sports Illustrated* and other things. But then people say, "I've never heard of it." But it's like anything else, all it takes is for somebody to do something one time, and then somebody writes about it and puts it in a magazine or newspaper, and then all of a sudden that's what it is. Whether is was that or not doesn't really matter. It's the perception. So when I saw Gracie I thought, "That's really cool." At the time I wanted to get into something that was like wrestling, since I'd been out of wrestling for quite some time and was doing something else – living in New York City living an unhealthy lifestyle – so I wanted to get into something that wa similar to wrestling, that wasn't exactly like wrestling. So logically, if you're going to learn anything as a wrestler, submission seems like the last one percent of wrestling since it is all the stuff that is illegal in wrestling – the joint locks, the chokes, et cetera. You can't even bring the arm past 90 degrees in wrestling. To me, you know, this is something I thought I could do. But were there any schools for this in New York City? So he had a tape that showed the positions, and we would practice to the tape after we did our workout. So that is when I really got interested in it. It's great. I love jiu-jitsu. It's a great sport.

**Q: You went to Renzo Gracie's school in New York first?**

A: No, I went to a bunch of different ones. I went to some guys that weren't so good and I rolled around with them. Then my friend said, "Lets go to this other school where they're better." And so we'd go there. And he would be all excited about the competition aspects of going in someplace new, but I was just into the learning aspect of it. I just wanted to find out more about it. Then I finally got around to checking out

Renzo's school. But Renzo wasn't there, Craig Kukuk was there. He had a really bad back so I was just watching him teach. So just from watching how he positioned himself I knew that he knew what he was talking about. I knew that he could show me something that those other people couldn't. Maybe a lot of them didn't want to show the position outright, or maybe they didn't teach it the way it should be done. I don't know why it wasn't right or what their reasoning was, but I knew Kukuk knew it and was teaching it.

So then when he saw that I had a little bit of talent he said, "You know, my partner is going to be back. And you'll love him. You guys will get along famously." But I went there 10 or 15 times at the most because at the time I was doing a lot of other things. But then every time I would go back they say "How come you only show up once in a while." Well, at that time I'd been wrestling for 29 years. I was finished doing anything like that every day – it was just too much for me at the time. But then I got really interested in learning. I learned a lot of the basic, basic stuff from those guys. And I showed him some of my wrestling tricks – so a lot of the time we were exchanging knowledge. And he was a really nice guy and Kukuk was a really nice guy, also.

*"I finally got around to checking out Renzo's school. But Renzo wasn't there, Craig Kukuk was there. I knew that he could show me something that those other people couldn't. I don't know why it wasn't right or what their reasoning was, but I knew Kukuk knew it and was teaching it."*

**Q: You've rolled with a lot of the top BJJ guys, right?**
A: I wouldn't say that I rolled 100 percent outright – the top BJJ guys don't really like to do that. It's not like in wrestling where you go into wrestling practice and the guys go as hard as if it was a real match. There's no ego in wrestling if you're wrestling with guys on your team. But Brazilian jiu-jitsu is a lot different than wrestling. I didn't know it at

*"The top BJJ guys don't really like to do that. It's not like in wrestling where you go into wrestling practice and the guys go as hard as if it were a real match. There's no ego in wrestling if you're wrestling with guys on your team. But Brazilian jiu-jitsu is a lot different than wrestling. That's where wrestlers come from. We're actively trying to find someone to beat us, basically, so we can improve. But the Brazilians will hold things back and they won't go as hard in practice."*

the time and I didn't understand it, even though Craig kind of tried to explain it to me. I was just this guy who came from a wrestling background where everything was totally open – everybody would train with anybody – you'd show anyone anything. I would tell guys, "I will show you every move that I'm going to do to you, and then I'll do it to you. And if you stop me that's great. And if you pin me then great – it would really surprise the hell out of me but more power to you." That's where wrestlers come from. We're actively trying to find someone to beat us, basically, so we can improve. How do you improve if you dominate everyone? But that's the competitive nature of wrestling. But the Brazilians will hold things back and they won't go as hard in practice. I think it is a different cultural basis.

**Q: Can you compare the personal styles of the different Brazilian champions you've trained with?**
A: Within any style there are millions of different approaches and interpretations. That's the way it is in any sport, not just in martial arts. Even in wrestling, for example, my style of wrestling is different from any style anyone else has ever seen. Everybody is built different. So it's really hard to pick someone's method of fighting apart and compare it to someone else's style.

**Q: So after you learned submission you went on to the stand-up game. Was it difficult for you to learn punching and kicking?**
A: That is the absolute hardest stuff to learn for any wrestler. Because we always want to be moving forward, and doing that was like being a little kid again and trying to learn how to ride a bike. Learning how to kickbox was like that – just completely foreign. But the foot movements are the same as in wrestling; intercepting some of the punches are the same as blocking an

arm grab; and some of the defensive movements are also pretty much the same. Once I went around in some other things, I came to the conclusion that all the martial arts are basically the same. Once you transfer your knowledge, and don't limit yourself by thinking that you're only a grappler, or only a striker then you catch on. It's all in the head and how you think about your self. I do other things as well, such as tai chi, and there is a big benefit to that too. Some of the footwork is the same – you can see the same things in aikido. Chris Campbell, who is a famous wrestler, used to tell me, "You wrestle like you're an aikido guy." He was one of the first wrestlers who started doing other martial arts as part of his training. And I just said, "What's aikido?" I mean, I just had no clue.

The martial arts are a wide field. But the entire focal point of wrestling is combat, because we fight and compete every day – that's why the base and the sensitivity is so good. Everything is just shortened. A lot of the martial arts are only real if the other guy isn't defending, or if the other guy is giving you his wrist and you're letting him lead you around. But wrestling is real because the other person is trying to defend what you're doing and is trying to beat you. When someone is attacking, you have to shorten everything up, which wrestling does – the circles are very short, the lines are very quick, it's not as wide and open as it is in some of the other martial arts forms.

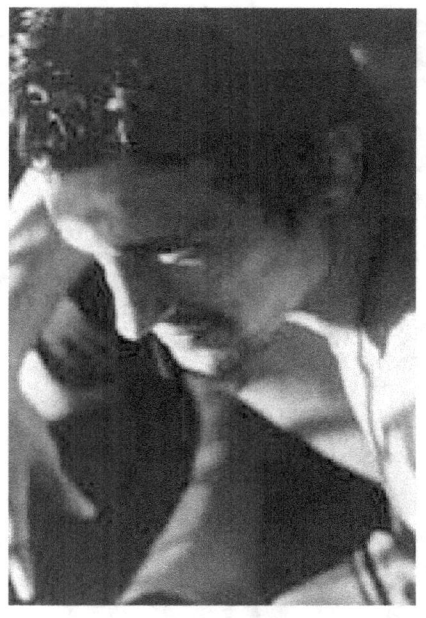

*"The martial arts are a wide field. But the entire focal point of wrestling is combat, because we fight and compete every day. That's why the base and the sensitivity are so good. Everything is just shortened. When someone is attacking, you have to shorten everything up, which wrestling does."*

**Q: You opened up the RAW Training Center in El Segundo, California. What is your vision for it?**
A: We opened this thing just so we could have a place to train. There are not that many places that are open where people can train seriously that have wrestling mats, a jiu-jitsu room, a boxing ring, weights, showers, cardio equipment and training bags and gear. This is like a stage for us to present NHB to people who don't know any better, and a place to improve

*"It's here to open people's eyes a little bit, and for me and others to learn more as well. I have everything here that I would personally want to do myself. The reason I came out here to do this is that L.A. is supposed to have all the top martial artists in the world living in a single city. So this is the place that's happening, and this is the place where we should be."*

people who do. This is how I ideally think we should treat this sport. We have many different combat arts here – jiu-jitsu, wrestling, submission wrestling. We teach Thai fighting, boxing, and cardio kickboxing for people who just want to stay in shape and not get into the combative aspects.

It's here to open people's eyes a little bit, and for me to learn more and for everyone to learn more as well. I have everything here that I would personally want to do myself. And eventually I want to have tai chi, and yoga, and a lot of other things as well. But we're just going to start small right now, and just have space for my guys to train, and for other people to come and train and to have some open space. The reason I came out here to do this is that L.A. is supposed to have all the top martial artists in the world living in a single city. So this is the place that's happening, and this is the place where we should be. I never try to get too rigid in what I plan and I never try to lock myself into an outcome. I just like to set up a situation and then see where it goes.

**Q: What would you say to people who are interested in training at RAW?**
A: This is a sanctuary for anyone who wants to live this particular lifestyle – you can come here and find your *way*. No one around here has an attitude. No one around here is trying to beat anyone up or is walking around with a bunch of tattoos trying to get into someone's face – you can bring the tattoos, just don't get into anyone's face. This is a place where you can walk through the door without any fear or apprehension – a place that is open to anyone regardless of skill level, what you train, or who you train with. None of that matters to me. If you want to come here then come. You're welcome anytime.

**Q: What has to happen in no-holds-barred fighting to bring it up to an international level and mainstream awareness?**

A: The main problem right now is with the majority of the promoters – not all of them – but the majority. They have an agenda. Obviously you have to make money, that's the number one agenda. In Japan, the agenda is to promote the particular form of fighting that they want to make popular. In America you just have unscrupulous people, because it's so unregulated, who couldn't do anything else so they went into NHB promoting. This is a new field that is treated almost like porno – people think it is dark and unwholesome. So it doesn't help that you get people running it who are not the top level of society. Most of them are not honorable and they try to get guys to fight for nothing, basically, or to even pay to fight. That hurts the sport. I'm sure many of them would say that me and my brother Louie are difficult to deal with. They say that simply because we try to protect our athletes and get them the price to fight that they should be getting.

*"The problem with NHB now is that it is not a sport. Nobody knows what it is. That's a huge problem. What exactly is NHB or mixed martial arts? The promoters don't know what it is they're selling, and most of them have never gotten their heart rate above two their whole life – so they don't have a feel for sports at all."*

The problem with NHB now is that it is not a sport. Nobody knows what it is – that's a huge problem. What exactly is NHB or mixed martial arts? The promoters don't know what it is they're selling – and most of them have never gotten their heart rate above two their whole life – so they don't have a feel for sports at all. But they think they're all tough guys – everyone wants to be the toughest guy on the block. But then they get into this and they find out they're not. "Well, then," they say, "How can we control these tough guys and make money off them." So a psychological thing happens where they want to control them just to prove they're somehow tougher than the fighters. So it becomes a problem because there are egos involved and strangely now, for some reason, you see fighters getting less now than they did five years ago – but yet there are more shows.

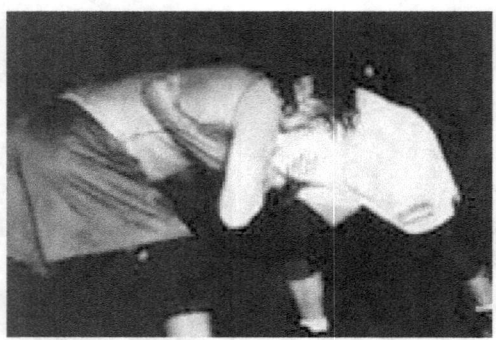

*"What I see is that most martial arts never become real sports because there's too many people who think they know everything. As a result, it becomes too fractionalized. That's what is happening in no-holds-barred. You have 100 different organizations and most of them don't even have real champions."*

**Q: So do you think that the sport is dying?**

A: Actually the sport on the grassroots level is getting bigger and bigger – so it'll never die – but whether it actually becomes anything important is another story. What I see is that most martial arts never become real sports because there's too many people that think they know everything – it becomes too fractionalized. That's what happening in no-holds-barred – you have 100 different organizations and most of them don't even have real champions. Most of them think you can get a shot at the title for doing nothing – just by having a couple of articles in a magazine or having your name mentioned in some obscure Web site. What happens is that a lot of people who don't know anything, team up with a different group of people who also don't know anything and prop each other up and become so-called experts when none of them actually know anything. Then they become the people that you have to talk to or have to go through to get fights in the sport. I refuse to let that happen to me or any of my guys. The people who know us know who is real and who isn't real.

What I'm trying to do is to promote the sport from a realistic standpoint. No promoter out there can sit down and talk to anyone and look directly into a camera and say, "Here's what our sport is exactly, here's why we do it exactly, here's why it's not wrong exactly – nobody can do that, not one of them. That's the biggest problem. Someone has to go before the government and explain it, or someone had to go on television and explain it but these guys look like fools when they're on television – it's really embarrassing for those of us who truly love mixed martial arts competition. Most of the people are probably not that educated, either – I don't know for sure but it's what it seems like when you watch them talk. One of the biggest problems is there is no name for it. It is just not treated correctly like a real sport. It's treated like half professional wrestling and half tough-man contest.

And therein lies another problem – people think that we have to be associated with professional wrestling in order to get an audience. That entire concept is a total joke. Professional wrestling was always popular with a certain fringe element, but it didn't become mainstream until a few years ago. Everybody in this sport because of their lack of patience or their lack of success in anything else they've ever done in their life expect this to be a sprint – well, it's not going to be, it's going to take a while to lay a base down. But it is picking up internationally and I'll tell you that mixed martial arts is going to eventually be the biggest sport in the entire world – quote me on that – because every country has their indigenous form of wrestling or martial art or self defense that people who do it will want to test. So this is the only sport that can ever truly be international – ever. Soccer is one that people say is international – but no one in the U.S. gives a damn about it so it is never going to be a global sport without the U.S. But you can see how mixed martial arts at the grassroots level is huge – it's going to survive and flourish because people love to do it. You might as well try to ban football. And no-holds-barred has spawned other things – the Pancrase style slap fighting and the ADCC style no-gi submission tournaments. There's a lot of different derivatives of it. It is obvious that this type of sportive activity had to have been around for thousands of years.

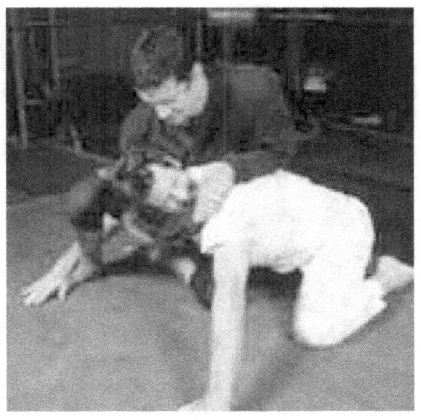

*"Everybody is in this sport because of lack of patience or success in anything else they've ever done in their life. They expect this to be a sprint. Well, it's not going to be. It's going to take a while to lay a base down. But it is picking up internationally, and I'll tell you that mixed martial arts is going to eventually be the biggest sport in the entire world."*

**Q: Why do you think that original style was lost?**
A: What I think happened is that some guys were good at standing and hitting and some guys were good at wrestling and so they split it up and started their own things and the fighting aspect got fragmented and stylized and watered down. But now in the new millennium its all coming back again – everything goes in circles and comes back in cycles. And now you have the original combat form happening again, but no one knows how to deal with it all, or how to put it together, or how to market it. The biggest problem with people who don't know about fighting – with people who haven't fought for real – is that they think a tough guy has to look a certain

*"Rickson knows that if you hold yourself back that you're going to get your price. He's very disciplined mentally. He's also done great with matchmaking himself to keep his record intact and to keep his name out there in front of people. He makes himself look like he's the No. 1 guy to people who don't really have an in-depth knowledge of the sport and who don't know better."*

way or act a certain way or be a certain way. They are drawn to the violent visual aspects of it. If you've done any combat form, any martial art, the actual combat part is meaningless, because the point is that you're supposed to do it to learn about yourself. But these guys have never learned any of that because they've never experienced it. They've never asked themselves any of the introspective questions – they've never looked within. They'v never laid anything on the line.

The reason anyone does anything now is to make money – that's not a good reason. The first thing I ask my guys, because a lot of people come here asking to fight, is, "Why do you want to fight?" If they say, "To make money," then I tell them that they'd better go somewhere else. Money is not a good reason to lay your whole life on the line – especially because now there's not a lot of money in fighting, just a little money.

**Q: What do you think of Rickson Gracie?**
A: He's the only person making real money in NHB. He has a knowledge of marketing and a feel for holding himself back and of not fighting in every event that comes along basically for free. There's guys who will walk across the street just to get on camera, or just to get their name in a magazine, or just to make 500 dollars. But Rickson knows that if you hold yourself back that you're going to get your price. He's very disciplined mentally. He's also done great with match making himself in order to keep his record intact and his name out there in front of people. He makes himself look like he's the number one guy to people who don't really have an in-depth knowledge of the sport and who don't know better.

But he is at the forefront of controlling the promoters, instead of doing what every other fighter does and let the promoters control them. Everyone should take a lesson from Rickson Gracie on how to market themselves, how to get your price, how to keep adding to your reputation. Basically what he did was to brand himself – he's his own brand name – he's the Rickson Gracie brand. When Rickson Gracie comes you know you've got to pay a certain amount for him to fight because he brings a certain image, a look that you can depend on, and will draw fans.

But with that being said, I think that most of the Japanese organizations he's dealt with have gone bankrupt. Pride changed their ownership after the first two shows; I've never seen Coliseum offer him another fight, and I doubt they ever will on the scale of the one he did. I wonder how much money these events make when he fights. But there is the beauty again – he gets people thinking that they're going to make a ton of money by having him fight. And to be realistic, they must make something. But you don't see him working with the same groups for very long. He started with Shooto twice then got out – they weren t making any money – they're still not making any money 8 years later – so maybe it wasn't him. Then he went to Pride and their first two financial backers have been replaced; with Coliseum he did the first show, but then the second show was with much more obscure Brazilian fighters.

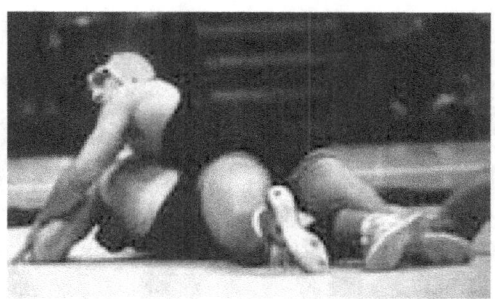

*"Everyone should take a lesson from Rickson Gracie on how to market himself, how to get your price, how to keep adding to your reputation. Basically what he did was to brand himself. He's his own brand name. He's the Rickson Gracie brand."*

But he's making money and he's doing it correctly for himself. Honestly, he's a guy who could do a tremendous amount of good for the whole sport because he has a certain look, a certain image, a certain something about him that ups the quality of whatever project he's associated with. Everything he does, as far as when you see it, looks really cool. And that's something that people need to do – bring that level of professionalism into the sport. That's what's incredible about what he's done. He started early and built his legend and image from an early age – and that's why he's where he's at right now. Now it's time for him to give something back – hopefully he will. But he has the jiu-jitsu schools as well, so to be fair he is helping to spread that particular art.

It's easy to sit back and talk about anyone. But who knows what's going on in their personal lives, in their heads, and in the life that they lead and with the people they're surrounded with. Who am I to criticize

*"It's easy to sit back and talk about anyone. But who knows what's going on in their personal lives, in their heads, and in the life that they lead and with the people they're surrounded with. You can't judge anyone else because you don't live their life."*

Rickson Gracie, or anyone for that matter, and say they're right or wrong? I can comment or observe, but that's it. You can't judge anyone else because you don't live their life.

**Q: Many insiders and experts think that you could win Abu Dhabi hands down. Why don't you compete?**
A: I have no desire to go over there and wrestle – none whatsoever. Because to me it is not a real competition. Who are the officials? Are they trained? Are they governed by an objective international governing body? Basically it's like when I went to Russia and dealt with their political system; or a lot like the John Dupont situation, where there was a rich guy paying a lot of people a lot of money to play monkey for him. At Abu Dhabi you don't know what the rules are, there is no official time clock that anyone can see, and there's no score displayed during the match. Who's ahead? Is it tied? Is it 2-0? Is there a minute left in the match? Is there 3 minutes left? You don't know. The first time I sent my guys over there – and I didn't know them all that well at the time – was the first year with Trigg and another guy. So Trigg went and wrestled Renzo Gracie and I don't know what happened firsthand, but everyone who saw the match said that Trigg lost because he got taken down. Well, I know for a fact that Renzo could never take Trigg down in a wrestling match. In a fight he could probably take him down, but never in wrestling. I would almost bet my life on it, just because that's the way it is. And yet Trigg lost. That is not right.

In the Olympics, for example, in the beginning of wrestling there were a lot of pins. But then guys became really, really good and you didn't see a lot of pins, and the outcome became dependent on the scoring system. But in wrestling there's a scoring system that's been around for years that's run by one international organization – FILA. Every country has its one national governing body that reports to FILA. So I laugh when an unsanctioned group with no uniform rules decides to hold a tournament and call it a world championship. It's not a world championship; how many countries are there? Who's the head of the organization? Are the rules written down? Are the judges impartial? Who made them? Can they change them on a moments notice in the stands? Of course they can. It's not a real competition as far as I'm concerned. My real interest is in no-holds-barred fighting. So if I did anything I would fight NHB or I would wrestle and try to be in the Olympics – because the Olympics are a real sport. It's been around for years.

*"My real interest is in no-holds-barred fighting. If I did anything I would fight NHB or I would wrestle and try to be in the Olympics, because the Olympics are a real sport. They've been around for years."*

Realistically, though, for guys who don't have the Olympic outlet to pursue, I think that Abu Dhabi is a good outlet – like the jiu-jitsu guys, for example, or people who do submission wrestling. Because maybe at some point Abu Dhabi could become real – I think the Sheik has genuinely good intentions. But at this point in time I don't think it has evolved to the point where it could be considered legitimate in the sense that Olympic wrestling is legitimate. Some of my people wanted to go this year and even though I'm not crazy about it I didn't try to stop them. I just told them to treat it like an exhibition match and to go hard, but to not get mad if they lost and not get too happy if they won. Personally, there's no reason for me to go and give credibility to it. If I wanted to make money I'd go. If I wanted to be Mark Kerr and go there and stall my ass off and make a lot of money for not doing anything, I'd go. But the way it is now, I personally have no interest. If some things were changed, then maybe. I mean, it's not personal – not by any means. I'm not against the concept, or the organizers, or the event – I'm mainly against the implementation.

*"I'd like to see the guys who are working their asses off get paid correctly and get the endorsements they should get from mainstream companies – just like a boxer would."*

Q: Would you do NHB?

A: I'd do a no-rules fight – one or two – just fo the hell of it. But again the price is not right. And they're not even paying my guys enough, and most of my guys are winning relatively easy, so I see no reason to do it. The problem I've got is that I got involved managing the guys, so that is my first responsibility. So me fighting would be a direct conflict of interest. But if the correct situation came up, I would step up. The only problem would be to get in shape in three or four months. That would be a problem – no, I could do it. What I perceive is that my international wrestling competition days are over – I'm old for a guy competing on an Olympic world-class level. NHB is another matter, of course. But I think that I can make more of an impact by trying to create a real sport and trying to bring a positive image to this no-holds-barred sport, trying to have regular people realize what NHB is all about and why it happens, and what it is, and why there's nothing wrong with it. I'd like to see the guys who are working their asses off get paid correctly, and get the endorsements they should get from mainstream companies – just like a boxer would.

When I wrestled in college we had guys in football, and they weren't even that good, and when they left for the NFL they'd be making millions. And here were the top in the world in our sport and we weren't making a dime. That's what drives me in this thing too. You see these fighters working their asses off in these obscure dojos and putting their life and their whole belief system on the line. It's a whole different thing when you go out there and they shut the cage and you're in there. It makes you learn more about yourself and why you are who you are – it's a defining moment. Anyone who's going to go that far and put that much on the line should be compensated in this world. It's not like a team sport where you play with a bunch of guys and if you lose it was their fault. In the cage there is place to hide and no one to pass the blame to – just you, your opponent, and a chain-link fence.

**Q: What keeps NHB from taking off?**
A: Self-interest. Guys like John McCain who is getting money from Budweiser through his wife's family. He has no convictions. He's a politician who does things for money and if all of a sudden his money started to come from NHB he'd turn on a dime. Just like in New York when it got the OK from the politicians and they were all behind it. Then Gulianni condemned it and two weeks later these same people were in the House of Representatives calling it a barbaric sport. Four-hundred people have died in boxing in the United States in the last 30 years, and there have been no serious injuries in no-holds-barred in America ever; but yet you don't hear McCain say anything about that because Budweiser makes money off boxing through sponsorships. Skiing is one of the most dangerous sports in the world but yet it's in the Olympics and there have been many tragic deaths from it – but yet McCain doesn't say a thing about skiing. So you can't really argue that NHB should be banned because of potential deaths or injuries. There are other reasons.

If people are queasy about NHB it's only because they would never do it themselves, and they don't understand the warrior mentality of those who do it. People want security and you don't get that in NHB. But then again many people do understand because you can see the overwhelming grass roots support this sport has.

*"If people are queasy about NHB it's only because they would never do it themselves. They don't understand the warrior mentality of those who do it. People want security and you don't get that in NHB."*

# Randy Couture

## *The Natural*

He makes everyone shake his head in disbelief and admiration. At an age that fighters are supposed to be retired, Randy "The Natural" Couture continued to step into the ring and destroed younger names like Tito Ortiz and Chuck Liddell. And he did it without leaving any room for excuses.

After graduating from Lynnwood High School, Couture moved on to military life where he found the love of his life... wrestling. After getting discharged from the military in 1990, he enrolled at Oklahoma State University and began to wrestle. His continuous victories in Greco-Roman collegiate wrestling made him the No.1 contender to join the Olympic team, but this never happened.

"When everybody expects you to achieve something and you fall short for various reasons, it is important that you re-evaluate everything in your life," says Couture smiling. "Take some distance and perspective and analyze why you are not getting what you are supposed to."

Despite the disappointment of not making the Olympic team, Couture, who once served as an assistant wrestling coach at Oregon State University, has had unparalleled success in the ring. And his winning ways are not coincidental. They are partially the result of a determined mind, which he inherited from his father. The remaining portion can be attributed to talent and hard work. Regarded as one of the true icons of MMA, Randy Couture is a quiet man, a focused fighter and an enjoyable human being. A true example of what a modern warrior should be.

**Q: How have events like the Ultimate Fighting Championship (UFC) influenced the sport of wrestling?**
A: Wrestling has been there for many years, but nobody ever looked at it as a fighting art until wrestlers started to compete in the UFC and win. That is when representatives of other martial arts styles opened their eyes and began to appreciate what we had to offer. I truly have a lot of respect for Mixed Martial Arts (MMA) and especially the UFC. It revolutionized

*"I have been surprised by the popularity I have received after competing in the UFC. Although I did a lot of wrestling competitions, both national and internationally, I never got the recognition I am now receiving."*

the martial arts world and brought realism to it. I have never been attracted to the more traditional martial arts systems so I think the UFC is a great forum for those whom advocate a realistic approach to combat sports.

I have been surprised by the popularity I have received after competing in the UFC. Although I did a lot of wrestling competition, both national and internationally, I never got the recognition I am now receiving. People stop me in the street and ask me for autographs and pictures. It is a great experience, and I love every minute of it. So I think events like UFC are positive for the arts and the athletes. Personally, I have learned a lot about myself competing in MMA. The exposure, being in the public... it's all being positive for me. The financial benefits have been fairly good as well.

**Q: Do you think MMA events are dangerous for the fighters?**
A: Those who believe that events like the UFC are dangerous don't know what they are talking about. We are athletes, and we are well prepared to face the demands and realism of MMA fights. They are not any more dangerous than football or hockey. Maybe in the past the things were a little different, but there are many differences between the first UFC and the last one. MMA are here to stay because they represent what many martial artists have been looking for and what they want. The training approach has changed drastically; kickboxing, grappling, wrestling, etc. have come together to create a format that is used by all of us. Wrestling is a little bit more limited because of the techniques, but both sports are totally safe for the athletes.

**Q: Do you believe in cross-training?**
A: Of course! The first thing a fighter should do is find a style he is comfortable with. He needs to create a base on which to build everything. For

me, wrestling was my base. From there, I went to boxing and then jiu-jitsu. I mainly wanted jiu-jitsu for the submissions and to learn how to pass the guard. In MMA, a fighter needs to know how to use his hands in every grappling situation. Unlike a grappler who looks to resolve the situation with a grappling movement, in MMA a fighter can use his hands to facilitate the escape. The strikes change the whole perception of the game, regardless how good he is on the ground. As I said before, it is important to keep an open approach to training. Try to learn as much as possible and try to overlap all the information. It's not wise for a fighter to jump from style to style because he won't get too far. He should try to be a well-rounded fighter but stick to what he does best. He should use the other styles to complement his strong points.

"When competing in wrestling at the level I did, I learned new ways to motivate myself. To do this, I didn't rush into things. I had to take one thing at a time. I rationally evaluated what I did; I tried to correct my mistakes and always looked forward."

**Q: Have you ever lost your motivation?**
A: Not really, although there are times when I've felt exhausted and tired and tried to find meaning in everything I do. After my fights against Barnett and Ricco Rodriguez, I could have quit. However, that's not my nature. This is logical [losing motivation], and I think everyone goes through this at some phase in life. For me, motivation is everything. When competing in wrestling at the level I did, I learned new ways to motivate myself. To do this, I didn't rush into things. I had to take one thing at a time. I rationally evaluated what I did; I tried to correct my mistakes and always looked forward. Going out there and proving that I am doing better than before is a key motivational factor. That really keeps me going. It is a constant internal challenge. Every time I step into the ring I feel I have to improve a little.

**Q: How do you prepare for a fight?**
A: I'm always training. So, when I have to prepare for a fight, I push a lit-

# Grappling Masters

*"One thing I never do is to think about my opponent as an individual. I don't get personal with him. I simply look at what he does. This allows me to better focus on the fighting aspects without getting involved in any personal facet of my opponent."*

tle bit more and re-arrange my training sessions to specifically fit what I need for that particular fight. I need about three months to be ready. If I have to, I can get ready in less time but three months is perfect. As I get closer to the fight, I train harder and push myself to the limits. It is important to evaluate an opponent. I watch tapes of my opponent and analyze what he does well and what he may lack in his fighting game. Based on this, I develop my strategy and game plan. Because of the limited amount of fighters, it is easy to get opponent's fight tapes. This is something that I did a lot in the beginning because I didn't know anybody. Now, I don't spend too much time watching tapes because I basically know the guys. One thing I never do is to think about my opponent as an individual. I don't get personal with him. I simply look at what he does. This allows me to better focus on the fighting aspects without getting involved in any personal facet of my opponent.

**Q: You are a type of fighter who doesn't respond to the mental games your opponents play. How do you keep yourself out of these games?**
A: Well, I'm a quiet guy and don't let these games get to me. I don't get intimidated. When they say these things, I tend to laugh. This pisses them off a little bit more.

**Q: What kind of martial art training you do these days?**
A: I stick to my wrestling training. Thus, I spend a minimum of two hours every day grappling on the mat. Most of this time is with bigger and heavier partners. When I want to improve my ability to adapt to the movements of a fast fighter, I will choose smaller opponents. Smaller and lighter opponents move and change positions faster than heavier opponents. I also train

several times a week on my boxing skills. Having good hands is a must in MMA. Occasionally, I train in jiu-jitsu. Not only do I want to learn new techniques, but I also want to take a break from my wrestling structure. This variety helps me to keep on my toes and stay mentally fresh. Basically, this is my MMA training. And, I do pay a lot of attention to my flexibility.

**Q: Why?**
A: Well, I train with weights and do a lot of power and strength training. The more I train, the more my body feels the stress and the stiffer it gets. That is when I need a lot of flexibility in my muscles and joints. This relieves the stress. Also, when fighting, sometimes I need to push a joint beyond its normal range of motion. For that, an extra amount of flexibility is required. Stretching also relaxes my body and allows me to recover from strenuous training sessions. I do my flexibility exercises before and after every training practice.

*"Cardio is the very basis of every athlete. No cardiovascular resistance and you are done in fighting. I consider this to be the most important part of any athlete's training program. When a fight is scheduled for 30 minutes, a fighter should have prepared with 90 minutes of non-stop cardio during his practice session."*

**Q: And your cardiovascular training? How do you approach it?**
A: Cardio is the very basis of every athlete. No cardiovascular resistance and you are done in fighting. I consider this to be the most important part of any athlete's training program. When a fight is scheduled for 30 minutes, a fighter should have prepared with 90 minutes of non-stop cardio during his practice session. When confronting an opponent, these 30 minutes fighting seem like an eternity. It's also imperative to have that conditioning to receive the punishment that inevitably occurs. When you get hit, endurance and resistance flies out the window.

I approach my cardio training in many different ways. I combine several exercises like running, skipping rope and stationary bike. When I run, I do a lot of sprints – usually from 8 to 12 – because that duplicates the change of rhythm and pace of a real fight. My long distance run is about

*"The idea is to strengthen my muscles to be prepared for the fight. The more muscle I have the better I can exert power. Stronger muscles also protect my joints. Many people think that fighters with muscles will be slow. Well, modern scientific training has proven this incorrect."*

four miles. As I said, I mix it with sprints using an interval training approach. I do the stationary bike and the rope for about 45 minutes, and I use them as a part of my warm-up.

**Q: And your strength aspect of your training?**
A: I work with weights three times a week, and I do it for specific reasons. I do bench presses and squats for power, but I don't do these as a powerlifter would. I also use free weights for several exercises. The idea is to strengthen my muscles to be prepared for the fight. The more muscle I have the better I can exert power. Stronger muscles also protect my joints. Many people think that fighters with muscles will be slow. Well, modern scientific training has proven this incorrect. It's important to balance strength with flexibility. Plyometrics are also critical because they will help to develop a power-in-motion quality, which eventually is what will be used in the real fight. Plyometrics are a very important aspect of my routine because they actually duplicate the action the muscles will be doing in the fight.

It's important that every aspects of the training has a purpose and perfectly overlaps with the rest to achieve the desired result.

**Q: Have you changed your training approach since the first time you fought in MMA?**
A: A little. I had to change and adapt to the new circumstances. The truth is that I narrowed my training, and I began to use a more analytical approach to understand my opponents. Every fighter has a strong point

that he capitalizes on when he fights. The key is to find what this strong point is and nullify it so he can't rely on it. When it's neutralized, it decreases his confidence. The key is to neutralize his strong points and capitalize on his weakness.

Personally, I have discarded what I call frivolous training and focused on the essential elements of physical conditioning. I have streamedlined my workouts to get the same benefits I did in the past but with a little less input. I cut down my weight training sessions, the running, etc. I train specifically for what I need, and I do the quantity of training that gives me what I need. No more, no less.

**Q: You have talked about confidence. Why is it so important for a fighter?**
A: Without it a fighter is nothing. If a fighter doesn't believe in himself, in what he has, in the hard training he went through, then it is better he doesn't step into the Octagon. A winning attitude is everything. A fighter needs a positive frame of mind to successfully confront his opponent. I use two methods that help me to reach the required state of mind. One, I visualize. Two, I do a lot of positive thinking. I can describe it as "fooling yourself positively." I learned all these techniques while training for the Olympics, and I keep using them in MMA.

**Q: I have heard you have a set of key phrases that you use. Is this true?**
A: Yes, it is true. I use them mostly to get back on track when things are not going the way I planned. Sometimes I get hit or the fight doesn't go the direction I expected. Then I need something that puts me back on track so I can regroup and keep going in the right direction. These phrases are very valuable in these situations. This is something I picked up from Olympic coaches. It is interesting because the Russians used this approach for decades and nobody knew. Now it is common knowledge.

It is important to know how to control negative thoughts. It is critical to intercept them and keep them at bay. This is a very important ability that can be used in any field in life, not just fighting. Focus on the positive and block the negative. This enables you to work in the right direction with the right mental attitude.

**Q: You always seem to be very calm. What about the final hours before a fight?**
A: I am a pretty laid back individual. I try to always be relaxed, even during the actual fight. It is a fight, but I look at it as a game. I focus on the positive aspects of my training and preparation. Once I feel confident about my abilities, the rest is pretty easy.

**Q: We have heard that you follow a specific diet that helps your performance. Tell us about it.**
A: I have always believed that the kind of food an athlete puts into his body determines the level of performance in any sporting activity. In order to have the proper energy for training and fighting, an athlete has need to know how his body reacts to certain foods and he has to learn how to combine them to get the best results. Eating the right food all the time is difficult. It takes planning and preparation, and that is not always possible. My diet is very simple. I try to eat five to six small meals during the day to keep my metabolism working. Sometimes I substitute a protein shake or sports nutrition bar for one meal. I also like to eat the carbohydrates in the beginning of the day and the protein later in the day. I do eat read meat, and I combine it with chicken, fish and vegetables. Pasta and rice are also important in my diet. I don't drink alcohol or sodas. In short, I keep a well-balanced diet and stay away from sugars and too many carbs.

**Q: In the press conferences before the fights, you don't seem to be altered by your opponent's comments. For instance, Tito Ortiz said very serious things about you, but you didn't seem to care. How is that?**
A: I'm an athlete. I don't get caught up in all that talk. I train, step into the Octagon and fight. That's all there is for me. They can say what they want. Now that you have mentioned Tito's comments, don't forget who won that fight and how. Facts speak louder than words. Period.

**Q: You have surprised fans because you – at an "advanced" age, at least for fighters – have defeated younger opponents. How do you defy age?**
A: If you take care of yourself, I don't think there is any reason you can't do the things you used to do. The one thing that really does change, however, is recovery time. I need more time to recover from training,

fighting and injuries. My body doesn't recover as fast as it did when I was 25. I have become more specific in my training. And this is something that I not only use in fighting but in other aspects of my life as well. As we grow older, we need to be more specific in the things we pursue.

**Q: What final advice would you give to the readers?**
A: Train hard and train smart. Don't forget that every aspect of preparation is important and that includes the physical training, the diet and nutrition, the rest, the psychological. Always be a gentleman, regardless if you win or lose. Don't forget that your opponent is the one who brings the best out of you. For that very reason, he deserves respect. Be gracious at all times, be honest with yourself and chase your dreams because your time is limited.

*"I have become more specific in my training. And this is something that I not only use in fighting but in other aspects of my life as well. As we grow older, we need to be more specific in the things we pursue."*

# HUGO DUARTE

## A History of Glory

HUGO DUARTE IS SYNONYMOUS WITH THE BRAZILIAN FIGHTING ART OF LUTA-LIVRE. MADE FAMOUS IN THE *GRACIE JIU-JITSU IN ACTION* VIDEO AS THE ARCH ENEMY OF JIU-JITSU, LUTA-LIVRE HAS A RICH AND PROUD HERITAGE SPANNING OVER SIX DECADES. AN EFFECTIVE GRAPPLING STYLE KNOWN FOR ITS ECLECTIC MIX OF JUDO, WRESTLING, AND JOINT LOCKS, LUTA-LIVRE HAS 54 SCHOOLS THROUGHOUT BRAZIL WITH A TOTAL MEMBERSHIP OF OVER 11,000. STARTING AS A YOUNG BOY, LUTA-LIVRE PRESIDENT HUGO DUARTE PARTICIPATED IN, AND NOW PRESIDES OVER, THIS EXPLOSIVE GROWTH. BUT GETTING RESPECT WASN'T EASY, ESPECIALLY IN A LAND WHERE JIU-JITSU IS KING. IN THIS FRANK AND HONEST INTERVIEW, DUARTE TALKS ABOUT THE TRIUMPHS AND DEFEATS THAT TOGETHER FORM LUTA-LIVRE'S "HISTORY OF GLORY."

**Q: What does luta-livre mean and who started it?**
A: It means free fighting and it is called that because it never used the gi. Luta-livre fighters always train and fight without the gi. It comes from wrestling with submission holds. Actually, luta-livre is just like Abu Dhabi. What they have been doing for one year, luta-livre has been doing for 60 years. Luta-livre is very respected in Brazil because they are the only group who has fought against jiu-jitsu thousands of time on their own terms. If you see a no-holds-barred event in Brazil the only style that beats jiu-jitsu is luta-livre.

Fausto Brunocilla and Mestre Tatu in Rio de Janeiro. They were both wrestling and judo fighters. So they used the judo joint locks and other submission holds and then a lot of freestyle wrestling throws. Around 1974 the great luta-livre names began to show up like myself, Eugenio Taudeo, Denilson, Carlinhos, and Joao Bosco. It is about the same time that jiu-jitsu started to get popular. There really weren't a lot of tournaments for luta-livre until recently. But now we are having them very often, without the gi of course.

*"I was a big kid, so I wanted to start training in something. At that time jiu-jitsu was popular, of course – not so big as today but still well-known because of Helio Gracie. It would have been easy for me to join with them, but they always had such an attitude towards all of the other martial arts that it turned me off."*

**Q: How did you get started training?**

A: I was a big kid and so I wanted to start training in something. In the section of Rio where I lived I saw some guys training in what turned out to be luta-livre and went in to check it out. At that time there was maybe only a handful of guys who actually trained in luta-livre. Even at that time jiu-jitsu was popular, of course, not so big as today but still well-known because of Helio Gracie. It would have been easy for me to join with them but they always had such an attitude towards all of the other martial arts that it turned me off. They wanted to control all the martial arts in Rio and would go into schools and intimidate the teachers and the students and fight with them. So I naturally did not like this bullying and so I did not want to join with them. I didn't want to join with the Lakers, but rather the Clippers.

**Q: How did luta-livre get the reputation of being jiu-jitsu's arch enemy?**

A: In the early '80s there was a guy in Brazil by the name of Flavio Molina who was a muay Thai teacher. A student of Flavio beat a younger jiu-jitsu student. So the Gracie guys invaded the Flavio Molina muay Thai Academy and beat up six teenage students who were happening to be taking a class – just unlucky guys who were not even top fighters or anything. In order to calm both sides and avoid a lot of street fights, myself and the Gracies set up a match between Flavio and Marcelo

Behring who was then the number two jiu-jitsu fighter next to Rickson Gracie. It was in the biggest soccer stadium in Brazil, in their indoor stadium called Little Maracana. But Flavio Molina was not a luta-livre guy but a muay Thai guy. But he was friends with all the luta-livre guys even though he didn't train with them. So to avoid getting beat up on the ground he asked his friend to train him in luta-livre to fight. So they taught him to fight on the ground and then he fought on the show. Eugenio Tadeo fought jiu-jitsu black belt Renan Pitangyi, the son of the most famous plastic surgeon in the world, Ivo Pitangyi, Marco Ruas fought Carlson Gracie's number one student Pinduca, and Marcello Behring fought Flavio Molina. In the end Eugenio won, Marco had a draw, and Flavio lost. So in the end it was even and it proved to the people on the streets that luta-livre was the equal of jiu-jitsu. For jiu-jitsu, it was the day the earth stood still.

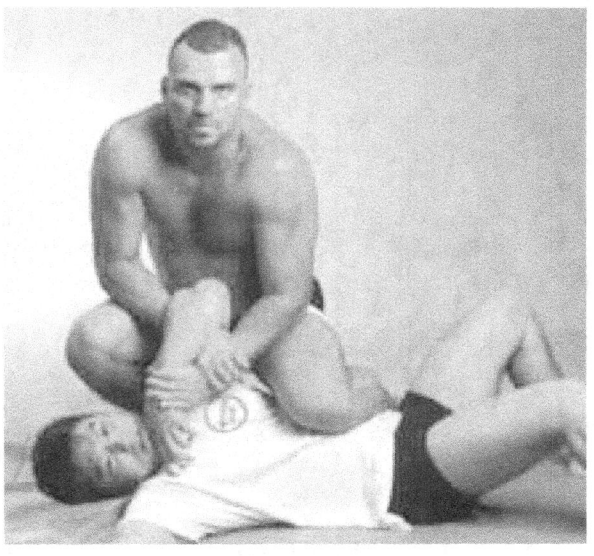

*"I was just having fun at the beach when 2,000 jiu-jitsu guys showed up in a giant gang with a video camera. Of course, we had a rivalry but I never expected anything like this. I did not have any of my students around – only a handful of friends."*

**Q: In *Gracie Jiu-Jitsu in Action II* there is a fight on the beach where Rickson Gracie fights a man whose face has been blocked out. Is that you?**
A: Yes, it is.

**Q: What happened in that fight?**
A: I had not planned on fighting and there was no warning that a fight was to take place. I was just having fun at the beach when 2,000 jiu-jitsu guys showed up in a giant gang with a video camera. Of course, we had a rivalry but I never expected anything like this. I did not have any of my students around but just a handful of friends to their thousands. So Rickson

*"Some other of his students threw sand in my eyes so I could not see. If those things had not happened, the outcome might have been different. Sometimes it does not matter if you beat the bully but only that you stand up to him. So I was proud in defeat."*

just came up and slapped me and said, "Are you ready?" I replied, "I'm always ready." And then we started to fight. The tape only shows the beginning and the end of the fight when Rickson had the superior position and forced me to tap. But there is a lot the tape does not show. For example, it does not show that I took Rickson down and mounted him. It also does not show that when I was mounted, one of Rickson's students came up behind me and pushed me off of him. Some other of his students threw sand in my eyes so I could not see. If those things had not happened then the outcome might have been different. A week later I went to his school with a bunch of my students to return the favor and fight again. Even though I did not beat him, what matters the most to me was that my students went with me and were not intimidated. We had the courage to go up against jiu-jitsu and show that we would not get pushed around. Sometimes it does not matter if you beat the bully but only that you stand up to him. So I was proud in defeat.

**Q: Is there a national organization?**
A: Yes, the Brazilian Confederation of luta-livre. It is comprised of about 54 schools all over the country. There are about 11,000 people who do luta-livre in Brazil. At the last tournament there were 3,000 spectators and the around 600 fighters. Luta-livre is famous for being very effective in foot and leg locks. They have many more leg and foot combinations that jiu-jitsu. The man difference between jiu-jitsu and luta-livre is the jiu-jitsu uses the gi and luta-livre doesn't. So many of the gi chokes in jiu-jitsu are not used in luta-livre so we concentrate on things that can be used without the gi. To us, it is funny now to see the jiu-jitsu fight so much without

the gi. In luta-livre we have always fought without the gi. In the old days, actually not that long ago, the jiu-jitsu players used to call us all kinds of bad names because we fought without the gi. They thought it was the stupidest thing they could imagine. Now, though, since Abu Dhabi started, they do not use the gi, look at Renzo, Rickson, et cetera. It just tells us that we were right all along. It makes me proud to think that luta-livre stood up to jiu-jitsu for all those years, and now jiu-jitsu is copying us.

**Q: Would you like to fight Rickson Gracie again?**
A: I've never chosen opponents and have fought all the tough guys out there, not just Rickson. My things with Rickson happened in the past and we fought then. But after I went to Japan for the first time I challenged him two or three times in a very professional way, with nothing personal – no hate, anger, or anything like that. But he chose not to fight me. He is in a position of influence as far as choosing his opponents because he is so popular. If it was up to me I would love to fight him again. I think we owe it to each other.

**Q: Do you think Rickson is overrated?**
A: I believe that Rickson's technique is an unquestionable matter. I have fought against him and I have fought against many of the people who say they are better than him and I can tell you that they just don't know. Anybody who knows anything, knows that he is very technical. And everybody in the world today is actually involved in no-holds-barred thanks to the Gracie family. The old myths that used to exist have all been destroyed. So when I go to the ring, now, I'm so much more relaxed than I was in the beginning because now no one is intimidated by reputation alone. But I can tell you that Rickson is much more than just an

*"To us, it is funny to see so many jiu-jitsu fights without the gi. In luta livre, we have always fought without the gi. In the old days, actually not that long ago, jiu-jitsu players used to call us all kinds of bad names because we fought without the gi. It makes me proud to think that luta livre stood up to jiu-jitsu for all those years, and now jiu-jitsu is copying us."*

*"If the top NHB guys fought each other, a lot of myths would be broken. But, unfortunately, a lot of guys choose not to fight. People would rather hide behind the curtain rather than fight, so you never know who the best really is."*

empty reputation. Rickson is the leader of jiu-jitsu and I am the leader of luta-livre, so a fight between us would generate a lot of interest and be very successful. I would be willing to fight for free just to see it happen.

**Q: Who do you think is the best NHB fighter?**
A: There are a lot of tough guys there today. Igor Vovchanchin is one of them. A very nice, humble guy out of the ring – so nice and polite – yet, he is able to become an animal in the ring. Mark Kerr, also, is a tough guy. But there are many other guys who are just as good I think. It is like the wind, you know. Sometimes it blows one way and sometimes the other so I think it is very hard to point out one fighter. I think there are a group of top fighters and it just depends on the night as to who will win. I believe that in NHB that if the top guys fought each other a lot of myths would be broken. But, unfortunately, a lot of guys choose not to fight. People would rather hide behind the curtain rather than fight, so you never know who the best really is.

**Q: Does luta-livre practice any stand-up techniques?**
A: Yes, we train boxing but for different reasons. One of them is to get accustomed to getting hit, and also to get the timing for the takedown – not really to learn to knock people out. But we have a lot of events that don't include vale tudo. We have five sport competitions a year, so if a fighter wants to fight and be active he can fight every other month.

*"People don't realize how hard it was to stand our ground in Rio against all the jiu-jitsu fighters. But I stood up for what I believed in, and it paid off in the end. I feel like a winner in life, along with all my fighters, who are also my friends."*

**Q: What does luta-livre mean to you?**
A: Today, I believe luta-livre is like a nation. The luta-livre I have believed in since I was a little boy has not changed. I've been rejected many times in my life but never by luta-livre. I have given my life to it. I stuck to it even though I faced constant discrimination and I had to fight a lot of people. People don't realize how hard it was to stand your ground in Rio against all the jiu-jitsu fighters. But I stood up for what I believed in and it paid off in the end. I feel like a winner in life along with all my fighters who are also my friends. We have a history of glory – wins and losses – and we're still around, stronger than ever.

## Grappling Techniques

*Hugo Duarte fights his opponent from the ground (1). Using his left leg, Hugo unbalances his opponent (2) and brings him down (3). Notice that Hugo secures his left leg between the opponent's right leg and arm. Hugo controls the opponent's right leg (4) and applies a reverse anklelock (5).*

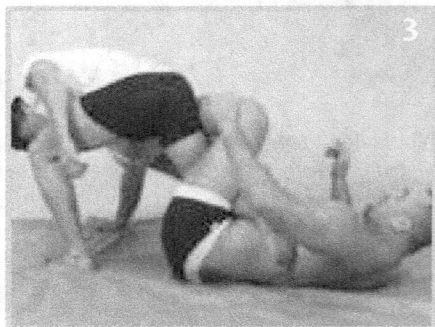
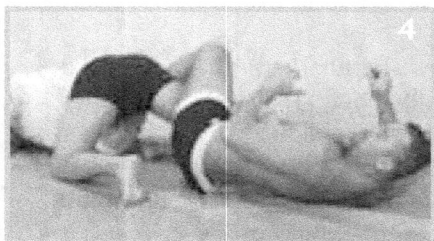

Hugo is on top of his opponent in the side-control position (1). As Hugo moves his right arm to the opposite side, he simultaneously secures the opponent's wrist with his left hand (2-3). Using his right hand, Hugo grabs his left wrist (4) and applies a straight armlock (5).

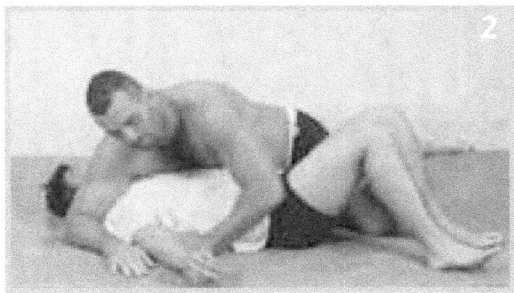
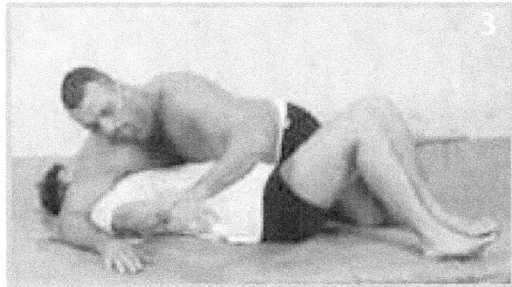
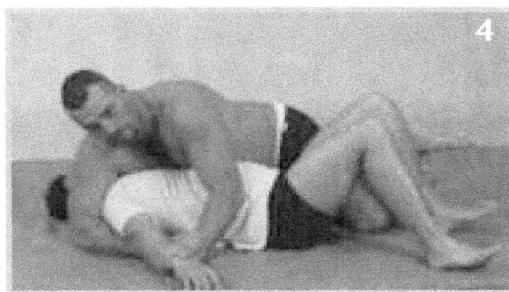
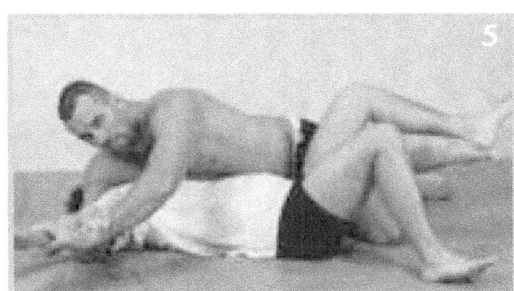

## Grappling Techniques

*From the side-control position (1), Hugo Duarte opens the angle by pushing the opponent's right arm with his elbow (2). He coils his right arm around the neck and applies a finishing choke (3-5).*

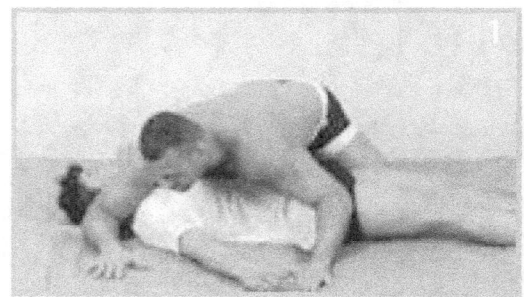

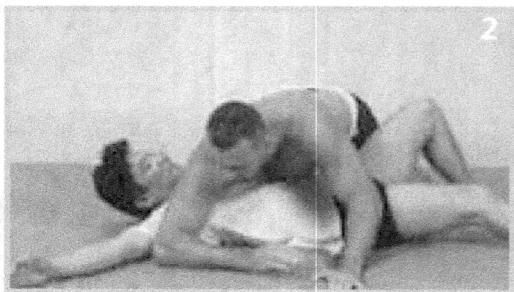

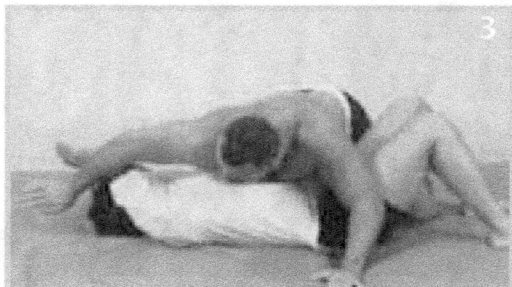

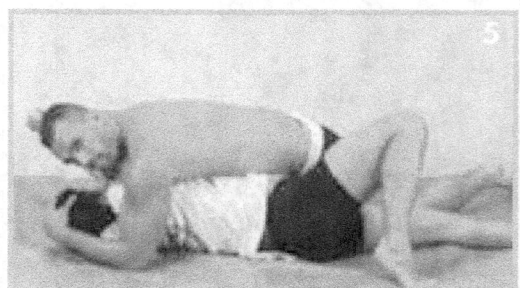

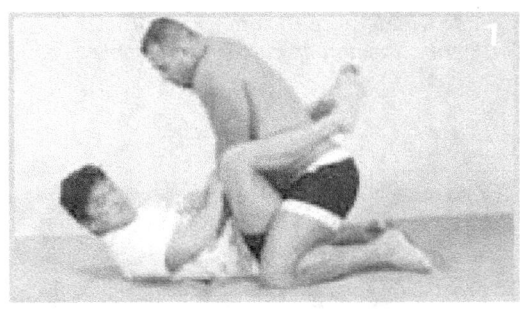

Hugo is inside the opponent's closed guard (1). Moving to the right, Hugo breaks the guard and passes as he controls the opponent's left leg with his body (2). He slides his right arm under the opponent's neck (3) and grabs the opponent's right arm (4). Hugo rises slightly and applies a painful and effective neck crank (5).

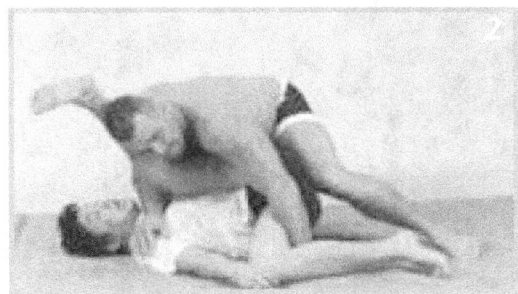
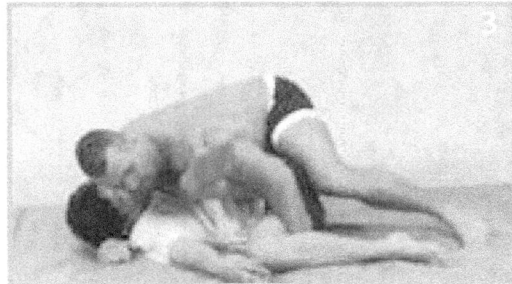

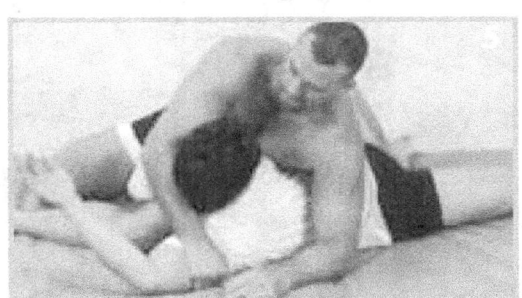

## Grappling Techniques

Holding Cacareco in the closed guard (1), Hugo Duarte traps the arm (2), reaches over the elbow (3), grabs his own wrist (4), rotates the arm upward (5) and applies a finishing lock (6).

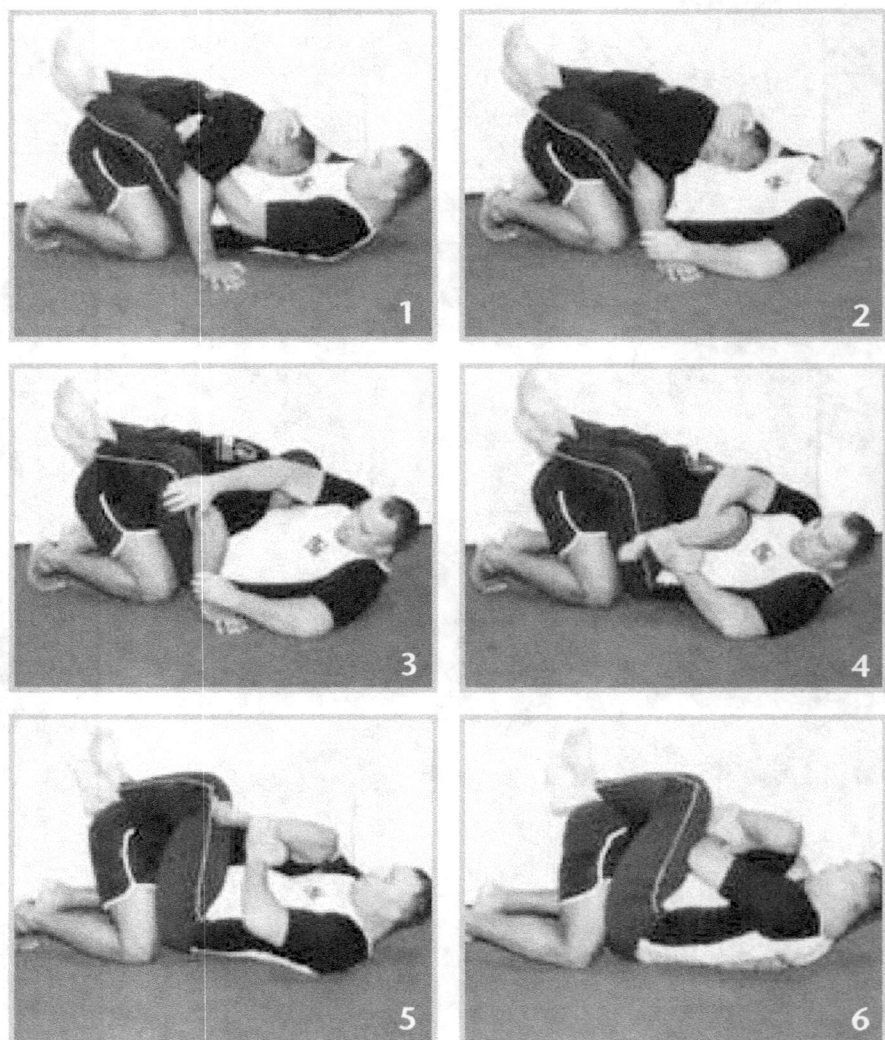

Working form a side control (1), Hugo Duarte lays out (2), traps the head (3), secures the arm (4), places his bottom arm on the head (5) and applies a painful neck crank (6).

# PAULO GILLOBEL

## *One of the Elite*

ORIGINALLY FROM RIO DE JANEIRO, PAULO GILLOBEL IS RECOGNIZED AS ONE OF THE MOST KNOWLEDGEABLE BRAZILIAN JIU-JITSU INSTRUCTORS IN THE UNITED STATES. HE RECENTLY WON THE 2003 PAN-AMERICAN CHAMPIONSHIPS, SETTING AN EXAMPLE OF HOW A DEDICATED INSTRUCTOR CAN ALSO SUCCESSFULLY COMPETE IN BIG TOURNAMENTS. A PERSISTENT DEDICATION TO SUCCESS, DESPITE MAJOR OBSTACLES, HAS ALWAYS BEEN GILLOBEL'S DRIVING FORCE. DISPLAYING THE QUALITIES OF AN ORIGINAL THINKER, HE HAS A VERY ANALYTICAL APPROACH TO BOTH LEARNING AND TEACHING: "REGARDLESS OF WHAT STYLE OF MARTIAL ARTS YOU ARE PRACTICING, YOU SHOULD ALWAYS ALLOW ROOM FOR ADDITIONAL KNOWLEDGE TO IMPROVE WHAT YOU HAVE. DON'T THINK THAT YOU KNOW EVERYTHING – OR THAT WHAT YOU KNOW IS ALL THERE IS TO KNOW – BECAUSE YOU'LL BE DIGGING YOUR OWN HOLE." BY COMBINING THE POSITIVE ELEMENTS OF ATHLETIC COMPETITION WITH THE DEEPER ASPECTS OF TRUE MARTIAL ARTS INSTRUCTION, PAULO GILLOBEL HAS TRULY TRANSFORMED HIMSELF INTO "ONE OF THE ELITE."

**Q: How long have you been practicing Brazilian jiu-jitsu?**
A: Since 1988. My first teacher was Jorge Pereira – a Carlos Gracie Jr. black belt – and I have been training with the Machado brothers for the last four years. During this time, I have successfully competed in many tournament and events. I won national and state competitions in Brazil, and since my arrival in the United States I have been competing in tournaments all around the country. In 2003, I won the Pan Ams. That was a great feeling because only the best compete in it. When I was in Brazil, I trained jiu-jitsu, judo and boxing, but I also started training in wrestling once I got to the United States. Wrestling is a different form of grappling that can create some problems for a BJJ practitioner due to its ways of attacking, defending, and controlling an opponent on the ground. It lacks submissions and other tactical aspects of jiu-jitsu, but it is very helpful in many aspects of ground control. I truly think that wrestling complements Brazilian jiu-jitsu very well. You need to know how to make both arts blend in a smooth way. Wrestlers have great training methods

*"Physical talent doesn't mean anything if you don't put in time on the mat. Talent, without passion and dedication, means nothing. But if you have natural talent and work hard, you can become a legend in any sport."*

and drills that any jiu-jitsu practitioner can benefit from.

**Q: Was jiu-jitsu easy for you to learn?**
A: When I first started jiu-jitsu, it was very easy to learn the techniques. I felt like it was my martial art. I was always one of the best in my weight at every belt, but to get really good you have to train and stretch a lot in order to avoid injures and to get your game flowing. Physical talent doesn't mean anything if you don't put in time on the mat. You may be better than another guy in the first stages of the training, but if he trains more than you he will make you tap regardless of your natural talent. Hard work and consistent training are more important than natural talent. Talent without passion and dedication means nothing. But if you have natural talent and also work hard you can become a legend in any sport.

Every day at the academy I learn something new. When I got my black belt, I felt like I was starting all over again. Plus, the Machado brothers have plenty of things to show and I feel very lucky to have a chance to learn from them. A lot of my previous perceptions of jiu-jitsu have changed with the years. Today, we have great instructors all over the world and you have to be more dedicated if you really want to be good at it. I have been extremely lucky since I always had great teachers and excellent training partners. With a great teacher next to you, it is easier to improve your technique and performance. You have to learn to be patient and understand that the good things take time. In any sport or activity excellence won't happen overnight – and jiu-jitsu is no exception. Jiu-jitsu is not an easy art, which is why it is one of the best martial arts.

**Q: What changes have seen in jiu-jitsu since you started?**
A: Compared to 20 years ago, there are BJJ schools all over the world now. There are a lot of people in different cultures who see the same concept in different ways – this gives BJJ different options to expand. But the bad news is that jiu-jitsu used to be more relaxed and technical in the past. Now we have a bigger tactical arsenal but a lot of people lack the basic foundation that helps you to reach the higher levels of the art. Evolution is good as long as we don't forget who we are and where we came from.

**Q: What should a person do if they want to train jiu-jitsu?**
A: The first thing is that you have to look for a good school, because not all academies offer a good training and teaching method. Then when you start, commit yourself to the training and go for it – that is way to have fun. The better you get the more fun it will be. Also remember to train smart and don't go crazy. Injuries will come very easy if you don't train wisely and these injuries will slow your progress.

In Mixed Martial Arts, you need a good trainer and coach to guide you. Unfortunately, too many people jump into a cage without proper training. Some teachers send their students to fight too soon because they want to become championship trainers, but they don't realize that you can't do that unless you truly prepare your students. What is really unfortunate is that the students don't know any better and follow their teacher's orders – even if these are crazy! A good teacher prepares a student the right way before sending him to fight Mixed Martial Arts or Vale Tudo.

*"Some teachers send their students to fight too soon because they want to become championship trainers, but they don't realize that you can't do that unless you truly prepare your students. What is really unfortunate is that the students don't know any better and follow their teacher's orders ... even if these are crazy!"*

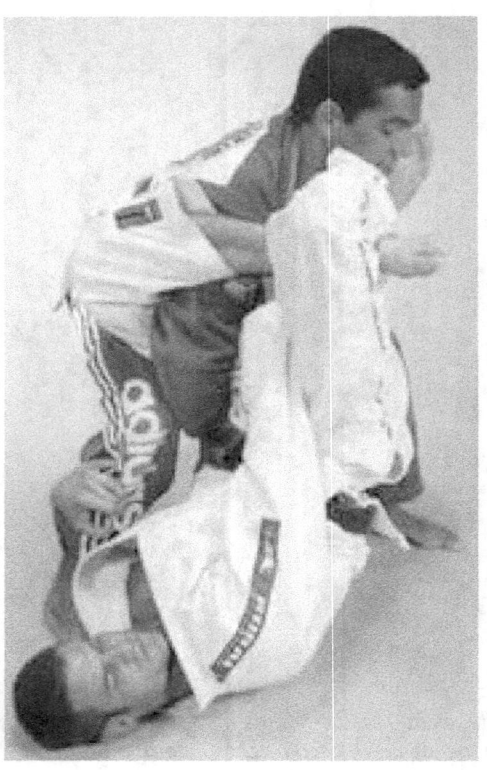

*"The bottom line is that jiu-jitsu has to be natural. If there is any technique that is not natural, you have a problem. You have to understand the principles of why and how the technique works and then adapt it to your own body structure."*

**Q: What drives you to keep training and teaching?**
A: I love what I do and I think this is the thing that pushes me day after day. The fact that I keep learning every day – there is always something new on the mat – keeps me on my toes. I love to compete and BJJ helps me to keep in shape, too.

**Q: Who would you have liked to have trained with?**
A: There are two people I would love to have trained with – Rickson and Royler Gracie. I am a huge fan of those two. I have been watching them fight my whole life, and they have been the motivation for my personal training and for my desire to compete. They are the number one examples of what all jiu-jitsu practitioners want to be.

**Q: How do you prepare yourself before a tournament?**
A: I meditate a lot. I always try to connect with my inner self. I also stretch a lot and try to relax, focusing on my breath and my heartbeat. I also do the "Ginástica Natural," which helps me a lot on my moves and my speed when I'm using jiu-jitsu techniques. The bottom line is that jiu-jitsu has to be natural. If there is any technique that is not natural then you have a problem. That's why BJJ is so different from other arts – you have to adapt the techniques to your own body to make them work. Not everybody can perform the same jiu-jitsu technique the same way. A jiu-jitsu technique is not a ballet movement that all the dancers have to follow exactly. You have to understand the principles of why and how the technique works and then adapt it to your own body structure. Only then can you truly express real Brazilian jiu-jitsu.

**Q: What fighter has inspired you?**
A: I have always admired Jean Jacques Machado. Every time I look at him or train with him I realize here is a guy who was born with a limitation – only half a hand in a sport where grip is everything – but yet became the best pound-for-pound fighter in the world. If he could overcome something like that, then all my petty complaints mean nothing. He is my biggest spiritual inspiration.

**Q: Why do you practice jiu-jitsu?**
A: That is a hard question because the answer involves many personal factors that are different for each individual. Everyone has a different point of view about this subject; some do to get more self-confidence, some to learn to fight, others because it is a good workout and simply makes them feel good. I think BJJ is a way of life, a challenge, a physical chess game. It is far more than simply fighting or grappling with another person. In Japan, the symbol of jiu-jitsu is water – that's because water is adaptable to any space, is unbreakable, and flows – but yet it is always water. It changes its shape but not its form. That is how I see jiu-jitsu and that's how the art should be used in competition. I also think it is how we should act in our personal lives.

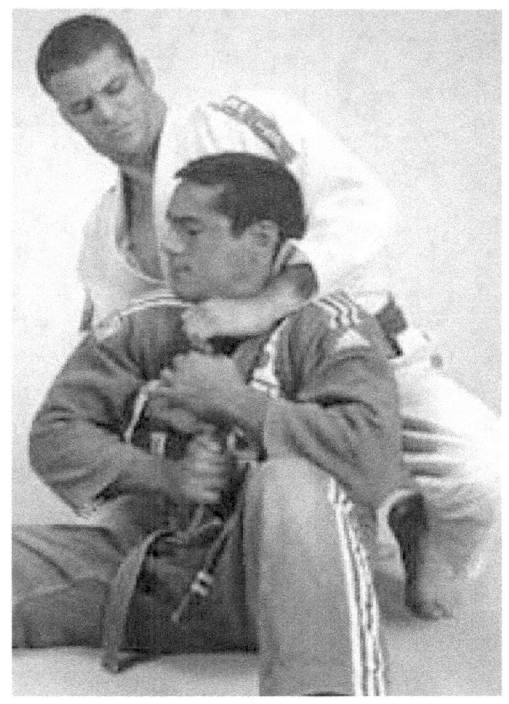

*"In Japan, the symbol of jiu-jitsu is water because water is adaptable to any space, it is unbreakable and it flows. Yet, it is always water. It changes its shape but not its form. That is how I see jiu-jitsu, and that's how the art should be used in competition."*

**Q: What are the most important qualities of a successful BJJ competitor?**
A: There are several. The first is determination – you have to focus on what you are doing and train hard to be the best. The next is humility – you need to be humble to respect who is at a higher level than you because you are going to have to learn from them. You have to respect

*"I have felt fear many times during my competitions. Fear of losing, of getting hurt, of not doing your best are all reasons why someone may feel fear. But you can use fear to your own advantage because you need fear to develop courage."*

everyone but fear no one. Finally, you need courage and lots of creativity.

On the physical level I would say cardio and flexibility are the most important aspects, but you also have to work also your strength – because sooner or later you are going to need it. You should never only lift weights, because you might get stiff and lose your endurance – which in jiu-jitsu is extremely important. Weeks before the competition, you got to work on sprints to get quicker; that will help you to gun your engine when you need it.

**Q: Is it beneficial for BJJ competitors to study other martial arts?**
A: That depends on your final goal. If you want to be a BJJ competitor, you have to spend all your time on the mat, training. Judo and wrestling will help in this. However, kickboxing, kung fu or karate won't do much for you. Therefore there is no need for a jiu-jitsu practitioner to spend time training in other arts. But if you want to be a MMA fighter, you have to study a martial art that teaches you how to strike and to defend against punches and kicks. This kind of training will give you more options when you are facing an opponent in the cage.

**Q: How does fear affect a competitor's performance?**
A: I have felt fear many times during my competitions. Fear of losing, of getting hurt, of not doing your best are all reasons why someone may feel fear. But you can use fear to your own advantage because you need fear to develop courage. A good fighter overcomes his fear, but if you let fear take control of you then it is going to be hard to succeed in a fight or in life. If something scares you then you should face it. If you do that, then

you have beaten fear. Courage is nothing more than having done something before.

**Q: What are your thoughts on the future of jiu-jitsu?**
A: I think we need more organization. We have the best product but we don't know how to sell it. We have to go after the big sponsors and get them to invest money in what we are doing – but in return we need to show a cohesive structure they can rely on. I like the way NHB is been managed, it is helping jiu-jitsu grow. Sport jiu-jitsu and submission fighting need events with credibility and professional referees, judges, and accredited organizations. We're starting slow but we will get there.

**Q: What's the key for beginning students to stay in the art?**
A: Keep training and believe that you are learning the best martial art ever. BJJ is growing fast and one day, for sure, it will be a very big sport. But in order to make this happen we all need to work together with the same goal in mind! New students should learn how to be patient and remember to always show respect for your partners. Try to focus on what you are doing with determination. Have the courage to train with everyone and to balance all the aspects of your life. All practitioners should develop these qualities from the early stages of their jiu-jitsu training. And like Jean Jacques Machado likes to say, "Leave your ego at the door."

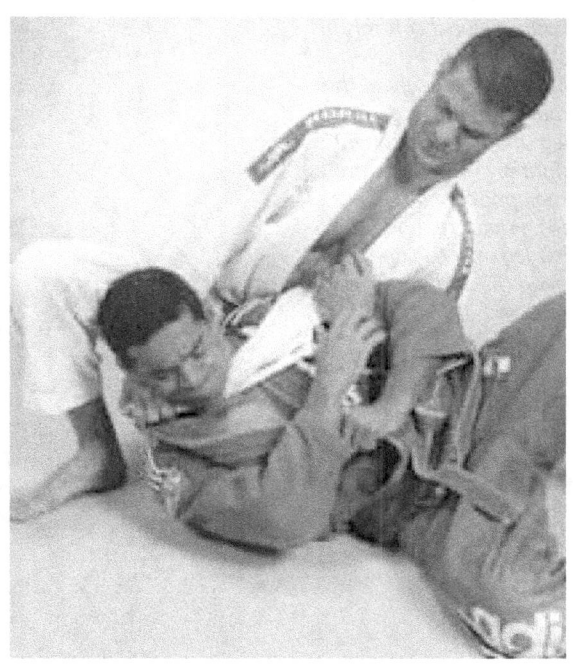

*"Keep training and believe that you are learning the best martial art ever. Try to focus on what you are doing with determination. Have the courage to train with everyone and to balance all the aspects of your life."*

## Grappling Techniques

Paulo Gillobel controls his opponent from the top (1). Spinning precisely to the mat (2), Paulo passes his leg under the opponent's right arm (3). This throws the opponent's balance off (4). Paulo then passes his left leg over the opponent's head (5) and applies the finishing armbar (6).

# GILLOBEL

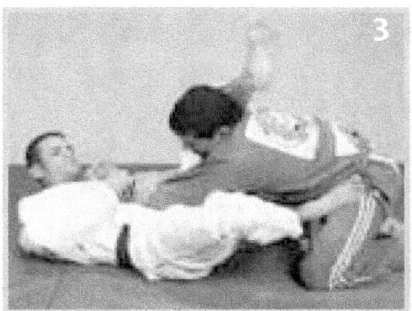 

Paulo Gillobel fights from the spider guard (1). As his opponent tries to pass (2), Paulo puts his foot on the right hip for leverage (3) and t applies the finishing lock (4).

Holding his opponent in the inside guard (1), Paulo shifts his hips to the side (2) and swings inside while applying the finishing elbowlock (3).

## GRAPPLING TECHNIQUES

*Paulo Gillobel operates against his opponent's open guard (1). He pins the opponent's leg to the ground (2), flips over (3), lands on his back (4) and settles into side control (5).*

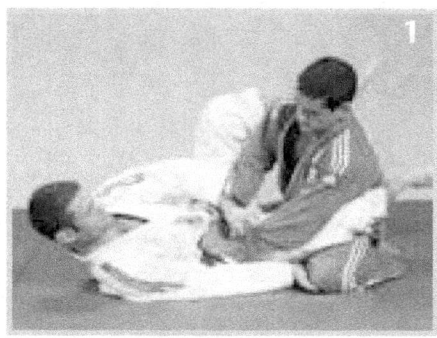

Operating from the open guard (1), Paulo spins on his opponent's arm (2), rotates onto his shoulder (3), controls the arm with his leg (4), rises and applies the omoplata (5).

# CARLEY GRACIE

## *The Brazilian Lion*

CARLEY GRACIE, A MEMBER OF THE FAMOUS BRAZILIAN JIU-JITSU FAMILY, KNOWS SOMETHING ABOUT THE REALITIES OF UNRESTRAINED PHYSICAL COMBAT. CARLEY IS THE ELEVENTH CHILD OF BRAZILIAN JIU-JITSU LEGEND CARLOS GRACIE, AND WAS BORN AND REARED IN THE FAMILY TRADITION OF DEDICATED JIU-JITSU TRAINING AND CHALLENGE MATCHES. CARLEY WAS THE FIRST PROFESSIONAL NATIONAL CHAMPION IN BRAZIL AFTER THE JIU-JITSU FEDERATION WAS ORGANIZED IN RIO DE JANEIRO, REIGNING FOR FOUR YEARS (1969 THROUGH 1972) BEFORE COMING TO THE UNITED STATES TO TEACH THE UNIQUE GRACIE STYLE OF JIU-JITSU TO U.S. MARINES. HE WAS THE LAST GRACIE FIGHTER WHO ACTUALLY LEARNED FROM AND WAS PERSONALLY COACHED BY HIS LEGENDARY FATHER CARLOS.

**Q: Carley, there have been somewhat varying accounts on the origins of the Gracie family art of jiu-jitsu. Could you give us your insight on how it all began?**
A: Everyone admits that our system started with my father, Carlos Gracie, in Brazil. My father originally learned jiu-jitsu from Conte Maeda Koma, a former Japanese and world champion who was visiting Brazil to help settle Japanese immigrants in the north. My father was only 17 years old when he first began studying under Conte Koma, and he opened his first Academy in Belèm (Northern Brazil) approximately four years later. The stories about my uncle Helio Gracie being the founder of our style are simply not correct; my uncle Helio was only about nine years old when my father started teaching jiu-jitsu.

My grandfather Gastão Gracie had nine children: five sons and four daughters. My father Carlos was the oldest. After my father opened his first Academy, he began teaching jiu-jitsu to his brothers Jorge, Osvaldo, and Gastão. Later he also taught my uncle Helio, who was the youngest brother and last to learn.

During this same time period, my father Carlos also established an open challenge. He used these fights to refine traditional jiu-jitsu tech-

*"I am known to be one of the most technical fighters in the family. This is partly because of my personality and dedication to jiu-jitsu, and partly because of the many hours I spent with my father and Carlson when they worked on fight techniques while Carlson was national champion."*

niques and develop the Gracie style. My father quickly became famous because of his small physical stature and the fact that he could overpower opponents of much greater size. My father and his brothers spread this powerful martial art all over Brazil and it's been proven since that time. Today our Gracie style is still undefeated against other martial arts.

My father Carlos was the first great fighter of the Gracie family. In addition to jiu-jitsu, he enjoyed boxing and was the Brazilian boxing champion. In the 1920's and 1930's he fought both Brazilians and foreigners. One of the most famous fights was against the Japanese jiu-jitsu champion, Giomori. The fact that my father was able to tie with Giomori, even though Giomori was much larger and heavier than my father, brought tremendous recognition to the Gracie style of fighting.

After my father retired from the ring, he continued the family tradition in his role as patriarch, brain and leader of the Gracie family. My father arranged all the fights and decided which of his brothers would fight against which challenger. Nobody fought without my father's permission. My father also acted as trainer and coach for his four brothers, constantly developing refinements and new techniques to make the system better and guiding each of his brothers as to which techniques would be most effective against each opponent. My father Carlos was constantly concerned with maintaining the good reputation of the family and the Gracie system of fighting in Brazil.

**Q: Can you describe your own background and training in the arts?**
A: I was born into a family of fighters. We were raised in a enormous house with 28 bedrooms and there were always many brother, cousins and students of the family around, practicing their jiu-jitsu, so I naturally learned how to approach a "fight" early. My father had 21 children and every one of them (even the girls) was trained in the Gracie style of jiu-jitsu. Even before any formal training started, the boys started to fight and practice with one another at home. The atmosphere was friendly but very competitive; if you didn't want to get beaten constantly, you had to learn how to fight well and defend yourself. It was the family way.

In formal jiu-jitsu training, my background is different than my brothers and cousins. My father began saying I would be a champion when I was very young, but because of my love for horses, I chose to stay at our country home (in the mountains above Rio) as long as possible. I did not begin my formal jiu-jitsu training until much later than the rest of the family.

By the time I came to Rio for my formal jiu-jitsu training, my father was coaching only my brother Carlson, who was at that time the champion of Brazil; teaching at the Academy was done by students that my father had trained over the years. However, unlike my cousins and the other brothers of my age group, I never studied under my Uncle Helio; I received my training directly from my father, Carlos Gracie, and my oldest brother, Carlson, who was also Brazilian champion for many years. Carlson's school has always been known for producing the toughest fighters in Brazil.

I am known to be one of the most technical fighters in the family. This is partly because of my personality and dedication to jiu-jitsu, and partly because of the many hours I spent with my father and Carlson when they worked on fight techniques while Carlson was national champion.

**Q: You mentioned earlier that you were Brazilian professional national champion from 1969 to 1972. When you say "national champion," how was that determined?**
A: When I began my fighting career, the champion was determined by consensus and acknowledgment, based on matches that were conducted by the martial arts schools. There were championship fights that received coverage in the newspapers, magazines and TV throughout the country. During my time, these championship matches were held approximately every three months. Yes, it was many years ago in the mountains of Rio where my father had a country home where the entire family got

together on weekends and holiday times. My father made a competition between people from the city and the people of the local town. I remember that I won that first competition – although that's just about as far back as I can remember. There was never any doubt about who was the champion when I was competing because no one could defeat me. I was still the reigning champion in 1972 when I came to the United States.

**Q: Do you fear anyone in competition?**
A: When it comes to a fight, there is no opponent whom I fear. My whole training has been to prepare me for the ring or the streets. Even though I have something of a disadvantage with my age and I no longer compete or train for competition, my extensive knowledge and the techniques that are now instinctive give me a tremendous advantage and the confidence that come with knowing I have the advantage.

**Q: How did they go about selecting fighters for the championships?**
A: The Gracies were always leaders in the martial arts, but every school sent their best representative to these matches. Originally, the Gracies got together with other schools to organize the matches and select the names of the fighters who wanted to compete. Later, after the Jiu-Jitsu Federation of Rio was formed in 1967, the Federation took an active role in organizing these matches.

**Q: What rules were these championships fought under?**
A: We fought two ways: with the kimono on and with the kimono off. When we wore the gi, we were not allowed to punch and kick. In some of the championship matches, we took off the gi tops, and then we were allowed to punch and kick in full-contact fighting. I fought and was champion under both conditions.

**Q: How did you win most of your fights?**
A: Usually on the ground, but it depends on the style of the opponent and the type of fight (with or without the kimono). For example, there are chokes you can use at the same time someone is trying to throw you; with judo practitioners, I could often finish the fight standing up by completing my choke before my opponent could throw me. But most of the time we went to the ground and I finished the fight there, especially if my opponent was a tough fighter.

**Q: Are there any fighters you can remember who particularly gave you trouble?**

A: Actually, the fighters who challenged me the most were two of my own brothers. Outside of my family, the toughest fighter I encountered was named Sergio Ines. He was originally trained by Barradas (who had been one of my father's top students). Barradas sent Sergio to fight me because he was the best in his area at that time. Later, Sergio continued to train and fight under my brother Carlson. Of course, there were many other fighters who trained hoping to overpower me, but none ever succeeded.

When a person holds the title of national champion, all the schools send someone to try and defeat him. It's just like in the old West; when a man is fast with the gun, all the young men want to challenge him. There were also matches with other family members. Fights within the family were private, and were usually held on Sundays, when the Academy was closed. I remember one of my relatives who were constantly training in the hopes of beating me. Each time he lost, he would go back and train for another six or eight months and then try again. This went on for years, but he never even came close.

*"When a person holds the title of national champion, all the schools send someone to try and defeat him. It's just like the Old West; when a man is fast with the gun, all the young men want to challenge him."*

*"There is no reason to go to the ground if you can finish the fight standing up. This is particularly important in street fighting and self-defense, because you are less vulnerable to a second attacker and can leave the scene much more quickly if you are already on your feet."*

**Q: Did you fight against opponents of other styles in open competition?**
A: Yes I did. I have sparred and fought matches with men who were very tough fighters or champions in their own styles, but their options are limited when they come up against the Gracie style. Once I close the distance and get them in a clinch, I simply put them on the ground and finish the fight.

**Q: The Gracie system is often perceived to be principally a ground fighting art. Do you agree?**
A: No. What's happened is that most of the other styles are weak in ground fighting techniques, so that's what students coming from other styles are most interested in learning. As a result, some of the Gracie members teaching in the United States have been focusing mostly on ground techniques. However, the style developed by my father, Carlos Gracie, actually places equal emphasis on standing techniques because we feel it's very important for a fighter to be well-rounded. While it's true that most fights wind up on the ground, they don't have to. As I mentioned earlier, the Gracie system has chokes and arm-locks that can be used to finish a fight in a standing position. There is no reason to go to the ground if you can finish the fight standing up. This is particularly important in street fighting and self-defense, because you are less vulnerable to a second attacker and can leave the scene much more quickly if you are already on your feet.

**Q: Why do you think your father's system of jiu-jitsu has become so effective?**
A: I think it's because of the development which my father made from the art he was taught. He constantly sought out matches against people trained in other styles of martial arts, and used that experience to help him to adapt and modify the classical techniques he learned so that they became more effective. Efficiency was also important, because my father was small in stature and looked ore like a scholar than a fighter. We use leverage and balance to overcome physically stronger opponents and our style make a point to deal with differences in size, weight and build. When I train, I like to take on people who are much heavier or stronger than I am, or who are skilled in other styles, but I have years of experience and training to use against them.

**Q: The Gracie challenge has been the subject of some controversy. How did it get started?**
A: The Gracie challenge started with my father Carlos Gracie in the early 1920's. When my father first started teaching jiu-jitsu, people questioned his ability as a fighter because he was small and not very muscular. There were fighters from other styles, such as Greco-Roman wrestlers, who looked much more powerful. My father fought with these other stylists to prove the superiority of his style of jiu-jitsu. He was so successful as a fighter that he began to have trouble finding opponents; no one wanted to lose. That's where the challenge came in. Eventually, my father put an advertisement in a newspaper that went something like this: "If you want to get your face beaten and well-smashed, and if you want broken arms, look for me at this address." It was an open challenge to all fighters and tough guys to test our system of fighting.

**Q: What do you think was his motivation for issuing that kind of open challenge?**
A: It was partly to promote my father's style of jiu-jitsu by showing its superiority as a fighting style, and partly to continue the process of improving the system. You see, once my father had learned traditional jiu-jitsu, from the Japanese point of view, he adapted it to a more practical style for street fighting. The advertisement was part of the method that he used to find out what worked and what didn't; as he practiced his art against new competitors, some of the traditional Japanese moves were completely eliminated, new ones were added, and others were modified

in order to make the system more efficient. For a smaller person, like my father and many of his students, it was important to use energy efficiently; the beauty of our system is that technique compensates for differences in size and weight, and allows the smaller person using the Gracie style to overpower a larger, stronger opponent from another style.

**Q: Some observers have put forth the idea that the Gracie Challenge is not budo-like, that it does not fit with the spirit of the martial arts, and you shouldn't go around challenging people. What are your thoughts on this?**
A: Well, I'm not really in favor of public challenge when it is used to humiliate other people and styles. However, I think the reason the challenge goes on here is that some martial artists live in a fantasy world. Some people go to school for years and when they get attacked in the street or the ring, they don't know how to defend themselves. The challenges wake these people up to reality. I believe that the martial arts are about fighting, not fantasy. The purpose of our style of jiu-jitsu is to prepare students to defend themselves in the streets as well as in the ring. The challenge is important to show the differences between the various martial arts styles, and also for the world to know the superiority of the Gracie style of jiu-jitsu.

**Q: Are you, in fact, the first Gracie family member to teach your system in the United States?**
A: Yes. I came to the United States and began teaching jiu-jitsu in 1972. I was actually invited here to teach by American marines. This happened because when I was in Brazil during my time as national champion, I was teaching a group of American marines who were in charge of security of the American consulate in Rio. After those marines returned to the United States, they continued to practice martial arts, and it turned out that the fighters I trained in Brazil were beating men returning from other countries. When the officers learned where my students had been trained, they contacted me to come to America to teach the Gracie system. Since 1972, I have taught the Gracie style of jiu-jitsu in Virginia, Connecticut, Maryland, Florida and California, where I have lived and taught jiu-jitsu since 1979.

**Q: Do you have a personal philosophy regarding martial arts training?**
A: Yes. I believe it's better to learn three things well than to know a little bit about a lot of things. One well-executed move can finish a fight, but many poorly-done moves will get you nowhere. As an example, I remember being on the second floor of a high school in Brazil overlooking a recreation yard when I saw a smaller boy with thick glasses being punched and kicked by a bigger boy. The smaller boy kept backing up and everybody was screaming for him to fight back. Finally, the smaller boy put one hand on the larger boy's collar and with the other hand, grabbed the opposite collar. Soon, the aggressor stopped punching and fell to his knees. The boy who was strangling was crying as he held on and all of a sudden, it became very quiet. I ran down the stairs and pulled the boys apart, because no one else seemed to realize what was happening. The strangle was so effective that the larger boy passed out and lost control of his bodily functions. That choke was the only thing the smaller boy knew; it wasn't very well put together, but even so, if you hold it long enough, it will be an effective defense. I tell my students this story because I want them to master each move I teach them, and this story illustrates the importance of doing so.

**Q: Finally, what do you think is your role now as a teacher in Jiu Jitsu?**
A: I have to explain clearly the principles of techniques of the art in a way that people can understand. I enjoy training professional fighters and teaching people how to defend themselves on the streets. I am also developing instructors who can pass on the knowledge correctly even if they are not black belts with many years of experience. I see teaching as an art within an art! You have something inside you, which you know, and your goal is to get another person to know what you know and do what you do. For me this is an art!

# Grappling Techniques

Carley faces the opponent (1). He deposits his right knee into the opponent's stomach (2), leans back (3) and allows himself to fall to the ground as he maintains control of the opponent (4-5). Next, he moves his left leg over the opponent's head (6), pushes down with the legs (7) and drops his opponent onto the floor (8). To wrap things up, Carley applies a finishing armlock (9).

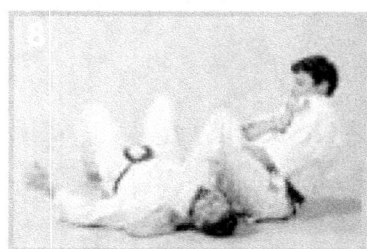
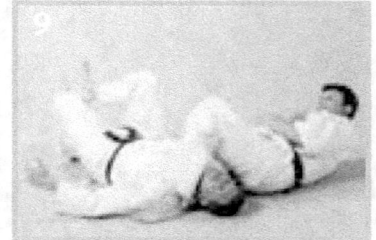

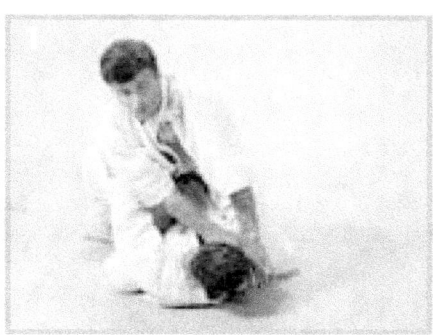

Carley mounts his opponent, who tries to escape by pushing him away (1). As soon as he feels the direction of the opponent's push (2), Carley leans to the side and moves his left leg over the opponent's head (3). Meanwhile, he secures the arm (4), so he can apply an armlock from the top (5).

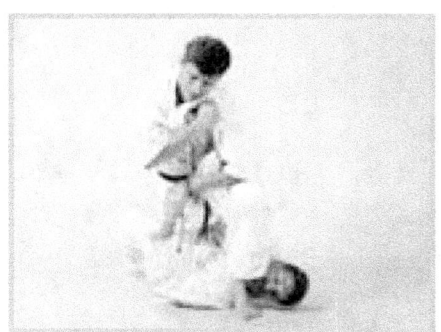

## Grappling Techniques

Carley Gracie has his opponent in the open guard (1). When the opponent delivers a punch, Carley blocks the strike from the inside (2) and moves attacking arm to the side (3). He switches his grip, and using his right arm to pull the opponent to the side (4), sweeps him (5-6). Carley ends up on top (7), where he can initiate his offensive maneuvers (8).

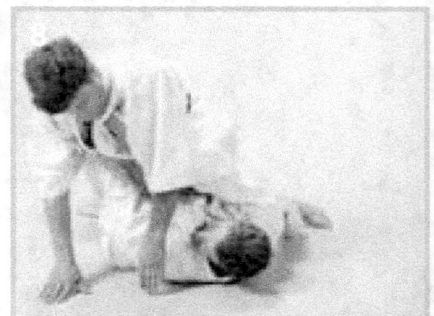

# GRACIE

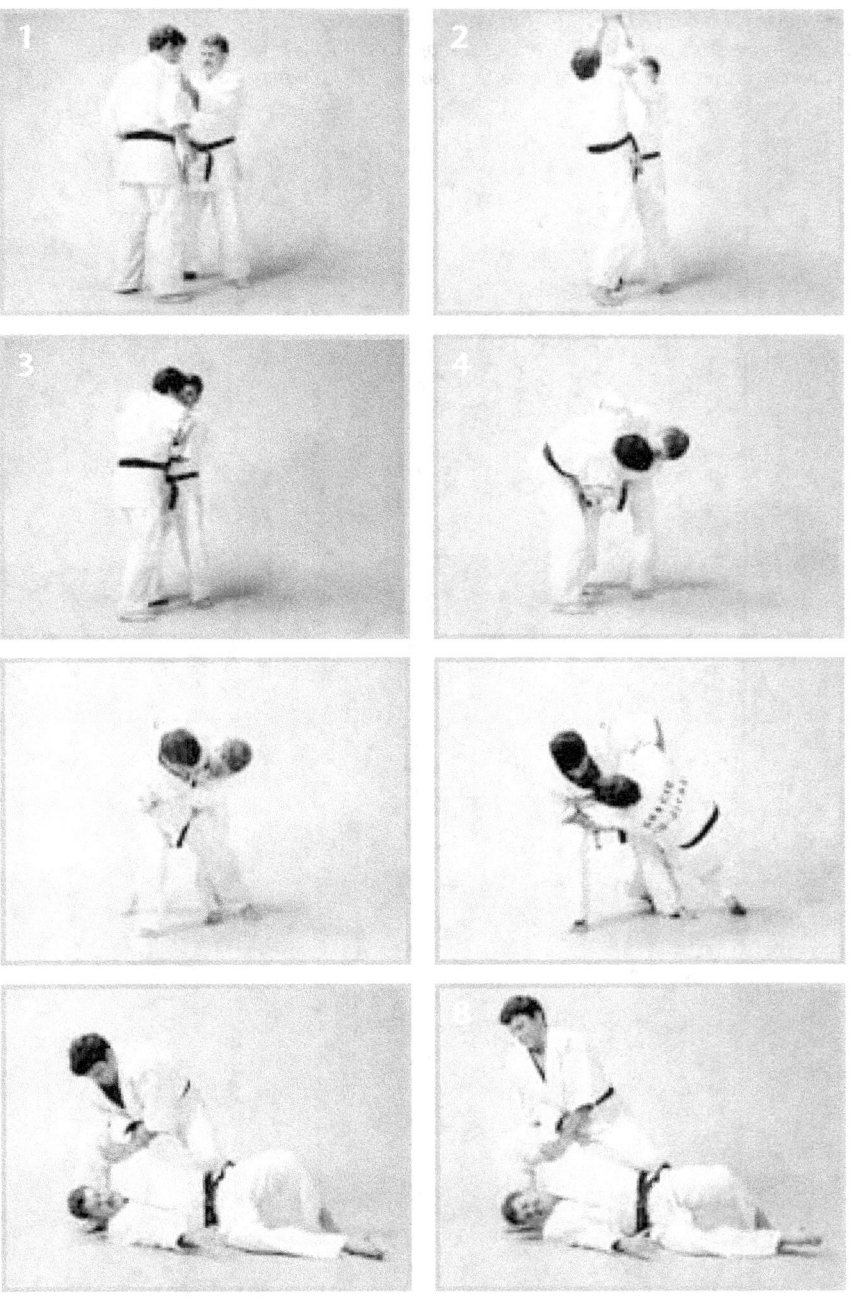

*The opponent grabs Carley Gracie's lapels (1). Gracie raises both arms (2), wraps them around the opponent's arms (3), turns to the side (4) and moves his left leg in front of the opponent (5). While controlling the arms, Gracie sends the opponent to the ground (6-7), where he finishes him with an armlock (8).*

# Grappling Techniques

*Gracie uses the same defense to escape form a double-lapel grab (1-2). He turns to the side and moves his right leg in front of the opponent (3-4). While controlling the arms, Gracie throws the opponent onto the ground (5-7), where he finalizes him with an armlock (8).*

# GRACIE

Gracie controls his opponent from the mount position (1), and he uses his right hand to control the opponent's right arm (2-3). He moves his right hand under the opponent's arm (4) and securely grabs his left wrist (5). This enables him to apply a painful bent armlock (6-7).

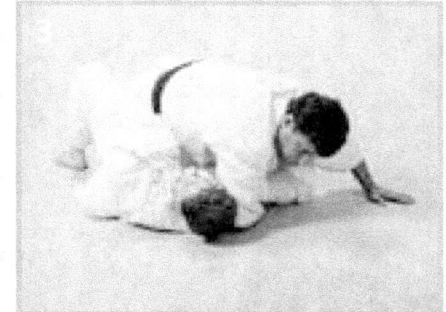

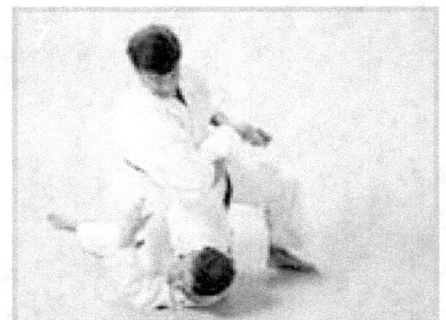

# CARLSON GRACIE

## *The Brazilian Legend*

A LEGENDARY JIU-JITSU EXPERT FROM BRAZIL, CARLSON GRACIE IS AN ACKNOWLEDGED MASTER OF AN ART THAT IS SYNONYMOUS WITH CHAMPIONSHIP GRAPPLING AND NO-HOLDS-BARRED FIGHTING. IN HIS YOUTH, CARLSON ASSUMED THE RESPONSIBILITY OF FIGHTING STYLISTS FROM OTHER MARTIAL ARTS TO PROVE THE EFFECTIVENESS OF GRACIE JIU-JITSU. HIS MOST FAMOUS FIGHT OCCURRED IN FRONT OF MORE THAN 20,000 SPECTATORS IN MARACANAZINHO STADIUM. AT THE TIME, HE WAS ONLY 20 YEARS OLD. HIS GOAL? DEFEAT WALDEMAR SANTANA, THE MAN WHO HAD PREVIOUSLY INSULTED GRANDMASTER HELIO GRACIE. AND A VICTORY MEANT THAT CARLOS COULD REGAIN THE FAMILY HONOR. AFTER THAT FIGHT, CARLSON GRACIE BECAME A NATIONAL HERO. FOR MORE THAN 30 YEARS, HE DEFENDED THE FAMILY NAME IN NUMEROUS VALE TUDO FIGHTS. IN HIS LATER YEARS, HE BECAME ONE OF THE MOST SUCCESSFUL TRAINERS IN THE HISTORY OF SPORT JIU-JITSU, AND HE HAS COACHED AND TRAINED A LONG LIST OF WORLD CHAMPIONS. NOW RESIDING IN THE UNITED STATES, CARLSON IS FOCUSED ON DEVELOPING HIS MOST SUCCESSFUL FIGHTING TEAM EVER, AND HE PLANS TO DO THAT WITH AMERICAN STUDENTS. CARLSON GRACIE'S TALENT, EXPERIENCE AND KNOWLEDGE GUARANTEE THAT THE BEST IS YET TO COME.

**Q: Professor Gracie, please introduce yourself.**
A: I was born in Rio de Janeiro on August 13, 1938. I began training in jiu-jitsu at age three under my father, Carlos Gracie, the oldest of the four famous Gracie brothers and the originator of Brazilian jiu-jitsu. I am the founder and head of the Carlson Gracie Jiu-Jitsu Team, and I created Carlson Gracie Jiu-Jitsu. My style differs from other styles of Brazilian jiu-jitsu in the sense that I am always inventing and evolving new techniques and fighting strategies, refusing to let my jiu-jitsu become stagnant or outdated. If you're not going forward, you're going backward.

**Q: What is your fighting record?**
A: At 16, I was the Brazilian jiu-jitsu champion in the open weight class, which was the only class at that time. I fought 18 no-holds-barred

*"Anytime I had a question about a position I would ask my father. He would always have an answer, but he would never directly come to me because he was so busy. He never gave me a formal class. I would just watch him and then practice."*

matches, ending up with a record of 14-1-3. My 14 wins were by submission or knockout, and my three draws included two against Waldemar Santana. My one loss was a controversial decision that caused a riot when I was not awarded the victory. During the fight, my opponent tapped, so I released the finishing hold. Afterward, he denied he had submitted. My most well known victory was against Waldemar Santana. I was 17, and Santana was 24. Santana had beaten my unc Helio Gracie.

**Q: How did your family get involved in the art of jiu-jitsu and what do you remember about your training days under your father, Carlos Gracie Sr.?**
A: Esai Maeda, also known as Count Koma, was a jiu-jitsu champion who was head of a Japanese immigration colony to Brazil. Gastao Gracie – my grandfather, Brazilian politician and scholar – helped Maeda establish the colony. As a show of friendship, Maeda taught jiu-jitsu to my father, who then taught it to his younger brothers. Anytime I had a question about a position I would ask my father. He would always have an answer, but he would never directly come to me because he was so busy. Nevertheless, I wanted to learn so I would ask. He never gave me a formal class. I would just watch him and then practice. This not only helped me to think on my own, it also helped me come up with new techniques based on things that I had seen others do. It trained my mind as well as my body.

**Q: Tell us about the fight against Waldemar Santana.**
A: Santana was actually a good friend of mine, even though he was older

than me. We liked each other very much. After his fight with Uncle Helio, however, I called him and told him that we now had a big problem! I was 20 at the time. Normally, the authorities would not have allowed me to compete. However, I lied about my age and was eventually given permission to try and restore the family honor. None of Helio's sons was old enough to fight. So even though I was young myself, I was the only family member available. I could have finished the fight earlier because I had many chances for submission. Normally, I would not have punished a man so much, but I wanted to make an example of him for the disrespect he had shown to Uncle Helio. I wanted his face to tell the story of the fight – not his words.

*"I lied about my age and was eventually given permission to try and restore the family honor. None of Helio's sons was old enough to fight. So even though I was young myself, I was the only family member available."*

**Q: Did you enjoy fighting from the bottom?**
A: Not at all! For quite awhile I was the only one fighting for the Gracie family. There wasn't another Gracie fighting except for my brother Robson. Robson was a phenomenal fighter – outstanding really. But at 118 pounds, he was too light to face many of the big and strong men who challenged the art of jiu-jitsu. I was always fighting against people who were bigger than I was, so naturally I would end up on the bottom. Fortunately, I could dish out a lot of punishment from there.

**Q: Rolls Gracie, your brother, died in a tragic hang gliding accident. He is regarded as one of the four greatest jiu-jitsu fighters ever. The others are Helio, Rickson and you. Did you have much to do with training Rolls?**
A: Rolls originally trained with Helio, but he didn't do very well. In a challenge match that many people watched, Rolls fought Cicero, a fighter from Nitorei, which is an island off Rio. Cicero, who weighed one kilo less

*"My greatest joy has come from producing numerous world champions from all races and walks of life. I would never prepare a fighter to face a Gracie family member in a no-holds-barred match, but everybody knows I have prepared many to fight against other Gracies in jiu-jitsu tournaments."*

than Rolls, beat him badly. Because it was submission only, it was ruled a draw. Using modern scoring it would have been 20-0. I was cheering for Rolls, but I was very upset when he was beaten so badly. I told Rolls that Cicero was nothing, and that he should not have lost to him. I opened a school a few months after that in Copacabana. Six months later Rolls left Helio's academy and came to train with me. Later, he became my partner in the school. Rolls bugged me all the time about how to do things. He would bother me constantly, so he learned a lot. After 18 months of training, he became a phenomenon and beat everybody. He is by far the best jiu-jitsu man who ever lived. Before me he wasn't learning all the updated techniques. He was frozen in time. To be good in jiu-jitsu you have to be always moving forward.

**Q: How has your teaching changed since you became better known in America?**
A: I have taught jiu-jitsu classes and seminars in the U.S., Canada and Brazil for more than 40 years. I have popularized jiu-jitsu in Brazil by spreading it beyond my immediate family and teaching the general public. My greatest joy has come from producing numerous world champions from all races and walks of life. I would never prepare a fighter to face a Gracie family member in a no-holds-barred match, but everybody knows I have prepared many to fight against other Gracies in jiu-jitsu tournaments. Don't forget Wallid Ismail, who beat Royce Gracie.

**Q: How do you see Brazilian jiu-jitsu competitions these days?**
A: Jiu-jitsu is so competitive now that it is hard to predict who will win. In my school, for example, I consider everyone above purple belt to be at the same skill level. In Brazil, the technical level is very good. It is no

longer the privilege of only the Gracie family to know the best techniques. All the academies have great knowledge.

**Q: Do you think no-holds-barred fighting requires different skills from jiu-jitsu?**
A: No. 1, I require my fighters to be good at jiu-jitsu, because that is the basis of what I teach. After that, I adapt the style to whatever the rules are in the particular event. I personally have done a lot of boxing, so I show that to my fighters. You see, you always have to be moving forward and learning different things. If you fight a boxer, you better know how to slip a punch or you're going to get nailed. Being successful in jiu-jitsu is as much about being open-minded to learning new things as it is about learning a particular set of techniques.

**Q: How close is Brazilian jiu-jitsu to Japanese jiu-jitsu?**
A: Japanese jiu-jitsu at one time was the best jiu-jitsu, but they began hiding so many techniques that they forgot them. In Brazil, we were lucky that Count Koma, who came to Brazil from Japan, knew the original jiu-jitsu and taught it to my father [Carlos]. He then passed it down to everybody. So that is why I don't hide anything. I have to be intellectually honest and show everything I know. Otherwise, how can I live with myself?

*"Japanese jiu-jitsu at one time was the best jiu-jitsu, but they began hiding so many techniques that they forgot them. So that is why I don't hide anything. I have to be intellectually honest and show everything I know."*

**Q: Is there any position or technique more important than another in Brazilian jiu-jitsu?**
A: All positions are important. You should not concentrate on just one thing and neglect another. You might start out learning slowly, but you'll eventually be well rounded then when you catch on. And don't get too specific as far as learning techniques. Learn them all equally as you go, and don't get impatient. One day you will wake up, and you will be comfort-

"Of course, Royce Gracie's victories were good for everyone, and he is probably the single reason you see jiu-jitsu everywhere. Because of Royce, everyone knows about jiu-jitsu now."

able [performing the techniques]. Don't try to force your learning. It should be natural.

**Q: What has made Brazilian jiu-jitsu so popular in the U.S.?**
A: Of course, Royce Gracie's victories were good for everyone, and he is probably the single reason you see jiu-jitsu everywhere. Because of Royce, everyone knows about jiu-jitsu now. He did everyone a great service, and he deserves to be admired for what he did.

**Q: Who is the greatest fighter in the world today?**
A: People ask me this question all the time, but it is honestly hard for me to say. There are so many great fighters that it is not fair for me to mention one because I admire so many. I don't want to disrespect the ones that I don't mention. I could name 20 fighters I consider champions and that I like to watch, and they are not just Brazilians, either.

**Q: Some of your previous students broke away from your "Arrebentacao" (Demolition) team and created the Brazilian Top Team. What happened?**
A: All these guys studied and trained here with me. The members of this so-called Brazilian Top Team were all my students, and I taught them everything. They never paid any money to train at the academy, and I taught them everything. But what can I do?

**Q: How do you see the American students?**
A: They have excellent backgrounds. Many of them are already wrestling champions, and they have tremendous physical qualities. Best of all, they are very determined and focused. You only need to tell them what to do once, and they go off on their own, following your instructions to the letter!

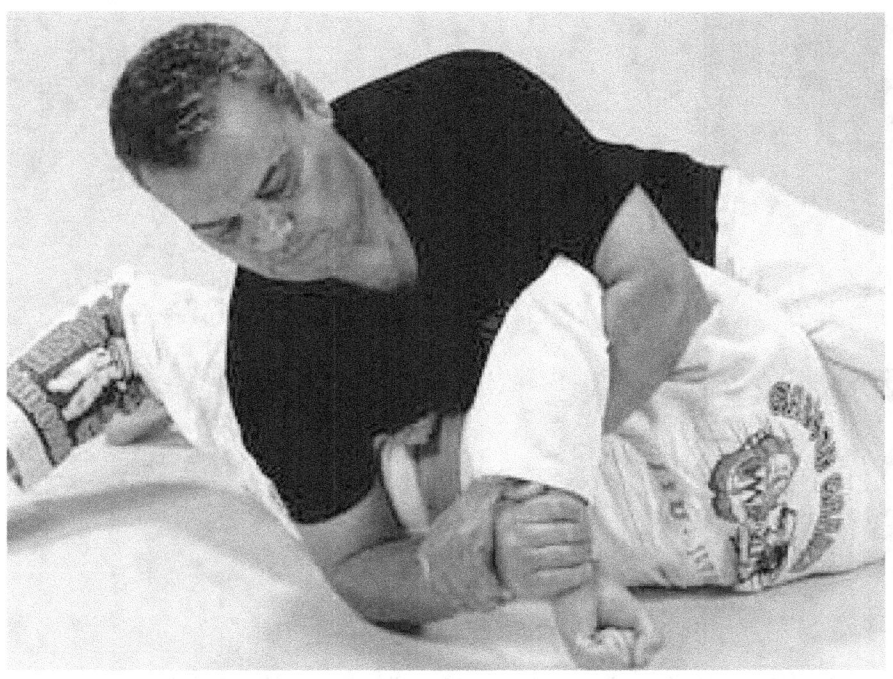

*"The Gracie name was low at the time, and I was able to bring it to the top again. I take great pride in the fact that I was the only one able to defend the family name for quite some time."*

**Q: You had great moments in your life. Which ones were the worst and the best until this day?**
A: By far, the worst moment of my life was the death of my father. It is the single most striking moment of my life. That loss was enormous. To this day I still feel it as if it occurred yesterday. The biggest joy and my most important moment was my win over Waldemar Santana. The Gracie name was low at the time, and I was able to bring it to the top again. I take great pride in the fact that I was the only one able to defend the family name for quite some time. There was my brother Robson, but as I told you he was very light. There were many women in the family but no fighters. There was a long gap there, and I carried the torch for all those years against one and all. Now I look to my new crop of future champions to defend my name in the years to come.

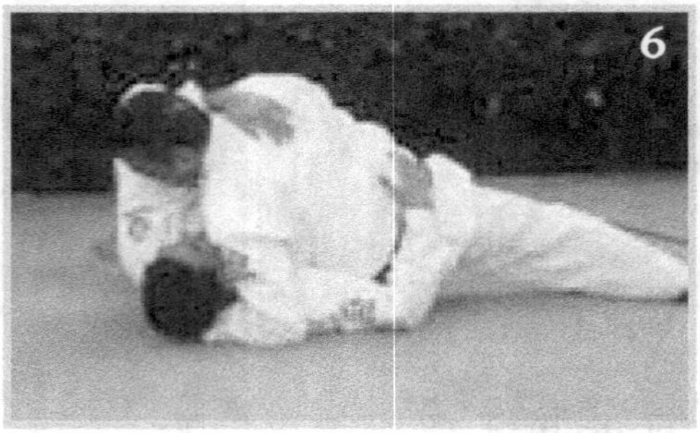

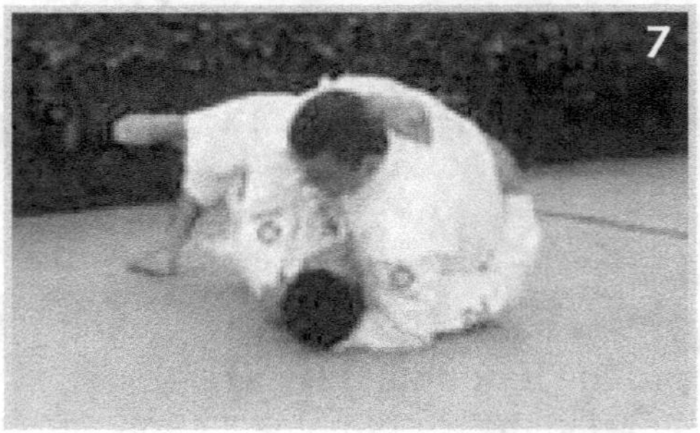

## Grappling Techniques

Carlson finds himself in the opponent's open guard (1). He straightens up, controls the opponent's right arm and passes his left arm around the right leg (2). Using his left hand, he reaches the opposite lapel (3), twists his body (4) and adopts firm side control (5). By switching his legs and changing his body weight (6), Carlson is ready to pass his right leg (7) and end up in the mounted position (8).

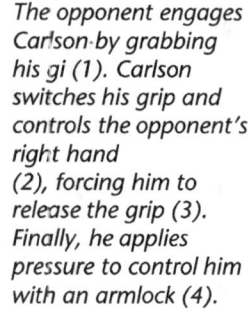

The opponent engages Carlson by grabbing his gi (1). Carlson switches his grip and controls the opponent's right hand (2), forcing him to release the grip (3). Finally, he applies pressure to control him with an armlock (4).

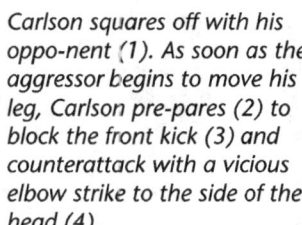

Carlson squares off with his oppo-nent (1). As soon as the aggressor begins to move his leg, Carlson pre-pares (2) to block the front kick (3) and counterattack with a vicious elbow strike to the side of the head (4).

# ROYCE GRACIE

## *The First Cut Is the Deepest*

This Rio de Janeiro native shocked the martial arts world on November 12, 1993, when he ran over all his opponents in the first Ultimate Fighting Championship. While fighting flawlessly in the Octagon, he impeccably represented the legendary tradition of the Gracie family to all those viewing the event on TV. Many things have happened since that cold night in Denver, Colorado, and Royce Gracie's life has drastically changed. After many years of teaching out of the Gracie Academy in Torrance, California, Royce recently decided it was time to pursue his dream of taking jiu-jitsu to a new level. Thus, not only did he begin conducting classes on a more international level and traveling more and more, he began to develop what is now known as the "Royce Gracie Network."

Married and with children of his own, that young kid who impressed the world with the grappling techniques developed by his father, Helio Gracie, is as busy as it gets. After a few years of observing MMA and no-hold-barred events progress in different directions, Royce decided to go back to fighting. When he was ready, he chose Japan. Experts measure the size of a man's body – not the size of his heart, spirit and soul. If they did that, he would be a super heavyweight. This is Royce Gracie, a true living legend who changed the world of martial arts forever. After him, nothing has been the same. The first cut is always the deepest.

**Q: How was it growing up in Brazil in a jiu-jitsu environment?**
A: It was fun and something very natural. My father never wanted us to do weird things so we studied, went to school, trained in jiu-jitsu, played on the beach, etc. It was very relaxing and nice. My jiu-jitsu training was always with my father, my brothers – Rickson and Rorion – and also with Rolls Gracie. For me, training jiu-jitsu was a normal thing in my life. I never felt pressure because my father understood that kids don't like to learn…they like to play. So training in jiu-jitsu was play for me. That's what I'm trying to pass onto my kids. When they go to the Academy, it

*"The only reason the Gracie family had to do these kind of matches was to put to test what we were developing and to prove to others that what we have works against an uncooperative opponent, regardless of the style he practices."*

will be like going to the playground.

**Q: You have been an icon, especially for those people who believed that size was relevant in a self-defense situation. How do you feel about it?**
A: Many people, when they saw me winning the UFC against bigger and stronger guys, realized that there was hope for them. If they knew the necessary techniques, they realized that they could actually protect themselves against bigger opponents. I probably opened doors for some other people and brought hope for those who didn't know that it wasn't necessary to be a monster with huge muscles to defend yourself effectively.

**Q: The Gracie family started a tradition with the vale tudo fights against practitioners of other styles. Why do you think some people never liked that approach?**
A: Well, to begin with, most people don't want to match what they know with what others know. The reason for that is they don't really believe in what they practice. The only reason the Gracie family had to do these kind of matches was to put to test what we were developing and to prove to others that what we have works against an uncooperative opponent, regardless of the style he practices. The UFC brought that to the rest of the world, but the Gracies were doing it in Brazil for more than 65 years. That's the reason why I got into the UFC. I believed in the art.

**Q: In the first UFC, you were skinnier and lighter than all the fighters. Nevertheless, you beat them all using pure technique and not brute strength. It is true that jiu-jitsu works without using brute force?**
A: It is true if the opponent doesn't know how to defend himself. In that case, you don't really need to use strength. Instead, you use leverage and

positioning. If you face an opponent who knows jiu-jitsu, then the physical characteristics could make a difference. Even if the other person knows jiu-jitsu you should look for the right technique based on leverage and correct principles instead of relying on your strength. The key is, as my father, Helio Gracie, likes to say, "We don't apply the technique, we ask for it." By this, he means we prepare the situation for that technique to happen. Don't force it. Create an environment in which the technique will be there naturally.

**Q: In the very beginning, some members of the Gracie family entered judo tournaments but then they stopped. Why?**
A: Well, it was a good way of proving a point. Many of the techniques and maneuvers we do in jiu-jitsu are not allowed in judo competition. Judo is mostly a game these days, and our approach to fighting is different. jiu-jitsu is not about sport, and we are not judo players.

**Q: After you stopped fighting in the UFC, many people said that you were afraid because things were different and people knew how to fight. How do your respond to that?**
A: People talk sometimes because they don't have enough important things to do. Of course, everybody is entitled to express an opinion, regardless if that opinion is based on facts or a stupid affirmation. I have never been afraid of fighting. Things in the UFC changed, and I realized that the way the event was going was putting me at a big disadvantage against all the big guys because they (organizers) were reformatting the event to fit the TV audiences. And that was fine with me, but I was not going to enter an arena in which everything was against me. I only ask for fair rules and regulations. After the UFC, I went and fought in Japan because they did accommodate the weight difference in a much better

*"I have never been afraid of fighting. Things in the UFC changed, and I realized that the way the event was going was putting me at a big disadvantage against all the big guys because they (organizers) were reformatting the event to fit the TV audiences."*

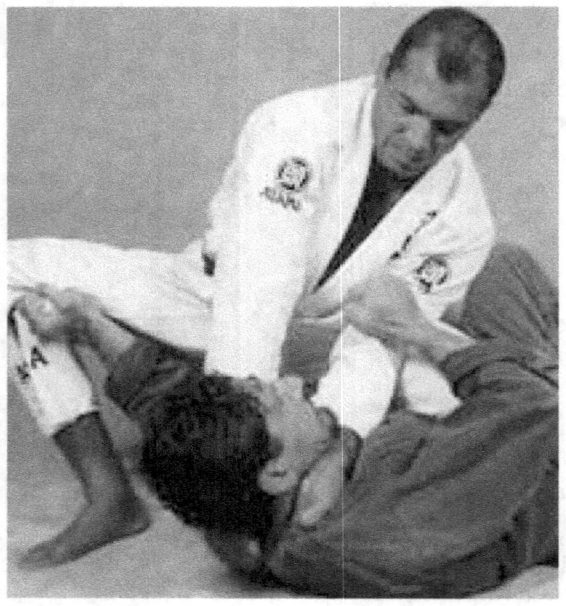

*"I give all the credit in the world to Wallid for what he did, but I wasn't focused enough or angry enough. And that was my mistake. I wasn't sharp enough. The three-year layoff from fighting dulled my blade, and I paid the price."*

way. They were fair and square, and I had no problem fighting other people. At no moment have I ever been afraid of fighting.

On the other hand, promoters and fans want me to fight every other month, and that can't happen. How many times does the boxing world champion fight in a year? Once, maybe twice. That's it. I can't be fighting all the people who want to fight me. It doesn't go that way. Things don't happen that way in any sport. So people should think before talking. Some of those things they were asking for at that time were very unreasonable.

**Q: Do you realize that you have changed the martial arts forever?**
A: I was simply a vehicle for that. Rorion was the mastermind behind the UFC and the Gracie revolution in the United States. I simply did what I have been doing all my life. I stepped into the ring and fought.

**Q: Your loss to Ismael Wallid was one of the major upsets in the history of martial arts.**
A: I know. I give all the credit in the world to Wallid for what he did, but I wasn't focused enough or angry enough. And that was my mistake. I wasn't sharp enough. The three-year layoff from fighting dulled my blade, and I paid the price. I was teaching and sparring with people but not with a goal in my mind. Wallid beat me clean and square. I learned a lesson that day. If you are not 100% prepared and focused, don't fight.

**Q: Your father was there with you. What did he say?**
A: He made technical comments on my performance and told me to be totally focused next time.

**Q: Did Wallid say anything to you?**
A: Yes, he came to me the day before and said, "You are a very nice guy. I don't really want to fight you." I said, "Thank you and good luck tomorrow." He is a tough guy and very respectful. I still believe he was very lucky that day.

**Q: What was your most memorable moment in the UFC?**
A: I would say winning UFC IV. The first one was a surprise because people didn't really know what was happening and hadn't seen jiu-jitsu. In the second one, people were saying that it was a set-up and a fake, even though I had to win four fights in one night, which was very tough. When I didn't complete the third tournament – even though I didn't lose – that opened a lot of people's eyes. At that point, they didn't question the reality of it and didn't think that it was arranged for me to win, which it never was. The fourth one is when I can back and beat Dan Severn, who at that time was just terrifying everyone with his power. That was when I got back to the top and validated myself in front of the whole world. That was my most satisfying win in the UFC.

*"The first one was a surprise because people didn't really know what was happening and hadn't seen jiu-jitsu. In the second one, people were saying that it was a set-up and a fake, even though I had to win four fights in one night, which was very tough. When I didn't complete the third tournament – even though I didn't lose – that opened a lot of people's eyes."*

**Q: What was your toughest fight?**
A: Probably with Kimo, because I fought the wrong way and gave him a lot of chances that I shouldn't have. I fought totally wrong. I tried to use strength and push him back and beat him with power instead of using his own power against him. He's a very strong fighter, and you're not going to beat him that way. I did get the submission, but it took a lot out of me. I got dehydrated after that match and passed out right before I came back for my next fight. I still got into the Octagon hoping that I would recover, but then I lost my vision and couldn't see. The referee asked me if I was ready, and I said I was. Then I turned around and told my brother, "Do something. I can't see a thing." That was tough.

# GRAPPLING MASTERS

"Bigger and bigger guys were coming into the UFC and limiting the time really hurt me. I thought it created a huge disadvantage for me. People who know me know that I don't fight in weight divisions. Size doesn't matter to me. My opponent's have mainly always been bigger than me."

**Q: What happened in the locker room that night? Did you pass out?**
A: To be honest, I never had the chance! My father and my brother Relson had me up and moving all the time. I took a shower to cool down, and they tried to keep me loose for the next fight. The heat and humidity were terrible, and all the fighters took oxygen back there. I was trying to rest as much as I could to get ready, but there wasn't enough time. The fights back then did not have time limits and there were no rounds. It was a whole different ballgame, to say the least.

**Q: Did you accept that as a defeat in your record?**
A: The old rules in the UFC said that if your corner throws the towel, you lose. So yes, I accept that fact. It is true though that Harold Howard never beat me because we never got into the fight. Technically, however, I lost. I only have respect for Howard because he said that my attempt to fight – considering how I felt – was one of the classiest gestures he'd ever seen in his martial arts career. I have to thank him for these words. He came to compete and there is a lot of respect in that. I truly appreciated his words. He could have reacted another way because I didn't fight him, but he didn't.

**Q: Why did you leave the UFC? Was it because of the rule changes?**
A: Yes. It was the rules and mostly the time limit. Bigger and bigger guys were coming into the UFC and limiting the time really hurt me. I thought it created a huge disadvantage for me. People who know me know that I don't fight in weight divisions. Size doesn't matter to me. My opponent's have mainly always been bigger than me.

**Q: Was it tougher then?**
A: Back then it was style against style – not fighter against fighter. But with the tournament format you had to fight three or four times in one night. You would always get injured during the first match and then have to fight hurt for the rest of the night. You never knew who you were going to face in the next round so you couldn't just train for one person like you can now. From a purely technical and physical perspective, it was much more challenging. Today, because everyone knows so much more, each individual fight is probably tougher. Back then the format was much more difficult.

*"You would always get injured during the first match and then have to fight hurt for the rest of the night. You never knew who you were going to face in the next round so you couldn't just train for one person like you can now. From a purely technical and physical perspective, it was much more challenging."*

**Q: Why have you always fought with the gi?**
A: I trained with the gi all my life. I'm comfortable with it. Plus, the gi always helps you grab your opponents better when they get sweaty and slippery. It helps to control your opponent and to keep your position. Plus, you can circle your arms or legs around him and then grab the gi. That helps to reduce fatigue in long fights. Because I've trained with the gi all my life, why would I take it off the day of the fight? It doesn't make sense to me. So I'm used to it, but it doesn't mean that if I use the gi that I'm a sport fighter only. My father and uncles always fought with the gi in their vale tudo matches. I don't think that I'm doing anything differently than them. It's just something that we use everyday in training and teaching and so we use it when we fight.

**Q: Did your father encourage you to wear it?**
A: Oh, yes. He was always in favor of me wearing the gi. He thought that it gave me advantage over people who didn't wear it. It worked for him

*"Every opponent is different and presents different challenges. It matters more who they are and what their tendencies are in the ring. Strategy is always a matter of a lot of different factors. Even when you don't know who you're fighting or what they like to do, you will find out quickly when you press an attack."*

so he thought that it would work for me. It wasn't so much tradition as much as he thinks it is good strategy.

**Q: In your UFC years, did you ever feel that the gi was a disadvantage?**
A: No, because my opponents didn't know how to use the gi against me. For it to be a disadvantage, they would have had to have known a lot of strategies that just weren't common when the UFC started. Now, perhaps, that might be different because so many people know jiu-jitsu. Back then the knowledge just wasn't out there.

You don't want to suddenly change the strategy that got you there and won a championship for you. When I won the first UFC with the gi, I just naturally left it on and kept going with it. Someone had to give me a reason to take it off in a fight. I never felt that happened.

**Q: Is it harder to fight a grappler or a striker when you're wearing the gi?**
A: It's just a matter of different strategies. There's no such thing as an easy fight, regardless of what you're wearing. A grappler might use the gi to hold you, stall the fight, choke you or use it for his own advantage in some way. A striker won't know how to do that. He just doesn't think in those terms because all he wants to do is to land a big bomb and end the fight. But he can always hold onto the gi with one hand to keep me away and then try to hit me with the other hand. If the guy knows what he's doing in either case, it can be tough. So it's mainly a matter of who you're fighting, not so much if he's a grappler or a striker. Every opponent is different and presents different challenges. It matters more who they are and what their tendencies are in the ring. Each shirt has to be custom made to fit whomever your opponent is. Strategy is always a matter of a lot of different factors. Even when you don't know who you're fighting or what they like to do, you will

find out quickly when you press an attack. They will sprawl against a takedown, tie-up with you, try to knee you, go for a takedown and/or force you to react. Even in a match your strategy will change depending on what your opponent does.

**Q: What about submissions? Is it harder to get one when you are wearing the gi?**
A: No, it's always hard... no matter what! Wearing the gi or not wearing the gi is less of a factor than what your opponent gives you. Jiu-jitsu is a very adaptable art and there are no pre-set moves against specific attacks. There are sets of options that you learn to consider from certain positions, but what really matters is how quickly you can evaluate those options and then change and react. That is always what gives jiu-jitsu an advantage over other martial arts that have pre-set moves and kata or whatever. Jiu-jitsu is built around learning to react – not just learning certain moves. Although you need both, mental agility is probably more important than physical agility. All the time on the mat sparring teaches your mind to work quickly as well as your body. Once you become instinctive in your reactions and don't have to think about your counters or your attacks, then you're getting the true essence of jiu-jitsu. This can take years to get to that point. Once you get there, you definitely know it. I like to train against really big and strong guys, because most of the people I fought were bigger than me. So I wanted to feel weight, strength and power during my preparation. Some of my training matches were harder than my actual UFC matches. I would rather train hard and have the fight seem easy to me, rather than to do the opposite and be shocked and overpowered.

*"The time on the mat sparring teaches your mind to work quickly, as well as your body. Once you become instinctive in your reactions and don't have to think about your counters or your attacks, then you're getting the true essence of jiu-jitsu."*

*"I really don't care what they were saying because I was extremely busy and concerned about how to heal myself. When you are dealing with something serious in your health, do you really think I pay attention to those comments? No way."*

**Q: Royce, you got injured and took some time off. Some people speculated that you weren't really hurt. What really happened to you?**
A: One day I started to feel numbness in the fingers of my right hand. This [sensation] went all the way down to my right leg. After doing some exams, the doctors said that I had a pinched nerve and a bulging disk, and he said I shouldn't be doing any kind of exercise, let alone jiu-jitsu. The problem with these kind of injuries is that you never know what caused them. Simply by sleeping wrong you may get it. I could have gotten it from lifting weights, running or simply by practicing jiu-jitsu. I had to carefully resume training. You simply can't rush these things.

**Q: Some people said it was an excuse to not fight Mark Kerr.**
A: People always say things. I really don't care what they were saying because I was extremely busy and concerned about how to heal myself. When you are dealing with something serious in your health, do you really think I pay attention to those comments? No way.

**Q: When did you leave the Gracie Academy?**
A: I left the academy in September 2001, after 16 years with Rorion. It was a very difficult decision for me to make, but I was teaching at the school from 9 a.m. to 1 p.m. and from 4 p.m. to 9 p.m. Monday through Saturday. It wasn't a bad schedule, but I was also doing seminars. If there wasn't a seminar, I'd teach Monday through Saturday. If there was a seminar, I'd only teach until Thursday night. I would leave town on Friday morning, teach the seminar on Saturday and Sunday and return home

late Sunday night. On Monday morning at 9 a.m., I'd be back at the academy to start all over again. It was a comfortable schedule, but I simply wasn't able to see my family! Every day I was able to give breakfast, lunch and dinner to my kids, but we couldn't spend any time together. Whatever time I had with them, I was in such a rush that I really couldn't enjoy it. In order to do that, I needed to have a schedule that I could fit around my seminars and my family. My family is very important to me. What good is it if I gain 10,000 students but lose my own kids?

**Q: Was it hard to be on your own?**
A: There were many opportunities coming my way when I was at the academy, but I never paid attention to them. I simply let Rorion take care of everything. So it was difficult for a short while to adjust to all the details. But I started to pay attention to things. I started reading more and learning more about business. I also started to spend more time with my family. In a way it was hard but in another way it wasn't.

In the past, the father taught his children how to survive. In modern times, it became the mother who taught the kids. Actually, sometimes in the modern days it is not even the mother who can do that; it is the babysitter who teaches the kids how to become adults. I wanted to teach my own kids. Any free time I have I want to spend with them. I don't want to be just a fictitious father; I want to be there for them. I want to teach them about life, and I want to teach them how to become adults. When I was growing up, I spent a lot more

*"In the past, the father taught his children how to survive. In modern times, it became the mother who taught the kids. Actually, sometimes in the modern days it is not even the mother who can do that; it is the babysitter who teaches the kids how to become adults. I wanted to teach my own kids."*

*"If you don't know how to escape from a bear hug or a headlock on the ground, a new half-guard move won't help you at all! Brazilian jiu-jitsu was developed by my family as a way for a small person to defend himself against larger opponents. I went to the UFC to show that those techniques worked and everyone saw that they did. I didn't go there to show my spider-guard!"*

time with my mother than with my dad because my father was always at the academy. For all my school functions – my homework and personal duties – it was my mother who helped me. I really missed having my father around, so I want to be there for my kids. But I also wanted to have time to pursue my personal vision of an international jiu-jitsu organization.

**Q: In the seminars, you're mainly teaching sport moves?**
A: Not by a long shot. The primary reason that people learn a martial art – any martial art – is to be able to protect themselves. After the UFC, a lot of people started learning Brazilian jiu-jitsu for self-defense. What they actually got when they went to classes was how to win a sports tournament with rules. They learned how to do a sweep and get two points, then a half-guard move and a reversal for two more points. They didn't learn how to defend themselves in a real situation.

Don't get me wrong. I am all for sports jiu-jitsu, but we need to remember why people started to learn martial arts in the first place! If you don't know how to escape from a bear hug or a headlock on the ground, a new half-guard move won't help you at all! Brazilian jiu-jitsu was developed by my family as a way for a small person to defend himself against larger opponents. I went to the UFC to show that those techniques worked and everyone saw that they did. I didn't go there to show my spider-guard! So I wanted to bring everyone's attention back to the essence of the art, which is the self-defense aspect. I think I've really hit a nerve, because the response has been overwhelming!

*"Fighting is something that gives me real focus.
I like the training, the strategy, the preparation… the whole thing."*

**Q: Tell me about your first fight against Yoshida, the Japanese judo gold medallist.**
A: I wanted to fight him for the challenge. Everyone said that he was the best grappler in the world, but I wanted him to prove it to me. Fighting is something that gives me real focus. I like the training, the strategy, the preparation… the whole thing. In the fight itself, I got robbed. Very simple, Yoshida looked at the referee and said, "Royce is out. Stop the fight." Since when do you talk to a referee and tell him what to do… and then he does it? You can't do that in boxing or in any other type of competition. That's not right. They worst part is that he did not have a thing; he did not have a choke. I've lost before. I know how to lose, but don't rob me.

**Q: Did you tap?**
A: I didn't tap at all. Why should I when he didn't have a choke? There was no reason for me to tap.

*"If you don't go into a fight knowing that you will win, then you have already lost. It's a reality of life that men are competitive. And the most competitive game draws the most competitive men – and that's no-holds-barred fighting. Winning is not a sometimes thing, it's an all-the-time thing."*

**Q: Why did you decide to fight him again?**
A: I was disgusted by what happened in that fight. If it can happen to me, then it can happen to anyone. When they ask me if I wanted to fight again, the only person I had in mind was him. I had unfinished business because the first never really ended. This time I was satisfied.

**Q: When did you get the idea that you would take off the gi?**
A: As soon as I got the word that we were going to fight, I talked to my father, Royler and Rickson. I asked them all what they thought, and they all agreed with it. But we also kept the strategy secret. Royler worked on the technical part of the fight and Rickson worked with me on the mental part. Rickson told me to always keep my opponent uncomfortable in every position. This will make the opponent think that he cannot win.

**Q: Were you worried about the outcome of the second fight?**
A: If you don't go into a fight knowing that you will win, then you have already lost. It's a reality of life that men are competitive. And the most competitive game draws the most competitive men – and that's no-holds-barred fighting. That's why they are there. They know the rules, they know the score. The object is to win. Winning is not a sometimes thing, it's an all-the-time thing. You don't win once in a while, you don't do things right once in a while. You do then right all the time. Winning is a habit, but unfortunately so is losing. So you have to keep focused on a positive outcome and not get distracted or have self-doubt. But you have to pay the price in training in order to be No. 1. I really wanted to surprise Yoshida. He said the fight would be a war, so I decided to treat the training as a war, too. So I totally

kept it quiet. Didn't say a thing about what I was doing… just a few people who I trusted. If there were media or people I didn't trust present when I trained in public in the U.S., I would train with the gi on. In Japan, we didn't go to the training place they gave us to use. We got some mats and got a room at the hotel and trained there.

**Q: Were you nervous or angry right before the fight?**
A: Not angry or nervous. I was very calm and totally under control. I was prepared. First, he didn't show up in the line-up when they introduced all the fighters. So I knew he was coming in by himself. During the introduction to our fight, I knew that Yoshida was behind me. But I didn't give him the pleasure of turning around and seeing me. When I finally turned around, I saw him and went right to his back and breathed on his neck… just so he could get used to me being on his back.

**Q: What was the look on Yoshida's face when you climbed into the ring and took off the gi?**
A: He gave me a double look like he couldn't believe what he was seeing. It was like he was thinking, "This isn't part of the plan." It was total surprise. He said the fight would be a war, and I had the element of surprise. From that point on, I knew that it was going to be my night. Everything was on track, and I was in control.

**Q: Were you looking more to hit him or to submit him?**
A: I was looking more to embarrass him.

*"I totally kept it quiet. Didn't say a thing about what I was doing… just a few people I trusted. If there were media or people I didn't trust present when I trained in public in the U.S., I would train with the gi on. In Japan, we didn't go to the training place they gave us to use."*

*"Over the years, I have learned that you can't change people that much from how they naturally are. You can't turn a leopard into a lion. What you have to do is to take what they do best, improve on it and find their weakest points."*

**Q: Do you think vale tudo fighters have to cross-train now because jiu-jitsu isn't enough?**
A: To fight vale tudo, everybody has to cross-train. That's a plain fact. There is no other way now. I've been doing kickboxing for more than 10 years. So this wasn't anything new for me. How I fought was different but not the tools that I knew.

**Q: Everyone is saying that the Yoshida match was your best fight ever. What did you change mentally to fight so well?**
A: Like Rickson said, "Take a step back and look at your first UFC. Then play that kind of game. Don't try to hype yourself up as a mean fighter because you're not a mean fighter. That will just drain you and make you weak. Play a cool game and deliver what you know."

**Q: How has no-holds-barred changed from the first UFC until now?**
A: It used to be style against style. Now it is fighter against fighter. It's man against man. The fighter who wins will have done the best cross-training, prepared the best strategy, trained the hardest and had the best day. It isn't so much the style any more but rather the fighter.

**Q: What is your approach to training and teaching?**
A: Over the years, I have learned that you can't change people that much from how they naturally are. You can't turn a leopard into a lion. What you have to do is to take what they do best, improve on it and find their weakest points. Then you can help them find alternatives so the weak point gets stronger. I can't tell you to fight the way I fight because you are not me. You have your own style so I have to take your characteristics and make you better. To do that, I don't need that much time, because I am not trying to reinvent the wheel; I am just trying to improve it. To be able to

fight, you need to stay within your style. I won't try to change it; I'll just make the right adjustments. I have a lot of experience in fights and people know that I talk from personal knowledge – not from something that I have just heard or read about.

**Q: You mentioned once that you try to do everything naturally and in a very relaxed way. How do you apply this approach to your training?**
A: For all the supplementary training besides jiu-jitsu, I try to keep my own pace. If I'm running, even if I do it with someone, I follow my own rhythm, my own pace. I don't think that I have to beat a world record or anything like that. Depending on how I feel is how I train. I don't like to have anyone clocking me when I run because I like to monitor my own running session. I use this specific approach for my cardiovascular training. When I train with weights, I do it a little bit different. I try not to miss one single day. If I'm sick, I'm sick... so I rest. Sometimes I feel that I'm pushing too much. Before I overtrain, I intentionally slow down and do the same activities but with no pressure on my mind. When you are using a trainer, it is easier to overtrain because he will push you hard every single session. You have to be careful with what kind of personal trainer you have. If I feel I need to stop, I stop for a day or two. It won't be the end of the world because of that. You should learn to listen to your body and take care of it. More sometimes is not better. Especially when you are feeling tired. If you keep pushing, you may end up hurting yourself. It is better to take a day off and come back stronger and more motivated than before. As far as jiu-jitsu is concerned, that is more of a technical training, although the intensity of my sparring depends on how I feel on a given day.

*"When you are using a trainer, it is easier to overtrain because he will push you hard every single session. You have to be careful with what kind of personal trainer you have. If I feel I need to stop, I stop for a day or two. It won't be the end of the world because of that. You should learn to listen to your body and take care of it."*

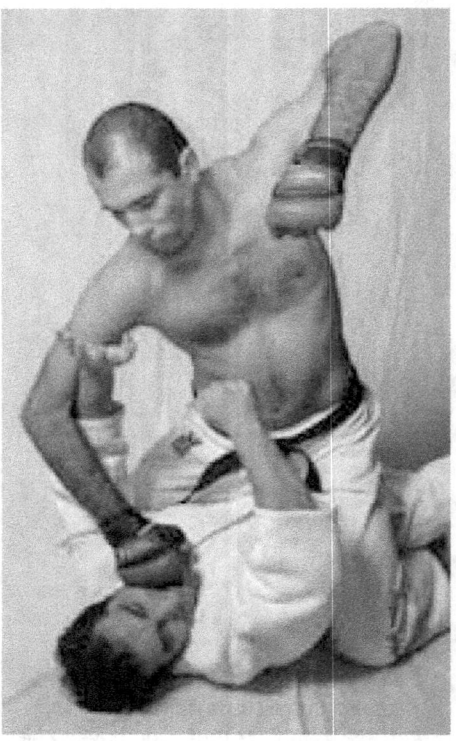

*"I think that a wrestler's takedown and counter is something that a lot of people have absorbed. I think this is a very interesting element for a grappler, regardless of his style. I definitely looked into it and picked up some tricks here and there."*

**Q: What keeps you so motivated to fight and to test yourself after all these years?**
A: I just don't like it when people try to tell me what I cannot do. I love a challenge, and I love jiu-jitsu. When people tell me that I can't fight again, that makes me want to do it. I think fighting should be fun... a fun challenge that you take seriously.

**Q: Today everybody seems to learn from everybody. Have you incorporated elements from other grappling arts into your jiu-jitsu repertoire?**
A: Not really. But I think that a wrestler's takedown and counter is something that a lot of people have absorbed. I think this is a very interesting element for a grappler, regardless of his style. I definitely looked into it and picked up some tricks here and there.

**Q: What has changed from the Royce Gracie who stepped into the Octagon for the first time to the Royce Gracie of today?**
A: I'd like to say that nothing has changed, but it is not true. I was single and now I'm married with children. I was teaching and working out of the Gracie Academy and now I'm on my own traveling around the world teaching seminars and spreading the art my father developed to every possible corner of the world. Inside of me, I'm still the same person. I enjoy the same things, and I haven't changed much. I don't have too much time to do other things, but I'm the same Royce Gracie who fought in the first UFC that night in November 1993.

**Q: You have published several books on various topics, such as Brazilian jiu-jitsu, physical conditioning and nutrition. Why did you do that?**
A: First, I wanted to leave a printed legacy, and I think these books are a

good example of that. Then I realized that it was an excellent way of answering many of the questions that students ask me every time I teach. The idea came from the necessity of answering the students' questions. And I think these books have accomplished that mission. The information is great and the quality of the work is indisputable.

**Q: Who do you think is your toughest opponent?**
A: Always... my toughest opponent is always the one I imagine inside of my head.

*"Being a Gracie doesn't just mean being a family member, it also means being a student and a member of the world jiu-jitsu community. All my students are members of the Gracie family – not just myself or my cousins or my brothers."*

**Q: Do you have any regrets about your career or life?**
A: I don't. Everything happens for a reason. Good or bad you can use everything to your advantage – just like in fighting. If you have the right attitude, then there is no bad in life. There are just different opportunities to do well and to become better. Happiness and success is within us all, regardless of outside influences. Each of us can choose how we want to feel. Attitude is everything.

**Q: What does it mean to be a Gracie?**
A: It's a very heavy name to carry. Being a Gracie doesn't just mean being a family member, it also means being a student and a member of the world jiu-jitsu community. All my students are members of the Gracie family – not just myself or my cousins or my brothers. To a certain extent, we all share common values and goals. For us all, it is just like my father says: "Everything that I am is jiu-jitsu. I will uphold the honor of jiu-jitsu in my everyday life with proper actions and morals, and I will defend the family name with my sweat and blood." That's what being a Gracie means.

# FABIO GURGEL

## The Lion of Jiu-Jitsu

A veteran of many tournaments, Fabio Gurgel has left his mark just about everywhere he has competed. He decided to put himself to the ultimate test by competing in the Ultimate Fighting Championship against Jerry Bohlander from Ken Shamrock's Lion's Den. After running out of time inside the Octagon and losing, Gurgel decided to tackle an even bigger foe.

Against the advice of nearly everyone Gugel faced Mark Kerr, the giant American wrestler. This match would go down as one of the greatest fights in the history of no-holds-barred. Giving away over 50 pounds, Gurgel took Kerr to a decision. Although Gurgel lost the match, his incredible technique earned him a moral victory. Watching Fabio Gurgel perform jiu-jitsu is like watching a ballet dancer — he is graceful, effortless, and precise.

Gurgel retired from competition to devote his time to turning out fine martial artists and promoting the art of jiu-jitsu around the world. For him, spirit and heart are the most important attributes in martial arts training. "In order to be the best," Gurgel says firmly, "you must have the warrior's spirit and the warrior's heart."

**Q: When did you start training?**
A: I was born in Rio de Janeiro, January 18, 1970. When I was 13 years old I started training in a small gym with Professor Toninho, who I trained with for 10 months. Coincidentally, this was the same master that Romero "Jacare" Cavalcanti started training with – Jacare later became my instructor. I was taken to Toninho's gym by a friend who used to train with Carlos Gracie Jr. He thought I should start in a smaller gym so I would get more personal attention. My original goal was simply to learn self-defense, nothing else. But I quickly fell in love with jiu-jitsu and just couldn't stop. I finally received my black belt from Jacare at the age of 19, after being a Brazilian champion several times in all the lower ranks.

*"At that time, all the Brazilian jiu-jitsu teams were united with the goal of proving that jiu-jitsu was more effective than luta livre. We all trained together, proving that a union makes a group stronger."*

**Q: What titles do you have?**
A: I have all the titles a jiu-jitsu fighter can have. To begin with, I am a four-time world champion. For my first title I defeated Murillo Bustamante. In 1996, for my second title, I defeated Daniel Gracie. Then in 2000 I won again against Ricardo Arona. Then in 2001 I got my fourth title defeating Fabio Leopoldo in the semi-finals and then Rodrigo "Comprido" Meideros in the finals, even though he was much younger than me and was considered the favorite. After that I decided that I had nothing left to prove because I had beaten everyone, and so I decided to stop competing.

**Q: What was your first big vale tudo fight?**
A: It was against Denilson Maia and was very important since it was my debut and I had the responsibility of defending the honor of Brazilian jiu-jitsu. At that time all the Brazilian jiu-jitsu teams were united with the goal of proving that jiu-jitsu was more effective than luta livre. We all trained together, proving that union makes a group stronger. The fight went 100 percent as planned – training for the fight was way harder than the fight itself. It was an unforgettable night for myself, Murilo Bustamante and Wallid Ismail as well as for all the people who watched it.

**Q: How did you get involved in the UFC?**
A: At that time the UFC was the biggest vale tudo event in the world. I was invited to participate and that alone was already an honor and a great responsibility too, since in those days jiu-jitsu had the reputation of being unbeatable, I trained very hard for that fight. I moved to Los Angeles and trained with Rickson Gracie for two months, plus I trained

boxing with Claudinho. I was truly in top shape, but unfortunately I did not fight well and my opponent, Jerry Bohlander, held the fence the entire time and left me with nothing to do. Since that fight, all events in the world have made it illegal for a fighter to hold the fence. If you watch that fight you will understand why. I had to keep him in my guard in order to control his movements. At the final bell, I knew I given everything I had and had done my best.

**Q: Some people said that you should fought with an open guard.**
A: It's very easy to make comments from outside the Octagon. I saw the fight on video and saw some mistakes. Jiu-jitsu is a perfect art, but it doesn't mean that everybody can use the art perfectly. Since I made some little mistakes, I ended up losing the fight. After that fight I went to train with Rickson Gracie to correct the mistakes in the positions. I'm sure that if I knew about those aspects before, that the fight would have been completely different. I was very frustrated by what happened and a promoter later brought Jerry Bolander to Brazil when Ruas had his revenge against Oleg Taktarov. That night they brought us both into the ring and I challenged Bolander to a rematch. He agreed but later on backed down from the deal. I learned later that the UFC had offered him an easier opponent. To me, however, I was freed from my frustration because he backed down from the fight. I did what I had to do and he did what he thought was the best for him.

*"Jiu-jitsu is a perfect art, but it doesn't mean that everybody can use the art perfectly. Since I made some little mistakes, I ended up losing the fight."*

**Q: Was the criticism hard to take?**
A: Nobody likes harsh words. But the point is that everybody likes to talk. Some people think that because they do few leg press repetitions with 300 pounds they can control Mark Kerr with an open guard. Why they

*"It was 30 minutes of fighting without rounds or breaks. I weighed 200 pounds and Kerr was 245. It was the first time I had faced a world-class wrestler who also trained as a professional bodybuilder. He was heavier and stronger than any of my sparring partners. I was very comfortable and had total control of the situation."*

don't they try to keep pushing the leg press with 300 pounds for thirty minutes nonstop?

**Q: You then won three vale tudo fights in a row in Brazil, right?**
A: I had to fight three opponents on the same night. The first one was Pat Smith, the UFC II runner-up and a great stand-up fighter at the time. He had just KO'd Andy Hug, the late K-1 champion. He was very explosive and strong when the belt rang he came ready to fight. But then shortly into the fight he started holding the fence, and the rules were clear. so he was disqualified, My second match was against Michael Pachoulik, a wrestler who had just defeated luta livre's Denilson Maia in Japan. I fought a good fight and brought him into my guard and punished him as much as I could. After five minutes, he tapped out. This brought me to one of my greatest tests in life as I then had to face Mark Kerr.

**Q: How do you remember that fight?**
A: It was 30 minutes of fighting without rounds or breaks. I weighed 200 lbs and Kerr was 245. It was the first time I had faced a world-class wrestler who trained as a professional bodybuilder as well. He was heavier and stronger than any of my sparring partners. Even though I felt he was strong in the beginning, I was very comfortable and had total control of the situation. Since my strategy was to take the fight the distance, I waited for him to get tired, hoping I could capitalize on any mistakes. Everything was going as planned, and then 15 minutes into the fight Kerr bit my finger real hard – I still have the scar to prove it. So I turned to the referee, who was new at vale tudo, and showed him my bleeding finger. Kerr then headbutted me right above my eye. After that he spent the last half of the fight punishing that eye. During that fight I experienced every single feel-

ing from tiredness to pain to the will to survive. It was a great feeling to hear 1,200 people cheering my name. It was a great fight and a great experience that taught me a lot about myself.

**Q: Is it true that Mark Kerr visited you the day after the fight?**
A: Yes, he did. He had a problem with his hand. Dr. John Keating asked me if I knew a specialist on infections. So I recommended a doctor that lived very close to my house. They visited him and Kerr got better. Mark then came to my place to express his gratitude. We talked about the fight and he told me that he knew I was not going to quit and that at a certain point he didn't know what to do. We respect each other very much.

**Q: If you had to fight Mark Kerr again, what would you do differently?**
A: I would not change positions as much as I did. I would adopt one and let him get tired. I would also try to stay on my feet longer. I have better coordination and could have done more damage on the feet. He needs the ground to win.

*"It was a great time because everybody was together, training and working for the good of all jiu-jitsu. Carlson was teaching all the time, and I learned a lot of tactics on the ground. He knows a lot about jiu-jitsu and how to use it properly."*

**Q: Didn't you also train under Carlson Gracie?**
A: Yes, I did. It was a great time because everybody was together, training and working for the good of all jiu-jitsu. Carlson was teaching all the time and I learned a lot of tactics on the ground. He knows a lot about jiu-jitsu and how to use it properly.

**Q: What was your most important sport jiu-jitsu match?**
A: There are many fights that were important and unforgettable in my career as a sport jiu jitsu practitioner, however one that I truly remember happened in 1990 in the Rio de Janeiro Championships against Amaury

*"Nowadays, vale tudo is about the best man. Styles help, of course, but today you see jiu-jitsu people beating wrestlers and wrestlers beating jiu-jitsu fighters. This is because it's about individuals. If you are not willing to change, you are going to lose."*

Bitetti. I was losing the match by two points and there were 30 seconds left in the match. I took him down and immediately won the match. He made his two points in the first minute of the match and I spent the rest of the fight trying to score. Fortunately, I was able to win. It was without a doubt a great moment in my career and I keep this fight in a very special place of my heart. It is a great memory.

**Q: Do you think Brazilian jiu-jitsu is the best style?**
A: Nowadays, vale tudo is about the best man. Styles help, of course, but today you see jiu-jitsu people beating wrestlers and wrestlers beating jiu-jitsu fighters. This is because it's about individuals. For me, jiu-jitsu is the best because it can help you in your life. Vale tudo events are a very small part of the whole picture. You can't educate kids with no-holds-barred events but you can help kids with jiu-jitsu.

**Q: What is your opinion about the new techniques compared to the old basics?**
A: The technical evolution of jiu-jitsu techniques is based on sport competition. Many people criticize sport jiu-jitsu but they never participated in a competition. New ideas and concepts are always hard to accept. It is natural not to accept them. The level of the game has increased and keeps evolving so that new ways of preventing attacks have to be developed. If you are not willing to change you are going to lose. Your approach is going to die out because what works is what people will use. This applies not only to jiu-jitsu but to everything in life including business. Anyone running a business for more than ten years knows that changes have to

be made to adapt to changing market situations.

Problems can arise, however, when someone with not enough skill in the basics wants to invent and create new moves. This is stupid. The basics movements of jiu-jitsu are the ones everybody should use and apply. The new techniques are mostly the product of high-level champions. They are capable of executing these techniques but most can't do them. So if your are not a full-time competitor, stick to the basics and you'll be surprised how good you can perform.

**Q: What is your opinion of Rickson Gracie?**
A: Rickson is a different fighter from anyone. He is a scientist of jiu-jitsu. His knowledge and skill is far and away above everybody else – not only in America but in Brazil as well. There's another level in the art of jiu-jitsu and Rickson lives on that level. I would like to reach it some day. He sees things in a fight that nobody else can see. Training under Rickson is a very revealing experience even if you're a world champion. With him I began to understand the 'real' essence of jiu jitsu principles. Some people say that I talk a lot about Rickson but let me tell you something, if you haven't been with Rickson on the ground, you don't know what jiu-jitsu is all about.

*"The basics movements of jiu-jitsu are the ones everybody should use and apply. The new techniques are mostly the product of high-level champions. They are capable of executing these techniques but most can't do them."*

**Q: Is jiu-jitsu strong or weak in Brazil right now?**
A: The jiu-jitsu situation in Brazil is not a good one, because the sport has split into two separate groups. It is an ego fight between those who want power at any cost. In this ego fight, the people involved do not realize how much damage they are doing to our sport. It is sad to see that hap-

*"If history teaches us something, it is that human beings never learn from their mistakes. We are no longer trying to prove who is a bigger man, what we are trying to accomplish is to professionalize the sport of jiu-jitsu and find new ways of making it more profitable for the competitors and sponsors."*

pen right in front of our eyes. It seems that other martial arts styles went through the same thing and have gotten weaker. Even with plenty of examples, jiu-jitsu does not seem to have learned from it. If history teaches us something, it is that human beings never learn from their mistakes. We should work together and try to push the sport in a strong direction instead of weakening it by fighting and arguing among ourselves.

**Q: What is the future of jiu-jitsu?**
A: I believe that jiu-jitsu will never stop being part of the lives of the people who have dedicated time and effort to it. However, as a sport, I am not sure what the future holds because there are too many variables. I hope the work that has been done by the Confederation of Brazilian Jiu-Jitsu (CBJJ) keeps growing and those who are trying to destroy the sport for personal gain lose credibility and eventually realize that it is better for all of us to stay together. On the other hand, I am a believer in submission fighting as a sport. I truly think it has huge potential, even though is still in the beginning stages. It is practiced in many countries around the world, which brings a healthy balance to the sport. I believe it does not help nor hurt jiu-jitsu. It is simply another grappling sport for the jiu-jitsu practitioner to enter, just like a judo or sambo tournament.

**Q: Do you like the new fighting rules?**
A: I believe any attempt to improve the sport by making changes in the rules is good and positive, since they make it possible for the art to develop. We are no longer trying to prove who is a bigger man, what we are trying to accomplish is to professionalize the sport of jiu-jitsu and find new ways of making it more profitable for the competitors and sponsors. I

agree with any new rules for the simple reason that anyone trying to improve the sport will eventually bring something new and good – it does not matter what kind of rules they are. If a participant does not agree with the rules they should find another tournament or create another event that they agree with and compete there.

**Q: How has Brazilian jiu jitsu and vale tudo developed in the last decade?**
A: The major change I see is that in the old days we used to fight for the simple pleasure of defending our art and to be recognized as a fighter – fighting for your style was the main reason for vale tudo fights. Today, the events have become professional and the fighters focus only on the money. Since the industry generates so much cash, it is logical for fighters to take advantage of that for their financial security. Another important point is that the jiu-jitsu that was only known by a very few 15 years ago has now become popular and everybody knows the art. Today, the art of Brazilian jiu-jitsu is practiced by all fighters. Without a knowledge of jiu-jitsu, no fighter has any business being in an MMA event. However, and this is a very interesting point, jiu-jitsu fighters also had to add strikes and kicks to their arsenal – which was unheard before. So now all fighters know a little of everything, and the best man wins, independent of their style of fighting. A true mixed-martial-arts style has been developed due to the UFC and other similar events.

*"Today, the art of Brazilian jiu-jitsu is practiced by all fighters. Without a knowledge of jiu-jitsu, no fighter has any business being in an MMA event. However, and this is an interesting point, jiu-jitsu fighters also had to add strikes and kicks to their arsenal, which was unheard of before."*

*"No style needs to prove that their fighting method works. Everyone has matured and realized that times have changed and that there is no room for the childish rivalries we had in the past. Everyone is trying to improve what they do."*

**Q: Is there still a big rivalry in Brazil between jiu-jitsu practitioners and other vale tudo fighters?**
A: Definitely, it is not the way it used to be. Before, luta-livre fighters wanted to compete directly with jiu-jitsu practitioners in Rio de Janeiro and there was a big rivalry between them. Today there is room for everybody, and luta livre fighters are respected all around the world. No style needs to prove that their fighting method works. Everyone has matured and realized that times have changed and that there is no room for the childish rivalries we had in the past. Everyone is trying to improve what they do and all the problems are solved in the ring now, with no hard feelings after the fight.

**Q: Can you talk about the Professional Jiu-Jitsu League that you have created?**
A: In my opinion, the Professional jiu-jitsu League is the best vehicle to have jiu-jitsu seen as a professional sport. It pays the fighters to participate in the tournaments, and it keeps the big jiu-jitsu stars fighting with the gi for the sport of jiu-jitsu, instead of going to Abu Dhabi and no-holds-barred which eventually will distance them from the art they learned in the beginning. In the event that took place in 2000, we had the cream of the crop from the jiu-jitsu community. The best 50 athlete in the world participated, going through a very clear and fair formal selection process.

The formula to participate is very simple. The fighter must be among the top eogjt athletes that have the biggest number of gold medals in each weight division. The champions were Robinho, Leo Vieira, Roleta, Comprido and Nino plus other great champions like Vitor "Shaolin" Ribeiro, Roberto Traven, Murilo Bustamante, et cetera. The Brazilian media said it was the best jiu-jitsu tournament ever. And the other interesting thing was that it was on TV and they received money to be in it. You have to come up with a complete package that allows the competitors to make money and became professional. This is the only way to keep them in the sport and away from vale tudo. Don't get me wrong, I love vale tudo and MMA, but sport jiu-jitsu is a great art that everybody can practice for the rest of their lives.

**Q: In your opinion, who are the best Brazilian jiu-jitsu and vale tudo fighters today?**
A: This is a very hard question to answer because there are many good guys out there, especially after the push the sport experienced in the last 10 years or so. The sport is moving in new directions and this simple factor opens more opportunities for all the new practitioners. The same thing happens with mixed martial arts and vale tudo. However, in the vale tudo circuit, I believe that Antonio "Minotauro" Nogueira is probably *numero uno* in the heavyweight division. In pure jiu-jitsu, "Pe de Paro" Cruz is currently the top jiu-jitsu fighter. The sport is evolving so fast that new great champions are coming out all the time. Sometimes it is impossible of keeping track of everything is happening.

**Q: What is next for you?**
A: I am involved in the production of professional events, will continue giving my seminars in Brazil and around the world, and managing the several gyms that I own. All these things keep me very busy and I'm the kind of guy that I think the busier you are the better you'll be. In short, keep your eyes open and your mind busy!

# JOHN LEWIS

## *The Invincible Warrior*

JOHN LEWIS IS NOT ONLY RECOGNIZED AS ONE OF THE FIRST AMERICAN NO-HOLDS-BARRED FIGHTING CHAMPIONS, BUT HE IS ALSO ONE OF THE MOST PROLIFIC AND SUCCESSFUL FIGHTERS. A VETERAN OF DOZENS OF COMPETITIONS – RANGING FROM EXTREME FIGHTING, TO VALE TUDO, TO BRAZILIAN JIU-JITSU TO EVERYTHING IN BETWEEN – LEWIS HAS TRULY PAID THE PRICE TO BECOME A SUCCESSFUL FIGHTER AND MARTIAL ARTS TEACHER. AS IMPRESSIVE AS HIS TEACHING CREDENTIALS ARE, HOWEVER, WHAT SETS LEWIS APART IS HIS UNCANNY ABILITY TO RELATE TO AND UNDERSTAND PEOPLE FROM ALL RACES, CULTURES AND BACKGROUNDS. LEWIS BECAME ONE OF THE FIRST TWO PEOPLE EVER GRANTED A MIXED-MARTIAL-ART PROMOTER'S LICENSE IN NEVADA. BUT LEWIS IS NOT ONE TO STAY IN ONE PLACE. "IF YOU'RE NOT MOVING FORWARD," HE SAYS, "THEN YOU'RE GOING BACKWARDS. I ALWAYS TRY TO CHALLENGE MYSELF WITH NEW IDEAS AND NEW PROJECTS."

**Q: How long have you been practicing judo, jiu-jitsu and the martial arts in general?**
A: Almost 20 years. I started with Gene LeBell. I have also trained in judo, Brazilian jiu-jitsu, Japanese jiu-jitsu, sho kon do (Japanese kickboxing), aikido, Northern shaolin, kali and boxing.

**Q: What is your family background?**
A: My mother, who is white, is originally from New York, and my father, who is black, is from Gainesville, Florida. I was born in Hawaii on February 8, 1968. My father is an executive chef, and he moved to Hawaii for a job. After four or five years in Hawaii, we moved to Daytona Beach, Florida for three or four years. In Florida, during the late 1960s, racism was very obvious. In elementary school I got into a lot of fights because of the racism. Therefore, we moved back to Hawaii after I got out of the fifth grade. I've always been a calm person at all ages. I wasn't a punk or a rabble-rouser. I tried to be as friendly as I could be in school. However, if someone was unfair to me or to my sister, who is two years younger, I had no qualms

# GRAPPLING MASTERS

*"In Hawaii, the testosterone level is very high, and the people are very fast to fight. People will fight at the drop of the hat. If you don't stand up for yourself and fight, you'll get a reputation as a punk and will get picked on more. So I got into a lot of fights because I never backed down."*

about standing up for myself. In Hawaii it was different. There is no real racism because the society is so multi-cultural. Of course, if you weren't a local, you got a lot of attitude. I was constantly called *haole* (outsider). In Hawaii, the testosterone level is very high, and the people are very fast to fight. People will fight at the drop of the hat. If you don't stand up for yourself and fight, you'll get a reputation as a punk and will get picked on more. So I got into a lot of fights because I never backed down. Being of mixed race, though, I grew up with a lot of tolerance for everybody. I never viewed myself as black or white – just as myself. My friends were just my friends, and I always treated people based on how they were as human beings – not on the color of their skin or their ethnic origin.

**Q: Did you take any martial arts as a kid?**
A: No, but I was always really athletic and I could naturally fight well. The only street fight I lost was in the sixth grade. I didn't really know anything formal, but I always had a strategy of how I'd fight. It may have looked like it, but I never just put my head down and fought. Although I never picked fights, I realized that I became more accepted and popular when I was victorious. Looking back on this, it certainly doesn't make me proud. At the time, however, it was all I knew, so that gave me reinforcement in the fighting mindset. In the eighth grade, I got into "popping" or street dancing, which is like stand-up break dancing. It was very popular at the time. Because I was very athletic, I was good at it.

**Q: Did you stop fighting?**
A: No. In the ninth grade, we had our own high school version of fight club. We would meet below a bridge near the school and a bunch of guys from all the local schools would meet and fight one-on-one. There were no weapons or anything, and no one ever got hurt beyond a black eye or a bloody nose. I never lost one of those fights, and it made me start analyzing

how I was fighting and what worked and what didn't work. That is when I started to get a formal interest in the martial arts. A lot of guys whom I fought did take martial arts. I still beat them, but it did make me think that I should get more formal training. As a result, I started kickboxing, and I got better and better. My dancing probably helped me to progress fast. During high school, I was dancing professionally. I opened for Menudo three times at the Blaisdell Arena and many other shows. At the end of my senior year, a friend of mine (Steve Silva) called me from the mainland and invited me to audition for a show in Las Vegas. This was big step for me because I had just turned 17. Because my parents always supported me in what I wanted to do, they let me go. I got accepted for a show at the Riviera called "Splash," which was the No. 1 show in Vegas at the time. During this time, I was still training in kickboxing. It was definitely second to my dancing, but I still did it because I liked it. After two years of doing the show, I decided that I wanted to get into writing and singing music so I moved to Los Angeles where the music business was.

*"A lot of guys whom I fought did take martial arts. I still beat them, but it did make me think that I should get more formal training. As a result, I started kickboxing, and I got better and better."*

**Q: With whom did you train?**
A: When I came to L.A., I met a man (Dan Koji) who would change my life. He was from Japan and had his own system that I can best describe as muay Thai for the street. He called it "shokondo." It was the first intense, philosophical and real martial art that I could respect. As good as I thought I was at fighting, Dan could take me out at will. To me, he was every bit as good as Bruce Lee. He's back in Japan now, but he is still phenomenal. He liked my talent immediately and started teaching me privates. Within two years I had earned a black belt in his system, and this was the first black belt he ever awarded. I was living in Culver City at the time, and my backyard was set up like a training center with heavy bags, double-ended bags, a mat area, a wing chun dummy and sticks for Filipino martial arts. I was exposing myself to as many arts as possible because I felt that no art was complete

"Bruce Lee's *The Tao of Jeet Kune Do* influenced me greatly. He was the first guy who realized you had to know different things. I felt the same way before I ever read his book, but this reinforced my feelings after I read it."

and that they all had important aspects. I would go to a lot of different schools for several months as a time until I felt that I had the essence of what they were teaching. Then I would incorporate what I liked and move on to something else. Bruce Lee's *The Tao of Jeet Kune Do* influenced me greatly. He was the first guy who realized you had to know different things. I felt the same way before I ever read his book, but this reinforced my feelings after I read it. I wasn't necessarily trying to become a JKD artist, because — after reading Bruce's book and notes — I felt that even that would be too limiting.

**Q: Who else influenced you?**
A: While I was doing all this experimenting, a friend of mine wanted me to meet his teacher from New York, a wing chun instructor and a former kickboxing champion. His name was John Peretti. John told me about Gene LeBell. Later, John introduced Gene to me when we were in Gene's mountain cabin. Gene is great guy, and he would have a select group of students come up to train at the cabin. A lot of the best martial artists in the world have learned and trained at Gene's cabin. So I started grappling with Gene, and it soon became a real passion. I ended up training consistently with him for five or six years. I still consider myself to be his student, and I go back and train with him when my schedule permits. While I was training with Gene, a friend of mine told me about the Gracie family. Eventually, he took me to Rickson Gracie's school in Los Angeles, and I started training in jiu-jitsu with Rickson.

**Q: Was Brazilian jiu-jitsu different from Gene Lebell's style?**
A: Gene knows a tremendous amount so none of the [Brazilian] techniques were new to me. The main thing I learned in jiu-jitsu was the smooth transition between positions and submissions. In jiu-jitsu, the smooth transition between positions is unique to the art. So I started accelerating at a fast rate in jiu-jitsu because Gene had taught me so

much, and I had the basics down. I became the first person to go from white belt all the way to black belt with Gene, and that was a great honor. Gokor [Chivichyan] was there before me, of course, but he was already a master grappler. Gene just fine-tuned him. It was special that I was given that rank.

**Q: A lot of people know your academy as J-Sect or J-Sect Jiu-Jitsu. How is that?**
A: Based on the flow of natural movement, J-Sect is a system I developed combining a multitude of techniques and philosophy's from my history and studies of the martial arts. The motto is "Strike first, strike fast and strike last." When you know combat is inevitable, strike first, take your opponent out and don't stop until it is finished. When I moved to Las Vegas to open my school in June of 1995, I was teaching J-Sect and Brazilian Jiu-Jitsu. Somewhere over time the "and" got lost, and the names merged to become J-Sect Jiu-Jitsu. Although my system of BJJ is André Pederneiras' Nova Uniao BJJ, we have no limitations to what we add to the core system. With all that I have learned from the grappling master, Gene LeBell, as well as my students and creative desire, my J-Sect system is very versatile. I have detailed leg locks, cranks and anything else that works. We also have a strong focus in wrestling and other takedown concepts. These days it is important to be skilled in all ranges of the fighting game. The majority of today's fighters can both strike and grapple. At the same time, it is important to know your strengths and weaknesses. For example, if your game is ground fighting, it is important for you to understand the striking arts. The most common mistake is thinking you are an expert striker after just a few months of training. This is just as ludicrous as an accomplished striker thinking he is an expert grappler after a few months on the mats. When a ground

*"The main thing I learned in jiu-jitsu was the smooth transition between positions and submissions. In jiu-jitsu, the smooth transition between positions is unique to the art. So I started accelerating at a fast rate in jiu-jitsu because Gene had taught me so much, and I had the basics down."*

*"Watch any combat sporting event from the UFC to Extreme Fighting to pancrase, and you will see that nearly every fight goes to the ground. If you are a strong stand-up striker, it is extremely advisable to learn as much about ground techniques as possible."*

fighter learns to strike, he has to understand the mind of a striker. At the same time, he has to work on making the takedown (his strength and primary goal) easier. In the same light, when a striker learns to grapple, he has to learn how to survive the grappler's attack and, [assuming they went to the ground], eventually regain his feet so he can employ his strengths. Watch any combat sporting event from the UFC to Extreme Fighting to pancrase, and you will see that nearly every fight goes to the ground. If you are a strong stand-up striker, it is extremely advisable to learn as much about ground techniques as possible ... if for nothing more than to know how to defend your weaknesses and keep or bring the fight back to your feet where your strengths lie.

**Q: Were you a natural at judo and jiu-jitsu. Did the movements come easily to you?**
A: I learn things very quickly. I was also a professional street dancer ... breaking and popping. I was very used to remembering combinations and internalizing movement. I am sure that has a lot to do with it. The same goes for my students. Each one who has had a break dancing background has taken to BJJ very easily.

**Q: When did you start fighting?**
A: I began my career in a Hawaiian show called UFCF. Matt Hume put it on. I fought a pancrase fighter who was one of Karl Gotch's top students. I won in 1:42 with an armbar. John Peretti and Gene LeBell were both in my corner. When I got back, I got a call from John Peretti. He said that if I really wanted to test myself that I should fight Carlson Gracie Jr. in a new show he was starting that was called Extreme Fighting. At the time, I was training with the Gracies. I was only a blue belt, and everyone was telling me not to take the fight because they were sure there was no way I could beat

Carlson. But I knew that I had lot more than just jiu-jitsu to bring to the table because of my stand-up experience and my years with Gene. I think I might have been a little tentative for that fight, but even then I controlled the fight and fought Carlson to a draw. And this was when the Gracies were dominating everyone. Therefore, I felt very good about it.

**Q: What did the jiu-jitsu community think about your fight with a Gracie?**
A: Well, before the fight everyone said how great Carlson Jr. was and that I didn't stand a chance. Afterwards, those same guys told me he wasn't one of the top jiu-jitsu men. So I have to laugh about that. It isn't that Carlson Gracie Jr. is not a good fighter. That's not true at all

*"Well, before the fight everyone said how great Carlson Jr. was and that I didn't stand a chance. Afterwards, those same guys told me he wasn't one of the top jiu-jitsu men. So I have to laugh about that. It isn't that Carlson Gracie Jr. is not a good fighter. That's not true at all. He's very, very good."*

… he's very, very good. I just think that he was expecting someone who was a jiu-jitsu blue belt, and I was actually a black belt under Gene LeBell and had also been training Brazilian jiu-jitsu for two years. I had eight years of grappling and even more years of kickboxing. I think I took him by surprise.

**Q: Did you continue to train in BJJ?**
A: Of course! After that fight I was introduced to a person I consider to be one of the top jiu-jitsu instructors in the world – Andre Pederneiras. Andre is a black belt under Carlson Gracie Sr., and he is also the founder of top jiu-jitsu team in the world, Nova Uniao (New Union). I trained with Andre in the U.S., and I was so impressed that I eventually went to Brazil and trained with him there. I'm now a second-degree black belt under him, and I give him 100 percent credit for my rapid progression in jiu-jitsu and my current technical level.

*"There are certain things that you can only learn from stepping into the cage. My biggest lesson was that no single technique or strategy works best in cage fighting. You have to be flexible and adaptable. Most importantly, if you ever want to be great, you have to have a strong sense of strategy."*

**Q: Did the Carlson Jr. fight lead to more offers?**
A: Quite a few. I learned from every fight. Each time I fought it seemed like I had someone with different skills and different strengths. I would always concentrate on the skills I needed to compete successfully with them. There are certain things that you can only learn from stepping into the cage. My biggest lesson was that no single technique or strategy works best in cage fighting. You have to be flexible and adaptable. In the cage, you can never be at a loss in a ground position – you have to know how to attack and defend wrestling takedowns, and you have to understand kicking and punching. Hopefully, you can learn to attack like a professional. If not, you have to learn to defend like one. Most importantly, if you ever want to be great, you have to have a strong sense of strategy. A lot of my current stand-up strategies come from my current mentor and trainer, former pro-boxer "Saigon" Skipper Kelt. Skipper was a top-level boxer who fought for the welterweight title many times.

**Q: What led you to open a martial arts school in Las Vegas?**
A: I love martial arts so it was only natural for me to come to Las Vegas to open a school because of my connections from the time I was a dancer. As soon as I opened the school, students enrolled and it started moving forward. I was a little nervous when I opened it, of course, but I felt that I had something important to teach. I was very gratified when it went so well. I met Chuck Liddell a couple of years after I opened the school. He told Tito Ortiz about me, and Tito joined the training group. We got along so well that Tito asked me to be his trainer and cornerman for his title fight against Wanderlei Silva.

*"As soon as I opened the school, students enrolled and it started moving forward. I was a little nervous when I opened it, of course, but I felt that I had something important to teach. I was very gratified when it went so well."*

**Q: How did you help Tito prepare for Wanderlei?**
A: Well, Tito and I both knew that Wanderlei would be a tough match, so we devised a strategy that we felt would give Tito a 90 percent chance of winning. We planned on using Tito's wrestling skills to neutralize Wandelei's striking power. Wanderlei always comes forward aggressively with very bad intentions. So knowing that, we decided that Tito would stand straight-up like he was going to punch, then drop under Wanderlei's punches at the last second and shoot for the takedown. That didn't give Wanderlei a chance to sprawl and counter the takedown because he was coming forward to punch. This worked the entire night. In our ground training, we attacked Tito from our guard constantly, doing sweeps and trying to get to our feet – just as we thought Wanderlei would do. We did this over and over. With this strategy, we felt that Tito could take him down at will at the beginning of each round, then ground and pound and work from there. In my mind, there was no way Tito was going to lose except to a lucky punch. That didn't happen, and Tito dominated for the decision victory.

"If you're a strong kickboxer, for example, I'm not going to try to turn you into a jiu-jitsu fighter. Instead, I'm going to teach you how to avoid being taken down. I try to make people great at whatever they're good at."

**Q: Did this victory attract more students?**
A: After Wanderlei, a lot of guys wanted to train with me and start fighting. I now have hundreds of students. I don't let anyone even think about fighting until they're at least a purple belt in jiu-jitsu. They also have to have a 'high intellect' and athletic ability. Nowadays, I have people moving to Las Vegas from all over the world to train with me. To qualify for the Lewis/Pederneiras Vale Tudo Team, they first have to be very strong in one area. That means that they have to be a strong kickboxer, a jiu-jitsu man, wrestler or whatever. They have to have a special skill I can build on. The success of our team doesn't come from making a generic mold that I try to fit all my students into. It comes from my ability to recognize and build on people's individual talents. If you're a strong kickboxer, for example, I'm not going to try to turn you into a jiu-jitsu fighter. Instead, I'm going to teach you how to avoid being taken down. If you are taken down, I'll show you how to fight from your back so you can get to your feet and attack with your strength again. If you're a strong submission artist, I'm going to teach you superior takedown abilities so you can take your opponent down and implement your submission skills on the ground. I also work to develop everyone's stand-up game, because everyone in vale Tudo needs striking skills. I try to make people great at whatever they're good at.

**Q: You are one of the martial arts most popular figures. Why?**
A: Part of what makes fighters feel comfortable with me and contributes to the team's success is that I'm not so egotistical to think I am a god-like

instructor. I exploit the strengths of the best guys on the team and they teach the other guys. I let the experts be the experts, and I learn from them also. The end result is that there is no situation in the mixed martial arts game that we don't have an answer to as a team.

**Q: Do you have any general advice you would care to pass on to the practitioners?**
A: The martial arts should be more than having the ability to beat someone up. To find the right teacher, look for a person who you can respect as a man or woman. These days – with the new generation of mixed martial artist and reality fighting – it seems that the martial arts have lost a lot of the building blocks of life and morality. If you go into a school and find that the students are cocky and full of ego, in most cases you will find that the teacher is the same way. Find a teacher that can help you develop your mind and heart, as well as your physical skills. A strong mind and good heart will take you a long way in your life. When you walk into a school and find a teacher that says he has no more to learn, turn and run the other way. All things are impermanent. Everything changes and grows. To stay cutting edge, a system needs to progress and adapt to the ever-changing environment. This is why a lot of very traditional art forms don't hold up against some of the new dynamics that more contemporary systems throw their way. No disrespect intended. If I ever feel I have nothing more to learn it, will be time for me to stop teaching.

**Q: What do you consider to be the major changes in the world of grappling arts since you began training?**
A: Like I said earlier, things are always changing and progressing. I have seen things go from BJJ prevails over all, to wrestlers dominating after learning submission defense, to wrestlers learning just enough submission to get them beat again, to the new hybrid of BJJ and wrestling, which is also known as submission wrestlers who can do it all. It is doubtful that you will ever master – or even hear of – every single one of the vast number of groundfighting techniques. It is much more likely you will gravitate to several techniques that you find most complementary to your style of fighting. Thus, you should always keep an open mind to variations and techniques from other styles. You may well prefer your version of a technique but learning how your opponent performs the technique may give you an insight on how to defeat that technique and opponent. Learning a technique and mastering that technique are two different things. You can

learn a key lock, but mastering it means you can do it even if your brains have been scrambled and fatigue has you on the verge of unconsciousness. When your body is in pain and you feel you cannot go on, a mastered technique could save the day. A technique that you have mastered will be available to you as easily as walking or breathing. Study hard and turn your techniques into natural reactions.

**Q: With whom would you like to have trained that you have not?**
A: I would have liked to have trained with Bruce Lee. Not so much for his technique but for his philosophy, which was way ahead of its time. He had a great mind, and I am sorry that I will never have the chance to sit and talk with him.

**Q: What keeps you motivated?**
A: The love and mutual loyalty that most of my students have demonstrated to me over the years. I love watching a new student arrive – maybe a little passive and inverted – and watch him blossom over the years into a confident and effective martial artist. That's what keeps me going.

**Q: Do you think it is necessary to engage in free fighting to achieve good fighting skills in self-defense?**
A: No, I don't believe that at all. But I do believe that the person who teaches you should have a legitimate fighting background if he is going to teach you how to fight. There are a lot of intricacies that happen during a fight that can totally mess up a technique that you have been taught. A teacher with real experience will be able to address those kinds of things while you are learning. A lot of great, technical martial artists get beat in street fights because they lack those experiences. You need to be very good at something before you try and master too much. It is better to be great at one thing than mediocre at everything.

**Q: Do you have any particular mental or psychological preparation that you use before a fight?**
A: The mental preparation before the fight is as important as the training regimen. Thus, let me tell you how the day of the fight goes for me.
I try to sleep in. Sometimes my mind takes over and I begin to think too much, and that disrupts my sleep. If this happens, I try to relax my thoughts and go back to sleep. Counting my breaths slowly from one to

10, over and over again, works. This enables me to focus on the numbers instead of the night at hand. I never begin my day too early. By the time the fight arrives, I don't want to feel fatigued. After I casually get up, I have a nourishing breakfast. I stay away from sugar. I also want to keep my energy level steady throughout the day. I stock up on carbs during breakfast and lunch because these are usually my only significant meals of the day. My trainers have a good supply of energy snacks and water to take with me to the event. I never count on the show to stock these items for me. In fact, I have yet to see that happen. After lunch, I head back to

*"There are a lot of intricacies that happen during a fight that can totally mess up a technique that you have been taught. A teacher with real experience will be able to address those kinds of things while you are learning."*

the room to relax. I may take a little nap or rent a movie from the hotel's selection. Whatever. I just relax. I like having positive people around me. People I respect and whom I understand what is on my mind without a hint from me. A little humor never hurt anyone either. Laughing is good. It keeps things light and takes my mind off the fight. I avoid negative people and anyone I straight out can't stand in my room. Fight day is a constant, slow build of mental focus and confidence that should not be distressed by anyone. If you like to stroll around and do things to keep your mind relaxed, that's fine. Just don't tire yourself or your legs out doing so. I often find myself in a large dressing room with a bunch of other fighters, hours before the show begins. I try to stay relaxed and focused on my objective. I lie on a bench and envision my strategy. I never – even for a second – let a negative thought enter my conscience. If that happens, I bombard it with 100 positive ones. My whole life has led to this day. This is my moment in time to shine ... to prove to myself what I am all about. This is when I remember all the pain and suffering my adversary caused by making me train so hard. Time to make him pay. How dare he step into my house, my ring. These are just a few of my favorite thoughts. When the

*"The martial arts are like dancing. You have 100 percent control of your body and mind, and you are able to command it to move, bend and flow with no hesitation at any given moment. It is my ultimate form of expression. It is who I am."*

battle draws near, I begin to repeat the above thoughts with increased intensity and more focus. It is now time to prepare my body for the battle. While training, many fighters have probably noticed that the first five to 10 minutes or so are usually more fatiguing than the latter 20 to 30 minutes. This is because your heart and respiratory system is going from a totally relaxed state to a faster heart rate without much warning. You definitely do not want to make that adjustment during the match. That is why it's important to break a sweat just before the match begins. This does not mean that you should go all out and wear yourself down before the fight. I just break a nice sweat, relax and maintain it. When I get into the ring, I make sure that my body is wet, my mind is focused and I'm ready to go. My eyes are fixed on my opponent, calculating any sign of weakness. This is what it is all about. Only someone who has been there can appreciate the intensity of that moment. The only comparison I can make is driving a car downhill with no brakes ... wondering what is at the bottom.

**Q: After all these years of training and experience, could you explain the meaning of the practice of martial arts for you?**
A: The martial arts are like dancing. You have 100 percent control of your body and mind, and you are able to command it to move, bend and flow with no hesitation at any given moment. It is my ultimate form of expression. It is who I am.

**Q: What are the most important qualities of a successful MMA and submission-grappling fighter?**
A: First and foremost, you have to be brave enough to expose yourself to the world. It is easy to talk about what you could do, but quite another thing to put it all on the line and step into that cage in front of everyone. You have to have a little bit of fearlessness and a lot of heart to make it through the tough moments. You have to be able to take your falls like a

man and your wins like a champion. You have to have a well-rounded arsenal, including stand-up, grappling and wrestling skills. You have to be courageous and intelligent with a sort of calmness of mind during hectic situations.

**Q: Have you ever felt fear, and how does that emotion affect a fighter's performance?**
A: I don't ever feel fear in an altercation. However, before fights, I do get nervous. I believe the nerves keep you alert. The key is to know how to channel that nervous energy and use it to your advantage.

**Q: How should competition training differ from practice at a regular class?**
A: It is a totally different thing. A class setting is where you develop new skills and techniques. A class is where you make your mistakes and try new things. Training for a fight should initially entail four to five hours of intense training focusing heavily on conditioning and endurance. Swimming, running, sparring, etc. It is a time to develop a strategy for the upcoming opponent and time to be selfish and focus only on yourself and the task at hand.

**Q: Do you have any final advice you would care to pass on the practitioners?**
A: Be invincible in what ever you do! Being invincible means much more than not being able to be defeated on a physical level. Invincibility begins and exists within an unbeatable mind. If your mind doesn't believe that you are invincible, you remain beatable because your mind accepts the possibility of defeat. If your mind is strong and free of all negative influence, the battle is 75 percent won. All that remains for this warrior is to achieve his optimal physical level of external conditioning and make sure that his weapons are sharp and ready for combat.

**Q: You are talking about warriors. What's required to become a warrior and what are the differences between a common fighter and a warrior?**
A: The common warrior can be defeated by the sheer presence of the invincible warrior. As a common warrior stands before the invincible warrior, he is overwhelmed by the invincible warrior's confidence. The invincible warrior stands tall and expressionless because he is free of all internal

battles. He stands there, aware of only that very moment, knowing he is totally prepared for whatever is to come. The invincible warrior has no fear of failure within him. This is possible because he has conquered his awareness of self, his ego. The common warrior is consumed by the fear of losing. He is afraid of losing his public stature. He is afraid that he will reveal his true nature to the greater public and even more afraid that he will confirm to himself what he already knows. He is just a common warrior. There is no fear of death in the invincible warrior. He has found within himself a belief structure that allows him to let go of his current level of existence if need be. This does not mean that he doesn't value life, but rather that he accepts the impermanence of all things and welcomes his next level of existence. The common warrior is afraid of death. Thus, he holds back during battle, and this allows him no freedom of physical or technical expression. The invincible warrior is mindful of every action he makes, always living in the present moment, aware of his every step. He meditates, looking deeply into all things and seeks a clear understanding of existence as a whole. He sees things as they truly are, not as they present themselves to be. The common warrior lives in his past and in his future, unaware of the path in between. He proudly boasts about his past victories, embellishing them to impress others. Inside he cannot stop dwelling on his past defeats. He safely maps out his future, taking only the safe turns in the path of life. The invincible warrior never stops seeking knowledge and finds a teacher in a piece of paper. He is always bettering his craft and educating his mind. The common warrior is satisfied by his current level of knowledge and is too proud to be seen as a student, so he encases himself in a stagnant tomb of mediocrity. In reality, no one is truly invincible, but you must learn to approach each battle, each test in life with the outlook and intensity of the invincible warrior. The mystery of life is free choice. With every step you take you reach a fork in the road, two paths from which you must choose one direction. Left or right, fast or slow, safe or exciting, common or extraordinary. You never really know what is to come of you in either path, so it is best to just pick one and go forward with no regrets. In the end, if you can say that you have attacked life with all that you are, then you are an invincible warrior.

*"The invincible warrior never stops seeking knowledge and finds a teacher in a piece of paper. He is always bettering his craft and educating his mind."*

**Q: Is there anything you would like to say?**
A: Yes, I would like to thank a few people who are very important to me. First, Dan Koji for setting the precedence for what a great teacher really is. Next, my second father, Gene LeBell. Thank you for the priceless gifts you have given me. I feel honored and blessed to call myself your friend and student. Third, to my partner, teacher and one of my best friends, Andre Pederneiras. You are always an inspiration to me, and I respect you more than you will ever know. To my brother and trainer, Saigon Skipper Kelp. Thank you for your loyalty and friendship. You can always count on me. To one of my "oldest" and truest friends, Steve Silva, thank you for always being there. To my students, I love you all and I am very proud to be your teacher and friend.

# Grappling Techniques

Operating from the mount position (1), John Lewis feints the collar choke, forcing the opponent to use left his elbow to defend (2). Lewis then traps that elbow (3), wraps his leg under the arm (4), traps the head and applies an armbar (5).

Lewis controls the opponent from the back (1). Using his left hand, Lewis loosens the gi and moves his right hand inside the collar (2), as he leans to the side (3). This creates enough pressure (4) to finish his opponent off with a one-hand choke (5).

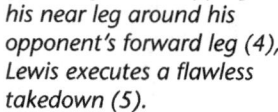

John Lewis is locked up with an opponent in a Brazilian jiu-jitsu match (1). When his opponent reaches for his collar (2), Lewis ducks under the arm (2) and quickly grasps his leg (3). Wrapping his near leg around his opponent's forward leg (4), Lewis executes a flawless takedown (5).

Placing his knee on his opponent's stomach (1), John Lewis secures the situation and traps the arm (2). He moves his leg over the opponent's head (3) and falls back into an armbar (4).

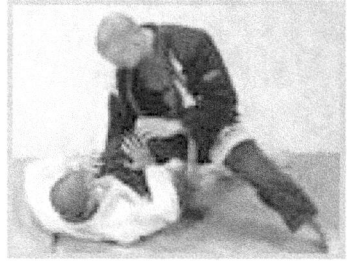

# DEAN LISTER

## *The World's Greatest Grappler*

Dean Lister is on a tear. After winning the ADCC 2003 Absolute division, in the most prestigious grappling event in the world, Lister returned home to San Diego and defended his King of the Cage world title with a submission victory over the tough Brian Sleeman. But that should come as no surprise. Lister loves submissions and at ADCC 2003 won three of his four Absolute matches by submission, setting an all-time ADCC Absolute record.

The humble and friendly "Machine" credits his recent spectacular success to his new support team. Since breaking-up with his first jiu-jitsu instructor, Lister has relied heavily on the support of close friends and training associates Jocko Willink and Brent Stuchlik, along with a dedicated group of training partners who keep the new champion in peak physical and mental condition.

Dean Lister's fascination with the combat arts started as a young boy. The son of an American Marine who was stationed in different parts of the world, Lister lived in Venezuela, Costa Rica, and Panama while growing up. "I was 13 years old and Panama was in civil war," Lister recalls. "I saw many people get killed in the crossfire." A foreigner in Latin America, Dean was always seen as a "Gringo" and had to face many physical challenges as a teenager. "The foreigner is usually seen under a bad light," Lister says, "so I had to learn to defend myself at a young age."

Now just coming into his prime as a fighter, and with his best years of competition still ahead, expect Dean Lister to be a permanent fixture on the winner's podium for years to come.

**Q: What is your background in martial arts?**
A: I did three years of wrestling at Hill Top High School. I was a high school division wrestling champion and I continued with other martial arts. I ended wrestling about the time I started learning jiu-jitsu – three months short of my 20th birthday, in December 1995! I had already trained in sambo. I was already U.S. National Sambo Champion before I

*"I am a national champion in sambo, but I am very proud of my jiu-jitsu accomplishments. I was four-time Machado National Brazilian Jiu-Jitsu champion, winning the Absolute division twice; a National Gracie Jiu-Jitsu champion; a Pro-Am Invitee and the 2003 Abu Dhabi Absolute Champion."*

started to learn jiu-jitsu. I took my second title after I started training jiu-jitsu. I trained sambo three times a week. This guy was teaching a free sambo class and I attended it. He was showing a basic arm-lock, a basic foot-lock, and then a lot of wrestling – so we mostly wrestled. I am a national champion in sambo but I am very proud of my jiu-jitsu accomplishments. I was four-time Machado National Brazilian Jiu-Jitsu champion, winning the Absolute division twice, a National Gracie Jiu-Jitsu champion, a Pro-Am Invitee, and the 2003 Abu Dhabi Absolute Champion.

**Q: Three years ago you started to focus on no-gi competition and fought Ricco Rodriguez twice in Neutral Grounds, right?**
A: Yes, at the time I weighed 175 pounds. The reason I was so light is because at that time I was going to college and I was very poor. I was broke and I lived on bread, milk and cereal – that is all I ate. I fought Ricco and he was 300 pounds and it is very hard to fight someone twice your weight.

**Q: But the second time around you gave him a hard time, right?**
A: It took 19 minutes and 30 seconds for him to beat me. I got to his back twice and took him down, but he eventually got to my side and got my head and arm. And he put all that weight on me and I tapped. He was very good at that position then, and he used his weight very well and

I just couldn't breathe. That move doesn't work as well when the weight difference isn't so great.

**Q: Why did you start focusing on submission grappling without a gi?**
A: I was always told that the gi was technical and no-gi was not technical, but I disagree, I think that is not the case, they are use different techniques. They are both very technical if you do them the right way. In my view, in no-gi there is more action, there is a lot more movement, a lot more slipping out of submissions, and more things happen. It is more fast-paced and is closer to a real fight. And since I am doing NHB now, I can't be in the habit of grabbing someone's lapel or their sleeve because it will not be there, so I have to concentrate on no-gi submission grappling. Not that I don't respect the gi; I love the gi and would like to train with it more. But I don't really have anyone to train with the gi now, and I'm focusing on NHB at this point in my career. Given where I want to go and what I want to accomplish, submission grappling makes more sense.

*"I was always told that the gi was technical and going without the gi was not technical, but I disagree. They are both technical if you do them the right way."*

**Q: I remember when you started training submission grappling it was kind of hard because there weren't that many people doing it at the time.**
A: Even after my regular class, my instructor used to get mad at me because I was training submission grappling without a gi. He wasn't helping me, to be honest, and was actually a big hindrance. You figure that if someone doesn't want to help you that's OK, but they don't need to make it harder for you either.

*"People are afraid of changes but they're usually for the better. Intelligent people get used to change more quickly than others. It does upset them initially but they accept and embrace it."*

Q: You have a core group of friends you workout with on your own and self – teach and develop new techniques, right?
A: Yes, guys like Jocko Willing, Brent Stuchlik, Jeff Higgs and James Nielsen. We all love submission grappling and train together and learn together.

Q: When you started training, I remember a lot people, myself included I'm sorry to say, used to tell you, "Dean, don't do sambo foot-locks! They are no good!" I'm glad you didn't listen to me! Did you ever think of giving up your sambo foot-locks?
A: Nah, I just thought it was different from what people knew and that they would eventually adjust. I'm sure Helio Gracie got frowned upon by the Japanese when he changed their techniques, but it didn't stop him! And now he is highly respected there. I just figured that people would evolve and adapt. It's like wrestlers – if you show them a different way to do a takedown they get very defensive! If you can beat them at their own game with something different it really upsets them. They think there is something that has always worked and that is the way it will always be. When you bring something new to wrestling they get defensive and it upsets them. It happens in every sport. I always figured that if you bring something new to the sport, that eventually people will embrace it.

Q: So change is good?
A: People are afraid of changes but they're usually for the better. Intelligent people get used to change more quickly than others. It does upset them initially but they accept and embrace it. You've seen that

yourself. You've seen Royler do foot-locks. He has adapted them to the jiu-jitsu game and has become a better fighter. I'm not saying that I created the change, but ADCC and the evolution of the sport forced everyone to change. Even if you don't like to use foot-locks you need to practice them to learn how to escape from them.

**Q: Were you nervous about starting your own gym, City Boxing?**
A: If you take a few guys that have a solid – I mean solid – background in gi jiu-jitsu with solid positioning, and solid knowledge of how to escape positions like cross-side, guard and mount, then add a few wrestling takedowns and adapt submissions to work without a gi, then you basically get what we teach at City Boxing. It is called City Boxing but it could just as well be called City Jiu-Jitsu, as we do some great submission training there. We are a good gym for jiu-jitsu, with good techniques, good camaraderie, and a good team.

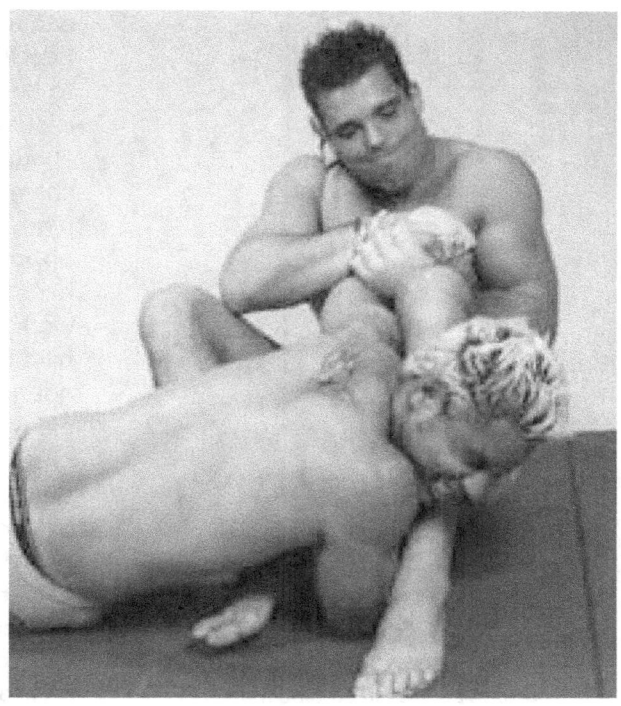

*"The truth is, if you train hard and stick with something, you will get good at it. I see a lot of people who give up too easily. They don't see themselves as being a champion one day and they never had anyone tell them they could be a champion."*

**Q: What is the key to being successful in submission wrestling?**
A: It's basically the same keys as gi work. Of course, there are a few different techniques, but you just adjust and adapt. I can say a lot of things, but the truth is if you train hard and stick with something you will get good at it. I see a lot of people who give up too easily. They don't see themselves as being a champion one day and they never had anyone tell them they could be a champion. I never had anyone telling me that I could be a champion. I

*"Genetics, opportunities and friends all help, but hard work is what really matters ... hard work and persistency. You can work hard, but if you quit in one month, you are not going to get anywhere!"*

had to decide that for myself. Fortunately, I decided early on. But if someone wants to be a champion, they have to train like a champion. Whether you're talking about being a local gym champion, a city champion, a state or even world champion, you have to work hard. Genetics, opportunities, and friends all help, but hard work is what really matters – hard work and persistency. You can work really hard but if you quit in one month you are not going to get anywhere! It is the people who don't quit who become champions. I even went through a few girlfriends that quit on me because they couldn't handle me not having any money. I'm a professional fighter and I have money now. But even when I didn't, I never quit and never stopped working hard. Most everyone quits, but if you continue to stay focused and follow your dreams you will win. If you don't quit at whatever you do, you'll become a champion in something one day.

**Q: Did that attitude lead you to your ADCC win?**
A: Exactly! I almost felt like it was fate. In 2001 I won my first fight and lost the second. Then this year, we were on our way to train with Royce and you had to convince me to enter the ADCC Trials in San Diego because there was a last-minute opening. I took your advice but then had very little time to prepare for it. Then I injured my knee in my first fight and still fought a couple of matches to win the event. Then when I was going to Brazil I almost couldn't catch my flight because the lady at the airport didn't see the visa stamp on my passport and gave me all kinds of problems. In Brazil, on the first day of ADCC, I didn't feel very good – I didn't feel like myself. I had a lot of anxiety and ended up losing my second match to Xande Ribeiro. On the second day I hadn't rested and entered my name for the Absolute just for the heck of it. I was the fourth alternate and just managed to get in and fill the last open spot when

everyone above me dropped out. I think that is what makes this sport great, it is not an exact science. It is not even about who the best fighter is, but rather about who gives the best artistic performance on a given day. If I can put on a great performance on a certain day, then that's great. There is no such thing as the best artist in the world, that is a purely subjective thing. In fighting it is the same thing – it is an art. The person who performs better on that certain day or at that certain moment is going to come out on top. The sport of grappling is basically an artistic achievement. I hope that people realize that there is no real "best" in the world. There is just a "best" on a certain day, and you can be great one day and not be great on another. I was not good the first day at ADCC but I was great on the second – and that was the best moment of my life.

*"There is no such thing as the best artist in the world; that is a purely subjective thing. In fighting it is the same thing; it is an art. The person who performs better on that certain day or at that certain moment is going to come out on top."*

**Q: At what point did you start thinking, "Hey, I can win this thing!"**
A: At the end of the first overtime with Saulo Ribeiro. Saulo is someone I have always looked up to, I have always had a lot of respect for him. But there have been times in my life when my confidence has gone up and down and I have had doubts about myself, I think everyone has that sometimes. At that moment, at the end of the first overtime, I began to realize that I can fight with these guys and do well. At that point I said to myself, "I'm here, I might as well win this whole thing!" I had Pe de Pano next and then Cacareco, and all of them are very tough opponents, but I decided to play my game – and my game is submissions. That is what myself, Jocko and Brent do at City Boxing; we train to submit, we don't train for points. At that point I played my game and ended up winning the whole thing. At first, my game used to bite me in the butt and I would lose

*"In my first fight, I had six guys back out on me. I am not a scary-looking guy – or maybe I am – but somehow my potential opponents get injured a lot. I've always just thought of myself as a submission machine."*

some fights because I didn't go for the points and I would lose by one point – but they would not submit me. But because of all the mistakes that I made in the past, I got better at the submission game and it all came together. Even with Pe de Pano, I was looking for a submission when time ran out. Then Cacareco was next in the finals. He is a super tough guy. He submitted six or so of his opponents with a guillotine and I knew he was going to try it on me. So I went out there and he tried it, but I have very good resistance to submissions. It was just my day and I am very happy with what happened and with my performance.

**Q: In NHB, you've had an inordinate number of opponents back out on you. How difficult is that?**
A: I guess that's why people started calling me "The Boogyman." In my first fight I had six guys back out on me. I am not a scary-looking guy – or maybe I am – but somehow my potential opponents get injured a lot. I've always just thought of myself as a submission machine. I know some were

legitimate injuries but I also know that some weren't. I even had an opponent in Japan back out!

**Q: Tell me about that one.**
A: I went all the way to Japan. When I got there they told me that I had to be under a certain weight, so I ran my butt off to cut weight. I get to the weigh-in and my opponent stares me down really bad. He gets off the scale and he is staring me down. I get on the scale and make weight and I think, "We are going to fight for sure. This guy really wants me." So the next day I'm warming up – I'm the fourth fight on the card – but during the third fight the matchmaker comes into my locker room and says that my opponent injured his head and can't fight! I got paid, and everything was great, but I didn't get to fight.

*"The next day I'm warming up – I'm the fourth fight on the card. During the third fight, the matchmaker comes into my locker room and says that my opponent injured his head and can't fight!"*

**Q: Even for your last fight you had the same problem, right?**
A: The last fight, two of my opponents in King of the Cage got injured and Brian Sleeman took the fight on a very short notice. I give him a lot of credit for doing that – that is very tough to do. He's a tough fighter but he made the mistake of taking me down to the ground, and so I took advantage of it of it to submit him.

"I like Pride a lot. The show is at a very high level, and I have a lot of respect for them and their fighters. I want to help out NHB in general. Things are looking bright right now."

**Q: What do you see for submission wrestling and NHB in your future?**
A: In submission wrestling I am really looking forward to my match with Ricardo Arona. I think he is a great part of the sport, really good at wrestling and really good at submissions and I have a lot of respect for him. He has always been my friend. Actually, It will not be a fight but rather a grappling match. so we are not going to lose our friendship over it. Of course, right now we are not talking and we're both training for this match in two years at the next ADCC, but that is really the only thing I am looking forward to in submission grappling. I'm completely dedicated to NHB right now and I am expanding my game by training muay Thai and boxing. I figure that no one is going to want to go to the ground and trade submissions with me, so I have to make them let go to the fence and get them off their feet and into my game. Right now, guys are doing that to me and giving me a lot of openings for strikes. So I want to take advantage of that. The future is in NHB.

**Q: Has your team been a big help to you?**
A: Of course! I have a very solid team at City Boxing. Robert Garcia and Mike help me with my boxing and muay Thai. Jocko and Brent, my great friends from submission grappling and jiu-jitsu, really know a lot. They are fast learners and they have helped me a lot with my training and my conditioning. Royce Gracie has put time into me to help me out with the

*"I am a trainer at City Boxing, but I get to train myself as well. I don't run anything, but everyone puts time into each other. We are a real good team, and we are a very successful gym."*

fighter's mentality and the inside aspects of the industry. My friend Ron Bergum has really taken care of me. There was a time I needed a knee operation and Ron was the one who made it possible. If it wasn't for Ron Bergum I wouldn't be where I am today – honestly, I wouldn't. He has really helped me tremendously. Right now I want to thank everyone who has helped me and the people at City Boxing, especially Mark Dion, for giving me the support to be my best! The main thing at City Boxing is that I am a trainer but I get to train myself as well. I don't run anything, but everyone puts time into each other. We are a real good team and we are a very successful gym.

# CLEBER LUCIANO

## *The Brazilian Volcano*

CLEBER LUCIANO IS ONE OF THE MOST WELL-KNOWN AND RESPECTED JIU-JITSU FIGHTERS AND TEACHERS IN THE UNITED STATES. A CHAMPION IN BRAZIL, WHERE HE BEGIN TRAINING AT AGE 5, LUCIANO TRAINED AND COMPETED AGAINST THE BIGGEST NAMES IN THE SPORT. HIS EXPERTISE WAS REWARDED BY A BLACK BELT BEFORE HE REACHED AGE 20. WITH COUNTLESS MATCHES IN JIU-JITSU TOURNAMENTS WITH THE GI, AND GREAT EXPERIENCE IN NO-GI SUBMISSION GRAPPLING, LUCIANO IS VERY FAMILIAR WITH WHAT TECHNIQUES WORK WITH THE GI AND WITHOUT. BUT MORE THAN THAT, HE IS FAMILIAR WITH HOW LIFE WORKS WITH JIU-JITSU AND WITHOUT IT. A "HYPER" KID WHO LIKED TO FIGHT ON THE STREET AND WHO WAS HEADED DOWN THE WRONG PATH, JIU-JITSU GAVE LUCIANO AN OUTLET FOR HIS AGGRESSION AND A STRUCTURE THAT GAVE HIS LIFE NEW MEANING. NOW SETTLED IN HUNTINGTON BEACH, CALIFORNIA, AND RUNNING TWO SCHOOLS, LUCIANO'S PASSION FOR JIU-JITSU HAS LED HIM TO ATTRACT NEARLY 300 STUDENTS – 60 OF WHICH ARE KIDS BETWEEN THE AGES OF 5 AND 15. "KIDS NEED JIU-JITSU AND JIU-JITSU NEEDS KIDS," LUCIANO SAYS. WITH A COMMITMENT TO GROW JIU-JITSU IN THE U.S. AND TO USE IT TO HELP KIDS BETTER THEMSELVES, CLEBER LUCIANO IS AT THE FOREFRONT OF THE MODERN JIU-JITSU AND GRAPPLING REVOLUTION.

**Q: How did you get started in jiu-jitsu?**
A: I started because I was very hyper as a kid in the Rio area. So my mom wanted to put me in sports to calm me down. So I had two friends who did jiu-jitsu and the mother of one of them took me to watch the class one day. So I went and checked it out and liked what I saw and so I started training. This was with one of Helio Gracie's students who was a very high black belt. I was just a kid, only six years old, but I knew that it was fun. I loved to train, I loved jiu-jitsu, and I loved grappling. So I just kept going. So I also took a lot of judo classes, because judo is also very popular in Brazil. So I eventually got my black belt in judo also.

**Q: Did you start taking judo after you started jiu-jitsu?**
A: I started both at about the same time. Because I figured that judo

*"When I was 15 I was a blue belt, and I went to the Gracie Academy and started training with Carley Gracie and got to know Royler, Rolker and all the rest. Everyone really accepted me and made me feel like I belonged and was part of the family."*

would help me in my jiu-jitsu. But I always liked jiu-jitsu the best between the two. It was just more fun for me. Now, even though I have a black belt in judo, I've forgotten most of my moves. I probably still do some of them without thinking, but I don't compete in that or teach it formally or anything. Part of it was just that I got a little bored with judo. When you do a match you just start to get going and they end the match after only a minute or two. I didn't like how fast it was. One takedown or throw and the fight was over – even when you were not hurt or in any real danger. So it was too far removed from a real situation for me. So I figured out that jiu-jitsu was more complete. You can do everything – takedowns, throws, pass the guard, get points, get submissions – everything.

**Q: When did you become closely associated with the Gracie family?**
A: When I was 15 I was a blue belt and I went to the Gracie Academy and started training with Carley Gracie and got to know Royler, Rolker, and all the rest. Everyone really accepted me and made me feel like I belonged and was part of the family. So I continued to train there with some of the top guys in the world like Royler Gracie, Saulo Ribeiro, Carlos Barreto, and all the top guys. I got my black belt together with Saulo and Carlos and several other guys. I guess that I was at the Gracie Academy for nearly 5 years before I got my black belt. I felt like I really got a great jiu-jitsu education and got my black belt just before I turned 20. I was very proud of that because it is very young in jiu-jitsu to get it then.

**Q: When did you decide to come to the United States and teach?**

A: I did some tournaments in Brazil – some really big ones – and in one of them I beat Leo Vieira, who is really good. We were both at the same level and the two top guys, so everyone really wanted to see us compete to see who would win. I won that – and don't know how – but I beat him. After that I started getting a lot of calls from people wanting me to go to different places to open a school. A few of the calls came from this area, and I knew that there was already a lot of Brazilians teaching in Southern California, and I decided to come here. I wanted to come to a place where my students would have a chance to compete against other schools. Los Angeles probably has the most jiu-jitsu schools in the United States of any city. So that was a big part of it for me.

*"I wanted to come to a place where my students would have a chance to compete against other schools. Los Angeles probably has more jiu-jitsu schools than any other city in the United States. That was a big part of it for me."*

**Q: What it hard when you first came?**

A: Yeah, it was. But I knew I wanted to be in Huntington Beach the moment I got off that plane and came here. It is a great area with the water very close and a lot of nice people and also a lot of people who want to train jiu-jitsu. So I just immediately loved it here. I want to be here forever. When I first came I started the school with two American guys and that didn't work all that well because I was working for them at a school called Brazilian Martial Arts. But I was the one who knew jiu-jitsu and knew how to teach. So after a year I left to open my own school –

*"I was the one who knew jiu-jitsu and knew how to teach. After a year, I left to open my own school – Cleber Luciano Jiu-Jitsu. With my own school I can teach the way I want to on my own schedule. For me, it is better. I have more freedom."*

Cleber Luciano Jiu-Jitsu. With my own school I can teach the way I want to on my own schedule – so for me it is better. I have more freedom. So I've been here at my own school for five years now and I have over I'm very grateful to my loyal students and I'm committed to teaching them the best jiu-jitsu in the world to show them my appreciation.

**Q: You're known as one of the world's top tournament fighters. What is your philosophy of competition?**
A: My strategy is to be very relaxed. In all my fights I relax and make sure in the first two or three minutes that I don't make a mistake and get behind on points. So I'm very careful early in a match. I don't want to get taken down, let someone get to my back, let someone get cross-side on me – things like that. I just try to figure out my opponent's game and get a feel for what he likes to do and what he is trying on me. It is very important to be patient. Once I get an idea of what he is doing, I can play my strategy and decide which attacks to use. I don't want to get crazy early, try to hard, and then get points scored on me or, even worse, get submitted. Relaxation and breathing is my game.

**Q: What do you do once you've figured out your opponent's game plan?**
A: Then I start to attack. But I always attack with good balance and good grip. Those two factors are the most important things to establish when you start your attack. As soon as you have a good grip and good balance then you can go for the takedown. If you're grappling with a good wrestler, for example, you can really feel his balance and so you need to be rock solid in your base.

**Q: In a tournament situation do you like to fight from the guard or do you like to operate from on top?**
A: You need to go for a superior position from the top. I don't believe in falling back into the guard and pulling your opponent on top of you. I teach my students to try to establish a strong top position during the first two minutes. In your first minute, if you put somebody in the guard, they are very fresh and will be alert and able to defend any submissions you might try. So if you work for two or three minutes, then you can get your opponent a little tired and also confuse him a little so when you get the position you want, you have a much better chance of your attacks working.

*"It is important to be patient. I don't want to get crazy early, try too hard and then get points scored on me or, even worse, get submitted. Relaxation and breathing is my game."*

**Q: What is your favorite position to work your attacks from?**
A: I like the cross-side position a lot. There are more opportunities for submission from this position. The good thing about the cross-side is that you can apply it with equal success whether you are fighting no-gi Abu Dhabi rules or fighting with jiu-jitsu rules with the gi. This is because you are able to use the weight of your chest to pressure your opponent, but

*"I like the cross-side position a lot. There are more opportunities for submission from this position. The good thing about the cross-side is that you can apply it with equal success whether you are fighting no-gi Abu Dhabi rules or fighting with jiu-jitsu rules with the gi."*

yet your hips and legs are free to move with him when he tries to escape. I work a lot of neck cranks and a lot of arm-neck combination chokes so it doesn't matter to me if I compete with a gi or without one. Of course there are a lot more moves that you can do with the gi – I can make a thousand moves with it. My whole life I trained with the gi for tournaments in Brazil. Plus you have material to grab at the lapel and the elbow and the back of the neck, et cetera that you don't have without the gi. So you have a lot more options. Without the gi I can do my basic positions, but I can't do all the advanced moves that I can do with the gi. With the gi it is really more fun because there are a lot more options.

**Q: Is it difficult to transfer submission sport techniques into no-holds-barred?**
A: My techniques are very effective in vale tudo fighting. So I don't have a lot of problems transferring them over. But kicking and punching do add a lot more dimensions to the grappling game, so while the sport techniques do work when you get into position, you have to be much more careful coming in, so you don't get caught during the entry. Plus, when you get on the ground you can use strikes to set-up your submissions. If you're cross-side, for example, and going for a choke, and your opponent is tightly guarding his neck, then you can drop a few elbows on him to make him block, which will then expose his neck for the choke. The same thing can done in different situations with the knees. The old technique of circling and then shooting in on him just doesn't work as well as it used to. People practice against it. Three of four years ago it was much easier to take strikers down. Now with everyone

practicing kickboxing and Thai boxing there is a lot more danger coming in. So timing is the more important aspect for grapplers now. Saulo Ribeiro got caught with a knee by Yuki Kondo in an NHB match when he was shooting in and lost by a cut. I remember Renzo Gracie had the same problem a couple of times. You have to come in behind a kick and you have to time your entry very carefully.

**Q: Do you think the guard still works for no-holds-barred?**
A: If you lock somebody in the closed guard, but then only defend from it, you are going to have problems. You can defend for two or three minutes but after that you will get tired and the punches will start to get though. So you can't stay in a defensive guard for a long time like a sitting duck. However, if you work from the open guard, where you move your hips, use the inside hooks, and use sweeps and half-guard moves to keep your opponent off-balance, then you can survive and potentially even submit your opponent. The key is to be active from the guard – you have to have mobile hips, legs, and feet.

*"If you lock somebody in the closed guard but then only defend from it, you are going to have problems. You can defend for two or three minutes. After that, you will get tired and the punches will start to get though. So you can't stay in a defensive guard for a long time. Otherwise, you'll be like a sitting duck."*

**Q: What is best way to mentally prepare for a tournament?**
A: In any tournament I do now I am very relaxed beforehand because I have done so many. Ten years ago I was really tense before a competition but I did so much that I don't worry about it so much anymore. Mental relaxation is as important as physical relaxation. The more you compete, the more relaxed you will be. When I was younger I made a big mistake of going into a fight as if my opponent was my enemy – I took the competition personally. I was like a volcano waiting to erupt and when I did I just

"Mental relaxation is as important as physical relaxation. The more you compete, the more relaxed you will be. When I was younger, I made a big mistake of going into a fight as if my opponent was my enemy – I took the competition personally. I was like a volcano waiting to erupt. When I did, I just forgot everything and I would not do well."

forgot everything and I would not do well. I don't want anyone to make this same mistake and I don't want to make this mistake again, either. Every time you go into a fight you should worry about yourself, and not worry about your opponent. Your goal is to fight the fight, not fight the opponent. If you do your job the outcome of the fight will take care of itself. What happens is that you get so intense that you forget all your techniques and your entire game plan and you just brawl mindlessly. It happened to me. Everything went out the window – all I could think was "Kill! Kill Kill!" When I fought it was as if I had never taken a single jiu-jitsu lesson. But I learned from that mistake big time. Now when I fight I don't care if my opponent is screaming and cursing at me – it doesn't matter. Let's just do the fight in a professional manner and then forget about it when the fight is done.

**Q: Do you see a big potential for jiu-jitsu in the U.S.?**
A: Of course! The key to the future of jiu-jitsu is the kids. Jiu-jitsu is great for kids because it teaches them respect and discipline and gives them something positive to do. I have about 60 kids who train in jiu-jitsu now, and as those kids grow up they are going to compete in tournaments. They will tell their friends about it and they will want to compete. I see so many kids who are as young as 5 years old and they already know how to move on the mat really well! These kids are going to be very hard to beat as they get older and move into the higher divisions. But more than that, it will help kids to become better much better persons. When I was a kid,

*"When I was a kid, for example, I was really hyper and I loved to fight on the street. Jiu-jitsu took me off of the streets and gave me an outlet for my aggression. Jiu-jitsu calmed me down mentally and gave me a much more cooperative attitude towards my family and people in general."*

for example, I was really hyper and I loved to fight on the street. So jiu-jitsu took me off of the streets and gave me an outlet for my aggression. Jiu-jitsu calmed me down mentally and gave me a much more cooperative attitude towards my family and people in general. Jiu-jitsu teaches fighting techniques to kids but it also teaches kids not to fight. It will change your attitude for the better. Without jiu-jitsu I don't think I would be here today.

## Grappling Techniques

Facing an opponent with a gi (1), Cleber Luciano is caught with a single-leg takedown (2). Luciano responds by pushing the opponent's head (3) and then trapping his arm (4). Lifting his leg to trap the elbow (5), Luciano executes a forward roll (6), comes to an upright position and applies the finishing shoulderlock (7).

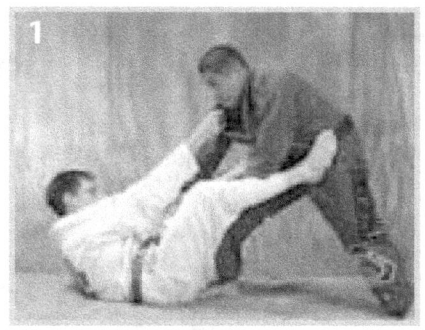

Cleber tries to pass his opponent's open guard (1). His opponent neutralizes the initiative by sitting and grabbing Cleber's right leg (2). As soon as Cleber realizes his opponent is contemplating a takedown, he grabs the collar (3) and simultaneously latches onto the right leg (4). He leans forward (5), and rolls over the opponent without releasing the grips (6), which provokes a finishing choke (7).

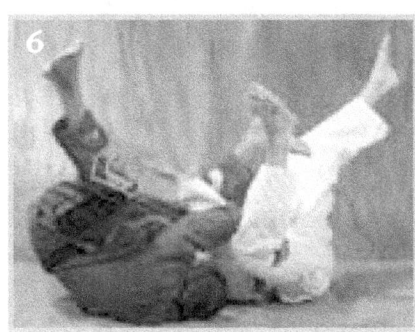
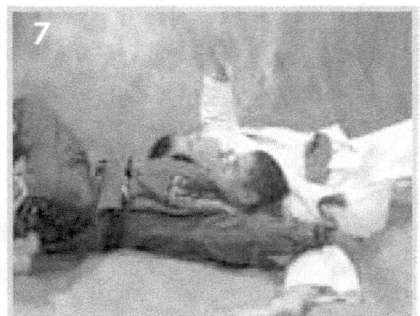

## GRAPPLING TECHNIQUES

Cleber Luciano is caught in his opponent's mount (1). Turning to his side, his traps the opponent's outside leg with his foot (2) and then puts his other leg in his opponent's stomach (3). This creates distance. Scissoring his legs, Luciano throws his opponent to the side while maintaining control of his ankle (4). Stretching his legs to deter any possible counters, Luciano applies the finishing heel hook (5).

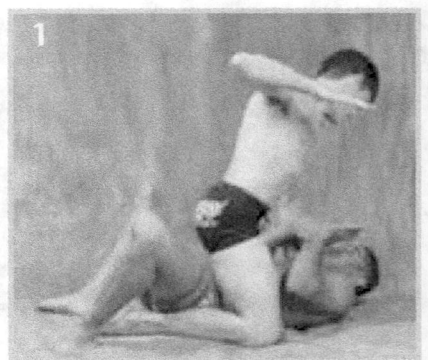

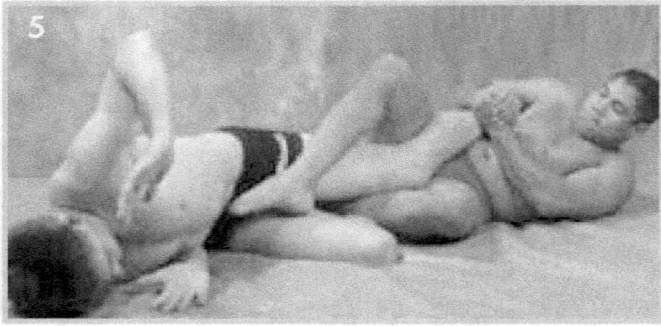

Cleber Luciano controls his opponent from the side mount (1). Swinging his outside leg over, Luciano traps the opponent's head in a single-leg scissors (2). From this position, he can either finish his opponent with a front choke (3) or trap the wrist and apply a straight armbar (4).

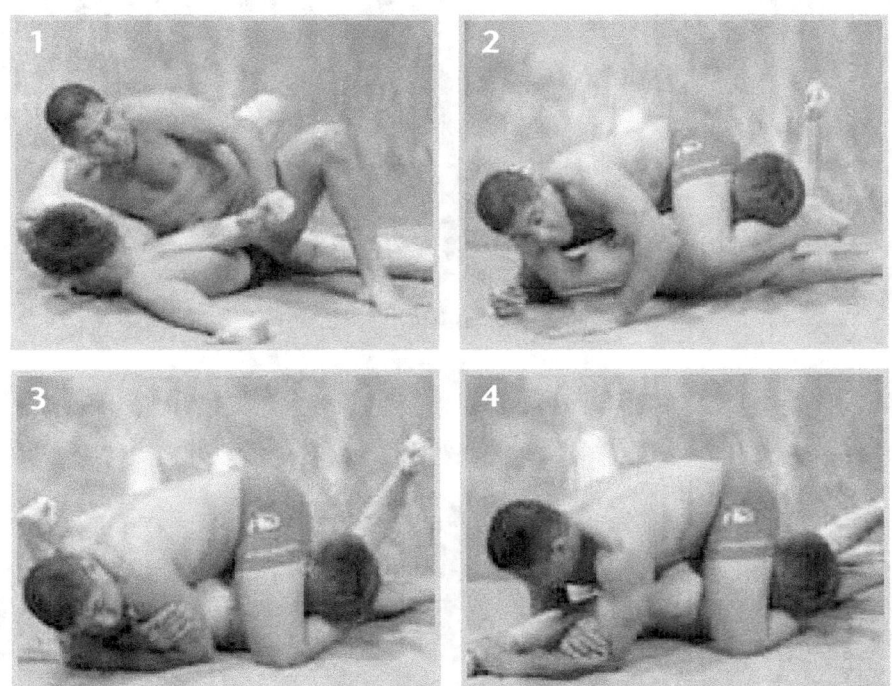

# RODRIGO MEDEIROS

## Going for the Kill!

ONE OF THE MOST DRIVEN AND TENACIOUS OF ALL OF CARLSON GRACIE'S WORLD CHAMPIONSHIP FIGHTERS, RODRIGO MEDEIROS TRAINED IN RIO FOR 14 YEARS BEFORE BEING AWARDED THE COVETED BLACK BELT FROM MASTER CARLSON HIMSELF. TRAINING DAILY WITH THE TOP JIU-JITSU FIGHTERS IN THE PLANET, MEDEIROS DEVELOPED AN ATTACKING STYLE THAT CLOSELY MIRRORS THAT OF CARLSON HIMSELF. BUT JUST AS HE ALWAYS GOES FOR THE KILL IN TOURNAMENT COMPETITION, MEDEIROS ALSO GOES FOR THE KILL WHEN EVALUATING THE PRESENT STATE OF WORLD JIU-JITSU AND ITS POTENTIAL FOR FUTURE GROWTH. NOW OPERATING TWO SCHOOLS UNDER THE CARLSON GRACIE FLAG, MEDEIROS HAS PLANS FOR FUTURE EXPANSION AND FEELS THAT JIU-JITSU WILL ONLY GET BIGGER. WITH CHAMPIONSHIP STUDENTS OF HIS OWN, IN BOTH JIU-JITSU AND NO-HOLDS-BARRED FIGHTING, MEDEIROS GENERATES THE SAME LOYALTY AND ADMIRATION THAT CARLSON GENERATED IN HIM DURING THEIR MANY YEARS TOGETHER. AND TO THOSE WHO SAY THAT BRAZILIAN JIU-JITSU IS NOT AS EFFECTIVE AS IT ONCE WAS, MEDEIROS HAS A TYPICALLY STRONG REPLY: "ONE HUNDRED PERCENT OF ALL NHB FIGHTERS TRAIN IN BJJ. IF THEY DIDN'T THEY WOULDN'T EVEN KNOW THE GUARD OR THE MOUNT – BUT THEY ALL DO. IN ADCC, 99 PERCENT OF FINALISTS ARE ALSO BJJ FIGHTERS. SO TO SAY BJJ IS NOT EFFECTIVE AS IT ONCE WAS IS JUST PLAIN SILLY AND IGNORES THE FACTS." ENOUGH SAID!

**Q: How long have you been practicing jiu-jitsu?**
A: Since 1982, so over 22 years. I actually started martial arts before that in judo, when I was 5. I went through it to the brown belt level, but when I discovered jiu-jitsu I focused myself more on ground training and just stayed with that. When I moved to U.S. in 1996 I did start to train in other styles such as boxing, kickboxing and wrestling, just to help round out my complete fight game. I started training with Maneco, a Carlson Gracie black belt, and then after that I studied with Carlson when I was 16 and already had a blue belt. Carlson's academy was a like boot camp! The eliminations inside the academy for the right to compete was harder than the actual tournaments themselves!

*"Brazil is a great place and a lot of fun, but I don't really stand out there. Here, people respect you as an athlete and a jiu-jitsu teacher. In Brazil, that respect is mainly reserved for the soccer players. Now, in Brazil, a lot of jiu-jitsu players are getting a lot of respect."*

**Q: So was Maneco good at jiu-jitsu?**
A: Maneco was one of the best black belts in the '80s in sport jiu-jitsu. Judo had a little bit on the ground but nothing like jiu-jitsu, and I really liked the ground. In 1996 I came to the U.S. to compete in the Pan American Games. I won my division and after I was going to leave I spent a week here on vacation. I went to San Diego and I went to Hawaii. And when I got back, on my last few days, I stayed in Carlson's house. And he was ready to open his academy and he invited me to teach with him. He helped me out my entire life. So he said he needed an instructor and asked me to stay though the end of the year. I called my father and told him. I had a pretty good life back in Brazil. I had an academy, I had a girlfriend, I had a nice apartment. But I told my father that I was going to be here through the end of the year and I thought it would be a good chance to meet people and to learn English. But then I just ended up staying. For me it was a great experience.

**Q: What happened to the school?**
A: It went away. When that happened he was ready to leave the school and close the building and I was ready to go also. But one of my students said, "I have a nice place where you can open your own school, so why don't you stay?" So I agreed. Brazil is a great place and a lot of fun, but I don't really stand out there. Here, people respect you as an athlete and a jiu-jitsu teacher. In Brazil, that respect is mainly reserved for the soccer players. Now, in Brazil, a lot of jiu-jitsu players are getting a lot of respect. But back then 1996 – 1997 they weren't getting that respect. Even no-rules fighters weren't that big then. The tournaments, you know, were

very small and no magazines really covered it. Now it is getting to be a big sport.

**Q: What is the difference between the American and Brazilian style of jiu-jitsu?**
A: I think the best teachers are here. Rickson Gracie, the Machados, and a lot of other good teachers are here now. The only difference is that in Brazil jiu-jitsu is more popular. And right now they have more magazines and more fight wear and better organization. In America, jiu-jitsu is still growing. I think in few more years that jiu-jitsu here will be like it is there. In Brazil you don't have a lot to do. So a kid will go to the academy at nine o' clock in the morning and leave at nine o' clock at night. But here the kids have to study, have to work, have to pay all the bills. He lives by himself. So you have to find time to train and it's hard. So the people in Brazil train more. They train much more, that's the difference. They have more options to train and more tournaments they can go to in a lot of different places.

*"In the United States, potential students have to be careful with whom they train. You have a lot of people who leave Brazil with a blue or purple belt, but when they get here they magically have a black belt. They give themselves a black belt and they start teaching."*

**Q: It seems like there are a lot of Brazilian blacks belts, but yet not that many top teachers. What makes a black belt a good teacher?**
A: In the United States, potential students have to be very careful who they train with. You have a lot of people who leave Brazil with a blue or purple belt, but when they get here they magically have a black belt. They give themselves a black belt and they start teaching. My opinion is that you have to have a background in every belt, like I did. I spent 4 or 5 years in each belt I earned. I competed in every tournament in each belt. When I was a brown belt, I already had about 15 years of experience in jiu-jitsu. So that is very important. If you want to teach, if you want to have a team, you have to have that experience. You have to be able to relate to each belt, because you spent a lot of time at that belt level.

*"You have to stress the basics and always keep going back to the basics. All the basic positions are where everything comes from, so I make my guys learn the base well. The simple things are hard to teach and to learn."*

**Q: What are the actual qualities that make a good teacher?**
A: I think that you have to be very patient with everyone. You have to know how to divide the players. Some guys you can't press hard, because they are just doing it for a hobby and for fun. Other guys train to be competitors or fighters – so these guys you can push harder. But you can't treat everyone the same. I think the methodology you use to teach is very important. You have to stress the basics and always keep going back to the basics – the mount, the guard, passing th guard, defense against knee on the belly. All the basic positions are where everything comes from. So I make my guys learn the base well. The simple things are very hard to teach and to learn. For example, how you move the hips. You think it is easy but it's very hard. You have to visualize every student. A student might come into my class and check out the school and right away I can tell if that person is going to be a good student or not. I can just tell.

**Q: It seems that in no-holds-barred at least, that wrestlers have caught up with jiu-jitsu fighters on the ground. Do you think that jiu-jitsu is still enough to win no-holds-barred matches today?**
A: No. In Royce's time, for example, no one knew jiu-jitsu. So it was very easy to fight against opponents who had no idea what was coming. But today, everyone knows jiu-jitsu. People have a background in boxing, muay Thai, and also wrestling – and they also train jiu-jitsu. So they have more skills in the no-rules fights. So today jiu-jitsu fighters have to learn takedowns and also defenses against takedown, and they have to learn how to punch and kick and to defend that also. If not, they are going to lose. Before it was a martial art against another martial art. But that day is gone. Today it is

fighter versus fighter. It is hard to find a pure jiu-jitsu guy beating everyone, or a pure wrestler beating everyone or a pure puncher and kicker. Everyone cross-trains. You have to be complete or you are going to lose.

**Q: From your many years of judo, do you incorporate some of its techniques?**
A: Yes, I teach some judo too. I have been training judo since I was 5 years old. I don't train anymore but I took it for 20 years before I just got tired of it. But I still teach it. And also since I've been here I've been teaching wrestling. So I mix a lot of things up. So when you have a little distance between your opponent then I like to see people shoot in with a wrestling takedown. When you are in grappling range with no distance, then I try to use judo because I think it is more simple.

*"I teach some judo, too. I have been training in judo since I was 5. I don't train anymore, but I took it for 20 years before I just got tired of it. But I still teach it. So I mix a lot of things up."*

**Q: What kind of overall training schedule would you recommend to someone who is just starting in jiu-jitsu.**
A: For guys starting out, I tell them to study at least three time a week in a two-hour group class if they really want to learn it. They I tell them to stretch every day, and also do some cardio like bike, or swim, or run twice a week. That is just for starts. Of course, if you're going to compete you have to increase all the training amounts. But it is very important to tell people that what I think makes jiu-jitsu so great and what attracts people, is that every martial art except jiu-jitsu has a limit. After five years in judo, for example, you have learned all the techniques there are. The same way with muay Thai of kickboxing. There are only certain amounts of techniques they possess. Not true with jiu-jitsu. You always have new techniques. That what's amazing about jiu-jitsu. Jiu-jitsu is infinite – anyone can

*"I think that diet is very important, not just for jiu-jitsu, but for you entire life. You are what you eat. The way you eat is connected to your success. As a jiu-jitsu fighter you eat, you train and then you rest. Everything is connected."*

teach you a new move. A white belt of two months can teach you a new move they've seen or learned. They can show you a new situation and you have to study it. So if anyone says he is a master and has learned it all, he's lying. In jiu-jitsu you have to die learning.

**Q: So if someone stops learning then they are not doing jiu-jitsu?**
A: I think that if you are a black belt, and you stop training jiu-jitsu and stop learning, then in three or four years when you try to come back all your techniques are going to be old and out of date. Some new move is always coming, and if you don't keep learning you're going to be obsolete.

**Q: Do you pay a lot of attention to your diet?**
A: I think that diet is very important, not just for jiu-jitsu but for you entire life. You are what you eat. The way you eat is connected to your success. As a jiu-jitsu fighter you eat, you train, and then you rest. Everything is connected. If you train, train, train, and then afterwards go get a burger and then sleep to 2 p.m. and then try to train again, you've never going to be at your full potential. You have to have the right diet. You have to mix the right amounts of protein, carbs, and fiber.

**Q: Aside from the physical aspects of jiu-jitsu, have you gained any mental benefits from it?**
A: I always tell all my students that if you're just taking jiu-jitsu in order to just beat someone in a fight, then you're thinking small. Jiu-jitsu is for life – it teaches how to treat people. Because you're so confident in yourself after taking jiu-jitsu that you naturally become more calm and respectful without realizing it. Also, in martial arts in general, you make very good friends. When I was young I was a really hyper kid. I was born and raised in the streets of Rio. You have to be tough to be born there and to survive

there. So today I can tell you that it is something very important because it made me a different person. I've traveled to Europe, to Saudi Arabia, and Japan, and I've always made good friends through jiu-jitsu.

**Q: So you feel jiu-jitsu helps to make you a complete person?**
A: I see people who don't attend any academy and you can see that they have no confidence and no self-image and have a lot of stress. I also see guys that are very violent. But over time I see all these people change for the better. All the time I had students come to me and say, "Thanks a lot for changing my life." They didn't have any direction or purpose or guidelines for living and jiu-jitsu gave them that.

*"I had students come to me and say, 'Thanks a lot for changing my life.' They didn't have any direction or purpose or guidelines for living, and jiu-jitsu gave them that."*

**Q: Did jiu-jitsu come easy to you?**
A: It came very natural to me. I never had a hard time with any technique or situation. I fell comfortable in any position. It's funny, in jiu-jitsu you always change. Every different time you have a certain position that you do well in and is your favorite move, your opponents will eventually notice that and learn to block it. So you have to constantly change your game and develop new parts to it. When you're a competitor you always want always to come up with a surprise to gain an advantage. But the basic parts of jiu-jitsu are always the same, so you never really feel lost.

**Q: Is there a point where you can ever stop learning?**
A: I don't think so. Jiu-jitsu is the only martial art that you'll die still learning about it. When you get the black belt, if you think that you know

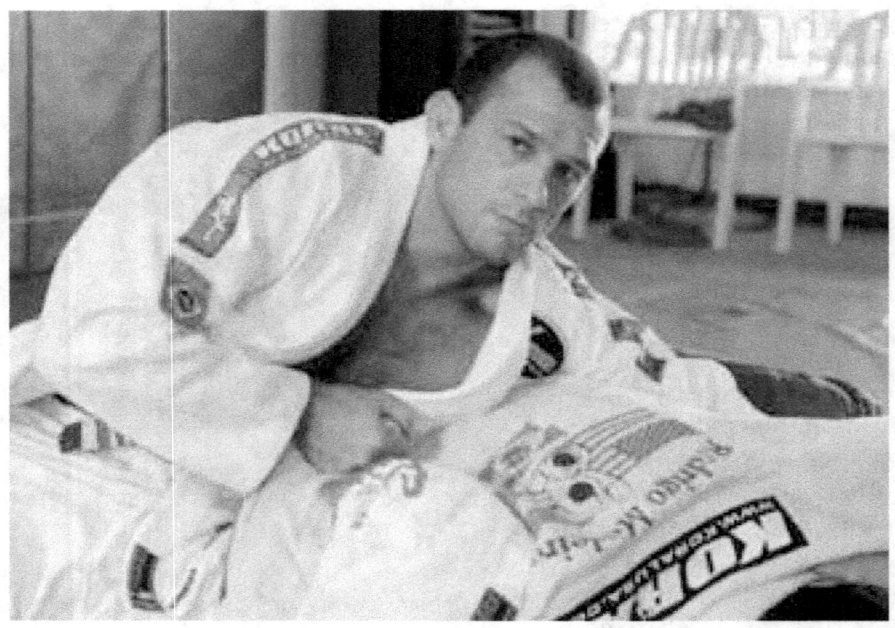

*"In jiu-jitsu, you always change. Every time you have a position that you do well in and is your favorite move, your opponents will eventually notice that and learn to block it. So you have to constantly change your game and develop new parts."*

everything you are wrong. This martial art is infinite. That's why you always want to learn more and more. I think learned more after I got my black belt than before

**Q: What are the keys to continuous learning?**
A: Be focused and learn the basics very well – everything will come from there. It is like the root of a tree. It is also important to learn in stages – don't step longer than your leg.

**Q: Has jiu-jitsu changed since you started?**
A: Right now it is a lot more organized than it used to be. There is the World Championships, the Pan Americans, and magazines that cover it them all – everybody knows what jiu-jitsu is now. When I started compet-

ing, just your family and the other athletes were really interested in it. But now a major tournament is a big event. I think that the Confederation of Brazilian Jiu-Jitsu (CBJJ) has helped to take jiu-jitsu to a higher level in Brazil. I hope the U.S. can also get organized in the same way.

**Q: Who would you like to have trained with that you haven't?**
A: Rickson Gracie, but not just for technique alone. BJJ will give you a lot more than just the ability to fight. It will also give you discipline, confidence, self-esteem, and respect for others. There are many things Rickson teaches that go beyond his techniques. But if you're talking about technique only, leave your ego at the door and be ready to tap for the rest of your life. No matter how good you are, Rickson can elevate his game to the next level and keep pushing you to become better. This is the same for white belts or for world champions.

*"BJJ will give you a lot more than just the ability to fight. It will also give you discipline, confidence, self-esteem and respect for others."*

**Q: What keeps you motivated after all these years?**
A: The fact that I'm still learning something every day. It also makes me very happy to change people's lives teaching this phenomenal art. To hear a student say "thank you" always makes my day. To be able to teach jiu-jitsu is a privilege that not many people have. I never forget that.

**Q: Do you have any particular preparation method before a big tournament?**
A: I just train hard, Carlson always said that he prepares his students to fight

*"You have to determine your strong points and emphasize those. Personally, I mainly train positions I can effectively adapt to my game."*

against a lion – then if a kitty cat comes along it will be no problem. So when I know I'm well-prepared I feel very confident. I don't fight if I don't feel that I've prepared myself well enough. I have also done transcendental meditation for more than 10 years and that has helped my concentration a lot.

Q: **Is it possible for a grappler to learn every move there is?**
A: You have to find what your strong points are and then emphasize those. Personally, I mainly train positions I can effectively adapt to my game. Of course, I try to learn everything and experiment a lot for fun, but when I'm training for a competition I concentrate on putting my opponent into my game and don't get drawn into his.

Q: **What do you remember most about training in Rio?**
A: I grew up watching the best guys train for no rules and BJJ. In the '80s, jiu-jitsu had more rivalry betweens academies, but at the same time more union against other styles. I will never forget when we had the challenge match between jiu-jitsu and luta livre in Rio. I was about 18 years old then and all the top BJJ fighters of that day guys on that time train together in Carlson Academy, Murillo Bustamante, Marcelo Behring, Rosado, Pinduka, Fabio Gurgel, Amaury, Wallid and others. I was there everyday to watch them and sometimes train when Carlson let me.

Q: **Is jiu-jitsu more than just a sport to you?**
A: For me, jiu-jitsu is a way of life and it changed me. When I started to train and compete I felt more confident, healthy, and ready for the tough

*"When I started to train and compete, I felt more confident, healthy and ready for the tough streets of Rio and anywhere in this crazy world. Jiu-jitsu for me is more than a martial art and more than my work; it is my hobby and my life!"*

streets of Rio and anywhere in this crazy world. Jiu-jitsu for me is more than a martial art and more than my work – it is my hobby and my life!

**Q: What are the most important qualities of a successful BJJ fighter?**
A: More than the technical skills, it is your attitude, your loyalty, and your respect. Jiu-jitsu is natural, so you shouldn't do anything artificial. You can have good results in a short time but only if you pay the physical price, eat healthy, don't use steroids, and do a lot of natural exercises such as yoga or swimming, and don't think in the next month and yes in all you life time. I respect the art more than everything, so I know that if you close a lock on me you will hurt me – whatever belt you are. Respect in

# Grappling Masters

*"Jiu-jitsu is natural, so you shouldn't do anything artificial. You can have good results in a short time but only if you pay the physical price, eat healthy, avoid steroids, and do a lot of natural exercises such as yoga or swimming."*

training and for the art means not hurting your classmates. That is an important thing that new students sometimes forget.

**Q: What are the main areas an instructor should focus on?**
A: I usually train together with my students and not just give them coaching from the sidelines. Right now, I have a very good quality of training at my school – the same level as the top academies in Brazil. When I first started teaching here in 1996, I had to create training methods that would push me, since there were no high belts that I had trained yet. I put the students on my back and let them get in the choke and let them started mounted or in cross-side control. Now I have very good students and I

can't go easy anymore. If I slack off they will make me pay! Overall, I focus on making the students learn the basics very well, and then after that help them to develop their own style and adjust it for their own body style. For vale tudo fights I think cross-training is good, but for the basic skills it is always BJJ with the gi.

**Q: Do you feel that BJJ is no longer as effective as it once was?**
A: I hope people still realize that the Gracie family was the first to start this kind of event, back in 1930 in Brazil. Today what I see is people just trying beat the BJJ guys and then saying that BJJ doesn't work anymore. What I see a lot of people who just start training without the gi, and have a small knowledge of jiu-jitsu and a background in something else, and open academes and invent names for it like submission wrestling, freestyle grappling, submission grappling, luta livre, etcetera. But they are all the same thing – BJJ without the gi. It is a part jiu-jitsu just as judo is a part of jiu-jitsu. I honestly don't know why they do this. Maybe to be able to open a school and make money even though they are not qualified to teach. I believe these people are trying to make BJJ loose its reputation for their own personal gain. The funny part is that 100 percent of all NHB fighters train in BJJ. If they didn't they wouldn't even know the guard or the mount – but they all do. In ADCC, 99 percent of finalists are also BJJ fighters. So to say BJJ is not effective is just plain silly and ignores the facts.

*"The funny part is that 100 percent of all NHB fighters train in BJJ. If they didn't they wouldn't even know the guard or the mount – but they all do. So, to say BJJ is not effective, is just plain silly and ignores the facts."*

## Grappling Techniques

*Caught in a potential anklelock (1), Rodrigo Medeiros steps between his opponent's legs (2), falls back (3), turns inside to control the body (4) and clears his back leg to establish side control (5).*

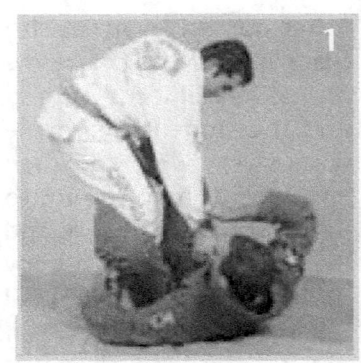
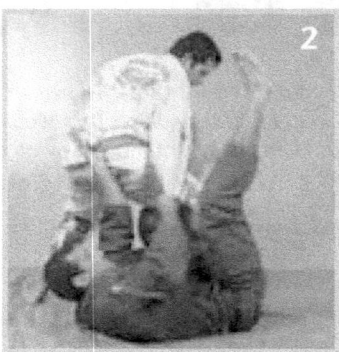

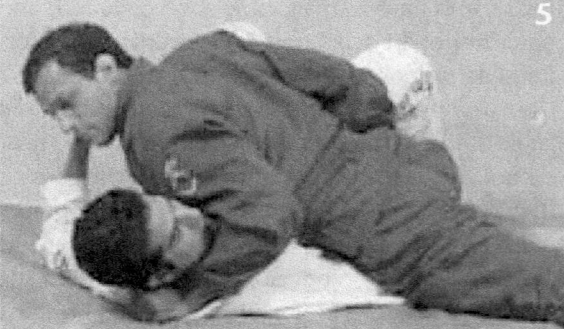

*Holding his opponent in the half-guard (1), Rodrigo Medeiros slips to the side (2), hooks his own ankle for better leverage (3), grabs his opponent's ankle (4) and applies nasty pressure for the submission (5).*

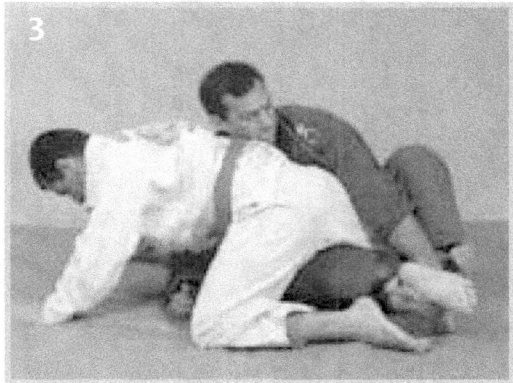

# Helio "Soneca" Moreira

## High Energy Jiu-Jitsu

When you meet "Sonequinha" you will feel nothing less than the energy of someone seriously devoted to the study of Brazilian jiu-jitsu. Although Helio Moreira started his training a very early age, he is extremely understanding, approachable and respectful – not only as a jiu-jitsu instructor but as a human being as well. His long years of experience have allowed him to internalize the important moral aspects of jiu-jitsu and use them in his daily life. Internationally recognized as a martial arts authority, he currently makes his home in the U.S. where he teaches and shares the knowledge he has spent a lifetime acquiring. Born in Rio de Janeiro, he first became involved in the art while looking for a method of self-defense. Instead he found a way of life and became obsessed with sharing his discoveries with students both young and old, regardless of their ability. What sets him apart is that he is ready and willing to not only train hardcore martial artists, but also individuals interested in personal development as well. He is a knowledgeable and fascinating man, full of interesting stories, and brimming with a positive attitude towards teaching and to life. In the modern world of disillusionment, he is truly a unique individual.

**Q: When did you start training Brazilian jiu-jitsu?**
A: When I was 9 years old. My main teachers were Cirilo Azevedo, Zé Beleza, the Machado brothers, Renzo Gracie and last but not least, the president of the Brazilian Federation, Carlos Gracie Jr. Although all of them practice the same martial art, they are very different in the way they teach and perceive jiu-jitsu. Even the same techniques have a different flavor depending of who is teaching it.

**Q: Do you recommend training under different teachers?**
A: Not in the beginning, because students can get easily confused and their progress will be slowed by all the information coming from different people. Later on, once the student has a brown or black belt, it is okay to

*"It is important to get the basics from one instructor and develop a deep understanding of them. Later, if you have the opportunity to expand your training under other instructors, you may get some personal points to add to your previous knowledge."*

learn different approaches to the same techniques and positions. It is very important to get the basics from one instructor and develop a deep understanding of them. Later, if you have the opportunity to expand your training under other instructors, they may give you some personal points to add to your previous knowledge. This can not only improve your techniques but also your level of understanding.

**Q: What attracted you to Brazilian jiu-jitsu?**
A: In Brazil, it is simply jiu-jitsu and it comes from the Gracie family. But I know it is important to use the term "Brazilian" in order for people to differentiate the system created and developed by the Gracie family from Japanese forms of jiu-jitsu. The reason I got involved in jiu-jitsu is very interesting and amusing. My mother has always been a very beautiful woman who attracted a lot of attention because of her looks. When I was in high school some of the guys started to joke about my mother, saying things that were offensive. One day I decided that I'd had enough and I confronted them. I fought all those guys at the same time and they were all older than me and much bigger. I got the worse part of that fight! I tried to face them again but they just got mad again and I got beaten again! It was then I decided that the only way out was to learn how to fight these guys with my bare hands, and jiu-jitsu was the answer. I spent three months training really hard with only the idea of getting revenge. After this time I went back to them and gave them what they deserved. They became my friends after they got their beating. We stayed friends all this time. I know this is not the reason an individual should learn a martial art but that is the way it happened to me. In a way, I'm very grateful things came out that way because jiu-jitsu became a way of life to me and opened a lot of doors.

**Q: Have you ever trained in other martial arts?**
A: Only boxing. I really like it and I feel it is a very good complement to jiu-jitsu. It is a very efficient art for those who want to learn to use their hands for fighting.

**Q: Was it hard for you to learn jiu-jitsu techniques?**
A: I started when I was a kid. At the age of 9 your body absorbs and learns in a way that you can't believe. Give a kid a bicycle and leave him alone for a week – then you go back you'll find the kid doing things you have never seen. Kids learn at a very fast pace and this is what happened to me in jiu-jitsu. Because of the age I

*"Because of the age I started, all the movements seemed to fit perfectly into my body. Because my physical structure is slim and limber, I had a lot of advantages when performing the techniques and positions. The way I learned was basically by playing."*

started, all the movements seemed to fit perfectly into my body. Since my physical structure is slim and limber, I had a lot of advantages when performing the techniques and positions. The way I learned was basically by playing. I loved to play, and when a kid plays without any pressure they learn really fast.

When I began to understand more about the art, I became more involved in the learning process. I believe that after all these years of training I have acquired the most important secret of the art – good basics and strong fundamentals. I have seen a lot of black belts with very weak and poor knowledge of the basics and this is very bad for the art. Some of them are what I call "three-position black belts." By this I mean those black belt who only know a few positions and everything they teach is based on what they do best. A teacher can't teach only the movements he likes. He needs to have a complete knowledge and understanding of the art and share all its possibilities with his students. Later on, the students themselves will decide which positions and techniques are better for them. It is the instructor's responsibility to give all his knowledge to the students. If a teacher saves a little here and there, eventually it will weaken the art.

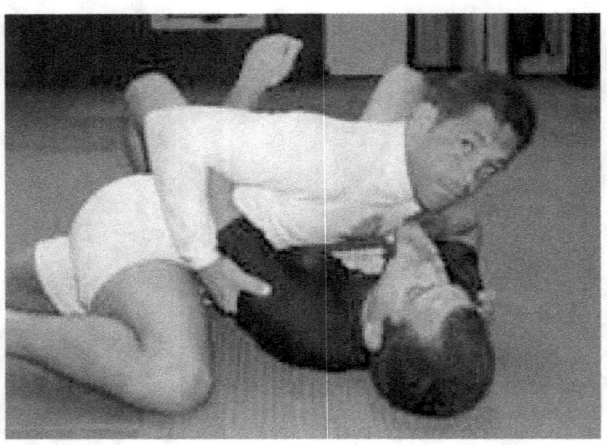

*"If a teacher doesn't want the students to learn, all he has to do is give a lot of technical information in a random way. This will confuse the student but nobody will be able to blame the instructor for not giving information."*

**Q: Why do you think some instructors do that?**
A: I can only guess! Definitely there is insecurity about what they may know or not know. If you really know the art, you are not afraid of giving knowledge to students. But I don't agree with giving tons of information to a student too early, because the only result you'll get is to confuse them! A good teacher knows how much information should be given at any point in training, so the student can naturally absorb all the technical knowledge. If a teacher doesn't want the students to learn, all he has to do is give a lot of technical information in a random way. This will confuse the student but nobody will be able to blame the instructor for not giving information.

**Q: How should a student's daily training be conducted?**
A: Jiu-jitsu is an art that evolves constantly. It has to do with the way the art is practiced in Brazil and the great number of competitions every weekend. New movements and technical changes appear all the time. This is good because it makes the technical aspects of the art grow constantly. On the other hand, we have to be careful because many people who are not interested in sport competition may end up trying to duplicate the latest techniques developed by the champions. Training for competition is a completely different thing than training for yourself and focusing on the true art of Brazilian jiu-jitsu. Competition goes away and disappears from your life when you reach a certain age, but the art stays with you forever if you are really interested in it. My advice for those who are not interested in competition is to focus on developing great basics. Don't try to learn 20 different ways of passing the guard. Learn three or four basic techniques that encompass all the fundamental principles of passing your opponent's guard and work hard until you have mastered

them. Analyze the principles and then try to combine them according to the situation you find yourself in. You'll be surprised how strong your game will become, focusing on a limited amount of techniques instead of chasing thousands of movements without taking time to master any of them.

Since the art is based on a logical and progressive approach to techniques, it is very common to find new movements while training and sparring. Sometimes you get caught in a technical dilemma, and the natural way the body escapes from a position will allow you to develop a new movement. But it is important to keep in mind the essence of how jiu-jitsu acts and moves. See how you can escape or do a movement without using strength – use technique and not muscle. This is the main reason why basics are so important.

*"Sometimes you get caught in a technical dilemma, and the natural way the body escapes from a position will allow you to develop a new movement. But it is important to keep in mind the essence of how jiu-jitsu acts and moves."*

**Q: What should a student look for in a school?**
A: Students should be dedicated and loyal to their teacher and not jump from one instructor to another for no reason. They should be honest with themselves and keep training hard regardless of what their goal may be. Before starting to train under any given instructor, check his credentials and find a little about him. Check a class and see if what he is teaching is what you want to practice and train in. Many instructors put too much emphasis on one aspect and forget others – too much competition, too much fitness, or maybe too much self-defense. The teacher should have a balanced approach to jiu-jitsu and not teach only one aspect. There are also differences depending on the country. For instance, in Brazil almost every academy focuses on training to compete in tournaments because that's what jiu-jitsu is there. In the United States, 95 percent of the students are interested in self-defense and exercise. Your approach to teaching should be different then. Rice is rice but Brazilian and Chinese don't cook it the same! Jiu-jitsu is jiu-jitsu but it should accommodate the culture of the country where the instructor teaches.

*"You simply start training because you want to learn self-defense or to be in good shape, but after years of dedication you realize that you have gained many other more important benefits during this great journey. Jiu-jitsu and my family are the two most important things in my life."*

**Q: Do black belts only need to train with other black belts to improve their game?**
A: Not really – not if the black belt wants to develop certain specific things. A technical jiu-jitsu practitioner, even if he is a high belt, can train with lower belts and get a great workout – but he will always be lacking something. For instance, an experienced and knowledgeable blue belt who has practiced for three years and is close to purple won't get much benefit from training with white belts all the time. He needs to train with higher belts because the way a purple or brown belt moves is more technical, polished and has more meaning and strategy behind each movement that he does. Jiu-jitsu is about technique and strategy, and the blue belt won't get much of that with white belts. He can train basics drills with the white belts but that will be it. The white belts will improve but not the blue belt. Now, picture the black belt. Of course, he can train with purple or blue belts but all he can really do are some basic drills and low-intensity sparring. If you want to seriously improve your game, you need to find the right sparring partners.

**Q: What are the major changes in jiu-jitsu since you began training?**
A: The rules established by the Brazilian Confederation under the guidance of Carlos Gracie Jr. is the major improvements in the sport. With these rules of engagement, practitioners have been able to face each other under safe regulations that allow the technical elements to keep evolving. Combat jiu-jitsu is a martial art that can't be trained unless you hurt your partner – but sport jiu-jitsu allows practitioners to test their skills safely. Of course, the Ultimate Fighting Championship brought everyone's eyes to Brazilian jiu-jitsu and spread it all over the world.

**Q: Who would you like to train with that you haven't?**
A: Rickson Gracie. I think any serious jiu-jitsu practitioner would love to train with him. He is a living legend to jiu-jitsu fighters and fans and the most technical practitioner of all time.

**Q: What keeps you motivated after all these years?**
A: My students are my best friends and I consider them like my brothers. Jiu-jitsu has helped a lot of us to find friends who become like a family. This is one of the many things the practice of a true martial art brings to your life. You simply start training because you want self-defense or to be in good shape, but after years of dedication you realize that you have gained many other more important benefits during this great journey. Jiu-jitsu and my family are the two most important things in my life.

*"A technical jiu-jitsu practitioner, even if he is a high belt, can train with lower belts and get a great workout, but he will always be lacking something. If you want to seriously improve your game, you need to find the right sparring partners."*

**Q: How do you mentally prepare for a fight?**
A: To be honest I don't have a special mental and philosophical preparation for a competition. I know that whatever I may accomplish is coming from God, so I simply consider myself a vehicle. In both jiu-jitsu and life sometimes you win and sometimes you lose and you need to be prepared for both. Embracing everything we have in life, good or bad, is something that helps everyone have a better existence. We are only taught to win, and so we are only happy when things go our way and not when things come out differently than what we planned. If you accept the fact that things can go the other way and don't try to engineer your life too rigidly, you'll find out that you are happy with whatever comes your way.

**Q: What has inspired you in your training?**
A: Some time ago I had the opportunity to train with a student of Carlos Gracie Jr. This individual only has one arm. I also trained with a student of Jorge Pereira. It happens Pereira's student is paraplegic and has no movement in his legs. With the first student I sparred using only one of my arms – and with the second I tied my legs. I lost against both of them!

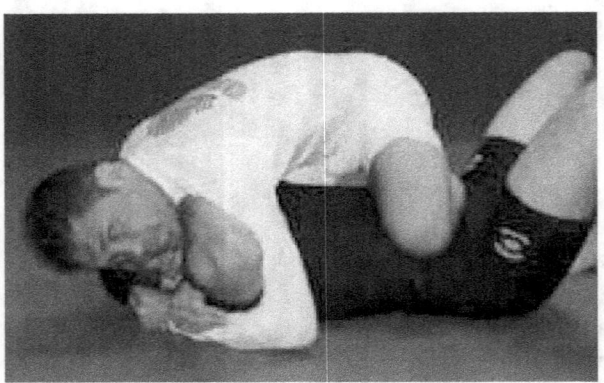

*"What is important is to find a teacher who understands this and will guide you to reach your goals according to your personal situation. Teachers can't teach the same to all their students; they have to vary their classes according to the type of students they have."*

This single experience allowed me to realize many things and opened my eyes. You have to learn how to use what you have and make jiu-jitsu work for you under your own circumstances, not somebody else's.

In 1995 I had a serious back injury. My doctor said I should start thinking about stopping jiu-jitsu completely. The back is a very important part of your body if you train jiu-jitsu. It is like having a shoulder injury in boxing; yes, you can use your hands but not the physical support system. That is what the back represents to a jiu-jitsu student. I had to re-evaluate my training, select the people I could train with, and what kind of techniques I'd do. My movements couldn't be as explosive as before. I needed to develop a new game plan so I could establish a more convenient position every time I sparred. I had to limit the weight of my sparring partners because heavier guys would seriously hurt my back. I also had to avoid training with people who used only brute force and pure strength. The funny thing was that I think that I improved my jiu-jitsu because of that and became a better teacher.

The moral of the story is to learn your limitations and then work around them. Jiu-jitsu has something to offer everybody, but we need to know how to find it. If you are a 40-year-old lawyer or an architect you can't train as crazy as a 20-year-old student. Also, you can't afford to get injured because you don't make a living with jiu-jitsu. Does it mean you can't get a black belt? No. Of course, you can! What is important is to find a teacher who understand this and will guide you to reach your goals according to your personal situation. Teachers can't teach the same to all their students – they have to vary their classes according to the type of students they have.

**Q: How important is proper nutrition for competition?**
A: One of the most important things a tournament competitor should have is a good diet. But this is true not only for a competitor but for every single student as well. A good diet is good for everybody! The right food is extremely important because if you don't put the right food into your body, it won't matter how many hours you train on the mat. Maybe when you are 20 years old your body will perform pretty much the same, but when you start getting older the proper diet will make a difference because your body will perform better. Once you take care of your body, then you need to put in many hours of training and do it intelligently, setting goals and improving at a steady pace. I used to love to eat junk food, but now I know I should have taken much better care of myself.

*"Train jiu-jitsu first, if it is jiu-jitsu you are interested in. Keep in mind that this supplementary training should be specific or you'll be wasting your time. Everything you do must have a purpose or an application to enhance your skills as a jiu-jitsu practitioner."*

**Q: Can weightlifting, running, swimming, et cetera replace time on the mat?**
A: First of all, I don't think supplementary training will ever compensate for a lack of mat time. Train jiu-jitsu first, if it is jiu-jitsu you are interested in. Then when you get some extra time, use it for additional training that allows you to improve the physical aspects necessary to excel in the art. Keep in mind that this supplementary training should be very specific or you'll be wasting your time. Everything you do must have a purpose or an application to enhance your skills as a jiu-jitsu practitioner. Remember that there is no substitute for hard training and it is not the quantity of time spent training but rather the quality.

**Q: How does fear affects a competitor's performance?**
A: There are many psychological aspects that can really mess-up your performance in a competition. There was a time when I though I couldn't

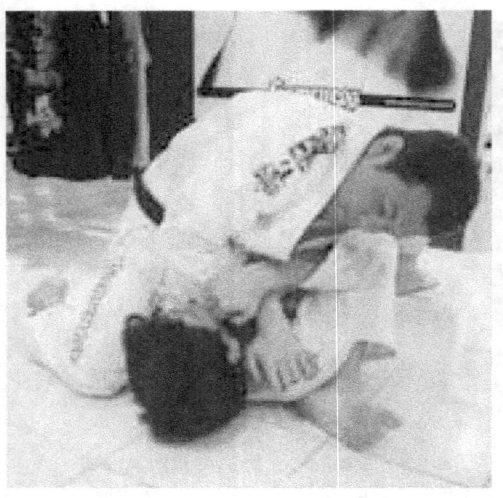

"Many people don't realize that proper breathing and relaxation come from a state of mind in which you are confident with your jiu-jitsu skills. When you are not sure of what you know and what you can do, that is when you start to get nervous and your breathing becomes ragged and tense."

lose. I was winning every championship and I thought I was unbeatable. Well, it took a very short time for me to find out that I was wrong. I was putting too much pressure on myself because I thought I had an obligation to win. When you feel obligated to win you perform at a very low level. Jiu-jitsu is an art and a sport. In any sport sometimes you win and sometimes you lose, so be prepared for defeat, accept it and move on. This will take a lot of pressure off and you'll be able to perform at a much higher level.

Q: How important are proper breathing techniques?
A: Extremely important! Breathing is the key to relaxing, and relaxation is the key to performing jiu-jitsu techniques correctly. Many people don't realize that proper breathing and relaxation comes from a state of mind when you are confident with your jiu-jitsu skills. It is when you are not sure of what you know and what you can do, when you start to get nervous and your breathing becomes ragged and tense. The only way you can be confident of what you know is to have very strong technical fundamentals. Students need to reach a technical level where they can control the timing of their breathing in relationship to their physical movements.

Q: Where do you think Brazilian jiu-jitsu is going?
A: Jiu-jitsu is an art which doesn't need to prove anything. It is accepted that Brazilian jiu-jitsu is one of the most effective fighting methods known to man. The Gracie family, and especially Royce Gracie in the UFC, opened everybody's eyes to what the art has to offer. That happened in the early '90s. In the future, I would like to see the art become an Olympic sport, but I also understand that there is much work to do before this can happen. It is important that all practitioners, instructors, federations, and associations work together for the benefit of the art.

**Q: Is it necessary to add other fighting skills to jiu-jitsu for mixed martial arts?**
A: Definitely! In vale tudo, it is important to add some other combative elements – forget about doing only jiu-jitsu. You need to know how to kick, punch, and close the distance to get into grappling range. MMA is not jiu-jitsu and therefore some modifications should be made to cover all the necessary basics. Martial arts cross-training is necessary for any fighter who wants to be successful in mixed martial arts.

**Q: What should jiu-jitsu practitioners mentally focus on?**
A: Don't let anyone to steal your dreams and take attention away from your goals – because those dreams are pretty much all you've got. Work hard to reach those goals and remember that battles do not always go to the stronger man. It is important to believe in yourself, but do it realistically and with common sense. One should know his own limitations and work hard to at least reach those limits. If you give your best to anything in life, you will surprise yourself and find that you can exceed the limitations that you thought were impossible to pass. Professor Helio Gracie, for example, is more than 90 years old but yet still trains and challenges people to get on the mat with him. Many people say that he is an old man, but they are wrong. He is far younger than many others who are not nearly as old as him. He has proven that age is just a self-imposed limitation that can be exceeded. What a great example and what a courageous mind.

*"Don't let anyone steal your dreams or take your attention away from your goals, because those dreams are pretty much all you've got. Work hard to reach those goals and remember that battles do not always go to the stronger man."*

# JASON MORRIS

## A Focused Mind

Jason Morris' amazing journey in the art of judo started in 1975 at the age of 8 and ended after his fourth Olympic appearance in 2000. His dedication and competitive spirit carried him through hard times when things weren't quite like he expected. Currently focused on training new judo talent for competition, Morris still finds time to be the editor of *Real Judo*, a publication dedicated to his beloved art. His work as a judo coach is recognized worldwide and his reputation in the international grappling community is second to none. Morris advocates proper training to get the right state of mind for elite competition: "Practice makes your feel confident in your abilities and this confidence will put you in the proper gear to fight. There is no other way you can step onto the competition mat with the right attitude if you haven't done your homework." His knowledge and understanding of the technical aspects of judo make him one of the best coaches in America and he brings hope to grappling fans everywhere when he says, "The best is yet to come for U.S. judo."

**Q: How long have you been practicing judo?**
A: I have been practicing for three decades and I have never trained in any other martial art or combat sport. It isn't that I haven't been curious or interested, but just that I started judo when I was very young and focused all my time and energy there. I knew that in order to achieve something in life you have to put everything into your chosen sport and not jump from one thing to another. Instead of spending three days a week doing judo and another three days doing something else, I dedicated six days a week to learn and perfect the sport I liked the most. Don't get me wrong, I'm not saying that a practitioner shouldn't train in anything else, only that it wasn't the right approach for me at that time. To be an elite competitor at the Olympic level you have to dedicate all your time to the sport you choose.

*"I was a natural athlete, so judo came fairly easily. Winning didn't come easily, though, and I had many ups and downs... mostly downs in the beginning. I have always looked for quality over quantity and maybe this is the reason why I succeeded in judo."*

**Q: Who were your teachers?**
A: I started at the Parkside YMCA in Glenville, NY under Warren Harris. Those were memorable times and I have many great memories of the time I spent with Sensei Harris. When you are young and begin martial arts training almost everything is absorbed immediately and stays with you for the rest of your life. The beginning phase of any martial art sets the foundations for who and what you'll become the rest of your life.

**Q: Was judo easy for you?**
A: I was a natural athlete so judo came fairly easily. Winning part didn't come easily, though, and I have many ups and downs – mostly downs in the beginning. But from the technical point of view I was very good early on. I have always looked for quality over quantity and maybe this is the reason why I succeeded in judo. I learned to train smart and get the most out my time in the dojo. I try to pass this approach and mentality to my students so they can get the most of their mat time.

**Q: Tell us an interesting story about your early days.**
A: OK. This is a story about my father, Bernie. I was scheduled to compete in the Austrian Open in the summer of 1987. I had just won gold medals at the Pan Am Games and Pacific Rim Championships and was extremely tired after both competitions. I was dreading the trip to Austria and was bitching to my dad about it, but I went anyway because he taught me to honor my commitments. As it turned out, it was a comedy of travel. To get there, it was literally planes, trains and automobiles. That trip was a real nightmare. Once I finally arrived, I was 10 pounds over my 172-pound weight class. I threw on my plastics and tried to lose the weight, but my motivation was low and everything I had to do was almost an impossible task. Finally, I decided to bag it. As I was walking down the hallway of the hotel to tell the organizers to pull my name from the event, I looked up and there was my dad! In total shock, I yelled, "Dad, what are you doing here?" He simply and calmly replied, "You seemed really bummed at home so I thought I could cheer you up." Needless to say, I was very happy to see him. In

response to him going through all that trouble to see me, I lost the weight and went on to become the first American male to win the event.

I like to tell this story because the situation one finds himself in is often the result of his mental state. For example, I was in the same physical situation when I was walking down the hallway right after I met my father, but my state of mind was totally different. I suddenly felt both motivated and ready to do what it took to compete. The mind is a very powerful tool, and a competitor should learn how to use it and channel his thoughts in the proper direction.

*"Professor Kano had a different cultural background, and the times were substantially different than today. His goal, I believe, was to develop an activity that could help an individual grow in society without the old warrior precepts used in the war times."*

**Q: Has judo changed from what Jigoro Kano originally intended?**
A: I don't know what Kano intended when he created judo because I never met him, but it has developed into one of the most dynamic sports in the world. Professor Kano had a different cultural background and the times were substantially different than today. His goal, I believe, was to develop an activity that could help the individual to grow in society without the old warrior precepts used in the war times. This has helped judo to develop into a very demanding and exciting sport for all to enjoy. I have always been all about the sport of judo. I love athletics and categorize judo as I would baseball, tennis or any other sport. Its practice definitely brings many mental and spiritual benefits, but the student has to look for those to find them. It has to be a personal journey.

**Q: What is your opinion of events such as the UFC and Pride and the judo fighters who compete in them?**
A: It's interesting to see how they do, but it doesn't prove anything. Many of the judo guys who try it are way past their prime and just pick up the no-holds barred thing later in life. Judo is sport with its own rules. A judo player entering a fighting ring is almost the same as a tennis player entering a basketball court. The no-holds-barred arena is its own thing and judo is its own thing – they are two separate and very distinctive activities. I

*"Judo is the ultimate athletic activity to create coordination, strength, speed and self-confidence. It's a perfect athletic base for any sport. I love the sport, so every time I think of it I feel motivated."*

have no problem with judo practitioners trying it out and I find myself rooting for anyone with a judo background. Personally, I haven't given much thought to the ramifications of mixed martial arts, but I definitely enjoy it as any sports fan would.

**Q: Do think these events are positive for grappling in general?**
A: It doesn't do much for judo, to be honest. Judo needs to promote itself on its own merits as does any other sport. Other than judo, I think these events are good for all martial arts and certainly give them more exposure to the general public.

**Q: What's your opinion about mixing styles? Does the practice of one nullify the effectiveness of the other? Or, on the contrary, can it be beneficial?**
A: To begin, there is not one style or grappling method that will make a good student or instructor. There may be an instructor teaching judo and another teaching BJJ. If the student is dedicated and motivated, the final quality of the product (student) will be the same. If an instructor has sound motives and is well qualified, then it's more likely that the student will develop good quality. Remember, working all these things will help a student improve. As he gets better, however, he will need to concentrate on one style and put most of his available time into it to really excel. It won't improve his game if he divides his training time in three or four different styles. He needs to learn how to add what it is necessary and completely discard the rest. Otherwise, he'll waste his time and won't ever achieve any major victory. The technical addition of any other element into the sport of judo has to be very subtle and specific. Please note that I am saying very specific because it has to fit into the judo format. It is not an addition for the addition's sake; instead, it has to make a certain aspect better or more complete. If this isn't done in the right way, learning and mixing grappling styles won't be of any benefit. Of course, maybe the student will feel happy when he goes home, but he'll never win and Olympic medal with this approach.

**Q: Do you think that the technical level in the West has caught up with Japan?**
A: Europe has caught up and in some ways passed the Japanese, but the U.S. is nowhere near the top in judo. We need a lot of training and have a long way to go. This is the truth, unfortunately. The Japanese still set the standard worldwide.

**Q: What are the major changes in judo since you began training?**
A: There are more wrestling and sambo type moves now. For instance, the amount of leg attacks has increase tremendously due to the addition of sambo techniques. Judo is a consistent and established art by itself and doesn't have a need to add more and more techniques. However, there are certain technical elements found in other grappling methods that can be very useful for a judo competitor.

*"Preparation has been the key word in my life, not only in judo but in everything I do. The practice of judo means the same as practicing any other sport. All sports teach many of the tools necessary for success in life if you know how to look under the surface."*

**Q: What would you say to someone who is interested in learning judo?**
A: Judo is the ultimate athletic activity to create coordination, strength, speed and self-confidence. It's a perfect athletic base for any sport. I love the sport so every time I think of it I feel motivated. For me, training is fun, but I understand that some students may need to make judo more enjoyable. My advice is to change the approach to your training and make it more interesting by choosing certain elements and focusing on them. Don't think about trying to get better overall, just think more about a single throw or a pin. There is so much to learn in judo that it is easy to get overwhelmed. Attend classes promptly and focus on what the teacher is sharing. Train with sincerity and the right spirit. Consistency will bring results – don't forget that you learn judo by doing judo.

**Q: What has been the main factor behind your tournament success?**
A: My main philosophy has always been to prepare myself. Preparation has been the key word in my life, not only in judo but in everything I do. The more prepared you are the better chance you give yourself to win. The practice of judo means the same as practicing any other sport. All sports

*"I find that sometimes the traditional instructors tend to impose unnecessarily harsh and structured attitudes on their students. This approach can intimidate the students and make them nervous, confused and inhibited. You have to use a more modern approach now."*

teach many of the tools necessary for success in life if you know how to look under the surface. I run an elite program so it's always geared toward competition. This puts additional pressure on every single decision I make for my players. I can't make mistakes because they will be the ones paying for them. Just like in life you have to be focused, prepared, and mistake-free or you'll pay for it.

**Q: Did you have any particular psychological preparation method that you used before an important competition or match?**
A: Not really. I was best prepared mentally when I knew that I had prepared physically and had done my homework on my opponents. My mind was ready because I knew that I had done everything to prepare. Because of that, my psychological state was always of readiness. That's why it is so important to put time and energy into training sessions because they are the trigger factors for your mental state.

**Q: What is the most important quality of a successful competitor?**
A: Character. That word best defines a person or a fighter. A person's character defines them and all the additional things necessary to be a champion like commitment, desire, focus, and determination. Character is what makes an individual – it is what sets him apart from the rest of the crowd. The instructor plays a tremendous role in the student's development but the instructor is also a student in many aspects and so must also learn and grow. When I train competitors I try to meet the needs of my students with my own perspective of the sport. I find that sometimes the very-traditional instructors tend to impose unnecessarily harsh and a structured attitudes on their students. This approach can intimidate the students and make them very nervous, confused, and inhibited. Instead of treating the students like robots, I'd rather allow them to discover and express their individual characters in the sport. When students feel happy they are more eager to learn, and more likely to train hard – which is the only way to be skillful in whatever activity you do. Today if you teach a student the rigid, traditional way you are

going to lose 90 percent of them. You have to use a more modern approach now.

**Q: How do you think fear affects a competitor's performance?**
A: Fear is a good thing and it partially is what drives athletes to train. When fear gets too strong, however, it can prevent an athlete from performing his best. So, the best way to prevent that is to prepare. The better prepared he is, the easier it is to keep fear at a manageable level so that he can control it and use it to his advantage. Tournament competition teaches a judoka not so much how to fight but how to apply a variety of techniques in a safe environment so that he eventually transcends fear and develops self-confidence. Once he has achieved a realistic level of proficiency in judo technique, confidence and self-knowledge, he can deal with almost any situation that arises in a competition arena... and in life.

*"Currently, judo is in the Stone Age and doesn't allow winners to celebrate. A winning competitor is only allowed to bow and walk off the mat. Half the enjoyment of watching sports is sharing the thrill of victory with the winner."*

**Q: What advice would you give to students about supplementary training such as weights, running, stretching, etc.?**
A: The best thing for judo is judo. Period. Beyond that, an athlete needs to find a coach who can create a training plan that allows him to reach the top. An athlete also needs to educate himself on the best programs out there. Then he should try them to see if they fit his needs or provide him with the desired results. The program chosen can and should assist with the overall total program, which may or may not include lifting, running etc. After all, every athlete is different and has different needs. Nevertheless, any additional training should be done in a very specific way to complement and help the sport of judo. It should not be done as an entity by itself. All these subsidiary exercises have their place in competition judo, but none of them will make a judo expert. The only way to do that is to put in many hard hours of technical judo practice. Supplementary training will, however, bring a new high level to judo practice. But, of course, they won't produce miracles overnight. As mentioned before, only through an intelligent application will they be beneficial for the judoka.

*"An athlete also needs to educate himself on the best programs out there. Then he should try them to see if they fit his needs or provide him with the desired results. Nevertheless, any additional training should be done in a very specific way to complement and help the sport of judo."*

**Q: What is the future of judo?**
A: Modern judo is blend of the most effective grappling techniques and principles into an organized and integrated structure that meet Olympic requirements. Judo is a sport that adapts with the times and grows and improves. The foundation, philosophy, training principles, and movements all make judo unique. One thing that would make judo more fan-friendly is to change the scoring system. The scores are currently in Japanese and are hard to understand. Making it easier for fans to know who is winning would make judo more accessible. Another thing that should be allowed is a celebration after a win. Currently judo is in the stone-age and doesn't allow winners to celebrate. A winning competitor is only allowed to bow and walk off the mat. Half the enjoyment of watching sports is sharing the thrill of victory with the winner. Judo should also develop a world ranking system so they can seed the top events as they do in tennis. As it stands right now, many of the best players meet in the first and second rounds. Nobody wants to see Pete Sampras play against Andre Agassi in the first round at Wimbledon. That match should be a final. The same thing should be used to make judo more exciting. We should look at successful sports and copy the good things to take judo to the next level.

**Q: Has judo ignored ground techniques in favor of throws?**
A: For the past 20 years, the ratio of ground techniques in judo has stayed about the same. The rules set the direction for training and scoring. People will use the methods that score the most points. It is only logical. So the techniques are pretty much the same as we have used in the last two decades.

**Q: After judo became an Olympic sport, did many of the classical techniques disappear?**
A: Judo has evolved as has every sport. Athletes are bigger, stronger, more prepared and better coached and the techniques reflect that. The techniques we use today are not weaker or worse than those used in the past.

The athletes are simply different and different things work now.

**Q: Is judo is gaining in popularity?**
A: Judo is currently the second most-practiced sport in the world and still growing. There are over 92 countries that have national governing bodies. Unfortunately, while judo is gaining popularity around the world, it has gone down in the United States. USA Judo needs to help clubs at the grassroots level get students in the door. They should create a national advertising and awareness plan. To do that, USA Judo would need to organize itself on more of a professional level. It's currently mostly based on volunteers and not professionals. It wouldn't hurt judo if we could produce more champions to get public notice, but that falls under the professionalism category. There needs to be a development plan to help athletes succeed at all levels. The current plan is that the athletes must do it on their own, which means there is no plan for judo in America. It's up to each individual athlete to make their way and this is very difficult.

*"Judo has evolved as has every sport. Athletes are bigger, stronger, more prepared and better coached and the techniques reflect that. The athletes are simply different and different things work now."*

**Q: Do you feel that you still have further to go in your studies?**
A: Absolutely. There is always room for improvement in anything. If an athlete thinks that he has arrived, then he is done. I am a professional judo coach now and am constantly learning and trying to improve all aspects of my judo and coaching techniques because I want to become a better coach. I want to take my students to an elite level. Elite competition, such as the Olympic Games, requires a highly sophisticated approach to training and psychology.

**Q: What is the best way to get benefits from the grappling arts?**
A: Stick with it. The martial arts – and judo especially – teach that there is no such thing as instant gratification. What they do teach is that if you work hard and stay with it, it will bring long lasting positive results to your life. Hard work and dedication will pay off in judo and more importantly in life. Martial arts teach that lesson very well.

# B.J. Penn

## American Prodigy

B.J. Penn is not a titanium cyborg, constructed by the Pentagon to be the perfect fighting machine. B.J. Penn is not the crowning result of years of genetic engineering in a secret CIA laboratory. B.J. Penn is not an alien life form, sent to destroy all life on earth. B.J. Penn is not even from the planet Krypton, with powers and abilities far beyond those of mortal men. No, B.J. Penn, according to his latest physical, is a mere human being, composed of ordinary flesh and blood. Yet in a martial art where many students take a decade or longer of daily training to reach the highest level of technical achievement, it took Penn a paltry three years and four months to get his black belt in Brazilian jiu-jitsu, and less than four years to win a world championship.

No matter where B.J. Penn goes in his career, and regardless of any future wins or losses he may have in no-holds-barred fighting, he has already made history by becoming the first and only American to win a world title in the black belt division of the Brazilian Jiu-Jitsu World Championships in Rio de Janeiro.

In comparison, B.J.'s name, like the fighter himself, is uncomplicated and simple. There is a directness of mind and purpose, and a refreshing simplicity of thought about B.J. Penn. It is this extreme single-mindedness that has driven him to the highest level of his chosen sport. One cannot help but wonder what mountains he will yet climb, what dragons he will yet slay, and what rivers he will yet ford. But Penn himself, seems strangely unconcerned about his destination, choosing instead to focus only on the the journey.

Born on the Big Island of Hawaii, B.J. Penn is the second youngest in a family of five. He grew up in the Islands with a big dose of determination; because in Hawaii, growing up is sometimes a game of survival.

While training for his fights, Penn is wearing the same tee-shirt he wore at UFC 34 after he knocked-out Uno. The shirt says, "What Brah Like Cracks!" Which is Hawaiian slang for, "I'm going to kick your butt!" Simple. Direct. Honest. And just a little scary.

*"I never did amateur boxing, but I was always into sparring. You have to know how to take care of yourself on the islands. You can't grow up in Hawaii without getting into fights."*

**Q: When did you start training martial arts?**
A: I always boxed at home in Hilo, Hawaii. I never did amateur boxing, but I was always into sparring. You have to know how to take care of yourself on the islands. You can't grow up in Hawaii without getting into fights. You know Hawaii. But my formal martial arts training didn't start until 1997.

**Q: Is this when you started learning Brazilian jiu-jitsu?**
A: Yes. A taekwondo teacher moved a few houses down from me. He had taken a few private lessons from Ralph and Cesar Gracie. He saw all of the neighborhood kids playing outside and started using us as sparring partners. He didn't want to teach or anything – he just wanted to practice with us to have training partners. After a while he tried to get us to do jiu-jitsu with him so he'd have some bodies to train with. We didn't want to do it. We kept saying, "It is such a waste of time. Jiu-jitsu is nothing!" But he kept asking my dad and insisting. Finally my dad said: "You know what? Why don't you guys just go and train with him a little. Otherwise, he will never leave me alone!" So we went there – and after a few times on the mat my mind just started rolling like my body and it seemed so natural to me. I haven't stopped since.

**Q: When did you meet your first real BJJ black belt instructor?**
A: He was going to the mainland to do belt testing for taekwondo and he said, "You know what? Ralph is just down the road. You should go train there." So I did and Ralf really encouraged me. He said, "You have a lot of potential. You should come train here." So I trained at Ralph's for a while, and then I moved back to Hawaii and started to train with Renato "Charuto" Verissimo. I'm still training with him.

**Q: Have you gone to Brazil often to learn?**
A: Only when there was some big competitions. I'd go there and train in order to prepare. I competed three times in the *Mundial* world championships, once in the *Brasileiro* national championships, and once in the *Brasileiro de Equipes* national team championships.

**Q: How did you do?**
A: In the blue belt division of the Brazilian National Championships I got fourth place. In the National Team Championships our team won. Then in the World Championships, in three successive years, I got second place in the blue belt division, third place in the brown belt division, and then first place in the black belt division. In the blue belt finals of the world championships I lost to Joao Vitorino in the finals, he is also from *Nova Uniao.* Then in the brown belt worlds I lost to Fernando "Terere" by advantage. Then in the black belt division it was a really tough field. I faced Fredson in the semifinals and I managed to win. When I did that I felt that I had a good chance of winning the whole thing because Fredson's guard is ridiculous! It is just unbelievable.

**Q: Have you had memorable wins in any American tournaments?**
A: In the Copa Pacifica I fought the guy who won the Pan Ams that year – the one I got disqualified on – Francisco Neto from Yamasaki. I never got to fight him again until the Copa Pacifica, so I was happy to win.

*"I got my blue belt in six months and my purple belt in 18 months. Seven months later I got my brown belt. Eight months later I got my black belt. So, it took me exactly 3 years and 4 months to get my black belt."*

**Q: How fast did you get promoted through the Brazilian jiu-jitsu ranks?**
A: I got my blue belt in six months and my purple belt in 18 months. Seven months later I got my brown belt. Eight months later I got my black belt. So, it took me exactly 3 years and 4 months to get my black belt. I got it from Andre "Dede" Pederneiras, the head of Nova Uniao. But getting any belt from Andre Pederneiras is not easy, so I was very proud of that. For my black, for example, I got it the week before the world championships. I was a brown belt and I had to fight a black belt. Dede told me that if I won that, then I would get the black belt, then I'd make the competition A-Team and get to enter the *Mundial* as a black belt.

**Q: Which jiu-jitsu fighter do you admire and try to model your career after?**
A: The same as everybody else – Rickson Gracie. I've never met Rickson Gracie or trained with him but I've trained with plenty of people who

*"The stories you hear about him are just incredible. Rickson Gracie is just the man. I've seen almost every good guy there is, but the name that keeps coming to mind all the time is Rickson Gracie."*

have. The stories you hear about him are just incredible. Rickson Gracie is just the man. I've seen almost every good guy there is, but the name that keeps coming to mind all the time is Rickson Gracie. It is a shame that he has never fought in the UFC and given the American fans a chance to see him.

**Q: At Nova Uniao, who were the top competition fighters?**
A: Renato "Charuto" Verissimo, Shaolin Ribeiro, Robson "Robinho" Moura, Leo Santos, Andre "Dede" Pederneiras, and a bunch of others. Nova Uniao is incredible. They have all the top guys in the world in the lighter weights. Outside of Nova Uniao I like to look at everybody. Particularly, though, I like to watch Antonio "Nino" Schembri, Leo "Leozinho" Vieira, and Royler Gracie – I love to watch Royler in jiu-jitsu or no-holds-barred. No one matches his intensity or aggressiveness. I believe that you learn a lot by having an open mind. The way I improve quickly is by copying champions. I watch what a champion does and then I try to do what they do. Then I just add my own style and flair.

**Q: You had tremendous success in jiu-jitsu and then you suddenly went into NHB. Did you have any full-contact matches before your UFC debut?**
A: Just one fight. I fought someone while I was still at Ralph's school. It was a pankration rules match with open hands. I was 18 years old – it was a long time ago. Then in my first match in the UFC I fought a tough match against Joey Gilbert. He's a really good wrestler and a good puncher. Before the fight I really didn't know if I belonged in the Octagon. I went there to answer a lot of questions I had about myself. I wanted to gage myself and see where I belonged in the scheme of the world fighting scene. But I went on to win via referee stoppage. I took him down twice – and he is a good wrestler! I couldn't believe it afterwards – I was as surprised as anyone! That did a lot for my confidence and self-belief.

**Q: So in your first fight you beat Gilbert very quickly. Then you knocked-out Din Thomas in your next fight. Then you also knocked-**

out Caol Uno, whom many considered to be the best lightweight in the world. How are you doing this?

A: I just have been training in everything all the time. I have been trying to improve all aspects of my game all the time. I try to improve my boxing, but I don't forget that I have to improve my wrestling, so I work on that too. I also try to improve my jiu-jitsu. I am always trying to improve. I also study my opponents, I watch tapes, I plan a very detailed strategy. I am committed to doing everything that I need to do in order to become a champion. I am not closed-minded; I am not one of those guys who says, "Jiu-jitsu is the only thing!" I don't want to stop learning – I want to learn everything – whatever I need to learn in order to make my game more complete. If I ever have to learn sombo to beat someone then I will learn it. I don't just want to learn how to defend against boxing – I want to learn boxing!

Q: You are known for preparing yourself very completely for a fight. Where did your work ethic come from?

A: Well, the truth is that I really don't like to train all that much. When I was preparing for the various *Mundials,* for example, I would not do any extra training – just my normal once a day for two or three hours. I look at sport jiu-jitsu as something fun to do, and I really don't care all that much whether I win or lose. A lot of times I will try out new moves or strategies and not get so focused on the outcome. Perhaps that looseness has been an advantage to me. But if you lose the fun part of sport jiu-jitsu then you have lost the true essence of the sport. When it comes to preparing for no-holds-barred, however, I am very determined. I will train twice a day for three or four hours each time, and I'll do it for two months in advance. If I have to get up at five in the morning to go running, I'll do it because it needs to be done.

Q: Which NHB match was your toughest?

A: Din Thomas posed the greatest test. He was really strong. As soon as I

*"The truth is that I really don't like to train all that much. When I was preparing for the various Mundials, for example, I would not do any extra training... just my normal once a day for two or three hours. I look at sport jiu-jitsu as something fun to do, and I really don't care all that much whether I win or lose."*

*"When it comes to preparing for no-holds-barred, however, I am determined. If I have to get up at five in the morning to go running, I'll do it because it needs to be done."*

grabbed him I could tell he was one of the strongest guys I have ever felt at my weight. People think I lost my footing or got taken down, but the truth is that I pulled guard and pulled him to the canvas to try to submit him. He felt really strong. He was my biggest test and my biggest growing experience. I felt like I really grew as a fighter because of that match. I got a chance to feel what it was like being in the Octagon, and I learned how to relax in there. It's a lot different from a street fight. I felt like I really matured after that one. When you beat a top contender, it really makes you feel like you belong in the fighting scene.

**Q: What about your match with Uno?**
A: He came out with a big flying kick and I immediately nailed him. He was wobbled right after the first punch, then the left and the right uppercut sent him down for good. I really didn't feel the punch in my hands, though. Just like when I hit Din with the knee – I didn't really feel it either. But that is what they say – when you hit the guy right, you don't feel it. I really didn't feel myself hitting Uno. He felt really light – the same as when I kneed Din. It felt as if I went through him and didn't hit anything.

**Q: What do you attribute your meteoric success to?**
A: Training hard and constantly. Initially, I only did jiu-jitsu just because I liked it. After I started getting good and winning a lot of tournaments I thought I trained hard. Even at the Mundial, when I won as a black belt, I thought I trained hard – but compared to now it was nothing. After I started in the UFC I really stepped-up – now I understand what the words "training" and "dedication" mean. Now I train like a professional – you have to be committed if you want to be successful. The sport is growing in that direction. I believe that Frank Shamrock was the first fighter to do things that way – to really commit himself to constant training. When he

fought Tito and beat him, he just pushed the whole time until Tito broke. Now Tito trains that way to. All the top guys do.

**Q: What is the strongest part of your game?**
A: My jiu-jitsu, no doubt, coupled with my ability to be open-minded about learning new styles. I still train with a gi at least once a week while I am training for a no-holds-barred fight. But if I am not training for a fight, then I grapple with a gi every day – just because I love it. Whether I ever compete with a gi again is a question, though. I'll just have to see what happens with my professional career. But in the future, who knows? I might just do it for fun. I'd like to teach someday, and when I do, it will be with a gi. Right now, I have a lot of goals. My first one was to win the Mundial as a black belt, and now my main goal is to win the UFC title. But after I reach all my fighting goals, I can definitely see myself competing with a gi for fun. I also see a possibility of fighting at Abu Dhabi without a gi in submission wrestling – although that is a different game.

*"Train hard and practice the martial arts for fun, because if you don't enjoy it, you are never going to be any good at it. For NHB, you really have to have an open mind. Brazilian jiu-jitsu is great, but you need to learn everything. Be ready for anything and never give up."*

**Q: What advice would you give to someone who wants to be an MMA champion?**
A: Train hard and practice the martial arts for fun – because if you don't enjoy it you are never going to be any good at it. For NHB you really have to have an open mind. Brazilian jiu-jitsu is great, but you need to learn everything. If you come from a striking martial art, you need to learn jiu-jitsu. To be a total fighter you need to learn how to strike, grapple, and wrestle in order to be ready for both the ground and the stand-up game. Be ready for anything and never give up.

## Grappling Techniques

B.J. Penn operates against Renato "Charuto" Verissimo from the open guard (1). When Verissimo lowers himself to pass, Penn secures the collar (2), rotates to the side (3), lays back to get a better angle for leverage (4) and applies a clock choke with precision for the submission (5).

B.J. Penn immobilizes Renato "Charuto" Verissimo by trapping both arms from side control (1). Pressuring the neck to create space (2), Penn secures the arm (3) and applies a painful Americana for the submission (4).

B.J. Penn controls Renato "Charuto" Verissimo from the top (1). Grabbing the collar (2), Penn applies pressure, going for the clock choke (3). When Verissimo counters by grabbing Penn's leg (4), Penn switches up and applies a straight armbar submission with his legs (5).

B.J. Penn establishes side control on Renato "Charuto" Verissimo (1). Snapping up, he puts a knee on Verissimo's stomach (2), grabs the collar (3) and swings his leg over the head (4). He falls back into the classic straight armbar submission (5).

## GRAPPLING TECHNIQUES

*B.J. Penn attacks the opponent from the back (1). He slides his right hand in to grab the lapel (2), but the opponent blocks this by grabbing Penn's wrist (3). Penn slides his left hand under the opponent's left arm (4), moves to the side (5) and applies an armlock (6).*

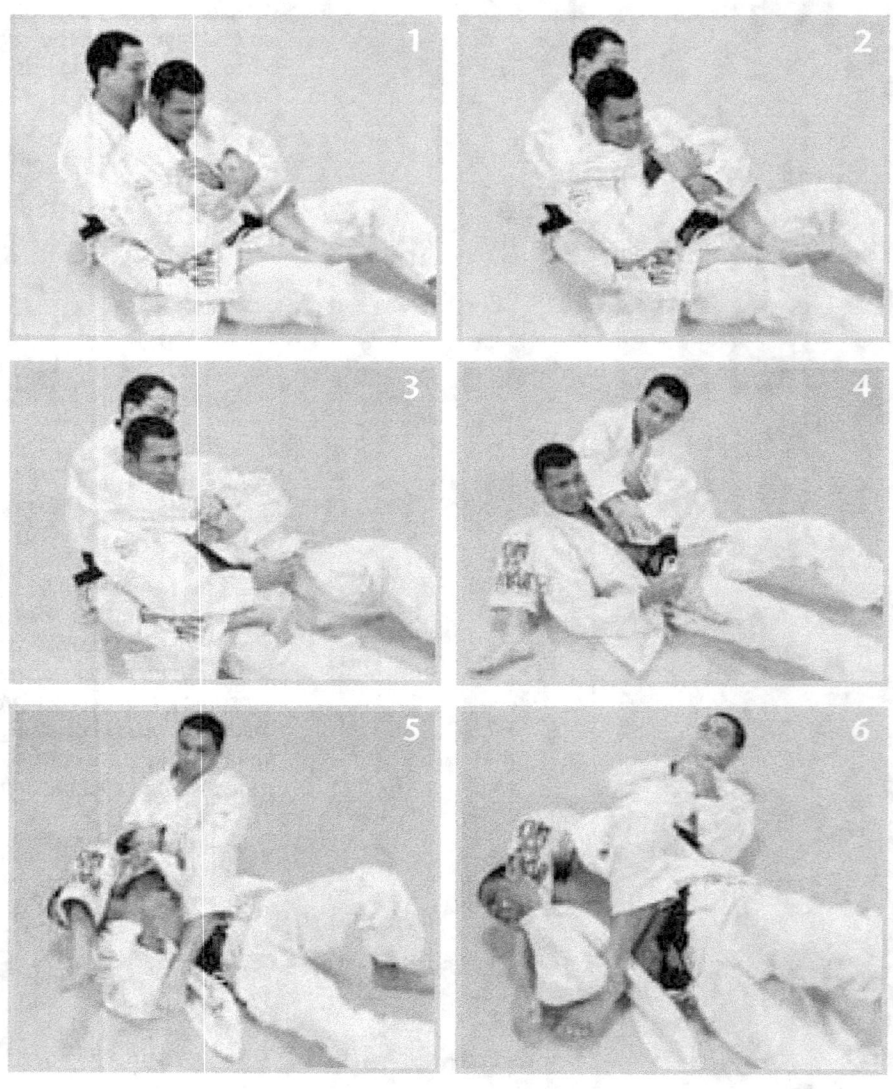

B.J. Penn faces his opponent's open guard (1). The opponent reaches for Penn's left arm, attempting to get a kimura (2). Penn follows the momentum of the technique, turns to the left (3) and moves his left leg over the opponent's head (4). He quickly stands so he can pass to the other side of the opponent's body (5). Without releasing the opponent's left arm, Penn applies an armlock (6).

# ANTONIO "NINO" SCHEMBRI

## *The One and Only*

It's August 16, 2000, and Nino "Elvis" Schembri is on a plane to the U.S. to attend Rickson Gracie's second international tournament. As the plane streaks through the sky, halfway across South America, with nearly everyone onboard slumbering, Nino prowls the aisles, finally stopping beside the seat where martial arts writer Kid Peligro sleeps. Holding a glass of Chablis in one hand, Nino prods Peligro with the other. Kid awakes groggily and looks up. "I just wanted to let you know that today is Thursday," Nino says quietly, raising his untouched glass of wine in a toast. "Elvis Presley died 23 years ago on this very day. I just thought it was important that you know." Without another word, Nino walks somberly away.

A riddle wrapped in a mystery inside an enigma, Nino Schembri walks to beat of a different drummer. With his ever-present sideburns, which he wears as a tribute to "The King of Rock and Roll," Schembri is one of mixed martial arts most easily recognizable figures. Nino's everyday path in life is the road less traveled, and every fork he takes is usually a direction not chosen by anyone else.

But Nino's good-natured originality doesn't obscure that fact that he is one of the top sport jiu-jitsu competitors in the world who is also 3-0 in mixed martial arts. He established himself as an international star with a KO win over Japanese superstar Kazushi Sakuraba in Pride. But to Nino, jiu-jitsu is not only about fighting, it is far more than that. It is philosophy, principle, power and strength — it is history and art — it is life itself.

**Q: How long have you been practicing jiu-jitsu?**
A: I started with Sylvio Behring when I was 6 years old, and I trained for one year under his supervision. I came back at 13 to train with Jorge Pereira, who was the instructor at my condominium in Nova Ipanema at Barra da Tijuca. When I was 17 years old and a blue belt, I went to Gracie Barra to train with Carlos Gracie Jr. and Renzo Gracie. It was then my career in sport jiu-jitsu really started. I have been very fortunate to have

*"If your base is jiu-jitsu, learn other arts to complement what you have, but don't be so naïve as to try to beat an experienced kickboxer when you have only trained stand-up for a few years. If you're a grappler, stick to what you know best and make everything else work around it."*

received instruction from excellent teachers who were great human beings, too. All together, I've been training for a long time.

Besides Brazilian jiu-jitsu I have also been training in boxing, karate, and muay Thai. These are very good fighting systems and I think they complement jiu-jitsu very well. I never felt that adding them to my fighting arsenal would take anything away from my jiu-jitsu. Definitely my main art is jiu-jitsu and everything else I do revolves around it. Unfortunately, I have seen great jiu-jitsu fighters train kickboxing for a few years and then go into a fight and forget all about jiu-jitsu and just punch and kick! It is hard for me to believe that. If your base if jiu-jitsu then learn other arts to complement what you have, but don't be so naïve as to try and beat an experienced kickboxer when you have only trained stand-up for a few years. If you're a grappler, then stick to what you know best and make everything else work around it.

**Q: Were you aggressive as a child?**
A: Not so much. When I was 7 and only a yellow belt, Sylvio and Marcelo Behring took me and my brother to fight in our first tournament. When we got there, I got extremely nervous and would not leave my parent's

side for a second. My brother fought and won, but that wasn't enough to give me the courage to fight. While waiting for them to call my name, I grew even more nervous and started clinging to my father's legs. I was so frightened that my father just couldn't bring himself to force me to fight. I still remember how relieved I was when I ended-up not having to fight. Who would have thought that eventually I would become one of the most active jiu-jitsu sports competitors and compete in mixed martial arts as well.

The lesson this taught me is that we all have fear and insecurities, but it is up to us to overcome that fear and try our best. I was frozen with fear and after that day I had to learn to deal with my fear and insecurities on the jiu-jitsu mat. Long hours of hard training brought me confidence and self-esteem, and I used those qualities to go forward in my competition career. The only thing that can beat fear is the confidence gained from experience.

*"Long hours of hard training brought me confidence and self-esteem, and I used those qualities to go forward in my competition career. The only thing that can beat fear is the confidence gained from experience."*

**Q: Were you a natural at jiu-jitsu?**
A: I think I can honestly say that jiu-jitsu was a very good physical fit for me, since my natural ability lies in my flexibility and strength. Of course, I have also worked very hard to achieve, maintain, and create effective techniques. You can have all the natural talent in the world but if you don't cultivate them then they are worthless. I have studied and still do all the basic jiu-jitsu positions, trying to adapt them and find new ways of moving from one position to another. I try to be creative and the only way I can do that is by keeping an open mind. I love to look at other competitors and grapplers and study what they do. The knowledge is out there for all of us to take. I do think that my exceptional flexibility helps my game flow more naturally. I have better control and awareness of my overall body mechanics with less effort than many other fighters.

To develop your own game you have to find what really works for you based on your physical characteristics. I have great flexibility and I use it to get the most possible benefits from certain techniques. Other people shouldn't necessarily try to copy my same exact movements because there are movements that one person can do and others can't. Find out how your own body moves – what your strong and weak points are – and then develop a game that works specifically for you.

**Q: Is your jiu-jitsu game constantly evolving?**
A: Nowadays, my personal game has more power and subtle techniques than in the past. I constantly create new techniques in order to always surprise my opponents. But don't misunderstand my words – I'm not saying that everybody should go out and create their own advanced techniques. That's stupid. You need many years of hard training and experience in the basics before you can really understand what works for you. It takes years to find that out. Sometimes you may think that a certain technique doesn't work for you and not work hard to learn it, but all what you are doing is justifying your own mental limitations – your mind is limiting your body. You need to work hard for many years before you can truly say that a certain technique is not good for you. At that point you'll have the understanding to develop and create your own movements. My personal game is a reflection of Brazilian jiu-jitsu in general – it is always growing and always being perfected.

**Q: What is the most important quality for a new jiu-jitsu student to have?**
A: My main advice is to have discipline and to follow the advice of the experienced teachers. There are experienced martial artists with a great deal of knowledge and it is up to new students to listen and learn from them. That way they save time and avoid making the same mistakes their teachers made. The young always think they know everything, but 20 years later they will realize that they simply didn't know anything when they started! I know because I've been there myself! For instance, new students always want to learn several new techniques every single day. They don't want to spend endless hours repeating the basic techniques because that's boring. In a few years, though, they'll realize that working hard on the basics is the secret to becoming a true champion and a great instructor.

**Q: Is it necessary to fight no-holds-barred matches to achieve good self-defense skills?**
A: I don't think a martial artist should ever use street fights to train them-

selves. Use martial arts for your own well-being and personal advancement. The satisfaction of overcoming your own weaknesses and expanding your physical ability will be enough to lead to confidence in the ring and self-defense skills on the street. I don't agree with the idea of going out to bars and parties and looking for fights. If you do that the only thing you show is your stupidity. Many people get into fights because they are insecure and deep down inside need to prove something to themselves. They have some kind of issues going on. A professional fighter does fight – but he does it in the ring with proper rules and respect for his opponent, not in the street. Martial artists who need to fight in the street only degrade their technical ability and show their immaturity.

*"Professor Helio is an example of a true martial artist. He is humble, he keeps teaching and training, and he is always open to evaluate and analyze any new movement or technique."*

**Q: What motivated you to train for so many years?**
A: My motivation comes from the fact that I need to keep learning because I think that no one knows it all – not even Professor Helio Gracie, the creator of Brazilian jiu-jitsu. Look at him, he still trains and is still learning in his 90s! The person who practices jiu-jitsu or any other martial art needs to be humble enough to keep learning. Professor Helio is an example of a true martial artist – he is humble, he keeps teaching and training, and is always open to evaluate and analyze any new movement or technique.

**Q: How do you prepare yourself before a fight?**
A: To get myself ready mentally, I listen to Elvis Presley backstage. He was a pioneer and broke many barriers in the music world. He set the pace and opened the doors for what *Rock and Roll* is today. One of the most important things a man can achieve is to leave a legacy and create or write something that in 200 years people will still talk about. That's why musicians, writers, artists and filmmakers are truly the building blocks of all cultures and societies. That is why I have so much respect for Elvis Presley and why I get so much inspiration from him.

*"If a fighter thinks that all he has to do is train, he is definitely wrong. He needs to keep an open mind and be aware that he doesn't know everything and needs to keep learning."*

On the physical side, I try to loosen up by doing a lot of stretching exercises. Those two things keep me at peace inside and prepare me to deal with the outside world. We all need to find those things that bring us peace and tranquility. Only then can we face the challenges of daily life. It is that way with martial arts. Jiu-jitsu is not something that you can leave at the academy – you need to take it hone with you, feel it, and then go back to the school to make it grow inside of you.

**Q: Who has been you biggest inspirations?**
A: Elvis Presley and Renzo Gracie are both great inspirations to me. I never met the King of Rock and Roll, but I was fortunate enough to meet Renzo Gracie and learn many things from him. These two men have been examples and inspirations to me.

**Q: What are the most important qualities of a successful fighter?**
A: I think that it is the sum of many things, however, discipline and humility are fundamental. If a fighter thinks that all he has to do is train, he is definitely wrong. He needs to keep an open mind and be aware that he doesn't know everything and needs to keep learning. Some fighters keep repeating what they know and they don't realize that the fighting game has changed and new techniques are being developed. You can get caught in a new technique simply because you think that you know everything there is to know. I have seen this to happen many times in sport jiu-jitsu competitions; someone develops a new choking technique, for instance, and chokes several of his opponents with it. Of course, the only way to prevent this from happening again is to study the new technique and find efficient ways to avoid and counter it.

A jiu-jitsu champion thoroughly knows the rules of the competition. He has a lot of genuine competitive experience, is in excellent physical condition, demonstrates superior attitude and character, is an expert at controlling his opponent's tempo and timing, and can change his game relative to the strengths and weakness of his adversary. All these qualities are developed through a dedicated training program that requires years of sacrifice and work. Championship performance comes only from the champion himself. A thousand perfect lessons cannot guarantee improvement. Winning is not found by who you learn from in the academy, but rather in the heart of the fighter who brings dedication and intelligence to a realistic and complete program.

**Q: Do you think fighters should cross-train or just do jiu-jitsu?**
A: Cross-training is necessary if you want to become a professional fighter. Look at the sport today – athletes are bigger, stronger and better conditioned than ever. In the past, martial arts techniques were the only thing we really cared about, but today you need to have technical skill, good nutrition, proper rest, solid cardiovascular endurance, a regular weight training program, and a stretching routine specifically designed for mixed martial arts. You need to supplement and support your pure jiu-jitsu training with any other aspects that will make you better and stronger. In sport jiu-jitsu there are various weight classes that in some ways limit the differences between the fighters. But the classes are fairly broad and sometimes you can be at the bottom range of your weight class and your opponent at the top. You also might be fighting up a class. So you need that extra edge. Then you need to combine your fight training with nutritional habits and enough hours of rest. You body needs these two as much as it needs the hard physical training.

*"Championship performance comes only from the champion himself. A thousand perfect lessons cannot guarantee improvement. Winning is not found by whom you learn from in the academy, but rather in the heart of the fighter."*

**Q: You have developed a personal training system, would you describe it?**
A: First of all, I am a very disciplined athlete and I maintain a rigorous training routine. My daily practice is comprised of Brazilian jiu-jitsu, muay Thai and boxing. I also supplement my technical workout with strength exercises done with elastic rubbers, which effectively prevents the injuries

# Grappling Masters

*"As human beings, we have many fears about a lot of different things in life, and we have to learn how to not be frozen by it. Defeating fear is a result of facing that fear head-on, again and again, as you do on the jiu-jitsu mat every day."*

usually related to weight training. I also spend time maintaining my flexibility, which for me is a very important aspect of my jiu-jitsu game.

**Q: How can a fighter control fear and nervousness in the ring?**
A: When someone starts to feel too much fear in training or competition, that means that they are not controlling themselves mentally. To reach the mental level required for successful competition you have to learn to rely on your mind to defeat that weakening fear. Fear is not a bad thing if you know how to use it to your benefit. You need to use it as a spark to start the fire inside. Unfortunately, many people get frozen, as I did when I was a kid, and can't get out there and perform. In the very end, defeating that fear inside of you is a reflection of what you are going to do in the other aspects of your daily life.

As human beings we have many fears about a lot of different things in life and we have to learn how to not be frozen by it. Defeating fear is a result of facing that fear head-on, again and again, as you do on the jiu-jitsu mat every day. If you run away from fear or give into it, then you will always be a slave to it. So don't run. Stand tall. Even if it is hard for you. You might not conquer it the first time or even the fiftieth time, but the important thing is to mentally resist and struggle against it. Over a period of time, if you resist your fear again and again, you will finally get used to it and then eventually conquer it. That is how the human brain works. The main thing is to face it.

**Q: You beat Kazushi Sakuraba in Pride 25 in a very tough fight. How do you remember that?**
A: Before the fight some people said, "Sakuraba was not that good anymore. He is not the same fighter he once was." Well, I didn't believe that. He has had some injuries lately but he is still a great fighter and he turned

out to be one of the toughest opponents I have ever faced. His kickboxing skills are first rate, even compared to K-1 kickboxers. And when you go to the ground he has a really good defense. He is not that good in submissions, but he knows how to defend against them. He is a very calm and strategic fighter and doesn't lose his head in the ring. Of course, once in a while he does crazy things and the audience goes wild. That's why people love to see him fight, because of the excitement he produces. But when you do crazy things, instead of focusing on your opponent and finishing a fight, you run the risk of eventually getting caught – and that's what happened in our fight. He landed a really good hand to my face and broke my nose. I started bleeding but that didn't bring me down. But then he relaxed and that gave me an opening. I came back up and landed a hard knee to his face and knocked him down. He was caught totally by surprise. Sakuraba didn't know that Elvis was a karate black belt. He thought that because I had a broken nose everything was over. But he was wrong.

**Q: What are your plans for the future?**
A: Keep doing more of the same – teaching and competing in jiu-jitsu, and fighting in MMA events whenever I get a good offer. I try to stay calm and relaxed and to balance all my opportunities in life. I don't want rush into anything, because when you rush you always end up crashing.

**Q: What does jiu-jitsu mean to you?**
A: The true meaning of the practice of jiu-jitsu is having respect for yourself and others. Respect for your training partners creates the friendly and unique environment in the world of Brazilian jiu-jitsu that everyone loves. The practice of jiu-jitsu in our daily lives and gives us energy and also fresh approach to things. I truly believe that by incorporating a physical discipline such as jiu-jitsu into our lives, we can balance and improve our overall existence.

*"The true meaning of the practice of jiu-jitsu is having respect for yourself and others. Respect for your training partners creates the friendly and unique environment in the world of Brazilian jiu-jitsu that everyone loves."*

# Grappling Techniques

*Using the open guard, Nino controls his opponent (1). By grabbing both sleeves and placing his right foot on the opponent's left biceps (2), Nino controls the opponent's balance at will (3). Then, he uses the left leg to push away the opponent's left knee and his right leg to push the opponent's left biceps (4). This forces the opponent onto the ground (5), where Nino mounts him and establishes control (6).*

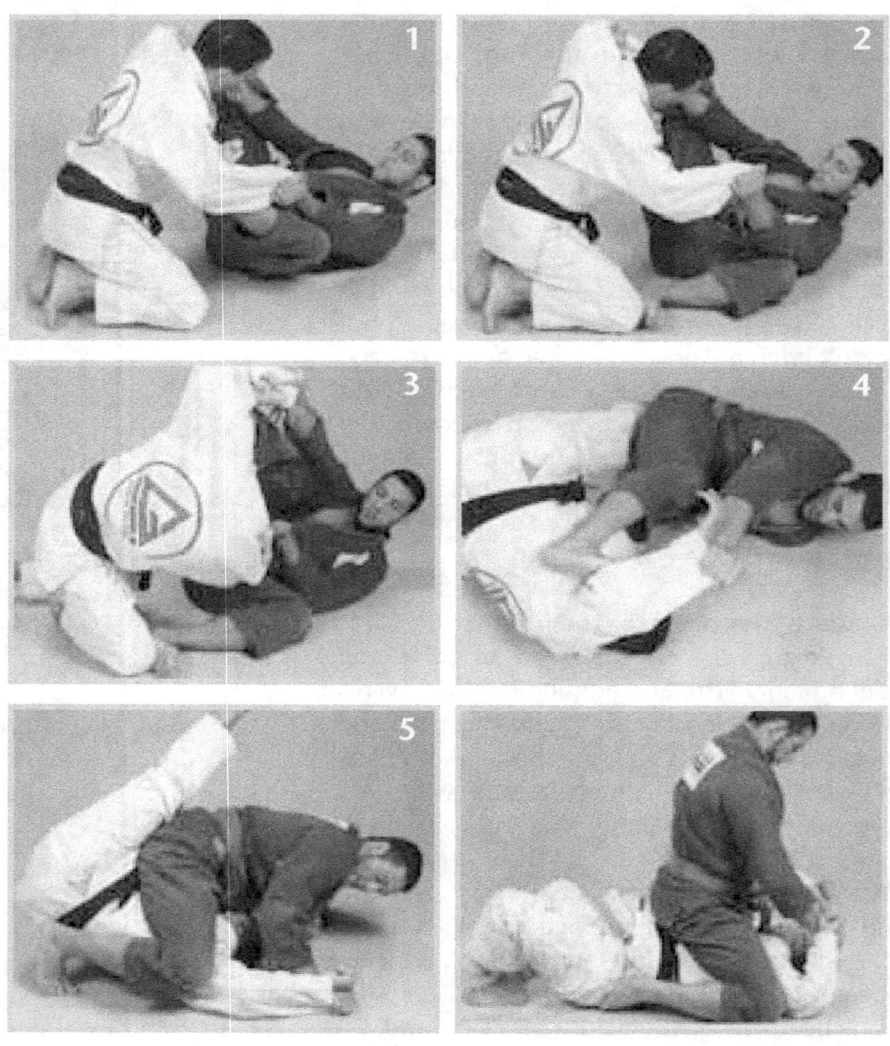

Nino controls Gerson Sanginitto inside his closed guard (1). Nino slides his left arm under the opponent's right arm (2), grabs his own hand (3) and then moves to the right to secure the grip (4). He pushes Gerson's right hip with his left leg (5), as he pulls down to apply a straight and gnarly armlock (6).

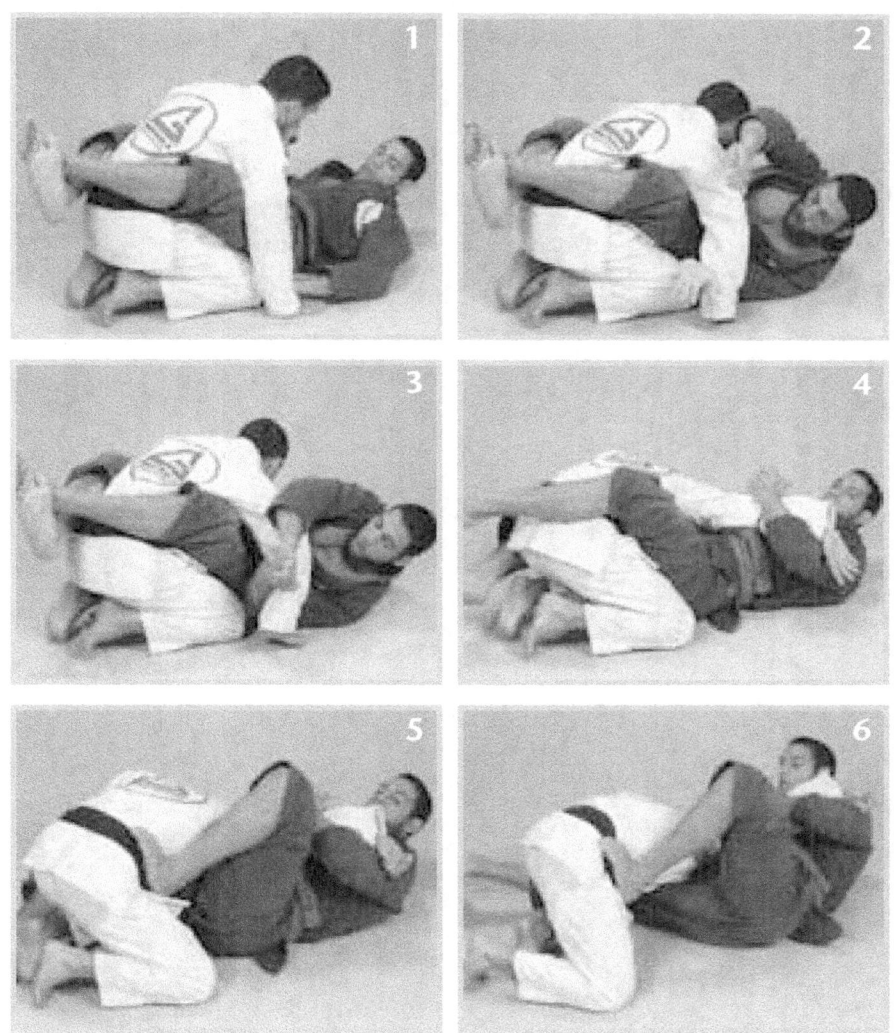

## Grappling Techniques

*Nino Schembri holds Gerson Sanginitto inside his closed guard (1). Nino breaks down Gerson's arm (2), puts his foot on his hip (3), shifts to the side (4), passes his leg over the head to gain a leverage point (5) and then applies pressure for the finishing armlock (6).*

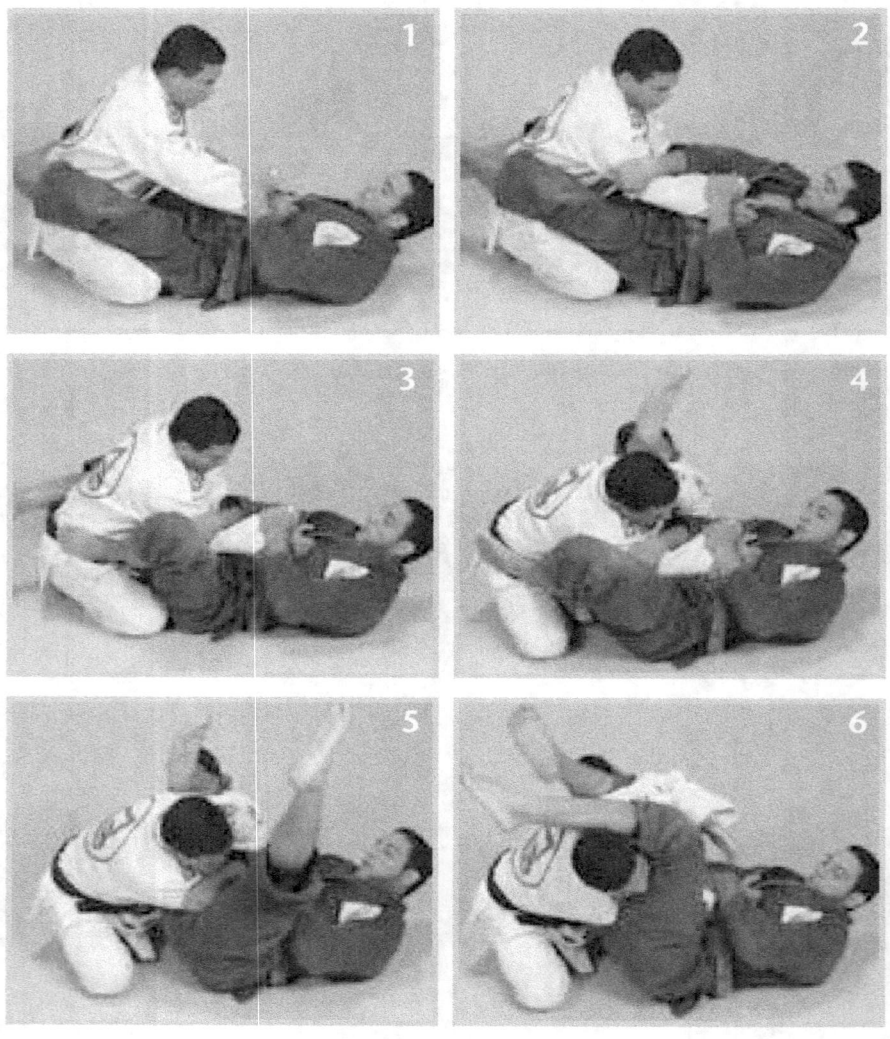

Nino Schembri holds Gerson Sanginitto in his butterfly guard (1). He shifts his weight back (2), propels Gerson into the air (3), unbalances him to the side (4), brings him down between his legs while securing the arm (5) and then applies pressure for the finishing lock (6).

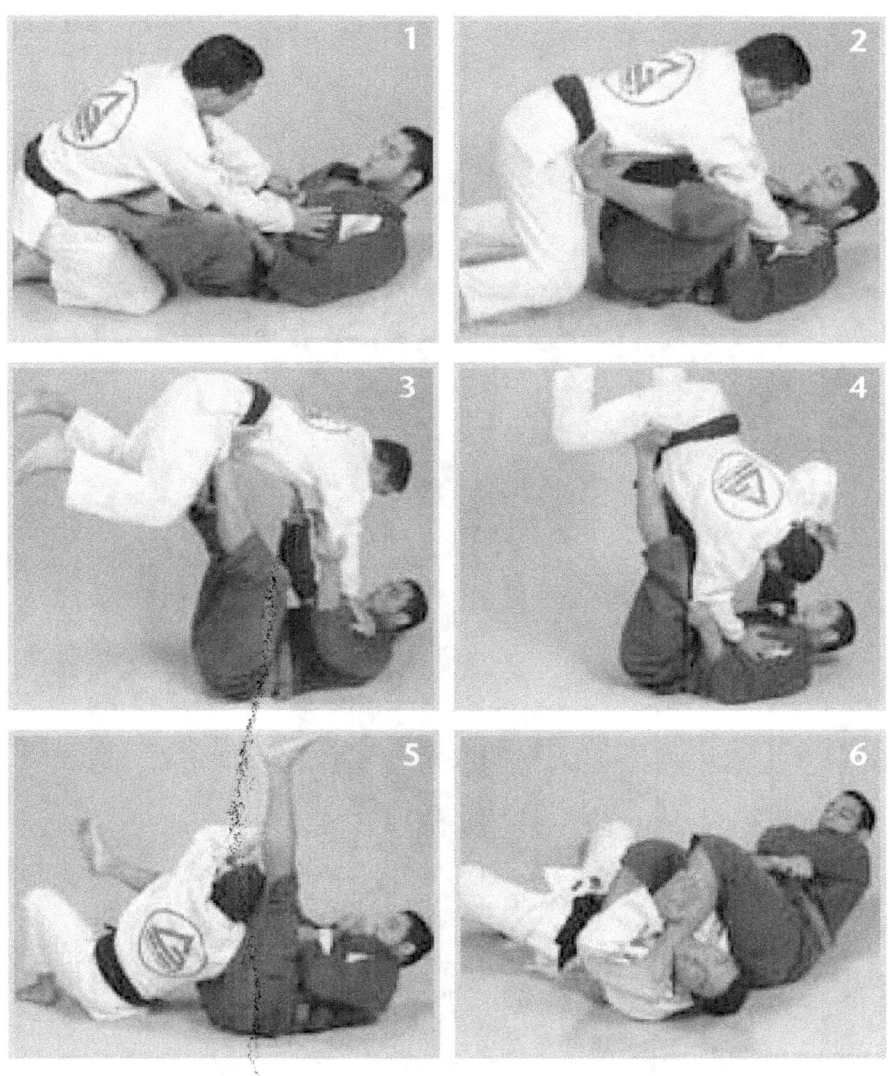

# KEN SHAMROCK

## *The King of Beasts*

AFTER FIGHTING IN JAPAN FOR THREE YEARS BEFORE HIS APPEARANCE IN THE VERY FIRST UFC IN DENVER, COLORADO, IN 1993, SHAMROCK FACED ROYCE GRACIE IN A MATCH THAT WOULD RESULT IN THE FIRST GREAT NO-HOLDS-BARRED FEUD TO POLARIZE AND THEN ENERGIZE THE WORLD OF MIXED MARTIAL ARTS. WITH MORE THAN 300,000 PAY-PER-VIEW BUYS FOR THEIR FAMED RE-MATCH, SHAMROCK ESTABLISHED HIMSELF AS A MARQUEE NAME WITH WORLDWIDE DRAWING POWER. SOON AFTER, WITH GRACIE RETIRING FROM THE UFC, SHAMROCK'S COMPETITIVE NATURE WOULD RESULT IN THE SECOND GREAT MMA FEUD – THIS ONE AGAINST DAN "THE BEAST" SEVERN – WHICH SHAMROCK SETTLED, AS USUAL, INSIDE THE OCTAGON... MAN-TO-MAN.

LEAVING THE UFC TO PURSUE A LUCRATIVE WWF PRO WRESTLING CAREER, WHICH SAW HIM GAIN EVEN MORE RENOWN AS "THE WORLD'S MOST DANGEROUS MAN," HE STILL HAD TIME TO ENGAGE IN ANOTHER FEUD WITH TITO ORTIZ. YEARS LATER, SHAMROCK RETURNED TO NO-HOLDS-BARRED WITH THE PRIDE FIGHTING CHAMPIONSHIPS IN JAPAN. HIS APPEARANCES THERE GAVE GREAT CREDIBILITY TO THE JAPANESE FIGHTING ORGANIZATION AND HELPED IT TO BECOME THE MOST POPULAR MMA SHOW IN THE WORLD.

BUT SHAMROCK HAS A LONG MEMORY AND THE THOUGHT OF TITO ORTIZ GNAWED AT HIM AND CAUSED HIM TO LEAVE PRIDE TO MEET ORTIZ IN A LONG-AWAITED UFC CHALLENGE MATCH. THE FINAL CHAPTER OF THE KEN SHAMROCK STORY IS FAR FROM BEING WRITTEN. ALWAYS LEARNING AND TRAINING, HE IS BETTER THAN EVER AND CLAIMS, "THE KEN SHAMROCK OF TODAY COULD DEFINITELY BEAT THE KEN SHAMROCK OF YESTERDAY."

**Q: American fans were introduced to you in the first UFC in 1993 in Denver, Colorado, but you had actually been fighting mixed martial arts long before that.**
A: That's true. I fought in Pancrase for three years in Japan prior to coming back to the United States to fight. When I came into the UFC, I did know some submissions. But I tell you... it was a totally different thing than Japan. For one thing, it was closed-fist punching in the UFC. In Pancrase, it was closed fist to the body but open fist to the head. When

# GRAPPLING MASTERS

*"In my first match in Japan, I defeated Yogi Anjoh. It was really fun and was definitely a good time. I was basically – by nature – a fighter. I was forced to learn how to protect myself at a young age so I was always down with defending myself."*

you hit the ground, it was just basic submissions. In the UFC, it was bare knuckles. You could punch on the ground and throw elbows. Really pretty much anything you wanted. So it was definitely a wake-up call for me as far as level and intensity.

**Q: How did you end up going to Japan in the first place?**
A: I was doing a little pro wrestling in North Carolina and a friend of mine showed me a tape of the UWF, which was a submission fighting organization in Japan. I watched the tape, and it looked really good. So I went down to Florida and tried out with a guy from Japan named Sammy Saranaka, who was their agent in the U.S. He watched me and said, "You got it. Let's do it." So as simple as that I was on my way to Japan. In my very first match in Japan, I defeated Yogi Anjoh. It was really fun and was definitely a good time. I was basically – by nature – a fighter. I started when I was 10 years old and that continued as a teenager. I was forced to learn how to protect myself at a very young age so I was always down with defending myself. During those days, I was usually facing two or three guys with knives, baseball bats, bottles or whatever they could get their hands on. Before I would fight a match in Japan, people would ask me, "Are you nervous? Are you scared?" And I'd just laugh and say, "Not compared to what I'm used to. This is a cakewalk." I mean there was no danger of two guys holding your arms on the ground while another guy kicked you in the head, or smashed you with a baseball bat, or pulled out a tire iron on you. Walking into the ring knowing it was

one-on-one with no weapons or foreign objects besides your opponent was actually a relief.

**Q: How were you approached about fighting in the UFC?**
A: I'd actually seen a UFC flyer that one of my students brought to me. It said they were looking for fighters for their first event. My student said, "Hey, man, look at this. They actually have this no-holds-barred fighting event coming up in the U.S." Now I'm very used to the entertainment world of pro wrestling, so my first reaction was, "OK, where's the catch?" At the time I was fighting over in Japan and I'd just won the *King of Pancrase* title. I was the champ over there. Anyway, I just sent it in and thought, "I'll just see what the catch is." There was no way that I thought it was for real. So a few weeks later I got a call from Art Davie. He said that they'd accepted me and that they would really like to have someone like me in the event. I told him that I'd do it. The whole time I was thinking it wasn't real. Eventually, I figured, something would come up and they'd tell me that you can't do this and you can't do that. I fully expected to hear that this guy had to win by knockout and that guy had to win by submission. I was looking for the set-up. I wanted it to be real, but I didn't believe that it would be.

*"I'd actually seen a UFC flyer that one of my students brought to me. It said they were looking for fighters for their first event. A few weeks later I got a call from Art Davie. He said that they'd accepted me and that they would really like to have someone like me in the event. I told him that I'd do it."*

**Q: When did you finally believe the UFC was real?**
A: The first time I knew it was legitimate and said, "Oh, wow! This is real!" was in the locker room during the first fight. Gerard Gordeau and the sumo wrestler were in the ring. This was the very first fight in the UFC... ever. Gordeau hit him with a right hand and dropped him to the mat. He followed that with a roundhouse kick that hit the sumo wrestler right in the face. The sumo wrestler's front teeth went flying out of the cage and

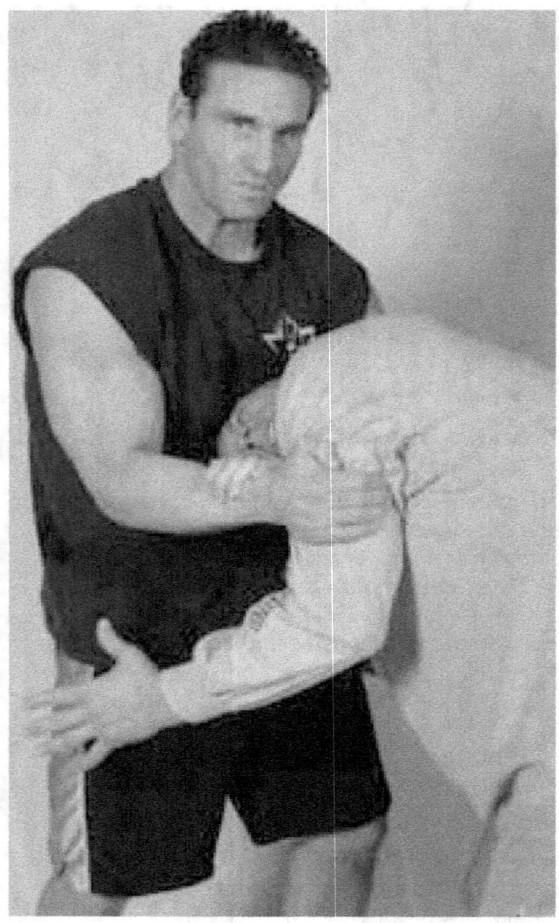

into the front rows. The crowd and everyone in the locker room were silent when that happened. Prior to the fight, everybody was all loud and up in arms. When the teeth went flying out of the ring, everybody just became dead silent; there was no noise at all. I swear it seemed liked forever. In reality, it was probably only for two or three seconds. Then the announcer, Bill Wallace, screamed out: "Oh, my God! His front teeth just went flying into the front row! Did you see that?" When he said that, the locker room went nuts and the crowd went nuts... and that was the very first fight of the UFC. In my mind, that was the very best way that the UFC could have ever been started. I mean, I know it was brutal and a tough fight and that guy got genuinely hurt – and we've fixed the sport since then – but that match left no doubt in anyone's mind, either in the audience or the locker room or the living room, that the fights in the UFC were real.

*"I know it was brutal and a tough fight and that guy got genuinely hurt, and we've fixed the sport since then, but that match left no doubt in anyone's mind – either in the audience or the locker room or the living room – that the fights in the UFC were real."*

**Q: Did seeing that make you feel nervous about going into the Octagon?**
A: Man, that didn't scare me. There were no firearms involved. He didn't get stabbed, he didn't get shot, he didn't get jumped by five guys with motorcycle chains. I had been fighting over in Japan in front of 40,000 people so this was no big deal to me. I walked into the Octagon through Patrick Smith's entourage and they were all dressed up in red and screaming that they were going to kill me.

Then Pat Smith said to me: "I'm gonna kill you, man." It didn't mean a thing to me. I just thought, "I've seen this crap before. So what?" We got into the cage, and I finished him in less than a minute with a heel hook. It was fun.

**Q: When you stepped into the Octagon for the very first time, did you feel that you were a fan favorite?**
A: Not at all. It was quite the opposite. My very first fight was in Denver, Colorado, against Patrick Smith, a hometown boy, and the crowd was screaming at me. That part got me a little nervous. I was thinking, "What the hell is going to happen if I actually beat this guy? Is the crowd going to riot and lynch me?" But the fight itself was no big deal. I can fight anybody one-on-one and deal with what happens afterwards. But when I won the crowd booed. I caught him with an anklelock and nobody knew what that was back then. Pat was screaming at me, "What the hell is this crap?" as he was hobbling around on one leg. I was public enemy No. 1. I broke his ankle. But what did they expect? That I would t use my best move? I watched it later on tape and Wallace was on TV saying, "He caught him with some type of leg hold or ankle twist or something." No one had any idea what it was. When I fought Royce in my second fight of the night, I almost caught him with the same thing. But he had his gi wrapped around my left arm and I'd never fought anyone with a gi before. So when I fell back to lock the ankle I just pulled him on top of me and gave him the mount. I just had no idea what he was doing with the gi.

*"Pat Smith said to me: 'I'm gonna kill you, man.' It didn't mean a thing to me. I just thought, 'I've seen this crap before. So what?' We got into the cage, and I finished him in less than a minute with a heel hook. It was fun."*

**Q: When people talk about the early UFC, it always turns to the fights between you and Royce Gracie. Why?**
A: Royce and I were the first great rivalry of the UFC. I really think it was

"Royce and I were the first great rivalry of the UFC. Fighting has never been about the rules or the event. What matters most is that the fans have an emotional attachment to the two guys in the ring. Rivalries define the sport."

the thing that got fans all around the world involved in the sport. Fighting has never been about the rules or the event. What matters most is that the fans have an emotional attachment to the two guys in the ring. Rivalries define the sport. We helped the UFC to get crazy numbers in the buy ratings – more than 300,000. The feud really made the sport grow. In that second fight I really blasted the hell out of him. It was somewhat slow paced, I'll give you that, but at that point in time they had no stand-ups or points. They'd just put in a time limit for that fight. Thank god they did – for Royce's sake – because they carried him out of the ring after that match. They put the time limit in for television schedule reasons. They didn't want to do it, but it was lucky for Royce they did.

Q: **When rules were put into the UFC, it seemed like a lot of fighters went onto other things. Was that one of factors that made Royce move on?**
A: Royce didn't move on because the rules changed. He moved on because the competition was getting tough and everyone was learning his game [Brazilian jiu-jitsu]. It was harder for him to win. They may want to say it was about the rules, but that's bull. He had a tough fight against Kimo. I really punished him in our fight. He came up against a tough, big wrestler, Dan Severn, and barely won. The competition was just getting better. They had a lot to lose if Royce Gracie got beat, so they got out when the getting was good. But with that being said, the truth of the matter is that Royce Gracie set the stage for how mixed martial arts fights are supposed to be fought. Things just changed

after a while, but it wasn't just about Royce. This was a change that came over the entire sport. When people started learning how to defend the clinch and beat the takedown and strikers started doing better against grapplers, you saw a shift. It went from grapplers winning all the time to guys like Maurice Smith, a kickboxer, winning against Mark Coleman, who was considered an unbeatable wrestler at the time. Guys started realizing that grapplers were short-handed when standing. So, they knew if they could keep the fight on their feet that they could beat the ground specialists – and that's just what happened. From then on, a grappler had to learn to use and throw his hands; otherwise, he was going to get beat. So Royce set the standard for the ground, and guys like Maurice Smith set the standard for blocking the takedown and throwing counters off the clinch. The game has so completely changed now that if you go in knowing only one thing you're at a huge disadvantage before the bell ever sounds.

*"Things just changed after awhile, but it wasn't just about Royce. This was a change that came over the entire sport. Royce set the standard for the ground, and guys like Maurice Smith set the standard for blocking the takedown and throwing counters off the clinch."*

**Q: Do you consider yourself a grappler or a striker?**
A: I'm definitely a grappler, but I also strike heavily. My hands, my feet and my takedowns are all coming together now. I've been doing a lot of training with Erik Paulson. Without a doubt, Erik Paulson is one of the most knowledgeable trainers in the world when it comes to combining different aspects of fighting into an integrated game. He knows everything, but he's a specialist in transitions between different phases, such as going from standing to a clinch and from a clinch to the ground and then back the other way.

*"Without a doubt, Erik Paulson (above) is one of the most knowledgeable trainers in the world when it comes to combining different aspects of fighting into an integrated game. He knows everything, but he's a specialist in transitions between different phases."*

**Q: You've gone from being hated to being a crowd favorite. When did the shift take place?**
A: I don't know exactly. I just think it got to a point that more people heard how unbeatable and how great jiu-jitsu was. That created a backlash. That happens in anything, and it happened to them. After our second fight, Royce kept saying things like he couldn't fight someone who didn't want to fight him. But it was obvious in the fight that I was the one on top who was landing punches. Then he left the UFC with no explanation... other than he didn't like the new rules. I think it made people respect me more, because I was the one who stayed and kept fighting. So from that point on things were different for me. Royce was tough, I'll give him that. He took a beating and didn't quit. But he didn't come back for

several years. When he did, it was in Japan. He won a fight and then got beat by Sakuraba and then by Yoshida. After that, Royce finally learned that you can't be one dimensional. He had been saying jiu-jitsu was all you needed for years. In the rematch against Yoshida, however, he came out as a kickboxer. This opened his grappling game, and he beat the crap out of an Olympic judo champion who had very nearly beaten Wanderlei Silva. It was like my last match against Royce. Even though it was ruled a draw, everyone knew who won. Royce's match against Yoshida was also ruled a draw but anyone who saw it knew who won. You can't just rely on jiu-jitsu, brother. People know that stuff. You've got to put your hands and feet together with it. At his weight, Royce is very good. No doubt about it. But his other big problem is that he still doesn't have the power he needs to fight top strikers. He needs to hit the weights, power up and put on some size. Until then, he's better off fighting ground specialists.

**Q: Why did you leave the UFC?**
A: I left the UFC purely for financial reasons. There was a lot of political pressure on them. They had lost their pay-per-view contract and just couldn't pay a living wage. I talked to the owner at the time and explained that I had four kids and a mortgage and that I couldn't fight for the money he was able to pay me. Therefore, I had to go do something else. So I went into pro wrestling, and I had fun as an entertainer. After a while, I just got the feeling that it was time for me to make a change. That's when I left pro wrestling and went to Japan to fight for Pride. They offered me the best deal. In my first fight back, I did very well. I then went through some personal things with a separation and divorce that affected my ring performance. I also had some injuries, and everything kind of snowballed on me. But I made it through, kept fighting, lived up to my commitments, then signed with the UFC to fight Tito

*"Royce's match against Yoshida was also ruled a draw, but anyone who saw it knew who won. You can't just rely on jiu-jitsu, brother. People know that stuff. You've got to put your hands and feet together with it. At his weight, Royce is very good. No doubt about it."*

Ortiz. That was just an awesome experience and an awesome set-up. It felt like I was going back into one of the first UFCs with those big shows we used to have. I walked in there and the feeling in the arena and the crowd was just amazing. And when I lost that match, even though it was tough and I was injured, I still felt like I gave it my all and it was all still good between the fans and me.

**Q: It seems now that the fans respect your effort more than they care about the actual outcome.**
A: People know me now. I've been around forever. I took the sport of mixed martial arts into the mainstream... or was always there with it, at least. I had the first great feud with Royce, then the second great feud with Dan Severn, then the third great feud with Tito. So I'm the history of the UFC. You can define its timeline with the timeline of my fights. People remember that passion more than they remember who won or lost, and I've won more than my share. And I've stayed with the UFC. I left for a while, but I came back to help the sport grow again in the U.S. The fans remember that. I've always respected my sport and the fans who support it. So they may support me, but I've also supported them with my effort and with my passion. The biggest live gate for the new UFC was between Tito and me. Before that it was Dan Severn and me. Before that me and Royce Gracie. I think people like to see me fight because I just want to go out there and battle. I have a lot of heart because I choose to have a lot of heart. I'll find a way to win. If I don't win, people will definitely get their money's worth. Against Tito, I was confident, but that's because I made myself confident. So even though I was injured going into the Tito fight (with a bad knee that didn't allow me to go side to side and kept me from shooting in), I still willed myself to take the fight. The UFC had set it up for me, and the fans wanted to see it. I felt an obligation to the sport to go into the Octagon, regardless of my physical condition. I made myself think I could win that fight, and I almost did. I came very close in one exchange to knocking him out.

**Q: Where do you see the MMA going? It started strong, faded away and now is back in the mainstream.**
A: There are just a few more little steps before the MMA blows up bigger than ever. It's just a matter of getting it in front of people so they can see it and fall in love with it. The MMA world now is just so much better that it ever was. If you watch the UFC now and then go back and watch an

early tape, you'll just laugh. A lot of those guys never should have been in there. It's 100 percent better technically, and from a promotional standpoint it is run 100 percent better. In the old days, you could never depend on who your opponent would be. Your opponent would be changed on the day of the event because the fighter you were supposed to face got drunk, or missed his plane, or just plain got scared and pretended to be hurt. Now, the guys who are in there want to be there. They're well trained, in top condition and are mentally ready. Even looking at myself, I'm much better now than I ever was in the early UFCs. Obviously, back then I was younger and had more jump in my step, but my approach to a fight, my set-ups and my understanding of my opponent is far superior. The Ken Shamrock of today could easily beat the Ken Shamrock of yesterday.

*"Obviously, back then I was younger and had more jump in my step, but my approach to a fight, my set-ups and my understanding of my opponent is far superior. The Ken Shamrock of today could easily beat the Ken Shamrock of yesterday."*

**Q: Who would you like to fight that would be good for the sport?**
A: Royce Gracie for sure. Can you imagine a rematch between us? Everybody would tune into that one. Royce and I are definitely not friends and it would be a worldwide phenomenon. It would exceed the buy ratings of our second match. If I wasn't fighting in it, I'd buy it myself. That match has everything – history, revenge, controversy and emotion. It would be legendary.

# MIKE SWAIN

## Throwing High

HE IS MORE THAN A JUDO ICON; HE OWNS AND OPERATES SWAIN SPORTS INTERNATIONAL, AND HE BREATHS JUDO 24 HOURS A DAY TO THE POINT THAT EVERYTHING HE DOES IS DONE FOR THE ART TO WHICH HE DEDICATES HIS LIFE. MARK SWAIN IS JUDO. AFTER BEING THE FIRST-EVER MALE JUDO WORLD CHAMPION FROM THE WESTERN HEMISPHERE, FOUR-TIME OLYMPIAN AND FIVE-TIME WORLD TEAM MEMBER FOR THE UNITED STATES OF AMERICA, MIKE SWAIN SWITCHED GEARS AND BECAME THE COACH FOR THE U.S. OLYMPIC TEAM. NOT ONLY DID HE PUT ALL HIS KNOWLEDGE AND EXPERTISE TO WORK FOR THE TEAM, BUT HE ALSO FOUND TIME TO CREATE AND DEVELOP A NEW APPROACH TO JUDO THAT HE CALLED PRO JUDO, AN ACTION-PACKED FORM OF JUDO COMPETITION THAT IS DESIGNED TO BE MORE SPECTATOR-FRIENDLY.

"JUDO OFFERS MUCH MORE OF WHAT WE CAN SEE TODAY IN THE MAIN INTERNATIONAL EVENTS, AND THAT'S THE GOAL OF PRO JUDO... TO BRING THESE ELEMENTS BACK SO PEOPLE CAN ENJOY A WONDERFUL ART AND AN EXCITING SPORT," SAYS SWAIN WITH PROFOUND PASSION AND LOVE.

WHEN NOT WEARING A GI, MIKE SWAIN CAN BE FOUND RUNNING HIS COMPANY, SWAIN SPORTS, A PROFESSIONAL BUSINESS PROVIDING HIGH QUALITY MATS, INSTRUCTIONAL VIDEOS, DVDS AND BOOKS RELATED TO THE SPORT. THIS IS MIKE SWAIN, A TRUE AMERICAN ICON IN THE INTERNATIONAL WORLD OF JUDO AND ONE OF THE MOST INSTRUMENTAL MEN IN THE DEVELOPMENT OF THE SPORT IN THE WESTERN WORLD.

**Q: How long have you been practicing judo and who were your teachers?**
A: I have been practicing judo for more than 35 years. I started when I was 8. My instructors were Rick Meola, a drill sergeant in the Marines, and om Seabasty of Colonial, NJ. Both were students of Yone Yonezuka Sensei at Cranford Judo & Karate Center. Yonezuka Sensei came to the United States of America from Japan in the early 1960s. I can honestly say that Yonezuka Sensei was my main teacher from the time I was 12 to 18, and he was the Olympic Coach in 1988 and 1992. During my Olympic and world competition days, I trained mostly at San Jose State University founded by Yosh

*"This experience helped me understand the training that goes into striking. The conditioning was great and different from all the previous conditioning routines I had as an elite competitor in judo. I think a good solid boxing and kickboxing background makes anybody a real fighter."*

Uchida. I also spent three or four years in Japan training at Nihon University and the Tokyo Police Academy. I learned from many great judoka and teachers.

Japan was my turning point for understanding the sacrifice required to become a world champion or compete at the Olympic level. I sold my lovely Chevy Nova in 1979, got the cash and took a plane to Japan with almost no money in my pocket. I told my parents that everything was taken care of once I landed. In reality, my contact never wrote back, so I didn't know what to expect. I didn't know what was going to happen to me. It was scary at first and very hard for a while, but I did learn a lot of things necessary to survive in life and also the demanding sacrifices you need to become a good judoka and a champion in the sport.

**Q: Have you ever trained in other martial arts styles?**

A: After my competition career in judo was over, I tried a little boxing and kickboxing with world champion Javier Mendez from San Jose, California. This experience helped me understand the training that goes into striking. The conditioning was great and very different from all the previous conditioning routines I had as an elite competitor in judo. I think a good solid boxing and kickboxing background – combined with knowledge of grappling arts like wrestling, judo and jiu-jitsu – makes anybody a real fighter.

**Q: How has your judo training changed over the years and what is your evaluation of the art's evolution?**

A: First of all, I would not say that judo was easy for me. However, because

I started at a very early age, this made things smoother for me... at least from the physical point of view. You learn better when you are young than when you are 50 years old. I began competing very soon, and I did place well in tournaments. This gave me a lot of motivation to train hard. Judo is a tough sport with little recognition for achievement at the Olympic level. It really is a sport that is practiced from the heart. I always remember my sacrifices in Japan and the hours of training each and every day included judo, running, weight training and other forms of exercise. These really built my fundamental character to be the best I can be at anything in life. This is the essence of what judo really is about. It is a vehicle to get the best out of you in every aspect of life.

Judo has evolved with the proliferation of the sport throughout the world because of the Olympic Games. Each region of the world brings a little of its own flavor, such as the Soviet Union with sambo and wrestling. Judo is now a combination of many styles. However, pure technique still prevails. The rules have been changing to push more action and they give a little less time to get ground techniques off, but you still see the top players able to perform beautiful throws and submissions because the timing and technique are perfected.

*"Judo is now a combination of many styles. However, pure technique still prevails. The rules have been changing to push more action and they give a little less time to get ground techniques off, but you still see the top players able to perform beautiful throws and submissions because the timing and technique are perfected."*

**Q: What is your opinion of fighting events such as the UFC and other submission grappling competitions?**
A: I think they have had a big affect in putting martial arts back in the spotlight. It made people really look at what they study and why they

# GRAPPLING MASTERS

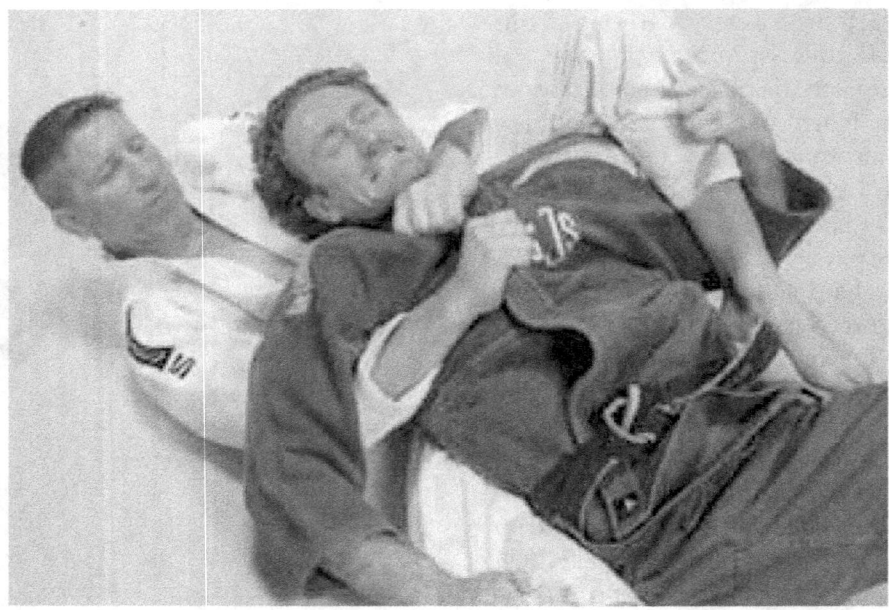

*"Jiu-jitsu and judo are close in techniques. Yet, because of the rules, they are two different games. Both arts have been developed based on different premises. That is the main reason why – although they seem to be very similar – they are in fact very different."*

study. It forced people to cross train in different areas of standing and the ground game because you really need both to enter that arena.

Jiu-jitsu and judo are very close in techniques. Yet, because of the rules, they are two different games. You can take a great judo player, and he will struggle in a jiu-jitsu match and vice versa. Both arts have been developed based on different premises. That is the main reason why – although they seem to be very similar – they are in fact very different. Yamashita Kashiwazaki, a 10-time All-Japan champion, is one of the best judo fighters I have seen take advantage of the ground. He was one of my mentors while I competed. In today's competition, I like Flavio Canto from Brazil. I am not sure if he competed in jiu-jitsu events. However, in the transition from throws to the ground, he is as smooth as they get.

**Q: Do you think that these events are positive for the overall spectrum of martial arts systems or only for the professional fighter?**

A: I think that any time you step into a fighting ring you challenge yourself and become a stronger person for trying, regardless if you win or lose. As long as you do not underestimate the commitment and are prepared at that level, it is all right to go for it. These events require a lot of training and a certain mental approach that you should find out if you have or not. It is important to research this internally to see if these types of competitions are for you or not. Once you have it clear, then it is all up to you.

**Q: Do you think that the judo level in Europe and the U.S. has caught up with Japan's or is there still a major difference?**

A: Judo is an individual sport. If you want to become a world champion, you have to travel and train where the best are training. The unique thing about judo is that you are welcome in Japan, Europe, the U.S. and virtually anywhere in the world you want to train. The attitude is pretty much, "If you can handle the workouts at that level, then come on over." That attitude of the judo philosophy has produced world champions from everywhere... big and small countries alike. There are more than 182 countries participating in the Olympics for judo alone. That is one of the biggest participation levels of any sport. Japan overall still dominates because of how things are organized. I talked about that before. Technique and timing will prevail in the end. However, the old Soviet countries produce some very tough fighters with unorthodox styles

*"Any time you step into a fighting ring you challenge yourself and become a stronger person for trying, regardless if you win or lose. As long as you do not underestimate the commitment and are prepared at that level, it is all right to go for it."*

*"The old Soviet countries produce some tough fighters with unorthodox styles so you had better be in shape and ready to fight. Their style is a combination of sambo, wrestling and traditional judo. The grips and other elements are different. Unless you know how to deal with them, those techniques can represent a serious threat to you."*

so you had better be in shape and ready to fight. Their style is a combination of sambo, wrestling and traditional judo. The grips and other elements are very different. Unless you know how to deal with them, those techniques can represent a serious threat to you.

**Q: Nowadays, judo is considered a sport. Do you agree with that idea or do you think it is a martial art?**
A: I think judo is a martial art first. To become a champion in the sport of judo, you must understand that judo is about making your character stronger through tough physical and mental practice on the mat. You also have to have mutual respect for your training partner to help each other become better. You need training partners to get better. If you do not respect them, they will not be there for you. That's the bottom line. I have not ever met a world or Olympic champion who does not understand this philosophy.

**Q: Do you feel that you still have further to go in your judo studies?**
A: Definitely! I became the first world champion from the U.S. in Essen, Germany in 1987. Since then, I have learned a tremendous amount about judo techniques and philosophy. Also, by teaching judo, I have been able to see things in the art that I wasn't aware of in my previous stages of development. I find I learn the most about judo from teaching beginners because it brings you back to the absolute basics of making a technique work against a defending opponent. You have to be able to break everything down in such a way that the beginner understands what he is doing and why is doing it. By doing this, you have to constantly review and revisit your knowledge and technical foundation of the art. Every time you

teach a basic movement to a beginner, you learn something new about the technique. It is a very interesting process that I recommend to all those who are truly interested in reaching the higher levels of understanding in judo.

**Q: What do you consider to be the major changes in the world of judo since you began your training?**
A: A lot of things have changed during the time I have been training in the art. The uniforms have become bigger and easier to grip because of the rules, the fighting area is smaller and the break-up of the Soviet Union has resulted in many smaller countries having some very strong fighters. From the technical point of view, the art has evolved tremendously. The conditioning methods used around the world are a thousand times better than the ones we practiced when I started to train. Things improved greatly, although other things have been left along the way. I guess that happens in every aspect of life. To win something, you must leave something behind.

Another aspect that has been introduced in many countries is mixing or adding elements from other grappling arts to judo. Cross-training is great when properly done; it keeps things fresh for the fighters and students. Just make sure your core techniques in the sport come first before any other type of training. First develop strong basics and fundamentals. Then you can build upon that and add elements that help to improve certain technical areas of your game. Three decades ago this was unthinkable. I have to say that I consider myself a modern instructor, but I try to keep all the good traditional values and principles taught in the classical art of judo as conceived by Professor Kano. I don't see any conflict at all by

*"Cross-training is great when properly done; it keeps things fresh for the fighters and students. Just make sure your core techniques in the sport come first before any other type of training. First develop strong basics and fundamentals."*

*"In training, you do not always face someone who you can control. Sooner or later you'll have to face someone who is better than you and who is capable of controlling you."*

doing both things; in fact, I believe that combining those two approaches is what makes judo a real and valuable vehicle for personal growth in our modern society.

**Q: What would you say to someone who is interested in starting to learn the art of judo?**
A: First, you learn by falling so be prepared to take a lot of falls. Second, you also need to leave your ego outside the dojo. Being thrown all the time is a very humbling experience, but it prepares you psychologically for what is ahead of you in the path of judo. As a beginner, you should be the one falling. At the same time, it is a way of learning how to protect yourself when someone applies a good throwing technique on you. In training, you do not always face someone who you can control. Sooner or later you'll have to face someone who is better than you and who is capable of controlling you. Thus, as I mentioned, it is better to know how to fall. Next, all students should always be humble and focus all their energy in training. Try to rest as much as you can and follow a good diet because the fuel you put in your body is extremely important. Also, try to stay motivated. For me, working out in judo leaves me with a different feeling than going for a run or weight training. There is a certain spiritual fulfillment that I get from doing the martial arts. I am not sure I can explain it, but it is very satisfying. Striving to be the best at whatever I do – at work or on the mat – is what keeps me motivated.

**Q: Do you think it is necessary to engage in free fighting to achieve good self-defense skills?**
A: I do not think it is necessary. If you want to be a good street fighter, then you better have a lot of fights in the street with no rules. It certainly cannot hurt to be in good condition and have fighting skills, but sport competitions won't prepare you to be a street fighter. A real self-defense situation has almost nothing to do with a tournament. The street is a completely different environment that brings many other elements into the equation. Judo is a sport under certain regulations for the competitor's safety. A self-defense situation is everything but safe. From the technical point of view, when facing a real danger, you need to know how to use your whole body to defend and attack, and that includes your hands, legs, elbows, knees, etc. In sport competition, that is a totally different scenario. You must take yourself outside the comfort zone. One example of this is to go to Japan or Europe and train in an intense, more difficult place with a different culture and food. It sounds easy but many people come back quickly to their comfort zone. You are going to win and lose. The question is how well you come back from your defeats.

*"A real self-defense situation has almost nothing to do with a tournament. The street is a completely different environment that brings many other elements into the equation. Judo is a sport under certain regulations for the competitor's safety. A self-defense situation is everything but safe."*

**Q: Did you have any particular method of psychological preparation that you used before an important competition or match?**
A: I think having your own personal method is the key. There are some

*"The day of the competition I had a certain way to warm up, and I used set breathing patterns before I went out on the mat. The key is to focus on your own techniques and visualize yourself completing these techniques, and you have to forget about your opponent."*

things you do that make you relax before a big event. For me, it was always to go for a short run the night before. I always did this alone. The day of the competition I had a certain way to warm up, and I used set breathing patterns before I went out on the mat. The key is to focus on your own techniques and visualize yourself completing these techniques, and you have to forget about your opponent. There are some phrases I like to keep alive to motivate the students and myself. For example, "The harder you try the luckier you get." "Pain is only a sensation." "If you use one excuse, you will use every excuse." "You learn by taking falls." It is important to have a strong mental framework that allows you to face any challenge with enough security in yourself.

**Q: What do you consider to be the most important qualities of a successful judo competitor and how does the fear factor affect a good fighter?**

A: Good conditioning, good technique and – most importantly – an awesome fighting spirit. I think these three characteristics sum it all up. Competition training should be shorter and more intense than a regular training session. As you get closer to a competition, all phases of your training – including weights, running and judo – should all be on the same page... shorter and more intense. Intensity is the key word here. You have to go for quality.

Fear is a definite motivator for any competitor. I can say that everyone feels fear at one time. The ones who channel it into a positive training tool with confidence will come out on top. Most importantly, I believe it is a matter of how you control the fear.

**Q: What advice would you give to students about supplementary training, including weights, running and stretching?**

*"Competition training should be shorter and more intense than a regular training session. As you get closer to a competition, all phases of your training – including weights, running and judo – should all be on the same page... shorter and more intense."*

A: At the world and Olympic level, all these supplementary aspects of the training are a must. I teach at San Jose State University. We have about 50 black belts training for national level and above. They all have a program that includes weight training, running and judo practice. Today you simply can't make it to the podium without a professional training program that involves cardio, strength and technical aspects in it. Technique is what you actually use in competition, but all the other aspects of the physical conditioning are the elements that make the technique work under pressure.

You need these additional elements in your training if your goal is win competition titles. Today you have to be an athlete – not only a good technical judoka to win in a world or Olympic event.

**Q: What are your thoughts on the future of judo competitions and what do you think should be done to improve the sport?**
A: I have tried twice to promote a more entertaining style of judo for the public. The first was called New Sport Judo. I did this with the help of Scott Coker, the K-1 promoter. The second was Pro Judo. Both made it to ESPN 2. They were very entertaining in the eyes of the spectator because the rules were in English and the point system easy to follow. The key is to have the funding to keep it going and keep it in front of the public long enough for them to catch on.

**Q: Why did you start Pro Judo?**
A: The truth is that judo is very popular in Europe and Asia, but it hasn't yet caught on in the U.S., and that's a fact. On another side, the Olympics are controlled by television interests and networks that do not necessarily work for the benefit of the sport. My idea was to create something that was more spectator-friendly with more action and much more fast-paced. This will eventually help to promote judo through television. Pro Judo is not meant to compete with the Olympics in any way, shape or form but to bring the sport closer to the audiences. Spectators look for action and entertainment in any sporting event. That is why football, basketball and baseball have changed their format over the years to fill what the audiences require.

**Q: After judo became an Olympic sport, many of the old and classical techniques have been forgotten because they have no place in modern competition. What is your opinion about this?**
A: I think Kano Sensei would be very proud that judo was the first martial art accepted into the Olympics and has grown into more than 182 participating countries. Many people may criticize where judo is now and complain that many things have been lost. But if you look carefully, you'll see a great evolution in the art and the immense popularity gained throughout the years. This is worth the effort and the changes that have occurred. I truly believe that we have gained more that we have lost along the way. It is true that to go forward you have to leave things

behind, but I'm happy because what judo represents today is something bigger that what it was in the past.

**Q: Whom do you consider to be the most relevant names in judo history?**
A: I think there are many great competitors, but there are several who stand out. First, there is Isao Okano, the 1964 Olympic champion, the lightest person to win the All-Japan Championships and twice world champion. We have had the pleasure of him teaching at San Jose State a few times a year because his son, Tetsu Okano, graduated from San Jose State and trains with us. Another is Yamashita, the Olympic and world champion and 10 time All-Japan champion. He never lost a match in international competition. That is simply unbelievable. Another is Anton Geesink, a fighter from Holland who won the heavyweight title in the 1964 Olympics. He has been a pioneer of judo in Europe and a true legend not only in the old continent but all over the world.

**Q: And finally, do you have any advice you would like to give to the judo fans and martial arts practitioners in general?**
A: Never give up and train as hard as you can. This is a very basic principle in all the budo arts, and I know it sounds very simple. But it is extremely difficult to understand and to apply in our daily lives. And that's the real challenge ahead of us.

*"Never give up and train as hard as you can. This is a very basic principle in all the budo arts, and I know it sounds very simple, but it is extremely difficult to understand and to apply in our daily lives."*

## Grappling Techniques

Mike Swain faces his opponent in an orthodox guard (1). Swain releases his left hand and moves his left leg behind the opponent's left leg (2). This throws the opponent's balance off (3), and he tumbles to the floor (4), where Swain falls on top (5). Swain adjusts his body (6) and finishes with a complete s control (7).

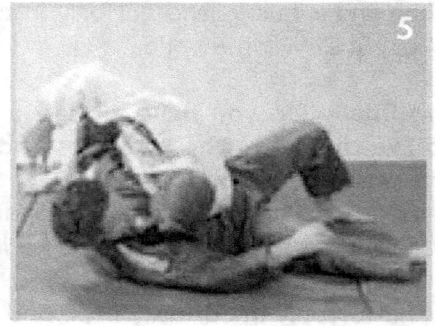
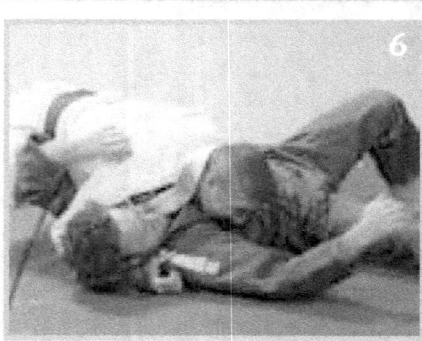

Swain faces his opponent (1). To unbalance his opponent, Swain takes a step back (2). This also creates momentum (3) for Swain to rock and roll onto his back (4) and launch his opponent (5-6). Once the opponent hits the floor, Swain mounts him and finishes him off with a frontal choke (7).

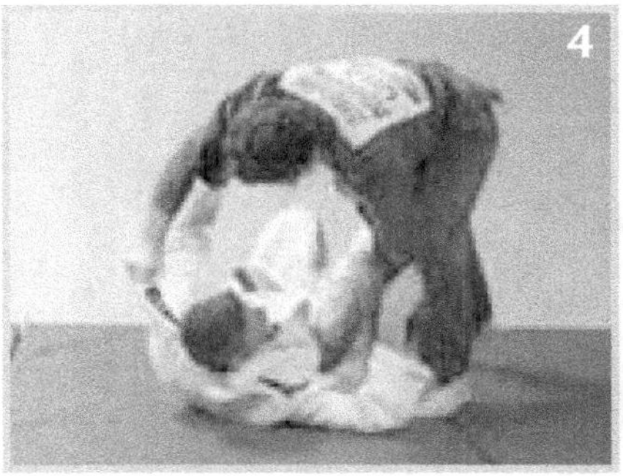

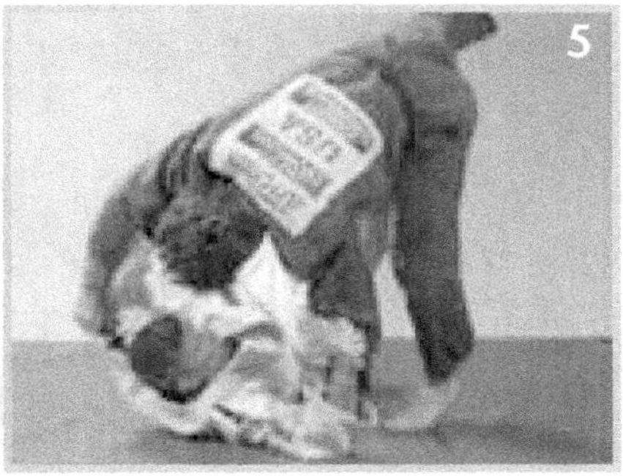

## Grappling Techniques

*Using an unmatched side grip (1), Mike Swain pulls the opponent close (2) so he can reach around and grab his belt (3). Swain moves his left leg inside the opponent's (4) and then sends him airborne (5-6). The former Olympian ends up in the mount, where he applies a front choke (7).*

Swain attacks his opponent from the back (1). He puts his right foot around the opponent's side and starts to pass his left arm between the opponent's neck and right arm (2). Without releasing his grip, Swain rolls forward (3) and falls on the opponent's side (4). Swain then grabs the opponent' left leg (5). He quickly passes to the other side (6) and applies an armlock (7).

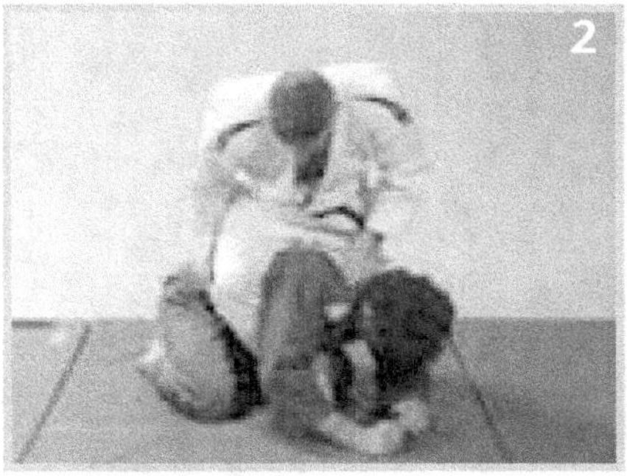

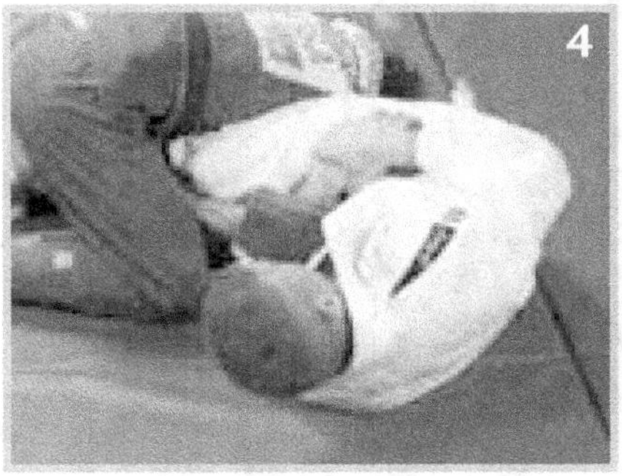

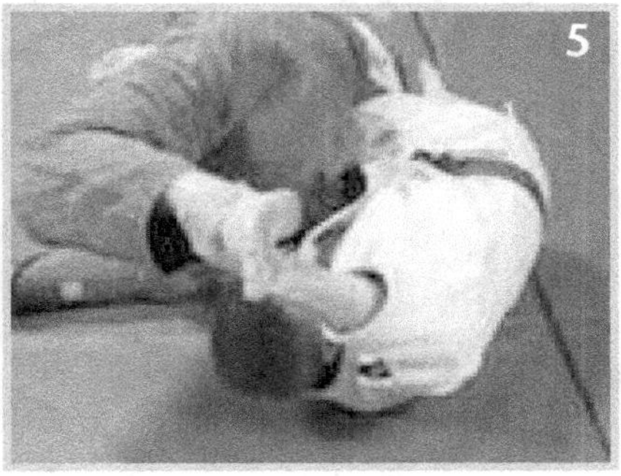

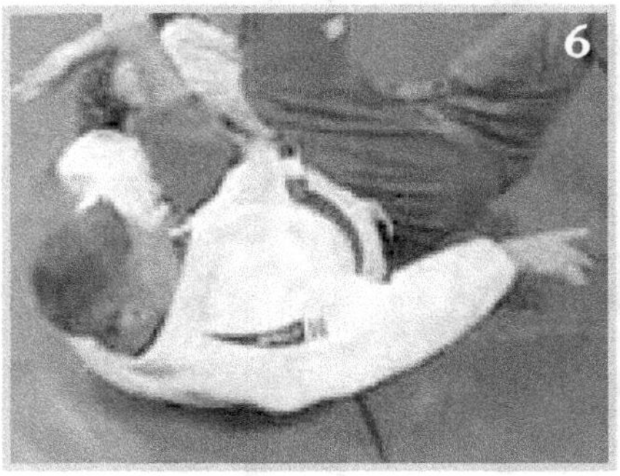

# LEO VIEIRA

## *The Young Gun Of Brazilian Jiu-Jitsu*

LEO VIEIRA'S SPECTACULAR VICTORY AT ABU DABHI 2003, WHERE HE GAVE A CLINIC ON JIU-JITSU TECHNIQUES TO THE BEST GRAPPLERS IN THE WORLD, MADE THE NAME "LEOZINHO VIEIRA" STAND ALONE. AS INTENSE AS HE IS ON THE MAT, HIS FRIENDLY MANNER AND GREAT SENSE OF HUMOR HAVE MADE HIM JUST AS WELL-LIKED OFF OF IT. STRONGLY ROOTED IN TRADITIONAL VALUES, THIS YOUNG GUN OF BRAZILIAN JIU-JITSU IS A LIVING ENCYCLOPEDIA OF THE MOST ORIGINAL AND UNEXPECTED TECHNIQUES OF THE "GENTLE ART." THROUGH MANY YEARS OF DEDICATION AND TRAINING, LEO VIEIRA HAS DEVELOPED A DYNAMIC WAY OF ADAPTING AND INTEGRATING THE FUNDAMENTALS OF BRAZILIAN JIU-JITSU WITH UNIQUE, ACROBATIC MOVEMENTS THAT FIT HIM PERFECTLY. EXTRAORDINARILY TALENTED, HE HAS REACHED A LEVEL WHERE "AVERAGE" OR "MEDIOCRE" IS NO LONGER ACCEPTABLE, AND "EXTRAORDINARY" IS HIS MINIMUM ACCEPTABLE STANDARD.

**Q: How long have you been practicing jiu-jitsu?**
A: I began training in jiu-jitsu when I was 7. My instructor is Romero "Jacare" Cavalcanti. He is one of the best jiu-jitsu teachers in the world with a very special skill to bring out the best in a student. There are teachers who only teach, but Jacare can look at you and see all the aspects you need to improve on to reach your potential. He is very analytical and a very giving person. I have learned from him how to deal with situations where the pressure is extremely high, when a fighter usually gets very nervous and can't his emotions. His knowledge of the art is amazing and his ability to show how to make different technical concepts work together is really amazing.

**Q: Have you ever trained in other martial arts styles such as karate or kickboxing?**
A: Not really. In Brazil, if you start training jiu-jitsu is very uncommon to go into another martial art. Only those who want to fight *vale tudo* train in other styles like Thai boxing or boxing to complement jiu-jitsu. I have

*"I know there are people in Brazilian jiu-jitsu who don't like to change, evolve and create new things. I am the opposite. I like to analyze and study different ways of improving whatever technique I'm doing. You must keep an open mind to be able to see and adapt new movements."*

always felt attracted to jiu-jitsu and so never felt the need to go to another martial art. I don't recommend that anyone jump from style to style to find the perfect style. I believe this is not a good way to bring out your best, especially when you don't have a strong foundation in any. Only when you have a high level in one art can you add other things effectively.

**Q: What was your early training like?**
A: I remember a long time ago that I was watching white belts train. They were doing something weird so I asked them to show me what they were doing. They started laughing and showed me. There was common sense in the position, so I took that movement, added some logical elements of jiu-jitsu, and started practicing it. As it turns out, that particular technique is now one of my favorites. Some of the details had to be changed, but the funny part is that two white belts, using common sense, created a new position! I know there are people in Brazilian jiu-jitsu who don't like to change, evolve, and create new things. I am the opposite. I like to analyze and study different ways of improving whatever technique I'm doing. You must keep an open mind to be able to see and adapt new movements.

**Q: But don't people sometimes train too many techniques instead of sticking to the basics?**
A: Unfortunately this is something that I see all over the world. Blue and purple belts see techniques used by world champions in tournaments and they try to learn and sue them immediately. This is not bad, but beginners need to work the basics to the level of a black belt. Only then can you start to add variations from other people. For instance, I have seen people that started to use the open guard, simply because they didn't take the time to master the closed guard! If you train hard and develop a

strong closed-guard then you won't necessarily need to open your legs all the time and work from the open position.

Of course, there are times when you face a bigger and heavier opponent when your leg can't wrap the opponent's waist. Then you need to use the open or spider guard. My advice is to stick to the basics and work very hard until you can make these basics work any time and under any circumstances. This way you'll have very strong basics and will be capable of surprising your opponent with strong techniques. Train the basics first because they are the foundation for everything else.

**Q: Has your personal jiu-jitsu developed over the years?**
A: I have never stopped learning! The fundamental techniques are the same for everyone, but after many years of training you develop a personal way of doing jiu-jitsu. I always compare this to cooking – rice is rice, chicken is chicken, and carrots are carrots, wherever you live. What makes a difference is the way a good cook combines and prepares these elements. Jiu-jitsu is the same. We all know the same techniques but we spice them up with a personal approach that gives each game an individual flavor. Then when you start competing, your jiu-jitsu becomes more streamlined and direct. You start using only those things that really work. It doesn't mean that you don't train all the moves, but when you compete you have to become really good at a few things in order to win.

*"My advice is to stick to the basics and work very hard until you can make these basics work any time and under any circumstances. Train the basics first because they are the foundation for everything else."*

**Q: Has jiu-jitsu changed over the years now that so many people are cross-training?**
A: Jiu-jitsu has evolved a lot in the last few years with new techniques and positions that have been developed by young champions. There is nothing wrong with that because that's the nature of competition. When you test yourself in different environments like Abu Dhabi where we fight

*"It is difficult to say where the sport will be 10 years from now, but the truth is that mixed martial arts is not a sport that everybody can play. It takes a certain kind of individual, with the right attitude and the time to train properly."*

without a gi, you need to incorporate technical elements like takedowns and reversals used in wrestling. Later on, when you go back to a jiu-jitsu tournament, you may end up using these techniques even though they were not originally from jiu-jitsu. Personally, I don't see a problem with this. It is a logical evolution based on achieving your competition goals. I don't spend time arguing philosophically about whether it is pure or impure. I leave that for the philosophers. I just know that you have to do it to win.

Q: What is opinion of no-holds-barred events?
A: Vale tudo fighting is not Brazilian jiu-jitsu. Jiu-jitsu practitioners do very well in these types of events because of the effectiveness of the art, but it doesn't mean that vale tudo exemplifies the essence of Brazilian jiu-jitsu. This type of fighting has been very important in giving credit to the art of jiu-jitsu. Royce Gracie made a tremendous world impact fighting in the UFC and defeating all his opponents with jiu-jitsu. In short, I believe these events are positive for jiu-jitsu but we can't mistake one thing with the other because they are very different.

Q: Do you think that the ADCC competition system is the future of the sport?
A: It is very difficult to say where the sport will be ten years from now but the truth is that mixed martial arts is not a sport that everybody can play. It takes a certain kind of individual, with the right attitude and the time to train properly. Many jiu-jitsu champions don't feel like entering MMA – they simply don't like it. It is here when grappling competitions like Abu Dhabi come into play. You can be a wrestler, a jiu-jitsu guy, a judoka, or a sambo practitioner and compete with a good chance of winning. Different grappling methods can compete against each other under basic rules that are fair to all styles. Regardless of your original method, you have to understand and even learn technical aspects of the other grappling systems you'll face. In MMA, a simple wild punch can finish the fight, but in a grappling compe-

tition like Abu Dhabi you have to be very technical or you will lose your first match.

**Q: Is no-holds-barred good for martial arts?**
A: It's a double-edged sword. Martial arts get recognition through these events, but people then assume that jiu-jitsu and other martial arts are simply an MMA style for cage fighting. The true art of jiu-jitsu embodies much more than vale tudo, MMA, and cage fighting.

**Q: Do you think that jiu-jitsu level in the U.S. has caught up with Brazil?**
A: The skill level found in American jiu-jitsu practitioners has improved substantially. There are more competitions in the United States and more Brazilian champions are invited to compete, which also increase the level. The main difference lies in the fact that in Brazil we have competitions every weekend. Practitioners are competing all the time in regional, state, or national tournaments. The level is very high and practitioners are used to the pressure of elite competitions. This makes a difference. It is difficult to say when the U.S. will catch Brazil. If you ask me when Brazil will catch the U.S. in baseball, it is impossible to say. In Brazil, jiu-jitsu is like baseball in the U.S.

*"Jiu-jitsu is more than a simple sport. It has a certain philosophy to its practice. It can be used as a sport but the right jiu-jitsu training develops more than the practitioner's body. Jiu-jitsu is something that you can practice all your life and always enjoy."*

**Q: Do you consider jiu-jitsu to be only a sport?**
A: Jiu-jitsu is more than a simple sport. It has a certain philosophy to its practice. It can be used as a sport but the right jiu-jitsu training develops more than the practitioner's body. I don't want to sound religious, but the deeper aspects of any martial art bring a certain spiritual meaning and benefit to the student's life outside the academy. A sport is simply a sport.

*"I'm far from being a master. It doesn't matter if you win 10 world championships and everybody tells you that you are the best. That means nothing to me. I try to keep my center even and my focus consistent... not only in my jiu-jitsu but also in other aspects like family, friends and business."*

Once you can't play it anymore you are done. Jiu-jitsu is something that you can practice all your life and always enjoy.

**Q: Do you feel that you have further to go in your training?**
A: Of course! I keep training because I see that I still have to improve many aspects of my jiu-jitsu. I'm far from being a master. It doesn't matter if you win ten world championships and everybody tell you that you are the best. That means nothing to me. I try to keep my center even and my focus consistent – not only in my jiu-jitsu but also in other aspects like family, friends and business. I would like to have the opportunity to spending more time with my teacher, because every minute I spend with him gives me information that stays with me forever. Since I can't train with Jacare all the time, I value every single minute that I spend with him on the mat or simply talking about jiu-jitsu. I also enjoy spending time with my brother, who is a great reference for me in the art of jiu-jitsu. He complements me greatly and we are good friends, too.

**Q: What would you say to someone who wants to learn jiu-jitsu?**
A: I would tell them to find out about the teacher the are planning to train under. Find out what his reputation is, not only in competition but also in life. You are going to spend a lot of time with him in the Academy, so check out some of the classes and observe his teaching. How does he speaks to his students? What kind of attitude does he have about life? That person is going to be someone that you look to for jiu-jitsu advice, but who will also influence you in many ways that you won't even notice. Make sure he is a good human being, not only a good jiu-jitsu instructor.

**Q: What keeps you motivated to train?**
A: Motivation is something that you always need to work on – not only in jiu-jitsu but in everything in life. I'm Christian and I believe in Jesus Christ. I don't want to sound too religious but I truly think that man needs a philosophical or religious belief to guide him through life. I have found that anchor in a particular belief – someone else can find it in Buddhism, Zen, Taoism, et cetera. Motivation usually is based on a reason to do something. If you have a strong reason to do a task, then the motivation is there. In jiu-jitsu, my motivation is in the joy of training and competing, challenging myself every time I step into a mat. In life, it's another story. It is important to have a reason to do things in life – to have a destiny and a destination. Unfortunately, I see people living and passing through life with no sense of leaving a legacy. I think this is sad.

**Q: Do you think street fighting is necessary to develop good self-defense skills?**
A: I don't look for fights. I don't need to brawl in the streets to prove that I can fight. I don't need it and I don't think it brings a good reputation to the art of jiu-jitsu either.

**Q: Do you have any particular mental or psychological preparation that you use before a fight?**
A: I think about what I'm going to do, but I don't stress or put unnecessary pressure on myself. I like to surround myself with people who say positive things and who have the right attitude towards life and training. I try to keep people who bring negative energy, far from me. As I said before, I'm a religious person so I read the Bible and try to keep focus and relaxed all the time.

**Q: Do you feel that breathing exercises are important for jiu-jitsu?**
A: Jiu-jitsu is an art based on using leverage, not brute force. In order to use leverage you need to position yourself in the right place so you can exert leverage. In a grappling situation, you can't position yourself in the right angle without subtlety. In order to place your body in the right position to use proper leverage, you have to pace yourself. You can't force it. Breathing allows you to stay calm, to control your body properly, and to save energy for later use. You need to understand when to inhale and when to exhale while performing the technique, because this is a very important factor in producing momentum and creating additional space

for the technique. It is difficult to explain without physically showing a technique. That's the reason it takes a knowledgeable instructor. There is more to the art of jiu-jitsu than simple physical techniques.

**Q: How important is finding the right training partner?**
A: In Brazilian jiu-jitsu you practice with a partner all the time, from the very first day. The effectiveness of the techniques lies in making it work against an uncooperative opponent. No motions are performed in the air. It is true that we have several solo drills that help to develop the necessary body mechanics for grappling, but this is neither the essence nor the basic training method of jiu-jitsu.

Training with a partner involves relating to a moving body all the time. You learn to "feel" another person and to adjust to your opponent in order to make a technique work. While in punching and kicking methods timing is the secret, in jiu-jitsu "feeling" is the key. You have to develop specific physical attributes to make the techniques work. Wrestling is similar. With no partner, there is no way of making the techniques really work.

The importance of having the right training partner is extremely relevant to improving. During all my years of jiu-jitsu I have seen many practitioners who didn't know how to help and cooperate with their training partner. They try to fight instead of cooperating, and never create the right circumstances for their partner to improve and master techniques. Unfortunately, many practitioners fight too much; they approach training like a competition or a fight, and make of a training session a nightmare where many students get hurt. I have seen people cracking elbows in training and breaking bones. I have seen people getting choked-out because they don't tap. All these attitudes are nonsense and stupid. Find a training partner who helps you to train and improve your technique, not a brainless tough guy who is going to hurt you.

With the right kind of training partner you can train hard and safe. It is the instructor's responsibility to control these situations so the tough guys don't hurt the rest of the students who are there to learn. In Brazil, a purple belt helps a blue belt, a blue helps a white belt, and a brown and black belt helps all the students. Unfortunately, I have seen blue belts badly beat white belts and purple belts punish blue belts instead of helping them to progress. If you want to play "tough guy" then enter a vale tudo competition or do it against a black belt.

In Brazil, the training is harder because the 90 percent of the practitioners compete. In the United States maybe only 20 percent the students compete; the rest simply train for pleasure and fitness and to enjoy learning the art. In order to attract people to jiu-jitsu schools instructors need to make everyday people feel comfortable and safe whatever their reasons for coming are.

**Q: You are known for having very creative and unorthodox techniques. How did you develop these amazing moves?**
A: I have to tell you that all these creative movements are very natural to me. I am not doing anything that doesn't fit my body and my physical attributes. If doing these techniques were something unnatural, then I wouldn't be doing them. You have to find what it works for you – the things that you can naturally do. These movements will be your basics, the foundation you'll build your jiu-jitsu on. In training I advise students to work and experiment with all types of techniques, but in competition to stick to the things that are natural for you.

*"You have to find what it works for you... the things that you can naturally do. These movements will be your basics, the foundation you'll build your jiu-jitsu on."*

**Q: How much strength is necessary in order to make jiu-jitsu techniques work?**
A: The key to making jiu-jitsu techniques work is leverage, but strength is also necessary. Don't think that technique will work by itself because it will not. A certain amount of physical strength is necessary to make leverage possible. What jiu-jitsu students must understand is that before applying force to the technique in order to make it work, they have to work on pure technique and leverage until they master the movement and can apply it with only technical skill, without using more than the required strength to make the body move. Then when they master this phase of the technique, they can start to add strength accordingly, but never try-

"Hardcore weight training, running and stretching are not beneficial for a jiu-jitsu practitioner. More exercising does not necessarily mean better results. You have to be specific in what you do and how you do it; otherwise, you risk wasting your time."

ing to substitute a lack of skill for brute force.

**Q: Can you imagine life without jiu-jitsu?**
A: Training jiu-jitsu for me is both a mental and physical therapy. It is an important part of my life. Honestly, I can't picture myself without jiu-jitsu being part of my life. But don't get me wrong, life is bigger and more important than jiu-jitsu.

**Q: What advice would you give to students about weight training, running, stretching, et cetera?**
A: I study physical therapy, and definitely all these supplementary aspects of physical training can help any practitioner of Brazilian jiu-jitsu. What is important is that the student knows how to apply these other elements to jiu-jitsu. Hardcore weight training, running and stretching are not beneficial for a jiu-jitsu practitioner. The weight training, the running and the stretching exercises have to be adapted and fit into the jiu-jitsu format of moving the human body. If you simply run, stretch, and lift weights you won't necessarily be improving your jiu-jitsu. More exercising does not necessarily mean better results. You have to be specific in what you do and how you do it, otherwise you risk wasting your time.

**Q: Has fear and nervousness been difficult for you to overcome?**
A: Fear is not something anyone should be affected by. If you know how to transform that fear into a useful tool to boost your training and skills then you're on the right track. Unfortunately, many practitioners let fear take them over, and then they cannot react quickly to an opponent's moves. They freeze and all the hours of training are useless. Fear makes you be cautious, and this can ruin your performance. Use fear for your own benefit.

**Q: What did your ADCC 2003 win mean for you?**
A: That victory was a very important moment and a turning point in my career. From the outside it might have seemed that I won easily, but all my opponent were very tough. I only had two weeks to prepare for that event because my university studies take a lot of my time. Then I have my regular day job, so I didn't have that much training time. I had a good group of people who helped me in every aspect of the preparation. I was confident of my ability but also very respectful of my opponents. My team, my friends, my wife and my family were really important in keeping me relaxed and focused for that tournament. They all had a great deal of patience with me and supported me in each and every way they could. Of course, the advice and attention given to me by my teacher, Jacare, every step of the way, was priceless.

**Q: What advice would you give to new students?**
A: I can only say the things that work for me. Find a teacher that is a example to follow not only in jiu-jitsu, but also as a human being. Have faith in everything you do, leave room to learn from others, and always be humble.

**Q: What does the future hold for you?**
A: I really don't know what the future holds for me but I'm sure of what I want. Regardless of how far I go in jiu-jitsu as a competitor, and eventually as a teacher for future champions, there is one thing most important to me – to spend time with my family and close friends. When you are on top everybody loves you, but once you start losing then nobody but your family will stick around. I take popularity for what it is and nothing more. Family and true friends are what really counts in life.

## Grappling Techniques

Leo controls his opponent from the side (1). He loosens the opponent's gi, forces the tip towards the adversary's neck and grabs the uniform with his other hand (2). Leo lowers his head (3) and raises his hips (4). This creates a strong base for him (5) to propel himself to the other side of the opponent (6-7). He can apply a choke simply by not releasing the grips on the gi (8).

Leo controls the opponent with the butterfly guard (1). By grabbing the opponent's pants at the knee and hooking with both feet (2), he sweeps the opponent up (3) and to the side (4). Then, he slides out from under the opponent and moves to the back (5), from where he prepares to apply a finishing choke (6).

"A true martial arts practitioner, like an artist of any other kind – be this a musician, a painter, a writer or an actor – is expressing and leaving part of himself in every piece of his craft. The need for self-inspection and self-realization of who he is becomes the reason for a journey in search of that perfect technique, that great melody, that inspiring poetry, that amazing painting or that Academy Award performance. It is this motivation to reach that impossible dream that allows a simple individual to become an exceptional artist and master of his craft."

– Jose M. Fragua

www.ingramcontent.com/pod-product-compliance
Lightning Source LLC
Chambersburg PA
CBHW081739100526
44592CB00015B/2237

# MASTERS
# Martial Arts
## Writings

*Edited and Compiled*
**Jose M. Fraguas**

EMPIRE BOOKS/AWP LLC

**DISCLAIMER:** Please note that the author and publisher of this book are NOT RESPONSIBLE in any manner whatsoever for any injury that may result from practicing the techniques and/or following the instructions given within. Since the physical activities described herein may be too strenuous in nature for some readers to engage in safely, it is essential that a physician be consulted prior to training.

First Edition published in 2022 by AWP LLC/Empire Books.

© Copyright 2022 by AWP LLC/Empire Books. All rights reserved. No part of this publication may be reproduced or utilized in any form or by any means, electronic or mechanical, including photo-copying, recording, or by any information storage and retrieval system, without prior written permission from AWP LLC/Empire Books.

Library of Congress Catalog Number: ISBN-13: 978-1-949753-50-9
22 21 20 19 18 17 16 15 14 13 12 11 10

Library of Congress Cataloging-in-Publication Data:

Master's Martial Arts Writings by Jose M. Fraguas = -- Compiled & Arranged ed. p. cm.
ISBN 978-1-949753-50-9 (pbk. : alk. paper)  1. Martial arts-- philosophy. 3. Large type books. I. Title.
GV1114.3.F715 20148861.815'3--dc22
20060103222

PRINTED IN THE UNITED STATES OF AMERICA.

## TABLE OF CONTENTS

*Introduction* .................................................... 1

- **Tony Annesi** .............................................. 5
- **Jiang Bangjun** ........................................... 27
- **Robert Chu** ................................................ 39
- **Fumio Demura** ........................................... 75
- **Jose M. Fraguas** ......................................... 83
- **Rorion Gracie** ............................................ 107
- **Chris Kent** ................................................ 119
- **Rigan Machado** ......................................... 127
- **Cass Magda** .............................................. 137
- **Tony Massengill** ........................................ 157
- **Ed Otis** .................................................... 171
- **Robert J. Ott** ............................................ 185
- **Avi Rokah** ................................................ 195
- **Hal Sharp** ................................................ 213
- **Tony Somera** ............................................ 221
- **Steve Tarani** ............................................. 265
- **Koss Yokota** ............................................. 279
- **Kam Yuen** ................................................ 287

# INTRODUCTION

In a magazine publishing company, every year we receive literally hundreds and hundreds of story submissions. These manila envelopes (or its email counterpart) contain works ranging from fascinating to—well, to put it diplomatically, "fanciful." Yet we open nearly each and every piece of mail to separate contents from the envelope while doing our best not to commit an eco-crime.

Kidding aside, what we look for in the mail is the best martial arts writing in existence. To be considered "the best" there are some basic criteria which must be met. As the Chief Editor at *Masters Magazine,* I carefully evaluate the articles and columns we receive to finally decide those which will be published on a regular basis. It is not an easy task since many variables are involved in the process.

Needless to say, while we receive a lot of good submissions we also, as an occupational hazard, have to read a lot of "really bad stuff." Fortunately, after years of working as an editor you develop an instinct and can quickly identify an unusable submission.

That's what this specific series of columns by great martial artists is all about bringing you the "best", without prejudice in terms of the writer, the source, or the subject. The aim with this work is to provide the readers with a wide selection of styles and systems. The collection includes many different authors who offer their own perspectives of the arts and the influences of their respective styles in the field. A wide spectrum of point of views and knowledge about all martial arts is presented in this compilation. All of them have expressed their ideas in a very different way. But whether expressed in the language of the teachers, the language of the students, or the language of the thinker, there is truth in concepts, philosophies and techniques that so many martial artists have believed and lived by for decades.

I have made every effort to present each column and work as accurately as possible within the limitations of the book format. In addition to being a resource for researchers, writers, students, and teachers, we hope this collection of works will provide comfort and inspiration for all those who love the martial arts. There are many excellent books about the martial arts writings, but my hope is that this book of collective columns will prove a worthy companion to them in two main ways: first, in its size and scope; second in its practicality and ease of use. When you work with individual pieces, you must also view them as a whole. It's not that you necessarily have to connect the articles. You do, however, have to consider how they will read in book form.

There have been many changes in the world of martial arts, but some things are still the same. A well-written column is one of them: precise, short and to the point in a few hundred words. Like a perfect punch or kick aimed to the target. The real responsibility as the world leaders in the publication of martial arts book is to inform and educate the reader, promoting all the styles and approaches without being limited by any of them. The credit of this compilation work goes straight to the masters who wrote these great columns. I just compiled them and edited for content. Magazines go away but hopefully this work will stay and future generation will be able of benefit from the wisdom and knowledge of the masters featured here.

Meeting and knowing these great martial arts writers and having long conversations with them allowed me to do more than simply scratch the surface of the technical aspects of their respective styles. It also helped me to research and analyze the human beings behind the teachers. And these columns show that.

As the philosopher Bertrand Russell wrote: "There is no more reason why a person who uses a word correctly should be able to tell what it means than there is why a planet which is moving correctly should know Kepler's laws." I respectfully would like to advise the reader to *listen* not to the words of the masters but to *what* they really meant when they said those words through these columns. The way of the warrior produces a practitioner torn between the art and the

# INTRODUCTION

mystic. The way of the artist and the way of the mystic are similar, but the mystic lacks a craft... the physical techniques. The craft (physical training) keeps the artist in touch with the remarkableness of the world and in relationship to it. Therefore, philosophy without hard physical training is useless.

As early as I can remember, my house was filled with martial arts magazines from around the world. For many years, I gathered publications and became curious about many of the authors who wrote columns for them. The more I researched, the more I realized that those "great people" were a lot more like you and me than they were different. Today, I have written over a thousand articles in magazines around the world, more than three dozen of books under my own name and a couple under some else's. At *Masters,* we have read, written, edited, and re-written more articles and books than one could possibly imagine. Although it is unlikely any of us will ever be awarded the Nobel Prize, the writing that we like is the writing that we like. Nothing can change that.

Most of what passed as human wisdom is merely the post-examination gabble of excited individuals trying to guess how the new lessons will explain the old questions of life and martial arts training. Anything is fresh on the first hearing... even though others may have heard it a thousand times through a score of generations.

I bring all this up because I believe all the martial arts masters who have submitted material to be published have followed similar paths.

Enjoy the reading and walk on!

— *Jose M. Fraguas*

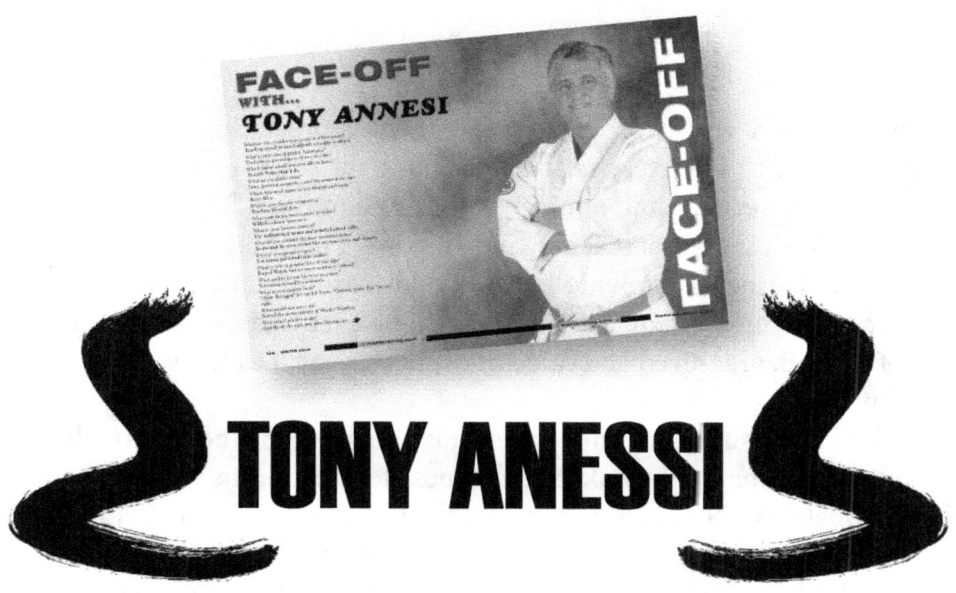

# TONY ANESSI

## THE AGONY OF THE FEET

In high school, I was not a rebel, but I asked questions to which no adult seemed to have answers. No adult was able to explain that students take advantage of relaxed dress codes. In less than a decade, the halls were filled with unwashed jeans, unwashed sweaters, and unwashed bodies. No teacher explained that young minds opt for irrelevant electives. In less than a decade, courses included pottery and comics (and unaccredited tutorials in avoiding growing up).

The culture rapidly became less uptight but more anxious, less intolerant but more disorderly, less demanding but more neglectful. A defense of standards was replaced by lack of concern. Regulation of any sort seemed like an intolerable force.

In burning old standards, we neglected to set reasonable new standards. In fact, reason itself was scorched in the process. In the turbulent 60s, martial arts were a bastion of unyielding standards. The order, discipline, and meritocracy of the martial arts attracted me as much as the physical exercise or self-defense. True, for some of us, budo seemed a little restrictive; but, for many, the martial arts were a safety net of sanity and reason.

When I taught English at Phillips Exeter one summer, I also offered a judo program. A young couple, instructors at Exeter during the year, also enrolled. They had previously served in the Peace Corps. I felt they were members of the "liberated generation." After the program was over, they spoke their appreciation not for the techniques or the exercise, but for "the tight ship" I had run. "The kids really needed that, and you were right on them." Frankly, I had not noticed. I was just teaching judo the way I had been taught. There had to be rules to provide both a good learning environment and personal safety. What a revelation! No one ever told me people learn better in an organized and safe atmosphere, even if that means a little conformity.

At aikido summer camp, an enthusiastic Aikido student attached silver sequins and pink rhinestones to her uniform jacket to personalize it. No one told her that the whole idea of a uniform is to make things...well...uniform. Evidently, she did not notice that no one else had a bejeweled uwagi. The instructors tried not to involve themselves with student concerns; that was the province of seniors. With 300 practitioners on the mat, a hundred of them black belts, no one mentioned a thing to Ms. Rhinestone. No one wanted to train with her, either. It was not just embarrassing but dangerous. If she pulled you into her ample bosom to swing an *irimi nage*, you arose from the mat with several none-too-shallow pockmarks on your face.

After a long, uneasy weekend of trying to get a partner for her Sunday exam, she found a kind heart named Sally. Sally hoped to find the right time to mention the rhinestones. But the exam came, and the sequins and stones still glittered in the bright gymnasium. Then, a flash of brilliance! Sally grabbed Ms. Rhinestone's lapel as the standard *ikkyo* technique required. Her grip dislodged a few small stones on the mat near the three senior instructors. When the exam was over and it was time to bow off, one sensei stepped on a fallen rhinestone. With a quick limp, he suppressed a Japanese oath.

During that evening's practice session, Ms. Rhinestone, having left the ranks of the uninformed, wore an unadorned gi-top.

Self-control is the key to self-respect. If one does not control oneself, some control inevitably will be provided from the outside. Such an outside source is where both laws and customs originate. That is what they didn't tell me in high school in the mid-60s. The summation of a collective social wisdom should not be disregarded lightly. That is why, at the expense of some conformity, we bathe regularly and wear no sequins on our gi.

## DIONYSIAN AND APOLLONIAN BUDO
## *AND A* NEW YORK STATE-OF-MIND

Like the yin-yang, martial arts have two opposing but complementary parts: hard and soft, defensive and offensive, physical and mental, as well as the martial and the artistic (known in academic circles as the Dionysian and Apollonian). The Dionysian is the raw, emotional, visceral force of bu-jutsu. The Apollonian is the ideal and artistic budo. Without the Dionysian passion of down and dirty combat, there would be no Apollonian art to analyze, to exercise, or to aid in self-development. Without the Dionysian, the Apollonian becomes misdirected, unverifiable, perhaps even unfulfilling of its own promise of self-development — in a word: effete.

I was one of many martial artists asked to demonstrate for a "Friendship Demonstration" in New York. Most of the attendees were hard-style practitioners. The afternoon was filled with slam-dunk techniques that showed the self-defense ability of their advocates. I showed a minimal-motion version of aiki. Most of the spectators, fellow martial artists all, did not receive my demo well. In their Dionysian passion for self-defense, they simply did not believe minimal aiki would work "on the street." The martial artists, many from less than sedate areas, wanted to know that what they learned today, they could apply tomorrow. The quickest, most effective way to apply waza was fast and hard, i.e., passionately Dionysian. Two visitors from upstate, however, loved the demonstration and came to see me afterward. They knew what I showed would take a long time to perfect but could, indeed, be effective as well as aesthetic. In their relatively safe suburban dojo, they could dare to be Apollonian.

Sabrina caught me after class and asked if we were going to learn stuff she could use on the street. I explained that traditional aiki is an art that teaches form and principle, so one can adapt it to many different self-defense situations. "What type of self-defense did you have in mind?"

Sabrina related a specific incident. She was in her SUV waiting to take a left turn in the city. Two young women behind her blared their car's horn and yelled threats from their open window. Sabrina said, "I wanted to get out of my car and pound them, but there were two of them and I didn't know any self-defense."

I gave her a lecture about trying to maintain a passive state of mind and choosing one's battles wisely. She responded that, because I didn't come from the city, I didn't understand. Appropriate or not, she wanted instant self-defense from her martial arts study. It was not that aiki could no*t* give her that ability, but that it could not give it to her quickly. In order to learn that ability, she had to be dispassionate. It was the passion she did not want to give up.

The Dionysian-Apollonian theory explains so much. Years ago, I noticed inner-city martial artists who, having learned a Japanese samurai tradition, wore hakama (formal divided skirts) with African designs. My first response was chuckling, then queasiness, and later, an attempt to understand. These big city budoka felt intuitively, and accurately, I think, that what they practiced was based on, but was not true to, the Asian forms. African designs on Japanese style garb expressed this. For pure Japanese stylists, African hakama seem inappropriate. For African American martial artists whose pride in their heritage overlays the Asian art they have studied, their unique uniform appropriately expressed their passions. Passion is quite personal, after all. And it is passion that self-defense is really about.

So, what about artistry? What about the Apollonian aspect? The Apollonian creates the arts all martial artists are passionate about. The Apollonian makes the tools of passion. The Apollonian instructs those who want passionate self-defense while teaching them to apply self-defense dispassionately. The Dionysian state of mind may be the motivation, but the Apollonian art is what civilizes Hell's Kitchen until it becomes the Met.

## MASTER OF PRESUMPTION

People came from several states to attend the Ju-jutsu Friendship Festival: one-hour seminars topped off with demonstrations by senior instructors. After his demonstration, each instructor did a two-minute interview for the local TV station.

In the middle of one demonstration, there was a small hubbub at the entrance. A large young man wearing a sport jacket and sunglasses insisted that, if this were truly a friendship demo, all styles should be represented. The fact that it was an invitational friendship demo was lost upon the gentleman.

In an attempt to be polite, minimize any disturbance, and subdue a negative buzz in the media, the sponsor graciously allowed the outsider in. Out of the hallway trooped six assistants and their oversized equipment bags. They were shown the locker room while the sponsor tried to figure out how to work even a ten-minute segment into the full afternoon of fifteen-minute demonstrations and two-minute interviews. Two masters kindly agreed to cut short their times to make room for the Master from the Outside.

Instructors will watch their peers demonstrate to get a feel for what their own emphasis should be. If Instructor A finished his exhibition with a huge *kata-guruma* (shoulder-wheel), Instructor B will not finish the same way. If Instructor C emphasizes knife defense, Instructor D will do gun defense. The Outside Master would be Instructor Z that afternoon, but he had not witnessed any of the previous demonstrations. When he duplicated four of the items done by other instructors, the audience was polite and tolerant. Master Outside was a little puzzled. Where was the friendship he was led to expect by the title of the event?

He showed knife defenses — techniques done earlier in the afternoon and done better. He showed gun defenses — repeats again. One sensei sidled over to me and whispered, "What d'you think of this guy?" I suppressed a wince.

Ten minutes passed like thirty. The host came onto the mat clapping his hands, thus giving the signal to applaud politely. The Outside Master reached out an arm. "Wait! One more thing — you've got to see this! It is a demonstration of Ki."

A demonstration of Ki! Holy Moly, Billy Batson! We martial artists ain't never seen no demonstration of Ki before! Couldya please do it two or three times?

He started with The Unbendable Arm, the Koichi Tohei technique known to American martial artists since the sixties. Mild applause. Then he had students punch his stomach, the "iron shirt" stuff that had been around far longer. Even milder applause. He showed the one-inch punch, a Bruce Lee demonstration famous since Ed Parker's 1964 Long Beach Internationals.

Once again, the host came out on the mat clapping his hands loudly and the crowd cooperated. We all stood up and continued the applause an artificially long time. The host pointed the master toward the waiting TV camera. The interviewer's spotlight went on and the mat was free again. A hundred martial artists gratefully reclaimed the training area. When Master Outside went outside, he was puzzled and somewhat disgusted.

No matter what his stature, no matter what his talent, a visitor has to be careful. The advantage of politeness is that it shows you do not take someone's kindness for granted. If you do, you are not a master, save perhaps a Master of Presumption.

A high-ranking teacher from Ohio once told me that he would not invite back a very, very famous martial artist, known for his happy-go-lucky attitude, because he kept pinching the girls. Admittedly, I heard only one side of the story, but I will bet it was presumption on the famed fellow's part that set the stage for his curtain call.

On the flipside of this, a Floridian sensei sang the praises of a former women's full-contact champion and movie star. He extolled her as quiet, polite, and modest, as well as a master of her martial art. I can't help thinking that his estimation of her mastery was helped by her quiet, polite, and modest lack of presumption.

## BLOWING ONE'S POTENTIAL

One of the saddest things for a teacher is to see good students drift away.

Many martial arts instructors of thirty- or forty-years duration, like myself, would like to produce just one or two really fine masters. The difficulty of this task depends on many factors: the complexity of the martial system, the standards for promotion, and the quality of the student who walks in the door, among others. We all would like to believe that our systems can themselves produce masters, but t'ain't that easy. Often when we have a candidate who has taken full advantage of the system, works hard and excels, he ends up taking advantage of the teacher as well and is expelled. Or maybe he just drifts away. In either case, he is, as we used to say in college, "blowing his potential."

In the martial arts, the teacher does not generally drift away. Rather, the student drifts away. Some die. Some know too much and leave. Some dojo-hop looking for new stimulation.

Matt was one of the brightest and most fun kids for me to teach. He was always enthusiastic, was able to make eight-year-old jokes that were both clever and appropriate, and just loved judo. During a Christmas break, Matt traveled with his mother and father to Australia to visit relatives. Bike riding in the warm southern winter on an unfamiliar road, he tumbled off an embankment hitting his head. He was rescued, hospitalized, and stabilized. The prognosis was positive. Then, one night, he died in his sleep of a blood clot to the brain. As his judo teacher, all I could do was sit in shock at the phone. We named an annual children's tournament for him. We remember Matt every year, but he would never realize his potential despite of any curriculum or teaching skill I may have had.

Elliott was a physician who had studied karate in another state. He was looking for a good, traditional school but did not expect to find one that satisfied him as much as his original school. For several lessons he was a little resistant, perhaps dubious. We did not do things as he was used to. Then, he settled in. Overnight, he became our biggest fan. He bragged about BUSHIDO-KAI to friends. Called out on a rescue mission during a flood, his helicopter crashed before it arrived on site. His enthusiasm is remembered in our annual Elliott Strom Memorial Award. His potential, however, as an intelligent, active, loving, appreciative, hardworking student will forever be unknown.

Jim almost never missed a class. He had just turned twenty and was enjoying life. He and his friends might have gotten into trouble had they not chosen to train in the martial arts. They made the right decision. We did not hold classes on Saturday evenings, however, and that was party time. Jim was driving from one party to another when four toughs decided to step in front of his car. Jim made the mistake of getting out and facing them. He had been drinking. They had been drinking. He had his karate. They had knives. The only thing I could do for Jim was testify at the murder trial. The defense subpoenaed a dojo video to show that Jim was a lethal weapon. Obviously not lethal enough. Thanks, in part, to my testimony, the defendant was sentenced to life imprisonment. Later, his conviction was overturned on a technicality, and he went free. If we cared to, we could trace the development of his potential. We will never know Jim's.

There are, sadly, many more stories where students "pass away" without dying. They take the path they think they need to take. Perhaps they are young, perhaps older but inexperienced. Perhaps they are afraid of full achievement, perhaps what they wish to achieve is not what the teacher wishes to teach. In any case, they drift away.

I can only suggest that, to a teacher, the loss of a good student, for whatever reason, is a smaller version of losing a son in a bike accident or a husband in a helicopter crash. One loss may not change a teacher's life but a career full of human potential blown away with the winds of fate and the vicissitudes of personal maturation, take their toll.

A teacher's real reward is being able to develop an excellent student. One of the saddest things for a teacher is to see good students drift away. It leaves that teacher without potential.

## THAT WON'T WORK!

Because most martial arts work in theory and occasionally in the simulated reality of drills, no one really knows what really, really works. But everyone thinks he knows. The traditional martial artist is sure his style has the techniques that will, when push comes to shove, be effective. Many know this so undeniably that whatever does not conform to their style they deem ineffective. Few, if any, have thought of setting up controlled tests to at least estimate effectiveness within a specific context. Having had years of experience with controlled tests, I suggest there are two reasons why others do not test.

The first reason: having invested in their own art, many martial artists have difficulty accepting that their investment may not have represented the absolute best use of their time, effort, and money. Consider the multi-thousand-dollar investment you make in a car. Do you want some yahoo to show up with another model that gets twice the mileage, has twice the horsepower and cost half as much? No way! You can barely tolerate the yahoos with cars that have 10% more efficiency and cost 10% less. If these fellows show up, you have already thought of ready defenses: your vehicle has a better repair record or a higher resale value. It is hard to admit, however, that all of this is just comparing apples and oranges. What you really want to believe is that you bought the absolute best vehicle that you could possibly afford.

The second reason that martial artists do not test their techniques: they are afraid that if reality has a rude shock in store for them, they would not know how to cope. Would coping mean having to change style (see reason #1, above) or having to conflict with their tradition by adapting something from the outside? They already put in ten years work! Now they might have to put in another ten and feel like a white belt again! No thanks.

Before seminars became popular in the United States, I ran early proto-seminars called BUSHIDO-KAI Weekends. Few outside students attended, but outside instructors were glad to oblige. They usually brought two or three assistants with them, but never stayed for anyone else's seminar. Knowing that they knew what they wanted to know, there was no use learning what they did not need to know, y'know?

One guest was a guy who reminded me of Snake Pliskin from Escape from New York. He did not have an eye patch but did have the hair and the confidence. Most of what Snake did was familiar to my students from their aiki or karate training, but Snake was convinced that all of what he did must be foreign to us and was invested in opening our eyes.

He asked the small group, "How would you defend against a side head strike?" Most karate-ka drill against straight punches and seldom consider round blows, but aiki deals with them regularly. Snake pointed to one of the smaller women in the dojo, an aiki black belt. "Show me what you would do."

He delivered a medium speed side head strike and Laurie, a characteristic smile on her face, responded with a typical circular reception that not only avoided the strike, but also looped Snakes arm in front of his body, in position for Laurie for a follow-up.

"That won't work," said Snake, matter-of-factly. But it had worked! Everyone saw it. Snake went on to teach what he felt was the correct response. I am sure it would have been equally effective, but I could not help asking myself, "Why would a martial artist deny the evidence of his senses and be so absolutely sure that he saw the reverse of reality?" I figured that I needed to re-read Eric Hoffer's *The True Believer*. Maybe Snake had been taken over by a mass movement, a cult, or maybe a martial art.

Would you be as proud of your martial arts seniors if they had not tested for their ranks? If martial arts schools gave outranks without exams (publicly, privately, or through personal evaluation), you might rightly wonder on what basis the rank was determined. If a martial arts instructor told you that a technique would work without his having tested it, on what basis would he know? You don't know what you know until you see how you test. After you have gone through some objective tests, you might honestly be able to say, "Oops. That doesn't really work!"

## NERVOUS STRENGTH AND THE IMITATIVE FALLACY

If success in the martial arts depended on size, martial arts would come from Sweden. If it depended on strength, karate-ka would bench-press bricks instead of breaking them. Instead, success depends on developing attributes, skills, and a willingness to keep on keeping on. That does not ignore the advantage of strength. "Other things being equal, a big man will beat a small man every time" implies the stronger man will beat the weaker man. Attackers are likely to be bigger or stronger. A victim that does not know technique will use fear to augment his strength.

The coordinator of gym introduced me to Harry, a 42-year-old inner city shop owner who looked 62, was of moderate height, somewhat overweight with a forced smile. Having been robbed at gunpoint six times, he was here to learn some basic self-defense and, as importantly, to feel comfortable among strangers.

I told Harry to grab me and indicated my lapel. He looked at me as if I had told him to sacrifice a firstborn. "Y'know, like this," I said reaching out my hand to his chest. Automatically, he shivered, coiled, and slapped my hand like an allergic person batting a bee. "Okay. Let's try this. You hold my wrist and I'll show you how to escape. I won't do anything fast or hard."

I once took my blood pressure on a self-serve machine, the inflatable cinch of which kept swelling, crushing my arm to my growing panic until I pushed the emergency button. If the cinch had been on my wrist and made of constricting carbon-steel, that would approximate Harry's grip. He was not trying to show me up, put me down, or brush my lesson aside, but was holding on for dear life.

Had this been a real attack, I would have back fisted him and proceeded with a release, but I was responsible for his safety, for making him feel at ease, and for keeping my promise of "I won't do anything fast or hard." His grip weakened my knees, so I gave into it. It probably looked to Harry like I was feinting. Eyes widening, he loosened slightly as my head dropped below his eye-level. The lower position gave me the leverage to release the grip.

"Now let's talk about the concept of leverage..." I covered my momentary panic well, I thought, but in my head some concerns were churning. Had I underestimated the strength of attackers? No question that a person can get much stronger when adrenaline flows. The incredible force emanating from a nervous attacker can easily overwhelm a victim. Did this mean that real miscreants, nervous in their crimes, would be as strong as Harry? The fact is that sometimes you cannot out-muscle the strong. If the martial arts did not offer alternatives to strength, those of us in sensitive situations would either be power lifting or freebasing coffee all day in anticipation of a potential attack.

There is a literary technique called The Imitative Fallacy. If, for example, the writer wants the reader to understand boredom felt by a character, he might write in a boring manner. Martial artists use a sort of imitative fallacy by imitating the opponent just enough to regulate the interaction and take away the opponent's advantage. That is when the opening occurs. There are wrist releases that apply this idea physically. Someone grabs your wrist with Harry-strength, you respond by spreading your fingers and tensing your forearm. His grip tightens not so much because of his strength but because you have expanded into his grip. You then relax your hand reducing its girth and proceed with your release. You imitate to regulate.

Contrast wakes us up. You may have taken fire fighters for granted...until the events of 9/11. You may have taken the value of self-defense for granted...until your shop gets held-up a half-dozen times. You may have taken budo for granted until you realize the richness of its teachings.

I am not sure which I learned first, the concept of tense-then-release in technique, the imitative fallacy in literature, or appreciation-by-contrast in human psychology, but for me, they overlap. Russell Hoban, the American author, said, "When you suffer an attack of nerves you're being attacked by the nervous system. What chance has a man got against a system?"

Simple. Counter it with another system — a system of martial arts.

## ALISLIM'S STABILITY

Any teacher can turn a jock into a good martial artist. Even in a hoakie system, a good athlete can make the art and thus the teacher look good. In most dojo, the members are not all jocks. Some are overweight, some underweight, some older, some in less than tip-top shape. The teacher must do his best, whether or not the student has inherent athletic gifts. The rewards for his efforts are not trophies or a tournament record, but little unexpected victories.

Allison was a cellist, but the cello weighed more than she. "Slim" was her nickname and then later, "Alislim." At another school she had been intimidated by a sparring emphasis and frustrated with a lack of instructional detail. A stickler for precision, she developed very good kata but was still unsure of her self-defense ability. Part of the problem was her wanting to get everything perfect. No musician wants to provide a mediocre performance. This made her a sincere, hard-working student that any instructor would love to teach, but it also meant that she had a mild case of paralysis-by-analysis. She could not react naturally because she was afraid that she would react incorrectly.

I suggested developing both ends of the detail-reaction spectrum. When I taught conscious, meticulous training, her attention to detail would prove valuable. When I taught reaction training, it was time to let go and trust that the previously accumulated details would allow an accurate response. What she did was important, of course, but that she did something was more important.

Vacationing in Montana while I was doing a seminar in Washington, she drove across Idaho to attend. Ali was excited but nervous about being our dojo's only representative. Most of the seminarians were black belt men, tall, large, or both.

At hombu, we often work on stability and "structuring," testing both blocks and stances in three or four different ways. During the Washington seminar, I taught a basic middle block and showed variations from various styles, then tried to reduce these to the elements that actually made the block function. The next step was for each student to make the block work against a sincerely delivered middle punch. Alislim was used to this and could block the attacks of her larger opponents. Outweighing her by as much as 100 pounds, they also were successful in applying their block against her, but they could not move her stance when they blocked. They could have more easily picked her up bodily. Two or three guys were shocked enough to tell both her and me about it. Her emphasis on detail had paid off.

Okay. She had worked a great deal on detailed basics but still was uncertain about her reactions. Back in Montana, she was having dinner with her sister and brother-in-law, a tall, wiry cowboy who had been in several street and bar confrontations. When the subject of martial arts vs. street fighting came up, Alislim was curious. She knew that budo was not intended to be black-and-blue-do, but she wanted to understand how the real world differed from the formalities of the dojo. After dinner, she asked, "If I guy wanted to really get in your face and deck you, what sort of punch would he use?"

Her brother-in-law stood her up in the living room and got close without giving her any specific indications. Them cowboys ain't exactly talkative types. He swung. She rotated inside and automatically delivered a controlled backfist that arched brother-in-law backwards making him lose his balance. When he righted himself, all he said was, "Been thinkin' of takin' some of that martial arts stuff." The evening ended with mutual respect and with Alislim finding a deeper level of self-respect.

Any teacher can turn a jock into a good martial artist because jocks train themselves. It takes a more experienced teacher to turn a non-jock into a good martial artist. The teacher cannot take all the credit, however. The non-athletic student has to work more than twice as hard for less than half the rewards. The rewards are usually not big victories like tournament trophies or real-life self-defense. The harder one works, the more one appreciates what one earns: little victories like delivering an un-programmed backfist and Alislim's stability are not the medals, ribbons, trophies, and plaques of the jock martial artists, but they are so much more appreciated.

## GETTING OUT-AND-ABOUT

When I was an only-child, weeknight entertainment consisted of visiting relatives and playing with cousins my age. My parents, concerned that I would not meet new people, took me to visit an old friend they had run into. I didn't want to meet people just for the sake of meeting people, especially people without children my age. The adults would give me the unavoidable four- or five-question interview before they began to talk with each other, referring me to the TV or some 14-year-old son who was uneager to baby-sit. Not my idea of a fun evening.

This attitude was reflected years later in my martial arts.

In earlier decades, most dojo kept to themselves. It was difficult to share with each other except for the monthly tournament. I thought in exactly the opposite way. I preferred to see martial artists in their own surroundings practicing seriously rather than in a public venue vying to get the judges' attention. In order to become familiar with other martial arts, I read books (there were no videos as yet) and respectfully visited dojo. When seminars became popular, I attended eagerly until I found myself coaching my training partners rather than learning. After decades of seminar attendance, I had become the teenaged boy babysitting the visiting kid.

Some students will not leave the dojo no matter what the attraction. They seem happy "at home," but the happiness is untested. Is this dojo their first infatuation? Would they have married their first girlfriend or boyfriend? Conversely, a few students spend too much free time connecting with other schools. Like a confirmed bachelor who does not see the value of commitment, they seem always to be looking for something better.

We live at a time when students are used to getting what they want on demand. If they are interested in Plum Duk Kung-fu, they will go out and sign up for a month. If they have a momentary fascination with Mud Stuk Buk, they will buy a DVD. This can be healthy curiosity — a desire to understand the entire field from which their art is drawn. Too much of this curiosity, however, is dilettantism, a fickleness born of the thrill of new experiences.

In the '80s, I knew a woman who wanted to skydive, deep-sea dive, visit Asia, do martial arts, become a model, go on Safari, be a dancer, etc. She fulfilled her own dreams, each with a boyfriend who could show her the ropes. As a result, she had many experiences than other women her age. She also had experienced more than 40 lovers by the age of twenty-two. By the age of twenty-four, one of her more exciting experiments ended up in a near-rape. "One thorn of experience is worth a whole wilderness of warning," said Lowell. The butterfly, like my former girlfriend, trades experience in depth for experience in breadth. Breadth gives one the whole world; depth tells one what to do with it. If it were not for a concentrated effort in one subject, there would be no mentor in the activities she had wished to experience and no boyfriend to show her the ropes.

Still, a martial artist also needs some breadth. A martial artist cannot defend himself in all situations with just an excellent upper block and counter punch. He must have experience in various types of martial artistry, but there is a limit. I cannot tell you how many schools I have visited in which students learn dozens of blocks, kata, throws, strikes, and kicks, however, when you attack them with a simple lunge punch, their upper block fails, their counter punch bouncing off your belly. Having traded depth for breadth, they have visited many skills, but have not spent enough time in one art.

Some students study martial arts as a sort of weeknight entertainment. To the extent they wish to be entertained, visiting other schools seems the thing to do. Other students study martial arts as a way to self-improvement. They also like getting out-and-about but enjoy it much more when the encounter has something in common with their goals. Getting out-and-about is collecting the material of knowledge. Studying at home is integrating that material into a single martial artist.

## TESTING THE TOURNAMENT TROPHY

My career with martial arts competition began in 1964 with collegiate judo. The referee called "Hajime!" I approached my U. Mass. adversary. Upon our mutual touch, I threw a right Sasae-tsuki-komi-ashi, felling my foe. The referee called "*Ippon! De-ashi-barai!*" and I was victorious in my first five seconds of play with a misidentified technique. Understandable, I thought, but also my first experience with a judge's imprecision. My next two matches were horrifically slow. I had drawn a larger, more experienced competitor. At the end of regulation time, we were tied. In the second overtime, still a draw. The referee asked for a corner judge's decision and the match went to the older guy. After about fifteen minutes, my third match was called. Evidently, I had made it to the quarterfinals. By the end of regulation time, my hands could barely grip, and my arms felt like they were carrying wet laundry. Draw! Overtime again. If this was what they meant by sudden death, why was it taking so long? A judges' decision and another near miss for me. I couldn't figure out why they didn't simply score my matches as ties.

The next month, I was out of the tournament early. My opponent had used a supposedly illegal choke across my windpipe. I was slowly losing my taste for competition, not because I did not win consistently, but because I could not depend on consistency from match to match. After college, I joined a local martial arts club where the judo we did was not competition but practice randori.

A couple of comfortable years not worrying about referees, not having my hands cramp up and not going home dragging my sweaty *gi* had made me soft. When Al, who was my size and rank, came to the dojo, I was faced with the undeniable conclusion that although experienced, I was not in shape to spar. Immediately I designed a new goal for myself: to never be more than a few weeks out of competitive shape for my age.

In my karate dojo, we were not allowed to freestyle until green belt. In my first match, I swept Richard, my senior, feeling immediately confident about my karate skills, but a year later, when a visiting brown belt did some light sparring with us, my confidence dissolved. His dojo sparred every class, and he would go to tournaments nearly every weekend. He scored on me with ease. Okay, another lesson learned, just the opposite from what I had learned years before in judo: even though I was in shape, I did not have the experience to engage in karate matches. Still, I favored my sensei's emphasis: karate was for character building and self-defense, not trophies. Many years later, I wondered, while sparring my students in class, if I had been missing something. I certainly had more experience now but had never officially entered a tournament. I wondered if, down deep, I was just plain scared — not of getting hit, not even of losing, but of not doing well — all the more reason to enter a tournament at age 42.

When I won the kata competition doing Unsu, the tournament director gave me a thumbs-up. He especially liked some dynamic tension at the end of the kata. "That's what karate is all about," he said. I was not sure if he meant dynamic tension or doing respectable kata. Then came the senior sparring division. I sparred younger men, managing to make the finals, then scored my third point on a round kick my opponent did not expect. First place. Not convinced that my win was anything but a fluke, I entered again the next year: eliminated in the first round. Then the third year, first place again. Okay. Test complete. I knew the following: (1) win or lose, I was not afraid of karate tournaments, (2) I could get ready for a tournament with a month or so of preparation, and (3) one cannot build character without testing weaknesses.

What about self-defense? Surely, I still believed that tournaments have little, if anything, to do with self-defense. Well, almost. Tournament sparring is, in my opinion, a very small part of self-defense. It helps build reactions, develop strategy, and may even help with conditioning, but does not simulate a realistic self-defense situation. However, it does put one on the line. It gives a little hint of the pressure one might feel if faced with a no-goodnik. It provides a test. Passing that test is not required for learning karate but ignoring the test because of fear or even a little uncertainty is not advantageous to the development of the self.

And that is what karate is all about.

## FOREST FOR THE TREES

I often tell beginners who claim to be self-conscious in class, "Don't worry, the other novices are too concerned with themselves to notice you." Generally, this is true for new students, not for seniors. Good seniors keep their eyes open and somehow manage to be aware of themselves and, at the same time, aware of others. Sensei is supposed to be aware of everything: the dojo atmosphere, individual students' needs, student-to-student interactions, if uniforms are clean, if the mat has been cleaned, if the trash has been dumped, and what he said last week about a certain technique. It is rather amazing how this skill grows in a good teacher. He or she may teach on one level, simultaneously suggest another level of study, observe beginners at a third level, and still time the lesson so that everyone receives adequate practice and attention. More amazing is that he doesn't screw up more often.

It is important that a new instructor teach his students as well as possible so a few of them last into the teacher's old age. That way he has some backup if he slips. In a very mature dojo, the seniors have the seasoning to start a dojo for themselves but choose not to. Sometimes this fidelity is because their priorities lie in a different area, sometimes they simply want to be loyal to the person who taught them how to tie an obi (belt.) Good seniors make an adequate sensei look good and a good sensei look great.

In the '70s, I did a stint as lifeguard for a summer camp. I was in tip-top shape and had passed a combined Red Cross/YMCA lifesaving course. I was looking forward to overseeing the single, moderate-sized pool for five 50-minutes shifts, five days a week. I had the ring buoys and aluminum poles at the ready, knew how to throw a coiled lifeline if necessary and, most importantly, could jump to any corner of the pool in a matter of seconds. Most of the staff had been briefed in water safety by previous lifeguards. All I had to do was set the pool rules, blow my whistle for buddy-drill occasionally, and look authoritative (and tanned). I let everyone know, however, that each person was responsible for everyone else's safety. "Everyone should be aware of everyone else at all times."

Late one Friday afternoon, I looked over to the far side where counselor Paul was flirting with counselor Nancy and thus not observing the pool. Just a yard away at my lower right, Robyn, a 13-year-old junior-counselor, was consoling a 6-year-old girl. The youngster was half crying, half coughing. Her counselor found her and walked her out of the swimming area.

"Robyn, what was that about?" I inquired.

"I thought you saw. She's okay, just scared."

A senior counselor leaned to me and whispered, "Robyn just pulled her out. She was struggling. You were looking across to Paul and Nancy." Only three or four seconds had passed between Robyn's noticing the girl and pulling her out by the arm. They were three or four seconds which could have been tragic. Luckily, Robyn had done her job well and simultaneously had covered my backside.

Referring to Joseph P. Kennedy's influence on his sons, Theodore Sorenson wrote, "The ambassador was never present, but his presence was never absent." So it is with teachers. Any teacher. Anytime.

It is for this reason that I am so thankful for the wisdom of senior students who share the instruction in the dojo. A woman whom I had been coaching in a difficult takedown visited my office after class. "I got it! I just want you to know I can do the takedown now. You've been trying to tell me, show me, teach me every way under the sun, but I just didn't get it. Sempai Tom just said that I was trying to see the whole picture and I needed to look more at the detail. It clicked! Now I can do it."

This was precisely what I had taught Tom ten years before. Sometimes, you have to look at the forest, sometimes just the trees. In either case, Tom might have said precisely what I needed to say to the woman but had not. He backed me up well. It was not that big a deal, I know. Not life threatening, nothing that would make the difference between life and death. One hopes.

# JIANG BANGJUN

## UNLIMITED WUSHU: NO BASICS, NO WUSHU!

The basic skills of Wushu, generally referred as Basics (Ji Ben Gong), are the essential fundamentals — the building blocks — to become an accomplished Wushu practitioner, regardless of the type of Wushu that you practice, whether it is traditional or contemporary, focused on forms or sparring. Basics encompass a wide array of techniques, exercises, and drills divided into eight areas of instruction. They are: stretching and flexibility exercises, hand forms and hand techniques, stances and footwork, leg techniques, basic combinations, balance techniques, jumping techniques, and tumbling techniques. In order to gain proficiency in Wushu, the objective should always be to build up a strong foundation first and work later on integrating and refining all the independent parts as a whole.

The process of learning basic skills is a long-term commitment. Beginners should practice the basic skills of Wushu at a comfortable level, with an emphasis on understanding the requirements of each movement while building up athletic attributes, such as strength, flexibility, balance, agility, and coordination. It is imperative to learn to execute all techniques in a correct and clean manner prior to thinking about adding speed or power. Correct technique and quality repetition is the key to learning skills. This is not to say that hard training is not necessary, but sometimes the wrong kind of training can do more damage than good.

Bear in mind that "basic" skills are not necessarily "easy" skills. For instance, let's take one of the most popular Wushu techniques — the jumping inside slap kick. This movement consists of a vertical jump, a spin of the waist, an inside slap kick performed in midair, and an accurate jump reception. For each part, numerous skills are involved. For example, explosive force and good spring to acquire the ideal jump height; strong waist, stomach, and back muscles to facilitate the spinning motion; good flexibility and leg power to kick close to the body and make a loud slap; and many more.

Ironically, a proper jumping inside slap kick can be completed in a split second by an experienced practitioner, but gaining such proficiency usually takes several years of continuous practice. Again, the teaching/learning process of the basic skills of Wushu is a long one, and unfortunately, there are no shortcuts. Following a systematic and integrative training program is the only way to guarantee a successful and safe Wushu career.

## OLYMPIC WUSHU: REALITY OR DREAM?

Wushu has a very long history in China; in fact, its long process of evolution predates recorded history. In ancient times, Wushu originated directly from the productive labors of China's ancient ancestors, since early men were forced to develop the ability to defend themselves against animals and other men just to survive. When the Xia Dynasty (2100–1766 B.C.) came into power, Wushu was well developed to meet the real needs for military use in the endless conflicts and battles that were to follow. Over the centuries, Wushu adapted to the changes of society closely related to the production, work, war, and entertainment needs of each era, gradually becoming an integral part of China's traditional sports.

During the Republic of China period (1912–1949), many Wushu experts started pugilistic and sportive societies across the country. In 1928, the Central Guoshu Institute was established in Nanjing, gathering many famous masters from several regions to coordinate and disseminate martial arts. Guoshu, literally National Methods, was the official name of Wushu during that period. In 1936, a Chinese Wushu delegation performed at the XI Olympic Games in Berlin, which was the first time that Wushu was displayed in the Olympics.

Upon the establishment of the People's Republic of China, the government set up a Sports Commission that engaged in efforts to rescue this important cultural legacy. In 1958, the Chinese Wushu Association was founded in Beijing, and masters worked upon the improvement of the sportive qualities and difficulties of Wushu, combining the principles of sports science with the skills and theories of traditional Wushu. Soon, the first Modern Wushu Competition Rules were published, and national competitions began to be held every year.

In the 1970s, legendary martial artist and movie star Bruce Lee took the world by storm with his martial arts movies, setting the path for international action stars like Jackie Chan, Jet Li, and others, but most importantly, letting the whole world know about Chinese Wushu. In 1985, the first International Wushu Tournament was held in Xi'an, China, and the Preparatory Committee for the International Wushu Federation was elected. This was an important milestone in the development of Wushu as an international sport. In 1987, the city of Yokohama held the first Asian Wushu Championships. In 1990, Wushu was included for the first time in the 11th Asian Games. The 1st World Wushu Championships were held in Beijing in 1991. Developments continued at all levels, and in 1999, the International Olympic Committee granted provisional recognition to the International Wushu Federation.

In 2001, following Beijing's successful bid to host the 2008 Olympic Games, and confident that the sport would finally be included in the official Olympic program, the International Wushu Federation stepped into a new era of development to meet the strict Olympic standards. In 2002, the International Olympic Committee officially recognized the International Wushu Federation and accepted its application to be listed as a medal event in February, alongside other sports. A few months later, 18 of those applications were formally rejected and Wushu was confirmed for further study. At this point, the Olympic dream seemed still attainable, and the Chinese Wushu Association and the International Wushu Federation ventured into different initiatives to further accelerate the popularization of Wushu in the world. However, despite all efforts, in 2005 the International Olympic Committee announced that Wushu will not be part of the official medal events of the 2008 Beijing Olympic Games. Instead, the International Wushu Federation will organize an international Wushu Competition, parallel to the Olympic Games and with International Olympic Committee approval, called "2008 Beijing Olympic Wushu Championships."

As reforms and modifications carry on, the great sport of Wushu will continue to develop more and more, and perhaps our Olympic dream will become reality in the not-too-distant future. I strongly believe that Wushu will be included into the Olympic Games one day.

## WUSHU: NOT YOUR TYPICAL "SOFT" STYLE!

During my years living in the United States, I have been invited to numerous tournaments and martial arts festivals of all kinds. I quickly noticed that some venues offer forms of competition that include divisions for "soft" and "hard" styles. In the beginning, I wasn't too sure of the meaning of such classification. Later, it was explained to me that styles like Karate and Taekwondo were generally referred as "hard," while "Wushu" was considered a "soft" style. I understand that having "soft" and "hard" divisions at these venues may simply be done as a way to provide a method to distribute competitors of similar types of arts when competing against each other, perhaps to facilitate the judges at their work. But, nevertheless, I consider that this distinction can be misleading for other martial artists and the public in general.

In terms of grouping martial arts, Wushu styles generally are classified into various categories according to all kinds of parameters. Among these, the most frequently used are:

***By Geographical Location*** -- Styles are divided into Northern and Southern, having the Yangtze River or Chang Jiang as the delimiter;

***By Originating Region*** -- Meishanquan is the style of the Mei Mountain in Hunan; Shaolinquan is the style that originated at the Shaolin Temple in Henan;

***By Family or Clan*** -- Hongjiaquan (Hung Gar) is the style of the Hong family; Yuejiaquan is the style of the famous General Yue Fei family;

***By Combat Approach*** -- Changquan is a long-range style; Yongchunquan (Wing Chun) is a short-range style; Chuojiao emphasizes leg attacks; Houquan is an imitative style that incorporates monkey movements;

***By Type of Strength or Power Used*** -- Taijiquan or Baguazhang are internal styles; Changquan or Fanziquan are external styles; and,

***By Religious Connotations*** -- Luohanquan is the style of Arhats (Buddhism); Chaquan is the style of Chamir (Muslim); Baxianquan is the style of the 8 Immortals (Daoism).

Granted, some of these classifications are not free of contradiction and ambiguity, as it is very hard to come up with parameters that clearly define mutually exclusive categories. But is it correct to divide martial arts into "soft" and "hard"? And moreover, why is Wushu considered a "soft" style?

Every style of martial arts may have its own appearance, preferences, and qualities, but we cannot forget that all of them share the same objective—to work as an effective method of attack and defense. Therefore, I dislike the idea that martial arts can be classified as "soft." On the other hand, a martial art should not be classified as "hard," either. Before, I mentioned that Karate and Taekwondo are considered "hard" styles because they are based mainly on punching and kicking techniques. But what makes a punch or a kick really powerful? Is it all based on muscular tension? No, actually, power is directly related to speed, distance, and mass, so the right amount of relaxation will speed up a punch and make its impact more explosive. The whipping motion of a good roundhouse kick clearly is not a "hard" movement. So, it is clear that softness and hardness are always interacting together in all martial arts.

Now, in regard to Wushu, this factor becomes even more evident. In order to promote Wushu in the United States, I have competed on a few occasions at these venues, preparing special routines with elements of various schools of Wushu, namely Changquan, Eagle Claw, and Taijiquan. Changquan allows me to show high speed and explosiveness with fast and extended punches and swift jump kick combinations. Eagle Claw incorporates the imitation of an animal spirit, slow and serene like an eagle floating in the air watching its prey, with sudden fast and fierce attacks, just like an eagle does.

With Taijiquan, an internal method of force generation can be demonstrated with slow movements that are "soft" only in appearance, but also integrate hardness within them. This is better described in the classic texts as "an iron bar concealed inside cotton." The softness of Taijiquan does not mean total looseness; there is active force of different kinds working behind every movement, and when power is released, it is complete power from the whole body, as well.

I will close with an old Wushu saying: "Gang Rou Xiang Ji" (literally: Hard Soft Mutually Aid) that highlights the importance for every Wushu practitioner to understand the skills and effects of the relationships between hardness and softness. This is just an example of how the concept of the Yin and Yang—the unity and interaction of two opposites—is borrowed from Chinese philosophy and applied to Wushu. In fact, Wushu stresses the integration of such opposites as motion and stillness, emptiness and fullness, softness and hardness, opening and closing, tightness and looseness, etc. And I am sure these are universal principles that can be found within all martial arts and combat methods around the world.

## WUSHU SHOUT: MORE THAN HOT AIR

Probably one of the most common ideas associated with many different styles of Martial Arts in general, apart from the punches, leaps and kicks, is that practitioners always use some kind of personal shouts or yells while carrying out their techniques. As we know, this not totally a misconception, but definitely not a rule of thumb either. Some Martial Arts use it and others not so much; therefore, I decided to dedicate this column to offer a brief explanation about this interesting subject.

Martial Arts shouts, called *fasheng* in Chinese (literally, release shout), can be great theater at competitions, movies, and demonstrations. They never fail to please the audience, but they are much more than that. Within the vast realm of Chinese Wushu, there are many traditional schools that emphasize the use of shouts, grunts, and exaggerated breathing patterns with physical, mental, and health implications. Perhaps most famous for this, but not exclusively, are those styles from the south of the Yellow River. Take for example Hung Gar, the style associated with the Cantonese folk hero Huang Feihong. During practice, Hung Gar experts use a wide array of sound emissions such as "Hah," "Wah," "Hee," and many more, forcing air from their abdomen and diaphragm, each said to have a specific effect in the body's internal organs.

Another example could be the hybrid style of Choy Lee Fut, which also originated in the Guangdong province. Choy Lee Fut fighters scream "Sik" when executing sweeping punches, "Yik" when rotating the waist, "Tik" when kicking and "Wah" when using a tiger claw technique, and others. Consequently, when modern *Nanquan*

(Southern Boxing) was compiled based primarily on these traditional styles in the 1960s, standards for *fasheng* also were incorporated into the program; in fact, failure to use screams in a competition routine according to the specifications will result in point deductions.

Back on topic, screaming actually is a method of channeling your mind, body, and spirit into a technique. This is demonstrated in many sports that require quick exertions of explosive force, and not just in Martial Arts. Research indicates that shouting can positively affect physical or mental performance. As you exhale forcefully (shout), you can amplify your strength by rapidly contracting the transverse abdominals and other core muscles, providing better support for striking techniques. Also, the scream can momentarily block diverse sensations on your nervous system that could slightly increase your threshold of pain, and thus allows you to continue with the exercise and carry out greater efforts than normal.

Finally, a point often overlooked is that by screaming at certain points of the execution of a form you can regulate your breathing, pacing your exhalations in coordination with those energy-consuming movements. Not to mention releasing any unnecessary tension and even intimidating your opponents. Now ou too can become a master of the fabled "Lion's Roar" skills.

## MODERN WUSHU *VERSUS* MARTIAL APPLICATION

During my years as a professional Wushu competitor and coach, I've often been asked about the functional applications of several of the typical movements found in Contemporary Wushu routines. I could even go further and say that I've noticed how Contemporary Wushu often is derided for its perceived lack of practicality. For that reason, I feel the need to comment.

Wushu initially evolved as a mean of military training closely linked with the ancient military struggle. This implies that Wushu had clear attacking characteristics used to conquer enemies by employing such fighting skills as hitting, kicking, wrestling, and holding as basic offensive and defensive techniques. Because of its long history of incorporating and blending with different regional cultures, ideologies, and usages, Wushu developed into a great variety of schools and styles. Most importantly, it broadened the horizon of mere martial arts, becoming one of our earliest sporting exercises, health improvement methods, and artistic forms. Upon the establishment of the New China and the development of Contemporary Wushu, many of these ancient ways and methods have been collected, refined, and standardized, and Wushu has been classified into several different areas of specialization. Yet, it still maintains its offensive and defensive skills; after all, how could it be different? Otherwise, Wushu would have been deprived of its essence!

Today, Contemporary Wushu can be grouped into two major divisions: Competition Routines (Taolu) and Free Sparring (Sanda). Taolu competition is a unique form of Wushu that could be defined as a fascinating interpretation of traditional martial arts within the characteristics of an elite performance sport, whereas Sanda is a complete and realistic combat discipline that preserves the martial values and heritage of traditional Wushu, both in its sportive and military versions. Therefore, if we want to talk about the actual combat skills of Contemporary Wushu, we first should understand the underlying differences in nature and purpose of both Taolu and Sanda. Since the martial implications of the latter are obvious, I will focus on the former for the rest of this column.

Originally, traditional Wushu methods were codified into routines, for multiple reasons. Routines represented core techniques to be preserved and passed down from generation to generation. They were training tools to allow practitioners to familiarize themselves with several different attack and defense skills while increasing their strength, improving their balance, etc. They also could be used for demonstrations in cultural festivals, early sportive events, and other forms of entertainment. Consequently, we can observe that elements of physical culture and performance always have been present among traditional martial arts.

Contemporary Taolu competition is no different. It comprises solo routines, both barehanded and with weapons; Group Sets, a collective event in which several competitors perform routines together, barehanded or with weapons; and Sparring Sets, which, as the name suggests, involve two or more contestants going through a prearranged combat routine that can be classified into three categories: barehanded, armed, and barehanded against armed. Evidently, some of the technical specifications of certain traditional movements, such as the amplitude of motion, the speed, the height of the jumps, etc., needed to be modified, subject to a specific competition format and rules, but the attacking characteristics of dozens of styles of traditional Wushu have been preserved. For instance, northern styles with long-range techniques such as Chaquan, Huaquan, Hongquan, and others, are present within the contemporary Changquan routines. The compact footwork and powerful hand techniques of the southern styles, such as Hongquan, Cailifo and others, are present within the contemporary Nanquan routines, and so on.

In general, Contemporary Taolu competition emphasizes agility and speed, stressing continuity of movements, clean and accurate actions, and sudden changes of rhythm. In addition, there is a need for a well-balanced choreography that includes the most important movements of the style that is being represented well-knit together. As a performance-oriented sport discipline, there also is room for movements and actions that may not represent attack and defense techniques, for example transitions between other movements or technical requirements such as high difficulty moves; however, the main components of a Wushu routine still are kicks, punches, grabs, throws, and other attack and defense techniques. And even though the main objective of a Taolu competitor is not to apply these techniques in combat, his or her representation will be improved greatly by understanding them.

In my opinion, without knowing the functional application of the movements, there cannot be real martial intent in the performance; without real martial intent, the performance then turns into a mere representation of a sequence of physical movements, more akin to gymnastics or modern dance. Only when the nature and true meaning of the movements is grasped will the movements become true to their origins. Attack and defense is the essence of Wushu.

# ROBERT CHU

## FIGURE IT OUT

My training brothers and I have often discussed our master's teaching methods. Sometimes we can see benefits and sometimes we feel there are better ways of teaching and making points. Early in my wing chun career, I was faced with some of the feudal methods of closed-door teaching: outrageous fees, curtains, secrecy, and oaths. I also met some false masters who did not have the proper credentials to teach or were not honest about their own training. Some will say that my criticism is unwarranted and goes against tradition. Some people look at my background and try to find out who these people are, then accuse me of being disrespectful to these "masters." It is not the masters I criticize, but the outdated teaching methods that inhibit true learning and block true understanding of the martial arts.

If you spent 27 years learning martial arts and found a way to encapsulate all your important teaching in a shorter period of time, would that not be more efficient? Why don't we look for that? Manufacturers do that all the time when building computers or cars – better, faster, and cheaper. Should we not also improve the training methods used to teach the martial arts? The traditional method basically has the student figure out the style for themselves by following the master's vague and unclear teaching. I have often said that if grade school were taught using the methods of the old-fashioned sifus, no one would ever complete high school! Perhaps because I grew up in the United States, I have come to believe that one should feed a student as much information as possible and have them prove the principles and concepts themselves. This way, a student wastes less time with theories, endless forms and techniques, and unstructured classes. Using this method, martial arts training in the next century can be revolutionized. In America, masters cannot expect a student to follow them for 10 or 20 years to learn their "secrets." A master in America should think of shortcuts and training methods to shorten the learning curve, This, while still imparting important skills and attributes to students of all levels by arranging the subject matter in a logical and easy-to-follow manner.

The late xing yi and ba gua master, Kenny Gong, once told me, "If a sifu really wants to teach a disciple everything, he can accomplish that in about two years, regardless of the martial art, provided that the student is diligent in his practice and reasonably intelligent." I believe this to be true. Teachers should all strive to teach as much important material as possible in the first two years of a student's education. To me, advanced training is simply the applied basics. Even if a system of martial arts has many forms, like choy lay fut, for example, a study of the core forms, and main principles and concepts of the art, is enough. If a student wants to learn more forms after this core training they may elect to do so, but that does not add to the kernel. This is the same with wing chun, or other martial arts systems like praying mantis, tai ji, xing yi, or ba gua.

My hope is to one day see a revolution in the teaching of the martial arts, and to have modern masters better systemize their teaching and training methods. Identify what prevents a student from learning a particular skill. If it is terminology, make it simpler to understand, if it is a series of complex movements, break them down to their basic components. This is the best way to teach martial arts. Teachers today can help create a new generation of practitioners who will later applaud and appreciate these helpful contributions to the martial arts.

## CIRCLE AND LINE DRILLS

Often, martial arts schools do not properly teach self-defense methods for dealing with multiple attackers. In this situation it is best to avoid using grappling skills and to not go to the ground. The idea is to stay on your feet and "hit and run" to immediately get out of harm's way. Self-defense is not dueling, and it is very important to distinguish the two. Self-defense requires that you stop an attack and then retreat and run away from danger. Dueling is a situation where both combatants mutually agree to do harm to each other. The only purpose of self-defense is to get out of a bad situation as quickly and efficiently as you can. Early on, I introduce my students to two very important drills which gives them a sense of how to face multiple attackers and escape quickly. I call these the circle and line drills.

The circle drill is done with the entire class in order to practice and develop timing and positioning skills while under the stress of facing multiple attackers. The circle drill begins with one student at the center of a circle formed by his fellow classmates. Each student along the circle is assigned a number. A number is randomly called, and the corresponding student attacks the person in the center with a single unexpectedly move. The person in the middle must spontaneously react to this attack and deal with it properly. Each member of the class has a turn being in the center of the circle. Variations of this drill include calling numbers out in random order and moving the position of the attackers around the circle to keep the defender mentally off-balance and unable to anticipate who and where the next attack will come from.

In the line drill, the class forms a single line with the defender at the end facing forward. Each person on the line, in succession, launches a single committed attack at the target defender. The object of this drill is to pressure the defender to react spontaneously to multiple attackers and to link attacking and defensive maneuvers. It also serves to train the mind to not lose composure in a real situation like this. This drill also develops timing and positioning.

As a variation to the line drill, the students form two lines and alternate making left and right attacks at the defender. They can also attack simultaneously. In my classes, both drills have been very well-received by the students. They are a lot of fun and are great aerobic exercise as well.

## MARTIAL ARTS LESSONS

It has been said that from a small *dao* (way), one can learn the *dao*. Learning martial arts introduces students to another culture and teaches them how things are done in another country. In learning about another culture, we can clearly reflect on our own culture and values. This can open our minds to a more cosmopolitan world view and free us from a limited, ethnocentric perspective. This is probably the single greatest benefit that comes from learning another culture's native arts. Learning about a salutation, or the history of a particular form, or lion dancing can give you unique insights into the Chinese mind.

In martial arts, sometimes teachings are metaphors for life's lessons. In wing chun, students are taught the value of the centerline. We want to protect and attack the centerline. Taking it a step further, the centerline is also a means of entry between the defender and the attacker and a metaphor for the center of gravity. It also refers to a philosophical base of being neutral and seeing issues from both sides, or clearly seeing where you are in relation to your adversary.

Lessons also include a means of understanding how one can become successful. The training that I give to my students does not just reflect in their fists and body, but in their minds, their social life, their work, and education as well. My students are taught to be successful in any endeavor. This is because you have to have a goal or target, make a plan to reach that goal, evaluate your plan, and adjust it to reach your destination. I look at martial arts as a means of developing positive strength for my students to be successful throughout their life.

When faced with sparring or sticking hands practice, I expect a student to learn how to problem solve and how to analyze, dissect, and summarize. When they are faced with adversity a student must ponder with an open, inquisitive mind and never just blindly follow teachings, but question them. A student should want to question and always learn, and I want them to not be tied down to the old, traditional, secretive instruction so prevalent in Chinese culture. I ask that they actively participate in the mastery of the arts by combining 50 percent of my instruction, with 50 percent of their own introspection and practice.

Martial arts training can also lead to one to find peace and inner harmony. Many of the philosophical notions of martial arts are based on the teachings of Buddhism and Taoism and lend themselves to a practice of spiritual enlightenment. Even the Chinese words "*wu shu*" (martial arts) have a deeper meaning. "*Wu*" means to stop a halberd, which relates to stopping conflict. "*Shu*" refers to "art" or "science." I always teach my students that if they can master the art of stopping conflicts, whether their own or others, they can live a better life. This is one of the deepest teachings of martial arts.

Martial arts training is also healthy. To maximize the potential of using the body flexibly and powerfully is one of the strongest lessons one can learn. In Chinese martial arts, the training of *qi* can also lead to understanding the body and health. The study of body mechanics, kinesiology, anatomy, physiology, physics, and the vulnerable areas to attack, led me into the study of Chinese medicine where I can now better understand how to heal the body. My teachers, Yee Chi Wai, Chen Tai Shan, Kwan Jong Yuen, and Lui Yon Sang influenced me by encouraging me to learn more about meridian points, herbal medicines, and the value of Chinese medicine.

The values of martial arts lessons are deeper than violence or self-defense. Martial arts can make you into a better person. With them, you can reach your full potential as a person. As the Greeks idealized, "Make savage the body and make civilized the mind." Through the practice of the martial arts, we can unlock the secrets of our own minds, bodies, and spirits to achieve true understanding and inner peace.

## **TEACHER, TEACH THYSELF**

Many martial arts teachers don't take the time to learn how to teach. Some may be great fighters, know forms, knowledge, and history, be champion sportsmen, or possess the deepest secrets of their systems, but learning how to teach is an art unto itself. Teaching is a separate ability that requires knowledge in language, social skills, and communication. All students learn differently. Many think it's easy to earn their black belt, open a school, have their own students, and collect tuition. But they realize it's not that easy when they see their students drop out one-by-one. When students lose interest, words alone will not motivate them to continue practicing.

A teacher of the martial arts must possess a genuine love for the art and not look at it as only a potential moneymaker. A teacher owes it to the students to make learning fun and successful by helping students reach their personal goals. I taught for my teachers for many years in order to develop a personal style of teaching. Many teachers bestow a certificate that says a student has reached the rank of "sifu," "master," or "instructor." A certificate, however, doesn't automatically make a person a good teacher. Teaching, and learning from teaching, is how one becomes a great teacher.

Interaction, communication, and humor are good ways to get a message across. Sharing personal anecdotes and experiences also works. This not only makes teaching fun, but also hard training enjoyable for the students. Minds should be developed along with bodies, and keen spirituality as well. The curriculum needs to be varied. There should be lots of drills and exercises that explore and emphasize different facets of the art at different times. Because different students learn differently, it is best to have a mix of practice, lecture, equipment training, partner exercises, forms and weaponry.

I have a list of subjects that I prepare lessons from. Sometimes I will brainstorm ideas with my students. I will even create a list of topics and then ask my students which looks most interesting. Some topics for wing chun classes in my Los Angeles school have included applications of wing chun against other arts, distance applications, taking the outside gate, body structure, throws, joint locks, long and short weaponry, and body connection. I even like to include unusual topics like Chinese terminology, history of martial arts, or Chinese medical theory. The list is endless. I review these subjects on a regular basis and make sure I prepare for them in advance. In this way, the classes never become stagnant or unimaginative.

Teaching is sharing and communicating. Boring teachers will lose students. Being too strict will also cause students to flee. I have learned to teach by the students I attract. I originally wanted to teach only Chinese students, but later found that I could teach anyone really interested. I was faced with having to also teach my students a bit of Chinese culture, history, and language so they could understand the context in which the martial arts developed. I have found that this makes for a better, more educated martial artist and does not take away from skill development, but rather, enhances it.

I always interview prospective students to understand what they want and why they train. I have to be in-tune to better know how to teach that individual. Often, people email me to ask what classes cost, what the schedule is, and where I teach. They are often put off because I question them about their goals and background. In essence, it's a screening process to see if that individual will be a good fit for the class. In the past, martial arts' training was only between people of close relationship and good character. I still think this is the way it should be.

It is an unfortunate fact that many people do not have a knack for teaching. They talk a lot but say nothing. Some just drill too much, paying no attention to their student's goals. A Chinese martial art should not taught like a Marine boot camp with barking commands and endless, mindless repetitions. Training should be hard but fun and emphasize understanding the essence and functionality of the art in a family setting.

A good teaching style will result in good students. Teachers shouldn't put themselves on a pedestal. The way to attract motivated, intelligent students, and keep them, is to be approachable, perceptive, and flexible. Most importantly, when teachers help students reach their goals, they also help themselves accomplish their own objectives.

## FOUR OUNCES

One of the most famous Chinese folk sayings is *"Si liang bo qian jin."* This is often poorly translated as "Four ounces can repel a thousand pounds." This saying is so common that it resounds in literature written on tai ji quan, xing yi, and ba gua. Many of the practitioners of these arts say this ability what makes their art "internal." Even Chinese knowledgeable in *cheng yu* (common Chinese sayings) are familiar with this phrase. But, under careful analysis, should it be taken literally?

We will start by analyzing the weights and meanings of the words. "Si liang" is a measure of four *liang*. A liang is a standard of weight from the Tang Dynasty. Often, a liang is called a *"tael"* in English. One liang was equivalent to 31.25 grams in the Tang Dynasty. In 1979, the People's Republic of China (PRC) set a standard of one liang equal to 30 grams. Four times 30 grams is 120 grams. For you metrically challenged individuals, that's 4.23 ounces. Not precise, but close to "Four ounces," roughly the weight of a McDonald's Quarter Pounder before cooking.

A *jin* is a standard of weight equals "16 liang" from the Tang dynasty. Sixteen times 31.25 grams equals 500 grams, or by today's PRC standard (16 times 30 grams) equals 480 grams, or roughly half a kilogram. "Qian jin" would be 1000 jin, or 1000 times 500 grams, and equals 500,000 grams or 500 kilograms. Again, for you metrically challenged individuals, 500 Kilograms would be 1103.75 pounds. Again, not precise, but close to the "thousand pounds" of the saying.

This leaves us with the word *"bo"*. In the Pinyin Chinese-English dictionary, the word "bo" (first tone in Mandarin) refers to "moving with the hand, stick, etc; turn; stir; poke." Now, that does not sound like a definition for the English word, "repel." When put together, "Si liang bo qian jin" actually means "4.23 ounces moves/turns/stir/pokes 1103.75 pounds".

What does this really mean? How can 4.23 ounces move 1103.75 pounds? It doesn't sound possible from a physics point of view. Maybe it's "qi power" or that special "internal power" from the "internal arts?" Perhaps that is one of the storied "internal principles" it takes 20 years to learn? Personally, I don't believe that. If it is a "principle," and we are not mentally challenged and a person can explain it to us adequately, we should be able to learn it quickly.

For many years I have studied martial arts and have met many real masters and many more pseudo masters. I have typically asked most of them this question and have gotten many answers. My belief is that a true master of tai ji quan should be able to demonstrate this principle all the time, as this is one of the defining points of tai ji quan and is related in the tai ji "Song of Striking (Push) Hands" attributed to Wang Zongyue, and Li Yiyu's "Five Word Secrets." The truth is, I have met few masters who could really demonstrate this. Many were excellent at the form, push hands, weaponry, qi cultivation, health, meditation, and philosophical aspects of tai ji quan, but never were able to satisfy me with their definition of "Si liang bo qian jin." If I, a Chinese, could not find a "real master" to show me how four ounces moves a thousand pounds," how is the average American going to learn?

Cheng Man Ching, in his writings from his 13 chapters (I use Douglas Wile's translation here), clarified it best, "...only four ounces of energy is needed to pull a thousand pounds, then the push is applied. Pulling and repelling are two different things. It is not really that one uses only four ounces to repel a thousand pounds." Cheng's writings then go on to describe an analogy of a thousand-pound bull. Regardless of pushing and pulling, one cannot move a bull if he does not want to move, yet by putting a ring in the bull's nose, pulling a rope with only 4 ounces of force can cause the bull to move. Strategically placed, and causing pain to the bull, the ring illustrates how one must lead the bull to move.

In my own art of wing chun, we have sticking hands (*chi sao*) which is akin to tai ji's push hands in developing and neutralizing power and developing sensitivity. In sticking hands practice, I may poke at, push, pull, press, move, stir, lead, or entice my opponent with what is called "*mun sao*" (asking hands). Once I get my opponent to move, I can guide, lead, or borrow his momentum to use his own force for my opponent's demise. When a force is upon you, let's say 100 lbs of pressure, you need to be able to equalize it with 100 lbs of your own pressure. The resultant force is neutralized, and we both stay where we are. When I reduce my force by a mere quarter pound, the opponent's force will begin to move toward me, and from there, I can change the direction of my 99.75 pounds and add on or change the direction of our resultant forces to other directions. This will lead me to create or find a technique to fit in accord to the circumstances. This illustrates the principle of "4 ounces moving 1000 pounds" in action.

In my opinion, to find someone who can really use the principle of "four ounces to move 1000 pounds" is rare. You will rarely find this in practitioners who do not engage in some form of sensitivity training like push hands or sticking hands. When a principle is fully understood, it moves away from the realm of theory. When one can actually use the principle in application, this is a person who has sought out the true function of the form. When I realized the true significance of "Si liang bo qian jin," I was able to use it in combat or practice and not hurt my opponents, by just using just enough force. How much exactly? About 4.23 ounces.

## WHAT KIND OF STUDENT AM I?

You can only teach a few students completely and can easily spot those who will stay with you the longest. Some come for information, some for technique, some for curiosity, but very few come for a complete transmission.

Teaching in the old days meant being part of a guild. To learn a craft, you had to find a master. *Sifu* means "skilled father of your craft." In Chinese culture, you can learn from anyone more skilled than you and call them "sifu."

Once you were accepted into the guild you began learning. You would move from apprentice to journeyman and finally, after much time and hardship, become a master and accept your own apprentices. The parallel between Chinese martial arts and society is clear. People have romanticized the teacher-student relationship as a form of adoption by a better parent, spiritual advisor, or healer with divine powers. These people need to face a bit of reality.

Some have wanted private lessons, saying that if I taught them everything about my art in a weekend, they would open a school and teach in my name. I usually laugh and say that nothing surpasses true physical skill in martial arts. One may develop strong theoretical and technical skill in a short time but turning the theories into principles and techniques into concepts takes years.

Some come to see if I can correct martial weaknesses. I try to provide pointers on the martial arts way so that these students can develop eyes to "see" the truth and develop a means to improve. In this way, they can train on their own.

Some want to learn a part of wing chun kuen they don't know. Others want to learn a weapons set because so few people specialize in it. I try to show them variations and give them a sense of "aliveness" with the weapon, as well as tie-in the core principles of wing chun. I am happy to help these *tong mun* (followers of the same art). I am not, however, as willing to teach wing chun outsiders as they could easily confuse the art, lacking a strong background in it. But I always try to give the student the best that I can and fulfill their desires as much as possible. I am glad to help fellow wandering knights along their path of self-discovery.

I have even had experts of other systems visit me to supplement their training and to discuss various general points of the martial arts. I enjoy this very much as I can learn more of another's art and get a fresh view of another system. A more enlightened practitioner should recognize that all martial arts are good and that we must understand the context of their use. For those seeking truth, there is nothing wrong in seeking it – but be fair and willing to pay your dues. Ultimately, one must solve the puzzle of their martial arts for themselves. If you need expert opinions, consult with an expert. If there is a fee, gladly pay it, as it will save you time and money in the long run.

I wrote a chapter in *Complete Wing Chun* on the gulao wing chun kuen system and people contacted me to learn the system long distance, through videotape. I rejected this idea because I did not know them personally and did not have a relationship with them. In all martial arts, it is best to have a personal relationship with an instructor. Nothing replaces human interaction and relationships. I tell prospective students to develop a relationship with their teacher, learn their personality, and develop open communication. Only then can they understand why the teacher chose to teach them in a certain manner, for their specific needs.

When I accept a student, I interview them to find out what their goals are. I find out their background, their experience, their profession, what have they learned in martial arts before, and why they want to study my art. I also ask them if they have any questions about me. In this way, I get a sense of who I am dealing with.

It is important to be honest with the student in fostering a good relationship, so that there are no unexpected disappointments in what they learn. I may be able to make a few months tuition on a particular student, but why deceive him if he is looking for ground-fighting skills and I teach standing techniques? It would be a detriment to me in the long run. I never try to put myself up on a pedestal and claim to be something I am not.

An early instructor of mine was very secretive and later I found out he was bluffing his way through teaching the system. The fact that my *si hing* (senior brothers) did not complete the entire system led me to believe that this instructor had not completed the highest levels of training. Sadly, some of his disciples are probably still propagating secrecy as tradition and not teaching the complete system to their students. What do we have here? A tradition of lies, cheating, and deceit. A knowledgeable teacher should be willing to teach everything openly and generously.

I believe that a student-teacher relationship must be kept honest in order to grow strong. A martial arts brother of mine, Hendrik Santo, said, "With strong roots one can grow tall. If one does not have strong roots, one can never stand tall on their own." Human interaction and relationships are the best ways to both teach and learn martial arts. As students of life, we can learn about living in the same way. Winning hearts is the best way to teach and opening your heart is the best way to learn. Each of us should always ask ourselves, *"What kind of student am I?*

## A CHINESE PERSPECTIVE ON OKINAWAN KARATE

My introduction to Okinawan Karate Do came at age 11, when I began training with Robert S. Weinberg, then 4th dan Shorin Ryu Karate Do, under Eizo Shimabuku, Hanshi of Shorin Ryu Rendokan in Okinawa. I studied Shorin ryu intensely for 7 ½ years, and later I pursued full time studies in Chinese martial arts, including Hung Kuen and Wing Chun Kuen, as well as the internal arts of Tai Ji Quan, Xing Yi and Ba Gua Quan. But I never completely gave up my Karate practice and did all the major kata of my system, including *Seisan, Naihanchin, Ananku, Wanshu, Gojushiho, Chinto, Passai, Kushanku, Sanchin* and *Seiunchin*.

Our first kata in Shorin ryu was *Seisan*. Through my long years of research and studying Okinawan roots in Chinese arts, I found that in *Seisan* kata there were many similarities to the Fujian fist arts, notably White Crane, Lo Han Quan, and other Fujian Shaolin derived arts.

As a researcher and writer, I often visited other martial artists and learned and spoke to them for their insights. As I grew up in NYC, there were always a plethora of many martial artists all with unique systems and methods. Throughout the years I had exposure to

Shotokan, Goju Ryu, Uechi Ryu, and other forms of Shorin Ryu. Of course, I also had access to Chinese Southern fist and Fujian fist systems as well.

In recent years, there has been a popularization of many Okinawan arts coming out and explaining the meaning behind *kata (forms)*, *bunkai (Dissection of forms)*, *oyo (follow up)*, *henka (transitions/variations)*, and *kakushite (hidden hands/hidden applications)*. In my opinion, many of these are made up and go overboard and do not reflect realism in the martial arts.

In the Chinese arts, we either practice two-man forms (*Dui Cha*) or extrapolate moves from the sets and practice their application called *San Sao* (Separate Hands). The two-man sets are often quite dramatic and showy, and may or may not reflect actual application of a particular system. These have a tendency to showmanship and performance. The *San Sao* often reflect the key words of a system and show the idea behind the system and its forms.

Since Okinawan martial arts are derived from Chinese Kenpo/*Quan Fa* in general, it is good to look at the source and how the fist arts are practiced by the Chinese. In the past, very little high-level information was passed on from the Chinese to the Okinawans, unless they were fluent in the Chinese language and *kanji* (written Chinese), and held status. In Matsumura Sokon's (founder of Shorin Ryu) case, that was completely possible.

There are some key points I would like to share from my years of practicing both Chinese and Okinawan martial arts:

1. **Don't defend from the inside gate.** A block to the inside of the wrist will get you struck by the other hand immediately.

2. **The hand that goes out does not come back empty.** You must be able to grab, pull, push, press, wedge against your opponent. This is the proper use of *meotode* (husband/wife hand).

3. **All kata actions are to go to the outside or behind the opponent.** At the first level, they may seem that the opponent is in front of you, but as you advance, it makes more sense to outflank your opponent.

4. **Stances are not poses; they are steps.** They are for transferring and receiving vector forces, energy, body weight and momentum.

5. **Steps should be against the opponent's stance to break his balance,** or through the legs to control the opponent's balance.

6. **Steps are often hidden kicks.**

7. **Poorly taught Okinawan martial artists mainly do a lot of wasted tension in the limbs.** The focus should be more on the *tai (body)*, *koshi (waist)* and *dachi (balance)*, which move with *chinkuchi (body connection)*.

8. **A vector line should be imagined** originating from your heels, through your *tanden*, to your striking or defending hand.

9. **Many blocks are not blocks,** but movements of crossing, entering, and controlling the bridges of the opponents, which leads to their off balance. Striking an opponent when you control their balance is the key to "one punch kill".

10. **Lack of understanding of *hojo undo* leads to overdone body development**. Instead, learn what these devices are supposed to train you to do – use your body optimally for leverage. What you are doing is throwing out your center of gravity and extending it out of your body with the training device to simulate offsetting an opponent.

11. **There should be proper timing when you do kumite**. It is reasonable to think that you only have time for one move if the opponent attacks with one move. The use of one step kumite which emphasizes a block, then a strike are suitable for beginners, but in reality, many kata motions use one movement to defend and attack simultaneously.

12. **There is no one true way of doing a kata**. It is subjective to the particular system you follow. When Chinese look at forms, they don't go crazy insistent that there is only one way – there are interpretations and we look at things as "*Da Tong Xiao Yi*" -- "The big things are the

same, the small things are different." This would end the political differences in performance of kata.

13. **Application is in the moment.** Try to drill multiple applications for one particular segment of the kata, as the Chinese do with *San Sao* (separate hands) extracted from the forms.

14. **You should not be able to dissect a corpse.** No opponent will simply stand there and let you finish him off, unless you are in complete control of his balance, and he has no ability to recover.

The above short list of points will go a long way to help your Okinawan Karate. Japanese Karate or Karate offshoots like Tae Kwon Do, will have to make major adjustments because of the length of stance, or distance they train in. Okinawan Karate is primarily infighting distance, and shares much in common with the Southern Fist Chinese boxing.

## BRUCE LEE'S GENIUS

By adapting and modifying his traditional Wing Chun skills into his personal art of Jeet Kune Do, Bruce Lee proved himself a true master and changed martial arts forever.

Because I have studied wing chun kuen in depth, I am often asked to give my opinion on Bruce Lee. My usual response is to say that Bruce Lee was quite talented and gifted. My background in researching wing chun allows me to view Bruce Lee as a practitioner of the art, a student of total combat (striking, kicking, joint locking, throwing, and ground fighting), and as one seeking liberation from the technical constraints of traditional martial arts. Of course, being from the same Yip Man wing chun system and being a student of Hawkins Cheung, his close friend and training partner, I probably view Bruce Lee differently from people not so well-versed in wing chun.

Many in the wing chun system say that Bruce Lee created jeet kune do because he was not a great practitioner and never completed the system. In all fairness, there is some truth to that. Bruce Lee probably only learned the *siu nim tao* and *chum kiu* forms (two of the three empty-hand sets), part of the wooden dummy set, and never formally learned the two weapons of wing chun – the long pole and the double knives. Despite these limitations, however, Lee did have a profound connection to the art of wing chun. His father had been a member of the Cantonese Opera (the ancestral source of the wing chun system) and, at a young age, sent him to study in Hong Kong directly under grandmaster Yip Man. Lee also had the opportunity to learn from his seniors, the late Wong Shun Leung and William Cheung. Later, in Seattle, Lee had a chance to see wing chun from a different perspective thanks to Yeung Fook, a friend of his father from the opera, who practiced the Gulao system.

## A True Master

Although Bruce Lee may not have been a master in the traditional Chinese sense, he is still deserving of high praise – not for being the founder of a martial art, a movie star, an early pioneer of wing chun in America, or even a role model for Chinese people everywhere, but rather for making his wing chun come alive.

My sifu, Hawkins Cheung, a close friend and training partner of Bruce Lee, stated to me, "The classical wing chun system doesn't teach you how to fight, it's up to your own experience. The three forms, *chi sao*, dummy, pole, and knife sets are there as reference material, and it's up to you to put it together in combat applications. Many create wing chun patterns to sell, but wing chun has no pattern. Many sell their patterns as wing chun – but wing chun is beyond that. Real wing chun is formless – practitioners create patterns based on their opponent's pattern. We study for years to reach a formless state. When one has reached a high level in wing chun, one discovers the changes that are possible in application. We call this *"bienfa"* (variations or changes). How many people spend the extensive time and do the intense research required to develop their wing chun to this point?

Bruce Lee did.

I believe the founders of wing chun named the first set *"siu nim tao"* (focus on the small at the foundation) because they wanted students to develop the imagination needed to utilize the art. *Siu nim tao* contains the majority of the wing chun tools, and someone who masters the form, in my opinion, has about 90 percent of the art already. With *chum kiu* (seeking/sinking the structure), the second form, and the first half of the wooden-dummy set, a student has about 95 percent of the tools used in the art. When people say Lee didn't learn the complete wing chun system, I agree with them in the classical sense, even though in the functional sense they're not entirely correct. How much does one really need to learn to truly understand what they have?

With some people, it takes longer to realize the tools are all there. Most are deluded by their teachers into thinking they need to learn the entire art of wing chun, and many other additional arts, to reach the point where they can create your own techniques. In my opinion, "mastery" is an unrealistic ideal and a very subjective individual attainment. Most martial artists are just technicians – they never reach a point where they become an "advanced" martial artist. I define an advanced martial artist as a person who can create his or her own patterns and techniques to adapt to the situation at hand while still following the structure of their own system. Bruce Lee reached this creative level in martial arts. Because of this, it can be said he was a true martial artist and a true master.

### Jun Fan Kung Fu

When Lee created his Jun Fan kung fu, he was marketing a modified form of wing chun that he created, which bore his name. Many buy into the concept Jun Fan, but in truth it is neither jeet kune do nor wing chun. I believe jeet kune do was Lee's term for his path of research for making wing chun come alive – he focused on the core principle important to him – the timing and ability to intercept his opponent's motions. Hawkins Cheung told me that Bruce and he had a motto, "One *pak da* to strike down everyone under heaven!" Jeet kune do was his expression of the combat applications, with variations and changes, of the wing chun *pak da* (slapping strike). The jeet kune do practiced today is not Lee's jeet kune do, but rather someone else's path. Wing chun contains a core concept called *"jeet kue"* – the central phase of wing chun where you cut off or intercept an opponent by proactively closing off or sealing their ability to continue. You deliberately place your body front of your opponent to limit and control his next motion. *Jeet kuen* is a way of meeting, capturing, and controlling your opponent's centerline and center of gravity in the most simple, direct, and economical way.

I believe Bruce Lee's celebrated fight with Wong Jack Man showed him many things. It showed him that he was not in top shape and that his understanding of wing chun (not wing chun, itself) was too rigid to deal with an opponent in a real encounter. In wing chun you are never told you must fight in a particular way, it's up to you how you choose to utilize it. Wing chun is like a toolbox: if you use a hammer like a screwdriver, then you're not using it for its designed purpose. But if you lack a screwdriver when you need it, and the hammer fits, why not use the hammer? One has to improvise to fit the situation at hand.

Wing chun can also be viewed like a racing car, If an "little old lady" drives the race car to the supermarket to do her weekly grocery shopping, she doesn't make maximum use of the machine. However, if Mario Andretti drives the car, watch out! How fast a race car goes depends on the person behind the wheel.

I think Lee also realized the American market liked sizzle and flash, so he jazzed up wing chun with such trappings, while still retaining wing chun's functional essence. The main concepts behind Bruce Lee's "real" JKD are derived from wing chun's motto: "Receive as the opponent comes, escort him when he leaves, rush in upon loss of contact." Hawkins Cheung said to me, "I can destroy you in one second, or I can destroy you in a few minutes. The simple, direct, and economical way is to do it as quickly as possible. That's the goal of wing chun."

By themselves, the wing chun forms are dead – only timing, attitude, and experience will make your kung-fu come alive. As a student on the path of totality in combat, Lee gained experience, and researched timing and attitude, to utilize his personal wing chun tools for his goal of "intercepting." In essence, he made the tools come alive in order to support his own personal philosophy of how to fight. Wing chun's tools are designed for maximum efficiency with minimum effort. With Lee's teachings now interpreted in so many diverse (and often opposite) ways, it complicates things and makes politics run rampant. In my opinion, however, Bruce Lee was just a student of totality in combat – a goal that all martial artists seek. He simply stressed a concept of martial arts which came from his study of wing chun – interception.

## New Patterns

I have been involved in wing chun now for many years, and I'm just beginning to realize the effort it takes to do the research and development required to make new patterns. The required effort is far greater than simply mimicking another style. In wing chun there is a saying that "there are no seniors, the one who attains it is the senior." I don't mimic Hawkins Cheung's wing chun because he's my sifu – his goal is to give me enough insight to enable me to create my own patterns. I believe Lee studied other styles to learn their weaknesses, not to incorporate them into a new system. *The Tao of Jeet Kune Do* was an unfinished collection of his notes, from various sources, to explain the art of intercepting. Many take it to be *his* writing or *his* truth. They mistake "the finger pointing to the moon," as the moon.

In my opinion, Lee used fencing terms to try to gain acceptance into the American market. Modem fencing terminology of the "stop hit" is universal - it means to "*jeet*" (intercept), as in wing chun terminology. Many martial arts styles and systems have a "stop hit," Lee was not unique in discovering that intercepting is one of the quickest counters. Attacking when the opponent is just preparing to strike is even faster but is dependent upon your ability to recognize complex situations and be proactive. Not many know the wing chun term "*huen sao*" (circle hand). In fencing, this is called a "bind" or a "crossover." *Pak sao* is the wing chun equivalent of fencing's "stop hit." I find that the Western public can't always relate to everyday Chinese wing chun terminology like "*tan*" (disperse), "*bong*" (wing), or "*fuk*" (subdue) so easily. In fencing, you have the terminology in French or English, so I believe Lee tried to substitute those terms. Now, many take it that Lee studied fencing to incorporate into jeet kune do. Others think that Bruce's stance was highly influenced by fencing, as well, but I am sure he really emulated the wing chun pole stance and weapon's footwork used by his seniors, which are nearly identical to fencing.

Many say that wing chun gave Lee the tools to make a sculpture – but Ed Parker said that without the ability of Bruce Lee, you could sculpt all day and come out with nothing. Parker realized you need a system. I think Lee was more interested in his own development than with the development of a system. He already had his foundation in wing chun and didn't need to spend time giving it to others. Instead, he gave them shortcuts and glimpses of what he was personally working on. Those who try to follow in his footsteps, without having a basis in wing chun, have no foundation to build upon or sculpt. They spend too much time chasing new styles and ways, without giving the wing chun foundation a chance to develop. When a building lacks a strong foundation, it collapses. Wing chun was Lee's strong foundation.

## "A Wing Chun Man"

The four stages of human learning are "unconscious incompetence," "conscious incompetence," "conscious competence," and, ultimately, "unconscious competence." Unconscious incompetence is not really a stage – a person is simply unaware that a subject, idea, or skill exists. Conscious incompetence is just the opposite, a person becomes aware that they are painfully lacking in a subject, idea, or skill. Carl Jung wrote that there is no coming of consciousness without pain. Conscious competence is the stage of gathering technical resources and learning about the subject – it is the stage most martial artists are at. Unconscious competence is the level of the expert or master. Without thought or delay, the expert can respond to a situation instantly with the correct fighting tool or teaching method.

Lee reached the stage of unconscious competence and could create changes in his existing tools to fit the situation at hand – he was able to create flowers from dirt. Lee borrowed a Zen term and warned, "Do not take the finger pointing at the moon as the moon." These days, people focus only on the artistic flower Lee created, and get caught up with copying his colorful petals. If they spent more time building the root, then they could grow new petals of their own whenever they wanted. If the flowers are cut and left without their roots, they soon die. Wing chun is named "in praise of the spring," an appropriate name for an art whose goal is to help the practitioner leave the dead of winter behind and travel into the spring of new creation, adaptation, and change.

The ideal wing chun artists, according to Hawkins Cheung, are the researchers and the thinkers – those courageous spirits who try its tools in different situations and find new uses for them. Yip Man often challenged Hawkins Cheung and Bruce Lee by saying, "Maybe I'm tricking you, go out and test wing chun for yourself."

Before his death, Bruce realized "he was a wing chun man." As Hawkins Cheung noted, "He made his peace with Yip Man after a long, silent feud." Jeet kune do was Lee's personal research and development vehicle to make his wing chun come alive. That is why he eventually regretted coining the term "jeet kune do." Jeet kune do is Bruce Lee's personal philosophy, research, and development and reflects his own personal genius – jeet kune do was Bruce Lee's way of making his wing chun come alive.

## FUTSHAN BAK MEI

Shrouded in myth and mystery and often not taught to outsiders, the Bak Mei (White Eyebrow) martial art is a very quick, efficient, economical in motion and generates force by using body power, emphasizes striking at vital points, and close quarters combat. The art is a swift, quick, and economical fighting system. It is hoped that this article can explain some of the nuances and unique features of this rare and unusual Southern fist system of martial arts.

### A Brief History

The Bak Mei (pronounced Bahk Mei) Pai, or White Eyebrow system of martial arts is shrouded in secrecy and legend. According to common gung fu lore, the martial art is attributed to the Daoist monk Bak Mei (who was noted for his white eyebrows, hence the name) during the Qing Dynasty in China during the time of Qing emperor Jia Qing (1796-1820). Bak Mei allegedly trained at the

Fukien Shaolin Temple at Jiu Lian Mountain in Fukien province and was one of the five elders that survived the legendary destruction of the Southern Shaolin temple, according to the fictional work, "Wan Nian Qing" (10000 years Green).

Some have depicted the Daoist Bak Mei as a traitor to the Shaolin and working on the side of the Manchus. Others say he was a spy or double agent who worked for the Qing but had loyalties to the Ming loyalists and rebels. While doing research on my previous work, "Complete Wing Chun", I came across legends of the related Southern Fist systems that were depicted as being descended from the Venerable Five (Jee Shim Sim Si, Ng Mui Si Tai, Fung Dao Duk, ak Mei Dao Yan, and Miu Hin) that survived the ravaging of the Fukien Shaolin. Some have twisted stories that have even put Bak Mei as a fantasy killer who killed his fellow monks with his suction and iron belly, or state he was in a conspiracy with Ma Ning Yee (a traitor to the Southern Shaolin that helped in the destruction of the temple). All of this is fictional and draws from the fictional work "Wan Nian Qing" and are just variations of the stories. With regards to who Bak Mei really was or if he really existed is doubtful. It is quite possible that Bak Mei Dao Yan (Daoist) is really a metaphor for a rebel or group of rebels that developed this system to fight the Qing. The salutation of a left fist and right open palm still signifies that, "From 5 lakes and 4 seas, all men are brothers" – a sign of loyalty to the Ming and the secret Hung Mun society that was created to overthrow the Qing dynasty.

The legends state that the Daoist Bak Mei traveled to Ngor Mei (Emei) Mountain where he refined his art to include the internal aspects of Qi cultivation and refined body mechanics after the destruction of the Shaolin temple. His art was a combination of both Shaolin Buddhist fighting techniques, along with Daoist arts of internal cultivation (Noi Gung). Bak Mei's martial art was passed on to monk Gwong Wai, the heir to the system, who named the system "Bak Mei Pai". The system was then passed to monk, Jok Fat Wan, who traveled with his disciple Lin Sang from Sichuan Emei Shan to the Gwong How Temple in Guang Dong province. Jok Fat Wan, during a trip to Guangzhou, eventually accepted a layman disciple named Cheung Lei Chuen. Cheung Lei Chuen, a long-time martial arts enthusiast, mastered several martial arts, including Lee Gar under Lee Mung Sifu, Wanderer's style under Lam Shek Sifu, and Lung Ying Mor Kiu (Dragon Form Scraping Bridge) under Lam Ah Hap a third generation disciple of the Dragon Form school. Grand Master Cheung Lei Chuen began training in Bak Mei Kung-Fu in the Gwong How Temple at the age of 24 after being introduced to Jok Fat Wan by Lin Sang. After undergoing his training in Bak Mei martial arts under Jok Fat Wan, he spread this system to the martial arts world. Cheung Lai Chuen was undefeated throughout his martial arts career, became famous as one of the "Three Tigers of the East River Region", and earned the title of "Seven Southern States Champion". In 1949, Grandmaster Cheung Lei Chuen moved to Hong Kong and spread Bak Mei there. In the fall of 1964, he died at the age of 84 in Hong Kong.

In contrast, the Futshan Bak Mei system traces its origin to Fung Fou Dao Yan (Wind Fire Daoist). Since we do not know Fung Fou Dao Yan's real name, or who he was in his layman life, we do not know the complete connection to Cheung Lei Chuen, if there is any, or if Fung Fou Dao Yan was connected to any of Cheung Lei Chuen's 18 schools in Southern China prior to the Communist takeover in China. We do know the system he handed down to his disciple in Futshan named Lau Siu Leung. Lau Siu Leung was a very selective teacher and only passed down his Bak Mei art to people of good moral character. One of his selected disciples was Li Yong Jian (Lee Yung Kien) in Futshan. The Futshan Bak Mei school long been established and Li Yong Jian, has selected to pass on the art on to Eddie Chong of Sacramento, CA.

## Several Versions

There are indeed several versions of the Bak Mei martial arts, as each had a background and varying curriculum based on what Cheung Lei Chuen taught in his eighteen schools. The author had previously seen many Bak Mei schools in New York City, including that of Kwong Man Fong, Chan Tai Shan and Chan Jor, seen Yau Gung Mun (an offshoot of Bak Mei), and a branch of Bak Mei that has descended from Vietnam. It was at the urging of my good friend and brother in Wing Chun Kuen, Eddie Chong, that I finally write about his particular Bak Mei art and focus on his unique school from Futshan.

In the Futshan Bak Mei training, the training consists heavily on forms and fighting applications. Through the forms and applications, one can develop and refine the art. Throughout the years and differences in the curriculum of Bak Mei, there are some 40 empty hand routines in White Eyebrow, which include: Sup Ji (Cross Pattern), Sam Sing (3 Stars), Chut Dim Mui Fa (7 Points Plum Blossom), Gou Bo Tui (9 Step Push), Sup Ba Mor Kiu (18 Touching Bridges), Fu Bo (Tiger Step), Diu Jeung (Carving Palm), Sin Lui San Fa (Fairy Spreading Flowers), Sup Ba Feng Seung (18 Crazy Monks), Si Ji Kwun Kau (Lion rolls the ball), Dai/Siu Ba Gua (Large and Small Ba Gua sets) , Fei Jum Jeung (Flying Dust Palm), Fa Lung (Fancy Dragon), Fa Fu (Fancy Tiger), Fa Pao (Fancy Leopard), Sup Ba Lo Han Kuen (18 Buddhist Guardian Fist), Lo Han Kuen (Buddhist Guardian Fist), Lo Han Ji (Buddhist Guardian Fingers), Jor Lung (Left Dragon), Kuen Long (Fist Corridor), Ye Fu Chut Lum (Night Tiger Emerges from the Forest), Fan Chien Jong (Pre-meal Bell), and Fan Hou Jung (After-meal Bell). There are also the Poon Lung Gwun (Coiled Dragon Pole), Poon Long San (Coiled Dragon Umbrella), Fei Fung Dan Yiu Dao (Single Phoenix Single Waist Sword), Cern Yiu Dao (Double Waist Broadswords) and other traditional Chinese weapons such as the spear, tiger fork, butterfly knives, and other weapons indigenous to Bak Mei.

At a quick look, the Futshan Bak Mei system has many forms. I believe the differences in curriculum are a matter of personal interpretation amongst the schools, newer forms being added to the curriculum, and the fact that master Fung Fou DaoYan may have taught a previous curriculum consisted of sets from various Southern Shaolin fist arts. This is only personal speculation of the author.

## About Eddie Chong

Eddie Chong has been involved in the martial arts for a lifetime. He is known for his Wing Chun and is the student of Ken Chung, a student of Leung Sheung, who was the first disciple of Yip Man. Wanting to do more research in Wing Chun, Eddie traveled to Futshan and became a disciple of the late master Pan Nam. While training with master Pan Nam, he was introduced to a fellow training brother, Lee Yung Gien and discussed the latter's expertise in the Bak Mei Pai system. After numerous years of dedicated study and the

Futshan system of Bak Mei is now introduced in the United States by Eddie Chong, who has a complete endorsement to teach by his Sifu and training brother, Li Yong Jian.

## Bak Mei Martial Arts skills

Bak Mei Kung-Fu is one of the few martial arts systems that combines both Shaolin and Daoist practices into a single fighting art. It is classified as an internal and external system that emphasizes the combination of the science of combat along with the Daoist principles of using the qi (breath), to maximize the generation of power from within the body and to maintain health. In Bak Mei, Qi Gong is incorporated into every aspect of the art to maximize the flow of energy to every move.

Beginners are taught individual exercises that include waist twisting, loosening and stretching exercises, stepping with advancing, retreating, left and right stepping. Punchig and stepping drills with the basic tools Bui Gim (Back carried sword), Bin Chuie (whipping punch), Pao Chuie (uppercut), Cup Chuie (downward blow) and Chung Chuie (Thrusting punch) are also drilled.

The Futshan Bak Mei system has a unique stance with a 50/50 weight distribution. The stance is called the "But Ding But Baat Bo" (literally, "Not 8, and not T Step"), because it looks like a cross between the Chinese character for 8 and the Chinese character "ding" which resembles a "T". Footwork is practiced in eight directions and the heel never touches the ground in this system. The contact point with the foot is the kidney one acupuncture point known as "yong quan" (bubbling well). It is this footwork which leads to the speed and mobility of this system.

Bak Mei is a highly sophisticated, fast, and aggressive system that is rarely seen in today's Chinese martial arts. Bak Mei practitioners use geng ging (scared power), a type of explosive power that enables a technique to change quickly from a soft and relaxed movement into a powerful strike upon impact. To the untrained observer can look quite external or using brute force. The motto of Bak Mei is to chain movements of heavy strikes, using the straight to go out and receive with the horizontal, use complementary powers generated by the body, and combine offense and defense as one. The six powers of Bak Mei include straight, pulling, raising, sinking, whirling, and splattering. Practitioners are advised to use the spirit, intention, breath and power. The form is round, and practitioners are advised for leading and calmness when practicing. The high level of Bak Mei is to use this concentration, overcome challenges faced during practice, stick to the principles, and develop spontaneousness of movement in the advanced and deep stages of this art.

Bak Mei techniques are executed between short and mid-range distances and hand movements are fast and powerful. Bak Mei also has a large repertoire of kicks including the side thrusting, front heart piercing, jumping, and ground rolling maneuvers. Bak Mei emphasizes the tiger form motions and emphasizes the structure of the body and steps to make it practical. The movements are small and precise, yet have the qualities of light, sharp, circular, and alive. Body motions including floating, sinking, swallowing, and spitting are evident in this art. The four body motions emphasize power executed in an upwards, sinking, pushing outwards and drawing inwards and is the major source of power for this art. When combined with one another and varied in direction, duration and intent, the different powers are manifested, and the practitioner can "Faat Ging" (Fa Jing – issue force) in many ways.

Bak Mei emphasizes the six harmonies of the 3 internal harmonies of visual acuity, listening skills and concentration with the external 3 harmonies of waist, bridge, and horse. At the highest levels of Bak Mei, the spirit radiates from the eyes, and one can go from fixed methods to flexible methods, utilize softness to dissolve, and hardness to push out. The advanced practitioner shows spirit and intent arriving; intention and breath arriving; and breath and power expressed throughout the system.

## Fundamentals

An old adage in martial arts states, "Before learning the forms, one must practice the stance." Without a firm foundation in stance training, there is no solid foundation and root. Typically, advanced practitioners display excellent basic skills in rooting, and from there will be able to differentiate methods of issuing power and adapt to different circumstances. At least three years' time is a good measure of laying down a foundation. A ten-year commitment will produce even greater results. In learning Bak Mei, a student should perfect his basics, practice individual basics, forms, and combat skills. One should also practice freestyle using the imagination, as in shadow boxing. A Bak Mei practitioner should permeate his being with the hard practice of the art. One is advised to:

1) Clarify and ask to better understand

2) Practice regularly to develop proficiency

3) Think more to develop a deep understanding and analysis

4) From understanding and analysis one can spring forth creativity and spontaneousness

This is the way for a Bak Mei person to advance to higher levels.

## The Curriculum

Chong Sifu teaches a core group of sets that include: Sup Ji Kuen, Fa Pao, Chut Dim Mui Fa, Gou Bo Tui, Sup Ba Mor Kiu, and Fu Bo Kuen. For the beginner, Sup Ji Kuen is the basis. An old adage states that "Sup Ji Kuen is the foundation and can be used as defending the name of Bak Mei. If one does not know Sup Ji Kuen, how could one claim to know Bak Mei?" Sup Ji Kuen consists of 72 important points that is performed in a cross shaped pattern, hence the name. The set consists of all the basic offensive and defensive, open and closed motions of the art combined with body movement, footwork and proper hand positions that are clearly laid out.

Chut Dim Mui Fa is also another fist routine that emphasizes a small circle and is useful for close range combat and quick attack training. It is important for beginners to learn this set to develop variations in the use of the triangular horse steps and chained motions.

Fa Pao is a set that emphasizes kicking and strikes that use the Geung Ji Chuie, (Ginger Fist) and maneuvering. It is important intermediate set, but very short.

Gou Bo Tui is the first of the advanced Bak Mei sets. Gou Bo Tui trains the importance of the pressing horse and actions that emphasize the floating, sinking, swallowing, and spitting powers. The importance of Gou Bo Tui is to change frrom one tactic to another. Bak Mei practitioners reserve this set as it teaches surprise tactics in emergency situations, and it is rarely shown to outsiders. The core of this set is to guard the centerline and attack your opponent with close power generated from the four body motions. Close power, or inch power (Chuen Ging) is not easy to develop and may only be reached through dedicated hard training.

Sup Ba Mor Kiu is a set that emphasizes the touch and feeling aspect of Bak Mei and is often used in Mor Sao (touching hands), a form of sensitivity arm practice. This routine places emphasis on the use of the waist guiding the bridges. The "hands do not come back empty" is a core principle of this set, that is, when a bridge is touched, one rubs or scrapes the bridge and traps the opponent's arms, pressing inward s to your opponent and controls the centerline. Movements to attack the head, chest and abdomen are both linear and circular in this set.

The key points lie in the touching, locking (aka trapping), straight issuing of the connected motions of swallowing (defending) and spitting (attacking). In Sup Ba Mor Kiu, the tactics of subduing and issuing, springing and receiving, entering and jumping, rolling and slapping, dragging and locking, touching and trapping and inside and outside bridges are emphasized. Combined with the six powers, the practitioner reaching this level of training will be a formidable foe.

Fu Bo Kuen is the most advanced form in the Bak Mei system with 108 motions emphasizing the tiger form. It represents the highest level in Bak Mei and emphasizes the changes of body structure with the four body motions and clawing maneuvers. In this level of training, there are many tiger motions: fierce tiger rushes from the forest, tiger enters the pig stuy, upper and lower mountain tiger, hungry tiger seizes the lamb, tiger sepeartes its prey, black tiger steals the heart, tiger returns to the lair, and other tiger motions. The forms also emphasize inch power, and it is rare that a Bak Mei teacher teach this form openly.

It is not important to learn all the sets of Bak Mei. It is even conceivable that some of these sets may have been added in from influences in other systems and have added in principles from Bak Mei into sets from other systems. Also, certain forms were created to emphasize different points or to emphasize a particular body type or limitation. What counts is the development of power and to know how to use and apply the movements in the core sets you know. Typically, the forms are either done with full power at top speed, or with little power emphasizing relaxed and fluid movements.

## Combat Methods

From the sets, San Sao (separate hands) are extrapolated and used during two-man prearranged sparring, Mor Kiu (sticking hands), and free fighting practice. Practice is often done at a quick pace with combat speed as it helps a practitioner develop timing, positioning and reflexes needed in combat situations. Chong Sifu has added in a dimension of training from his many years of experience in Wing Chun Kuen and teaches many of the Bak Mei applications through the platform of Wing Chun's Luk Sao (Rolling Hands practice) and Chi Sao (sticking hands) practice.

Bak Mei practitioners believe one must attack the outer gate of the opponent. They call this principle "Boon Bien Lien" (Half Face Attaching) which is to attack on a consistent basis, the opponent's flank, where he is weakest and unable to defend. Since the system is a close quarters combat art, there is a strong emphasis on bridge crossing. An adage of Bak Mei is, "If there is a bridge, cross over; if there is no bridge, touch and feel." The stance is used to trap the opponent's leg and control it in case of leg attacks.

To prepare a practitioner for use in combat, a Bak Mei practitioner should stay calm and focus, never panic or be nervous. These are the keys to victory. Being relaxed and calm allows one to know the openings in your opponent and know your surroundings and for you to act accordingly. A Bak Mei person overwhelms his opponent with courage and resourcefulness, and attacks after, but arrives first. It is important to be proactive and never give up and avoid risky moves. Unity of the techniques, footwork and trained strength are demanded. One must always focus on linking damaging motions against the opponent and to combine offense and defense as one. Ideally, one should move like lightning and strike like thunder. The quickness in Bak Mei is from sudden starts and relaxation and one is advised to reach the opponent in one movement and never withdraw the hands without controlling or touching an opponent's bridges.

## Conclusion

Futshan Bak Mei Pai is an art that stresses Mo Duk (Martial Arts Chivalry). One should never show off or bully others. In Bak Mei, there is a creed:

"Respect the Founder, respect the teachers, and respect the martial arts; Learn to be kind, righteous, and practice martial arts. Once accomplished in martial arts, use it only for self-defense and not to bully others. If someone is not loyal, devoted, or honest, don't bother to teach a person even if ten thousand taels of gold are offered to you. Those who disrespect relatives or are dishonest with friends should never be taught." The Futshan Bak Mei system is a fascinating system in learning how to use the body in combat and has a rich culture behind it. It is fortunate to have an authorized representative of this great Southern Chinese fist art introduce it here to the United States.

## REFRESHING HONESTY

If a martial artist has created, modified, or changed something in his system and teaches it to his students, he should be honest. This holds true for forms, drills, partner exercises or whatever. That a sifu or sensei should say, "I learned it like this, but because of my experience, teaching strategy, desire to be different, preference, or because I couldn't do that move correctly, I changed it to this." Wouldn't that be ideal? It would be refreshingly honest.

Now you're probably asking what's the big deal?

Many teachers pass down a lineage or a tradition from a long line of their predecessors. When they add or modify what they were taught, they are breaking that tradition and they are fooling their disciples. These disciples will be thinking that what they are doing is exactly what their *si gung* (teacher) is doing, or even their *si jo* (founder), when it is clearly not. If you don't care about lineage, it's not a big deal. But if you're a traditional martial artist, it's a very big deal.

Loyal students are sometimes tricked by the lies and non-disclosure of the truth by their sifu. They will fight to the end to defend their sifu's honor, even when they are wrong. Maybe this is Asian loyalty, but it is misplaced when defending a liar. It's quite common since many students place their sifu on a pedestal and think, "Sifu would never lie to me!" I want to share a tale of deceit that happened in the wing chun art.

One wing chun instructor I know of came to the United States as a teenager. He was a top student of a well-known Asian sifu. When he came here to attend college, he found that teaching wing chun was better than working in a Chinese restaurant. The only problem was that he did not complete the curriculum set forth by his teacher and grandteacher. What he did was decide to modify the system that he taught because he did not complete the system and presented it as his teacher's system. He deliberately modified the three forms, made up a second half of the wooden dummy and made up his own pole set. He also paid his respects to other *si bok* and *si suk* (kung-fu uncles) and learned a knife set which he modified also with pieces of this and that person's knife set. He taught many students and had many loyal followers and modified his curriculum to have many flashy moves outside of wing chun. One of this "master's" students inadvertently found out that his curriculum was modified after a visit with his grandteacher in Asia. The result was that this student was expelled from his school and branded an outcast.

The grandteacher was so mad about the changes to the system that he made a trip to the U.S. to straighten this out. The result was that the grandteacher taught a series of seminars, with the intent of presenting the correct art as taught by Yip Man. The mistake was that the grandteacher spoke no English and had to rely on the "false" sifu to translate for him. Even when translating, the sifu did not want to reveal the truth. So, when demonstrating the actual forms, if a student asked, "Why are the forms different?" -- the sifu's response was, "These are the basic forms; I taught you the advanced ones!" Instead of being truthful, he used more deception and lies to hide the fact that he had not fully learned the curriculum and had made modifications to the art.

When this was discussed by several wing chun students on an Internet discussion list, one of the sifu's senior students vehemently denied that his teacher made any curriculum changes and modifications and was teaching the art exactly as his grandteacher did. I assure the reader that this is not the case. I tell this tale and mention no names because it sets forth a new standard in fooling students and grandteachers. I find it a disgrace because it violates a student's basic trust in his teacher.

Another instructor I know of created a marketing story that his art had secret footwork patterns, death touch, and special forms and weaponry that everyone else in the system lost, and that his art was part of some secret conspiracy. He strung together history derived from Chinese pulp fiction and claimed himself the successor and grandmaster of this particular art. Paraphrasing little-known Chinese fiction in English, teaching fiction as fact, learning from some secret relative, monk, nun, or unknown grandmaster are also means some Chinese martial arts instructors use to elevate their status and make you believe that they are a "gift from God" to have preserved this rare art and passed it down to you. Some are con men who use distorted facts, lies, deception, trickery, and other means to part you from your money while teaching you trash. I again urge the student, "Buyer beware!"

Jack Kornfield wrote an excellent book called *A Path with Heart*. In it, Kornfield discusses the spiritual romanticism between a student and a teacher. A student not only is happy to learn a teacher's craft, but also a romantic notion of the greatness of his teacher. Perhaps it's that many are looking to belong to something or are just searching for a spiritual connection. As a teacher, however, I do not want to be put on a pedestal by my students and let them think I have the answers to everything. Many are looking for the Mister Miyagi of the *Karate Kid* movies, or the Master Po of the *Kung Fu* series. As a person with limitations, I cannot elevate myself to such omnipotent status.

As a teacher myself, I have to avoid "Godliness" and "emotional baggage" thrown upon me by students seeking to better themselves, and act and work as a partner or guide in martial arts, not the giver of truth or ultimate realization of the Tao. Honesty is what can differentiate a good martial arts practitioner from "grandmasters" and "gurus" with all the answers.

Often there are feelings transferred upon a teacher by a student. It's important for a teacher have to be aware of transference issues with students and always appear as a real person, with human deficiencies. Perhaps the idealization can help some in learning, but when it gets carried too far, it will detract from the teacher/student relationship by creating false hopes, expectations, and outcomes. Some have said that power corrupts, and absolute power corrupts absolutely; therefore, I advise that teachers remain close to their true nature and realize the limits of what a sifu can do and always express simple, refreshing honesty. I believe if one can keep this balance, they will never have students suffer unrealistic delusions of their teachings, nor be placed in a position to hide their true self. Wouldn't that be ideal? It would at least be refreshingly honest.

## DOUBLE-WEIGHTING

Often in martial arts, the terminology and language which describe movements are misinterpreted. This can cause confusion and a loss of clarity when the movements are executed. One of the most misunderstood concepts in martial arts is that of "double-weighting." Called *shuang zhong* in Chinese, this term is often spoken of in tai ji, xing yi, and ba gua but is often misunderstood. Very simply, "double-weighting" refers to the exchange of force between yourself and your opponent.

Cheng Man Ching in his book *Thirteen Chapters*, which presents his simplified form of tai ji quan, thought that being double-weighted was when you had your weight evenly distributed between both legs. He wanted to avoid this so much that during the transitional movement of "cross hands" and "return the tiger to the mountain," he deliberately put all his weight onto one leg. This makes me suspect that Cheng had misinterpreted the concept. All martial arts begin with the practice of the horse stance. Because the weight is distributed evenly, does this mean that the horse stance is teaching the error of double-weighting? I don't think so. Double-weighting does not refer to the weight being distributed on both legs, nor is it of any concern during solo forms practice. The main problem with being double-weighted is when your opponent puts pressure on you.

Many tai ji players have gone to the extreme, thinking that a stance with weight equally distributed between both legs is not desirable. They have mistaken what double-weighted means and cannot see the advantage of why a 50/50 stance is preferable. In my opinion, a 50/50 stance gives you more options on the direction and speed of your transitions and allows you to go from one side to another very quickly. In application, however, the advantage you get from a particular stance depends where your opponent is and how much pressure he puts on you.

Most tai ji players do use a 50/50 stance in *zhan zhuang* and other postures such as *shi zi shou* (cross hands). People who avoid the 50/50 stance in tai ji are missing the picture. *Shuang zhong* (which can also be translated as "double emphasis") means that if you shift your weight onto your back leg, your opponent can simply push you, which adds force onto your weight shift, and topple you backwards. Similarly, if you step forward and your opponent pulls you, which adds force onto your weight shift, you fly forward. In both circumstances you direct your weight, and your opponent adds to it, causing you to have one weight (your own), plus another (your opponents). Hence, the term "double-weighting."

Practically speaking, if you cannot keep your balance in a tai ji push hands match, you will lose. This is the error of double-weighting as mentioned in the classics of tai ji and ba gua. It has nothing to do with a 50/50 stance, but rather is a mistake in not equalizing your opponent's forward energy (*peng jing*) and guiding it to the ground, thereby rooting yourself. When you have control of your center of gravity and your moment of inertia, you can be agile and easily avoid this error.

# FUMIO DEMURA

## KOBUDO-BO

The real origin of the Bo, kon, or straight staff, is still obscure in the Kobudo history. The Okinawans had to rely on farming instruments to protect themselves since the inhabitants of the island were barred from owning any sort of weapons, and it is believed that this weapon was developed from the tenbin, a staff held across the shoulder that was used to carry buckets hanging from each end with water or food. When attacked, the farmer would drop these and use the staff for self-protection.

The size and dimensions of the Bo will vary depending on the practitioner, but the regular Bo is about six feet long or as described in Japanese roku shaku-bo. There also are other lengths and shapes for the Bo, like the four-foot (yon shaku-bo) and the nine-foot (kyu shaku-bo). As far as the shape is concerned, some traditional teachers still use the square and hexagonal shape because these multiple edges provide a more destructive effect. Some of the most common circularly shaped types of Bo are:

1. Maru-bo (round);
2. Kaku-bo (four-sided);
3. Rokkaku-bo (eight-sided); and,
4. Take-bo (bamboo).

The thickness also varies due to personal preferences, but it typically measures 1¼-inch thick at the center (Chukon-bu) and around 3/4-inch at the end (Kontei). This difference in thickness facilitates strong and powerful whipping actions and guarantees that the Bo's fulcrum stays at its center as rigidity is simultaneously reduced, which helps easy handling.

To determine if the Bo possesses the correct shape and handling qualities, we can simply roll it across a flat surface; if it is properly constructed, it will roll smoothly. If it is bent or warped, the weapon will roll unevenly, making a loud clatter. Modern Bo manufacturers use strong wood like red or white oak to produce the weapon. These have replaced the old bamboo and increased the sturdiness of the weapon.

There are four basic holds when practicing with the Bo. You should develop a familiarity with all of them so you can switch holds at will and at high speed when performing kata and sparring combinations. Almost all Bo-jutsu actions [both single and complex] are executed by grabbing the weapon with the basic grips. These are:

1. Jun Nigiri (Basic Hold)
2. Gyaku Nigiri (Reverse Hold)
3. Hasami Nigiri (Palm Hold)
4. Yose Nigiri (Double Hold)

Remember, no matter how proficient you may be using the Bo, your technique will never be perfect because perfection is something unattainable in the Martial Arts. It is a goal we all must strive for but that we'll never achieve.

## KOBUDO – NUNCHAKU

My good friend and Martial Arts icon, Bruce Lee, was responsible for bringing the nunchaku into the spotlight. He used it in his movies as a new "attraction" for the viewers, and his skills were second to none. Although popularized by Bruce Lee, the forerunner of the nunchaku was an instrument used as a bit for horses; it was not used as a weapon until later on when Okinawan farmers converted farm implements into protective devices. This weapon was constructed of two hardwood sticks connected by a rope braided from horses' tails. Because of its simple appearance, the nunchaku easily was mistaken for a harmless bundle of two sticks. The Okinawan karateka saw the efficiency of this tool as a protective weapon and immediately incorporated into their arsenal.

The length of the nunchaku should equal the distance from the middle of the hand to the elbow, but it also should be adjusted to fit the practitioner's height and arm power. The weapon is divided into seven different parts:

1. The rope/chain (Himo or Kusari).
2. Top (Kontoh).
3. Hole (Ana).
4. Upper Area (Jokon).
5. Middle Area (Chukon).
6. Lower Area (Kikon).
7. Botom Area (Kontei).

Every part of the nunchaku can be used as a weapon and has a certain utility. For instance, the bottom and top can be used to jab or spear, the middle area is used to block and control in close-quarter range, and the rope or chain is very practical to pinch or choke the opponent.

When analyzing the different designs of the weapon, we will find out that there are many different "shapes" used for the nunchaku. The main categories are: a) Maru-gata (Round); b) Hakakukei (Octagonal); c) So-setsu-kon (Long and Short); d) Han-kei (Half-size); e) San-setsu-kon (Three Piece Nunchaku); and f) Yon-setsu-kon (Four Piece).

The grasping methods are simple, but they require diligent training and practice. The weapon can be grasped at the bottom, the middle area, and the top, and these grasping methods can be combined and altered on both sides, which gives us several possibilities of maneuvering the nunchaku. The possibility of changing grasps and gripping methods during the action provides this weapon with great versatility and a high degree of deception for our opponent. Although the basic grasping-change action involves two hands, it is the true mark of a master to change grips with one hand while using the nunchaku to attack or defend.

Due to its nature, the nunchaku is mainly a swinging weapon, and this dictates the type of defensive and attacking actions that we can do in combat. The "snapping" techniques allow for a faster recovery to the on-guard position, but the swinging actions are more difficult to control specially after hitting the target. Constant practice should be allocated in the training time to learn how to recover the weapon; the idea is to hit the target and recover the weapon safely so we can use it again. The recovery action in the most important technique for a Kobudo practitioner when using this weapon.

We can state that all the techniques developed for the use of nunchaku are self-defense oriented. Please do not mistake the "flashy" and "attractive" swinging actions that you can see in movies and TV with the "real" use of this weapon for self-protection. Once you understand the use and essential principles of the nunchaku, you will be able of developing a limitless amount of efficient and practical techniques.

## KOBUDO – SAI

The sai is one of the most popular weapons in the art of Kobudo. Its shape and unique versatility offer a great training challenge for any dedicated practitioner. Originally, the sai was used to drag the soil by one farmer, while another would plant the seed. The farmer, when attacked by the Samurai, would use this tool to protect himself against the sword. It was normal for a farmer to carry even three sai with him. This was based on the fact that sometimes the farmer could actually throw one sai toward his opponent. This surprise action was the key for victory in many encounters. The third sai usually was carried in the belt.

In the beginning, the tip of the sai was sharp and only lately has been blunted and rounded for training purposes. Its techniques are very dangerous, and a thrust to the neck or the face can be lethal in a real fight. Since it is no longer used as a real weapon for combat, the material has changed and now we can find great steel and chromed-plated sai in many martial arts stores around the world.

The sai is formed of two important parts, the curved prong and the main stem. When this weapon was introduced to Japan it was called "jutte" and it bore a single prong at the handle. Japanese police found this weapon to be very effective in controlling aggressors and they started to use it more and more.

In many ways, the techniques used in sai training are very similar to the movements used in Karate. They follow similar principles, and they require a sense of "kime" like the empty hand actions. One important point that the practitioner should develop in training with the sai is dexterity in the fingers. The fast change of grasps and different gripping methods require from the practitioner a high level of proficiency in maneuvering the weapon. This is the reason why, usually, no beginners are taught the use of the sai.

The complete anatomy of the sai involves seven parts:

1. The point
2. The blade
3. The prongs
4. The guard
5. The guard center
6. The handle
7. The butt

All these parts have a function in the use of the weapon, and in order to give the user a better grip, the handle usually is wrapped with a cotton ribbon for a more secure grab.

The gripping of the weapon is very simple when compared to other tools; the sai can be held in only two ways: pointing the tip outward or pointing the tip inward. These two methods will dictate what kind of flipping action we are going to do with the weapon. The flipping action is a very important movement when training, and the wrist and elbow should be properly conditioned to precisely execute the snapping movement of the technique. Try to relax and don't try to put too much body weight when you snap the sai; the secret for the right snap is speed and control. Any additional tension on your shoulders will decrease the power in the technique. It is important that we correctly train to develop the right feeling of a whipping motion when using the sai. These flipping motions have no real counterpart in empty hand Karate; therefore, they must be learned separately. Never forget that good technique stems from good form. The ideal technique is always perfect in form and places you in the best position for the next movement in combat.

## KOBUDO – TONFA

The tonfa originally was a wooden handle fitted into a hole on the side of a millstone used by the Okinawans for milling grain. This handle became a very effective weapon for self-protection. The main part of the tonfa is a large hardwood body about 15–20 inches in length, with a cylindrical grip secured to the main body about six inches from one end.

Karate and Kobudo are mutually supported arts and many of the tonfa actions reflect principles used in Karate. The practice of any Kobudo weapon improves coordination, strength, and balance for the Karate practitioner.

The tonfa is a great training tool by itself. It develops strong hands, wrists, and forearms, since all the actions are generated using these parts of the human body. For instance, the snapping action of the tonfa originated in the wrist is similar to the wrist action of a Karate punch. In many ways, training with this weapon will increase the karateka's empty hand skills in a very short time.

The correct length of the tonfa is determined from the grip to the back head, and the back head should extend past the elbow by one-half inch. Once this important distance is determined, we can adjust the balance of the weapon by reducing the length from the grip to the front head. Based on these requirements, every practitioner should choose a length and balance to fit his/her personal characteristics. Although the basic configuration of the weapon is the same, the main body of the tonfa can have different shapes.

Two of the most popular materials for tonfa manufacturing are oak and cherry wood. Many people like their torfa varnished for better look, but if you are using it for practical combat techniques and training, this varnish soon will go away. No matter what, remember to clean it periodically with a cloth moistened with olive or other vegetable oil.

The tonfa is composed of seven parts:

1. Front head
2. Grip
3. Grip head
4. Top of main body
5. Bottom of main body
6. Side of main body
7. Back head

The basic grip of the tonfa is very similar to the Karate fist and is firm enough so the weapon doesn't drop while in use. Due to the twisting and snapping actions, the grip has to be very relaxed but firm enough to apply power at the moment of impact by squeezing and tightening up the fingers. This is the reason why, in order to be effective using this weapon, the practitioner must develop strong wrists. The key for a powerful swing of the torfa is to minimally bend the elbow when you are swinging the weapon. Always keep the arms extended when rotating the tonfa.

The blocking actions resemble those used in Karate and the principles are almost identical. The attacking maneuvers are varied, and they can be more complex when we use two tonfa at the same time. Always remember that an effective performance and use of the tonfa involves three different principles: maai, kime, and mushin, and perfect synchronized action of the hands, elbows, and hips.

# JOSE FRAGUAS

**THE ROLE OF THE COACH**

Karate is a sport that is considered a team sport, although there are sole competitors competing against another. Coaching karate is not unlike any other competitive sport where the goal is to win. However, in coaching athletes in the sport of karate, there are particular sport coaching tips that can make karate easier to adapt. It is important to teach the athletes how to think strategically and to try and sense his opponent's next move. They can be successful with pre-set milestones and expectations and with every available opportunity to practice their skill level and enhance it as much as is possible.

In a perfect world, a coach winds the athlete up outside of the competition venue, gives them a little shove through the door, and returns in a few hours in time to see the student collect a medal. There are some coaches that work this way, and there are some athletes that are capable of performing in this way. However, for the rest of us, we attend competitions to support our competitors, educated and help them, and gain insights into their competitive behavior. While at the competition, it is expected that you will assist the athlete during the day by:

- Engaging in pre-competition warm-up lesson or other activity.

- Providing information about opponents in the opening seeding rounds of the tournament, if that information is known to you, or based on your observations of the early matches.

- Offering reassurances during the pool about the correct choice of actions, choice of rhythm or speed of the bouts, and a reminder about any serious tactical errors your athlete is making.

- In the direct elimination matches, you can help your athlete develop a plan for the opponent, based either on observations of opponent's behavior in that event, or on previous encounters with the opponent.

- During the breaks, you have a chance to redirect tactical choices or provide additional information to the athlete.

- You can provide emotional and mental support to a struggling athlete who has the tools to score but may not have the belief.

- And last, but not least, you can provide feedback and reassurance (if needed) to the athlete after his/her elimination from the event.

## Coaching Points:

**1. Set goals and milestones for the athletes.** They're likely to all be at different skill levels, so it's important to assess each one accordingly and set goals for the team and each individual. In the absence of known and clear goals, some athletes will find it hard to make progress, especially if they're not at peak fitness.

**2. Teach, focus and coach on the basic karate moves and strategies so as not to overwhelm the athletes.** Make sure they have the foundational karate moves intact before showing them strategy moves or other complicated maneuvers. This breeds confidence and gives them a skill base to always refer back.

**3. Coach and play all of the athletes during practices and drills.** There will surely be a few highly skilled athletes, but also give the other athletes with limited skills mat time as well. This boosts confidence and helps the competitor to become acclimated to competition, the mat and a chance to strengthen their current skill level.

Even if you decide to do none of these things (and these suggestions are not followed by all coaches) attending the competitions of your athletes gives you the perspective of their true level in a real competitive environment. This information is invaluable in assessing the effectiveness of the athlete's training.

## TEACHING ELITE KARATE TECHNIQUE

These are some important aspects that karate coaches need to consider when they are helping an athlete develop a specific skill.

Demonstrating good technique from a sporting karate perspective involves applying optimal movement ability in order to accomplish or solve a particular task effectively. A young athlete, for instance, who demonstrates sound technical ability while hitting the target with a kick from point A (origin) to point B (target) in an effective manner.

The technical abilities demonstrated in a given sport – including karate -- can be categorized based on the rules or requirements of that sport or specific activity:

**Group 1:** An activity in which making a good impression on a judge is crucial (Kata competition) often involves coalescing intricate movements together. Within these specific activities, the techniques being demonstrated are described or clear (and therefore can be judged for efficiency). They are being performed within a fixed environment and without impediment, (i.e., no one is interfering with you). The athlete's task is to develop technical skill that can be showcased in a performance of pre-determined and practiced movements.

**Group 2:** The techniques in this grouping allow the athlete to attain maximal and impartially measured results; there is no consideration for how perfectly the technical abilities are displayed, just objective measurement for how effective they were (i.e., how fast did they run, how far did they throw the object, how much did they lift etc.). Sports in this category would include track and field events, swimming, and weightlifting. Outside impediment is not an issue in this grouping either. In this grouping of sports, one's motor abilities will define success - meaning, the fastest or strongest athlete will win. Karate division of kumite and kata do not directly apply to this category.

**Group 3:** The ability to display adequate technique within this grouping aids in overcoming an opponent (Kumite competition). This would include any combat sport, and virtually all team sports. In this group, technical ability is combined with tactical sense and reacting to a continually changing situation and varying conditions. In this category, motor abilities (strength, speed, endurance, timing, explosiveness and flexibility) are submissive to technical ability (karate proper technique). That is to say that the fastest or strongest athlete in this grouping of sports is not necessarily the most successful athlete. Motor abilities are developed in order to improve the application of technical skill.

## Skill Learning

How efficiently an athlete learns the technical skills of a sport (Karate), strength training exercise or movement is determined by several variables:

*Age* -- Complex skills are often understood and comprehended better by more mature athletes (although individual exceptions certainly apply).

*Emotional State* -- Relaxed and easy-going athletes tend to learn and reproduce new skills better than athletes who are uptight and self-critical.

*Motivation* -- So many parents, coaches and trainers just assume that the kids they are working with want to be at practice or in that training session.

*Natural Talent* -- Athletes with innate natural ability are far superior at learning and reproducing new skills.

## Coach's Philosophy

Critical to note within this topic are the methods being employed by the Karate Coach to teach new techniques. With the lack of stringent regulations at the youth sport coaching level and the youth training industry, it is certainly more than fair to consider the quality of instruction being given:

*What kind of personality does the coach have?* In a study released by the *Journal of Applied Sport Psychology* in 1999 (Youth Athletes & Parents Prefer Different Coaching Styles), it showed that adolescent athletes (ages 10 - 18) enjoyed coaching styles that involved concerns regarding the well-being of each athlete, a positive group tone and feeling, and supported friendly interpersonal relationships.

*Does the Karate coach have a solid working knowledge of the technique?* This goes right to the route concern of "*inadequately credentialed*" Trainers and Coaches - if you are not sure yourself how to correct the problem, how is the young athlete supposed to get it right? Remember, when working with kids, you are building habits, good or bad. Your job is to make sure that each repetition is forming a strong, positive habit in that young athlete. That can only be accomplished if the Coach understands what they are teaching and can instruct the technique properly

## Developing Sensory Skills

The core of technique development or learning is in the action of achieving perfect sensory-motor habits. A sensory-motor habit is simply a "learned activity of sensory and motor processes intentionally practiced to the point of automatization." From a physiological perspective, this entails creating a permanent conditional reflex connection that enables the exact same motor reactions to respond to the same stimuli. The development of a sensory-motor habit occurs through many stages:

### 1. *Generalized excitation of motor centers in the cortex*

When young athletes are first learning a new karate skill, they will often become overly tensed as they concentrate hard on performing that technique correctly. This often leads to needless additional movements and a lack of ability to 'zero-in' on movement of skill execution perfection.

### *2. Concentrated excitation in the appropriate motor centers*

This is when young athletes become much more comfortable with a new skill. The movements become much more economical, flowing and precise. Young athletes' attention is drawn more towards the rhythm and speed at which skills are performed as well as specific details of the technique.

### *3. Automation of the entire action*

There is no need for any sort of conscious effort with respect to movement control. The skill is performed in the right situation, in the correct way and all via automatization.

### *4. Sensory-motor habits are either "open" or "closed"*

"*Open* Habits" are variable or adaptable to unexpected situation changes. "*Closed* Habits" are suitable for when the movement is being executed in a static situation or environment. In sports involving closed sensory-motor habits like a Kata performance, training or competition, athletes practice precise and pre-programmed movements. The athletes learn via feedback from their bodies and are eventually able to detect very small divergences from proper execution, divergences that would lead to a poor result or performance. Elite figure skaters or world-class kata performers, for example, will know immediately upon executing a jump or throw weather or not it was their best effort based on the feedback their bodies give them in relation to an automatic understanding of what perfect execution feels like. They "know" at that exact moment.

In sports relating to open sensory-motor habits like Kumite training or competition, once the essence of the technique has been taught and perfected, the young athlete should be placed in constantly changing situations that will demand that the athlete learn to make quick reactive choices and maintain the ability to apply the learned technique in varying conditions. True aptness or perfection of open sensory-motor habits involves making them more plastic. This neurological reference means making these skills more adaptable to a variety of situations.

Coaches come from a variety of back- grounds and possess a range of qualities and experiences from which they develop their coaching skills and unique coaching styles. Then, they adapt these qualities to the specific needs of the athletes with whom they work. Yet, in spite of such individual approaches to coaching, it is possible to identify certain skills and attributes that underpin effective coaching.

For example, all coaches need to:

- **Communicate effectively with athletes** to ascertain their needs and ambitions, relay information and provide constructive feedback;

- **Plan and organize sessions and programs** to meet athlete's needs and guide their development; analyze and evaluate performance (their own and that of the athletes) to gauge and direct progress;

- **Create a safe environment** in which the well-being of the athlete is paramount; and,

- **Be open-minded** in developing their coaching skills and knowledge. This is perhaps the most important attribute of good coaches: the ability and willingness to evaluate their own skills and knowledge, and constantly work to develop and improve them.

## Communication

Effective coaching is not just about developing skills and improving performance; it is about building good relationships with athletes, refeerees, other coaches and parents when working with young athletes. The skills of good communication are therefore a central component of coaching. Communication is a two-way process where listening is equally, if not more, important as talking; this is especially true when attempting to establish each athlete's needs and goals. Coaches are often good at talking and giving information, but not so good at listening.They need to develop good communication skills both within and outside of the practical coaching situation, not just with athletes, but with parents, other coaches, officials and administrators.

## Planning and Organizing

Athletes can soon become bored and disillusioned with poorly structured coaching sessions and programs, so the ability to plan and organize effective and meaningful activities is vital to improving performance. This can only be done if coaches first identify each athlete's needs and goals and then use these as the basis for session and program planning. Where the plans form part of a series of sessions, a season or annual program, the goals of the specific session should represent one step in the overall plan. Such systematic planning is crucial to ensure progress and for the athletes to achieve their goals. It also offers athletes an appropriate level of challenge and ultimately promotes self-confidence and a sense of achievement.

## Analysis and Evaluation

Analysis is another component central to the coaching process and therefore a key coaching skill. Coaches need to analyze (within the session initially) the technical and tactical aspects of performance, the physical condition and mental skills of the athletes, the extent to which goals have been achieved, as well as their own coaching performance.

The skills, knowledge and experience of the coach are often required to revise practices to meet the changing needs and demands of the athletes. Analysis is also an important part of the overall evaluation of the coaching session or program, which strongly influences the planning of future sessions and goals.

## Creating a Safe Environment

The well-being of the athlete should be of utmost importance to all coaches. Therefore, coaches need to be aware of their legal responsibilities, especially with regard to child protection, negligence, risk and duty of care. They also have an obligation to con-form to accepted ethical codes of practice in terms of competence, responsibility, confidentiality, relation- ships with athletes, fair play and drug abuse.

## Keeping an Open Mind

An open mind is crucial to effective coaching and can be defined as being receptive to new ideas and amenable to change or different ways of doing things. Coaches should acknowledge their own strengths and weaknesses. Meetings, conferences, courses and workshops provide structured opportunities to learn and discuss current and future developments. In addition, a great deal of knowledge can be gained from observing more-experienced coaches and establishing a more formal mentoring relation- ship. All coaches, regardless of age and experience, should constantly strive to improve their knowledge, understanding and communication skills.

The true elite and professional coach never stops learning. This applies not only to "new" coaches but also to coaches who have been teaching and coaching for many years and who may have had many successful competitors. I have always been very impressed by Sensei Antonio Oliva; my mentor, a great international coach and trainer of many European and World champions and Head Coach of the Spanish Team which won the World Champion title in Madrid, Spain in 1980, and marked a 'turning point' in the history of sport Karate.

The professional coach is one who teaches to the room, and not for the paycheck or for ego feeding. This coach shows as much enthusiasm and gives as much effort to a class of five as he or she would to a class of twenty-five. This coach may not undertake every project offered but follows through on every project accepted.

Being a good and professional karate coach is more than just a title, paycheck, or certification, just like being a good doctor is more than certificate hanging on the wall.

## TACTICAL ACTIONS

Sport karate tactics are the proper application of karate techniques with precision to score points and not be scored against. On the average it takes from five to seven years to master the basic actions and footwork necessary to become a really competent competitor. This is a time of drilling with a coach and working independently to make essential actions muscle memory. In order to be practical and effective they must become instantaneous reflexes rather than the competitor having to think about each one as a possibility and then implement it. In other words, actions become instinctive rather than a selection process.

As an action takes place it must be executed in the most economical fashion possible. That is, it must be executed at the correct distance, the correct timing, and with no wasted motion. To accomplish this, all actions have to have been practiced through drills and actual competition so that they become absolutely relaxed and fluid. By experience after both training and competition an athlete learns not only how to evaluate his opponent but also his own action-responses as well.

A karate champion is a tactical competitor. When he approaches the competition area, he already has a plan in place. Tactical competitors are trained to follow through with a series of strategy-based actions that provide necessary information for both winning on the mat and success in the competition. A champion begins a match with what are called reconnaissance or exploratory moves. These test the opponent for patterned responses: attack situations, action preferences, footwork patterns, type of parries and blocks, type of counterattack, and responses to sudden changes in distance or timing. Such reconnaissance moves can include: attacks, false attacks, feints, changes of timing, footwork variations, attempted attacks or counterattacks, parry and counter exchanges, invitations, and responses to what are called "second intention" actions.

It is also advisable as a part of the reconnaissance procedure to observe potential opponents as they train or warm up with their respective coaches. Routine drill responses and actions will follow through in a match situation. In pool bouts also take the time to watch them compete. As this is being done check to see if by any body language (posturing) they telegraph their intentions prior to attacks, etc.

Champions conceal their intentions and mislead their opponents. The easiest way is during the reconnaissance phase of the match to respond in patterns other than normal routine and in so doing set the opponent up for responses that will not come, or footwork or feints that either will not be used or be implemented in ways other than expected.

Experienced competitors also make use of their feet. The attacking limb is delivered and withdrawn by the action of the feet. Changing tempo or cadence, and distance as using the width of the match area have a profound impact on the outcome of matches. In addition, it is advisable drive the opponent rather than being driven by him.

Body Evasions or Displacements and their accompanying footwork can be very effective as deceptive tactics especially if executed and timed to the very last cadence (part) of an incoming attack. They can also be used very effectively to intercept. Although technically considered as defensive actions, they can occasionally be used offensively to launch an attack at close distance.

Feints are also very effective tactical deceptions. Feints are always best delivered if accompanied with an acceleration or broken (rhythm) tempo/cadence footwork.

Karate champions use distractions or other methods to hinder the opponent's game. Using time between rounds in direct elimination matches by interaction with a coach so that the opponent at least thinks that either a definite strategy is being discussed or that he is the subject of conversation can also have a demoralizing and distracting effect on an opponent.

Tactical competitors control the bout by making the opponent respond by attacking or defending at inopportune times. In addition, a quality competitor uses as little energy as possible by setting up situations that cause the opponent to act or react and by so doing using their energy reserves. When it comes down to it in the end a match or a tournament can easily be won or lost because of energy reserves.

Lastly one of the most important karate strategy applications is the concept of "Second Intention Actions." To make the opponent do what you want him to do is to control the bout. Second intention is a coordination of both body actions and footwork to elicit a specific reaction from the opponent. The best and classic example is to initiate a short attack with no intention of scoring. The opponent predictably makes a parry followed by a counterattack. That counterattack is the setup action. It is parried and a counter-attack counter riposte is launched to score. Any action that elicits a predictable response from an opponent is second intention whether it involves just a body action or combines body action and footwork. "All" high level competitors fight in the second intention. It is one of the most important lessons that a trained intermediate level competitor can learn. To learn it however an athlete must have a good practical application knowledge of technique.

Tactically it can be said that a karate champion is not just a well-trained athlete or technician, but firstly is an astute student of human nature.

# AFTERTHOUGHTS

## Reflecting Images

Images are better than words in correcting errors and acquiring new skills. However, if one is unable to directly observe an art, reading will at least allow us to experience its essence.

Funakoshi Gichin believed that in order to become a man of accomplishment, one had to encompass *bunbu itchi* (the sword and the pen). Such parallel disciplines filled the life of the Japanese nobility. This age-old doctrine was also expounded by Plato in his *Timaeus*, in which he argued that balancing the mind and body was essential to the pursuit of excellence. Only when those two parts were exercised equally could one rightly be called a fully-developed personality. It is regrettable that Western martial arts puts so much emphasis on physical attributes and so little on mental development.

Philosophers do not, as a rule, have an easy relationship with their bodies. Descartes recognized that he had a body but insisted that it was not the same thing as himself. Plato sneered at the body's demands and shaped his philosophy from his desire to overcome them. Berkeley's body was a bundle of his own ideas, while Hume had great difficulty establishing that his body existed at all—which is why he got so fat. Socrates is remembered by his body, but largely on account of his ugliness. Nietzsche exercised, fruitlessly attempting to overcome the "blond beast" of his dreams with dumbbells. And Sartre exercised no more than was required to get from his downtown apartment to the bar across the road. For some people, mind and body do not connect.

We, as martial artists, train in such a way that a dual connection can be established. Our training reminds us that our bodies and our mental self-awareness are one and the same. Establishing this connection can sometimes take a lifetime, but the journey is as important as the arrival. So as we travel the path to enlightenment just remember: as we think, so shall we be.

Probably the most important thing in martial arts is to understand *why* we train. If we don't know precisely why we are studying a particular art, if we haven't clearly identified what we want to achieve

— either physically, emotionally, or psychologically — then it is impossible to set goals, plan our training, and measure results. If we want to develop a new mindset, or increase our self-belief, we have to employ procedures that directly affect the way we think. We cannot plan and set goals until we have assessed our present situation accurately. But it is very difficult to maintain a degree of subjectivity when practicing self-assessment because this is a process that requires the help of a reliable instructor. It is much easier to learn or teach someone physical techniques and skills than it is to implement a change in attitude.

Modern martial artists are very concerned about "what works" and "what's useful." Understanding is the key to deciding whether or not a particular art is "effective" or "works," because the answer depends on how you define these qualities. In other words, if a practitioner gains improvement in any aspect of his/her life, then the chosen art has been effective and worked for him/her. Different people want different things in life and as long as they enjoy their martial arts training and get something positive from it, that's all that counts. Hopefully, we'll finish with a clearer *understanding* of who we are and what we want to become.

Unfortunately, most of the things we do in our lives are things we don't necessarily enjoy, things we deem as meaningless, and there's nothing more unsatisfying than having to do a task with a feeling that it has no purpose – especially when the reason to do that task is only money. When money is what makes you do something, there is something intrinsic to that attitude that won't make you feel proud. You'll get paid but you won't necessarily take "vital" pride in your task. Sooner or later, when you look back to your past life, you will feel frustrated, disappointed, and empty as a human being; you will have a feeling that you haven't accomplished anything because it was not a deep sense of pride that moved you to do the things you did. Your best achievements in life will seem useless and wasted memories.

Money is the result of perfect work done with pride. Money shouldn't be the reason why we all must give our best in anything we do. Yes, we all have to pay bills, but that doesn't change anything for anyone. Bills, family, and other things only give these individuals excuses to justify their own failures and inadequacies.

If you're going to do something, do it right. Follow through to the very end. Don't just open the door and let someone else catch your inadequacies. Catch your own mistakes by showing what you are made of. Your work in all areas of your life is a reflection of yourself, representative of who you are and what you're about. This is true, whether you like it or not, and has nothing to do with how much – or how little – you get paid for doing something.

Sometimes, life deals us a very bad hand. But for the "right" individuals, sometimes the worst cards make the better players. It all depends on how you play with what you have. Some look at their blessings in life and see them as "responsibilities'" and "heavy weights" they carry on their backs, complaining constantly about them and wishing for someone else's life.

When your work ends up being less than top notch, your inherent value has changed, and you have to evaluate who you have become – and how alive you are. For good or bad, your quality of work reflects your values and demonstrates how much you ask of yourself. Every action can be purposeful and fulfilling, if we attach meaning to it.

In Martial Arts, there's an attacking principle that teaches us to deliver a "full-committed' offensive action with body, spirit, and mind. To be successful, the attack must be delivered with total commitment and lacking any hesitation, virtually ignoring the possibility of a counterattack by the opponent. Whether you are editing a magazine, filing papers in cabinets, putting labels on packages in a warehouse or cleaning bathrooms, make sure the work you do reflects your full commitment and shows pride. That attitude and behavior defines what kind of person you are.

When you have pride in what you do, you will work hard, even in the face of seemingly impossible odds and regardless of your paycheck. But when you just "don't care," you won't work nearly as hard as is needed, showing everybody the "real" you. Then, don't blame anyone for who and what you have become...since it is only your fault.

For too long we, as a society, have reached for happiness through money. And we have learned that the quest for material things won't bring us real happiness. In fact, if we analyze it carefully, we'll see it brings conflict, greed, and war.

These times of crisis present a good opportunity to ask yourself if the way you have been living is the way you really want to live – if your life is authentic and true. They open the door for us to focus more on the little and simple things. Focus more on your family and your own community. Live more creatively, do things from the heart, and you'll discover that simple not only is good, but it might even be better.

Today, the media is bombarding us with messages of fear. Don't base your state of mind on these messages, but on something deeper and more solid within yourself. If you can create deep pleasure and peace using your Martial Arts training, you don't need the world to provide it. You should remember that you already have what you need to get by in these times of uncertainty. Martial Arts training, in addition to supporting and calming you, will allow you to see a time of difficulty as an opportunity for positive change.

Budo teaches us to find a balance between taking care of ourselves and taking care of others. You have to nurture and strengthen yourself before you can give to others. Martial Arts practice is a journey much like life itself. Sometimes we find ourselves in times of transition. At those times, we need to ask ourselves, "What is really important? What makes me happy?" I am not talking about the instant rushes we get from an expensive meal or going shopping, but genuine deep-down happiness.

At the end, if you can enjoy Martial Arts for its own sake, you can change the way you relate to the world. And with that, comes power to change your destiny.

Anyone who seriously studies martial arts will eventually come to understand budo and bushido. As martial artists, we should try to avoid confrontation and strive to resolve conflicts without the use of force. However, if force is necessary, then we must do what we have to do. Survival requires the right attitude, and the right will. Without these, it is unlikely that superb technique, immaculate posture, or great timing will save you. You must be strong in the knowledge that you are doing the right thing, and dismiss any fear or doubt, for they are your worst enemies; this is bushido – the way of the warrior.

Black belts are no different from anyone else. They bleed and feel pain as readily as the next person. This doesn't mean that martial arts training will not increase self-defense skills – it will. But the superhuman qualities that Hollywood would have us believe in are not determined by the color of a person's belt.

In street survival, psychology is more important than technique. Keeping your head in a situation and not panicking is what matters. Non-martial artists can defend themselves quite well in a fight if they have strong will and character. It is a very interesting fact that most people who study martial arts are decent individuals who have no desire to involve themselves in acts of violence. There are, as we all know, many benefits to be gained from martial arts other than pure fighting ability. This means that many martial artists have little or no experience in real fights. If their training has not been designed to simulate reality, if it is not sufficiently stressful, if realistic scenarios are not considered and explored, they risk being unprepared if they ever have to defend themselves in the street. In short, you don't get what you don't train for.

Understanding *why* they train in a martial art is one of the major things most people lack. If you don't know precisely why you are studying a particular art, if you haven't clearly identified what you want to achieve – either physically, emotionally, or psychologically – then it is impossible to set goals, plan your training, and measure results. For instance, if you want to develop a new mind-set, or increase your self-belief, you have to employ procedures that directly affect the way you think. On the other hand, you cannot plan and set goals until you have accurately assessed your present situation. It is very difficult to maintain a degree of subjectivity when practicing self-assessment – this is a time and process that requires the help of a reliable instructor. It is much easier to learn or teach someone physical techniques and skills that it is to implement a change in attitude.

Modern martial artists are very concerned about "what works" and "what's useful." Understanding is the key to deciding whether or not a particular art is "effective" or "works," because the answer depends on how you define these qualities. To brand a particular art "ineffective," simply because it does not work in a limited environment, is narrow minded. Years of kata training alone may not prepare one for street fighting, but it can certainly result in greater character development. In other words, if a practitioner gains improvement in any aspect of their life, then their chosen art has been effective and worked for them. Different people want different things in life and as long as they enjoy their martial arts training and get something positive from it, that's all that counts.

Martial Arts are a way to understand the meaning of life (and death) from the warrior's perspective. It is correct to say that Martial Arts are supported by four pillars. In the first place, it can be understood as a life vision; second, as the proper spiritual way to realize this vision; third, as a set of physical techniques and specific tools for self-preservation; and finally, as a way to see a warrior's philosophy as the proper experience of freedom from death, which is its bigger objective. All these pillars act simultaneously to enhance our understanding of who we truly are.

The true way of Martial Arts places a practitioner in a process of self-discovery. The process is one of continually freeing himself of concepts about who he is and of letting go of all the limitations imposed on his mind, so that he can know and fully express his essential nature. What the philosophy of Martial Arts means to each practitioner who truly understands its meaning simply cannot be defined; it is something everyone must discover for him/herself. Attaining self-knowledge is not like discovering the law of gravity. There is no benefit possible in the process of self-discovery except through personal effort. No matter how much one man drinks, he can't satisfy the thirst of another. All he can do is recommend the process of drinking to those who are thirsty.

Quality in anything we do in life is never an accident but the result of strong intention, intelligent direction, and skillful execution.

There are no shortcuts in the process of character development in Martial Arts training. The practitioner of the arts has to develop as a whole, and, when only one of the aspects, such as the physical body, develops very quickly and the others are left behind, there are more obstacles and challenges in the medium and long run. Once a person awakens to his/her thirst for self-knowledge, the determination to succeed in life is reflected in the sincerity and strength of the search. Some like to talk about water but not look for it. Some like to discuss the available ways to search for water or hope that water will come to them out of the blue. Even some enjoy the process of looking for water so much that they avoid finding it. Only the sincere seeker feels keenly the thirst inside and determines not to stop looking for water until the thirst is quenched.

Regardless of what level the practitioner finds him/herself in, there really is only one teacher: experience itself. The true martial artist follows one abiding principle: pay attention to what is happening in one's immediate experience. And this is something that cannot be expressed in words. As the famous Japanese writer Yukio Mishima, practitioner of Martial Arts, personal friend of JKA Karate master, Masatoshi Nakayama and fifth dan in the art of kendo said, "Words are a medium that reduces reality to abstraction for transmission to our reason. In their power, they corrode reality. Inevitably, danger lurks that the words themselves will be corroded, too."

If one simply goes through the physical motions of Martial Arts, but omits the intrinsic elements of traditional training, such as framework, history, and ultimate purpose (self- improvement), then you can call what you practice anything you want – but you cannot say that it is "Martial Arts," because it really is only a collection of fighting techniques.

It is up to us to decide whether Martial Arts will become just one of many physical activities or – in accordance with the hopes of many practitioners – remain a unique art. Full of expressive beauty, philosophy, and respect for one's opponent, the true skill of Martial Arts lies in knowing how to move the body and mind along a path that lasts a lifetime, consummated in the contentment of a job well done. Experience is the best teacher and Martial Arts, in its instruction, adheres to this philosophy.

Our time on earth is limited, so don't waste it living someone else's life. Don't be trapped by living with the results of other people's thinking. Do not try to be like Buddha or any other leader – it is good to follow what is wise in their teachings but another matter entirely to try to wear their clothes. Don't let the noise of others' opinions drown out your own inner voice. Have the courage to follow your heart and intuition. Rather than fight to destroy others, we should fight to destroy the separation of mind and body within ourselves.

It is written that those "who increase the knowledge increase the sorrow." The more we know, the more responsible we are. It is that simple and it's all up to us.

The first and most important rule of the Martial Arts is dedication. To decide to fully embrace the Warrior's way forces us to leave some things "behind," and it requires significant commitment to change the very essence of us as individuals and move "forward" to develop some of the warrior's attributes.

One characteristic of a true Martial Artist is to know how to control one's emotions. Understanding emotions, not only ours but those of our opponent or aggressor, is essential. This is the only way we actually can use them for our benefit. Fear, courage, envy, anger, etc., have a wide, almost endless range of levels, and they are entwined into who we are as human beings.

Martial artists rely on their judgment and mental acuity to keep them safe and alive in a variety of circumstances, but many find that their judgment is less reliable when compromised by strong emotions. Emotional stress can dangerously impair our ability to judge an extreme situation and act accordingly. We should learn how to restrain our urges when we are upset – distracted by our emotions – and focus on acting with determination and purpose. Emotional factors may lead to risky decisions, not only in a self-defense situation but in life as well.

The Zen and Martial Arts masters of the past dedicated much of their lives to develop techniques and philosophies that we now have the benefit to enjoy thoroughly. Let's use them. Sometimes the ability to appeal and touch the other person's emotions is all that it takes to achieve victory.

Martial Arts training is an adventure. By definition, an adventure is something that has an unknown outcome. Life itself is an adventure. We know where we come from but we don't know how long the journey will be and where it will take us.

For many years [for a period of three months per year], I used to practice what I like to call a "mindful adventure." Going into a meditation retreat in the mountains of Kyoto, Japan, is not the kind of 'adventure' that our society would invite us to do. But one thing is certain: every time you do it, the outcome is different. These types of experiences take work and determination. But the payoff is well worth the commitment and the things you left behind. Many of the things you do there are treated with a "celebration" flavor. Every detail matters. With very little to do around you, one learn that our nervous system is designed to respond to the external fluctuations that occur outside [in our society], and that the act of meditation is a tool to recalibrate that. You learn to respond to your nervous system and to ride the waves of these emotional fluctuations, not only when things are going well, but especially when things are going badly in your life; not only when you are in solitude in the gardens of the Temple, but also when you are in stressful freeway traffic or a life-altering situation.

They say that Zen Meditation is virtuosity in being human. The important thing is that any kind of meditation – even the act of sitting quietly in your living room – should teach us about our role in the world, our relationships, our values, and the things we have passion for. It teaches us not to hold on to the fruits of our actions but to realize that the real transformation occurs when we find the unity of settling into ourselves. And that... is a great adventure.

# RORION GRACIE

## JOIN THE GRACIE REVOLUTION

The primary objective of my family is to teach Gracie Jiu-Jitsu to the world. What is unique about this objective is that, due to its magnitude, it had to be broken down into three phases and accomplished over three generations. Although phases 1 and 2 are complete, phase 3 is not — and that is where you can help.

### Phase 1: Create Gracie Jiu-Jitsu

When my father, Helio Gracie, first was introduced to Japanese Jiu-Jitsu by his brother Carlos, he couldn't use the techniques due to his small stature and frail body—so his determination to help his students with truly effective moves pushed him to change the system. As he began modifying the traditional techniques so that they relied more on leverage, patience, and precision and less on strength, speed, and coordination, he unknowingly started the greatest revolution in martial arts history; it was the birth of Gracie Jiu-Jitsu. In order to test the effectiveness of his new system, he issued challenges to all the reputable martial artists in Brazil, regardless of their size. The positive result of his test gave him tremendous confidence in his system. That was when he realized that his most valuable contribution would be to educate and empower others with the techniques of Gracie Jiu-Jitsu.

## Phase 2: Show the Necessity for Gracie Jiu-Jitsu

I know that I was conceived to carry on the family tradition of perfecting and perpetuating the techniques of Gracie Jiu-Jitsu. I realized long ago that the key to global exposure for Gracie Jiu-Jitsu lay in my ability to establish credibility in the United States. When I came to America in the late 70s, I noticed that the martial arts community placed very little emphasis on the importance of ground fighting. In 1993, I created the UFC so the viewers could see that even the most skilled strikers are helpless when the fight goes to the ground, and that an average size guy (Royce at 178 pounds) easily could defeat much larger opponents with the simple and effective techniques of Gracie Jiu-Jitsu. Over the years, with the help of my brothers, and many other family members, the whole world became aware and dependent on the benefits of this amazing system!

## Phase 3: Teach Gracie Jiu-Jitsu to the World

When high ranking officials in the U.S. Army saw the UFC and witnessed firsthand the effectiveness of Gracie Jiu-Jitsu, they quickly realized that their existing hand-to-hand combat system was outdated. So, they hired me to develop a program that would prepare soldiers during one week of intensive training to realistically defend themselves in life-or-death situations. The result was Gracie Combatives, a precise and objective selection of the 34 most effective and important Gracie Jiu-Jitsu techniques ever developed.

The unprecedented level of success of this course made us decide to teach it to civilians, as well. However, we realized that it would be difficult for most civilian students to commit an entire week to Gracie Combatives training.

***The Solution:*** Divide the 34 techniques of Gracie Combatives into 22 one-hour long classes. These 22 carefully designed classes then were laid out and printed on a monthly calendar so that students knew which class was going to be taught each day of the month. Each student would be assigned his or her own Gracie Combatives

Card that contains the complete curriculum and allows them to keep track of their progress. Once each class had been completed, they would qualify to participate in a Fight Simulation Drill class, in which they learned how to execute all 34 essential techniques in combination with one another to better prepare them for a street fight. With the implementation of this unique program here at the Gracie Academy, we suddenly were preparing students to defend themselves in less time than ever was thought possible.

## You Can Be an Instructor

Since the UFC took the world by storm in 1993, thousands of avid martial artists from all over the world have desired to become instructors certified by the Gracie Academy. To meet this demand, we originally developed an instructor certification program that required the instructor candidates to move to Torrance, California, to spend about four to six years learning all the techniques (several hundred) and how to teach them before they were certified. The problem was that this program was so demanding that only a few individuals ever could devote themselves long enough to actually complete it. With careful analysis of the techniques used by the second generation Gracies in all of their challenge matches, and the successful implementation of the Gracie Combatives program at all military bases and at the Gracie Academy, it became clear that you can defend yourself successfully in 99 percent of real street fight situations using only the 34 Gracie Combatives techniques. With this realization, we felt comfortable redesigning the instructor certification course to base it entirely on the Gracie Combatives program. As a result, we have been able to reduce the time it takes to certify an instructor from several years to *only two weeks*. If you have ever dreamed about being a certified instructor by the Gracie Academy, visit: www.gracieacademy.com

# THE GENESIS OF MIXED MARTIAL ARTS

I've heard it said that the first UFC was just an infomercial for Gracie Jiu-Jitsu but that's not really an accurate analogy. Infomercials are well-rehearsed, scripted presentations in front of paid audiences, whereas the UFC was closer to a "reality show" in which anything could happen. I think an even more useful way to look at it would be as an "experiment," or a demonstration, the Octagon being a giant mixing bowl and the wide variety of martial arts—sumo, boxing, kung fu, karate, shoot fighting, savate, kickboxing, etc., as the ingredients. Without judges, points, time limits or rules, I tried to create as pure an environment as possible to mix them all together and watch the results. What the audience might not have realized at the time was that they were witnessing the creation of a new sport, mixed martial arts.

On the surface, they saw the crowning of an Ultimate Fighting Champion, a skinny kid from Brazil, who had never fought professionally until then. But the truth was, he wasn't the best fighter in the world; in fact, he wasn't even the best fighter in his own family. But as I predicted, he was the ideal representative of the most effective martial art in the world, Gracie Jiu-Jitsu.

If it was like an infomercial in one small way, it was that I was confident in the results ahead of time. I had the advantage seeing it all before; decades earlier in Brazil, my father had already conducted the same experiment by challenging fighters of every discipline to help him fine-tune his jiu-jitsu and prove its effectiveness for his students. So, in a way, Royce was like a fighter from the future brought back to 1993 to fight all the old school martial artists who had no idea of what I already knew.

My father, Helio Gracie, grew up small in stature and prone to fainting spells. Due to his poor health my parents let him quit school early, but doctors warned against any strenuous physical activity. After my grandparents divorced, Helio looked to his older brother, Carlos, as a father figure. Carlos was an adventurer and a student of life. He was the first Gracie brother to learn jiu-jitsu. Then he taught the other Gracie brothers, and they soon opened their own school to teach others. My father would sit on the sidelines and watch his brothers teach, until one day, at age 16, when a student was about to leave because Carlos was nowhere to be found, my father volunteered to fill in and the student accepted. When Carlos arrived at the end of his lesson, he apologized, but the student told him, "No problem, but from now on I want Helio to teach me." Thus, in that small moment, began the evolution of traditional jiu-jitsu into Gracie Jiu-Jitsu.

The combination of his small stature, being warned not to exert himself, and having to learn jiu-jitsu intellectually first, led my father to approach jiu-jitsu as a science, a way for a smaller, weaker man to intelligently defend himself against a larger and stronger opponent—technique over brute strength—a way for David to consistently beat Goliath.

After discarding techniques that felt "forced," or required too much strength, and fine-tuning those that didn't, he sought to expand his knowledge base by challenging fighters of other disciplines. After all, what good is a fighting system that only works against other practitioners of the same art, as was the practice of most other systems?

Through my father's open challenges to all fighters, from world champion boxers to wrestlers, street fighters and judo champions, the sport of "Vale Tudo" emerged and became popular throughout Brazil.

I choose Royce to represent Gracie Jiu-Jitsu because I wanted people to look beyond the fighter and say, "Wow, if that skinny guy could beat all of those big, tough martial arts representatives, maybe I should learn it, too!" And it worked. We demonstrated the importance of ground fighting and today Gracie Jiu-Jitsu is widely recognized as the most effective martial art in the world. I give my father all the credit for being the first true pioneer of mixed martial arts. But the future is not here yet; there is still more to come from the world of Gracie Jiu-Jitsu.

## FOCUS AND POSITIVE ENERGY

Thoughts become reality. That's the message of a current best-selling book called, "The Secret." The premise is that this is an ancient secret passed down by the power elite and is only now being revealed as "something new" to today's readers.

Likewise in the world of Gracie Jiu-Jitsu this was a lesson passed down by my father. My father believed in the power of intention and positive thinking. He believed that just by being at his academy he attracted students who otherwise wouldn't stop in and that his positive energy set a positive "can do" atmosphere at his academy as well. As a child I remember trips in my father's truck up the winding mountain roads to the Gracie compound in Terezopolis. Along the way it was normal for my father to pull over many times to assist stranded motorist or offer rides to those in need. Those were happy times, and the sense of camaraderie was all around. He also told me that teaching jiu-jitsu was the best job in the world. Of course, at the time I couldn't see it, but I later experienced the good will that inevitably comes by helping others with sincerity and enthusiasm.

When I decided to open the first Gracie Academy, in Torrance, CA, I was told that it would be impossible. At the time I was barely able to make ends meet for my family but as it turned out, just by putting that intention into the air, friends I made along the way by sharing the knowledge of Gracie Jiu-Jitsu during the years prior opening my first school helped make my dream a reality. And now a new era is dawning as the new Gracie Academy, in Torrance. Once again it was the friends I made along the way that have come back and helped make my new dream a reality. The new academy is a modern building with state-of-the-art amenities and comes at a time when MMA is at an all-time high in popularity. And it coincides with our re-focusing on what Gracie Jiu-Jitsu had always been about: self-defense.

We will no longer host traditional sportive jiu-jitsu tournaments. While they're fun, they encourage "chasing points" to win, which can give competitors the illusion of effectiveness against the reality of punches and kicks of a street fight. Clear examples of this are often seen in NHB arenas when jiu-jitsu champions, are easily knocked out while attempting moves that would bring them points in a sportive competition. The focus on getting the point makes them forget the punches.

Our new system of classes, "Gracie Combatives," focuses on specific situations that are the most commonly encountered in a street fight. Once students go through that program, they qualify to join the "fight simulation" classes, which is focused on keeping you aware of the vulnerable spots you can be in during a street fight. This type of training is much closer to real fighting than tournament jiu-jitsu. The best way to find out about this amazing concept is stop by and check out a class. At the same time take the opportunity to visit the new facility which features a one of a kind 4500 square feet custom made mat, the beautifully redesigned Gracie Museum, comfortable and clean locker rooms, granite flooring and is conveniently located just 30 seconds off the 405 Freeway, at 3515 Artesia Blvd. in Torrance, California.

## WHY YOU MUST LEARN GRACIE COMBATIVES

*"If you perfect the 34 Gracie Combatives techniques, you don't need a Black Belt."*

In order to get a Black Belt in Gracie Jiu-Jitsu, you need to perfect over 600 techniques. What is amazing, however, is that studies have shown that you only need a handful of these techniques to be defeat a larger stronger opponent in a real street fight.

The Gracie Combatives™ course is made up of the 34 most important and effective Gracie Jiu-Jitsu techniques ever used by the Gracie Family. Of all the fights my family members have ever been in, these 34 techniques have been used more often and more successfully than all others combined. I originally developed the Gracie Combatives™ course exclusively for the U.S. Army but now it is being used to prepare civilian martial arts students for combat in less time than ever before possible!

If you are traditional martial arts instructor, you probably realize the importance of incorporating Gracie Jiu-Jitsu into your existing curriculum. The problem, as you may have also realized, is that the time it would take for you to get your black belt in Gracie Jiu-Jitsu makes it almost impossible to make this necessary change at your school. What you didn't know is that if you perfect the 34 Gracie Combatives techniques, you don't need a Black Belt.

Realizing that the most important techniques anyone could ever learn or teach are the 34 Gracie Combatives techniques, we have decided to certify existing martial arts instructors to teach Gracie Combatives at their schools upon successful completion of a 10 day, 80-hour Instructor Certification Course. This course is so comprehensive that I can confidently say that those who complete it will be able to execute and teach the essential Gracie Jiu-Jitsu techniques more profoundly than most of the existing self-proclaimed Gracie Jiu-Jitsu instructors who have never been certified by my family but use the name to add marketability to their school.

If you have ever considered teaching Gracie Jiu-Jitsu but were unable to commit to the years of training it used to take, the Gracie Combatives Instructor Certification Program is perfect for you. Upon successful completion of the course, you will be authorized to administer the Gracie Combatives course at your school in the exact same format that we offer it here at the Gracie Academy.

## Who Might Qualify to Become a Certified Gracie Combatives Instructor?

Our goal is to make Gracie Combatives available at martial arts schools around the world and for this reason we are only accepting applications from existing school owners. If you own a school, we highly encourage you to visit our website for more information on how you can become the exclusive Gracie Combatives Certified Training Center in your community.

To see if you qualify to become a Certified Gracie Combatives Instructor, visit: www.GracieAcademy.com.

## THE GRACIE DIET—A NEW OBJECTIVE

I came to America in the 1970s with a single objective — to establish my family's Brazilian style of jiu-jitsu as the most as the most effective self-defense system in the world. To prove my point, I challenged anyone — regardless of size, weight, athleticism, or martial arts skill — to defeat me in a one-on-one, no-holds-barred combat.

I quickly convinced the martial arts community in Southern California that the Gracie system was amazingly effective.

In 1993, I co-created the Ultimate Fighting Championship to showcase my family's art against all comers. The UFC was a pay-per-view extravaganza that pitted all varieties of martial arts against each other in the first modern fighting competition without rules, judges, or time limits.

The repeated victories of the Gracie Jiu-Jitsu practitioner against larger and stronger, opponent fighters sparked a revolution in the martial arts world that has continued to this day. I had achieved my objective.

Now, I have an even greater task — to expand the concept of self-defense beyond physical combat to include lifestyle changes that will enable you to defeat your internal assailants. That's self-defense in the fullest sense of the term.

Millions of Americans struggle with the challenges of diet, weight control, and fitness. We hear that the United States is the most obese nation in history, that childhood obesity is epidemic, and that poor nutrition is increasing rates of heart disease, diabetes, and cancer.

In the face of these alarming trends, many people simply surrender, just as they would if facing an attacker twice their size. But in the same way Gracie Jiu-Jitsu revolutionized thinking about physical combat, I believe the Gracie Diet will revolutionize your thinking about healthy eating habits and help you win the fight against internal assailants such as: obesity, disease, and frailty. I promise you that you can do it!

My book, "The Gracie Diet," outlines ways to take a good look at your current eating patterns and, smoothly and efficiently, ease into the Gracie Diet, which will lead to a healthier, more energetic life, for the rest of your life.

In fact, as time passes, you'll find the routine easier. As in Gracie Jiu-Jitsu, it's just a matter of consistently using the tools and techniques you've learned. But first, there are a few key principles you must understand.

First and foremost, you must embrace the basic metaphor: Weight control is a matter of defending yourself in a fight against a ruthless opponent who will use every trick in the book to harm you. Of course, we all know that there is really no external enemy. The person eating unhealthy foods is the same person who's suffering the consequences. That's you.

So, it's important to start separating your negative self-destructive impulses from the authentic "you" who wants to have a healthy and fulfilling life.

# CHRIS KENT

**MAKING BRUCE LEE'S NOTES
WORK FOR YOU**

Bruce Lee's intense thirst for knowledge and understanding was a prime factor that led to his growth and evolution as a martial artist. In his never-ending quest for personal development, Lee went to great lengths to gain insight and learning that would aid him in actualizing his full potential, drawing from all forms of combative arts, modern dance, bodybuilding, exercise physiology, kinesiology, philosophy, and psychology. And in the years before copy machines, computers and printers were part of the mainstream, Lee put pen (or sometimes pencil) to paper and recorded his thoughts, observations, and ideas on these as well as other subjects, leaving behind countless pages of written and typed notes. Many of these notes have been compiled into books over the years since his passing.

In order to get the most out of JKD it is essential to know how to make Bruce Lee's

notes work for you—how to bring them to life and use them to help you achieve your fullest potential as a martial artist. Lee's notes have been likened to guideposts, or clues, that can lead an individual to their own self-expression in the martial arts. But guideposts do a person little or no good if they don't know how to read or interpret them correctly. So, the first thing that needs to be understood is how to study Lee's notes. This is not as easy as it sounds. When reading

Bruce Lee's notes, three intrinsic principles should guide your study. These principles may, in the beginning, require several separate readings but in time can be done concurrently. The three principles are as follows:

### *Understand the Notes*

You need to comprehend thoroughly and perceive clearly the nature of what you're reading. What are the particular writings or notes you are studying saying?

### *Interpret the Notes*

The word "interpret" in this case means, "to bring out or explain the meaning of something." In other words, what do the notes you're studying mean? In martial arts it seems that many times people immediately rush to the application stage of Lee's teachings and bypass the theoretical stage. They want to know what the technique means to them before they understand what Lee intended it to mean.

### *Evaluate the Notes*

To evaluate something means to judge or determine its worth or quality. In other words, is the given principle right or wrong for them? Is it valid or not? Unfortunately, many people tend to skip over the first two principles and jump right into evaluating Lee's notes. They judge a particular concept to be right or wrong before they understand what it says or before they interpret its meaning.

The above three intrinsic principles are, however, by themselves, inadequate. To study Bruce Lee's notes successfully and get the most out of them, a person also needs three important extrinsic aids.

### Experience

Experience is the only way to interpret and relate what has been read. A person who has little or no experience in martial arts and/or philosophy is going to be at a distinct disadvantage in understanding, interpreting, and evaluating Lee's notes. I may be able to tell you what I like or don't like about a particular painting by a master like Van Gogh, but I will not be able to interpret and evaluate the painting like a person who has and education and background in fine arts.

But experience by itself is not enough. We need to research our experience. Experience that has been understood and reflected upon informs and enlightens your study.

## Other Books and Writings

Books and writings that precede or advance the subject you're studying can be very significant. Very often books or notes can have greater meaning when they are read in relation to other writings. I have had the privilege of perusing the books in Bruce Lee's personal library at great length on numerous occasions. But I have also established my own library that includes books on martial arts, Western fencing, physical fitness, kinesiology, philosophy, psychology, and various other categories of interest. Studying and analyzing these books has unquestionably helped to increase my understanding of Lee's notes. Bruce Lee always approached a subject wanting to know as much as possible about it and with an open mind ready to absorb new information. If he were alive today, there's no doubt that he would avail himself of all sources of information including books, videos, films, DVDs, and the internet to gain access to the most up-to-date information on whatever subject that interested him or that he was studying. And you should follow his example and do the same thing.

## Live Discussion

The final extrinsic aid is live discussion, which means the interaction that occurs among individuals as they pursue a particular course of action. My close friend Cass Magda and I have spent countless hours discussing JKD, sometimes amongst ourselves, and other times with other friends or students. When we discuss and debate certain issues, techniques, or philosophical attitudes relating to JKD, many times new insights emerge that might have never occurred without this type of exchange.

As important as it is to successfully research Lee's notes, however, it is equally important to know how to use them. The first step of this process is to read Lee's notes without trying to fit them into established categories. The goal here is to simply grasp the content of the material, the essence of what is being presented, and to understand it. Expect to hear new things in new ways when you read the notes at different times and don't be concerned if you don't get some things in the first reading. It might take several readings before you fully comprehend something. All of us have had the experience of reading something over and over and then suddenly understanding what it means. This "Wow, now I get it!" experience of understanding catapults you into onto a new level of growth and freedom. You might find it useful each time you read the notes to use a differently colored pen to mark certain things that stand out to you at that time. Another idea is to keep a journal or notebook handy to jot down thoughts and impressions that occur while reading.

The next step is to investigate why Lee drew a particular essence from an art or why he chose to absorb something into his own art. It's important here to recognize the difference between absorbing and simply adding. Bruce did not add something simply for the sake of adding it. To "absorb" something means, "to take in and incorporate; to assimilate." To "add" means to take in and unite so as to increase the number, size, etc. Ask yourself, "What is it about this particular technique that Bruce Lee felt was useful or valid to what he was doing?" Analyze it by breaking it down into its component parts and examining it to find out its interrelationship with other material in Lee's notes. Don't simply look from one angle, but from all possible angles.

The third step is to apply what you are studying. Theory without application means nothing. You've got to take the material you're investigating onto the floor and test it. You need to see if, and how well it works under pressure and in realistic situations. Keep in mind, too, that just because you may not be able to do it or use it at that particular moment, doesn't mean that it's not valid or that it's no good. If your instructor shows you how to do a technique and then you try it and you cannot do it, don't immediately respond with, "Oh, that's stupid. It doesn't work" and throw the technique out the window. Don't reject something until you know why you are rejecting it.

The final step is evaluation, in which you judge the value of the material for a given purpose. Ask yourself, "Is this particular principle or technique valid or not? How does it relate to me? Does it have application to what I'm doing?" If, for example, the particular style of martial art you practice doesn't believe in the use of hand immobilization attacks, then sensitivity training such as *chi sao* may have no application for you. Keep in mind, though, that just because something might not have an application for you, that doesn't mean it won't have an application for someone else. The following are some pitfalls you should try to avoid when studying and/or using Bruce Lee's notes:

**Simply memorizing and regurgitating Lee's words, ideas, etc.** -- Anybody can repeat someone else's words by rote. Remember, it's not how much fixed knowledge or information you have accumulated, it's what you can use and apply that counts.

**Taking the material in Bruce Lee's notes to be the "Bible" of martial arts** -- Some people approach JKD very dogmatically and with the fundamentalist view that "If it's not in the *Tao of JKD,* or if it's not in Bruce's writings, then it's not JKD." This is the very antithesis of Lee's teachings. Bruce was a seeker of truth. To him, each thing he wrote down represented *a* truth, not *the* truth. No one has a monopoly on truth. There is no "one way."

**Adding your own interpretation to Bruce Lee's material** -- I am not saying that you shouldn't interpret Lee's material. I am simply reminding you to keep things in proper context. Many times, people read something with an eye towards finding support for what they themselves are doing. For example, in Lee's notes it states, "Investigate into fighting from the ground...develop such mastery that one can fight safely from the ground." But Lee doesn't make a point of telling you to study any particular style of ground-fighting or martial art that includes ground-fighting. The point is to hear what Bruce Lee is saying, not what we want him to say.

**Solidifying Bruce Lee's guideposts into laws** -- Bruce changed his mind about publishing his notes when he came to the realization that trying to encapsulate fighting into words was like trying to capture something on paper that is alive and constantly changing. It was, he concluded, "like attempting to tie a pound of water into a manageable shape." So don't calcify what should remain alive and growing.

**Starting from a conclusion** -- Remember, to taste someone else's tea you must first empty your cup of preconceived ideas, notions, etc. Begin with an open mind.

Bruce Lee's notes are like an extension of Bruce himself. They describe the direction of his studies and shed light on his own process of intellectual growth and development as a martial artist. As such, they can serve as a pipeline to his way of thinking, feeling, and researching. Bruce's notes can also act as a navigational guide, like a compass, which can help direct you to where you want to be as a martial artist. If you know how to use a compass, even if the terrain changes, a road becomes blocked, or a detour arises, you can still remain on course toward your ultimate destination. In order to do that, however, you must know where it is that you want to go and whether the goal is physical, mental, emotional, or spiritual. Once you know that, then you can take all of the information in Lee's notes and consider it; debate it, turn it upside down; look at it from your own perspective; refine it to suit you; rearrange it; keep what you think will work for you; and even throw some of it out (just make sure you know why you're throwing it out).

Don't allow anyone to simply hand you the truth. It cannot be done. Take an experiential attitude and find out for yourself what works for you. See Bruce Lee's notes as a literary work in progress, not as something that was finished or completed. Remember, "If you understand it and can use it, it belongs to no one; it's yours."

# RIGAN MACHADO

## THE ART OF TEACHING

Being able to perform all Jiu-Jitsu techniques won't make you an instructor in the art. Doing and teaching are two completely different things and as such should be understood and separated. As student, you should be able of performing the physical techniques with a skill level accorded to your rank. As instructor, the physical ability won't make your student good Jiu Jitsu practitioners. It is your ability to communicate, breakdown and pass your technical knowledge what is important here. Many great champions, in all kinds of sports, lacked the ability to breakdown everything they were capable of doing, and teach it to their students. They were talented athletes but with no ability to make other practitioners good at it.

Teaching Brazilian Jiu Jitsu requires, in first place, an extensive knowledge of how all the pieces of the puzzle (techniques) fit and the fundamental principles that every single technique exemplifies. A good teacher will have a progressive program that will allow the student not only to physically improve, but also understand how the different techniques are inter-related among them and how those can be combined in a practical format. Although it is very common see an instructor giving techniques in a random manner, this approach is definitely not the most appropriate for the students to understand what they are doing. An instructor should start showing the student the basics of the art. The basic techniques develop the most fundamental principles found in the art and what is more important, teach the student the necessary body mechanics for future technical growth. Like any other martial art system, Brazilian Jiu Jitsu has a set of fundamental techniques that a good instructor should give emphases in the early stages of learning. These basic techniques should be backed up with several drills -- not fighting drills -- that improve the student's ability to move their body on the ground, and eventual will make possible to perform the technique properly.

Beware of instructors that show too many techniques in a randomly way without giving a strong foundation to the student. Be cautious with those teachers who put beginners to spar almost immediately -- focusing on a competition approach and how the techniques are supposed to be used in a tournament -- and force them to struggle in a grappling situation without a previous intensive training and understanding of the basics. These instructors will push the student to get the technique perform via pure strength and muscle use which eventually cut the student progress in the art since all the basic information added to the data base has been wrong. It is easier for this kind of instructors, to put students to spar, than dedicate time to correct and teach the art properly. There is a time for everything and sparring in Brazilian Jiu Jitsu should be incorporated into the student program at the right time.

A good instructor will make any student, regardless of their level of understanding and physical ability, learn and apply a basic movement. It is up to the instructor to be able of dissect the technique in little pieces and communicate the intrinsic principles of the movement to different level of understanding. An experience instructor will teach an arm-lock differently to a white belt, a purple belt, and a black belt, depending on their expertise and knowledge of the art. It is the ability of the instructor to breakdown the information according to their student's level (technical and understanding) what sets a master apart from an average instructor. There are no bad students, but incapable teachers of making the student good at Jiu Jitsu.

Find a teacher who dedicates time and attention to explain the art and the techniques properly; someone who has a teaching structure and the correct methodology. No art or subject of any kind can be properly taught without a correct structure and format. Finally, when looking for a Jiu Jitsu instructor, simply remember that the students are the reflection of what the teacher is. Pay attention to the students, analyze how they train, how they move and also how they behave with lower ranks and explain the techniques. See if they compete with the lower ranks or they help them to improve. If you are planning to join a school and find that all what the students do is to roll indiscriminately, fighting with not sense of technique or finesse and focus excessively on competing, maybe it is time for you to look someplace else.

## TOURNAMENTS AND COMPETITION

Tournaments are an important part in the promotion of any martial art style, but when practicing a martial art, we must take into consideration what the real goal of the art is - since ultimately a martial art is something different than a sport. Rules in competition, in any kind of competition, set the direction in which the physical techniques of the art/sport will evolve. The goal of Jiu Jitsu is to control and to submit your opponent. Only these aspects represent the true superiority of one fighter over another. The problem arises when two excellent competitors meet, and the ideal submission technique is blocked and countered by the other fighter. This situation provokes both participants try to stall and play with the rules -- using excessive force to get out of a position in which the opponent gets more points even if the fighter is not under any kind of real danger.

Jiu Jitsu competition rules vary and changed according to the specific tournament and those running it, but the essence of our Jiu Jitsu training -- when we practice at the school -- shouldn't be governed by the set of rules of the sport.

Training in the art of Jiu Jitsu and be good at it should be our main concern, not simply winning tournaments. Jiu Jitsu is first a martial art and a sport second.

When you step onto the mat and you are rolling with your partners, try to do your best regardless of how many points are awarded in competition for any specific movement that you are training. Develop your game plan based on the concept and principles of a martial art, and later, if you feel interested in competition, learn the rules, and try to use them appropriately without forgetting that trying to control and submit your opponent exemplify the main objective of the art of Brazilian Jiu Jitsu. In a perfect world, referees should only award points for either controlling the opponent clearly and with a full controlled technique for a certain amount of time (several seconds) or for putting the opponent into a submission and make him tap. This way, the competitors should have to train to fully control and totally submit their opponent. Once you get into a tournament, make sure you know the rules and how to play with the regulations in order to get the best out of them. There is nothing wrong with using the rules of competition to our advantage, that is why they are for. But remember sport competition has limits and regulations that don't measure your self-defense abilities and your personal involvement and complete skill in the art.

In competition, the majority of participants have a similar level of rank and skill. Therefore, the key element in sport jiu-jitsu lies in other surrounding aspects of the technical training. Physical conditioning, strength training, power training, cardiovascular training, psychological make-up, etc. are these key attributes that will make a difference at the end. It is pretty much like an iceberg: the tip of the iceberg represents the physical techniques of the art -- the basic movements. The rest, all the physical attributes necessary to make that "tip" work in a fight, are the other 8/9 parts of the ice. They are under the water, where you can't see them... but it doesn't mean they don't exist.

Every martial art system requires certain physical attributes from the practitioner to fully apply the individual techniques of the art. Standing fighting arts require specific attributes as timing, mobility, reflexes, eye-hand/foot coordination, etc. Grappling arts such as Brazilian jiu jitsu rely mostly on corporal (body) sensitivity, body positioning, isometric muscular strength, limberness, et cetera.

Since the perfect execution of a single technique depends on the practitioner's level at what the physical attributes are performing, it is important for the students allocate time to develop these necessary attributes for their chosen art.

Analyze the attributes that specifically apply to Brazilian jiu jitsu and work on hard on them. By doing this, you'll improve the effectiveness of your technique.

Do the attribute training once you have already developed a high technical level and not before. Attribute without a refined technique is useless. It is important to bring the 'building blocks' in the proper order to establish a strong foundation. Technique first, everything else should come after.

Nowadays, the competitors are more knowledgeable about all the technical possibilities available at their hand's reach. Hopefully, the knowledge of an additional technique may surprise your opponent and allow you to score a decisive point or completely submit your opponent, but with all the technical advancements, only technique is not enough anymore. The competitor needs to be an athlete if he wants to become a Brazilian jiu-jitsu champion. The physical techniques now must be supported by other supplementary aspects of fighting, due to the fact the game has improved tremendously in the last decade. Simply technique in a world-class competition level is not enough.

The hours you spent on the mat are what is called "flight time." Leave the ego at the door and don't try to fight with your partners. The school is not a competition or tournament, it is not a fight; it is the place where you learn the art. If your partner doesn't cooperate, then ask him to slow down and make him to understand that both of you are helping to each other. Anybody with enough muscle power can fight and force their way thru a technique. Doing it with refined technique and skill is reserved to a few. A good way of training intelligently is to roll with your opponent when no submissions are allowed. Neither you nor your opponent can go for a submission; arm-locks, chokes, or leg-locks. This takes the pressure out of trying to submit the training partner and allows the practitioner to smoothly roll with the opponent which eventually will develop many of the important attributes in sparring or competition. In this specific training drill, there is no destination (submission) so we can enjoy (learn) the journey more consciously and improve one of the most difficult aspects of the art of Brazilian jiu-jitsu; flow with your opponent.

Finally, set a progressive training plan that allows you to get better and improve your game. Start working hard on the basis, work on the small details that make the technique work; leave the brute force at home and think of finesse instead of strength. Try to discover how all the positions you are learning inter-relate to each other and how you can move from a defensive movement into an attack, how to reverse an arm-lock and end up submitting your opponent with a choke or how to escape from a headlock and finish your opponent with a leg-lock. All techniques are interchangeable, and you'll be surprised how the most advanced technique can be countered with a very basic movement. Most of the times the solution to a big problem lies in a simple answer.

Train hard, train smart, but at all times, train safe.

## MAKE IT WORK. MAKE IT FUNCTIONAL.

In any sport, long is the road to excellence, and Brazilian Jiu Jitsu is not an exception. From the very first moment when a practitioner learns a technique until he applies it successfully in a World Championship, there are many hours of hard training and progressive technical development. Four phases must be completed in order to achieve final mastery of any physical technique. We'll analyze each one separately and explain how the different concepts apply to each one of these training phases. To learn, practice, master, and finally functionalize are the four different phases of the complete 'mastery' of each single technique.

***Learn:*** This is the very first step. The instructor teaches the movement (technique) to the student and gives him all the technical details necessary to perform the technique correctly. He walks with the student through all the basic elements and principles that build the foundation of that particular movement. The student now has all the information about how to perform the technique correctly, but he still lacks the training on it. This is the reason why he doesn't perform it well and has problems when trying to do it. Don't be aggressive or use a "combative mind" in this phase. It is paramount to empty and relax the mind, trying to absorb as much as information as possible about the fine details of the movement.

***Practice:*** Now that the student has the basic information, the next step is to practice what he already has (in his mind). This phase is extremely important since all the fundamental body mechanics for that specific technique will be built during this phase. This means that he must pay very close attention to how he inputs the information into his system. Taking time to absorb and work on the little technical details of the movement is very important. The mind should navigate the body. Don't rush and try to use force because all the data that you'll be putting into your body will be incorrect. Relax and work slowly, little by little, paying full attention to each small detail that the teacher corrects.

Progressively, and only once the student has a fair amount of control on the little details, he should start to increase moderately the speed used to perform the movement. If he feels that he is having problems in achieving any segment or section of the movement correctly, he should slow down the pace and work on that particular aspect of the technique until it is correct. Paying complete attention to each detail is extremely important in this phase of training.

***Master:*** This is a tricky word that brings confusion to the practitioner. He already has a very good level of skill in performing the technique, as a mold, but now he needs to add a new element into the equation; different opponents give him different scenarios. Here, the practitioner doesn't need to think about the small details of the physical movement anymore – these already should be in the data base – but needs to be able to fit the technical movement into the structure of different uncooperative opponents. Uncooperative is the key word, because no two opponents in the world have the same way of moving, give the same energy back, or try to counter the technique in the exact same way.

This first aspect of mastering the technique has to do with the "operativeness" of the technique itself and your ability to understand how the technique should be used against different kind of opponents. You should research and go deep into the essential principles of the technique and its possibilities under different kind of circumstances (opponents). When facing a problem, don't try to find the solution outside the fundamental principles of the technique but analyze this new situation and try to find a way using the essence of the principles that compose the basic movement. Don't randomly change the technique for the sake of change but make the technique fit into the new scenario as you maintain the basic principles of it. In this phase of the technical development, the training-partner again is a very important element of the equation -- an extremely important one.

To a certain extent, your training partner should be at least as skillful as you are, and in a perfect world, be a much better Jiu jitsu practitioner than you are. Why? Simply because he is the individual that needs to set the environment for you and needs to think ahead of your technique. He is the person who will set the circumstances for you to improve your game. Ideally, your training-partner should be your instructor and teacher and that's why private classes are very important at this stage. Only someone with more understanding, skill and knowledge than you, can truly take you to the higher levels of this phase. No beginner will improve your technique at this level. Only someone with a deep and mature understanding of the art, its principles, and the complete spectrum of the training phases in the art will be capable of getting out the best of you.

***Functionalize:*** at this level, the practitioner already has (a) a sound technical foundation; (b) a deep understanding of the fundamental principles that rule that specific technique; and (c) the ability and precise body feel to use it against different kind of opponents. Now he needs to kick it another notch and develop a plan of how to use the given technique against different opponents in size, weight, and physical characteristics and, begin to incorporate combination attacks which involves to studying and analyzing how to interrelate and combine that specific movement with other techniques, creating a network of technical solutions for any problem we may face. Each one of the techniques composing that network should have been take to the master level. Otherwise, the technical network will have important flaws that will bring problems to the practitioner. For instance, let's take the "triangle" as the main technique. You have to learn to adapt this movement against someone who is skinny and against someone who is heavy with a strong neck and shoulder muscles that will impede the movement to be applied easily without any kind of alteration or minor modification in the delivery method. Then study how to interrelate that movement with, for instance, the straight arm-lock and omoplata. Now that you have three different options from one single given point in combat, you'll have to be able to attack with one and, as soon as your opponent blocks this one, move into the other successively, creating a constant menace for him. He will be only humanly able of cover a limited number of attacks. When one door closes, another gets open. It is in this stage when you develop a complete game plan that brings together the fine skill in techniques with the proper tactics and strategies of when and how to use the technique you know against any kind of opponent and under any kind of situation.

To reach this very advanced level the student needs to be able of modify the techniques to better suit against different opponents and how to inter-relate the technique and combine it with other in order to create a "tactical network." It is only here when you can really say that your Jiu Jitsu techniques are truly functional.

Unfortunately, and due mostly to the urgency of passing belt tests or winning sport competitions, these phases are overlooked and easily forgotten in many Brazilian Jiu Jitsu schools. It is true that without using this 4-phase approach, you can become a BJJ world champion anyway and you'll probably happy because you 'found' a shortcut. The truth is that you haven't take a 'shortcut' to excellence but cut yourself short in your true Jiu Jitsu potential allowing a great deal of understanding and talent be lost somewhere along the way. The road you'll take will depends on what degree of personal imperfection you'll settled with.

# CASS MAGDA

## SILAT – THE ART OF DIRECTING

The guiding philosophy of our method of silat is that of "being the director," not the "directee." This philosophy produces all the movements, strategies, tactics, and techniques that we use. *Directing* means to move the assailant into a position we desire. We control his body by forcing him to make moves he doesn't want to make.

The idea is to make him react to *our* moves. If we are reacting to *his* moves, then he is directing us. The attitude of trying to dominate your opponent is a natural result of being directed. The philosophy of directing is like a tree trunk secured in the ground with deep roots. The many branches of various tactics and techniques can spread out from this "trunk" in numerous directions yet are always related to the directing trunk and anchored in the combative truth of directing.

Directing the assailant can be expressed in many ways. Silat styles excel in directing the assailant to hit or move where the silat proponent "asks for it." You can direct people in a conversation by asking questions. The man who asks the questions controls the conversation. The same is true with silat. When we make fake attacks, false moves, and expose targets we are "asking questions," so to speak, of our assailant and thus directing him – we are taking command of the fight.

The silat fighter may invite an assailant to attack a target by purposely leaving a vulnerable spot open. When the attack comes, the silat fighter closes the opening and counters. The silat fighter may also force an assailant to make a predetermined counterattack and then close the trap. Faking with the eyes, shouting, thigh-slapping and hand-clapping feints are also used by silat fighters to psychologically direct their assailant. These special moves shake an opponent's confidence, creating fear and indecisiveness.

Three tactics comprise the philosophy of directing: "tenderizing," "making the way," and "keeping constant forward pressure in your technique."

Tenderizing comes first. Our method is a pentjak silat style called *pukulan*, which means "to hit," so the emphasis is on fast, rapid hitting. If the strikes don't finish the opponent, they soften or distract him so that you can now manipulate his body. More often than not, your assailant is finished after a *pukulan* blitz.

Once we are *in,* we manipulate his body with various techniques to follow up and finish him. Manipulating is expressed by the tactic, "to make the way," and "constant forward pressure in your technique." We can direct and "make the way" for our techniques with any part of our bodies – hands, arms, shoulder, hips, head, knees, feet, legs, elbows, etc., keeping the pressure on him the entire time – directing him to our finishing technique. For example, to go into a rear leg sweep we might push his weight onto his rear leg using our shoulder against his chest. This makes the way for us to step into position to execute the rear leg sweep. If we just tried to step into position without making the way to get there, our assailant could easily counter because he is still balanced. You must keep the pressure on him while you are making the way, so he is constantly unbalanced. It makes his hitting ineffective because he is always one beat or move behind you and is always trying to catch up.

Your sweep will depend on your ability to direct your opponent to your feet, *not* how you position your feet to him. This allows you to adjust in case you miss, because you will still have the pressure on and can make the way for the next technique.

The silat fighter also practices being the director of his own thinking. If not, then his thoughts are being directed by an external source. Ask yourself, "How good is my ability to direct my opponent? Am I making the way? Is each move making the way for the next move? Am I keeping pressure in my techniques and moves or are there gaps in my pressure he can counter? Do I tenderize enough? Am I consciously aware of all these things when I practice? Or am I trying to speed and muscle my techniques through?"

Refine your art. Always be the director, never be the "directee."

## BACKYARD TRAINING

I could hear the faint tinkling of the wind chimes in the cool, morning breeze. I pushed open the back gate and walked around the corner to see him sitting quietly on the patio, puffing on a half-smoked Chesterfield. His free hand lightly stroked Tiger, a very fat housecat who has been the stoic observer of my silat training for many years.

"Hello there," said Paul de Thouars, deftly knocking the ash off his cigarette. After a few pleasantries we headed into the kitchen for a cup of java. Food and drink before or after the silat training is customary and I learned to drink coffee this way.

As I sipped my morning wake-up call I listened to the master discuss the *langkahs* or footwork of the Indonesian art of pentjak silat serak. With pen and paper, a diagram was drawn to carefully explain where to step, sweep, and direct the opponent's energy so he will fall easily. I asked Paul, "Would this also work against a knife?" He smiled and lifted his glasses to the top of his head. "But of course," he said confidently. He reached into a nearby drawer, pulled out a huge butcher knife, and nodded for me to follow him This was not the first time I've encountered a real knife in training. Often in backyard training, the needs of the moment dictate what the lesson will be. The beauty of the Filipino/Indonesian styles is that the teacher tailors the training to fit the pupil. This allows students to become very good, very quickly.

I followed Paul outside and we stepped onto the cement patio where the *langkah* diagram was waiting. It was drawn full-scale with plastic tape.

He pointed to a line. "Stand there and do the move." I took the knife and attacked as he did the maneuver, stepping on the corresponding lines of the *langkah*. I hit the floor. "How sweet it is," he quipped, doing his best Jackie Gleason imitation. "You see, Cass, the lines are always true, they never fail." He shook my hand to congratulate me on his marvelous takedown – and my resulting fall, I suppose. We practiced this set of moves until he judged that my "feel" was correct.

In backyard training you get the teacher's energy and spirit. Terminology takes a back seat to learning by "feel," because it is a very intuitive art. Being able to "just do it" is the most important thing. As we practiced, Tiger came over to have a look and walk between our moving legs, somehow avoiding getting hit.

Informality is one of the great things about backyard training. People are more themselves at home. They let their guards down. No judgements, no appearances to keep, just being around friends and feeling free to share the martial arts and their accompanying thoughts and opinions. We learn as much about the man as the art.

The backyard is also very social. Visitors and distinguished guests often watch the training, shoot the breeze, or kibitz the teacher, offering advice about the training.

That was one of my favorite parts. Mr. Beijer, an older silat player of another style, would often come by and sit with my teacher, watching me train. He would inevitably ask if he could show me something. When he did, they would occasionally get into an argument over the effectiveness of a particular move. It was always great fun to hear them go back and forth and be demonstrated on, while trying to pick apart their respective opinions.

Every silat teacher sets his own standards. A silat school can be just a few students in a living room or a backyard. In Indonesia and the Philippines, you won't find them in the yellow pages. You have to be introduced privately. There is a certain protocol, and the teachers are very selective.

I really enjoyed my training in the backyards of all my Filipino and Indonesian martial arts teachers. There were all very personal experiences of philosophy in action, with a lot of freedom of experimentation and laughter, too. It's a fascinating way to learn the martial arts – just watch out for the butcher knives.

## JKD'S DISTANCE IN ATTACK

In *The Tao of Jeet Kune Do*, Bruce Lee lists the following principles of distance in attack. What follows is a more detailed, practical explanation of each.

**"The FIRST principle is using the longest to get at the closest."** This is to score the fastest hit when attacking from a distance to the nearest target. In kicking, JKD uses the lead shin/knee kick as the primary weapon. In punching, JKD uses the lead hand or finger jab to the eyes. In different ranges there will be an intuitive sense of which secondary tool to bring into play such as the elbow or the knee.

**"The SECOND principle is economical initiation (non-telegraphic). Apply latent motor training to intuition."** What he means here is to acquire instinctive initiation. This is done by repetitively training the initiating technique until it becomes automatic. Hundreds of repetitions per day emphasizing explosive acceleration will develop this.

**"The THIRD principle is correct on-guard position to facilitate freedom of movement(ease). Use the small phasic bent-knee position."** This means to keep the legs flexed and footwork slightly shifting, like a boxer or basketball player. Confidence comes from the ability to fire and return to the on-guard position ready for a counterattack. The correct on-guard position is important because the fighting distance you maintain and the confidence you have in it will depend on how well you cover yourself. The on-guard position becomes a safe haven to return to after a probe or attack sequence. Make it an unconscious habit and your mind will be free to think about tactics and strategy.

**"The FOURTH principle is constant shifting footwork to secure the correct measure. Use broken rhythm to confuse the opponent's distance while controlling one's own."** This means moving to keep a certain distance so that your opponent has to step to get to you. You should be just out of reach but close enough to take advantage of his misstep. You can confuse him by feinting an attack when he takes this step. Footwork variations in your distance will also make it difficult for your opponent to time his attacks.

**"The FIFTH principle is catching the opponent's moment of weakness. physically as well as psychologically."** You can determine this by conscious use of fakes and harassing blows designed to intimidate and get respect. Lee student Bob Bremer says that Bruce would tell him that, somehow, he could tell when "you just weren't with him." That momentary lapse in concentration is the time to strike.

**"The SIXTH principle is correct measure for explosive penetration."** This means taking aim at the distance where the opponent will be when the attack is completed, not at the distance before the attack. The strike should have enough momentum and power to drive straight through the target and not fall short or push against it.

**"The SEVENTH principle is quick recovery or appropriate follow-ups."** Study your balance after the attack and consider your defensive postures and covering moves. You may want to try to limit your opponent's ability to counterattack by cutting off or smothering some of his more dangerous options such as his foot position or his hand tools.

**"The 'X' principle is courage and decision."** In JKD we call this "X" because it is an unknown factor residing deep within each individual's psyche and the possibilities are unknown for any one particular situation. The confidence required for split-second decision-making ability and courage can be improved by careful progressive training.

## KEEP THE PRINCIPLE, NOT THE STYLE.

Many popular stylized systems of martial arts originated from the success of a talented individual. That person's peculiarities may not be suitable for everyone in that style. Many styles also have lost much in the process of being passed down generation to generation resulting in ineffective but stylized knowledge. Accumulating stylized knowlegde and patterns without understanding the underlying principles leads one to become trapped by the style. The principle is always more important than the style.

In JKD, liberation from the stylized way of technique does not mean abandonment of the principle that makes that technique work. It may mean you have a different purpose. For example, the style may dictate that it is important to always cover the groin while kicking. This may be good for self-defense, but if you are training for kickboxing and the groin kick is not allowed then it makes no sense to keep that as a habit and leave yourself unnecessarily exposed to the fury of your opponent. Your hand is better placed in the kickboxing on-guard rather than in front of the groin.

It is liberating to know we can change. The freedom to find another way to express the principle can mean to change the technique that originally illustrated the principle. For example, the wing chun principle of dissolving arm to arm pressure by folding the arm at the elbow and coming back with a backfist punch. The change of technique that illustrated the principle could be changed by pivoting at the waist to dissolve the pressure on the arm. The entire body turns, then comes back with a shoulder push, elbow smash, or even a leg-to-leg takedown. Same principle, different application.

We can learn much by researching other styles of martial arts. To understand the principles of their structures of defense, attack, and counterattack rather than getting hung up on the stylized patterns of movement they use will give you ideas you can modify and adapt to your own personal JKD structure. This allows you to change or modify your technique in the future because of a limitation such as age, injury, point of view or to solve a particular problem.

It opens up the need to see things differently and ask questions about the principles such as: Can it be found in other arts or different aspects of combat? Is it expressed the same way? Does it need to be? Is it important or not?

In JKD, the five ways of attack consists of Simple Direct Attack (SDA), Attack by Combination (ABC), Attack by Drawing (ABD), Hard Immobilization Attack (HIA) and Progressive Indirect Attack (PIA). Most were derived originally from Western fencing, but Bruce Lee applied these attacking principles to his JKD using hands and feet. Bruce used the lead leg and hand like a fencer's sword. The principles guided the movement. If you can use ABD in boxing by exposing a target to get a counter hit, the same principle applies to leaving an opening for the grappler to attack that you counter with your own lock or hold.

Some principles to look at are: Superior positioning; Slipping (evasion); Centerline theory; Substitution principle; Retaining energy; Dissolving energy; Constant pressure; Longest weapon to hit nearest target; Correct on-guard positioning; Constantly shifting footwork; Leverage; Timing (Styles tend to favor a type of timing for counterattack.); Bamboo (yielding) principle; Economy of motion – (defense/offensive structure); Broken rhythm; Bridging the Gap; Five Ways of Attack

The idea is not to be limited to the stylized way but to use the principle with other aspects of fighting. Keep the principle, not the style.

## ADAPTABILITY

Adaptability is the single most important trait a fighter can have. It is more important than power, speed, timing, balance, coordination, grace, fortitude, conditioning, aggressiveness, agility, precision, endurance, body feel, posture or form. To instantly respond to your adversary's every move and condition, and every fight environment, requires a flexible mind and a martial art suited to modification. Some say that conditioning is the number one trait, because if you lack stamina, you won't be able to use your art after a few seconds, anyway. But I think adaptability is more important because if you're huffing and puffing and still have to fight, you've got to adapt to that lack of conditioning.

So, what exactly is adaptability? The dictionary says it means "to make fit (as for a specific or new use or situation) often by modification." Adaptation also means "an adjustment to environmental conditions, or an adjustment of a sense organ to the intensity or quality of stimulation." A fighter's sense organs include his legs, feet, arms, and hands for sensing his adversary's movements by feel. The senses also include the eyes, for marking changes in the timing of movement, and the ears for adjustment to verbal harassment. Of course, there is the sixth sense of intuition, which senses intangibles such as fear. Being able to adjust the senses means training them to know what to expect. Adaptability training should involve all your senses.

The fighter must modify his martial art system for fighting under various potential conditions. This means adapting to the quality or intensity of stimulation in a fight – stimulation such as a screaming, crazy-man swinging a crowbar in a bus, or a group of bikers yelling at you, or a guy foaming at the mouth, impervious to pain, determined to bite your ear off. Could you adapt your psyche and your martial art to deal with these?

Environmental conditions could be a parking lot or a packed men's room at a rock club. Are there obstacles like cars, or tables and chairs? Are other people in the way like at a rock concert? Can you adapt the current structure of your martial art to such environments? If you can't, you could find yourself in serious trouble.

If your style is primarily kicking, could you adapt it to work? Could you continue to fight if your arm or leg got hurt? What tactics do you know? What have you practiced? The Filipino and Indonesian arts excel at training in these situations.

What if you picked up a weapon like a stick or knife? Do you know how to use it? What if they were used against you? A champion kickboxer might face a sixteen-year-old girl trained in kali knife-fighting. The kickboxer must adapt to the sharp razor facing him, and it isn't going to be easy because she is trained! One cut in the wrong place could mean instant death. Can he adapt? Try to figure out how to adapt your fighting art to a boxing, muay Thai, wrestling, judo, kali stick, escrima knife, or taekwondo attack. How would you change what you know so you can use it?

If you can't modify your art, you've got to modify your thinking: 1) Learn to counter everything – physical and mental; 2) Develop adaptive knowledge under fighting conditions; 3) Practice environmental awareness in the places you frequent most; 4) Learn to use your art against other style's attacks – prepare for the unexpected; 5) Develop a philosophy of adaptability and make it the centerpiece of your training.

## CONSTANT FORWARD PRESSURE

In pentjak silat, constant forward pressure means attacking your opponent to keep him in a perpetual state of unbalance. Instead of being able to counter, your opponent becomes concerned with trying to regain his composure, footing, and equilibrium. As he's trying to escape or counter, he's already *being* countered. Because has no base from which to renew his attack, you can trample him with your counterattacks. Constant pressure is a martial arts water-hose blasting punches, kicks, elbows, body shoves, traps, leg sweeps and trips. It is hard, brutal, unrelenting, and unmerciful. There is no good way to counter – it's even hard to breathe! Constant forward pressure allows you to find or create openings, set-ups, various follow-ups or footwork placements. This concept can also be found in other arts such as JKD which uses the equivalent "straight blast."

Constant pressure doesn't mean trying to move your opponent straight backwards, but rather pressuring them in the direction of your technique (you might lose contact by pushing straight back). Instead, your attack must guide your opponent into your future hits, locks, sweeps, and takedowns. It's safer because you are not waiting for incoming blows, but instead actively overwhelming your opponent. Psychologically, this also puts you into a superior frame of mind.

You cannot apply this pressure intermittently. If you do, your opponent will push forward into the space you give him. In an encounter, an attacker will constantly probe you – pressing, hitting, and trying to get in and find a weak spot. If he senses you've let up, he will move in violently, without compassion.

Constant forward pressure is a fundamental tactic taught at the Magda Institute. It means total commitment. If the enemy is physically off-balance and struggling, he is also mentally off-balance and struggling – often he is desperate. When he attacks in a wild frenzy you must not give in. Cracking under emotional pressure is the worst thing you can do because you'll end up covering-up, helpless, praying the attack will end. The emotional pressure to quit can be kept at bay by pressing forward; otherwise, when an opportunity comes to counterattack, you will have no emotional reserves left and will be unable to take advantage of the opening. Proper training and discipline will insure this never happens to you.

There are also enemies in life pressing you and looking for a weak spot. These enemies are indifference and procrastination. Take your health, for example. Those two enemies are always there, waiting for you to take it easy so illness can take over and destroy you and your happiness. This process doesn't happen all at once, it's subtle. It's not like a punch in the face, but it does hurt because before you know it, the days, weeks, and months will quickly go by. Five years later you'll be depressed and angry, wondering why you are overweight, sick, and unhappy with yourself. It's because you stopped pushing, let things slide, and procrastination pushed itself in and cunningly stole your health and happiness. You've got to push to keep the pressure on indifference and procrastination so they can never take control. They are so dangerous because they are so deceptive. According to an old silat saying there are two enemies – the one on the outside and the one on the inside. Keep "constant pressure" on both!

## THE CORNERSTONES OF JEET KUNE DO

In JKD we always search for ways to make ourselves more functional in combat. This can be done by researching other arts, fitting what is useful into our structure, putting what we learn through the rigorous test of full contact sparring, and then eliminating what doesn't work or modifying it so it does. In this research we use the criteria and theory of JKD as a method of study. JKD is our way to study other things to decide if they're functional or not. Dan Inosanto once told me that one of the most important things that Bruce Lee taught him was the ability to decide what was functional and what was not. He called it, "The Functional Eye."

"Simple, direct, and non-classical," is a phrase which describes the three cornerstones of JKD. These cornerstones are the criteria for our method of study and analysis of what is functional and what isn't.

They are used when analyzing other martial arts techniques or when trying to improve within our own system of JKD.

The first cornerstone is "simplicity." If a technique sequence against an attack takes six moves, then the chances of it being used successfully in reality are slim. It's a simple fact that the more moves one has to make, the more chances there are of something going terribly wrong. So, part of using simplicity as a criterion is to ask, "How can that six-move sequence be shortened to three moves? Can those three moves be shortened to two?" Ultimately, modifying and changing a six-move sequence to one or two moves and getting the same end result is a JKD way of thinking and studying.

"Directness" is the next cornerstone. The techniques of various martial arts can be simple but still not be direct. So, a simple counter such as blocking an attack then hitting back may be simple, but it is not direct. One way to improve directness is to improve the timing for the counterattack. Try to hit just before the opponent's blow lands. In other words, beat him to the punch or perhaps simultaneous block and hit. Interception is considered the highest stage of JKD. Directness can also be improved by minimizing preparatory movements. The less we have to move to hit the better.

The last cornerstone is "non-classical." This is the freedom to go outside the established classical system and break the rules of the techniques or theory. The classical system says there is only one way to do something. "Non-classical" in JKD means personalization. When we are being non-classical, we have the freedom to change things for our needs. We may absorb a theory or technique from another source but accomplish it in quite a different way. A lot of the time, as a result of these modifications, the finished motion may end up only faintly resembling or looking nothing like the original source. The modifications change the technique, principle, or training method into something unrecognizable from the style of origin, hence it becomes non-classical. It may also mean that we don't go outside our system to absorb from another source but instead modify what we already have or even create something new to solve the problem.

Just as a three-legged stool provides a steadier base than a four-legged chair, the three cornerstones of JKD can be used to improve the martial arts skill of any style by providing a steady base for using what works.

## MASTERY IS A MOVING TARGET

The wrong questions to ask are: What is the meaning of my life and training once I become a master? When will I get "it"?

A martial artist's frustration in training is about the lack of an answer to those questions. Instead ask: What's the meaning of my life and training today, NOW, before you get the skills and knowledge and become a master. Here are five things to think about.

### 1. You Get the Elusive "It" Before the Mastery

It requires a new mind set. You don't have the skill yet, but you are on the path working for it. You get the spirit first then the skill and knowledge. Focus on what you love about training and learning. You have no competition; you are the only player. There's no one to beat in a game of solitaire. As you move along, the spiritual-philosophical path opens up to you, and you get a taste of the power of your invisible self. You discover learning martial arts is a game that you play with yourself.

### 2. Trust Yourself, For You Are the Only Guru

If you meet Buddha in the martial arts dojo, kill him! Why? Because you are the only guru you will ever need. No outside authority can give you meaning. Of course teachers light the way for us and we need to be respectful to the martial arts traditions. But we need to keep hold of our own minds and trust our own intuition in this process. Systems and styles help only up to a point before the individual finds out enough about himself to know what is best.

We need to echo the Buddha: "Believe in nothing, no matter where you read it or who has said it, not even if I have said it, unless it agrees with your own reason and common sense."

### 3. Make Peace with Your Inner Enemies!

Kahil Gibran in his book *The Prophet,* said: "Bless the darkness as you bless the light." Embrace your martial art difficulties as you would your successes. You are always going to have problems on the path. Accept that! Face them, stop blaming and "get over it"! 19th century philosopher James Allen said, "Circumstances do not make a man, they reveal him." Your problems will be your greatest teachers.

### 4. Being A Master Is Nothing Special.

Zen masters remind us that enlightenment is "nothing special" and neither is the mastery of the martial arts. To paraphrase the ancient Zen masters "Before you become a martial arts master, you chop wood, carry water. After you are a martial arts master, you chop wood, carry water".

Most martial art masters live normal lives without flaunting their skill and live with a strong sense of responsibility in service to the world around them. They are surprisingly very ordinary. Being a master is nothing special.

### 5. The Martial Art Master "Just Is."

The ancient masters always regard themselves as beginners, with minds open to the experience, the momentary adventures of life, new things to learn and enjoy. In his book, *Mastery,* George Leonard writes: "Mastery is not perfection but rather a journey and the true master must be willing to try and fail and try again." Learning itself becomes an art.

The martial arts life is a moving target. Just when you think you've mastered it, it moves again. The beginner's mind is the only "technology" you'll ever need in finding solutions to the martial arts' never-ending stream of challenges.

So, ask yourself the right question: *What is the meaning of my life training today right now?*

## POLITICS IN MARTIAL ARTS

We hear again and again that martial artists are turned off by politics. Frustrated, they cry, "I hate politics, I just want to work out," or "He got that (rank, position, award) by brown-nosing," or, "All we do is waste time in these meetings." Pleeeease!! The fact is that nothing from running a school to organizing a tournament can be done individually.

Politics is life. It is the basis for getting things done as opposed to the fantasy brought to you by "strong leaders." Every relationship with instructors, training partners, friends, or spouses is political and depends on lots of give, a little take, and the acknowledgment of assumptions. Of course, splits regularly occur between instructors, students, people, and organizations – but the fact is that most such failures are caused by the failure to invest sufficiently in the relationship. Investing means paying the price of frequent compromise and, above all, spending time. I like to call that "hang time."

Some say they don't want to waste their time that way. Well, it may seem like a waste, but it's how you look at it. If we pay attention, we learn what's going on with so-and-so which led to today's surprise outrage over a trivial remark. Spending time is a gradual approach of feeling and "vibing out" the other person to see where they are really going. You get a sense of what they want and how they want it. Attending meetings and spending time together isn't always about getting things done. Under this veneer, they're also about understanding how so-and-so is feeling – which inches toward an eventual consensus about a future issue.

Some martial artists quit and move to small schools or garage groups to avoid politics. Nice try. The only place to avoid politics is in a cave by yourself. These small groups are more informal, so rank, rules, and procedures tend to be not so important. Everyone knows their place. That's an example of acknowledgment of assumptions. But assumptions must be constantly nourished and maintained. Even groups of three or more people have cliques. Some will feel that they are being ganged-up on or overlooked. Some people will use jealousy, backstabbing, character assassination, and hogging the limelight to get their way. Hey, it's called reality. But in my experience these people eventually get theirs. When the time comes for a special rank promotion, demonstration team opening, or other special recognition, the jerks are usually left out. They then inevitably run around screaming "I'm a victim...I hate politics!"

The fact is, no successful instructor or martial artist is unsullied by politics. Effective human beings are compromising human beings. In his book, *Leadership*, author James MacGregor Burns discusses the fact that inspiring leaders such as Ghandi and Martin Luther King spent a huge amount of time in a transformational leadership style, talking with their followers, especially their inner circles, mending bruised egos, soothing slights, meeting, talking, meeting, and talking, and meeting and talking...you get the idea. These leaders invested in relationships and became experts at reading people – they were super-compromisers. They bent, wiggled, twisted, turned over, and gave in – all to get things done.

To hate politics is naive. Without politics how could rank be bestowed, tournaments be run, schools exist, knowledge be spread, seminars be created, or higher standards be set? Politics is the art of getting things done with people. It's as simple and complicated as that.

## WHAT YOU NEED TO KNOW ABOUT JEET KUNE DO

To say we know what jeet kune do is and isn't, we must have three things: knowledge of JKD philosophy; the original, physical, technical curriculum; and a direct training lineage to a quality, first-generation student.

### The Philosophy Of JKD

To know and understand the philosophy of JKD, as Bruce Lee considered it, is to think the thoughts the thinker thought when he thought the thoughts. To arrive at one's own JKD point of view, we must first understand the philosophy of JKD as the founder, Bruce Lee, considered it for himself.

This would consist of his compilations, modifications of existing philosophies such as Taoism, Krishnamurti, and Zen that he thought was relevant truth that applied, i.e., they *were* JKD. It would also consist of his own original thoughts on JKD.

The philosophy of JKD is both pragmatic and abstract: pragmatic because it can be applied to physical fighting techniques; abstract because it can be applied on many levels relating to all aspects of one's life.

For example, JKD can be a vehicle for self-discovery, self-improvement, and self-realization. So how do you realize the self? Since only "self" can realize the self, the learning process of JKD involves stripping away at the individual's limitations. If, for example, you are not flexible or lack endurance (physical and/or mental) then that is the truth about yourself you face – in fighting and in life. When you do something about it you are removing that limitation, that burden, realizing a better self.

Important also is the *context* of the JKD philosophy. Familiar sayings such as "Using no way as way; having no limitation as limitation," once understood first in the context of JKD technique, can be then understood in the context of analyzing other systems and styles to make yourself a better, more efficient fighter.

## The Original Physical Technical Curriculum

A chronology of the changes in the curriculum – from the time Bruce called it "JKD" until the time of his death – is important to know. What and why changes were made show us the evolution of JKD as well as the principles of these technical elements and the science behind them. When a study is made of the various years of JKD's development, there is not a great deal of difference between the Oakland to L.A. Chinatown eras. The Seattle curriculum proves to be an important historical study of how the roots of JKD began and later flowered. It shows that the earliest years in Seattle seemed to emphasize more self-defense, while the Oakland and L.A. periods became more alive with full-contact free sparring. Knowing and practicing the structure of JKD is essential because it gives us the habits and movements we use for fighting.

## Training with a Direct Lineage Student

Some of the first generation spent a great deal of time in direct contact with Bruce Lee and are intimately familiar with the ideas, principles, techniques, philosophy, attitudes, et cetera, that were never written down. They are the recipients of the oral tradition of JKD. Since they gained their insight directly from the founder and were close enough to recognize, learn, and understand the thinking processes he used (i.e., why he discarded, modified, or added to his JKD), they are in a position to follow this method and do the same for themselves. They may expand but are still consistent with the philosophy and technical elements of JKD.

We can learn by observing and participating in this process with them. A direct lineage aids in this accomplishment because guidance along the way is vital to prevent sticking points or to prevent the student from wandering away or misapplying the JKD principles. It gives the student time to season and mature and to develop his ability to use his JKD in a variety of ways.

I think one has to be very careful studying the expanded versions of second or third generation students, as only a handful have studied directly, personally, and closely with the first generation. If their training was incomplete, inconsistent, thin, or lacking, then aberrant versions that violate the philosophy and principles will occur. An example would be the putting together of various techniques learned in an isolated manner and claiming this is a "JKD flow." Entering with a capeiora cartwheel leg kick, followed by a Thai boxing elbow, silat throw, and ending with a sambo leg bar is an entertaining flow, to be sure, but is definitely not JKD. The integrity of the JKD structure is gone. As Bruce Lee said, "A few simple techniques well presented, an aim clearly seen, are better than a tangled maze of data whirling in a disorganized educational chaos."

## DARE TO BE INCONCLUSIVE

Today's martial artists are knocking on the door for the personal experience of "something more" which is the heart of the essence of what it is to be a martial artist – a fighter. They want more of "it."

Many fighters have had this peak experience of finding flow, perfect harmony, the feeling of complete perfection and invulnerability that seems to lift them right out of themselves. Such experiences and personal development along these lines has to be disciplined and discovered anew, in a personal way. Such an experience cannot be taught or even described in a way that is easily understood. What can be taught is how to discover! The traditional way of teaching such discovery is through the use of repetition and progressive approximations to all-out fighting. These types of approximations include various levels of sparring and two-man drills that nudge one closer and closer to the truth until a discovery is made.

Any great style provides these levels of progression, different levels of understanding, and a spiritual experience of training and fighting. There is something useful for everyone and a further opportunity to rediscover new meaning and greater realization again and again. That's why it has survived – why it is cherished as a great system. This way is open-ended and inconclusive.

The "how-to-discover" requires one to be ready to abandon any fixed notion so that a new, more comprehensive view – a deeper experience of realization – can take its place. With all the various systems of martial arts comes the perplexity of choice, of alignment and partisanship as to theories and assumptions, even political and prejudicial beliefs. Many assume the beliefs of their instructor without thinking twice. Taken literally these various "truths" incorporated into a style become dogma. Dogma says, "Here is the only way to do it." Dogma is final, not inconclusive.

A martial artist trapped by such dogma will say that anything new has to be accounted for in terms of his own theories that are familiar and acceptable. If they don't fit then they are unacceptable. It is like a drunk looking for his keys under the light of a streetlight because that's where the light is – rather than where he lost them in the dark!

This leads to the peculiar attitude of martial artists being able to deny their own observations and experiences more easily, rather than deny the pet theories of their style. I once had a college friend show me how he blocked a stick attack with his *tonfa*. He said the theory was that the energy of his block was so hard that it would allow him to counter without worrying about a possible re-counter or combination attack. When we tried it and my stick combination was not stopped on repeated attempts, he refused to believe his theory wasn't true!

There are always some facts left out of any system, anomalies that do not fit into the framework of accepted explanations. The alternative to this is to be personally courageous and experiment and explore in a way that is open-ended. If you keep your program open-ended then that attracts new experiences and new ideas about them. Good teachers and good training partners certainly help too!

Inconclusive doesn't mean to be unsure, undecided or gullible about your style. It just means never to form a final judgement – to remain open and reaching for new experiences, ideas, and meaning. Spiritual experience realization and know-how are there to be discovered. In order to discover more of that "something more" try to be experimental and inconclusive.

# TONY MASSENGILL

## THE MOST DEADLY MISTAKE

There are many mistakes made during the training of the martial arts. Some are small, some are big. Some lead to a waste of training time, some lead to injury. But one mistake is catastrophic and can lead to a very violent and preventable death.

That egregious sin is mistaking fighting for combat.

In real life there is no such thing as a fight. A fight is a sporting concept. Anytime one individual is attacking another with the intent of doing bodily harm, that is combat. When you see two people in the street bouncing around throwing jabs at one another, they are suffering from a very deadly side effect to today's "martial sport" popularity.

Today the word "martial" has lost it's meaning to many training what they are calling martial arts. Rules involved in the ever-popular martial sports create several very bad weaknesses in the armor of the modern martial artist. Anytime one trains with the idea of limitations of any kind, they build weaknesses into their ability to respond to real world violence.

I worked as a police officer early in my public safety career. In learning strategy and tactics of the use of my gun, we used training scenarios which had us responding to the unexpected. We were taught close range deployment of our gun, the use of cover during a firefight, methods of weapons retention in the event of someone attempting to take our gun during a hand-to-hand confrontation, and many other very important real-life skills needed to survive the mean streets.

Now, compare the skills and tactics taught to police, with the individual who is into the "combat sport" of paintball. In paintball, if you are behind cover, firing at me from 25 yards away, and I am behind cover firing back, we are using the tactic of utilization of cover, just like the police tactic. But if I can't get a good shot at you, I may break cover and run across the open space, hoping that you can't hit a moving target, and hoping to get a better angle for a shot at you. If, on the other hand, we were shooting bullets instead of paint balls... I think you can see the problem with this tactic.

There are chances, tactics, and techniques that one will attempt in a sporting arena, where there are safeguards against catastrophic injury, that would be just as unwise in a real fight as the breaking of cover would be in a real gun fight. But unfortunately, these unwise methods become part of the "conditioned reflex" of the sport fighter.

This is the danger of losing sight of the real aim of the MARTIAL arts. This "sport leakage" is the side effect of training for sport. We react the way we train. Under the stress of a violent unexpected attack, you react, you don't think.

There is a saying among law enforcement trainers, which states "You don't rise to the occasion; you sink to your level of training."

## CHIN-NA: VERTICAL GRAPPLING FOR THE STREET

Ground fighting is a great strategy for the ring. It allows the grappler to smother and immobilize the striker. The grappler is able to take the striker out of his fighting range and reduce the dangers they face in a fight. On the ground, the striker cannot develop the power in striking available to him while standing. And if the striker doesn't have an extensive grappling arsenal of his own, chances are that he will be tapping out very quickly.

With the popularity of Mixed-Martial-Arts competitions, grappling has become all the rage. Ground and pound, arm locks, triangle chokes, the mount, the guard, all have become common terms in many martial art schools around the world. But how do these methods translate from the ring to the street?

In the ring there are rules that limit the weapons available to the fighters. Weapons that could easily turn the tide of the fight while on the ground. While the striker has a difficult time developing punching power while on his back with an opponent mounted on top of him, a thumb to the eye doesn't require striking power. As a matter of fact, the eye is such a weak target, rich with nerves, it takes a very small amount of force to create major pain and do extensive damage.

Biting is also a very effective weapon in a close quarters encounter such as on the ground, but it too is against the rules of these sporting events.

As you can see, in a real "No Rules" environment, the fight can be quite different than what we see in these competitions. So, we must ask, "Is there a place for grappling in a street environment?"

The answer is, "Yes, definitely! But the strategy of use must be "real world – street oriented" and take into account many factors that are not in existence in the matrix of the sporting arena. While a good grappling system must prepare one for the possibility of being taken to the ground, the terminology here is the key. There is a big difference in being taken to the ground and TAKING IT to the ground. If you are taken to the ground, it is not intentional on your part. But taking it to the ground implies intention. This is where we must draw the line.

On the ground in the ring there is a padded surface, and only one opponent. On the street, the surface is usually concrete, with obstacles such as curbs, broken glass, weapons of convenience that can be used against you like bricks, and bottles, and let us not forget the possibility of third or more party interventions.

Many in the current ground grappling craze are fond of quoting that 90% of all fights go to the ground. Here is the problem with this statistic. The author worked for over twenty-five years in public safety, serving as a police officer, firefighter, and emergency medic. In that career, there were hundreds of responses to street and bar fights. In the emergency setting, on the medical and police reports, there is no data entry for the fight going to the ground or staying upright. So where does this statistic come from? There is not some guy named Eugene at the U.S. Department of Statistics keeping track of the number of fights that go to the ground. However, this being said if you consider the number of fights that involve at least one party who is impaired by alcohol and/or drugs, it's not difficult to believe that many fights do go to the ground. In the words of Wing Chun Grandmaster Samuel Kwok, "All fights should go to the ground; at least your opponent should!" It would help for people to remember that 98.3 % of all statistics are made up on the spot with absolutely no statistical data. I just made that up. But it is as valid as the ground fighting statistic that many put their faith in.

The Chinese Martial Arts has a method of grappling that is combat efficient, economical in application, and focuses on "vertical grappling." Fighting from the ground is not ignored, but the strategy does not intentionally take the fight there. The method is Chin-Na the Chinese art of Capture, Control and Destruction. Chin-Na is the art from which modern systems such as Ju Jitsu, Aikido, and Hapkido have their origin. Chin-Na has many of the same type of techniques you see from some of the Mixed-Martial Arts practitioners but with one very important difference. The focus is on applying the techniques in an upright position and in staying upright in the fight.

The methods are meant for real life application in a violent encounter, not sport.

The purpose of Chin-Na is two-fold. One, after capturing the opponent's limb, damage it very badly and thus render him defenseless. Or two, utilize a locking technique to put the opponent in a position where you can deliver a fight ending strike or kick, and the opponent has no way of defending against the strike. As you can see, both work to achieve the same outcome, a quick efficient and victorious end of the fight. Basically, you can think of Chin-Na as Ju Jitsu on steroids, with a very bad attitude. Chin-Na also specializes on using the environment as a weapon against the opponent. As a martial artist one should be acutely aware of their surroundings.

There are many things that can be picked up to use as a weapon, and there are also many areas of the landscape that can be used to run the opponent into that can cause him damage. Virginia based Ba Gua instructor and Chin-Na expert Glen Moore explains, "If you can't find something to hit the opponent with, you find something to hit with the opponent!" This is a very good strategy.

## The Environment as a Weapon

In the TV series called *Burn Notice,* on Fox network, the main character is a former C.I.A. type agent who uses quite a bit of Chin-Na in the fight scenes. In the premier episode he encounters a couple of bad guys in the restroom of a restaurant. In the narrative of his thoughts running during the fight scene in which he is securing joint locks and running his opponents headfirst into sinks and urinals he states, "I like bathrooms, lots of hard surfaces!"

Unlike the ring, many real-world encounters occur in an enclosed environment with obstacles that can be used to your advantage, or against you. Environmental considerations such as stairs, curbs, changes in grade of the fighting surface, corners of walls, windows, mirrors, are just some of the things that can be brought into play in the encounter.

So, in parting I will leave you with words of wisdom I attempt to impart to my students: "In the street, ground and pound is a great strategy, except for the ground part!"

## Death by Political Correctness

*"In the field of observation, chance favors*
*only the prepared mind."*

--- Louis Pasteur (1822 - 1895)

Juan Williams, political pundit, and radio and T.V. personality was fired by National Public Radio for stating on Fox T.V.'s Bill O'Reilly Show that he became fearful when he sees someone in Muslim clothing enter an airplane he is on. The discussion was on

"Political Correctness" and "Profiling." Juan was fired and disparaged publicly by the big wigs of N.P.R. for expressing his true FEELINGS about the fear that the terrorists have caused with their actions and words.

We have become a society that is supposed to be blind to those who have hurt us, and overly cautious not to "hurt the feelings" of those we have cause to be cautious of. There are those who will tell us that we are wrong to be cautious of a people who have declared war on our people because, "Not everyone in that culture is bad," and they are right…but…

We have been under attack since the early 1990s by Muslim extremist, with the first Trade Center bombings, attacks on our embassy in other countries, the U.S.S. Cole bombing, 9/11, the shoe bomber, the "Fruit-of-Kaboom" underwear bomber, the Fort Hood shootings, the Time Square bombing attempt and as I am writing this column, an arrest has just been made in our Nation's Capital of a terrorist who was planning to "kill as many as possible" with bombs in rolling suitcases on the subway near the Pentagon.

So, yes...I agree that only a very small percentage of the Muslim people want to do us harm. Of this there is no doubt. So it may cramp your sensibilities, but since we cannot discern the good Muslims from the ones who have the declared the goal of "killing as many of us as possible," we would be making a big mistake not to pay a little closer attention until we have the opportunity to get to know individuals in order to know on which side they stand.

## Experience

We as human beings learn from our experiences. Good experiences bring us joy and create feelings of anxious anticipation at the thought of repeating the experience. Bad experiences teach us what to avoid or be cautious of in the future. This is a part of our natural survival extinct. To expect a human being to act otherwise is to ask us to act in an unnatural manner.

In law enforcement training, we teach officers a method we call active awareness. As martial artist we need have the same understanding. Being actively aware means to be mindful of what is going on around us.

## In Police Work They Call That Clue!

In order to know what to pay attention to, in addition to our experiences, we must train ourselves what to look for. This is awareness with a purpose. Anytime you enter a new environment, such as entering a restaurant, exiting an office building, going from home to your car outside, you must pay attention to ANYTHING that doesn't fit with your expectations as to what should be present and happening in this environment. If it is 90 degrees outside and you see someone wearing an overcoat, your mental alarm bells should start ringing very loud. In police work they call that a clue!

> *"The ability to focus attention on important things is a defining characteristic of intelligence."*
>
> --- Robert J. Shiller

## Area of Concern

Awareness will alert you to areas of concern. An area of concern is a specific person, or action that creates a mental alarm. These alarms should sound anytime something, or someone seems out of place, or is not acting properly for the circumstances or environment. Once you have identified an area of concern, your level of awareness must be stepped up a notch.

## Aware – Relax Cycle

We must train ourselves to be observant, and aware of everyone and everything. This doesn't mean being paranoid, but aware. After entering a new environment, visually scan the area, if nothing creates an area of concern, relax. If someone new comes into the area, check them out. If there is nothing that sets off your internal alarm bells, relax. But make awareness a habit!

## Awareness is a Habit

*"How use doth breed a habit in a man."*

--- William Shakespeare (1564 - 1616)

Awareness must become habit. If it is something you only do every now and then, it will not be reliable in your self-protection. Your skill of observation is a tool that must be continually sharpened. The only way to keep these skills sharp is through continual use. Man lives and dies by his habits. Make awareness one of the habits you live by!

## Your Experience programs your Internal Alarm System

Our experiences, both as individuals and as a collective (Nation, Culture) is what programs our Internal Alarm System. There are psychological and physiological responses to what we experience. This is just how we humans are wired.

This Internal Alarm System is what keeps us out of danger. To ignore these feelings in the name of "political correctness" is not only unnatural; it is one step towards suicide.

## "WING CHUN MASTERS" – THE BOOK

Wing Chun is a Chinese Kung Fu system which has captured the imaginations of many since the release of the first Ip Man movie several years ago. While most people recognize that Wing Chun was the system that Kung Fu superstar Bruce Lee learned as a youth in Hong Kong, and that the legendary Grandmaster Ip Man was his teacher, many have no real understanding of the system itself!

The Wing Chun system is physically simple. The system is comprised of just three empty hand forms, one additional form applied on a unique training apparatus called the Muk Yan Jong (wooden dummy) and two weapon sets, the Luk Dim Boon Kwun (Long Pole) and Bot Jam Doe (Eight Cut Knives) In comparison to other Kung F systems, it is relatively simple. The real treasure of Wing Chun lies in its operating system. The principles and theories upon which the system is built.

Author Jose Fraguas has just released what I believe will be the most valuable tome on the Wing Chun system ever written. The book, *Wing Chun Masters,* is a collection of interviews. This book is essentially a grand tour inside the minds of the most notable Wing Chun Masters of our time.

This is not the average step-by-step Kung Fu forms book. These are the insights on the operating system. The knowledge and understanding gained form lifetimes devoted to training with some of the great warriors of the past, as explained by the present generation of masters.

The book includes interviews with the two sons of Grandmaster Ip Man, Ip Chun and Ip Ching. An interview with the late Master, Wong Shun Leung, considered by many to be the best fighter to come out of the Ip Man lineage!

First generation Ip Man lineage students Victor Kan, the man known as the King of Chi Sao and William Cheung, classmate of Bruce Lee, explain what they have learned from decades of training and teaching. The reader is treated to their memories of learning directly from Ip Man.

Insights of such modern masters as Francis Fong, Jim Lau, and Robert Chu. Master teachers like David Peterson and Gary Lam give the reader insight into the lessons of their teacher, the great Wong Shun Leung. Their memories of what Master Wong learned from his fighting experience, and how it affected his teaching and training methods are simply enlightening.

This book is loaded with the secrets of these and many other Masters. Their photos, experiences, as well as their own research into this great system. These Masters explain their understanding of the lessons learned from training the three empty hand forms of Wing Chun. The reader is exposed to how the forms lead to the development of the weapon that each master becomes. The Masters explain how the unique training exercise of Chi Sao leads to the development of conditioned reflex, and how it teaches the Wing Chun student how to deal with an opponent without opposing muscular force with muscular force.

The mysterious Wooden Dummy is explained and its unique relationship to Wing Chun is explored along with its distinctive training benefits. The Weapons of the Wing Chun system are revealed, along with how the Pole and Knives relate back to the empty hand methods taught in the foundational forms.

Having been a student of Wing Chun since 1979, I have had the opportunity to train directly with many of the masters profiled in this book. Many of the ones with whom I have not personally trained, I have conversed with on many occasions, or read everything I could find on their methods. Just seeing the names in this book is enough to make any Wing Chun enthusiast salivate, but there are principles explained in detail that will enhance any systems application in fighting!

On a personal note, I would like to thank the author, Jose Fraguas for his decision to include a chapter on me in this project. In my years in Wing Chun, I have been blessed in the opportunities which have been opened to me. I have written two books on Wing Chun and the highlight to my Wing Chun career was having one of them placed in the Ip Man Museum in Foshan, China. Being included in this book is every bit the equal to that experience. It is truly a humbling experience to see my name included among the great "Masters" in this book.

## Conditioned Reflex: The Key to Application

In the self-improvement classic *Psycho-Cybercenics*, by Maxwell Maltz, which has been called an "owner's manual to the mind" there is an explanation of what Maltz calls the four stages of learning.

These four levels explain the progression from knowing nothing of the skill, to mastery of the skill. The careful study of these four levels reveals that they are present in any physical skill development. In Kung Fu, these levels are very important as they can outline exactly when a skill can be relied upon in a violent encounter.

In the Martial Arts, we begin by teaching the most basic of methods, and using a stair step process to advance to more advanced skills. Mastery is judged not by knowing, or being able to perform a technique, but in how the technique can be relied upon under surprise attack in a very dynamic and violent setting. The mere knowledge of, and ability to perform a technique when given time to think is utterly useless in a fighting situation. The technique must "perform itself" in order to work under the stress of a real-world assault.

Dr. Maltz explains the four stages of learning as follows:

1. Unconscious Incompetence
2. Conscious Incompetence
3. Conscious Competence
4. Unconscious Competence

As you review these four levels, you can see the progression. As a student of the Martial Arts, we come into the school generally thinking we know at least how to do a rudimentary skill like punching. But upon being taught the proper method of punching, which includes such considerations as balance, power generation, structure and alignment of the arm and wrist and angle of execution, we realize that we didn't really know how to throw a punch.

At this time, we pass from level one: Unconscious Incompetence, to level two: Conscious Incompetence. We now know that we do not know how to throw a proper punch. So, we go about learning the proper mechanics of the technique. As soon as we are introduced to the technique and are able to reproduce satisfactory results in performing the method, we have passed from level two into level three: Conscious Competence.

However, because we can only reproduce the proper technique with mental deliberation the technique will still not be a reliable method of self-protection that can be relied upon in a violent encounter.

In a fight, you seldom have time to think, but must react. This means that even if you are able to do a technique and reproduce satisfactory results with the technique with deliberate concentration, it is still not a tool that can be relied upon in self-protection. In order for the technique to be reliable, you must have entered the fourth level of learning, Unconscious Competence. This is when you will experience "Conditioned Reflex" in your technique. This is when the technique "Does itself".

The 25th anniversary edition of Bruce Lee's Martial Arts epic *Enter The Dragon* contains some scenes which were unfortunately deleted from the original theatrical version. In it there is a scene at the beginning, right after the fight with Sammo Hung, where Lee is walking in the garden with his teacher. The teacher is questioning Lee about his thoughts on the Martial Arts. He asks, "What is the highest form of technique"? Bruce Lee answers, "To have no technique." The teacher asks him to explain. Bruce explains, "A fight is like play, only played seriously. When the opponent expands, I contract. When he contracts, I expand. And when there is an opportunity, I don't hit... it hits all by itself!"

This is a great expiation of the way our martial art is supposed to serve us in the event of a self-protection event.

Conditioned reflex development is the major difference I found when I began Wing Chun training in 1979 after many years of training in other martial systems. Many of the seminars I teach are to martial artist outside of Wing Chun, in order to incorporate the Conditioned Reflex drills into their training systems. This has been so popular in fact that it is one of the subjects of my latest DVD series produced by Empire Video.

Training can sometimes become a little too mechanical. Application can become based on rhythm rather than reaction. This is dangerous because it can create a false sense of security. This kind of training can make us believe we are much better than we actually are. It is very important to examine our training methods and reach a good balance between reality and safety, with an eye on creating unexpected or non-rhythmic changes that require the training partner to react.

This examination of our training methods, and research on how to create more realistic training drills which are designed to develop conditioned reflex, can carry our skills to a much higher level. This conditioned reflex is the key to applying your martial skills in a violent encounter and may one day save your life!

# ED OTIS

## SAMURAI STORY:
## THE STUDENT AND THE TEACHER

*"The master in the art of living makes little distinction between his work and his play, his labor and his leisure, his mind and his body, his education and his recreation, his love and his religion. To him it is all the same – he is always doing both".*

*– Zen teaching*

I first heard my favorite martial art story when I was new to karate. I re-tell it now to my own students and, not surprisingly, to my personal performance and corporate clients as well. It isn't about dramatic feats of courage or sacrifice -- and it isn't about slaying a dozen enemies or fighting to the death for the family honor. The story is simple, yet it clearly illustrates how useful it can be to apply the martial arts' most fundamental lesson -- personal balance, to life's large and small challenges.

In my second column I'll share some of my thoughts about why we train.

**The Student:**

A talented young warrior goes to the school of a famous teacher, intent on being accepted as a student. The teacher invites the student in, and as they sit waiting for a pot of tea to steep, the student begins to tell the teacher about his enemies, about the battles he has won, those he has lost, and the times victory has been unfairly snatched from his grasp. He talks about the techniques he has mastered, his own students, and most importantly, what he expects this teacher to teach him.

The teacher smiles politely. He watches. He listens. He waits. Finally, the tea is ready, and the teacher begins to pour a cup for his visitor. The small cup fills to the brim and the teacher, still looking at his guest, keeps pouring. The cup overflows and tea begins to spill across the table, and down, onto the student's lap. After an uncomfortable moment, the student finally jumps up and yells, "Stop, Master! Stop! The cup is full. You can't put any more in." The master, still smiling and still looking at the student, slowly stopped pouring the tea, and says, "Yes. The cup is just like you. Already full. I will not be able to teach you anything until you come to me with a cup that is empty."

**The Teacher:**

During the first year of the apprenticeship, the master trains the student in the arts of war on a daily basis. Although much older, and not as strong or fast as the younger man, the master is many times more skilled and experienced. From day one, as the boy had expected, it is never an even match. The training is intense, the pressure is constant, and the old man's wooden practice sword is very, very, hard. Additionally, there is never a time when the student is truly safe. The master strikes him in the blink of an eye, anytime, day or night – whenever his attention lags or wanders.

In addition to his physical training, the student is also responsible for managing the master's household and affairs. This task isn't much easier. The teacher has many interests and arbitrarily changes his plans from day to day, all the while making countless unreasonable demands on the student's time and energy. Additionally, the student is sent to deal with an endless number of ignorant, stubborn and cruel people, and on one impossible mission after another. Always, no matter how a situation is resolved, it seems to the young man that it was never good enough for the master.

**The Student:**

At some point in his apprenticeship the student comes to doubt himself. For the first time in his life, he feels ashamed of his limitations. He becomes nervous and jumpy. His performance as the master's sparring partner gets worse – not better. There are many times that the student wants to just turn and run away. He has brief frightening moments where he thinks of taking his own life. On other days he is more tempted to take out his sword and kill the next person who looks at him in a funny way – the master included.

Finally, not knowing what else to do, the student goes to the teacher. He tells the old man that there must be something wrong with him. Maybe he is ill. The old man knows medicines and remedies – people come to him from across the region to be healed. "Please Master", says the student, looking down, "I am sorry, but I am sick. Please give me something to feel better. There must be some medicine..."

**The Teacher:**

The old man looks at the young one for a long quiet moment, and says, in a kinder voice then the student had heard in quite a while, "My son, you are not sick. You simply need to control your emotions. Right now, your anger controls you. Your fear controls you. Worst of all, you waste your energy worrying about what will happen tomorrow, whether you are good enough, whether you will survive here. You are a leaf blowing in a storm of your own making."

The student is stunned to hear this – especially after all he has endured. He becomes angry, he slams his fist down on the table, and through barely controlled tears of rage yells, "No, Master! That is not true! I am not a child who cannot control his anger! And, I have never been afraid of anything in my entire life! I have had many opponents, and survived many life and death battles..."

Eventually, with effort, the student stops himself, and regains his composure. The teacher, still looking at him, finally says, "I am not the one you need to convince. Your argument is not with me – it is with yourself."

**The Student:**

That night he lay awake on his straw mat, staring at the ceiling, thinking about tomorrow. Worrying, "what if I am not good enough?"

Eventually, as most do, the crisis passes for the young warrior and the apprenticeship continues.

At some point, as if by magic, the student gains control of his emotions. From then on, he is never angry, he is never afraid, and he never feels anxious. He is able to see the solution to every problem, defeat every opponent who challenges him, and find the answer to each of the master's riddles.

In practice, the old man can no longer toy with him like a child, but rather, finds a true challenge. Nor can the teacher catch the student by surprise and smack him sharply as he sleeps, or bends over the stove to cook their meals, or stands with his back turned to relieve himself in the river.

From one morning to the next the student never allows a single opening or a single lapse in his attention. His focus is absolute. It occurs to the young student that he has become very much like the master's one vanity – the strange "grandfather" clock the old man had received as a gift from a foreign patron. It is precise, exact, and although it moves constantly, nothing disturbs, or upsets, it. Of his few simple possessions, the master loves this object very much.

**The Teacher:**

One day, the young warrior returns home from completing a task for the master and sees something that shocks him. On the floor, smiling and working with the intensity of a fascinated child sits the master. The beautiful clock lies around him in sections. Slowly, and patiently, he is going about the task of taking it apart, piece by piece.

The student stands in the doorway for a long moment, watching, trying to figure if this is another test. Finally, he asks the teacher why he is ruining his prized possession. The old man laughs out loud, as if delighted that this wonderful student is once again missing the point. "My son", he says, "you have become very strong, and you are very efficient, but you have misplaced the joy of living and the curiosity that first brought you here. Tell me, why do you think I am doing this?"

## WHY WE TRAIN

In my first column, I recounted my favorite martial art story — the tale of a talented young warrior struggling with the challenges posed by his wise, stern, unpredictable master. I think this story is so popular in the martial arts because (accurately or not) we all like see a bit of ourselves in both the young warrior and the old master.

I'd like to expand a bit on the themes of the story and share some personal thoughts on the value of traditional martial arts training. Specifically, how do the lessons we learn in an intense traditional environment translate to tools we can use in modern times, facing modern challenges?

For those of you who are wondering, the student finally succeeds. Ultimately, he masters the one aspect of the martial arts he (and we) need(s) the most. No, not new and fancier tricks, not how to move more quickly, or how to wield a deadlier weapon, but rather, he learns *personal balance — the artful way of being.*

In many ways, personal balance (and there are a lot of different terms for this) is really the most important skill that martial arts training offers us. With it, we learn to do something that is both difficult and necessary: integrate two dramatically different approaches to life into one singularly effective way to live.

First, personal balance makes us acutely aware of our moment-to-moment relationship with the world of the present, giving us the ability to accept reality (what our current status is NOW) without hesitation. In this way, we remain free of expectations, so that we can deal with danger, bad trouble, or good fortune spontaneously decisively. We are able to respond to the immediate — immediately and with the full force of our spirit and without the hesitation and doubt that puts us in greater danger.

Second, personal balance gives us the confidence and poise to plan and strategize, and ultimately to act, in a way that moves us forward to a better position than we are now. To switch from defense (the position of reacting without thinking, struggling to get our breath, saving our butt, wondering if well survive) to offense, where we can strategize and maneuver our opponent (or our situation) to the outcome we want.

In the story of the young warrior, the teacher guides the student through the difficult process of developing personal balance, by teaching him three key martial art lessons. The first of these lessons is *to see solutions;* the second lesson is *to control emotions;* and the third is *to keep a beginner's mind.*

## The First Lesson—To See Solutions.

We see solutions when we are able to recognize the opportunity, instead of just the difficulty that is contained within each crisis, and to recognize the opening that is hidden within each attack, instead of just the danger. To see solutions, we must develop the talent to switch back and forth between "the forest and the trees" in the blink of an eye.

The essence of learning this skill lies in our ability to accept what is, while at the same time, realizing that where we are (in the best and worst of times), is never our final destination. It is a step on a journey, a moment in time — nothing more.

When life is good, we can take the opportunity to pause, rest, get our bearings, fortify ourselves, have fun, and enjoy what we have. When times are bad or dangerous, we may need to drastically change course, attack, run, hide, or just grit our teeth and persevere. Regardless, the task is the same: see the solutions that are there, recognize the options, and act on them — the more decisively the better.

As we learn in training, and the student learned in the story, seeing solutions is difficult when you are caught off guard or blindsided by the unexpected. Additionally, it is very hard for any of us to see solutions when we feel as if we have been pushed past our limits. How can we possibly hope to *make a plan* when we lack the resources to simply get by from one moment to the next, or the strength to just "come up with something" that will save us?

Training teaches us to ignore the pain, control the fear, and sidestep two common mind-sets that hamstring us when we attempt to focus on resolving a particular challenge. First, we frequently convince ourselves that there is only one perfect (usually unattainable) solution. While this is hardly ever the case, it does make a vast number of good alternatives *seem* like failures. And second, like a deer frozen in the headlights of an oncoming car, we often come to feel (usually in a blind panic) that there is no solution. Confused and paralyzed, we find ourselves in a kind of free fall— fighting without goals, like a rabbit caught in a trap.

The truth is that usually there are several solutions to any problem and several ways of besting an opponent. As evidence, I offer the following simple, universal, experience. How many times have you struggled to overcome a difficult challenge, worked hard to find the right solution, and acted on it, only to look back a year (a month, a week, an hour, even a moment...) later, and said, "Damn! I should have done... something else"?

## The Second Lesson – To Control Your Emotions.

The old teacher's second lesson is one of discipline. For us, this means the ability to keep a sense of purpose when we find ourselves "face-to-face" with tough situations. To deal with a crisis, cope with change, or win a conflict, we need to stay focused on the here, the now, and the task (the solution) at hand, no matter what. Usually, and here's the hard part, this is going to mean controlling three specific, balance-breaking emotions: anger, fear and anxiety,

Now, don't misunderstand, anger, fear, and anxiety, each are valuable parts of being human. They are your "fight or flight" emotions — the ones that flare when you are exposed to danger. You cannot function normally without them, and you don't want to lose them. And they are related to each other in complex ways. However, as the young warrior in the story finally learns, they are an unwanted hindrance when the only thing that will really save you is being able to act, not plan or feel.

Why? Because each of these emotions separates you from the present and puts you in a place that is anything but balanced. Briefly, this is how they work:

### *Anger traps us in the past.*

Anger locks your attention onto a real, or imagined, event in which you were hurt, scared, challenged, or disappointed. When you are angry, your attention focuses on that pain. Your struggle immediately becomes to make things "right" and come to terms with those feelings. Anger can be a flash that comes and goes in half a second, or an emotional companion that you have lived with for a lifetime. Regardless, focusing on the feeling of anger keeps you from fully paying attention and reacting in the present.

Try this as you sit and read these words. Think of something that makes you angry. It can be real or imaginary. Now, take a moment and actually let yourself feel the anger. (Just a little bit; go easy. There's no point in ruining your whole day.) Maybe it's a small thing: you've been insulted, someone cuts you off at an intersection, you spill coffee on yourself while waiting for a job interview, or your favorite restaurant closes. Usually, just stubbing your toe in the dark, losing your keys, or being put on hold when you're on the phone, is enough to do it for most people. Or, maybe, it's something big: your boss accuses you of something you didn't do and threatens to take your job; you are betrayed by your wife; or your child is beaten up by bullies.

Now, notice: as you feel the anger, you stop thinking of it as an idea, as something distant or as a memory, but rather, you experience it as if it were happening now. Regardless of where you actually are, it becomes your immediate reality. You go somewhere else in your head because anger always becomes the present. When you are angry, you are more aware of what was, and what happened than you are of what is, and the moment at hand...

There is no balance in anger because, no matter what, you can't be in two emotional places at once. When you cannot focus on what needs to be done in the present, since you are using what you do in the present to correct or avenge the past, you reduce your options, because you limit your ability to think and to act spontaneously. It destroys your timing.

Next issue, I will conclude my discussion on why we train with some comments on fear, anxiety, and the beauty of the Beginner's Mind...

### *Fear projects us into the future.*

Fear, on the other hand, focuses your attention forward to a place in your imagination where you anticipate being hurt, scared, challenged, or disappointed.

As you did with anger, try thinking of something that makes you feel afraid. It can be a big fear or small one. It can be immediate, taking only as long as it would for you to hear the squeal of tires and then jerk your head around to make sure your child isn't in the street. Or you can use a longer time frame, maybe thinking about being carjacked, planning to make a speech in front of thousands of people, losing all your money on bad investments, being abandoned by your spouse, or, crashing in an airplane.

Now, notice that the consequences of the fearful thing you imagine happen at some point in the future—not in the present. To actually experience the fear, you must leave the present and go to a place that you have created in your mind, where the "bad thing" is going to happen.

Fear, like anger, takes you out of the present and destroys your ability to respond as effectively as possible to the moment at hand.

### *Chronic Anxiety keeps us stuck in place.*

Chronic anxiety compromises your balance by pulling you back and forth between past and future, without ever letting you come to rest in the present. It creates an emotional reality in which you are not adequate to the task of living your own life.

You might think of anxiety as a combination of a fear you can't really identify, combined with anger about something that hasn't actually happened. The result is that you end up stuck in place, incapable of making decisions or developing an effective strategy.

Anxiety is a little harder to experiment with than anger and fear. This is because anxiety bypasses your conscious thoughts, memories and imagination, and manifests itself physiologically, with symptoms that are directly related to your natural "stress response".

For now, let's try this. Think of a person or a situation that makes you anxious. The key here is that, unlike either anger or fear, *you can't* choose a specific emotional event that actually has happened, or a specific one that is definitely going to happen. Where does that leave you?

Well, try thinking of having a relationship with someone that can affect your daily life, but is so unpredictable that you never know what to expect from them. (Hint: for lots of us, teenage children and aging parents fill this criterion very well.) Or try focusing on all the little things you need to do, all the things you are responsible for, and all the big things you need to accomplish, but haven't the time for. Or maybe just think of one or two things that are very important to you, but that you have no control over.

What happens? In order to do any of the above, you are forced to focus on all the things that *might* happen. If you look at this closely, you will find that you become emotionally hyper-vigilant, mentally pacing or spinning in circles — like an animal trapped in a cage.

Ultimately, anxiety focuses your attention on an endless series of life's "what ifs?" and "oh, nos." By focusing emotionally on everything that might happen, you are not able to focus on what is happening, or to plan for what you will do about it.

In a sense, martial art training prepares us to deal with emergencies, and is no different from other types of emergency training. I think we can learn something fundamental about controlling our emotions from those who must do just that in their professional lives. Emergency medical personnel, police officers, competitive athletes, soldiers, race car drivers, martial artists, and others, all must all learn one important skill — to put aside their feelings and concentrate entirely on the task at hand.

The key? They don't block their balance-breaking emotions by holding themselves back from the situation; rather, they do it by immersing themselves fully in action, in *doing the things* that will lead to solutions.

## The Final Lesson – Keep "A Beginner's Mind."

The first two principles of personal balance that the old master tries to teach the student — *to see solutions* and *to control our emotions* — are easier for some to master than for others. Generally, these are aspects of our personality that only can develop through a combination of experience, discipline, and maturity. They are active states that keep us focused and vigilant. The third aspect of personal balance — *a beginner's mind* — however, is different. It is about trust, and appreciation, and openness. It is about the joy of living. In many ways, it is the most elusive of the three. Yet, it is vitally important to the creation of true *personal balance*.

The "beginner's mind" is a phrase used by martial artists and Zen masters alike. It describes the ability to maintain a sense of wonder and excitement for life's normal daily events. The beginner's mind is open to new knowledge and new experiences. It is able to pay total attention to the task at hand, with a lack of ego, defensiveness, or the fear of failure (there is a lot of freedom in not being an expert).

Most importantly, the beginner's mind is non-defensive about what it knows, and what it doesn't know. This point alone gives it tremendous practical merit for one simple reason. By being flexible and non-dogmatic, the beginner's mind is free to approach any challenge, or any problem, from any angle. In a sense, it is programmed *to see solutions.*

The irony is that as children we are born with a beginner's mind. Unfortunately, the same combination of life experiences that make it necessary for us to see the solutions to sudden problems, and to control our emotions in emergencies, can harden us, and make us cynical and pessimistic. Ultimately, pessimism and cynicism are exhausting, and as far removed from personal balance as are anger, fear and anxiety.

How do we go about developing a beginner's mind? First, we must start to consciously take control of how we approach life and perceive events. For example, I ask my students and clients to perform one simple beginner's mind task a day, regardless of their circumstances. In fact, I strongly feel that this assignment becomes *more* important, not less, if they feel as if they are fighting for their lives against one of life's many challenges. The assignment is this: *Take a genuine, daily, interest in something that is not directly related to you, or your current situation.*

Clearly, this task can be satisfied in a wide variety of ways — some elaborate, some simple. For example: you can read a section of the paper you don't usually look at, watch a television show you don't normally see, read a book you wouldn't normally read. You can go to a play, or a concert, or professional wrestling — if those are new to you. Pursue a hobby. Eat somewhere new. Have a conversation in which you find out about another person's life. Go to your local courthouse and attend a trial. Go to a local church and sit in the back of a wedding or attend a funeral. Feel joy or grief for those people. Take a moment to enjoy something simple: the sunset, a flower, the bark of a tree (or a dog for that matter). Take a different way home. Your options are limitless.

The point is to immerse yourself totally, but briefly, in a new environment. Most importantly, the point is to let down your defenses, and enjoy these adventures for what they are, at that moment, and not for where they can take you, or what they can do for you in the future.

Really, it is all a variation of what we get to do every time we go to the dojo. We are lucky.

Eventually the young warrior and the master reach the same point. They understand that the ability *to see solutions, to control emotions,* and *to keep a beginner's mind,* are not separate goals. Rather, they are interrelated aspects of the martial arts' fundamental principle — *personal balance.* When mastered, they work seamlessly together to protect you from life's risks, as they allow you to enjoy its gifts. They are the horse, the sword, and the shield that we need to deal with the overwhelming crisis, the unwanted change, and intense conflict, of life. They must come as naturally to us as when we catch our footing walking across a wet tile floor.

# ROBERT J. OTT

## NOTHING MORE THAN FEELINGS

For some, *"Nothing more than feelings"* are the words from an old song. For me however, it is much more. In many different martial arts, the theory of the circle is a vital part of the system. Until one comes to understand and value this principle, very little progress in the study can be achieved. The first thing to learn is how both our offense and defense methods can be affected by the circle. It is clear that when one is defending him or herself that any attack that is performed outside of the opponent's circle is a waste of motion and energy. It is also clear that the body of the opponent will also be unable to attack yourself when they are not in your circle. Thus, it can be seen how detrimental the circular theory is in one's practice.

In my sharing of knowledge there are 3 different ways that one can learn to be in another person's circle.

1) Touching

2) Seeing

3) Feeling

Each out of the three that are mentioned are vital but often enough the third one is overlooked. Every day in life we use our capability of feeling to exist. When one sits in a chair, he or she can feel the wall behind them. They are not looking at the wall nor are they touching it, yet the presence of it is felt. When walking through a downtown city we are able to feel an incredible difference in energy upon arriving at an intersection, for prior to the intersection we were walking adjacent to a high-rise building. Once the building stopped and coming to the intersection the reflection of our energy ceased to be felt. My fellow martial artists this is the study of feeling. When defending and or counter attacking the energy from the opponent as well as the energy from yourself can be felt colliding in the air. It is energy that is neither seen nor able to be physically touched yet filled with significant power, because of our ability to see we often enough do not use our other senses. I will have to admit that I was at one time no different than the rest of the practitioners who are unable to utilize this great technique. However, that all changed when I became blind! I cannot say it is easy nor what I had wanted in my life but nevertheless it is what it is for me. So, as said long ago from one of our U.S. Generals, "some see it as a problem, but I look at it as an opportunity…" Through continuous practice of this technique, one will develop better speed and stronger focus. Ultimately, he or she will then have less distractions and greater results in their study.

## I CAN SEE MY DOJANG

In the year 1989, I made a transition in Martial Arts, from being the Chief Instructor and Office Manager of the Dragon Gym in Exton, PA., to becoming the Owner/Operator of the Traditional Martial Arts Institute in Somerdale, NJ. There were many reasons why this change happened, with the most vital reason, was to be closer to my family and loved ones. It was an hour drive each day from Southern New Jersey to Exton Pennsylvania and I easily worked 12 to 14 hours a day, 6 days a week. Even more so, I was growing as a Martial Arts practitioner, who needed to blossom into my own personal warrior.

It is clear that a true instructor is a true student but that is not always the case for the opposite. I lived and breathed my practice, and it was time for me to have my own dojang. I remember the street address of 409D White Horse Pike. It was adjacent to a U-Haul location and without question, the building was old and run down. However, it was all I could afford during those days and clearly, I knew in my mind and heart, that the passion and love, I have for the art, would turn this Dojang into the most traditional, attractive Korean Martial Arts school in the local tri-state area.

At the grand opening of my new location, we had over 150 people attend. For a small studio, it was a great number. The compliments on the furniture, mirrors, paintings on the wall, display of weapons, changing rooms, show case windows to even my office, came from all who entered the dojang. During my time of owning that business and teaching at that school, I explained to my students, that a part of the payment for learning from me and practicing in this studio, would be, that they would also do their part in maintaining our school. After every class the students would sweep, vacuum, window clean and adjust all the weapons to the exact area, where they originally came from. The students would empty the trash cans and make sure that the dojang looked as good when they left, as when they entered.

This became another way, in which, I taught my students to care for and be proud of our school. The Traditional Martial Arts School was the only Hapkido dojang in the Delaware Valley area, at that time and was only open for business one year. Tragically, this beautiful school closed soon after my blindness came in 1990, as a result of a change in my life, which no person could have ever predicted.

Today, I now live on the other side of the country and am once again a practitioner who owns and teaches at a Dojang. This one, however, is more secluded and not used as a business. It is one, that allows me to teach from the heart and train practitioners to be Warriors, such as myself. Even though I do not use the dojang to make money, the appearance and quality is just as vital.

Some of the most well-known fellow Martial Artists in the world, have come to visit and teach/train at my Dojang. This has been a truly great honor. I have heard that my Dojang is one of the most traditional, classy, and truest, from the heart facilities, that many have come to see, in their entire lifetime of study. Through this, I have come to realize that even though I do not teach for a living and am blind, the classiness and visual look of the Dojang, I have today, is just as critical as the appearance of my first Dojang. Each day after training, my students have the same responsibilities in cleaning and maintaining the quality of the dojang from his or her heart. Just like the Flowering Warriors, who unified the dynasties of Korea, many years ago cared about their swords, I care the same about my Dojang and everything in it.

When this Dojang was completed, I named it "Temple of Certain Victory." I planned each detail, and the details do matter, as they come from the heart. Every school is very different in appearance, but throughout each school/Dojang, I can only hope, that other Martial Artists, will teach and share their Martial Arts study, from their hearts and in so many ways, they too will demonstrate and share the same principles, with their students. For in the big picture, what ultimately comes from this, is self-confidence, discipline, pride and the understanding that what one puts out in life, one will get back in return.

## THE APPRECIATION OF FREEDOM

It was a minimum 3-hour drive to our destination in Bellingham, Washington. My mind was letting much of my daily responsibilities go while simultaneously filling up with thoughts regarding our current trip. I was traveling with 3 of my fellow Moosa. In actuality, they are my students, yet when referring to these folks, I often use the words "Fellow Moosa." The word "Moosa" is translated from Korean into English giving us the title of "Martial Artist." My students may be learning from me, yet I am no different than each of these; for a true instructor will always be a true student.

The mission we were embarked on was one that I had undertaken many times previously, yet truth be told, each one is unique its own way. The program coordinator, Debbie Himes called me several months prior to ask if I could serve as one of the motivational speakers for this year's Youth Leadership Forum. The distance and transportation requirements involved made it clear to me that the commitment to this project would require more than one day. In my dojang (studio for Martial Arts training) each student must not only give their hearts to each class that is instructed, but he or she must also donate time to the community. So, what started off as simply a speaking engagement went on to become a seminar and demonstration with all the logistics that entails.

Each of the 35 participants attending the week-long program lives with a disability of some fashion. I prefer to call it a challenge, for I believe challenge indicates something that can be overcome with effort. Today I maintain just as many abilities enabling me to give back to this world as I did prior to my blindness. The challenges that the participants had in this weeklong event were varied, and each earned my deep respect and admiration for their pursuit of excellence. The program participants ranged from the ages of 16 to 20, and the ultimate purpose of the event was to prepare each individual for the transition from high school to college.

As we drove north my mind found itself focusing more on the seminar and demonstration versus the speaking engagement. With each participants having various challenges, we as instructors faced our own challenges in how to present particular techniques. Upon arriving we checked into the hotel and did a little bit of driving around to get a feel of the community. The event was located at the Western Washington State College and the environment was the picture-perfect image of a small town on the coast overlooking the entrance to the great Pacific Ocean pouring into Puget Sound, where thousands of people, ships, and wildlife travel through each day. It was a small town with a true "Mom & Pop" feeling to it. My students pointed out some great locations where photos could be taken during our little tour of the town. When traveling, I always enjoy getting the most out of each trip. Having photos taken for the articles I write and or the advertising I do for my book is always an extra bonus. With fantastic weather and a positive feeling lifting our spirits, it clearly felt that victory was in the making.

That evening, I found myself tossing and turning in bed often thinking of how I could assist the participants in achieving the most in both confidence and a higher level of self-esteem. With myself being blind, I have had the opportunity of developing programs of "Martial Arts and or Self Defense" for others who are faced with the same and or similar challenges with sight. However, wheelchairs, deafness, inability to speak, lack of use of arms/hands and even blindness were going to be in this room looking to me for leadership and guidance. My previous experience has taught me that we would face those challenges and overcome them together the next day.

As we entered the room at the beginning of the lunch hour, there was nothing but a positive feeling of warmth, appreciation, and goodness from all who filled the space. Lunch had just begun, and the food was delicious. As I began to eat, the keynote speaker for the day was about to begin his presentation. I was scheduled to speak following this gentleman, and it was critical to listen to his approaches and main points of knowledge and experience so that I myself would not be repeating some of the same subjects. Often my approach is to share my journey in life and how I found the inner strength to go from a victim to a survivor and in conjunction share strength, courage, and indomitable spirit to all within hearing. As mentioned earlier, in this article my concerns and or focus of thought leaned more to the teaching than the speaking, yet little did I realize how much that was all about to change.

As I ate my lunch and listened to the speaker something began to tell me that this man is someone. I already know yet never had the opportunity of meeting. With each word, I began to eat less and focus more on his words. In less than 5 minutes time, it became clear who I was listening to as he continued to share his life store with all in attendance. It had been at least a year and a half prior when my wife and I sat in the living room and watched a movie called *Music Within*, that portrayed the story of how the American Disability Act had been enacted into law. His story reminded me of how far we have come in this country assisting individuals who face physical and or mental challenges. The movie shared that disabled people had been removed and or locked up and taken to jail for simply being in public locations via the embarrassment that others felt in as late as the 1960s to the early 1970s. The movie was one I never forgot, and it strengthened me to an entirely new level of humanity. His name is Richard Pimentel; he is 64 years of age and is living in Idaho. It is so hard to express to another person in words what difference this man has made to millions of people around the globe. As he ended his speech, the crowd erupted in a standing ovation. I made my way to the podium and as the cameras snapped away, I spoke in open, honest words about the impact he had had on my life. As I placed my hand in his, I shared that his life example brought more vision into my life than when I could once see.

After the photos had been taken and the handshake ended, I lost all concern about my teaching and or speaking. All of it came natural to me and my words of Certain Victory were shared with all of the participants with lust for life, passion for persistence and an attitude of never surrender. Later that evening, I held my seminar and demonstration and instructed these participants with various disabilities for over two hours. I ended the seminar/demonstration with a show of myself throwing and taking down attackers and lastly blowing through a stack of cinder blocks. My words struck with action rather than just thought. I shared with all the Flowering Warriors in attendance, the greatest truth of all. We must all understand that our own attitudes about the challenges facing us will either assist us in overcoming them or act as a barrier to our ultimate success and happiness in life. We must face these challenges individually and as a community in pursuit of our own individual and collective Certain Victory. If we believe and apply ourselves there is nothing that cannot be achieved. I shared with each how I learned to find vision in my blindness and how they too could find a path through their own darkness.

## A TRUE TEACHER IS A TRUE STUDENT

When hosting the event in 2009 I thought my experience and participation in seminars throughout my many years of martial arts study would have made the orchestrating of the event to be of little challenge, that my fellow martial artists was my first mistake. The truth is, different from all the events in the past this seminar was being hosted and constructed by myself and only myself, in conjunction I was advertising the event to fellow practitioners from all over the world. It is not possible for an artist to paint the exact same picture of another artist for each of us humans live under our own skin and walk in our own shoes, thus what may be a priority to me may not be for another. Ultimately much was learned from the 2009 event, throughout the numerous challenges, responsibilities, and various walks of life it became a success -- an experience shared through the testimonies of the participants.

As I write this article there are only few days left before the kickoff of the 2011 Super Summer International Korean Martial Arts Seminar. One of the greatest changes made from the 2009 event is the location, instead of the training, presenting awards, eating, sleeping and entertaining at different locations, I have brought it to one place. In conjunction with the beautiful summers in the great northwest (70s with no humidity) we have rented out a full facility called Camp Thunderbird. This beautiful campsite is located on Summit Lake on the outskirts of Olympia. As an owner of a summer home at Summit Lake I am confident to say it is a location of peace and tranquility. The water of Summit Lake is crystal clear making swimming, boating, and other water sports quite popular, along with BBQs and hiking of the surrounding trails. I have also decided for this event with all the beauty and passion to increase the time from two days of training (the normal) to a four-day event with an official opening and closing ceremony. While having the campground rented out for one week, I have added a women's self-defense seminar and a youth self-defense seminar before the official event that will be instructed by our special guest. All participants will be able to sleep in the wonderful cabins as well as enjoy breakfast, lunch, and dinner at the dining facility. With six designated Grandmasters/Chief Master instructors we will also be having speakers, entertainment from the international Korean dance school and well-known special guests attending. Further there will be custom traditional Korean martial arts products available to purchase that are one of a kind and normally out of reach for the dedicated collectors.

For those of you who have had the opportunity of learning about myself it is important to see I have put my heart into each and every part of my study, it is without question a way of life, I feel communication, positive relationships and brotherhood support is a critical part of the foundation martial arts sits on. Please take the time to read the advertisement here in this magazine for my event; it is one that would be a valuable addition to both your relationships and knowledge your practice currently provides. As I shared in the title of this article: "A true teacher is a true student" this event and all it takes to be a success will continue to teach and enforce that in life what one puts out, one will get back in more ways than ever imagined.

# AVI ROKAH

## BREATHING

**Intention, breathing, muscle action, then technique – this is the order in any karate technique.**

You must have a mental picture before movement, otherwise the muscles have no direction and cannot cooperate. Sensei gave the example of lifting heavy weight; you have to prepare mentally, or you can hurt yourself.

Where the eyes go the body follows. Therefore, whatever body action you make, do not change your eyes and face from the opponent. From in between the eye, "shoot" energy, project, give direction to your technique. The point between the eyes is called *Kami Tan-Den* (upper center of energy). The actual eyes are soft, seeing the total picture, so we have a wide picture and the focus -- the soft and the strong.

If the eyes don't give direction, the breath cannot guide the muscles.

The breath activates the feet through the body center to the technique. In order to do that, we have to use diaphragmatic breath -- breathing from the chest will activate only the top muscles.

Good use of the breath is only possible from a good posture, since in a bad posture the muscles are not in optimal length, and the breath is forced. Also, from a bad posture the muscles cannot be activated in proper sequencing.

**Reaction by breath, not by brain.**

If you walk in the street and a car comes at you surprisingly, you react with the breath: *Haaaaa...* and jump (before the brain realizes). You don't look at the car and decide to be surprised and jump. This is the reaction we use in karate. That's how we bypass the brain.

The breath control center is in the lower, more primitive part of the brain, an area that has to do more with survival and not conscious. We already explained that the breath controls the muscles and technique. Breath makes reaction, breath makes action. Reaction and action become one without space and the breath is the trigger.

**Karate technique should start quickest, without back motion. Otherwise, it cannot be used in application.**

Two methods to initiate technique quickest without back motion, breath is most essential for both methods.

*First,* body dynamics such as rotation and vibration have to initiate not from the hips, not thinking of rotation, but thinking of initiating from the spine, which is a smaller diameter and therefore can be switched quicker, expanding less energy to achieve more result. The intention is in the low spine and the breath controls the center.

*Second,* muscle reaction, creating a sling shot within the body, making the preparation internal by using the breath (reverse exhale) to draw the stomach back toward a stable back and buttocks which are the base, and then switch exhale direction, stimulating the muscles, using muscle reaction from the center, not chest, to drive the technique.

**Increase Energy**

At the end of the technique, the forearm twists sharply at the elbow joint as action center (in most cases). The sharp change from straight line to circular action increases energy sharply.

What is important here again is the breath that controls the whole body snap from the ground through the core, with the elbow being merely an expression.

## KIME: Focus and delivery of total energy to target at impact

***Pressure*** — At contact we don't rely on muscle strength, but rather on skill. If we relied on strength to achieve twice the power, we would need to develop twice the muscles. Instead, at impact we create pressure to floor with the breath, to accelerate the body weight. Twice the pressure means twice the body weight as reaction from floor.

As we make pressure, we must have strong intention of the reaction of this pressure being delivered to technique direction.

***Contraction*** — As we make pressure to produce energy, we need shocking power, meaning all energy delivered in shortest time (avoid pushing power). Therefore, we need sharpest contraction of total body musculature in proper sequence (ground to technique in most cases).

Again, breathing makes sharp contraction, or slower contraction. As the breath makes pressure, contraction starts from the ground up. But at the same time our intention is of contraction toward the spine, which then as chain reaction and with a stable spine as an anchor, the big muscles are working from the spine to the technique.

## Breathing controls type of contraction and type of energy

Depends on the purpose of the technique. If it is sharp shock, heavier target, smooth technique, the breath controls the way the muscles are activated, and making the contraction at kime.

## My Addition

At the beginning we learn form and a lot of detail, but the purpose is to be able to let go, to forget form, and do anything according to necessity, without violating the principles of the form.

Form is limitation, but through it we learn principle of natural, most effective way of using ourselves. Then we forget form, but in whatever we do the principles of natural movement are not violated.

Breathing is the bridge between form to no form. At certain levels, all that is left is intention and breath. Everything else does itself.

## YOU DON'T SEE – YET YOU SEE.
## YOU DON'T HEAR – YET YOU HEAR.

This is a Budo martial arts saying describing the highest level of intuition and awareness, and the ability of a person to perceive without interfering with himself without the interference of thoughts and judgment. It's an awareness in which our receivers are clear, not clouded.

At this level, without trying to see, without trying to know, you know the opponent's intention; you see his action before he moves.

This is not magic, anyone can get to that level, but it is tricky. The harder you try the more difficult it will become. The beautiful thing is that if you have the proper guidance and directions, and you understand the factors that are necessary to get to that level, you will get there.

I think that part of the difficulty lies in our beliefs. In our society, we are trained to believe in logic and to believe only to what we see and can confirm.

In karate, confirming and trusting what we see only will make us always late, behind our opponent. If we open our "receivers," there is enough information in the opponent's movement, body language, breath and rhythm, and the energy that he projects to us allows us to see the opponent's intention and movement ahead of time.

I believe that the ingredients that bring a person to such high level are: stable emotions under pressure, confidence, experience, proper use of the eyes, proper use of the breath, and proper movement. You also have to believe that it is possible.

### Confidence and Stable Emotions

Hard training brings confidence and confidence brings stable emotions. Of course, there are other factors that affect emotions, such as the breathing and even our posture and the way we move.

When we get excited or afraid, our breathing rises and becomes faster. When we try to focus, our breathing slows down, and that is also not good, since it is a narrow focus and what we need is attentiveness, which is wide and includes focus. So, our breath should be just natural.

Just the same way that emotions affect the breath, it works the other way, and we can affect and quiet our emotions using the breath.

## Breathing

The breath "catches" the opponent's rhythm and movement rather than the eyes. If we use the eyes, we are behind. We use the breath to "ride" the opponent, tune to him, rather than fight or compete with him.

We say that your breath and the opponent's breath should become one, and in the more advanced levels, your breath will conduct the opponent's breath and movement. You are the commander, and he is your soldier.

Through connecting to the opponent's breath, we connect to his intentions, since the breath is the connections between mental and physical.

We also react to the opponent's action with our breath rather than with the eyes. Light reaction is too late for us, since you have to look, analyze, decide and then act.

We bypass the conscious brain by reacting with the breath, which means reacting directly at the spinal level, and at the same time the breath also activates the body center.

The breath initiates reaction and action, so reaction and action become one, without space. (This needs deeper explanation that is beyond the scope of this article).

If a person's breath does not tune and match the opponent's, we say that he is "self-dancing," and that means that he has to rely on speed and force rather than skill.

## The Eyes

In karate we understand that the eyes affect the brain. If we look at the opponent too hard, we will judge, confirm and be behind rhythm and out of tune with the opponent. We will easily become overly excited and emotionally unstable. When we rely on the eyes, we become hesitant and have doubts.

There are many ways of describing the use of the eyes depending on the level, with the highest level being "you don't see, yet you see," or in other words, you don't try to look, yet you see inside your opponent without trying.

***Enzen No Metzke*** – Eyes back as if looking at a mountain from long distance.

This is one of the most basic and important methods of using the eyes. When looking from close, you can see a house, a tree, you get stuck in details. When looking from afar, you can see the whole without getting stuck in one place.

The feeling should be as if the eyes are monitoring the situation, observing, looking softly, and not trying too hard.

***Looking at the shining star*** – Looking to the opponent's eye as if looking to a star. When the eye shine changes you know the opponent's intention changes and he is about to move.

***Tani No Metzke*** – Looking through a canyon, looking through the opponent' eyes to his heart or feeling. You are looking to the opponent's eye level, not staring at the eyes but rather through and down to his heart.

Aiko San (a woman who has worked with my teacher for the past 40 years, and who understands karate more than anyone else) once gave me a great advice: "Look at your opponent as if he is a shadow; he has no details."

In the end, you don't look in any special way, you just see inside your opponent.

## Experience

Through experience of facing many people, we realize that most people have similar patterns in the way they react, and they project their energy before certain action. This is a very important component of reading our opponent without judging and analyzing.

Experience can also create bad habits. The way you respond mentally to a stimulus is similar to how we respond physically: nerve impulses travel in certain pathways, and once they travel in certain pathways, they are likely to travel in the same pathway in response to a stimulus.

So, if we are creating a habit of tensing up, getting nervous or angry when facing an opponent, we will block our ability to sense him and to respond to him in a flowing way.

How to use experience to our advantage need to be taught orally in the class and in accord to how a person interact with the opponent in a certain moment, here I only describe the general concept.

## Body Movement

If my body moves in the way it was designed to, from the center out, then my reaction (from the spine) and my action (from the spine) are one, without space of choosing or deciding.

If, on the other hand, my training is improper, and I move my arms and legs independently, in isolation, it's a different pathway of movement. The brain has to order the arms and legs to move. I could not bypass the brain, and I am going to be busy with many details and could not perceive my opponent.

In proper movement, there is one center control (mentally and physically) and the movement become simpler and the brain not so busy.

Details can be let go, and all is left is intention and breath. The proper movement will take care of itself and I don't know what I am doing until it's done

## Posture

In a good posture, openness and sincerity are expressed, and your body and mind are light and sensitive. We say that even a fly landing on you will set you in motion. When an opponent senses that you give yourself up, not holding anything, he will feel very difficult to attack.

## KARATE: TIMING AND APPLICATION TECHNIQUES IN COMBAT

From kata we learn principles of body movement and combat. For example, we learn to move the body from the center out as a unit, rather than moving the arms and legs independently. It is impossible to seize a split-second opening if there is extraneous energy or unnecessary movement in our technique.

From kata we learn to synchronize mental energy, breath, muscles expansion/contraction and sequence of joint movement: ki first, breathing next, then follow with muscle movement and technique. If this is not digested into our system, then we cannot react with our breath. In the kata we learn to make strongest, sharpest technique without back motion; we learn to wind-up internally. Against a skillful opponent, the technique cannot be applied if you need back motion. Kata teaches us continuity between techniques; if there is space between techniques, there is a chance for the opponent to counterattack and we will miss many chances for attack combinations.

An example of a combat principle from kata is that with few exceptions we always move in when blocking. There is no need to block when moving away from an opponent's attack because we use space to avoid the attack – *amashi waza*. We also learn that block and counterattack are one action – block is not a technique by itself unless the block is used as attack such as against a joint.

From here we understand how important kata is for kumite. Even if you favor kumite make sure that you always come back to kata and improve your kumite weak points. Always self-examine your kumite and come back to the kata to make good patterns in your nervous system. In kata you have low stimuli, no opponent, and no threat – that's your opportunity to make corrections. Kata is the base and is how the knowledge and experience of many generations is transmitted to us. Take it very seriously, otherwise your kumite and self-defense will depend on strength and speed alone, not skill.

Now, kata training by itself will not make you a good fighter. Only through timing and distance training can you bring the techniques in kata to life. Timing is the function of the kata and is the means by which the techniques can become useful.

There are a few elements that need to be understood so we can apply the technique in good timing.

## Qio and Jitsu

To understand proper timing for executing the technique we must understand *qio* and *jitsu*. When the opponent is in good posture and has stable emotions and a strong spirit, this is jitsu (complete). Attacking a skillful opponent in this condition is suicide.

When one of these conditions is changing, it is *qio* (chance). Physical qio is when the opponent show is inhale, when he shifts his center of gravity, or while he attacks. When the opponent moves there is in-between space to attack.

Mental qio is when there is hesitation and the opponent is afraid, has a weak spirit, or when his mind is stiff. He only thinks of one technique or worries about your one technique. His mind is in one place and he cannot adopt smoothly to the changes – this is chance.

## MAAI: Effective Distance or Timing

In karate, timing and distance are one. For a technique to be effective, the technique has to be strong, and the timing and distance have to be proper. At impact, feel as if your body center goes through the opponent. If the fist reaches the target and the body is stretched, the fist is dragged behind the body and is an ineffective technique. Therefore, get the feel of where the feet should be at impact. Think of the feet making the distance rather than thinking of the contact area reaching the target. In some sport karate competitions, you might get a point for touching the target with your fist or foot – in the street you might die. Remember, karate is based on *todome* (finishing blow technique), not scratching the opponent.

Know your own distance and your opponent's distance. This is called *mikiru* – to estimate your opponent's distance in relation to yours. Your distance is called *isoku-ito* (one-foot, one-technique) and is the distance at which you can hit your opponent in one motion. Your opponent's distance depends on his size and ability – a more explosive, coordinated opponent has longer distance. Basic distance is where you can reach your opponent with one technique, yet you can get out of his technique – you are on the borderline of his territory.

Many times, for strategic reasons, if you feel confident in your ability, you can close the distance to cause the opponent to move; after the first technique you will be in close range. We divide distance into short and long range. When two opponents face each other, each should try to get the advantageous distance. The first fight is to control the distance.

## Rhythm

Don't self-dance – don't jump around and think only of attacking. You have an opponent in front of you so adjust your rhythm and breath to his, but don't follow him. You have to assume leadership and be the conductor. Adjusting your rhythm to your opponent's by using your eyes is being behind, waiting. Look softly with the actual eyes and "shoot" from in-between the eyes (*kami tanden*). Use your breathing to set the rhythm for your opponent. When your ki from lower *taden* already hits the opponent, use your ki to give mental pressure to the opponent. Some people with less skill can beat more skillful opponents if they have stronger ki and spirit.

Only when you understand the rhythm can you catch the opponent in-between techniques. This means to break their rhythm – to be off the dance but still ahead and in control of the dance.

## Timing

***Oji Waza (response techniques)*** -- Notice that the word "response" and not "defense" is used because "defense" means being behind; it's the wrong state of mind. The best defense is offense, but not a wild rush. The spirit will not change – your energy is always passing through the opponent and your ideal is early timing – but your action in responding to the technique will be in accordance to how early or late your reaction is. You should practice responding timings and techniques over and over. This will register in your system, at the time of interaction. How you react is not a choice, it should happen by itself, depending on the situation. Your spirit and mind should not change.

***Shikake Waza (set-up techniques)*** -- Again, the word "offense" is not used because it's also the wrong state of mind. It means being mentally unbalanced, rushing in, and by so doing exposing chance to the opponent. When the opponent is in jitsu he does not move, yet he is ready so there is no space to attack, I have to do something to create movement, or mental or physical energy from the opponent so I have space between his movements to attack. I have to give the opponent something, move myself to encourage him to move. Depending on my opponent's inclination, I'm choose my set-up strategy. You have to check your opponent by giving him some pressure and than choose your strategy, don't be mechanical. Only when you are confident of your *oji waza*, will you know that whatever your opponent does you can respond to. Only than will you be comfortable setting up your opponent and be willing to take risks without hesitation, knowing that you can recover.

## Oji Waza

***Kake no sen*** -- "Sen" means "ahead of the opponent's action." "Kake no sen" means "early sen." This means atching the opponent between the decision to attack. When this happens, the brain gives an order to the nervous system in the spine, and nerve impulses travel to muscle ends before the physical movement starts.

***Tai no sen*** -- Catching the opponent while his technique.

***Koroshi waza*** -- Giving shock to opponert's technique as a stage on the way to our attack. Koroshi waza literally means "to kill," meaning to kill the opponent's technique or its potential before it starts. It can be use in *oji waza* or *shikake waza*.

***Go no sen*** -- Hitting the opponent between two techniques. Technically using *uke waza* or *amashi waza*.

***Uke waza*** -- Block and counter; moving in and attacking the opponent's attack as a step to our attack.

## AMASHI WAZA: Using space and shifting out of the opponent's attack and then counterattacking.

In all oji waza the base and the ideal is earlier timing, not defending and waiting. If I'm early enough I respond with a direct attack (*kake no sen*). If I'm slightly late then I use *tai no sen* using *koroshi waza*, which is a small early *uke waza*, attacking the opponent's technique rather than a direct attack as a step to my attack. If I am more late, I use *uke waza*, which needs more shock and therefore more base. Again, the feel is of attacking the opponent's technique on the way to my counter. If I am more late I shift to the back or side, or switch my hips out of the opponent's attack line on the way to my counterattack.

In any case the baseline of attack is already set and the spirit is of *aiuchi* (mutual kill). I don't shift back and then attack, and I don't block and then attack either. Rather I shift back and counter is one motion – block/attack is one action. Once I adapt to how early or late my reaction is, the base is already set and I have already passed through my opponent. I don't choose to use this timing or another; it should happen by itself because you should have enough experience, repetitions of different timing, and situations to sense it and it should be digested in your system. Just keep the right spirit, set the rhythm to the opponent with your breath, and allow your breath to react and the body to follow the breath – proper timing will happen by itself. If you try to consciously choose a response, there will be over-involvement of the brain. This will bring doubt and contradiction to your movement.

## Shikake Waza

***Sasoi waza (to invite)*** -- When you push your opponent and sense that he wants to anticipate with early timing (*sen*), you can fake in order to draw him to attack and then respond with any timing. If it's hard to move the opponent with a fake, or if you feel confidant, you can use *tsumi-ai* to smoothly close the distance. At some point the opponent cannot allow you to get closer and he has to attack – then you anticipate with any *oji-waza*.

***Koroshi waza*** -- You set the rhythm with your breath. When the opponent shows his inhale, give shock to his *kamai* and attack. Or when the opponent is between body shifting, give shock to his *kamae* and attack. Or when he is about to start his attack, give shock to his technique and attack.

***Combinations*** -- When you press your opponent and he backs up, and it's hard to attack directly, start a combination attack between his rhythm. You have to stay ahead of his rhythm until you close the distance enough for the finishing technique. You have to initiate the combination between his rhythm so he cannot recover his momentum.

***Break Balance*** -- Break-balance in karate is different than judo. In most cases the purpose is not to throw your opponent down but rather to create enough space for your finishing technique. Many times, break-balance is used in conjunction with sasoi waza or combinations.

## JUST TRY!

If you train under Sensei Nishiyama and you get frustrated about some subject, feeling that you cannot get or improve your technique, kata, or sparring, Sensei Nishiyama won't say much; he will simply say, "just try."

Most of the time, students will misunderstand him, and think that they have to work and try the same thing harder, not give up, and do more repetitions of the same. But this is not what he really means by "just try."

If you do something wrong and try harder, repeating this movement over and over, you will intensify the bad habit; you will instill a faulty movement pattern into the nervous system that will be harder to undo. The benefits of 'trying harder" sometimes are not positive results.

Keep trying means that if you want different results, you cannot do the same thing in the same way. You have to find other ways to make it better; you have to change what you are doing wrong that is bringing an incorrect technical movement. You have to think of different ways to get to the desired result and find ways to get the right feel of the movement, since your "feel' is inaccurate. You have to fine-tune your kinesthetic awareness, and to do that, you have to reflect constantly on yourself, and try often to get some kind of feedback. That feedback can be from a teacher or a fellow student, or by simply looking at the mirror or a video of yourself performing that technique or kata

Think of one of the most common faulty movement pattern for most people: head forward posture. The most common direction that we get to prevent head forward posture is "eyes back as if looking at mountain from far away," but that unfortunately does not work for everybody. Sensei Nishiyama gives many other images or ways to get the right feel, such as: "Head suspended" or "back of the head applies pressure to the back, support foot," or "slightly raise the eye line to look to the opponent's top of the head" or "the eyebrows shrink to each other and the eyes look softly," or that one I heard from Aiko-san: "the head is like a ball balancing on the shoulder; if it tilts, it will immediately fall down; if it should fall, it should fall through the body and between your legs."

Find an image that talks to you and when you internalize the correct movement pattern and you've got the right feel, the movement will be yours; then, you don't need the image anymore.

To change a faulty movement pattern or even to change the way you react mentally to a stimulus, you have to consider something else that Sensei Nishiyama often says, "In order to make a change, you have to feel uncomfortable for a while."

Obviously, if you are comfortable doing something in certain way, and that way is wrong, doing it the right way has to feel wrong for a while. It is common sense!

Sensei Nishiyama is a man of few words, but I realize that each word he says needs to be pondered upon, and not just taken literally.

When we cannot do this or that, and we give up or change direction, we are setting ourselves for future failure in other areas of life. We must learn to be persistent. Any karate technique, like anything important and valuable in life, requires patience and hard work along with openness and mental flexibility.

It's like climbing a mountain: you go up but sometimes you have to go down in order to go up again. You see a hilltop and you think that's it, "I'm getting to the top." But when you get there, you see the next hill. The true problem is that some people don't look up and they already think that they are at the top.

## HOW MUCH STRETCHING DO WE NEED?

The cave man did not stretch or went through yoga poses, his lifestyle kept his range of motion, he had to throw spears and use his torso in full rotational movement, he had to squad in order to gather foods or even to go to toilet, he sat on the ground rather than chairs and kept his range of motion in his hips, knees and ankles.

The primal man had to move in all plans of motions in patterns of movement such as squat, lunge, bend, twist, pulling and pushing.

When he woke up in the morning he stretched naturally, the same way that cats do to release any tight muscles (it's a problem if you don't do it).

We are lucky in karate that we have the kata, the kata is very special in that it has movement in all plans and including all primal movement patterns (those movement patterns that the cave man could not survive without), and all to the full range of motion. Research shows that there are two reasons for shortening of the tonic muscles and lengthening and weakening of the phasic muscles: inactivity, if a person is put in bed for 2, 3 weeks for example, and faulty movement patterns or bad training.

We have tonic muscles, those are mainly postural muscles with high percentage of slow twitch muscle fibers, those are muscles that hold us up against gravity and meant to work for a long period.

Tonic muscles have low threshold and are easily activated, and when someone develops faulty movement patterns or is inactive, those muscles will shorten and tighten and often will become hyper active and inhibit their antagonist muscles, when the brain sends a message to the lower abdominals the over active hip flexors will try to do the job instead. We also have phasic muscles, those are muscles that are mainly movers, and they have higher percentage of fast twitch muscle fibers, and are used when we have to throw an object explosively, when we have to jump or sprint.

Phasic muscles have high threshold, they are "lazy", and when someone develops faulty movement patterns or is inactive those muscles will lengthen and weaken, or the brain will lose communication with them.

Dr. Janda, a most respected rehabilitation expert from Czech Republic took 200 people with back pain that had weak abdominal relatively to the lumbar erectors muscles and put them on program to strengthen the abdominals, after a while he found out that those patients abdominals strength improve but the lumbar erectors also strengthened proportionally, so the imbalance remained.

An EMG showed that when the patients did their abdominal exercises their back muscles were as active as their abdominals, after stretching the lumbar erectors and then doing the abdominal exercises the EMG showed activation of the abdominals and quiet back muscles.

From here we learn that we need to stretch the tight muscles before strengthening the weak muscles to create balanced musculature, we have to stretch the tonic muscles before any skill movement training otherwise when the brain calls the abdomen to work the back, or the hip flexors will join. That means that we have an orchestra that makes noise not music, when the violin is called into play the tuba respond instead.

Much like the guitar player will not tighten all the strings or loosen all the strings to tune his guitar so do we should not stretch all the muscles or strengthen all the muscles, we will than just get out of balance in a loose way or a tight way.

Why it is so important to stretch the tight muscles and strengthen the weaker lengthened ones?

Since muscles act on joints from both sides, and if the muscles are out of balance, the joint mechanics will be altered, early degeneration or injury could result, and energy could not be transferred smoothly which means that the quality of movement will be compromised.

Stretching the tonic muscles before training is especially important, since the tight tonic muscles could inhibit their antagonist muscles, and become over worked, and we got faulty movement patterns.

Such as the lumbar erectors working when the abdominals are supposed to do the job, or the hip flexors inhibiting the abdominals and that can cause to lose of spinal stabilization.

## Things I Learned Lately

I am very excited, I was supposed to go to the World Cup in Poland on October 15th, and I had to cancel my participation at the last minute, since I hurt my knee and it is still not 100% stable.

I'm not excited about missing the competition or being injured, but until the last few days Sensei Nishiyama pushed me as if I am competing and I learned a lot.I did not learned a lot of new things, a few new angles and deeper understanding of some concepts, but mostly I learned the importance of the fundamentals and how easy it is to neglect what seem obvious.

What we hear all the time and is obvious to us logically is not necessarily internalized in us, and we have to continuously reflect on ourselves, I think that that is real learning, then we grasp a little more of that concept or another each time we come back to it.

I'll tell you few of the points that Sensei was pushing me with and you will see that you are all familiar with them, but I felt some kind of enlightment each time Sensei and Aiko San went into it.

***Project your energy to the opponent*** -- From the body center through the kamai arms, if you don't, you are one rhythm behind, you have to decide, confirm and then move, breath reaction without interference of the brain is not possible.

Projecting your energy include extending the kamai arms to the opponent, within the functional range, that give you bigger territory, and more space for your game, strategy.

# HAL SHARP

## THE TITANS OF THE KODOKAN

### Sumiyuki Kotani

Sensei Kotani was the ultimate person. In the 1930s, Japan needed a wrestler in his weight division to represent the country in the Olympics. Kotani was not a wrestler, but he was extremely good on the ground. He was trained in Olympic wrestling rules, and he went on to win the bronze medal. He was an excellent teacher because of the way he talked, the way he communicated with the students, and his ability to see what the student was doing wrong and immediately correct it—and always with a warm smile on his face.

Kotani became very close friends with the head of wrestling at the University of California, Berkeley. They brought a judo team and a lot of good will to judo tournaments. His friend at Berkeley helped to get judo into the AAU and eventually into the Olympics. Uchida asked him: What do we need to to do to be accepted in the AAU?" and he answered: "the first thing is weight divisions." Uchida had to convince the top people at the Kodokan to have weight divisions. Remember that at that time there were no weight classes in judo. It took a lot of hard work to convince the masters to include weight divisions. Once inside the AAU, judo got big, which eventually opened the door to the Olympics.

## Chu Kawakami

He was a very quiet man. He started his judo in the 1800s. When you did mat work with him, all that you could do was move your eyeballs! He could easily control your body at will. He was terrific in all techniques, but his footwork was exceptional. He was the man who taught me bojutsu...but just for fun.

When he was young, his older brother died of an illness, and he promised to become the best judoka ever. He took a pledge to have a super body and be super-healthy and strong. He loved sumo and bojutsu. In his town of Mito, a teacher came from the Kodokan and taught him judo. That's how he started. His physical build was amazing.

One day a group of masters came to Tokyo to demonstrate jiu jitsu. All of them practiced with the young Kawakami and he threw them all over. The jiu jitsu masters were so impressed that they asked him to go back with them and teach them. He became the captain of the judo and sumo teams at the Meiji University. Meiji was one of the strongest martial arts universities in those days. On another occasion, a member of an Agriculture Department came to Sensei Kano and asked for a judo teacher. Sensei Kano sent Kawakami. He went and became the teacher/sensei for judo—and at the same time a regular student at the University. It was a strange situation for him!

## Shinzo Takagaki

Takagaki was a very bright man and one of the main instructors at the Kodokan. He was a great technician. One day he approached me and asked if I could help him to write his book. He handed down to me an old manuscript he had written in India more than 20 years before. The manuscript was brilliant, but it was very difficult to read. For each technique, he had a great explanation of how and when to apply it, depending on the opponent's body movement at that specific time. It was brilliant, the way he analyzed and dissected every technique and the proper timing to apply it.

We had a great relationship, and he was a person with a very keen sense of humor. One day I asked him about 'kiai.' He looked at me and said: "I am going to tell you a story. During the war, the Japanese government thought it was a good idea that women were trained to defend the country. They took them to a training camp and gave each one a spear. At the other side of the field were some dummies that women should attack with the spear. The instructor yelled 'kiai' and the women started running across the field screaming 'yayaya.' They fell to the ground exhausted before reaching the dummies! So that's what I think of kiai. Keep your mouth shut!"

## Kiyoshi Kobayashi

He was only a few years younger than I and one of the youngest instructors at the Kodokan. He had a perfect body for judo, was an excellent technician, and his English was very good because he worked for the U.S. Special Forces in Japan. He was great at showing you the proper form of each technique. Of course, when you work with someone that good, you are the one being thrown all the time! The good thing about it is that you learn to 'feel' their bodies in combat. I may add that it probably was Kobayashi who really influenced me. The way he moved his body in fighting, the smoothness, the timing, the relaxation...everything was there.

At one point, I was struggling with one particular throw, so I went and asked for advice: "Sensei, I am trying to do it, but it doesn't work for me." And he answered: "Don't try. Just do it!" What a breakthrough that was for me. I didn't *try* anymore...and it worked.

Another anecdote concerns the time we worked out together the whole day. We were exhausted and it was a hot summer night. Kobayashi always threw me at will with his uchi-mata. I could never stop this technique when he applied it to me. So that night, when I felt it coming, I knew it was going to happen. I didn't fight it and...I stopped him cold without even trying! He was shocked...and I was, too. I asked him to do it again. And he really tried to throw me again and nothing happened. I realized that by not even trying to be defensive, you can prevent being thrown if you have the right posture, balance, and relaxation.

It was with him that I ended up writing a best-seller book called *The Sport of Judo*. It was the first technical book. I wrote the descriptions and took the photos. Kobayashi posed for the pictures. After that, all the Japanese at the Kodokan though I was a great author!

## Yakahiko Ishikawa

He was a marvelous man and a two-time Japan champion. He was the youngest person to become a *shihan* (teacher's teacher) in the Kodokan. He used to teach at the Tokyo Police Academy, where I got to practice with him. One day, Ishikawa came to me and asked me to help him to write his book. The pictures were already taken, and he wanted me to write the text and the captions. We spent many hours together getting the book ready, and one of his most important teachings was the power of the mind. He fought the great Kimura. In a previous match, he was fighting the legendary Daigo and became injured. Daigo smashed Ishikawa's testicles when trying to throw him with uchi-mata. Ishikawa continued fighting and beat Daigo. He should have gone to the hospital then, but he decided to stay there and fight the great Kimura. The first match with Kimura was a draw. Both fighters were trying to feel each other out and sense the right time to attack. The fought the second round (extension) and it still was a draw. Sensei Mifune declared a 'dual-championship'! Right after bowing, Ishikawa collapsed and had to be taken to the hospital. He couldn't even stand...if he wasn't at the mat fighting. That's how mentally strong he was.

### Kyuzo Mifune

He was a small man but very powerful, and a classic judo man. He was at the Kodokan every single day and trained in the classes. He was an old man at that time and I am sure they were cooperating with him, but watching him move so smoothly and relaxed against opponents with 60 pounds more than him was amazing. He controlled bigger guys with his grips. I remember that a great French judoka named Maurice attempted to throw him, and Sensei Mifune spun around and jumped on his back like a monkey, and then threw Maurice down!

One day, we had a tournament of a Japanese team against an American team. Sensei Mifune was there and did a demonstration of judo form. I was the captain of my team and I fought the captain of the Japanese team to a draw. After the fight, Sensei Mifune came and asked me to become his student, which was very unusual. I politely begged off. I didn't have time in my days to include another training session. I was working full time and training the rest of the day. Every day. Seven days a week. I was writing all these books and I had no time on my hands.

Looking back, I think refusing the opportunity to become a personal student of Sensei Mifune was something I shouldn't have done. What a great opportunity I missed!

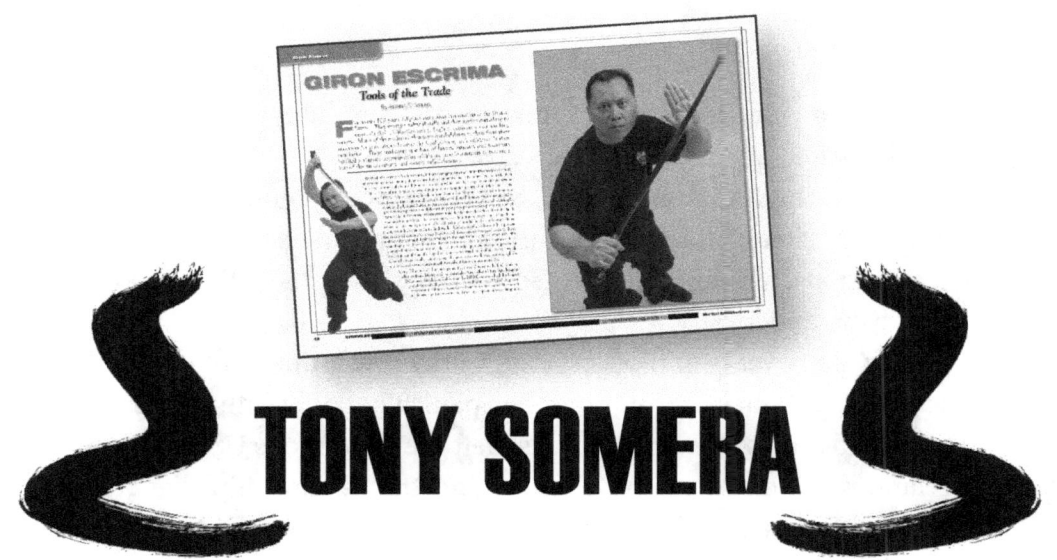

# TONY SOMERA

## COMING TO AMERICA

In the mid-1560s, the Philippine Islands became a territory of Spain. During the nearly 333 years of Spanish occupation the Philippines would go through many small revolutions in an attempt to regain their freedom from the Spanish imperialism. For instance, in 1892 a small body of young Filipino leaders secretly banded together and started to form and organize other groups of Filipino patriots with the aim to begin a coordinated struggle to retake their native homeland. This was the beginning of the Katipunan. The Katipunan was a Philippine revolutionary society founded by anti-Spanish Filipinos in Manila in 1892, which aimed primarily to gain independence from Spain by any means necessary including armed revolution. The word 'Katipunan" means simply "association" but the complete official name of this revolutionary force was "Kataastaasang, Kagalang-galangang Katipunan," or "The most high and honorable society of children of the Nation".

In order to gain membership to this secret society it was first thought out by the leader Andres Bonifacio to recruit within a "triangle" system. The triangle system of recruiting would start as such, the tip of the triangle would know the other two members, but the other two did not know each other. However, at the end of a year the system was abolished after proving to be too clumsy and complicated. A new system of initiation was then adopted which was modeled after existing Masonic rites. The new way to become a member of the Katipunan would be through completion of a set of initiation rites, resembling those of established Masonic organizations, which were created to test the applicant's courage, patriotism, and loyalty.

After many years of bloody struggle, the revolution was a limited success. Freedom was won from the Spanish but only with help from the United States. Once the Spanish left the continuous US presence became resented by many Filipinos and the relationship that was once helpful for the Philippines turned violent. It was only after a final short but bloody war with the United States of America, and not until well after the turn of the 20th century, that the Philippines would gain her independence. The US presence remained, but at an acceptable level for both the US and the Filipinos.

Mainly for economic and social reasons many young Filipino men began to travel to the United States beginning in the 1906 to 1932. This first wave of young Filipino men that came from the Philippines to America were truly sons of the Revolution. This early and sustained influx of Filipino culture set the stage for Filipino inclusion in what would become the thousands of young men that would make up and be counted as America's greatest generation, the WWII generation. These men came with a hopeful attitude and the revolutionary experience of life to make their dreams into reality.

However, life in American soon proved to be equally as difficult to the life they left because of discriminatory feelings within America for these young Filipino men.

Filipinos that travel to American would find out that life would not always be a land of opportunity but could be a land of cruelties and racism. But much like their forefathers of the Katipunan these young men would not be easily defeated. They wanted to belong to a greater America. One of the ways they were able to gain access to American society was to recreate and partake in established international fraternal organizations by banding together and forming their own groups of Filipino Masonic Lodges.

These Filipino Masonic groups formed their own secret social and society groups, with a focus on the working classes. Within these groups the Filipino immigrants created enclaves of brotherhood, friendship, and community. To this day there are still these same Filipino Masonic lodges that still carry out the same rituals and ceremonies that were practiced during the days of the Katipunan. These were the young men, in the Masonic groups, who would train and pass on behind the locked doors of the temple the martial arts of the revolution; the warrior arts of the Katapunan.

And out of these Masonic orders would grow the many modern day Filipino Martial Art Icon's that Martial Art giant Guro Dan Inosanto would seek out. His discovery revealed a hot bed of Filipino Martial art masters residing in his own hometown of Stockton California. Men like Angle Cabalas, Joe Papaco, Leo M. Giron, Jesus Corallas, Juanito Lacoste, Pasqual Ovales, Gilbert Tenio Victorino Ton, the eldest at 109 years young, and many more, who had made the journey from the Philippines to the US for the chance of a better life for themselves and their families.

# FILIPINO GENERATION: GROWING UP IN AMERICA

The years 1906 through 1932 saw the first wave of young Filipino men coming to the United States mainly to work as farm laborers. These young men came to America with little or no money with them and only what they were wearing as they left home in the Philippines, with maybe one change of clothing. As they went to their new job's most did not know exactly what they really would be doing in the farms and fields of central California and other US agricultural centers. Most did not know anything about asparagus, celery, or lettuce, but through hard work they would help create the agricultural giant of the Central California Valley, including the San Joaquin valley and the Sacramento-San Joaquin River Delta, that even now feeds much of the US and world population. However, it was not an easy path by any means for these early Filipino emigrants.

In their quest for a better life many young Filipino men saw America as the land of opportunity. After the Philippine Revolution of 1896-1898, and the Philippine-American War of 1899-1902 the country became a recruiting station for the US labor market and was inundated with labor contractors sent by the large agriculture facilities in the US. Filipino labor was in very high demand by the large farm companies because of the hard work ethic held and demonstrated by Filipinos.

Unfortunately, many of the American labor contractors turned out to be unscrupulous businessmen and many young men were lured into labor contracts which were often unfair and discriminatory. The sales pitch made telling of excellent working conditions and of the great wealth to be made were, at best, misleading promises that did not materialize once the relocation from the Philippines was finished and the work in the US was started.

For instance, often the migrating worker had to take a loan from the contractor just to make the move to the US which automatically put the worker in debt to the contractor. The average labor contract would last 2 to 4 years, but often times much longer because in the small print the contract made the labor last, "until their debt was paid."

Many of these young men would come to America with little or no money with them and only what there were wearing and maybe one change of clothing. As they would go to their newfound job's they would be unaware of what they would really be doing. Most if not all of them do not know what asparagus, celery or lettuce were.

Harvesting Asparagus would be the training ground for them to master their Martial Arts skills with the very tool they used every day to cut and harvest the asparagus, the Asparagus Knife. Depending on the height of the man, the type of soil and what type of asparagus would determine the type of asparagus knife. The knife has a short wooden handle that is connected to a steel rod with average length of 24 inches that ends in flat, razor-sharp tip. The ringing sound of steal on steal could be heard far off in the hidden corners of the asparagus camps as the secret escrima masters played the ancient Philippine warrior arts of their homeland away from prying eyes. You would be able to hear the clanging of metal against metal, thrusting, poking, sounds of the air being cut and hands parrying and slapping their townmates hand to the side. What is very common is for any of these young Filipino men would do is too be very quiet about their knowledge of what they knew about martial arts. If others would know many times they would be challenged or if other cultures would find out they would be an easy target of a group fight in which was very easy anyway because of their race.

Other times were more simple and quiet. These young men would stay in their camp, playing cards, washing clothes, or telling stories of back home in the Philippines. They would tell stories about their families as lonely young men will often do.

After working long hard hours during the week in the fields many of the young Filipinos would travel into Stockton, California to visit their friends or town mates and to try to find a little entertainment. This common search for community involvement or just the joys of "big city" life were the seeds of the "Little Manila" experience to come.

Also, in later years many of these same men would rush to join the U.S. Army during the outbreak of World War II to help recover their native homeland of the Philippine Islands. They would become heroes and return to America to start a new life and take a second chance of becoming part of American society.

## FILIPINO DREAMS COME TRUE

On April 1, 1942, the First Filipino Infantry was formed in San Luis Obispo. Every student of history knows of the bombing of Pearl Harbor, Hawaii on December 7, 1941, but few know that on the next day, December 8, 1941, the Imperial Japanese also bombed the US and Filipino forces in Manila Bay, Philippines. The attack was very effective and devastating for the allied forces and the foreign invaders soon took over the Philippines forcing the American and Philippine military out of the Philippines to relocate to other strong holds in the hope to live to fight another day. These events would inspire Filipinos living in America to petition for the right to serve in the United States military. After a hard political fight on January 2, 1942, President Franklin Roosevelt signed a law revising the selective service act. Filipinos were now able to join the U.S. Armed forces and many thousands of Filipino volunteers would rush to join the U.S. Armed forces in hopes of help in the recapture of their native homeland the Philippine Islands. There were so many Filipino recruits rushing to enlist, that orders were given to form the famous 1st Filipino Infantry Regiment that was formed in Salinas, California on July 13, 1942. Filipino recruits continued to volunteer in increasing numbers, so much so that the 2nd Filipino Infantry Regiment was formed on November 21, 1942, at Camp Cooke,

California. During one of the largest mass naturalization ceremonies at Camp Beale, California in 1943, Filipino American soldiers from the 1st Filipino Infantry Regiment were sworn in as United States Citizens. Although it would fulfill a lifetime dream of becoming an American citizen for many of these young Filipino men, citizenship came at a price. They were inducted into the military, naturalized as US citizens, and then off to war they went! The price was high, but none flinched from their duty to their country, the United States, or to their homeland, the Philippines.

It was out of these thousands of members of the 1st and 2nd Filipino Infantry Regiments that then commander and leader of the Pacific theater, General Douglas MacArthur, would hand select men to form a small group of secret elite commando group. These commandos were assigned to send back vital information setting the foundation for the retaking of the Philippine Islands. This secret group of elite fighting men was known as the 978th Signal Service Company. All became highly skilled in jungle survival, jungle fighting and were experts in the Filipino Martial arts of Escrima, Arnis and Kali. These special fighting men were dropped off behind enemy lines by secret submarines nearly one year before any American soldier landed on Philippine soil. Their assignment was top secret and has only recently been declassified. Their mission objectives were so secret and important that even at the time their orders were to "take no prisoners" in any encounter with the enemy. Bahala Na was their slogan, "Come what may".

The secret commandos would travel through the jungle and collect vital information such as the location of the Japanese military and the intricate troop movements. The commandos would also relay back to base their estimates of Japanese supplies and send eyewitness accounts of how the enemy was treating the local citizens, all in an effort to prepare the US intelligence forces and military units for the bloody battles to win back the Philippine islands.

Specifically, the 978th Signal Service members would send back this needed information through Morse code to Allied Headquarters. Often the commandos would encounter the enemy and be forced to use their own cultural martial art of Escrima Arnis Kali to defend themselves from by swinging their bolo knifes or machetes to silently cut down the enemy forces. No American commando could allow himself to be captured because this would be proof for their enemy that American commandos were already on Philippine soil preparing for the invasion by General MacArthur, the 1st and 2nd Filipino Infantry Regiment, and the entire US invasion force.

When the final invasion came it was a great allied success in no small part because of the efforts of these men from the 978th Signal Company. These highly skilled commandos trained in the Filipino Martial Art of Escrima Arnis and Kali were the first of their kind in American Military history.

These first-generation Filipinos came to America and set the standard for future generations. During WWII many earned their right to citizenship, and many made the ultimate sacrifice for that right. These men were proud Filipino Americans and also proud Filipino Fraternal Lodge members, like Leo M. Giron, Leon Ancheta, Secundio Bucol, Victorino Castillo, Raynaldo Domingo, Antonio Dizon Felicitas, Monico Luis, Juan Peralta, Ventura Serquinia, Cornelio Supnet, to name only a few of thousands that were there. These were some of the men who became known in time as "America's Greatest Generation."

## WHAT HAS BEEN LEARNED?

During the many years of our forefathers struggles and sacrifices they have paved the way in which we now know as our fathers of Filipino martial arts, this that bridges our generation to our fathers' generation and our heritage to our fathers' heritage and our fathers' way of life to our own way of life starts a new chapter in Filipino Martial Arts. All that has been pass down to us, the many hours of learning, the many hours of listening, the many ours of loving the very art that has influenced Americas greatest generation. We now are the caretakers of this ancient way of life and their ancient martial art.

Because of our interest and the wellness to try and understand our own culture. We need to ask the question and try to bring the knowledge and history of what our fathers had to endure. This was not an easy task; our fathers did not want to reveal the cruelties of a nation. They remain quiet, hardworking, proud, passionate, dedicated to their families, dedicated to their beliefs, and dedicated to their commitments. Many of them would say that they were also the "best looking" and the best dancers, and many would admit the best lovers, but very rarely would they brag about their skill in the Filipino martial arts.

What would we learn from these "Supermen," men that were thrown into manhood after leaving their families at such a young age, many in their teens to chase their dreams of being Americans, of being wealthy, being successful and being of family?

When we would call them uncle, manong (elder), ninog (godfather) and now today we are the uncles, we are now the manongs and we are now the ninogs. As time has quickly advanced, we are thrust into a new role for us but an old role for our uncles. They made it look so easy; their movements like swans that move in the water effortlessly -- a role which we would never have seen ourselves, a role in which we are now the elders, and we are the guros the manongs and now the ninogs.

Through the Filipino martial arts, they have taught us our history and our culture. By teaching us the techniques of self-defense they teach us the reasons why we call it a roof block or inside block. This culture of the art is the culture of a people. To learn more about our forefathers, we learn the Filipino martial arts. So, we take the time to listen, learn and love.

In order to continue this legacy of our forefather we must open our hearts to share what they have guarded by our forefathers for so many years, this the art that was held in such high regards and the highest of secrecy even their family members did not even know of the highly skilled art that they possessed.

We now have the role of sharing the art with those that would like to learn more about the greatest generation. We are the caretakers of Filipino martial arts this culture of a proud people and the teaching of our history that is deeply rooted by the soil of our forefathers known as the ancient ones. How do we do this? By the same tools our teachers had taught us, through the martial arts? We will tell the stories as they were told to us; we teach the Filipino martial art of self-defense as they were taught to us. And as we teach the art of self-defense as we teach our history and culture through the stories that we were taught. How do we do this, easy one movement at a time, one story at a time, one chapter of history at a time? This until it is time for our students to continue and to fulfill the legacy in which they will now be the new uncles, manongs and ninogs they will become the new legacy of Filipino martial arts, until it is time for the cycle will continue and repeat. So, who is next? Who will be up for the challenge? Who will take on the responsibility, who will be the next? Will this be your legacy?

## ESCRIMA LODGE

Filipino Martial Arts have been around for many generations and are as old as the history of the Philippines. Because of the deep cultural stresses from the Spanish occupation of the islands, the Filipino Martial Arts became a hidden and a secret treasure for the practitioners who had to practice the arts in secret. Since 1596, our forefathers were forced to practice the art by moonlight or candlelight to avoid persecution or even death at the hands of the Spanish regime. Later, the secret Filipino Martial Arts were used by the revolutionary forces and helped to liberate the Philippines from the Spanish who occupied the Philippines for more than 330 years

The revolutionary society was and is now known as the Katipunan. It was a secret society organized along Masonic lines; through skillful use of politics and warfare on varying fields of battle, it achieved its desire and obtained independence from Spain. The Katipunan would be the model and catalyst for later Filipino organizations to come, as Filipinos once again were forced to band together for strength and support in the new fields of America. Here, the determination and power gained through knowledge of the Filipino Martial Arts will again show its usefulness in liberating the Filipinos who keep the secrets of the arts.

After independence from Spain, and throughout the colonization by America, or what was called the new beginning of an American territory, the Philippines became a natural recruiting ground for large American labor corporations looking for a cheap labor source to work in the fields of the U.S. In the early 1900s, for many reasons, these offers of work at first appeared very attractive to young Filipino men who were looking to create a new and better life for themselves in a new country. But the rewards were long in coming and hard to win. The recruited laborers did backbreaking stoop labor for low wages for years and suffered greatly to create the bright future of their dreams. The labor corporations, in order to maximize the profits from the field work, would force the Filipino laborers to live in substandard housing in labor camps that had little or no running water or heat during the winter. These young Filipino men also would face racism and prejudice in order to maintain their dreams of a life of riches in the newfound home of America. However, through industriousness and perseverance Filipinos thrived in the new environment and began a journey to make themselves the equal of any citizens of the United States. For many of these first-generation Filipinos, the beginning of the journey started at El Dorado Street (the street of gold) in Stockton, California.

As the different Filipino groups began to solidify and occupy the area of Stockton, many social obstacles became obvious to them. For instance, Filipinos could note vote or own property at this time in the U.S. As in the old days of the Katipunan, they decided to form many different clubs, associations, organizations, and Masonic lodges that would be a unique feature of Filipino American society. The lodges became a place to conduct social affairs and business that the first-generation Filipinos could not conduct in other ways within the society of the time.

The "Big Three" Secret Filipino fraternal orders, as many Filipinos would refer to them, were the Caballeros de Dimas Alang Lodge, Grand Oriente Filipino Lodge, and the strongest and most powerful lodge, the Legionarios del Trabajo Lodge. The first of these lodges was started in 1924 in San Francisco. And on February 11, 1927, the Francisco Daguhoy Lodge was formed in Stockton California, which by that time was home to thousands of Filipinos.

Behind the locked and guarded doors, many of these first-generation Filipinos would "play" or train in their ancient Filipino Martial Art of Escrima Arnis. It was common in the early days that these young Filipinos would spend a Sunday afternoon after their secret lodge meetings to play and practice sharing the Martial Arts of their forefathers.

After the outbreak of World War II, many of these Filipino men would enlist into the United States Army to serve and fight to retake their native homeland the Philippine Islands. More than 12,000 Filipino men would join and create the 1st and 2nd Filipino Infantry. Out of these 12,000 men, General Douglas MacArthur selected nearly 900 to serve as his secret commandos; one of these men was Sergeant Leo M. Giron of Bahala Na Martial Arts Association. He would credit his membership in the Filipino Lodge, and his continued Martial Arts practice there, with much of his success in his military roll which helped to liberate his homeland.

It has been my pleasure to also be a member of this same Filipino Lodge for nearly 30 years. My Illustrious Brother Leo M. Giron, who became the founder of the Bahala Na Filipino Martial Arts Association after the war and his lodge brother, my father, Illustrious Brother Chester S. Somera Sr., both sponsored me to join this ancient brotherhood that maintains an active lodge to this day. In the Legionarios del Trabajo Lodge of Little Manila, Stockton, California, well over 100 years has gone by, with the secret rituals and ceremonies continuing within the lodge and through its members. To this day, you can find first-generation Manongs who remain after their regular lodge meetings to visit upstairs behind locked and guarded doors. You can hear laughing, talking, and sticks clanging as the ancient and secret Filipino Martial Art continues strong. As with the ancient Katipunan, the Filipino Lodge offers a model to the community and shows the new generation how to properly maintain the commitment and dignity forged by practicing the secret Filipino Martial Arts in the Escrima Lodge.

## ESCRIMA – THE HIDDEN TREASURE

It has been more than 30 years since Dan Inosanto introduced the world to the Filipino Martial Arts, and it took Guro Dan nearly 15 years before that to learn the martial arts of his ancestors. Encouragement from his late teacher and good friend Sifu Bruce Lee too seek out his roots of martial arts and to learn of the many unsung master in the arts was the mission of young Inosanto. Without a doubt, his groundbreaking book, *The Filipino Martial Arts as taught by Dan Inosanto*, would open the door and would be the reference book and inspirational guide for many students and teachers to seek out the masters and the many different styles of Filipino Martial Arts that Inosanto featured in this now hard to find collector's book. This powerful book was a wealth of information that exposed thousands of readers to an art that was lost from Filipino society here in America. This book truly would inspire countless readers to research further and to seek additional information on the Filipino Martial Arts.

The names of humble men that the world has never heard of before would become Filipino Martial Arts icons, a kind of Superstars to America and eventually to the world. These men also would become role models, father figures, and men who would change the life destinies of thousands upon thousands of people and would find a newfound respect for the Filipino community and its hidden Martial Arts.

The Filipino Martial Art treasures Inosanto uncovered for America and the world would be men by the names of Pepe Montano Arca and Vincent Arca, escrima instructors who came to the Hawaiian Islands and eventually would accompany the first Filipino immigrants who, without knowing it, would keep the art alive:

Pepe Montno Arca was Inosanto's grandfather; Master Pedro Apilado was known as one of the top fighters and would serve as head referee in the Hawaiian Islands in the days when full contact stick fighting was done without armor; Master Apilado also was a student under the great champion of the Northern Philippines, Santiago Toledo; the famous Canete family would have the largest escrima school in the Philippines; Grand Master Angel Cabales, considered the man responsible for the exposure of escrima to the American public, was most effective with the short stick and was a true master of the art; Master Regino Ellustrisimo a master in the Bohol method of escrima; Grand Master Leo M. Giron, a man with a wealth and knowledge of the combative art of arnis escrima whose combat proven style was tested during World War II for more than a year in the jungles of the Philippines (Inosanto would consider Leo Giron to be his second father).

Also, Grand Master Juanito Lacoste, considered by Inosanto to be the most well-rounded escrimador and a master of stick, dagger, long blade, and empty hands; Grand Master Ben Largusa, the most all-around Filipino Kali martial artist, according to Inosanto, and a student of the great Grand Master Floro Villabrille, champion of countless matches in the Philippines and Hawaii; Master Pasqual Ovales, the grandson of the great Santiago Toledo, a master in the Toledo-Collando style of escrima that uses the long stick and "escala" (stroking pattern) of training; Grand Master Braulio Pedoy, who taught escrima but also the awareness of the history of the Filipino martial art and culture; Master Narrie Babao, who holds the title of champion in the first weapons sparring tournament held in the United States; Grand Master Lucky Lucay Lucay, whose expertise is in "Sikara (Filipino Foot Fighting) and Panatukan (Filipino Boxing).

Also on the list are Master Dentoy Revillar, senior student of Grand Master Cabales and the first to train with both Cabales and Giron, making him highly efficient in both the short and long stick methods, and an organizer in the first escrima academy open to the public in the United States; Grand Master Jack Santos, who serves as an advisor to the Filipino Kali Academy in Torrance; Master Max Sarmiento, a man gifted with the use of empty hands, dagger, and knives, who was one of the first, along with his wife Lynn, to help organize the Cabales academy, the first open to the general public in the United States; Grand Master Telesporo Subing Subing, an expert in the Moro style and double stick style of the Southern Philippines; Grand Master Sam Tendencia, who trained under the great Deogracias Tipace in the Philippines and is expert in the art of Filipino nerve pinching and Hilot (massage); Grand Master Gilbert Tenio, who trained in many Filipino arts and was founder of the Tenio Dequedas system in Stockton, California; Grand Master Floro Villabrille of Hawaii, known as the undefeated champion in countless escrima and kali matches in the Philippines and Hawaii; And Grand Master Viliabrille, who at that time was the head of the Kali organization.

Add to the group Grand Master Richard Bustillo, who during that time was Inosanto's training partner and also was responsible for promoting and preserving the Filipino Martial Arts and Jeet Kune Do; Ed Parker, Inosanto's instructor in Kenpo karate and in Inosanto's opinion a "true Master," And last but not least the great Sifu Bruce Lee, who was Inosanto's instructor and good friend who guided him to the art of Jeet Kune Do. Under Sifu Lee's tutelage, Inosanto gained the educational eye to find out what was functional in the Martial Arts. Lee also encouraged Inosanto to look for his roots in the arts and to continue until he has found all that is useful.

Guro Dan Inosanto's book *The Filipino Martial Arts* was so powerful that many individuals followed in his footsteps in researching the Filipino Martial Arts. It is a virtual encyclopedia of unadventured knowledge exposed to the public for our own consumption. Thousands more would experience the art itself and would test the very foundation of the applications of techniques.

After all the research and information publish on the Filipino Martial Arts, you would think that we would have exhausted our wealth of individuals who would play the art of our forefathers. Digging a little deeper in my hometown that once was called "Little Manila" because of the huge Filipino population, Stockton, California, would be the small farming community that to this date still would have a few more hidden treasures.

These men now are the last of their kind, the ancient ones who set the foundation for us to have a better life here in America. These men are still active; some teaching the Filipino Martial Arts and others would be more than happy to demonstrate and tell stories about the many different styles of the Filipino arts.

Jesus Ragail Corales was born in Narvacan, Illocos Sur Philippines on December 25, 1910. Like Giron, Corales arrived in America in 1929. He immediately took a bus from San Francisco to Stockton and would work in the fields and farm labor camps in the San Joaquin valley. Due to his working in the many different Filipino labor camps, he would be exposed to a number of Filipino escrimadors. Corales would take the time to play or train in the art after a hard day's work in the fields.

He remembers that "after working so hard during the day, in the afternoon, during a cool delta breeze, my town mates and I would sit outside next to the barn away from everyone and play with our asparagus or sticks knives. I can remember the quickness of the weapon, but no one would get hurt." Corales' teacher was a man by the name of Hilario Ramolete from Santa Catalina Illocos Sur, Philippines. Corales played the cabaroan or new system of arnis escrima. His specialty was the cinco tero style or five strikes, and also the redonda style or circular striking, and close quarter hand-to-hand combat. Corales was a member of the 1st Filipino Regiment and served in the invasion of Lyette, Philippines, during World War II. Of the four in this article, Corales had the most energy. At times, it was difficult to interview him and also play with him because he would keep moving. He would explain his current movement and would already be demonstrating the next movement. His knowledge of the Filipino arts of self-defense is unlimited as his energy to demonstrate it. Corales is also a member of one of the "Big Three" Filipino Lodges of America, The Caballeros de Dimas Alang.

Joe Arruejo Pacpaco was born in Vigan Illocos Sur Philippines on November 24, 1909. He arrived in San Francisco in 1930 on the President Jefferson and went to Stockton by boat through the San Joaquin Delta. As did most of the Filipinos who arrived during this first wave, Pacpaco took his first job cutting celery. He also worked in the many different Filipino farm labor camps in the San Joaquin Valley and occasionally took work in Marysville and Yuba City, California. Pacpaco's teacher was a man by the name of Francisco Realin from Santa Catalina, Philippines. His system of play is the cabaroan or new style of arnis escrima. His style is Larga Mano or long hand/weapon style; he also plays abierta or open body style of arins escrima and he has an empty hand style that is similar to cadena de mano. Pacpaco's Larga mano is different from Leo Giron's larga mano. Pacpaco incorporates the abierta (open) body footwork to his larga mano. Pacpaco's footwork is attributed to his natural open foot movement. Joe Pacpaco has a unique gift of playing. He is left-handed, very graceful and to the point. Pacpaco and Giron would play together in the Giron's basement and at the Filipino Grand Lodge just half a block from both Pacpaco and Giron's house and a block from Inosanto's house. Pacpaco was the person that Giron had in mind to train the "killer" style to Dan Inosanto. Pacpaco is also a life member of the Legionarios Del Trabajo and member of the Worshipful Mabini Lodge with over 60 years of service to the Filipino lodge.

Victorino Ton was born June 29, 1895, in Lapaz Abra, Philippines. He arrived in Hawaii in 1924 and worked in the pineapple and sugar cane plantations for six years. After completing his work contract in Hawaii, he moved on to Stockton, California in 1930. Ton's first job in Stockton was cutting asparagus. To my knowledge, Victorino Ton is the oldest living arnis escrima player in America. At the time of this article Ton was 108 years old and lived at a Filipino lodge in Stockton, enjoying a very simple life, gardening, and playing cards. The first question he had for me was, "why are we so close?" and the second question was, "do I have a longer weapon"? This would lead me to believe he was a cabaroan (new style) escrimador. Ton plays the cinco tero (five strikes) and incorporates blocking and counter striking. He started playing with sticks in the Philippines at the age of 10; this would be 1905. This was without a doubt one of the most fertile times of escrimadors in Philippine history due to the Filipino revolution. Ton is truly a son of the revolution who fought against the Spaniards in the Filipinos' struggle to gain their freedom from Spain. Manong Ton also is a life member of the Legionarios del Trabajo in America and is a member of General Lim lodge with more than 60 years of service to the Filipino lodge.

I would like to mention a few factors that link these four incredible men together:

1. They all came to America during the first wave of Filipinos from the Philippines.
2. They all were farm laborers.
3. They all learned and still practice the Filipino Martial Arts.
4. They all are members of a Filipino Masonic Lodge.
5. They are all from Luzon, Philippines.

Amazingly enough, these hidden treasures are still with us today. My teacher, Grand Master Leo M. Giron, has encouraged to me to seek out the remaining masters or ancient ones of the Filipino arts.

Many thanks to our forefathers like Giron, Corales, Pacpaco, and Ton who endured so many hardships to make our life better. And for those Grand Masters and Masters of the arts, Cabalas, Elustrisimo, Giron, LaCoste, Largusa, Villarille, Canete, Tenio, Pedoy, Tabosa, Ovales, Santos, Revillar, Sarmiento, Lucaylucay, Babao, Paker, Subing Subing, Tendencia, (others that I have not mentioned please forgive me) and the legendary Bruce Lee.

And thanks to people like Inosanto, Bustillo, Lucaylucay, and Dentoy Revillar for helping our generation recognize our Filipino fathers and our heritage. The torch has been passed to us to continue with their work and to ensure the legacy of our forefathers will live on forever.

## SITUATIONS CHANGE

Any fighting style must essentially account for situational changes presented within the evolution of experienced combat. Responsible combatants must evolve and adapt to the acute needs of the battlefield as well as present practitioners of the style with enhanced training opportunities before going into any future conflict. This may be accomplished through diligent practice of the basic fundamentals of the art.

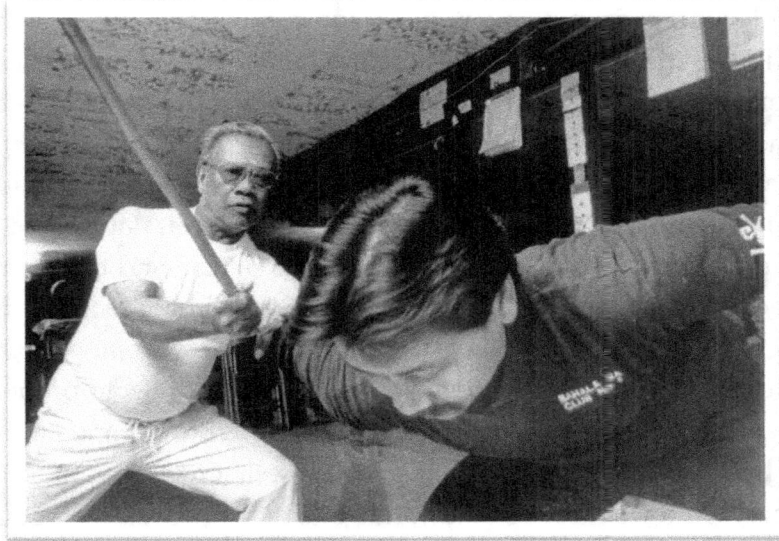

Upon survival of the encounter your mind will review and analyze your own fighting actions after each combat situation. When you do this you will be able to see clearly the changes or alterations that evolved during combat. Every encounter is different from any encounter experience before, and any experience in the future. Each evolution, whether it a new insight into the opponent's state of mind or his physical abilities, use or new type of weaponry, battle in an unknown environment or even subtleties in the elements such as terrain, wind, rain will need to be immediately processed and reviewed in time for complete success.

For instance, was the encounter during the day or during the night? What were the successful, or more importantly, the unsuccessful techniques or counters used and witnessed during engagement? This earned knowledge set is the secret knowledge of the warrior and it is this precious knowledge that is passed on between comrades, and among families and between brothers within the combative arts.

One common thread is that by nature the combat situation will change and so will the techniques and applications needed for success. This is because you cannot be certain that you will engage in a well-analyzed situation but must accept the risk of defeat if the wrong technique is implemented. In some situations, the style that you will use will be wrong and therefore fatal if you do not evaluate the terrain, the elements and most especially the ability of the opponent and instantaneously adapt.

Evaluation of terrain is important because a failure to recognize the uncertainties of the terrain may result in mission failure and be could easily become fatal. Evaluation of the nature and type of the opponent's weapon is important because if you do not evaluate the threat, for instance, if it is short or long, an edged weapon or a club of hard wood bahi or kamagong, you will not know how to properly counter the weapon. For instance, if he is using a short weapon would it not be to your advantage to use a longer weapon to keep at a safe distance? And would it be to advantage to apply proven techniques on your opponent if he has an edged weapon and you have an edged weapon? For instance, if you have the opportunity to block with the back or side of the edged weapon you will be able to maintain the integrity of you weapon and successfully counter the attack. But if you were to block the attack with the sharp edge of your bolo you would surely break or damage your weapon and invite disaster!

Often what we learn in our school or academy is a fixed pattern while the terrain we play on is among the most perfect of conditions. The training floor is free from debris, stones, rocks, roots, shrubs or fallen limbs from trees. The lights in the academy provide good illumination. The environment is dry and free from rain or snow. We are often wearing well-fitted clothing, maybe a special uniform, and eye protection along with form fitting shoes or boots. The most perfect conditions are comfortable and present a fine environment for study. However, such training environment may produce false product from our training, so a good practitioner needs to know both the perfect type of terrain or conditions to train and also the most difficult or most dangerous conditions to train. By training under various conditions, you will learn to correctly apply your style for combative advantage. This means we should incorporate training outside in the park, or perhaps in the parking lot, or even in a shed or furnished room.

For success we will need to understand and modify our body position and adapt and modify our footwork depending on the terrain. Everything will change under adverse conditions, and we need to understand that if we are in a perfect setting to train and the techniques we used, and the footwork and body position used, will change or modify when training in conditions that are dangerous or difficult. Just think if you were on a level and even floor, would your stance or footwork change if you were fighting on unnatural terrain or an uneven floor? What if you were sparing in the academy on a nice perfect floor or sparing in the field where there are rocks, potholes, slippery grass or if you were fighting in a muddy field? What if you were fighting on a stairway, on top of a car or over a desk? Will your strategy change? More than likely the answer is yes. So, the question then becomes what should you do and how will you handle the different action taken by your opponent under these different conditions? To best train in a traditional way learn the basics from your instructor and follow the direction given. This is the way to learn a style using the basics that your teacher will train you to do. These are known as the basic fundamentals of the art. Then we must take these basics and apply them in every different way possible to gain the widest knowledge of what will work or not work under changing situations. We should keep what works and discard what does not work.

A common goal for many fighting arts, and especially, within the Filipino Martial Arts, is to engrain within each student the ability to the apply techniques under stress. As everyone knows, all techniques work in practice, almost nothing works "for real". Training done between partners works well because we want to see what an "opponent" looks like as they prepare and execute an attack. How must a person stand to deliver an attack? What types of attacks can be delivered from a certain position? The options for the attacker are not unlimited, although in the gap preceding the engagement your mind can easily have you convinced you are dealing with unlimited attack possibilities. By gaining a demonstrated understanding through training of the attack options we may face based on the reasoned study of the physical abilities inherent in the attackers position we give ourselves the best chance to counter their actions.

On the other side, by playing the role of an "attacker" we are able to see what a defender does as a counter to our attack. We give ourselves a chance to see the options that the defender may have to counter our own movements and discover the limits to these counters as well. This give and take, attack and defense, training structure is a helpful tool because as partners we can begin to test each technique for weaknesses in its structure or in our application of it under pressure. Usually, it is the way we apply the technique that is the weak link, but through this partnership of practice we can correct mistakes and perfect our theories and assumptions through trial and error.

By acting out the different roles and situations available in attack and defend modules the student will be more able to adjust to situational changes in combat because he has specifically trained to adapt within his study of the basic, fundamental principles of the martial art.

## A HOMECOMING FOR GURO DAN INOSANTO

Once a year Grand Master Tony Somera of Bahala Na Giron Arnis Escrima sponsors one of the most highly shout after martial artist in the world. Guro Dan Inosanto makes his annual seminar stop in Stockton California the birthplace of Filipino Martial Arts in America. But is also unique is that Stockton is the birthplace of Guro Dan an icon himself in the world of Martial Arts. From his training of many of the mainstream Hollywood movie starts, like Denzel Washington in *The Book of Eli,* to Guro Dan's many appearances in a number of motion pictures and of course the famous appearance in Martial Art giant Bruce Lee's move such as the game of death to mention.

With many months of preparation, it all comes down to a great weekend of lessons of Filipino Martial arts, Filipino History, Filipino Culture and many of Guro Dan's childhood classmates, family and friends that come by to pay their respect to "Danny" or "boom boom" as they would address him. This seminar in Stockton holds a great deal of emotion and memories that every time an old friend or family member drops by a new chapter of history, or an old story of Guro Dan's childhood comes out from these meetings. This is what is called priceless by many of those that are lucky enough to be around while this is taking place.

As our first day begins, I drive to Guro Dan's hotel and pick up his assistants and Guro Dan for an early breakfast.

As the first day starts Guro Dan is in perfect form, revealing the history of what was at one time the Hub of Filipinos in America – Stockton, what is known as "Little Manila" worldwide (because of the it being the largest population of Filipinos in America, hence the largest population of Filipino Masters of Escrima Arnis Kali.) Many of Guro Dan's stories at the breakfast table would be of the early days of growing up in a neighborhood of mixed races in which no one would even pay any attention too.

Driving to our destination in which the two-day seminar would be held, Guro Dan would mention how Stockton has changed and how at the time he would get lost driving from street to street, trying to recall the names of the streets and remembering how Stockton has grown, with houses and strip malls are now that at one time this was all farmland, farmland that is the riches in the state of Californian. As we park the van, many onlookers and students of the Filipino Martial Arts are racing to get into the room in which Guro Dan would conduct his seminar.

Old friends would meet Guro Dan in the parking lot, greeting him and welcoming him back home. Handshakes and hugs with heartfelt greetings and the words of Guro Dan, "Wow, this is really Stockton weather; 100 degrees of heat," and remembering how it was to work in the fields of Stockton, California. As the day continues, Guro Dan's best friend from the old neighborhood and the early days would greet him before entering the seminar. "Billy," as Guro would call him -- they would talk about growing up in the southside of Stockton in which many of the Manong's Escrimadors would live. Filipino Martial Arts icons like Leo M. Giron, Juan Lacoste, Joe Pappaco, Angle Cabales and Victorino Ton. "Billy" would also talk about growing up with "Danny," playing on the same baseball team, basketball team, remembering there old and dear childhood friends and having the same teachers.

An introduction by Grand Master Tony Somera of the world famous Bahala Na Martial Arts and Giron Arnis Escrima Association, and with a huge roar and applause to greet the home grown and world-famous martial artist Guro Dan Inosanto, our formal salute that begins a day of memories of Filipino Martial Arts, Filipino history and a road to remember of Guro Dan's memories of growing up in Stockton. Guro Dan would start the seminar with several techniques, keeping his eye on his childhood friend, "Billy," with the anticipation of catching up of many years and of many memories. Guro Dan would work his way through the crowded room, helping the attending students until he would meet once again his childhood best friend "Billy." They would talk and laugh about the good old days in Stockton. Guro Dan would then rush back and call "time" and give another short history lesson of Stockton, show the next technique, and reveal early times of Stockton.

As the day continues, the door to the gym will open and in walks Guro Dan's two remaining aunties. The first one is Auntie Arca, wife of the late Albert Arca, in which is Guro Dan's mother, Mary Arca Inosanto. Also walking in is his first cousins Paul and Al and their children. Coming in also is Auntie Flora Arca Motto. This is the sister of Guro Dan's mother. Auntie Flora was the very first Filipino ever to be hired by the Stockton Unified School District. The room stops and Guro Run's over to embrace them with joy. This is truly a priceless moment in time.

Cameras and flashes take over as group shots of Guro Dan and his last remaining Aunties and cousins are taken. By this time stories and memories by Guro Dan's aunties are now taking over of Guro Dan or "Boom Boom's" childhood and early adult years. After a few minutes, Guro Dan rushes back to the head of the class and calls "time." He gives another short history lesson of his childhood and relates all of this to Filipino Martial Arts and honoring his teachers.

The next technique is now being given and is being shown to the room full of students, that is reflected in the technique that has not been shown in many years and is accelerated in the demonstration. As the first day comes to an end, Master Adrian of Tandez Martial Art Academy from Mountain View, CA, and Sifu Gonzalez of Western Martial Arts from Sacramento, CA, along with his students are all amazed that have been treated to a very special session of Guro Dan's own childhood history and his history of growing up in Stockton. Everyone in the room has been treated to the first day as not only a day of outstanding training by Guro Dan but also a day of history of Filipino culture, and also the personal life of Guro Dan.

As the second day begins the word must have spread throughout the San Joaquin Valley that Guro Dan is working his magic with many of his Filipino Martial Art teachers along with the history that only Guro Dan can teach. The lines are deep at the front door with the anticipation of Guro Dan walking up to the entrance door with all the knowledge of Filipino Martial Arts, but also the history of how it came to be; and even more exciting are the stories that Guro Dan will share of this early years in Stockton and the many masters of the Filipino Arts that he had discovered from this little town that is known as "Little Manila."

Once again, the room is packed with many students eager to learn from the world's greatest Filipino Martial Art historian and player. Grandmaster Art Mirlfor, who as a young man trained with Guro Dan during his training with Great Grand Master Angle Cables in Stockton, during the early years of research, was present with his school Knights of Escrima. With all eyes and ears ready to absorb what Guro Dan gives right away, Guro Dan picks up from yesterday's seminar. As the day begins, the room is full of eager students and in walks the Carrido family, in which Guro Dan grew up with.

As Guro Dan noticed the group of old friends that enter the room, a smile of joy takes over his face and with teary eyes Guro Dan rushes over to the Carrido family and embraces them all with hugs of joy. The first is Pat Carrido, the youngest sister about who Guro Dan would say, "When we were kids playing and during the time we would pick football teams, I would pick Pat first because she could catch and run faster than anyone." The next hug went to Gloria Carrido Nomuma, the retired Vice-Mayor of Stockton and the first Filipino every to hold this rank in city government. As Guro Dan goes to the next person, Coach Frank Carrido grabs Guro Dan to embrace him and share the good old times. Coach Frank Carrido is one of the greatest football coaches in our area and now is one of the most sought-after high school coaches in California.

What a great treat for everyone in attendance. Once again Guro Dan rushes to the front of the room and calls "time." As if his old town mates inspired Guro, his rate of play and intensity would be push to every ones limits. Guro Dan would review the technique and would explain the reason why this technique was done and why it was done nearly 100 years ago. By this time, Guro would not only give us one technique to review but several and at one time there was eight techniques to review. As the day moves forward, the door to the gym would open once again and in would walk Mel Suguitan, Jr. who was the father of Manong Mel Sr., which was one of Guro Dan's teachers.

It was only after Manong Mel, Sr.'s death that Mel, Jr. would be told by Guro Dan was his Escrima teacher, and Guro Dan's mother Mary Arca Inosanto would tell Mel Jr. of an encounter that Manong Mel Sr. had in Alaska, fighting off over 5 men that attacked him in which Manong Mel Sr. came out safe and sound, but Mary could not say the same for the men that attacked him. Mel Jr. is also one of the most sought-after choral teachers in the state of California. He is also famous for being in the all-Filipino singing group, "The Old Pinoys."

Mel Jr.'s wife, Addie Suguitan, was also present. Addie is also a who's-who of Stockton by being one of the Charter members of the Little Manila Foundation and an honored City of Stockton employee. Mel and Addie's Suguitan's daughters were also in attendance, with Tamara an MMA fighter, promoter, and writer along with sister Adrianna, an accomplished supporter of the Stockton Filipino Community. Along with the Suguitans, Pat Muraoka a member of the Filipino American Historical Society, would accompany family and the Stockton Buddhist Church which will host the largest Obon Festival south of Sacramento, California. Pat is also a supporter of the Filipino community and is involved with all that takes place with both historical societies.

Pat's son Alan was also there, with many accomplishments within the Stockton Asian communities and surrounding areas. After all the hugs and short stories of the early days of Stockton and Guro Dan growing up, many photos would be snapped and once again Guro Dan would rush back to the front of the class and call "time." Guro Dan would move on with the next technique with even more intensity. With a big smile on Guro Dan's face, he would reminisce about all of his visitors and would introduce them with rounds of applause. Amongst this day, we are also honored to have visitors like Master Carlito Bundoc of Mata Sa Bagyo Filipino Martial Arts Academy and Grand Master Max Pallen of Pallens Martial Arts, both coming to pay their respects and also train with the living legend, Guro Dan Inosanto.

What a great day that ended much too fast, with both days going by like it was in speed. To communicate this great weekend Guro Dan shared with us many of his childhood stories of growing up in Stockton along with speaking of the great Bruce Lee and many of his Filipino Martial Art teachers. As many of us know, Guro Dan is like a walking Google application that has endless information about martial arts in general, but also the love and respect of this teachers in which he gives all the recognition as he speaks about each technique that is given throughout both days.

Training with Guro Dan is an honor and privilege that all of us had experienced, and if you ever have the opportunity to train with this living legend Guro Dan Inosanto, this writer highly recommends this to any type of practitioner of the Martial Arts, for Guro Dan is a gift from God that has blessed us in a way that no other martial artist can describe or has given information so freely to all of us. The best time to visit Guro Dan is when he is in his hometown of Stockton, California, so that you can experience the things that all of has during his last visit here in the city nicknamed "Little Manila."

## BANDA-BANDA
## THE STAFF OF GIRON ESCRIMA

The Giron system of arnis/escrima has a staff system called *banda-banda*, meaning side-side. In the Filipino martial arts, the staff is thought by many to be "secret," as it is rarely taught to anyone. This is evidenced by the fact that most articles on arnis show only techniques with the single stick.

The Filipino staff generally is a length of rattan measuring six feet, with a diameter of one-to-two inches. In simple terms, *banda-banda* is a long-range weapon art that uses a two-handed grip to maximize striking power and force on impact. The Giron *banda-banda* staff system has approximately 70 basic moments, encompassing the elements of blocking, deflection, evasion, and direct striking.

The staff is used to put an opponent out of commission quickly. To use this weapon effectively, the practitioner must be strong and well-versed in the *estilo redonda,* or circular style of offense and defense. Since the staff is long, it is used most effectively in the street or the cleared area of a parking lot.

The Giron *banda-banda* system uses two staff grips. The first features two hands held at one end of the weapon. If you are right-handed, the right hand will be positioned above the left hand, and vice-versa. With this type of grip, the basic *cinco tero* pattern is used, along with the *redonda* style of striking. The blocking grip is used in much the same fashion. The theory behind this grip is that you must keep your opponent at bay, and only when the opponent closes the distance does the second grip comes into play. In this grip, your hands are held a shoulder's width apart, dividing the staff into thirds. Both of these grips are used for blocking, deflecting, redirecting, and direct striking to the opponent's body or weapon.

The striking patterns used with the staff vary, depending on the situation. Normally, strikes come from the traditional arnis striking patterns, known as *cinco tero* (five strikes) and *redonda* (circular strikes). In order to acquire the proper striking habit, each motion must be followed through to its completion. In other words, don't stop the strike on impact but aim past the target. Moreover, foot and body movements must work together to create the maximum amount of torque in each technique. Once these two striking sequences have been mastered, unorthodox movements can be developed based on the process of interpolation.

The novice also must learn how to relax and feel confident that the opponent's weapon may not necessarily inflict injury on him, and that such a painful experience can be avoided. Tenseness will result in slow reaction, impairing both timing and coordination. Until one becomes fairly skilled with the staff, one should not sacrifice safety by chancing an aggressive movement.

## LARGA MANO: THE WARRIOR STYLE

*Larga Mano* is one of the twenty styles of the Giron System of Arnis Escrima. Grand Master Emeritus Leo Giron defined Larga Mano by saying, "The term Larga Mano literally means "long hand," and implies the ability to extend one's reach. Reaching your opponent without jeopardizing safety is foremost because one can disable his enemy with less chance of getting hurt or killed. To employ this style, a practitioner must know how to use a longer weapon systematically. A person cannot just swing his longer weapon like a flail. It is an art and therefore must abide with the larga mano science. The practice of stretching far is the daily exercise of a larga mano practitioner. You need to understand the components of larga mano in order to maintain the control and accuracy of this combat.

## Basic Fundamentals of Larga Mano

***Body mechanics*** is an essential component of Larga Mano. When choosing the style of Larga Mano, the student must use proper body mechanics to use a weapon of such great length. Not only is a larga mano weapon extra long, but it also carries a significant increase in weight. Your entire body needs to work together in order to defend yourself. The feet need to be planted in a strong position in order to give you a solid foundation to strike. The legs need to balance and support the weight and force of your motion as you advance or retreat. Conditioning of your legs is mandatory in order to maintain your balance. Using your legs to stretch forward and back works in conjunction with operation of such a long weapon. Timing your legs with your hips also is necessary, much like a baseball pitcher when rotating his hips to deliver a pitch. The larga mano student must incorporate the rotation of his hips to deliver his ending strike to his opponent and his legs to retract the motion of his weapon in order to prepare himself for the next movement and oncoming enemies.

To simplify striking patterns, the larga mano system is adapted to only five strikes or what is called *cinco tero*. The striking patterns called cinco tero are taken from the term cabaroan, which means "new way" or "new style." The ancient warriors discovered that when swinging a long weapon, the first angle of attack is to the left side of the opponent targeting the base of the neck. Slicing down diagonally to the right side of the opponent's right leg, the return strike will target the opponent's right ankle and return to the original angle up to the opponents left side of the neck. The third strike will circle from the opponent's left side to the opponent's left ankle, striking up diagonally to the opponent's right-side base of the neck. The fourth strike will return in a downward strike to the opponent's right-side base of the neck, cutting back down to the chamber on the right side of your hip ready to deliver the fifth and final blow. The fifth strike is a thrust to the opponent's midsection, targeting the bellybutton. With the length and weight of the larga mano weapon, it can be used to cover all striking angles just by using cinco tero, and all that is needed is to lower your body to cover the mid and lower angles of attack.

**Terrain** is another essential component of Larga Mano. Naturally, the perfect terrain or area to use larga mano is in an area that is open and free from any obstacles that might interfere with the cinco tero kabaroan strikes. Also, the ground should be flat and free from any obstacles. But this is not always the case, as during World War II when then Sergeant Leo M. Giron would need to adapt to the different terrain when defending himself in the jungles of the Philippines. Giron would plant himself using the de fondo style of Giron Arnis Escrima and use the components necessary to gain the advantage to win in combat. Moving or jumping around could be very dangerous to you during an encounter. You may run the risk of twisting your ankle and falling down, cutting your own leg or falling down by losing your own balance. Grand Master Giron often would relate to us that terrain also may be your enemy if not used and thought of properly, but it can be your advantage if you know how to use it.

**Distance** is a major component of larga mano. Utilizing the length of your weapon is a must for any larga mano player. Keep in mind that even when using a shorter weapon, the concept of larga mano still is applied. Your body mechanics will apply, along with your striking pattern and the use of terrain fighting. But most importantly, your basic fundamentals will carry you through. You may have a shorter weapon but play larga mano by using all the basic fundamentals of a long weapon where applicable. Remember the true meaning of larga mano is using a longer weapon. While playing larga mano, keeping your distance is keeping you safe.

Finally, we must consider the fundamental of ***Timing.*** Timing your movement and strike to evade the attack of your opponent will allow for direct cuts into vulnerable targets of opportunity within the conflict.

In the middle of World War II, one year before any American soldiers landed on Philippine soil, then Technical Sergeant Leo M. Giron was dropped off by submarine with a secret mission directly from General Douglas MacArthur to be his eyes and ears on the Philippine Island of Luzon. Giron's mission was to send back vital information in preparation for the American invasion forces. Part of Sergeant Giron's mission was not to be detected. If he was detected, he was to eliminate any evidence of U.S. soldiers currently on Philippine soil. Armed with an M-1, a .45 colt, a 24-inch bolo knife, and a 36-inch talanason Giron and a small group of Filipino American commandos, along with a handful of native Filipino guerrillas, started their mission deep behind enemy lines.

During Giron's many encounters with the enemy, he had to use silent, deadly force. If Giron and his unit used their firearms, they would bring attention to their position, and also risk alerting the enemy that U.S. soldiers had landed with the intention of retaking the Philippine Islands and liberating the native Filipinos from their cruel captors.

Giron would depend on his 24-inch bolo knife and 36-inch talanason. The bolo knife was used mainly to clear brush, creating a narrow path through the thick jungle for his patrol. On rare occasions during close quarter encounters, Giron would use his 24-inch bolo knife to protect himself and his unit from the enemy. But, in nearly all of Giron's encounters with the enemy, he would use his 36-inch talanason to counter the long bayonets and samurai swords that were being swung at Giron's head to chop him down. Giron would counter his enemy with his talanason, using Larga Mano. By combining combatively body mechanics, cinco tero striking patterns, terrain management, larga mano distancing and timing, GME Giron was able to keep himself safe in the Philippine jungles and complete his mission.

Applying your basic fundamentals is the secret to defending any form of attack and can be used no matter what style of martial arts you are playing. Larga Mano encompasses many different components. In order for the student to play larga mano, students need to understand that the weapon of choice is one that will range in length from 30 to 36 inches. This understanding must include the knowledge of what it may take to handle a weapon of this great length. Just like any martial art that has its own style, you will need to understand the basic fundamentals in order to master the style.

Antonio Somera is the heir and leading authority of the Giron Arnis Escrima / Bahala Na Filipino Martial Arts system. Somera was promoted to the rank of Grand Master by Grand Master Emeritus Leo M. Giron.

## TOOLS OF THE TRADE

For nearly 100 years Filipinos have been immigrating to the United States. They brought cultural skills and their native arts along to maintain their civilization and to begin to cultivate a new working society. Many of the traditions that were handed down to them from their ancestors for generations became the focal point of their existence in their new home. These traditions of a love of liberty, equality and fraternity instilled a singular determination within the new immigrants to become a part of this great country and society called America.

With all the America's allurements, Filipinos migrated to the United States for variously important reasons, among them education, economics and adventure and to seek their fame and fortune of their all-American dream which would bring them riches beyond belief. One of the largest waves of Filipinos to American started in 1906 and lasted until 1934. Upon gaining freedom from

Spain the Filipinos embarked into a new land to earn their fame and fortune.

Many of those Filipinos were encouraged to come to the United States by American teachers and misleading advertising by predatory employers and different shipping companies which promised a much better life in America. Stories were told of gold and silver that lined the fields and mountainsides ready for the harvest. Unfortunately, this tale of gold and silver was in reality a story of backbreaking farm labor that only was offered if you were lucky enough to find work. Unfortunately, as history has proven the reality of coming to a new land to seek their riches was paid back to these unknowing young Filipinos ranging in the age from 14 to 22 years old, this would only hold for them the demand of stoop labor in which many of these young Filipinos found in the fields of the San Joaquin valley and in particular Stockton California. During these times work was hard to find, and you would take whatever would come along. In most cases work was just enough for survival and always just enough to make it through one more day.

Many Filipinos of this new generation would eventually find work in fields as farm labors and in particular the fields of the San Joaquin Delta near Stockton, California.

In 1930 California had the largest population of Filipinos in America with just over 30,740 Filipinos. Stockton California would dominate with the most Filipinos in California and at one time had the largest population of Filipinos in the United States and so earned the nickname of "Little Manila". The work these young Filipinos found was in the asparagus farm labor camps in which they would work countless hours of long hard backbreaking stoop labor and was so difficult that many people would not attempt to try this type of work. Immigrants, some who had been doctors or professional men in the Philippines, found themselves working in peat dirt that was itchy to the skin and burning to the eyes. These laborers would need to start their day in the early morning hours and had to endure the intense heat of the sun and the back breaking pain of running up and down miles of asparagus rows cutting it for our own human consumption.

These labor camps were often lawless and dangerous places. Fortunately, along with their strong will and hope the Filipino immigrants brought with them their proven systems of self-defense. History has proven that all the many different cultures in the world have had their own different martial arts and Filipinos were no exception. In self-defense the Filipinos applied their own types of weaponry that grew from their own type of domesticated tools, farm tools and implements.

One of the tools of the trade is called the "asparagus knife" and in those days this was the tool of the Filipino. The asparagus knife consists of a round steel shaft that is one-half (1/2) inch in diameter and 16 to 20 inches long. It has a handle for grabbing on one end and a razor-sharp flat tip 4 to 6 inches long and 2 to 3 inches wide on the other end which made this invaluable tool in the length of 20 to 30 inches long depending on the user. This tool was used for thrusting into the ground and precisely cutting the asparagus grass. After using this tool for hours upon hours, days upon days, weeks upon weeks these young labor warriors would become experts in the thrusting and cutting style of Sonkete (poking) much like the style of European fencing. Although some Filipinos would have some background in fencing and swordsmanship, they would practice their techniques on the application of precision thrusting and cutting while they earned an honest living in the fields of Stockton, California.

The style of Sonkete is one of the 20 styles that encompass the Giron® Arnis Escrima system. Estilo Sonkete is a thrusting and poking style using rigid weapons such as bolo knife, baston (Escrima stick), dagger, asparagus knife or any type of weapon that can be used for poking or thrusting. This style is used for thrusting the weapon into an opening in the opponent's guard. This is accomplished in several ways.

First, you can parry the opponent's oncoming weapon with your left or right hand and thrust your weapon into the created opening. Second, you can block the on-coming weapon and slide your own weapon along your opponent's defense until the point of your weapon makes contact with your opponent's body. Third, you can evade or sidestep left or right while thrusting your weapon into the body of your opponent. Fourth, as you opponent attacks you can deflect the oncoming blow and follow with the point of the weapon sliding it pass the opponents guard until it meets the target of the opponent's body.

The use of the asparagus knife is not limited to just the Sonkete style of poking and thrusting. This unique weapon can also be used in confrontations of normal applications of weapon fighting. It is an excellent weapon that can be used for cutting and slicing. The tip of the weapon with its flat razor-sharp tip is an object that commands the respect of a bolo knife or machete. Depending on the use of this weapon and the position of attack, it can be very difficult to see the flat tip. An experienced escrimador, a practitioner of the Filipino Martial Arts, can manipulate the position of this bladed weapon to use it to his advantage, more like the use of a sword. It is a very fast weapon with the ability to poke, thrust, cut, and slice. Using this type of cutting and slicing can be very effective.

First, you can strike the oncoming weapon to divert the course of the blow and return the strike using the razor-sharp end to disable your opponent. Second, as your opponent attacks you can apply blocking techniques to utilize the shaft or the shank of this weapon, your follow up or counter strikes would be the use of the tip to cut and slice the opponent. Third, when your opponent starts the attack, you can deflect an oncoming direct blow and force the oncoming strike to miss its intended target. In most cases the deflection serves its purpose best when done with a twist of the body. Your follow up strike or counter striking will be done with the flat edge of the weapon. Fourth, you can evade or move out of the path of an oncoming strike. This will not require the assistance of the asparagus knife. But for the maximum amount of protection an evasion is best done in conjunction with the weapon. Your follow up strike can now be a direct strike to the opponents nearest point of vulnerability. This will incorporate the Giron® Larga Mano striking system.

The Estilo Sonkete system can also be used to protect you from intruders that are trying to make their way into your home or office. Because of the thrusting and poking style, you do not need a wide angle of striking patterns as in the case in many deliveries or angles of attack. You can stand in a doorway with a right foot lead using the

Sonkete method to drive your attacker away or to keep your opponent at bay until help can arrive.

Also, in the outdoors and in different terrain, this style can maintain a defensive and offensive position by positioning your body between two objects, for instance in a parking lot between two cars or at a park or in your front yard between two trees. This style can restrict the opponent's aggression to just a narrow pathway of attack. By using this theory, you can eliminate attackers from your left or right side and focus on the forward attacker. This can give you the opportunity to maintain a position of offense by using the poke or thrusting style of Sonkete. Lunging forward and leaning backwards along with a weapon of any length or without a weapon in hand you can play this style with powerful counter striking and pinpoint accuracy.

A style that is called Estilo Elastico can also be an accommodating style to enhance Estilo Sonkete. Estilo Elastico, which means the rubber band style, can be used to increase the reaching ability and accuracy of Estilo Sonkete. This is a common fighting method among Filipino bolo men, who can use this stretching ability forward to reach their target and to lean backwards out of the opponent's line of attack. Fighters who indulge in this method are usually veterans of a few encounters. Their style varies from long distance fighting techniques, retreating techniques, or consequently both are woven into the Larga Mano (long hand) style. Estilo Elastico complements most combat methods especially Estilo Sonkete.

Although there have been many stories of fierce battles in the Filipino farm labor camps using these types of weapons, nearly all confirmations were between only two combatants. The two combatants were also allowed to choose their seconds to handle any problems that may arise or to take care of the wounded combatants. I have been told that these encounters were unspoken laws between the two warriors and was never brought up in conversation or bragged about. I was further told that the loser would disappear and was never heard of again. This reminds me of a saying that my teacher Grand Master Leo M. Giron would say was the slogan of those that train in the art of Arnis Escrima back in the days of yesteryear,

"Don't brag about what you know, you are liable to get a stick shoved down your throat".

Another tool of the trade used for self-defense would be the grape knife. The grape knife is a very small and short tool with an inward curving blade that could be maneuvered through the woven vines of the grape plant. Many of these short and deadly weapons would be two to three inches long with a slight hook or curve on the end so that the grape bunch can be hooked at the vine that is on the end of the grape knife and then cut with procession accuracy without damage to the grape bunch or grape vine. These small, hooked tools would be held using the reverse grip. The tool was so small it could be concealed without very much effort. After a long hard day in the grape fields these young Filipino men would clean up eat their dinner and dream of going into to Stockton, CA for some fun and pleasure. But only a select few would go deep into the grape vineyards to play with the very tools they used during the day of harvesting grapes.

In the Giron® System we would use this grape knife in the style of Cadena de Mano and an unlisted style from the Giron® Master Fan called Tabot. In some martial art styles this tool would be a near fighting weapon called Karambit. The tool would be put into your palm both in forward grip much like if you would hold a dagger but the most common and most deadly is the reverse grips much like an ice pick.

Grand Master Giron would relate this to Filipino Boxing in which had made a great impact to American contractors that came to the Philippines directly after the short lived Filipino American war of 1898. These American contractors would come to the Philippines looking for young Filipino men to work in horrible living conditions and in the fields as cheap labor in order to harvest the rich farmer's crops. During the American contractors' visits to the Philippines, they would witness during Sunday afternoons the traditional chicken or cock fights but also Filipino Boxing style that is now known as western style of boxing. The Filipino Boxing style was taken from Filipino's that would box using a reverse grip, derived from holding a dagger in both hands, and would incorporate the punch and cut method of fighting.

The American contractors were so amazed by this boxing style of Filipino's that they came back to America and contacted boxing promoters to return to the Philippines and watch this new style of boxing. One by one the boxing promoters would recruit these Filipino boxers and bring them back to American to show off their skills against European bareknuckle boxers. This Filipino style became what we know now as Western style of boxing.

From my research I found out that no two experts would be in one camp and most of them possessed a secret fighting style or folklore system called anting-anting, a magical power that was given to them by elder Filipino man. This magical power was handed down to them to keep the Filipino Fighting arts alive and is handed down from generation to generation. This mystical type of playing (training) was the most feared among the Filipino's because they would use prayer in their system to give them superhuman power. This power was only to be used for good, not evil, and would be the most sought-after training of all without ever speaking of it.

Also, many times there would always be one expert in each camp. Knowledge of who the expert was became much like a secret code amongst the camp workers. In many cases there would be one expert that would work many days or weeks in the camp until he would find a younger Pinoy to share his knowledge and skill. The expert Filipino would keep quiet and watch to find a match somewhat like himself that was loyal, hardworking and most of all a person that would not brag about his ability. The story was also told to me that there would be times that this expert would show one person the skill he possessed and that the expert and young Pinoy would become lifelong friends in which they would both travel together to different camps working together side by side. After each day of work, they would go deep into the grape vineyards, pear orchard or behind the barn or bunk house of the asparagus camp to play (train) in the deadly arts of Filipino Escrima, Arnis and Kali.

One well known expert that comes to mind is a man that was one of the teachers of world-famous Martial Artist Daniel Inosanto. He was a World War II veteran and war hero named Manong Juan Lacaste. Manong Lacaste was known for his supper human powers and as an expert in Filipino Martial Arts to the Stockton Filipino community. Guro Dan, in seeking out his out his Filipino Martial Art roots, was urged on by his teacher and best friend Bruce Lee to go back home to Stockton California. Guro Dan's mother and father were pillars of the Filipino community and was very well known by the city of Stockton, had natural connections to these hidden treasures like Manong Lacaste. His father ran a very successful Filipino Labor business, and his Mother Mary was a schoolteacher to many of the young Pinoy's teaching them English and working for the school district.

Because of the research and study conducted by Guro Dan Inosanto many other Filipino Martial Art Masters and world icons in Filipino Martial Arts have become known. Respected men from the Stockton area such as Pepe Montano Arca and Vincent Arca emerged as leaders and experts in the Filipino Arts. Giants like Angel Cabales, the man responsible for the emergence of Escrima in the United States was also from the Stockton area and a member of the Gran Oriente Filipino Inc. Lodge. Another, Regino Ellustrisimo was expert in the Bohol method of Escrima. Ellustrisimo claimed to have a power which enabled him, by putting his hand on your head, to know if you would be a good person to learn the deadly art of Escrima.

Leo M. Giron, a World War II hero that was a secret operative hand selected by General Douglas Macarthur was another master from the Stockton area. Giron was a member of the first group of Army commandos, called the 978th Signal Corps. Leo M. Giron is also known to all as the Father of Larga Mano in America.

His environmental training gained in the war is an invaluable perspective and personal knowledge has given much to the arts as a whole. Giron is a true combatant of hand-to-hand combat and an expert in terrain fighting. Leo M Giron was a member the most powerful Filipino Lodge on the west coast, the Legionarios del Trabajo in America in which he would hold many high positions. Giron would hold the office of Supreme Minister longer than any other member of the Legionarios.

Another Stockton martial expert was Juanito Lacaste. Lacaste was an expert in stick, dagger, long blade and empty hands. His expertise in hand trapping and checking and inner achievement of the martial arts such as love and peace towards all mankind and proper morality won him many devoted followers. Manong Lacaste was a member of the Filipino Federation, which even today is a very strong and wealthy Federation.

Jesus Ragail Corales, a well-known figure in town due to his working in the many different Filipino labor camps, was a master exposed to a number of Filipino Escrimadors. Corales played the cabaroan, or "new system," of Arnis Escrima. His specialty is the cinco tero style or five strikes and also the Redondo style or circular striking and close quarter hand to hand combat. Corales was a member of the 1st Filipino Regiment and served in the invasion of Lyette, Philippines during World War II. Corales is also a member of the Filipino Lodge of Caballeros de Dimas Alang.

Joe Arruejo Pacpaco also played the cabaroan or new style of Arnis Escrima. His style was Larga Mano or long hand/weapon style. He also played Abierta or open body style of Arnis Escrima and had an empty hand style that is similar to Cadena de Mano. Pacpaco's Larga Mano is different from Leo Giron's Larga Mano. Pacpaco incorporated the Abierta (open) body footwork to his Larga Mano. Pacpaco's footwork was attributed to his natural open foot movement. Joe Pacpaco had a very unique gift of playing. He was left-handed, very graceful and to the point. Pacpaco was also a life member of the Legionarios Del Trabajo and member of the Worshipful Mabini Lodge with over 60 years of service to the Filipino lodge.

Victorino Ton was born June 29, 1895, in Lapaz Abra, Philippines. Ton arrived in Hawaii in 1924 and then came to Stockton, California in 1930. Ton first worked in the pineapple and sugar cane plantations in Hawaii for 6 years. After completing his work contract in Hawaii, he moved on to Stockton, California in 1930. Ton's first job in Stockton was cutting asparagus. Victorino Ton to my knowledge is the oldest living arnis escrima player in America. At the time of this article Ton is currently 109 years. Ton lives at a Filipino lodge in Stockton California. Ton plays the cinco tero (five strikes) and incorporates blocking and counter striking. He started playing with sticks in the Philippines at the age of 10 this would be 1905. This was without a doubt one of the most fertile times of Escrimadors in Philippine history due to the Filipino revolution. Ton is truly a son of the revolution that fought against the Spaniards during the Philippines revolution to gain their freedom from Spain. Manong Ton is a life member of the Legionarios del Trabajo in America and is a member of General Lim lodge with over 60 years of service to the Filipino lodge.

Max Sarmiento is a highly skill empty hand expert and is credited of being among a group of Filipinos that brought together the first Filipino Martial Arts school open to the general public. The school opened with Sarmiento, Angle Cabales, Leo M. Giron and Dentoy Revillar. Max Sarmiento was a member of the Filipino Community and a Filipino activist.

Dentoy Revillar the top and senior student of Angel Cabales and man highly creative in his own right and without a doubt one of the top instructors in Escrima in the Cabales and Larga Mano systems.

Gilbert Tenio is expert in a number of Escrima styles and is proficient in disarms. Manong Gilbert Tenio was a member of the Legionarios del Trabajo in America.

All of these Filipino Martial Arts' world icons called Stockton California their home. And this is but a small example of all the Filipino Masters of that original generation from the area presently known as the hot bed of Filipino Martial Arts in the world. These are the names and faces of those that we are privileged to know. Now you need to ask the question how many of those names and faces of history did not tell anyone of the secret unknown masters of the Filipino Martial Arts? How many masters did not find the one young Pinoy to pass on their secret and ancient fighting art of the Philippines?

In honor of those that planted the seed of martial knowledge in the new world called Stockton California, and in honor of those men lost to history, it is now our turn to play and train in the arts of our forefathers. We must find the one deserving person to plant the seed so that we will ensure that our forefathers art will continue to live on. In this way we may live with the same dignity, using all the tools and gifts left to us by our beloved teachers.

# STEVE TARANI

## HISTORY OF THE KNIFE AND DAGGER

Researchers, relying upon archeological evidence, have isolated the birthplace of the knife and dagger somewhere in the northeast corner of the ancient African continent. The evolution of these weapons can be traced from the European Stone Age all the way up to the nuclear age. Significant modifications to basic knife design, materials, and functionality can be found in virtually every ancient and modern civilization, particularly during times of war.

The earliest recorded archeological evidence of prehistoric edged-weapon combat was discovered during the early 1960s at a burial site along the Nile River in ancient Nubia, located between Egypt and Ethiopia. The site contains remnants of several dozen human bodies dating from between 12,000 and 8,000 BC. The archeological record indicates that between these same dates there was a revolution in weapons technology. During this period four new weapons made their first appearance: the bow, the sling, the mace, and the knife and dagger.

About 40 percent of these remains were found buried alongside small bone-flake points and a number of points were found still embedded in some of the bones. Although no concrete evidence was uncovered via written record, researchers have observed that several individuals appeared to have been executed. Additionally, seven skeletons had arms fractured in a manner consistent with the warding-off of heavy, impact strikes at close-quarter range, thus indicating a struggle.

Cave paintings such as the ones of Lascaux, France and Teruel, Spain, which date as far back as 25,000 to 15,000 BC, illustrate possible evidence of man's earliest weapons. Prehistoric hunters equipped themselves with edged and pointed weapons to ensure basic survival. To use those same weapons on their own kind would have been a simple step if, like in modern politics, they believed the ends justified the means. Small hunting and gathering groups that weathered the last ice age undoubtedly had cause to attack each other for dominion over valuable resources like food, water, and firewood.

Although modern synthetic materials and stainless steels may have replaced the stone and bone blades of old, the purpose of today's knives and daggers is basically the same as that of the ancient stone-age people: a tool for survival and self-defense.

There are basically two types of knives and daggers: fixed blade (no moving parts), or folding blade (which can have as many as five or more moving parts).

Archaeological digs have unearthed folding knives from as far back as the late ancient Roman Empire (circa 2nd-4th century AD). We use the term "pocketknife" today, but back then, pockets had not yet been invented.

The earliest known folding knives had no back-springs in their handles. Reliable, crucible-cast, spring steel wouldn't be produced until 1742 as the invention of clock maker Benjamin Huntsman in Sheffield England. Interestingly enough, inexpensive folding knives, to this very day, are made in the ancient Roman style without back-springs!

Although the knife and dagger were considered secondary weapons (the sword dominated the ancient world), they were essential to the armory of the most powerful armies of antiquity. In fact, from the earliest times of issued body armor in the 3rd quarter of the 14th century, the dagger became an indispensable and visible part of a warrior's equipment. Daggers are displayed in famous weavings of old such as the Bayeux tapestry and can be seen in Le Moyne's sketches of the French in Florida in 1564. Indeed, just about every military monument from that same era displays a dagger of one type or another. Many civilian figures are also depicted wearing knives and daggers, which were as popular with citizens then, as our high-tech combat folding knives are to us now.

Perhaps the knife's enduring popularity can be explained by its compactness and usefulness. You can turn a screw with the tip, make a sandwich using the blade, and then clean your teeth with it afterwards. It slices, dices, fixes, repairs, and, of course, protects. But perhaps the real answer is that we humans just like to own bright, shiny, sleek objects. That would not only explain the knife, but also the 1956 Chevy Bel Air!

## TACTICAL CARRY AND DEPLOYMENT

How can you carry a knife? Well, the real answer is any way that you can think of. However, there are certain advantages and disadvantages to certain methods. For example, if you have a fixed-blade dagger and carry it as a neck-knife, under your shirt, the advantage is that it is concealed, most people won't suspect it's there, and that it provides easy access. The disadvantage is that not only might it be considered a concealed weapon, but you must also reach underneath your clothing to access the handle and pull it from its sheath – which takes time.

Another type of carry is the classic side-pocket carry. The classic folding clip-on can easily be carried in either your side or back pockets, in front or behind you on the belt, in the shirt collar or, if the knife is small enough, inside the shirt pocket. The advantage to this carry is convenience and legality. The disadvantage is that it may turn out to be a two or three-step process to access the folded unit, flip open the blade, and acquire a combat grip.

Another method of carry is called the "Dundee rig," named after an Australian character in a popular movie. This allows instant access to a large blade with one simple motion. The advantage is that you have fast access to a large blade. The disadvantage is that the legality of its size may be questionable in certain areas – plus, it may be uncomfortable to wear during business meetings.

As far as carrying a knife or dagger, the very best idea is to have it ready in your hand. Of course, other people may find this method of carry quite offensive and in most cases, you will be questioned by local law enforcement as to *why* you are strolling around with a Tennessee toothpick. The second-best carry method is a fixed blade located in a sheath external to any clothing, such as an exposed side sheath or boot sheath. While this make for instant access, there again may be certain legal restrictions depending on where you live. So, by default, the most practical knife to carry and deploy in modern society is the high-tech combat folder.

Deployment simply involves pulling it out and acquiring a combat-ready posture. The best method of deployment is to secure a solid grip on the handle – from its place of carry all the way through to deployment and operation. Certain weapon instructors refer to the act of deploying a weapon as a "presentation." In the case of a fixed-bladed deployment the presentation is simple. You just grab the handle, pull it out of its sheath, and stand there with the point between you and your mugger with a smile on your face.

In the example of a combat folder there's a few more steps: 1) Secure a firm grip on the handle; 2) Pull the weapon from its carry location; 3) Using either one or two hands unfold and lock the blade into its operational position; 4) Assume an effective combat posture. All four of these steps must be practiced many times to ensure proficiency when you need it most. You can practice while watching TV, on the phone, stuck in traffic, or just before you go to bed at night – just don't confuse it with your toothbrush. However, you practice, the secret to deployment is repetition. The number of times the move is executed will equal your degree of technical certainty in a combat situation.

A final word of wisdom: always carry your weapon in the same place. If you need it fast, you don't want to add the slow step of thinking, "now where did I put that darn thing?" Imagine getting into your car every morning and finding the position of the brake, clutch, and gas pedal had changed. Sure, you'd figure it out after a while, but in an emergency, you'd better know where the brake is. This also holds true for your knife: once you decide on a carry position that fits you – don't change it!

In our modern, politically correct society, it's almost a crime to defend ourselves either with or without a knife. However, if you chose to have the carry-and-deployment advantage of an edged weapon, support that choice with professional training. Most importantly, check with your local law enforcement agency to ensure that you are within the confines of the law.

## STANCES, GRIPS AND OPERATION

In the many different styles and systems of knife fighting, there are certain basics which are common to all systems. These are the basics of edged weapon combat – how to hold a knife, how to stand with a knife, and how to operate a knife.

Depending upon the origin of a particular system or the emphasis it places on a certain aspect, there are tremendous differences in philosophy and training methods. Much like comparing makes and models of sports cars, it's not a matter of one being better than the other, but an issue of which fits you the best. Some people prefer a BMW over a Corvette. Others might prefer a convertible Mustang over a Ferrari. Still others would choose a Jaguar over a Viper – it's truly just a matter of personal choice.

There are about a half-dozen ways to hold a knife in a defensive posture: the hammer grip (*langit* in the Filipino tradition), the saber grip (*la sabre* in the European tradition), the ice pick or reverse grip (*pakal* in the Filipino tradition), reverse grip with thumb support or canted reverse ("military" in the Western tradition) and the prison shank grip (where inmates duct tape a shank to their fingers and execute purely thrusting deliveries – said to have originated in Folsom Prison). There are others such as the Japanese *tsuki* grip (used predominantly with the tanto), or the Malaysian execution grip, et cetera.

Stances are simply how to posture your body while holding a knife. Much like the classic fencing postures of the famous sword-fighting schools of ancient Venice, Madrid and others, body position while holding a knife is just as important as the technique itself. In fact, your stance is the very platform from which any technique is executed. In order to have a strong building you need to have a solid foundation. The same goes for knife fighting – if your grip or stance is weak then you've already compromised the integrity of your technique.

Common sense tells us that if you are holding a weapon in your hand and you engage in mortal combat, then you want to keep that weapon between you and your adversary. Some systems promote holding the knife behind your back or at your side during combat. Although this may be a stylized function, it is purely a matter of time and distance. Simply put, if the knife is farther away from its target, then it's going to take longer to get there. Most Filipino, Malaysian and Indonesian styles place the weapon out in front of all appendages and in the closest possible position for a strike or defensive tactic.

Similar to classic European fencing, there are five general postures in which to hold during engagement: basic ready, high open, low open, low closed and high closed. Each of these can also be maintained with any grip of your choice based on style, system, or personal preference.

Operation of the blade can be broken down to six basic moves: thrusting (some systems call it "cut-poking" or *sungkette* in the Filipino tradition), hacking, scraping (tearing), coring, and puncturing. Slashing means moving the blade along an arc of attack so that the sharp edge makes contact with the target area along that arc with full follow through. Thrusting is to place the tip or point of the blade exactly at the point of contact and penetrate the target in a linear trajectory. Hacking is to snap the sharp edge of the blade at the target area, make contact, and literally "bounce back" from the point of contact to your starting position. Scraping is to place the tip or edge of the blade at the target area and drag the tip or edge at a 30- to 90-degree angle so as to tear. Coring is the same action as coring an apple. Puncturing can be likened to opening a can with a triangular can opener to create a triangular flap on the target area.

To be lacking in knowledge or skill in stances, grips, or operation can weaken the foundation of your overall combat effectiveness. Remember, a strong foundation makes for a strong defense. A solid proficiency in the basics will give you an advantage in any edged-weapon encounter.

## GEOMETRY OF THE MASTERS

Edged-weapon masters frequently teach and write about the geometry of combat including footwork and handwork. Examples of this are the *langkah* (angular footwork) of pencak silat or the *tatsulog* (triangle) of Filipino martial arts.

What secrets do these ancient traditions hold and how can they be applied to modern knife self-defense? The answer is a study in the geometry and trajectory of motion. Similar to a Physics 101 class in college, we must first understand the principles of attack with an edged weapon. If someone pulls out a knife and is moving toward you there are a couple of factors which require analysis. Freeze-frame the attack and draw a line from the tip of the attacker's weapon to your centerline (imaginary line drawn from your forehead to your groin) – this is the line of attack, or LOA.

Imagine you are standing on the face of a clock. If your attacker is at 12:00 and you are in the middle of the face, then he is directly in front of you. No matter where the attacker moves to on the clock face, you can still connect the line from his weapon to your centerline and call this the line of attack. The laws of physics hold that after he commits to a slash or thrust (or some other type of attacking motion) with the knife, he must follow along that same LOA to reach his intended target. Your response is to step off that line of attack as quickly as possible to reduce his chances of connecting.

The ancient masters figured out that the best way to step off the line of attack is to step-out 45 degrees either forward or backward from the attack. Using the clock face example, the assailant attacks from the 12:00 position. Now, if you're standing in the middle of the clock and you take one step straight back then you're still along the same LOA and it's just a matter of time before he closes the gap and hits his target. If, however, you were to step 45-degrees back, say to 4:00 o'clock, this would force him to change his direction and motion in order to pick up the new line of attack.

In other words, the closer you stay to the LOA, the better his chances are of hitting his target. The faster you move off that LOA (using 45-degree steps) the less chance he has of hitting his target and the more time you gain to react. In the condition where you have lost ground and cannot use footwork to escape, let's say from close to extreme close-quarter range, you have lost the advantage of using angular footwork and must now rely heavily upon use of the hands in breaking down the arc of attack.

The arc of attack can be viewed as that arc scribed by the tip or edge of the weapon as it approaches the target area. In other words, if you strapped a big green crayon to the tip of the blade and made your attacker slash at a huge piece of paper, then you would see a curving arc-shaped "C" on the paper. Optimally, you would like to avoid this arc of attack at all costs.

There are two ways to break this arc of attack. One is by pushing down and away from your body, and the other is by pushing up and away from your body. If you don't have a choice and must make contact with your arms or hands then you must effect the arc of attack – you have no choice in the matter – it's already too late for you too step off the LOA. A good suggestion would be to use any object at your disposal such as a grocery bag, jacket, trash-can lid, car door, distance, or whatever you can put between you and your attacker to defeat that arc of attack.

At long range you can affect the line of attack by either stepping 45 degrees forward or backward away from the incoming motion. If you fail against the LOA then you must deal with the arc of attack. This means you are in close quarter proximity or ECQ (extreme close-quarter range) and are already at an extreme disadvantage – especially if you are empty handed. Here, at this range it's up front and personal, and very ugly. You're going to get cut and nothing short of a miracle is going to keep you from bleeding. Your only recourse is to break down the arc of attack by keeping that point down and away from your centerline, or up and away from your centerline.

Remember, if you get caught in a knife fight, use your feet to step 45 degrees off the line of attack. If you get caught in hand-range, remember to break the arc of attack. It's all really just a simple matter of understanding angles and arcs – use the geometry of the masters to your advantage. Sometimes it's all that you have.

## GETTING A GRIP

One of the most frequently asked questions about knife fighting is "What's the best way to hold a knife?" This is just about the same as someone asking you "What's the best way to open a door?" There are many different ways to open a door. It is simply a matter of what kind of door it is that you want to open. For example, if the door has a doorknob on it, then you must first turn the doorknob and then open the door. If it's the kind of door that has a bar going across, then you simply grab the bar and then open the door.

Just as there are many types of handles on different doors, so are there many types of handles on different knives. Depending upon what type of knife it is that you're holding, determines how you are going to handle it. For example, if it's a modern combat folding knife (such as a liner-lock, bolt-lock or ridge-lock style), then the handle will tend to be very narrow and come with both a forefinger stop and some type of thumb rest. In this case, you would use a saber grip to take advantage of the design features. However, if the knife happens to be a fixed blade, where the handle is much thicker, such as the K-Bar, Scottish Dirk or Bowie, then perhaps a hammer grip or reverse grip may better suit your application. In simplified terms, *design determines grip*.

However, regardless of design, there are two key elements which forge a rock-solid grip. These are: 1. Creating friction and 2. Locking the wrist.

Creating Friction is literally producing enough friction where the handle of the knife is molecularly bonded to the skin of your hand. Have you ever walked across a room holding something in your hand and then accidentally bumped into something with your hand? The impact immediately loosened your grip and most likely, whatever you were holding fell from your grasp. The same principle applies to gripping a knife. If you've ever really stabbed a piece of wood or thrust into a training tire, then you know how much pressure is applied against your grip at point of impact. The last thing you want, when it really matters, is to have your knife blasted away from your hand because your grip was weak.

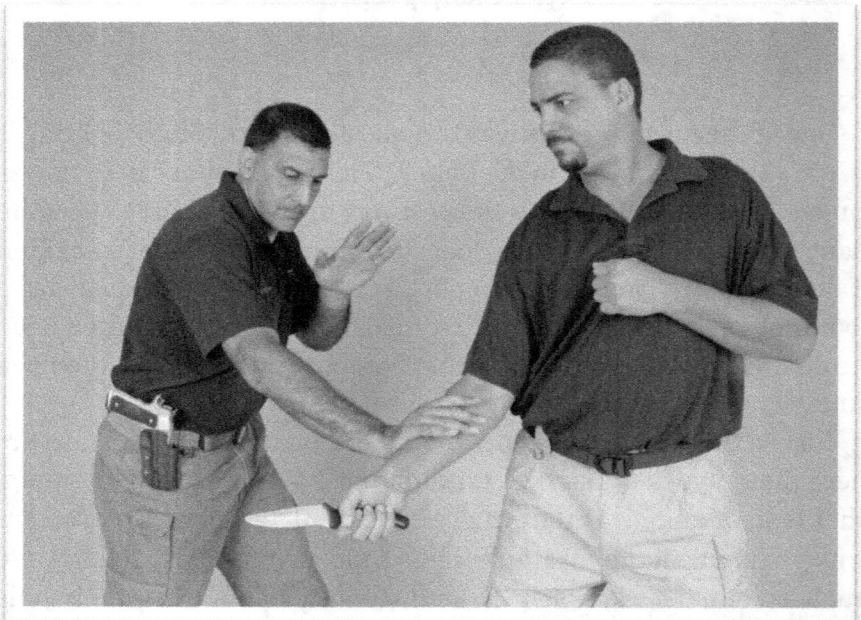

There are four points of contact that create enough friction to establish a "secured grip". These are considered primary points of contact and are: (1) Thumb, (2) Forefinger, (3) Pinky finger and (4) Surface of the palm.

Try this experiment: Grab your combat folder, open the blade and hold it in your hand. Take your thumb, place it on the thumb rest (located at the foremost position of the spine at the base of the blade).

Then place your forefinger securely on the finger rest (located opposite the thumb rest). Wrap your pinky finger tightly around the base (butt of the knife). Then squeeze the handle with the remaining fingers to eliminate any space between the flat side of the handle and the surface of your palm. What you now have in your hand is a secured grip.

With your secured grip, wiggle the knife around in the air. Now, lift your thumb off and wiggle it around. Does it feel different? OK, put your thumb back on and take off your forefinger and do the same thing. Now try it with the pinky. Finally, create a gap between the surface of the handle and the surface of your palm. What is the difference in handling with less friction? The more friction you can create the more solid your grip.

Locking the wrist is the second key element of establishing a secured grip. The Japanese have a term "kamai" which, when training with the Tanto, Wakazashi or Katana is applied to the wrist. Sometimes referred to as "Kamai Wrist", the alignment of the first two knuckles of the weapon hand with the base of the wrist joint, locks the bones of both the hands, wrist, and forearm in a natural alignment. This locking of the wrist combined with your secured grip gives you the best way to hold a knife – especially when you really need it.

The next question, now that you've established a secured grip, is how do you determine the use of your grip when operating the edge?

One of the greatest recorded fencing masters of antiquity (both rapier and dagger) was a Master Instructor named Giacomo Di Grassi who lived during the Eliabethan era. His famous book <u>His True Arte of Defence</u> (published in 1594) is one of only the oldest training manuals on knife and swordplay surviving. In it, the master describes how a wrist cut is quick but not so strong, while the force generated from the shoulder is much stronger but not so quick. The edged weapon fighter must be trained to always have at his disposal, the balance of the two.

Therefore, when delivering a slash or thrust, the Master recommends "he shall only use the compass of the elbow and the wrist: which as they be most swift, so are they strong enough, if they be orderly handled."

Even the blade masters of antiquity stressed the practical importance of employing a secured grip in an edged weapon encounter.

## DISTANCE IS YOUR FRIEND

The three most important elements of dealing with an edged-weapon encounter are distance, timing, and reaction. These three elements work together like gears in a motor to produce the best possible response to the action of an attack. The most important of all these factors is distance.

Whether you're trying to hit a bull's eye by throwing darts, or making a shot with a basketball, or even tossing a piece of crumpled paper into a wastebasket, the ability to gauge distance by feel is an absolute necessity. How much more difficult is it to hit a bull's eye if the target is moving? Now imagine that your target can cut, slash, hack, or even puncture you – this should give you a feel for the difficulties faced in a knife encounter.

The best range to be at in a knife fight is about 2,000 yards away, looking at your opponent through the scope of a high-powered rifle. Because most of us don't have this option during a surprise attack, though, we have to understand which response works best at which distance.

At conversational range, there are three basic distances to any edged-weapon encounter: long range, medium range and close range. Long range is when both the attacker and the defender are just outside of arm's reach. Medium range is when both the attacker and the defender can touch wrist-to-wrist if both stretched their arms (some Filipino knife-fighting systems refer to this range as *pulso y pulso*). Close range is when both the attacker and the defender can access a vital area of the body by simply extending their arms. Some edged-weapon trainers, law enforcement academies, and military training schools also refer to this distance as "extreme close-quarter range" (ECQ) or "close-quarter combat" (CQB).

Although it sounds simple, it is important to emphasize that the further you are away from the attacking blade, the more time you have to get away. This is the most important defensive knife tactic in the book – distance buys you time. The further you are away from an incoming blade, the more time you have to completely disengage – the closer you are, the less time you have to react. This proportional relationship is known as the time-distance variable.

At long range, the best technique to use is footwork; especially if you are unarmed and have nothing to place between yourself and your attacker. Again, the absolute best thing to place between you and your attacker at this range is *distance*. By using footwork to create distance, you can achieve the ultimate goal in any edged weapons encounter – to get out of there as fast as you can. You don't want to risk changing your distance to a closer range (which gives you less time to react) where you will have to deal with a razor-sharp blade – odds are *not* in your favor and you *will* get cut.

If you get caught at medium range, your best option is to again use your feet and create distance as quickly as possible. However, you may not be able to move quickly enough and may have to use your hands or elbows. At medium range you may need to employ a downward or upward deflection to gain time to escape via footwork. Remember you have increased odds of being cut at this range because of a decreased reaction time.

The worst position of all is close range. Here, you are at maximum risk of getting cut because your reaction time is almost nothing. In this case it is best to use your shirt, briefcase, shopping bag, or even your elbows to place a barrier between your vital organs and the incoming blade. This gives you that split second you need to move completely out of range.

The simple lesson of proper spacing has been taught by blade-masters of old and modern combat instructors alike. What was true for the powerful legions of ancient Rome is still true for modern commandos, and for any "normal" person caught in an edged-weapon encounter today: distance is your friend.

# KOSS YOKOTA

## ASAI KARATE

Sensei Asai's karate was not standard JKA or even Shotokan style. It was Asai style karate, unlike any other. There are more than a dozen points to describe his style, but I will list five points here so I can share some of his techniques and teachings.

**Understanding the Human Body**

Asai Sensei really understood the mechanism of our body. The following understanding is the key point of how our body is constructed now and its history or evolution.

Though it may sound far-fetched, to understand our body mechanism, we need to trace our evolution back to the fish. It is interesting to see how the fish use their backbones. The tail fin is positioned vertically, and the fish moves the backbone horizontally to generate forward motion. It is amazing how fast they can move in an environment of high viscosity: water. Some fish can swim as fast as 100 miles per hour and for many hours. Another interesting point is the surprising amount of power a fish shows when we try to grab one. We have difficulty holding a rather small fish like a salmon. It is impossible to think that we could handle a bigger fish like a tuna. It shows that a tremendous amount of power can be generated using the backbone movements.

The fish evolved into amphibians. The alligators move their backbone horizontally and they walk with four legs. Notice that their legs are set off to the sides of the shoulders and hip joints. They are flat on the ground and their motions on the ground are rather slow.

The next generation is mammals. Look at horses, dogs, and cats to see how their body mechanism differs from alligators. The mammals use their backbones vertically. Look at the backbone movements of a cheetah while it is running. We can clearly see the backbone is weaving and the movements are vertical. The legs of a cheetah are not that muscular, but rather slim. Therefore, it is obvious that the tremendous speed does not come only from the leg muscles. It depends on the strong backbone movements. Also, notice that their legs are set downward rather than to the side, like an alligator. Their chest cavity is oval shaped, stretching up and downward, rather than sideways as seen with an amphibian.

It is very interesting to see how a human is constructed. We are so different from all the generations of the past. Fish, amphibians, and mammals position themselves horizontally. We are unique, as we stand upright. As a matter of fact, it is a very strange position—to hold the heaviest part of our body, the head, on the top. And we walk on two legs, constantly balancing this heavy object. Bipedal mechanism itself is a topic we can spend hours discussing. We just touch the fact that we humans have a unique physical construction and mechanism. Our chest cavity is unlike most mammals. Ours is elongated to sideways, which is interestingly similar to that of an amphibian. Our arms and legs also are set differently, not only from the mammals but also from the amphibians. The legs are not set downward (at a 90-degree angle) but rather parallel to the backbone. Now the body is positioned vertically (including legs), rather than horizontally. The arms are set to the sides, like those of the alligator; yet, we have much more mobility as far as the shoulder joints are concerned. We can swing the arms in almost all directions, which is impossible for any amphibians and mammals. We gained a lot of arm mobility, but we also lost some capabilities.

The main capabilities we lost are: 1) balancing of the body mass with four legs (now we have bipedalism); 2) use of the backbones to generate power for body shifting (very little use now); 3) stomach breathing (most people do chest breathing, short and shallow).

Asai Sensei's training will recover the abilities we lost in the evolution process.

This challenges us to consider the changes from the fish age to our current body structure, and to appreciate the abilities we gained, but at the same time we need to understand that we lost some important ones and to figure out how to regain those lost abilities.

## Total Relaxation of the Body

Asai Sensei's body was very flexible. It was not just loose but it had elasticity and rebound power. In Western culture, we (mostly men) want to build and admire strong and stiff muscles. Body building is a good example of this trend. He explained that our body is 70 percent water, and it is held up with several sticks, bones, and covered with a thin elastic material, skin. It is not natural to make our bodies hard and stiff. He says: look at the body of a baby; that is the ultimate flexibility. But we as we grow older, we get stiff even if we do not lift weights. He says that to be able to relax and be able to use our body to a satisfactory level, we must start by understanding why our bodies become tight or stiff as we grow old.

Bipedal is like riding a bike compared to riding a cart with four wheels. It is much more difficult to keep one's balance to stand up with only two legs. As we learn how to stand up and walk, we learn to stiffen our body in order to keep our bodies like one stick. This action applies particularly to the inner muscles that are attached to the back bones, hip joints, and ribs. Having the backbones and ribs all being stiff and not mobile, the shoulders and their joints also get tight. Therefore, the relaxation must start from the backbones, hip joints, and ribs. When those main three parts are relaxed, the entire body is ready for the whipping movements of the fists and feet. However, relaxing those three parts are not easy.

What can one do to relax those parts? You start from moving the backbones in a way a snake does (swinging or winding sideways). Then you move the backbones in a forward and backward motion as a dolphin does as it swims. You do all these moves slowly and consciously to feel the movement of different backbones. Initially, your concept or feeling of the backbones is like one long stick. After several exercises, you will begin to feel them as a long, flexible chain. At the same time, you will expand your chest cavity to move the ribs and try to make it move like an accordion. The more flexible you can move your backbones and ribs, the better it is.

## Fist and Foot Whip Techniques

These are Asai Sensei's signature techniques. Such techniques cannot be achieved by simple arm moving exercises. One can throw a backfist strike a million times but will not be able to achieve a whipping technique without doing it correctly with good understanding of the mechanism behind it.

To enable a true whipping action with your fist, your backbones and ribs must have total relaxation and mobility. Then, you must have relaxed shoulder joints, as well as all the muscles that are involved and connecting between the backbones to the fist. For instance, a backfist strike movement must start from the inner body with a leveraging point at the backbones and not the shoulder.

The simple exercise for this technique should be practiced with both arms simultaneously. Hold the arms in front of your chest and swing them out to the sides. There are many ways to use the hands in this exercise. The easiest is to keep the hands open. Basically, there are three ways to position the open hand here. One is to keep the palms down as you would do a knife hand strike; another is to keep the palms up as you would be doing haito uchi (ridge hand strike); a third way is to keep the hands vertical, so you will be striking the target with back of your hands. When you feel comfortable with the open hand, you can do this with fists and you can position the fist in three ways, as you did with open hands. In doing this exercise, you must bring the hands back very quickly to your chest, as fast as, or faster than, the strike out. One set of exercises is about 20 quick strikes (from the chest position and back to the original position). If you do both open hands and fists with three different positions, you will be doing 120 strikes. That would be an excellent exercise if you have only five minutes to practice. Another important point is that the extended arms must be open wider than 180 degrees (meaning your arms are in a straight line). If you tense too soon, your arms will stop before they stretch to the 180-degree point. You get better exercise when your arms are extended 200 degrees or more.

If you become good at a whipping motion with your fist, your straight punch will change. You will not stop your punch too soon. You will learn how to deliver the energy when your fist is fully extended. Check this with a simple experiment. All you need is a bunch of old newspapers. Hold a sheet of newspaper (a half of the full page) with one hand fully extended in front of you and punch it with your other hand. The purpose is to make a hole with your fist. The idea is not to cut the paper in half but punch through it. Punching through one sheet or two sheets is rather easy. Try it with three sheets or more and it becomes challenging. If your punching arm is tensed, or if you try to punch with only the arm power, you will not be able to make a hole through the sheets. You must be completely relaxed and throw a punch quickly but lightly. It is a fun experiment, and you will make a lot of trash!

For a whipping kick, the movement must start from the pelvis joint. The pelvis joint must initiate the whipping action as the backbones did for the back fist strike.

## Tenshin (spin body shifting)

Tenshin is a body movement that requires a high level of body shifting capability. An easy example of basic tenshin would be a forward step from left front zenkutsu dachi to right front zenkutsu dachi. In a normal step forward, you simply step forward with your rear foot (right foot). In tenshin move, you pivot on your left foot and move your rear or right foot in a clockwise direction. By doing this, your upper body will rotate 360 degrees as you move forward. In a regular step forward, your upper body will rotate very little (maybe 30 degrees or so if you start from hanmi (half hip) and end up in straight hips.

A karateka must develop a good "center," which is an ability to keep the axis of your upper body straight, thus enabling you to keep your balance after a quick turn and spin. To develop a center, we practice the turning exercise, initially with a natural stance (shoulder width), then on to kibadachi (wider stance) to rotate our body by 90 degrees (both clockwise and counterclockwise). Then, we rotate by 180 degrees, then by 270 degrees and finally by 360 degrees (complete rotation). The rotation can be initiated from the head, shoulders, midsection of the body, hips, knees, or feet. Each method has its own merits and challenges.

To check your tenshin ability, try a rotation of 360 degrees from kiba dachi. The important point here is that you will NOT jump to get a complete turn. You will rotate quickly by using rotational power (head, shoulders, upper body, etc.) by only floating on the floor. Once you are able to rotate 360 degrees successfully, punch chudan at the moment of the completion of the rotation. This cannot be done unless the upper body and the stance complete the rotation in a coordinated way. There are two ways of punching. One is to punch with a fist of an outside turn (meaning a side that is moving forward). For instance, if you are rotating clockwise, you will punch with your left fist. The other is to use an inside turn (the side that is moving backward) fist or right fist as you rotate clockwise.

## Balancing

When Asai Sensei talked about balance of the body, he was talking about executing techniques from one leg. We find this is difficult to do as we are so used to doing things with both feet on the ground. Once a practitioner learns how to balance well on one leg, naturally, his moves using both legs will become more solid and stable.

There are some one leg moves in JKA kata, such as Gankaku and Jutte, to improve the one leg balance. Because standing on one leg is difficult, this movement of one leg stance (tsuruashi dachi and sagiashi dachi) purposely is done slowly in kata. Asai Sensei wanted us to practice the one leg stance in fast motions to build our balancing ability.

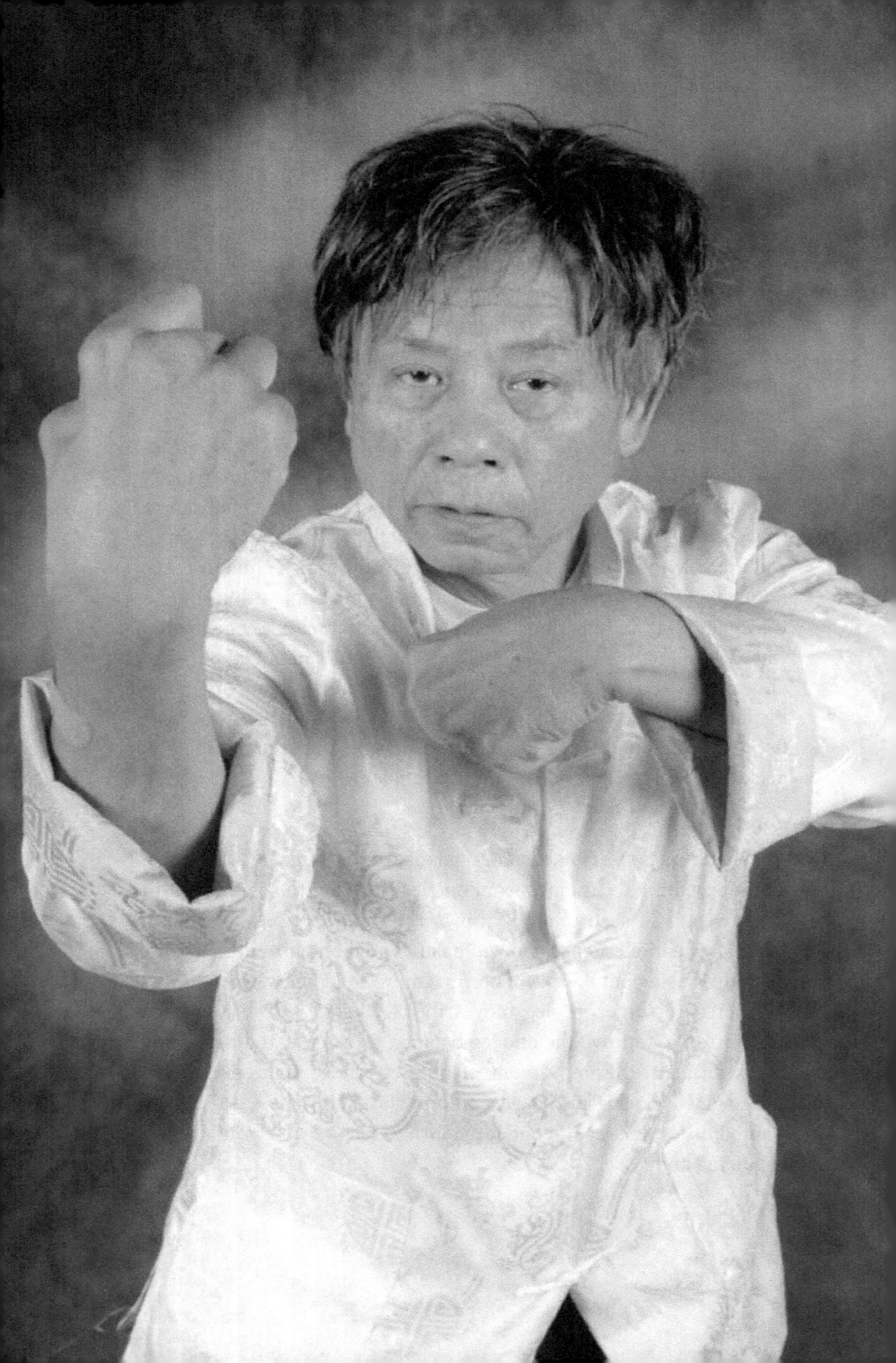

# KAM YUEN

### THE ART OF LIVING

Living is an art, not a science. If it were a science, we all will be in more Bunsen Burner flame, boiling hot water and centrifuge spin than we already are now. Science, in spite of its flamboyant and glamour status, creates more questions than answers.

Do we need to ask and be asked more questions with no answers or at best a few answers unrelated to the questions? Usually, science would have approximately one answer per a thousand questions. In such statistical probability, to have two or a second answer, science has to formulate an additional thousand questions. By the time, we get answers from science; we will be old and gray as I am now, if not already dead in which I am getting closer to.

Science's answers are not truthful because it needs empirical evidence whatever that means before they considered anything to be true. Gathering empirical data put everyone to sleep including those doing the gathering and interpreting them. It is difficult for science to recognize the answer even if the answers have been starring in its faces for decades. Their answer is not the truth because none of their answers are applicable in improve anyone's lives or anything else for that matter. Does science really care to get to the truth? It is difficult for science to get to the truth because it doesn't have a sense of humor. The truth is funny!

Even stones in caves have changed by the time it takes science to form a single postulate let alone a conclusion; carbon molecules would turn into diamonds by the time we get any useful answers from science for us to live by. Every few years, scientific theory gets discarded and reversed itself and even contradicted its own previous theory. It is difficult for science to make up its mind if it has one?

To improve the art of living, we can't depend on science; it is really technology that improves the standard of living not science. Science gets the credit as medicine gets credit for health when the standards of health improve through hygienic knowledge and practice. Under such premises, the art of living finds science to be unreliable as other human institutions. It should not give science more credence than any other limited human systems of experiences. The art of living sought to unchain itself from the yoke of science; to be treated as equal to science as all things being equal. There is a science and art of developing unparallel intuition unmatched by previous generations and setting a new baseline standard for the new and future generations. The art of living takes into consideration our intuitive access to our physical, mental and spiritual being.

It is only through intuition we get to the truth; logic can only point us in certain directions. There are infinite possibilities for science to deal with, but it is up to our intuition to choose the exact one that is applicable to the giving situation. Otherwise, we cannot siphon the truth out from the midst of untruths. Art is intuition and science is hard nose logic with a sinus problem.

Such new standard of intuition mentioned here can be taught and trained. This gives us the judgment without positive or negative judgment to know other's untruths even though everyone including all the king's horses supports infinite untruths as the truth. It is time people get off their high wooden horses and smell the aroma of wonton soup, not the chicken soup.

We have been led if everyone holds something to be truth, even if it doesn't do anything or if it does do something, it is only done by accident or from probability of random chance resolved one time, then we must accept it as always the truth. This is the result of great marketing strategy. If we can get one person out of a hundred better, we can convince everyone that the other 99 would get better or even have gotten better that no one else knows about including the person who supposedly have gotten better. There should be no argument about what is and what isn't the truth!

Remember whatever that have been said were truth, it would resolve whatever ails us in our lives more times than one. However, if what has been preached didn't resolve even one ailment of a person's life then there is no truth to what has been said even though all the gurus are saying the same as other parrots.

And you know what is worse than listen to one parrot? It is having to listen to a whole bunch of them!

## TAOISM AND ITS APPLICABLE TRUTH

After over 20 years of treating hundreds of thousands of patients by natural means as a Doctor of Chiropractic, a non-force, and no contact method was developed commonly known today as the Yuen Method. This method has been recently found to be running parallel to the principles of Taoism; even though there was not originally intention to do so. When it comes to wellness, such as health and fitness, Taoism intuitively has had established the methodology of longevity with less aging accompanied by fitness and other aspect of living.

The basic principle of yin and yang correspond to the strength and weakness of muscles in chiropractic kinesiology. It is in the perception of the yin effect that indicate what is truthfully taking place in all human disorders whether it is physicals, mental or spiritual. The Yuen Method however do not depend on finding the physical weakness of muscles, it does it intuitively by the separation of thinking from feeling, Emotions from thinking as well as feeling.

The Yuen Method is not wholly a physical discipline of treatment; it is similar to the Taoist's definition of the existence of both the physical and non-physical realities. Each does not limit one over the other; it accepted the matrix of countless physicals and non-physical influences leading to any human disorders. The yin effect similar to the weak response in the Yuen Method is the only true indication we have of the true reasons, causes and the sources of any dysfunction leading to the two leading wellness challenges of diseases and traumas.

When we get to the truth or to the Tao's truth path, ailments unbelievably disappear on the spot instantaneously. To get to the truth, there must be clarity, not affected negatively or positively, just the state of neutrality. This is the neutral line which separated the yin from the yang and is identical to the midline of our body.

In the Yuen Method just by placement of our thought to the midline of our body restores the state of neutrality in which center, balance and stability can be maintained.

The Yuen Method and Taoism are totally applicable to our daily life. We as humans can recognize, acknowledge, embrace and know how to get to the truth by perceiving it intuitively supported by 50% logical and not dominated 100% by it.

Essentially it is getting to the truth that resolves not just some but all ailments. Taoism encompasses every aspect of our human life. It can deal successfully to our personal and professional life when it's correctly applied. It is applicable for health, fitness, relationship, money /finance, career/purpose, and aging/ future.

This is what the Yuen Method also deals with. It searches for the weaknesses that affect us personally and professionally.

In this present magazine article, we can start with this new way in dealing with a back pain. This is new because many people are not familiar with this methodology.

The good news is we have a simple technique that'll rid you and anyone's back pain in as little as a few seconds "on the spot". As quickly as you can think or talk about it. This would save the US economy billions.

## THE MYTH OF AGING

Just want to dispel the conventional thinking that leads to creating aging myths. From a person who is about one year before hitting his 70th year mark, there must be something more I could say about aging than someone who is 50 and 60 years of age. I still have my hair on my head, my original teeth, no sagging skin, muscles, osteoporosis, overweight or mental dementia and know how to handle any stress and able to teach other seniors and would be seniors to do the same. This is more coming from a direction of demonstrable results than a lengthy dissertation and discussion on aging. More on this later, so please stay tuned!

Of course the number of years we have is always on the increase and despite our denial and forgetfulness, the years are still going to take place and add up. We are all caught in this forever treadmill: wondering if we could still walk without tiring ourselves out. Up to this point in human history, we have only dealt with aging but not resolving anything other than: suppression, denial, which was already mentioned, numbing, partial or near totally shutting ourselves down, not being truthful with ourselves and practicing forgetting, which also has already been mentioned. Wouldn't you say, these are some of the "common human tools" we have all used? As we progress in our time table, we actually become experts in their usage. We made them not just a part of us, but more and more a definition of us. Sad but true. Of course the common excuse is that we don't have any choices on the matter, which is one of three leading aging myths.

Since we are on the subject of three's, here are the three proverbial questions out of countless and endless issues pertaining to aging. Things that affect us more do come in threes more often than just one's or two's. If we can't deal with one issue, it would be unlikely we can deal with more than one at a time. Two and three or more would be overwhelming. This is kind of limiting and restricting. We are not aware of this and continue to practice limitation and restriction until we have no choice but to acknowledge and finally admit that we have aged.

Commonly, the only thing that is constant and consistent is that we, in every second of our long life, are constantly triggered by thoughts and events that have been going on and will be going on in and around our life, making us resort to using those "common human tools" that trigger our reactions and emotions inappropriately. This is the third item, which makes up the common triad of issues-triggers-choices that inevitably mess us up to no end. Until we can recognize them and deal with them quickly and effectively - preferably in "real time" - there are no hopeful promises in the future.

Of course, in my future writings and talks, I would make up more questions and get to the answer in real time, eliminating any necessity to debate about it since we "old folks" really don't have that much time left in our lives and energy resources to argue with everyone and anyone about their academic points of view that may not hold up much water in the practical sense -- in the physical "real" world of us "old folks."

- *Is aging weakening us or is it the weakness that causes us to age?*
- *Is aging slowing us down or is slowing down leading us to aging?*
- *Is aging making us forget or is forgetting making us aged?*

## IT IS TIME WE KICK DISEASE IN THE BUTT

Kicking disease in the butt comes as the result of truthfully at ease about diseases not just in your body and mind but your hidden culprit of disease, which is your spirit. When there is no ease in your life, it doesn't matter whom you have on your high price health dream team and what kind of spiritual drug journey you are on! All living beings warrant being at "ease" and having freedom from the "disease" state of body, mind, and spirit. The practice of those two dumb choices namely safeguarding your health and becoming spiritual will not save your butt.

Basically, when we don't have fitness, don't "fit" into our life situations, our clothes, family, and society, etc., having challenging relationship, difficulty paying our bills, don't have purpose with unrewarding careers, issues about aging and concern about our future all of these degenerated and messed up our body, we logically jump to the conclusion and assume it is our health that is being compromised. Please don't offer us to "live at the moment now", BS. Offering that is denying you have a past and future and perpetuate the limitation that you can't change the effects of your past and future at the present!

It is our countless spiritual experienced of trauma, illness, limitation, fear/phobia, and cause/effect that connected to our spiritual self that is highly detrimental to our wellness. Please note, it is wellness that is essential not health. When we consider health and spirituality as leading life choices then we acquired further "disease". We don't want more of those do we?

When it comes to our mind, we speak highly of how our mind accomplished what we want in our life. We speak how we excel in sports; make lots of money and perfecting our relationship by what we can program in our mind. Then we totally forget or have amnesia when it comes to the wellness of our life, practically more with our body and the physical environmental that affects us. Then we either consider everything important is physical, our diet and how we eat, cook our food, etc., which has nothing to do with anything or go in denial of our physical essence and speak only the vagueness of spirituality. Essentially when we can't get any concrete results, we choose only to speak of spiritual extracts.

Now whom have we been listening to; stupid educated people or self-proclaimed spiritual teachers from the past or at the present? Let's make sure there will be less of those candidates in the future!

# NOTES

www.ingramcontent.com/pod-product-compliance
Lightning Source LLC
Chambersburg PA
CBHW081740100526
44592CB00015B/2244